D1455548

THE YEAR'S WORK
IN ENGLISH STUDIES—1963

The Year's Work in English Studies

VOLUME XLIV

1963

Edited by
BEATRICE WHITE
D.Lit., F.S.A., F.R.Hist.S., F.R.S.L.

and
T. S. DORSCH
M.A.

Published for
THE ENGLISH ASSOCIATION

HUMANITIES PRESS NEW YORK

Printed in Great Britain by Cox & Wyman, Ltd.,
London, Fakenham and Reading

Preface

The Year's Work in English Studies once again pays tribute to the fruitful labours of scholars in the field of English. The number of books and articles included continues to grow annually and to bear testimony to the wide interest evinced in the English language and its literature.

In a survey of this nature and size overlapping is sometimes unavoidable. Material contained in one book or article is often relevant in different contexts in this volume and the same works may be found mentioned by more than one contributor.

There are three changes to record. Professor V. de Sola Pinto and Mrs Thompson, for whose long co-operation the editors are grateful, are both replaced, the first by B. D. Greenslade, the second by Margaret Willy and Howard Sergeant. Professor G. H. Moore is assisted by Professor T. R. Arp.

Offprints of works in foreign journals dealing with English studies should be sent to The Secretary, English Association, 8 Cromwell Place, London, S.W.7, for distribution to the contributors.

BEATRICE WHITE

T. S. DORSCH

Abbreviations

ABC	American Book Collector
AL	American Literature
A Ling	Archivum Linguisticum
Ang	Anglia
ANQ	American Notes and Queries
AP	Aryan Path
AQ	American Quarterly
Archiv	Archiv für das Studium der Neueren Sprachen
AS	American Speech
ATR	Anglican Theological Review
AUMLA	Journal of Australasian Universities Modern Language Association
BAASB	British Association for American Studies Bulletin
BC	The Book Collector
BJA	British Journal of Aesthetics
BJRL	Bulletin of the John Rylands Library
B.M.	British Museum
BMQ	British Museum Quarterly
BN	Burke's Newsletter
BNYPL	Bulletin of the New York Public Library
BSL	Bulletin de la Société Linguistique
Bu R	Bucknell Review
BUSE	Boston University Studies in English
C	Critique
C.B.E.L.	Cambridge Bibliography of English Literature
CE	College English
CL	Comparative Literature
CLA	College Language Association Journal
CQ	Critical Quarterly
D.N.B.	Dictionary of National Biography
DR	Dalhousie Review
DUJ	Durham University Journal
Ea	Études anglaises
EC	Essays in Criticism
EDH	Essays by Divers Hands
E.E.T.S.	Early English Text Society
EFT	English Fiction in Transition
EG	English and Germanic Studies
EJ	English Journal
ELH	Journal of English Literary History
ELIT	English Literature in Transition
ELN	English Language Notes
ELT	English Language Teaching
EM	English Miscellany
E.P.N.S.	English Place-Name Society
EPS	English Philological Studies
ESA	English Studies in Africa
ES	English Studies

ABBREVIATIONS

ETJ	Educational Theatre Journal
E & S	Essays and Studies
Ex	Explicator
HLB	Harvard Library Bulletin
HLQ	Huntington Library Quarterly
HR	Hudson Review
HTR	Harvard Theological Review
JEGP	Journal of English and Germanic Philology
JHI	Journal of the History of Ideas
JWCI	Journal of the Warburg and Courtauld Institutes
KR	Kenyon Review
KSJ	Keats-Shelley Journal
KSMB	Keats-Shelley Memorial Bulletin (Rome)
L	Language
Lib	The Library
LLM	Les Langues Modernes
LS	Language and Speech
MÆ	Medium Ævum
MCR	Melbourne Critical Review
MD	Modern Drama
MFS	Modern Fiction Studies
MLJ	Modern Language Journal
MLN	Modern Language Notes
MLQ	Modern Language Quarterly
MLR	Modern Language Review
MP	Modern Philology
MR	Massachusetts Review
MS	Mediaeval Studies
N	Neophilologus
NCF	Nineteenth Century Fiction
NEQ	New England Quarterly
NM	Neuphilologische Mitteilungen
NMS	Nottingham Medieval Studies
NQ	Notes and Queries
NS	Die Neueren Sprachen
O.E.D.	Oxford English Dictionary
PBA	Proceedings of the British Academy
PBSA	Papers of the Bibliographical Society of America
PMASAL	Papers of the Michigan Academy of Science, Arts and Letters
PMLA	Publications of the Modern Language Association of America
PQ	Philological Quarterly
P.R.O.	Public Record Office
PULC	Princeton University Library Chronicle
QJS	Quarterly Journal of Speech
QQ	Queen's Quarterly
QR	Quarterly Review
REL	Review of English Literature (Leeds)
RES	Review of English Studies
RI	Rice Institute Pamphlets
RLC	Revue de Litterature Comparée
RLV	Revue des langues vivantes
RMS	Renaissance and Modern Studies
RN	Renaissance News
RP	Renaissance Papers
R.S.L.	Royal Society of Literature
S	Speculum

ABBREVIATIONS

SAQ	*South Atlantic Quarterly*
SB	*Studies in Bibliography*
SCN	*Seventeenth Century News*
SEL	*Studies in English Literature* (*Rice University*)
Sew	*Sewanee Review*
Sh J	*Shakespeare Jahrbuch*
Sh Q	*Shakespeare Quarterly*
Sh S	*Shakespeare Survey*
SIR	*Studies in Romanticism* (*Boston University*)
SL	*Studia Linguistica*
SN	*Studia Neophilologica*
SNL	*Shakespeare Newsletter*
SP	*Studies in Philology*
SQ	*Southern Quarterly*
SR	*Southern Review*
S Ren	*Studies in the Renaissance*
S.T.C.	*Short Title Catalogue*
T	*Traditio*
TCBS	*Transactions of the Cambridge Bibliographical Society*
TCF	*Twentieth Century Fiction*
TCL	*Twentieth Century Literature*
TLS	*Times Literary Supplement*
TN	*Theatre Notebook*
TPS	*Transactions of the Philological Society*
TQ	*Texas Quarterly*
TS	*Theatre Survey*
TSE	*Tulane Studies in English*
TSL	*Tennessee Studies in Literature*
TSLL	*Texas Studies in Language and Literature*
UKCR	*University of Kansas City Review*
UMSE	*University of Mississippi Studies in English*
UTQ	*University of Toronto Quarterly*
UTSE	*University of Texas Studies in English*
VN	*Victorian Newsletter*
VP	*Victorian Poetry*
VQR	*Virginia Quarterly Review*
VS	*Victorian Studies*
YDS	*Transactions of the Yorkshire Dialect Society*
YW	*The Year's Work in English Studies*
YR	*Yale Review*
ZAA	*Zeitschrift für Anglistik und Amerikanistik*

Contents

CONTENTS

I

Literary History and Criticism: General Works

T. S. DORSCH

1. HISTORIES OF LITERATURE AND REFERENCE WORKS

It is questionable whether John Parry's *Guide Through English Literature*[1] will be found adequate for the needs of the Advanced Level candidates for whom chiefly he professes to be writing. It is true that from his book they may derive a reliable enough chronological outline of the main authors and movements—in this sense the book is a guide; but they could get this equally well from a number of more substantial single-volume works which are much more generous in supplying both background material and criticism. Beginning with Chaucer, he devotes only five pages to fourteenth-century poetry, and of these five pages one is in fact a survey of English literature and language before the time of Chaucer. The whole of the Elizabethan drama, including Shakespeare, is dealt with in a dozen pages. The novel since the Second World War receives a page and a half, and the only novelists discussed, and that of necessity in brief generalizations, are C. P. Snow, Henry Green, Joyce Cary, Graham Greene, William Golding, and John Wain, who is curiously described as an 'angry young man'; Parry ought to know that sixth-formers are avid readers of contemporary literature, and are anxious to have their tastes guided. He has followed a useful procedure in treating the different literary forms and genres separately in successive sections tracing the whole history of English poetry, drama, prose (of many varieties) and fiction; but his treatment is everywhere too sketchy to be of much value for the senior forms of the schools of today.

Enid Moodie Heddle's unpretentious little book, *How Australian Literature Grew*,[2] is designed largely for school children, but it may be read with pleasure and profit by more mature students. Within so brief a compass it can offer no more than an outline history of Australian literature in which comparatively important writers are dismissed in a few lines or a paragraph, and the main emphasis is laid on authors of the last few decades; anyone who wishes to consult an authoritative reference work on Australian literature will have to go elsewhere, to H. M. Green's massive *History of Australian Literature*, for example (see *YW* xlii. 11). The chief interest of this book lies in the background material which it presents, and which it relates to such writings as deal specifically with Australia and its life—the history of the first settlements, life in the

[1] *A Guide Through English Literature*, by John Parry. Univ. of London Press. pp. 244. 8s. 6d.

[2] *How Australian Literature Grew*, by Enid Moodie Heddle and Iris Millington. Melbourne: Cheshire, pp. vi+90. 16s. London: Angus & Robertson.

outback, and the lore and legend of the aborigines. The volume is pleasantly embellished with line-drawings by Iris Millington.

Darrel Abel's *American Literature*[3] tells the story of American literature from the beginnings to Henry James. Abel's purpose, to some degree a deliberate rejection of the methods of the American New Criticism of a generation ago, is 'to describe and interpret American writing in relation to the characters and personal circumstances of the men who wrote it and to the social and political tendencies which conditioned their writing'. In his 1350 pages he has room to be expansive, and his first volume, *Colonial and Early National Writing*, brings us down only as far as William Gilmore Simms. To central figures, such as James Fenimore Cooper, he can devote as much as forty-five pages, though it must be said that much of his material is narrative rather than criticism. Extended analyses and descriptions are given also of the writings of such authors as Benjamin Franklin, Thomas Jefferson, Washington Irving, and William Cullen Bryant. In Volume II, *Literature of the Atlantic Culture*, the main writers discussed include Emerson, Thoreau, Hawthorne, Longfellow, Lowell, and Poe, though there are of course many lesser authors as well. Volume III, *Masterworks of American Realism*, is devoted almost entirely to the works of Mark Twain, William Dean Howells, and Henry James, and again there is a good deal of summary. However, Abel is a sensible critic, and

[3] *American Literature*, by Darrel Abel. Three volumes. Vol. I: *Colonial and Early National Writing*. pp. vi+442. Vol. II: *Literature of the Atlantic Culture*. pp. vi+537. Vol. III: *Masterworks of American Realism: Twain, Howells, James*. pp. vi+370. Great Neck, New York: Barron's Educational Series. Each vol. $2.25 paperback. The whole in cloth $9.95.

although his work is aimed at American readers, English students could learn much about American literature both from his background information and outlines of particular works and from his comments upon his authors.

Frederick B. Artz's *From the Renaissance to Romanticism*[4] is one of those useful books in which an attempt is made to co-ordinate the study of several of the arts. As the title and subtitle indicate, it is a historical survey of certain stylistic trends which, between the early Renaissance and the Romantic period, affected the visual arts, music, and literature at much the same time. The rate and extent of changes in style are different in the various arts, and vary from country to country; but there are times when, although a variety of artistic currents are running side by side, certain specific tendencies predominate. Thus Artz divides the period under review into ages characterized, by and large, by common features of style: 'The Early Renaissance, 1300–1500'; 'The High Renaissance, 1500–1530 and Later'; 'Mannerism, 1530–1600 and Later'; 'The Baroque, 1600–1750'; and 'Neo-Classicism and Romanticism, 1750–1830'. To give an example of his method, under the heading of Baroque, he discusses, among many other figures, Rubens, Velasquez, and Rembrandt as painters, Milton as a poet, and Monteverdi as a musician. However, he recognizes that some artists, including Shakespeare, Milton, Goethe, Michelangelo, and Beethoven, 'made the long journey through changing styles' — Michelangelo's work, for example, embraced the styles of the High Renaissance, Mannerism,

[4] *From the Renaissance to Romanticism: Trends in Style in Art, Literature and Music, 1300–1830*, by Frederick B. Artz. Chicago U.P. pp. ix+311. $5. 37s. 6d.

and the Baroque, and Beethoven bridged Neo-Classicism and Romanticism. To such artists he gives special treatment. His book is extremely interesting, and could be read with profit by students alike of literature, of music, and of the visual arts.

The reprinting of the *Columbia Dictionary of Modern European Literature*[5] will be generally welcomed. This very useful work of reference covers thirty-one literatures ('because that is how many there are'). It provides authoritative historical surveys of these literatures, and of less familiar branches, such as Catalan, Flemish, and Icelandic, but the bulk of the volume consists of some 1,200 biographical and critical entries on authors of note who were writing between about 1870 and 1946, when the preparation of the volume was completed; these include 200 French authors, 150 German, 100 Russian, 100 Italian, 100 Spanish, 50 Polish, and 40 Czechoslovakian—which will give some notion of the ground covered. Admirable as the *Dictionary* is in its present form, it is difficult not to feel that it ought to have been revised rather than merely reprinted, in order to embrace, say, the first fifteen eventful years of post-war writing. Its usefulness could also have been increased by fuller, preferably complete, listing of the works of the authors represented.

The title of *The Concise Encyclopaedia of Modern World Literature*,[6] edited by Geoffrey Grigson, is misleading; it is not, like the *Columbia Dictionary*, concerned with biograph-ical and bibliographical facts, but aims at supplying 'brief introductions to various writers who are worth reading, in the not infallible opinion of the editor and the contributors'. Thus its entries consist of what are in effect short critical essays, varying in length from one to six columns, on the authors represented, and the contributors 'were asked to concentrate on the books which mattered, instead of giving the neutral itemized survey which you might expect from a conventional encyclopaedia'. A further restriction is that only poets, playwrights, novelists, and writers of short stories are treated. Then, 'Our time is the twentieth century,' says the editor; but exceptions are made in favour of a few writers, such as Gerard Manley Hopkins. Samuel Butler, who died in 1902, is included, but Émile Zola, who died in the same year, is left out. Where many lesser figures find a place, why are T. F. Powys, Angus Wilson, and Iris Murdoch forgotten? Are they not 'worth reading', and have they written no 'books which matter'? J. R. R. Tolkien is there, but not Charles Williams, or C. S. Lewis, for whom claims just as strong could be put forward. And surely, in a 1963 publication, Pinter, Arden, and Wesker could be regarded as 'established' playwrights. However, in spite of its many limitations, the volume has its value as a critical miscellany, and it gains further interest from its 200-odd full-page portraits of authors, sixteen of them colour reproductions of well-known portraits.

The scope of the *Concise Dictionary of Literature*[7] edited by I. A. Langnas and J. S. List is much wider; its aim is 'to provide a readily accessible source of basic information about the major

[5] *Columbia Dictionary of Modern European Literature.* General editor, Horatio Smith. Columbia U.P. pp. xiv+899. $10. 72s.

[6] *The Concise Encyclopaedia of Modern World Literature*, ed. by Geoffrey Grigson. Hutchinson. pp. 512. 50s.

[7] *Concise Dictionary of Literature*, ed. by I. A. Langnas and J. S. List. Peter Owen. pp. vi+526. 35s.

writers of the world from earliest times up to the present day'. Like almost any compendious work of its kind, this book has some worth. Among its 1,400 entries it includes many writers about whom it is not always easy to find information elsewhere; four successive entries relate to the Sanskrit writers Bhartrihari, Bhasa, and Bhavabhuti, and the modern Hebrew poet Chaim Nachman Bialik. But it commits many sins of proportion and omission. W. S. Gilbert is given a whole page, Sinclair Lewis a page and a half; Virginia Woolf receives eight lines in which the only novels mentioned are *Mrs. Dalloway*, *Orlando*, and *Between the Acts*. Much of the value of a 'dictionary' must surely lie in the completeness of the information it supplies. Jack Kerouac has a longer entry than Virginia Woolf, but only the most senior of living English novelists, such as E. M. Forster, are mentioned. John Lyly receives a six-line notice as an 'English novelist'; Dekker and Chapman do not appear. Students will be able to make up their minds from these few observations whether they think the volume worth possessing.

First published in Germany in 1958, and now translated into English by Margaret Shenfield, G. S. Wegener's *6,000 Years of the Bible*[8] is an excellent outline history of the genesis and development of the Bible, of its propagation over the face of the earth, and of Biblical archaeology and scholarship generally. Wegener begins by sketching the civilizations of the ancient world, particularly of the Israelites, since 'theirs is the soil that nourished the traditions, the stories, and the songs, which eventually became Holy Writ'. He brings his story down to recent research on the Dead Sea Scrolls, and is sufficiently up to date to include passages from the New English Bible. Of most interest to students of English will be the not inconsiderable sections devoted to the history of the Bible in England. The volume is illustrated with more than 200 beautifully clear photographs of old prints, title-pages, and sites.

The first volume of *The Cambridge History of the Bible*[9] to appear covers in considerably greater detail a much shorter span of time and of territory, as is indicated by its subtitle, 'The West from the Reformation to the Present Day'. In the words of its editor, S. L. Greenslade, the scholars who have contributed to the work 'have tried to give . . . an account of the text and versions of the Bible used in the West, of its multiplication in manuscript and print, and its circulation; of attitudes towards its authority and exegesis; and of its place in the life of the Western Church. And, with much reserve, something has been said of the impact of the Bible upon the world.' English versions are treated in two excellent long chapters: from 1525 to 1611 by Greenslade himself, from 1611 to the present day by Luther A. Weigle and C. F. D. Moule; and there is an extremely interesting chapter, by M. H. Black, on the printed Bible. Similarly authoritative chapters are devoted to the history of the Bible in Continental countries. There are appendixes on aids to study and commentaries, a long bibliography, and forty-eight excellent plates, and the work is well indexed. Another volume, 'From Jerome to the Renaissance', is nearly complete; a history of the Bible in English, 'more ample

[8] *6000 Years of the Bible*, by G. S. Wegener. Hodder & Stoughton. pp. 352. 35*s*.

[9] *The Cambridge History of the Bible: The West from the Reformation to the Present Day*, ed. by S. L. Greenslade. C.U.P. pp. x+590+pp. 48 plates. 45*s*. $8.50.

than any recent one', is envisaged; and further volumes 'may take up other aspects of the story or cover other areas'. The project is one which must interest all students of literature.

Since its first publication in 1870 Ebenezer Cobham Brewer's *Dictionary of Phrase & Fable* has been frequently revised, most extensively in 1952, when, among other things, it lost the Concise Bibliography of English Literature which was appended to earlier editions—no serious loss, since so many fuller bibliographies are now available. It seems now to be the policy of the publishers to keep the work up to date, for there were further revisions in 1959, and the present eighth revised edition[10] has again been enlarged 'in order to keep pace with the coinage of new phrases . . . and with advances in knowledge'. 'Beatnik', 'Guinea-pig', 'Mock-up', and 'Shoot a line' are a few recent coinages or usages revealed by a few minutes' turning of the pages. Brewer is a most agreeable companion as well as an invaluable reference work, and it is pleasant to think that he is unlikely to be allowed to go out of print or out of date.

First published in 1943, *An English Library*,[11] compiled by F. Seymour Smith, now reappears in a revised and considerably enlarged edition. The information provided by this volume is classified in ten groups (with subgroups) under such headings as 'Autobiographies and Memoirs', 'Fiction', 'Philosophy and Religion', 'Poetry and Poetic Drama', and 'A Bookman's Reference Library', and

more than 2,600 books are listed, with brief notes on their contents and character, and often on their authors. Living writers, other than editors, are excluded. This work is not designed for academic readers, but it should be helpful to general readers, and perhaps to school librarians.

Philip H. Vitale's *Basic Tools of Research*[12] is a descriptive guide to the kinds of reference book which the undergraduate student of English would find useful in the various branches of his studies. Its 285 items are listed under such headings as 'Guides', 'Dictionaries', 'Wordbooks', 'Encyclopedias', 'Histories', and 'Bibliography'. The work is geared to the needs rather of American than of English undergraduates. It all but ignores Old and Middle English studies, and while it lists several books of the type of *The American Thesaurus of Slang, Western Words: A Dictionary of the Range, Cow Camp and Trail*, and *Dictionary of American Underworld Lingo*, it omits such standard works as the *English Dialect Dictionary*. There are other surprising omissions, Alfred Harbage's *Annals of English Drama*, for example, M. P. Tilley's *Dictionary of the Proverbs in England in the Sixteenth and Seventeenth Centuries*, and a number of important specialized histories, such as those of Allardyce Nicoll; and there are some outright errors of fact, such as that *YW* 'excludes American literature'. However, for all its shortcomings, the book will be of service to American students, and perhaps to English undergraduates who are without tutorial guidance.

[10] *Brewer's Dictionary of Phrase & Fable.* Revised Edition. Cassell. pp. vi + 970. 42s.

[11] *An English Library: A Bookman's Guide*, by F. Seymour Smith. André Deutsch. pp. 384. 30s.

[12] *Basic Tools of Research: An Annotated Guide for Students of English*, compiled by Philip H. Vitale. Great Neck, New York: Barron's Educational Series. pp. vi + 173, $1.95.

2. ANNUAL PUBLICATIONS

Most of the contributions to the 1963 volume of *Essays and Studies*[13] are noticed in later chapters, and, as in the past, all that is necessary here is to give some brief indication of their subjects. Milton Waldman writes interestingly about the functions of a publisher, and among other things laments that present-day economic conditions make it increasingly difficult for a publishing house to develop or maintain an individuality of its own. Pamela Hansford Johnson's 'The Fascination of the Paranoid Personality: Baron Corvo' is a lively study of the *folie de grandeur* which gave 'a significant, penetrating quality', and at times 'a real touch of splendour', to Corvo's books. 'He is larger than life,' she concludes, 'much, much larger, and we have found him larger than death.' In 'The Hawthorne Myth: A Protest', Martin Green argues persuasively that Nathaniel Hawthorne has been greatly overrated in recent American criticism. Tony Tanner's study of *The Sacred Fount* sets out to show that in this novel Henry James 'was probing and exploring a profound aesthetic issue and that his notion of non-participatory speculation is related to the ancient and persistent idea of the artist as a man who creates forms which might be truer than the truth'. Arthur Mizener considers 'The Voice of Scott Fitzgerald's Prose'. In 'Beasts and Politics in Elizabethan Literature', Anthony G. Petti analyses beast allusions in this literature, and demonstrates that 'many Elizabethan writers saw in the animal kingdom a valuable commentary on the nature and state of man'. Harold Brooks's

subject is the role of Speed, Launce, and Crab in *The Two Gentlemen of Verona*. Finally, in an interesting paper Keith W. Salter discusses the treatment in English literature of the theme of 'The Right Use of Riches'.

This year's issue of *Essays by Divers Hands*,[14] which is edited by Joanna Richardson, opens with a paper, 'In Praise of Anatole France', by Robert Baldick. Baldick believes that France has too easily been dismissed as a merely negative writer, and that he 'deserves better of posterity than he has received' for his qualities of gentle irony and heartfelt pity. In his Wedmore Memorial Lecture, 'On Translating Poetry', C. Day Lewis offers some perceptive comments on the art of the verse-translator, drawing both on his own experience and on that of his great predecessors. 'A translation,' he concludes, 'cannot be poetry in its own right unless it has been subdued to the imaginative process of its original; nor can it be a faithful translation unless it is in some sense an original poem.' Discussing 'The World of William Golding', Peter Green claims that, despite all his self-imposed limitations, Golding 'remains the most powerful writer, the most original, the most profoundly imaginative, to have turned his hand to fiction in this country since the war; and if he never wrote another word his place in English letters would be secure'. The subject of Pamela Hansford Johnson's interesting lecture is Marcel Proust, whom she regards as one of the most lovable of authors. Margaret Kennedy speaks about 'The Novelist and his Public'; her witty paper, ranging over the work of many of her pre-

---

[13] *Essays and Studies 1963*. N.S. Vol. 16. Collected for the English Association by S. Gorley Putt. John Murray. pp. v+114. 13s. 6d.

[14] *Essays by Divers Hands: Being the Transactions of the Royal Society of Literature*, N.S. Vol. XXXII. Ed. by Joanna Richardson. O.U.P. pp. viii+144. 18s.

decessors, aims at showing that the novelist must have in mind a particular public, 'his *own* public, "an audience fit though few", capable of giving him, should he deserve it, the response he desires. He may get little applause from such readers, he may get scanty evidence that they exist, but he must fancy them to exist somewhere, if he is to write at all.' In 'What They Read' Carola Oman gives a lively account of the reading tastes of Lord Nelson, Admiral Collingwood, Sir John Moore, the Duke of Wellington, and Napoleon. Under the title 'The Critic and the Public', Joanna Richardson lays down the functions and responsibilities of the critic and the reviewer, chief among which she places the obligation 'to increase public understanding and appreciation and so to create an atmosphere in which the artist can work to the limit of his powers— and beyond his known powers'. Sir Steven Runciman's subject in the Katja Reissner Lecture is 'Medieval History and the Romantic Imagination'. Sir Steven speaks of the way in which our hearts are stirred by the deeds and the names of the medieval period, 'and if its echoes stay with us to illumine the past with poetry, then we shall have a deeper understanding of history, of the hopes and sorrows of humanity, of the passing of all worldly things, and the relentless governance of fate.' The volume closes with Enid Starkie's Tredegar Memorial Lecture for 1957, a moving personal portrait of Joyce Cary and a tribute to his achievement.

Four items in the 1963 *Proceedings of the British Academy*[15] require notice. Laurence Lerner's Chatterton Lecture on an English Poet is entitled 'W. B. Yeats: Poet and Crank'.

Lerner regards Yeats as 'the most eloquent, the most ecstatic, and the most splendid of modern poets', yet he finds much that is puzzling in his verse. 'How is it,' he asks, 'that the greatest poet of the century, a poet of wisdom and understanding of the heart, a sage as well as a singer—how is it that he expounded in his poems such absurd, such eccentric, such utterly crackpot ideas?' Yeats had a taste for queer religions, for Theosophy, Rosicrucianism, the Order of the Golden Dawn; for alchemy and spiritualism; for Plotinus, Cornelius Agrippa, and Madame Blavatsky; and he published his strange and complex system in *A Vision*, which perhaps most people find unreadable. Lerner is one of these; however, he believes, and indeed demonstrates, notably in an excellent analysis of the *Dialogue of Self and Soul*, that 'these crackpot ideas, when they are turned into poetry, are somehow able to slough off their eccentricity, to take on a form that bestows on them, or restores to them, a wisdom and seriousness they had lacked'. Kathleen Coburn's title for her Warton Lecture on English Poetry is Coleridge's phrase 'The Interpenetration of Man and Nature'. Miss Coburn sets out to show, in relation both to his poetry and to his prose writings, that this phrase embodies some of Coleridge's 'most vital and persistent preoccupations'. Harold Jenkins's Shakespeare Lecture, 'Hamlet and Ophelia', is a searching examination of the 'nunnery' scene and of its significance both in the relationship between Hamlet and Ophelia and in the thematic structure of the play. The scene has often been interpreted rather cynically, and doubts have been cast on Ophelia's sincerity and on the depth of her love for Hamlet. Jenkins brings out better than Ophelia's previous advocates her essential

[15] *Proceedings of the British Academy.* Vol. XLIX, 1963. Published for the British Academy by O.U.P. pp. xvi + 465. 84s.

purity and truth, and he convincingly defends her lie about her father's whereabouts as the only possible answer that she could in the circumstances have given. By the nunnery scene, although he sees the god in man, Hamlet has also learnt 'how the beast everywhere transforms him; . . . renunciation of Ophelia expresses in the action of the play Hamlet's rejection of the beauty and nobility of life because of what must be inseparable from it.' Brian Ó Cuív's subject in the Sir John Rhŷs Memorial Lecture is 'Literary Creation and Irish Historical Tradition'. Ó Cuív makes a careful study of the early annalistic sources for Irish history, and shows that much that has been considered fantastic in Irish literature is based on material of this kind. Other contributions to the volume are as follows: 'The Russian Revolution and the Peasant', by E. H. Carr; 'Descriptivism', by R. M. Hare; 'Bronze Age Architecture of Anatolia', by Seton Lloyd; 'On the Dionysiac Fresco in the Villa Dei Misteri at Pompeii', by G. Zuntz; 'The Debate on the American Civil War', by Sir Denis Brogan; 'Kant's Moral Theology', by W. H. Walsh; 'Leon Battista Alberti and the Beginnings of Italian Grammar', by Cecil Grayson; and 'Various Numismatic Notes', by Harold Mattingly. Among the obituary notices are three which will be read with special feeling by students of English literature: those by Basil Willey on E. M. W. Tillyard, by Herbert Davis on F. P. Wilson, and by John Butt on J. B. Leishman.

The invaluable *Annual Bibliography of English Language and Literature*[16] is again being compiled in England

under the editorship of Marjory Rigby and Charles Nilon; Nilon's work in its assembly preserves its long association with the University of Colorado. The present volume covers the year 1960. If this seems rather a long time-lag in a work published in 1963, it should be remembered that in recent years the *Bibliography* has had to cover retrospectively the big gap caused by the Second World War, and that in any case in a cumulative reference book of this nature completeness is of greater value than punctuality.

Dissertation Abstracts[17] becomes more valuable every year as it draws within its orbit further universities and colleges; more than 140 such institutions are now associated with it. It publishes digests of doctoral dissertations and monographs which are presented at the various universities, and which may be purchased in microform. Almost every academic discipline is represented, and among these disciplines English studies play a large and important part. Reference to the well-organized subject and author indexes enables a scholar to ascertain what is being done in his special field of study, and from the digests he may make up his mind whether it will be worth his while to purchase any particular work which is listed. Some 8,000 dissertations are listed in the 1963 issues, which appear monthly, as in the past; and that the work supplies a real need is attested by the fact that several hundred of its items are purchased every month.

In 1962 a considerably smaller work was published experimentally

---

[16] *Annual Bibliography of English Language and Literature*, Vol. XXXV, 1960. Ed. for the Modern Humanities Research Assn. by Marjory Rigby and Charles Nilon. C.U.P. pp. xvi+376. 80*s*.

[17] *Dissertation Abstracts: Abstracts of Dissertations and Monographs in Microform*. Vol. XXIII, Nos. 7–12, Pt. I (Jan.–June 1963): pp. 2269–4860+Indexes. No. 12, Pt. II, Subject and Author Indexes to Vol. XXIII (1962–63): pp. 415. Vol. XXIV, Nos. 1–6 (July–Dec. 1963): pp. 1–2635+ Indexes. Ann Arbor: Univ. Microfilms, Inc. $50. ($55 outside America.)

under the title *Masters Abstracts* (see *YW* xliii. 15). This provided abstracts of Masters' theses presented in the universities of the *Dissertation Abstracts* panel. A second volume[18] appeared at the very end of 1962. The innovation has been well received, and from now on *Masters Abstracts* will be published quarterly at an annual subscription rate of $6 in the United States, and $8 elsewhere. It should be pointed out that the theses digested in this work are very rigorously screened; they are not accepted without a recommendation from the relevant head of a department. This ensures that only theses which contribute significantly to their fields of knowledge are included.

Four of the six articles in the 1963 issue of *Annali*,[19] an annual publication of the Istituto Orientale in Naples, require notice. With illustrations drawn from Shakespeare, Sophocles's *Oedipus Tyrannus*, and modern American plays, E. S. Miller discusses 'Perceiving and Imagining at Plays'—the fact that, whereas the playwright can make a direct appeal to the eyes and ears of his audience, he can work only through their imagination in making an appeal to their other senses. E. Schulte's article (in Italian) brings out relationships between Keats's *Hyperion* and Goethe's *Prometheus*, and comments on Henry Crabb Robinson's admiration for Goethe, several of whose poems he translated. V. Sanna offers a study (also in Italian) of Henry James's *The Turn of the Screw*. In 'The Dialect of North Staffordshire' D. Plant provides interesting analyses of the pronunciation, the grammar, and the vocabulary of this part of England.

The 1963 volume of *Studies in Bibliography* is noticed in the bibliographical section of this chapter (see note 45).

3. COLLECTIONS OF CRITICAL ESSAYS

Scrutiny was first published quarterly in Cambridge between 1932 and 1953, its principal editor and driving-force throughout being F. R. Leavis. It has now been photographically reprinted[20] in nineteen volumes, together with a twentieth volume containing eight well-organized indexes compiled by Maurice Hussey and a twenty-four-page 'Retrospect' by Leavis. The 'Retrospect' is also published separately as a pamphlet. It is impossible in a short notice to sum up adequately the merits and deficiencies of a work so vast in scope as this; perhaps the simplest thing is to approach it by way of Leavis's 'Retrospect'. On this one's first comment must be that it is a very bad advertisement to the work as a whole —it seems deliberately calculated to repel any liberal-minded would-be reader of the journal who is ignorant of its nature and its history. It is written in the tone of defensive arrogance, rancour, and discourtesy that has characterized others of Leavis's recent public utterances. Nor is it easy to believe that anyone who writes as badly as Leavis can have been fully sensitive to all the virtues of the many writers on whom he pontificated in the pages of *Scrutiny*. No one in his senses would deny that *Scrutiny* had to contend with a good deal of ill-judged and at times wilfully perverse opposition—there is no need

---

[18] *Masters Abstracts: Abstracts of Selected Masters Theses on Microfilm.* Vol. I, No. 2. (Dec. 1962). Ann Arbor: Univ. Microfilms, Inc. pp. viii+64.

[19] *Annali* (*Sezione Germanica*). Vol. VI. Istituto Orientale di Napoli. pp. 181.

[20] *Scrutiny: A Quarterly Review,* variously edited (1932–53). Twenty volumes. C.U.P. pp. 7,658. The set £45, $125. Each vol. 50s. $6.50. '*Scrutiny*': *A Retrospect,* by F. R Leavis, C.U.P. pp. 24. 3s. 6d. 75 cents.

for Leavis to labour this point so persistently and insistently—or that it contained much excellent criticism, including some of Leavis's own. But Leavis's assumption that *Scrutiny* was always right, and that any opposition to the views it expressed resulted merely from 'the fierce (and unscrupulous) hostility of the literary and academic worlds', is absurd. Nor can other extravagant claims that he makes for the influence of *Scrutiny* be accepted: that it completely transformed the study of medieval English literature, for example, that it was solely responsible for all right-minded modern outlooks on the novel, or that by its triumphant slaughter of Bradley (who, however, has resolutely defied death) it brought health and sanity into Shakespearian criticism. Turning to the journal itself, one re-reads with pleasure and respect the work of many of the contributors: to give only a few examples, that of Miss M. C. Bradbrook, of Henri Fluchère, and of G. D. Klingopulos, of W. H. Gardner on Gerard Manley Hopkins, of L. C. Knights on many Elizabethan and Shakespearian topics, of W. H. Mellers and Bruce Pattison on music, of John Speirs on a variety of medieval writers, and, at times, of Leavis and Mrs. Leavis, particularly when they are discussing novels. It is scarcely necessary to add that what is sound or stimulating or adventurous in *Scrutiny* outweighs what is shaky or tiresome, and that no serious student can afford to ignore these volumes.

It is a pleasure to welcome the reissue, as a Peregrine Book, of Herbert Grierson's *The Background of English Literature*,[21] which first appeared in 1925. This is a book which has been read with profit and enjoyment by several generations of students of English; it contains the Edinburgh lecture from which it takes its title, the Leslie Stephen Lecture 'Classical and Romantic', and lectures and prefaces on, among other subjects, *Don Quixote*, the metaphysical poets, Byron, and Blake and Gray. The rereading of these papers prompts certain reflections in one who has recently spent a good deal of time with the volumes of *Scrutiny*. Grierson is just as perceptive (and practical) as the *Scrutiny* critics; but he possesses attributes of which there are very few signs in *Scrutiny*, notably a mind very well stored with the Biblical and classical learning which is fundamental to a full appreciation of a great part of English literature. His work has a breadth and a humanity that are very rare in contemporary criticism. It is always a refreshing and enlightening experience to return to the writings of a critic of the breed to which Grierson belonged.

In the words of its editors, Gerald Jay Goldberg and Nancy Marmer Goldberg, the main purpose of *The Modern Critical Spectrum*[22] is 'to "impose cosmos on chaos" by clarifying and categorizing the dominant critical tendencies of our age'. As the Goldbergs see them, these tendencies may be categorized under eight heads: 'The Uses of Formal Analysis', 'The Uses of the Socio-Cultural Milieu', 'The Uses of Tradition', 'The Uses of Biography', 'The Uses of Humanism', 'The Uses of Scholarship', 'The Uses of Psychology', and 'The Uses of Myth'. Their way of explaining and illustrating these various approaches is in each case to present an essay in

[21] *The Background of English Literature and Other Essays*, by Herbert Grierson. Penguin Books in association with Chatto & Windus, 1962. pp. 249. 8s. 6d.

[22] *The Modern Critical Spectrum*, ed. by Gerald Jay Goldberg and Nancy Marmer Goldberg. Englewood Cliffs, N.J.: Prentice-Hall, Inc., 1962. pp. xix+344. 56s.

which the particular critical method is discussed, and to follow this with a series of essays in which the method is seen in action. Thus the section on the socio-cultural milieu opens with David Daiches's essay 'Fiction and Civilization', and the practical application of the method here considered is seen in Christopher Caudwell's 'George Bernard Shaw', Edmund Wilson's 'Flaubert's Politics', Lionel Trilling's *The Princess Casamassima*, and Leslie A. Fiedler's 'Saul Bellow'; under 'The Uses of Humanism' the theory is expounded in Douglas Bush's 'The Humanist Critic', and the practice is illustrated by Irving Babbitt's 'The Problem of the Imagination: Dr. Johnson'; and the same procedure is followed for the other six categories. Inevitably there is some overlap between the types, but the volume as a whole serves as a useful guide to the techniques of criticism most frequently practised today. Its thirty-odd essays also make up an interesting anthology of contemporary critical writings, most of which are too well known to require individual notice here. In addition to those already named, the critics represented include Cleanth Brooks, Maynard Mack, John Crowe Ransom, Allen Tate, William Empson, T. S. Eliot, A. S. P. Woodhouse, Louis L. Martz, Herbert Read, F. R. Leavis, and Maud Bodkin.

Explication as Criticism,[23] edited by W. K. Wimsatt, Jr., is a collection of eight essays reprinted, with a few slight modifications, from early volumes (between 1941 and 1952) of the annual series of English Institute papers. The book takes its title from the opening essay, in which Wimsatt considers 'whether explication of a

poem is an act of criticism and hence of evaluation'. As the Institute volumes have been noticed in *YW* as they have appeared, it seems unnecessary to do more here than name the essays included in the present work. They are, after Wimsatt's contribution, as follows: 'Idiom of Popular Poetry in the *Miller's Tale*', by E. T. Donaldson; '*Troilus and Cressida*: Music for the Play', by Frederick W. Sternfeld; '*Macbeth* as the Imitation of an Action', by Francis Fergusson; 'Literary Criticism: Marvell's "Horatian Ode" ', by Cleanth Brooks; 'John Milton', by Douglas Bush; 'Blake: The Historical Approach', by David V. Erdman; and 'Wordsworth's "Ode: Intimations of Immortality"', by Lionel Trilling. In his Foreword Wimsatt outlines the early history of the Institute after its inauguration by sixty-four 'eager scholars' in 1939.

From the various journals in which they were first published John Wain has, in *Essays on Literature and Ideas*,[24] gathered together a score of interesting critical essays on subjects ranging in time from Shakespeare to the present day. The most substantial, 'Forms in Contemporary English Literature', calls for special notice; it is a study of drama, poetry, and the novel in the last decade or so. In spite of much mediocre imitation, Wain considers the innovations in recent drama 'entirely for the better', since modern plays offer their audiences 'scenes in which they can recognize their own life-style'; whether it is always a life-style that is worthy of serious dramatic presentation he does not discuss. Like drama, poetry 'is fighting for survival'; but Wain is hopeful of its future, for 'again like the theatre, it is fighting successfully, with the worst of its doubts and

[23] *Explication as Criticism: Selected Papers from the English Institute, 1941–1952*, ed. with a Foreword by W. K. Wimsatt, Jr. Columbia U.P. pp. xix+202. 33s. 6d.

[24] *Essays on Literature and Ideas*, by John Wain. Macmillan. pp. xi+270. 30s.

despairs behind it'. In the novel, too, there is healthy activity, and the most discouraging thing for the aspiring author is 'the increasing difficulty of keeping alive . . . the idea that such a thing as imaginative literature can exist at all'. Most of the other essays are as stimulating as this one, though not so fully developed. Writing on 'The Mind of Shakespeare', Wain has no difficulty in demonstrating that it is anything but the 'second-rate mind' that it is still sometimes declared to be. The essay on Pope is especially interesting for its discussion of eighteenth-century irony and for a sensible study of *The Dunciad*. Two papers are devoted to George Orwell, who, in Wain's view, will be kept alive not so much by the literary qualities of his writing as by the fact that he 'put the claim of his fellow-man consistently before his own'. Short surveys of the work of four recent critics (T. S. Eliot, Edmund Wilson, R. P. Blackmur, and Cyril Connolly) include a well-reasoned 'debunking' of Blackmur's methods. Among other writers treated are Johnson, Byron, Dickens, and John Betjeman. Wain is a balanced and courteous critic, and his book as a whole makes very good reading.

The fifteen essays brought together in John Sparrow's *Independent Essays*[25] consist of his British Academy lecture on 'Great Poetry', his prefaces to the Nonesuch edition of *In Memoriam* and to *Selected Poems by John Betjeman*, a *Spectator* article on Barrie, and a number of reviews that he has contributed to *TLS*. The British Academy lecture was noticed in *YW* xli. 14. The essays as a whole reflect a wide diversity of interests—among them medieval Latin poetry, seventeenth-century philosophy, the letters of Dr. Johnson and Sydney

Smith, Pope, Jane Austen, Oscar Wilde, A. E. Housman, and John Betjeman. Sparrow will not be to everyone's taste when he writes on such topics as homosexuality (in relation to Peter Wildeblood's *Against the Law*) or D. H. Lawrence's sexual ethics (in relation to the *Lady Chatterley* trial); but his judgement in purely literary matters is usually to be trusted and his reviews are interesting and sensible, as far as they go. As a generalization, however, it is questionable whether a scholar is likely to enhance his reputation by reprinting a collection of reviews that he has written for a quasi-popular journal; all too often, in reading this book, one feels that Sparrow could have increased the interest and value of what he has to say by developing his points more fully and expanding his reviews into full-length essays.

The Dyer's Hand,[26] by W. H. Auden, is a stimulating collection of some three dozen essays, mainly on literary topics, although a few are devoted to music. The most substantial, 'Making, Knowing and Judging', which was Auden's inaugural lecture as Professor of Poetry at Oxford, has been noticed in a previous issue of *YW* (xxxvii. 12). Several of the essays relate to Shakespeare. 'The Globe' draws some distinctions between the conventions of Greek and of Shakespearian tragedy. 'The Prince's Dog' is an interesting study of Prince Hal and Falstaff, and of their relations to each other and to society. 'Brothers and Others' has as its main subject *The Merchant of Venice*, which for a variety of reasons Auden classes as one of Shakespeare's 'Unpleasant Plays', and 'as much a "problem" play as one by Ibsen or Shaw'. In 'The Joker in the Pack', a sensible

[25] *Independent Essays*, by John Sparrow. Faber. pp. 209. 30*s*.

[26] *The Dyer's Hand and Other Essays*, by W. H. Auden. Faber. pp. xiv+528. 42*s*.

analysis of *Othello*, Auden argues that we feel pity for Othello, but no respect; 'our aesthetic respect is reserved for Iago.' Finally, there is an illuminating essay on music in Shakespeare. Byron is another author about whom Auden writes with great spirit; although *Don Juan* is the principal object of his attention, he ranges very widely in his treatment of Byron, as indeed he does in all his criticism, which manifests a great diversity of literary interests. He is especially good when he is discussing Byron's poetry as 'the most striking example . . . in literary history of the creative role which poetic form can play'. American poetry and detective stories provide the subject-matter for further studies which are, each in its own way, equally penetrating. Authors treated in other essays include Franz Kafka, D. H. Lawrence, Marianne Moore, Henry James, Robert Frost, and Dickens. Auden is often witty, often provocative, and always individual, and his volume contains much criticism which will set its reader thinking for himself.

Under the heading *The Critical Moment*, *TLS* (26 July) publishes a series of articles largely relating to current outlooks on literature and criticism. An anonymous introductory essay entitled 'The Critical Moment' prepares the way for the following articles: 'Humane Literacy', by George Steiner; 'Why I Value Literature', by Richard Hoggart; 'Some Principles of Criticism', by Réne Wellek; 'Are Purely Literary Values Enough?', by W. W. Robson; 'Notes on Imagination and Judgment', by John Wain; 'Leech-Gathering', by Harry Levin; 'In Search of Fundamental Values', by L. C. Knights; 'The Function of the Imagination', by Graham Hough; and 'Research in English', by F. R. Leavis. Most of the essays are interesting in themselves, and together they provide a very fair picture of what is going on in criticism today.

4. FORMS, GENRES, AND THEMES

Francis Berry's thesis, in *Poetry and the Physical Voice*,[27] is that, whatever attributes of other kinds we associate with it, a poem is essentially vocal sound, reflecting the voice, the actual physical voice, of the poet by whom it was written. Thus Tennyson, whose voice was described by Fitzgerald as 'deep and deep-chested', is seen at his most characteristic in poems that possess a 'deep-chested music'; his failures occurred when he wrote of things 'he had never experienced nor could experience, things which he neither had nor could convincingly vocalize' [*sic*]. Berry argues that Tennyson was, 'as a poet, confined within the limits of his personal voice'. Much is also known about the quality of Shelley's voice, and with Shelley again, in Berry's view, it is possible to hear the personal voice in the poetry. 'Dizzy soarings, rapturous ascents, precipitous journeyings, aerial cars or chariots in speedy motion, careering clouds—these are typical events in the poetry, requiring for their rendering a high-pitched, rapid, ecstatic, and scarcely varied vocal delivery.' A man's voice, though it remains essentially the same throughout his life, undergoes changes in the course of time, and in *L'Allegro* and *Paradise Lost* Berry detects Milton's voice at different stages of his career; the processes of maturing manifest themselves in diction, syntax, versification, and total effect. Such a development he sees also in poems which W. H. Auden recorded for the gramophone in 1936 and in 1954. As a dramatist, Shakespeare wrote, not for his own voice,

[27] *Poetry and the Physical Voice*, by Francis Berry. Routledge. pp. x+205. 28s.

but for the voices of fellow-players with which he was intimately acquainted; he 'used surrogates, or instruments', and it should be possible to identify many parts in his plays with the voices of members of his company. It will be recognized that Berry's discussion of his chosen poets is very largely conjectural and theoretical, and it raises many questions to which it is perhaps impossible to find answers. However, his approach has interesting potentialities, and it may be that it can with profit be further extended.

'It happens a score of times in the *Iliad* that an immortal has occasion to leave Olympus for the theatre of human action. Iris most frequently, but also Athene, Apollo, Thetis, Zeus himself, among others, descend to intervene in the theatre which seems to afford so large a part of the gods' amusement.' With these words, after an introductory survey of the structural and stylistic conventions of epic, Thomas Greene embarks upon the main sections of his book *The Descent from Heaven*,[28] which is a large-scale study of Western European epic poetry from Homer to Milton. The quotation provides a connecting-link between all the epics about which Greene writes, for in each of them he sees a special significance in the part played in the affairs of the human personages by celestial messengers: Olympian deities in Homer, Apollonius Rhodius, Virgil, and Statius; Michele in Ariosto; Gabriel in Sannazaro's *De Partu Virginis*; Mercury in Camoens; Mercury again in Spenser's *Mother Hubberds Tale*, and Mutability in *The Faerie Queene*; Raphael in *Paradise Lost*. Greene aims at showing that these visitations affect, not only the events of the poems in which they occur, but also the spirit in which the poets approach their task. Other works than those named are included in Green's development of his thesis, which on the whole he argues persuasively; and the incidental criticism of styles and themes adds interest and value to his work.

Joseph Raith's *Englische Metrik*[29] is rather more than a study of metre, since it contains discussion also of rhyme (including internal, double, and eye rhymes) and of such devices as alliteration, assonance, and consonance, which strictly speaking, apart from the integral part played by alliteration in Anglo-Saxon verse, have nothing to do with metre, except in so far as they may reinforce stress already indicated by a dominant metrical pattern. For the most part, however, the book is made up of examples of English metrical patterns, from the various types of Anglo-Saxon alliterative schemes to the *vers libre* of recent decades, and including a great many line and stanza patterns which have established themselves as standard English patterns. Analysis of the recurrent metres of English verse is confined to the introductory sections; the book would have been even more useful than it is if the sections devoted to individual verse-schemes had also contained some metrical analysis of these schemes which could be applied to the many examples offered. It might be added that an English reader would find the pages of this book uncomfortably and unattractively cramped.

The purpose of *Drama: The Major Genres*,[30] edited by Robert Hogan

[28] *The Descent from Heaven: A Study in Epic Continuity*, by Thomas Greene. Yale U.P. pp. ix+434. $7.50. 56s.

[29] *Englische Metrik*, by Joseph Raith. Munich: Max Hueber. pp. 203. DM 9.80.

[30] *Drama: The Major Genres*. An Introductory Critical Anthology, ed. by Robert Hogan and Sven Eric Molin. New York: Dodd, Mead & Co. pp. xiv+652. $4.45.

and Sven Eric Molin, is to introduce students to certain principles which have through the ages governed or influenced the composition of the three dramatic genres of tragedy, comedy, and tragicomedy, and to teach them the criteria by which any drama is to be judged. This it sets out to do by means both of precept and of example, in the shape of specific plays. Thus under the heading 'Tragedy', there are passages from Aristotle's *Poetics* and from the critical writings of Dryden, Dr. Johnson, Gilbert Murray, Joseph Wood Krutch, Arthur Miller, S. H. Butcher, Allardyce Nicoll, and a number of other authorities; the extracts are chosen to throw light on particular aspects of tragedy: the tragic structure, the tragic hero, the tragic style, and the like. The illustrative plays are Sophocles's *Antigone*, Shakespeare's *King Lear*, and Federico Garcia Lorca's *The House of Bernarda Alba*. Comedy and tragicomedy are similarly introduced by critical material. Comedy is exemplified by Jonson's *The Silent Woman*, Molière's *Tartuffe*, and Shaw's *The Six of Calais*; tragicomedy by Chekhov's *The Three Sisters*, O'Casey's *The Plough and the Stars*, and Gorky's *Yegor Bulychov and the Others*. Each of the nine plays is accompanied by a critical essay. Also included, without critical commentary, are Henry James's *The American* and William Inge's *Bus Stop*, on which students are expected to practise the techniques they have acquired by studying the earlier sections of the volume.

In *The World of Harlequin*,[31] a very handsome volume printed by the C.U.P., Allardyce Nicoll provides an important and valuable study of the *commedia dell' arte*. Nicoll is dis-

turbed to find how many works on this subject are based on an incomplete review of the existing documents, and how many are distorted by partial interpretations of the evidence. He himself takes into account all the documents, and it is his constant endeavour to interpret them as objectively as is humanly possible. His chief aim is, not to write a history of the *commedia dell' arte*, but to discover 'what was the basic force which kept this particular kind of theatrical presentation vital for more than two centuries and which, even after it had vanished, has caused many of its characters to live in our memories'. He begins by establishing the nature of 'the comedy of skill', and in doing so finds it necessary to dispose of a number of misconceptions held alike by some scholars and by the majority of laymen—for example, that it is essentially a drama of buffoonery. On the contrary, as he amply demonstrates, 'serious speeches and ridiculous clowning, merry servants and fervent lovers, old men and young, all have their apportioned parts in this comedy, all contribute to the general symphony, the art of all is controlled by the purpose of the play in which they appear.' Later in the book he shows that the form admitted also horrifying tragedy and well-developed pastoral themes. Some of the most interesting sections of Nicoll's study relate to the conventional characters of the *commedia dell' arte*: the four 'masks'—Pantalone, the Doctor, Harlequin, and Scapin, that is, the two old men and their servants—and the various characters, who include Pulcinella (Punch) and Pierrot. He has no difficulty in showing wherein lies the perennial appeal of these figures. Although he disclaims the role of historian, he in effect supplies a history of the *commedia dell' arte* in that he traces

[31] *The World of Harlequin: A Critical Study of the Commedia dell' Arte*, by Allardyce Nicoll. C.U.P. pp. xvi+243. £5.5s.

the various developments which it underwent from its rise in the sixteenth century until it ceased to exist presumably fairly soon after the suppression, in 1780, of the Comédie Italienne. His book is illustrated with 130 excellent reproductions of contemporary prints, drawings, and paintings, many of which have never before been reproduced, and some only very seldom; these have a very special importance as evidence in any study of the *commedia dell' arte*, as also have the scenarios, of which he gives a great many examples. Undoubtedly this volume will long remain the standard English work on its subject.

Four or five years ago Leo Weinstein, in *The Metamorphoses of Don Juan*, traced the origins and the literary development of the Don Juan legend from its first appearance in Tirso de Molina's early seventeenth-century *El Burlador de Sevilla* to versions in the literature of the last few decades (see *YW* xl. 20). Weinstein catalogued nearly 500 versions, representing almost every European and American country; to print all of them would require several massive volumes. In *The Theatre of Don Juan*[32] Oscar Mandel confines himself to a selection of the plays of which Juan has been either the central or an important subsidiary figure, reproducing many of them complete, and printing relevant acts or episodes from the rest. Thus from the seventeenth and eighteenth centuries he gives complete versions, where necessary in translation, of *El Burlador*, Molière's *Dom Juan ou Le Festin de Pierre*, Shadwell's *The Libertine*, Mozart's *Don Giovanni*, and a German puppet play. Later authors whose works are represented, either whole or in part, include Stendhal, Christian Dietrich Grabbe, W. T. Moncrieff, Alfred de Musset, Kierkegaard, Shaw, Edmond Rostand, Salvador de Madariaga, Henry de Montherlant, and Max Frisch. Mandel provides an excellent historical and critical introduction, and informative introductions to the individual plays and extracts; and for good measure he adds also a number of critical essays by authors of many countries and periods. The volume supplies a fascinating study of Don Juan, showing how each age has refashioned the legendary figure according to its own tastes and conventions—sometimes as hero, sometimes as villain, sometimes as gentleman, sometimes as ruffian, sometimes as mere sensualist, sometimes as philosopher; indeed he is legion in his manifestations, and in none of them does he seem capable of being dull.

There are nearly fifty active theatres in the West End of London and the 'Outer Ring'. In *The Theatres of London*[33] Raymond Mander and Joe Mitchenson provide interesting historical and descriptive accounts of these theatres, and notes on the types of production with which they have been associated. Certain theatres have a special interest for the theatre-historian, Covent Garden, for example, or Her Majesty's, or the Haymarket, or Drury Lane, and these naturally provide the fullest entries. The history of Drury Lane is almost, indeed, the history of the London theatre from the Restoration to the end of the eighteenth century, although it shares this century from 1732 with Covent Garden, and from 1720 unofficially, from 1760 officially,

[32] *The Theatre of Don Juan: A Collection of Plays and Views, 1630–1963*, ed. with a commentary by Oscar Mandel. Nebraska U.P. pp. x + 731. $10.

[33] *The Theatres of London*, by Raymond Mander and Joe Mitchenson. Illustrated by Timothy Birdsall. Hart-Davis, 1961. pp. 292. 30s.

with the Haymarket. The authors trace in some detail the history of the four Drury Lane buildings (1663, 1674, 1794, 1812); the first two opened with plays by Beaumont and Fletcher, and the fourth with an address composed by Byron. This theatre is associated with many of the great names of the English theatre—with Betterton, Garrick, Mrs. Siddons, Sheridan, Kemble, Kean, Macready, Irving, and Forbes Robertson, among others; and it is interesting to be reminded that the Adam brothers reconstructed the second theatre in 1775. To their descriptions of the public theatres Mander and Mitchenson add sections giving accounts of the 'Club' theatres, and of a number of theatres, such as the Carlton, the Dominion, and the Lyceum, which have now been turned to other purposes. Timothy Birdsall's sketches, more interesting than photographs, add to the pleasure that this volume will give to all devotees of the theatre.

Although it does not aim at being a work of scholarship, Sir John Gielgud's *Stage Directions*[34] deserves mention here. For most students of English the main interest of this book will probably be found in the short essays on Shakespearian characters that it contains; but Sir John also writes interestingly on productions of plays by Sheridan, Wilde, and Chekhov. However, he is accepted perhaps first and foremost as one of the great Shakespearian actors of our time, and he speaks with authority here on several of the Shakespearian roles he has played—Richard II, Benedick, Leontes, Cassius, Lear, and Hamlet. He has played Hamlet in five productions, spaced out over fifteen years, and although he feels that the part ought to be given to a young man (he himself was twenty-five when he first

took it), his experience has taught him that only an older actor can balance 'the neurotic youthful side of the part' with 'maturer qualities of strength, manliness and wit'. He feels, too, that 'the demands of the character are so tremendous that . . . no actor should be asked to play it more than once or twice a week. For in such a part the player must really live and die before our eyes.' The interest of his vivid reconstruction of rehearsals for *Lear* under the direction of Harley Granville Barker is heightened by the detailed production-notes and letters which he received from Barker, and which he prints in an appendix. Sir John writes modestly and sensitively; what he has as an actor to say about plays must be listened to with respect by scholars whose approach to drama is largely academic.

The purpose and scope of Dale B. J. Randall's book *The Golden Tapestry*[35] are indicated by its subtitle, 'A Critical Survey of Non-chivalric Spanish Fiction in English Translation (1543–1657)', that is, from John Clerc's fumbling version (from the French) of Diego de San Pedro's *Arnalte y Lucenda* to John Davies of Kidwelly's translation, again with the help of a French intermediary, of Quevedo's *Historia de la vida del buscón*. Randall begins with an interesting outline account of the development of interest in Spanish affairs and Spanish language and literature in Tudor England, an interest which was fostered by Henry VIII's marriage to Catherine of Aragon, and which was greatly increased after the defeat of the Great Armada. This interest mani-

[34] *Stage Directions*, by John Gielgud. Heinemann. pp. xiv + 146. 21s.

[35] *The Golden Tapestry: A Critical Survey of Non-chivalric Spanish Fiction in English Translation (1543–1657)*, by Dale B. J. Randall. Duke U.P. and C.U.P. pp. ix + 262. $8.75. 70s.

fested itself in a variety of ways, most interestingly in the translation or adaptation of a great many Spanish books. Part of Randall's thesis is that, at a time when English prose was stylistically immature and uncertain, the translation of works from countries with more firmly established prose traditions had a very beneficial effect on English prose, as may be illustrated from the influence of, say, Lord Berners's *Golden Book* or Sir Thomas North's *Dial of Princes*, both from the Spanish of Guevara, or Bartholomew Young's *Diana*, from Gaspar Gil Polo. Inevitably Randall devotes special attention to such works as Thomas Shelton's *Don Quixote*, or James Mabbes's *Exemplary Novels* (Cervantes), *The Rogue* (Mateo Alemán), and *The Spanish Bawd* (i.e., Fernando de Rojas's *La Celestina*); but he finds room also for fairly detailed discussion of many less well-known translators from the Spanish like Leonard Digges and William Melvin.

Since it is neither a reference work nor in any full sense a history, *The English Bible*,[36] by Donald Coggan, Archbishop of York, is noticed here rather than in the first section of this chapter. As a contribution to the Writers and their Work series, it is necessarily only a brief survey of its subject—English versions of the Scriptures from Caedmon to the publication in 1961 of the New Testament in the *New English Bible* translation, and their influence on the English language, on English literature, and on English life and thought. Within the space at his disposal the Archbishop has had to concentrate on the most significant and influential translations; but he has managed to include some interesting observations on the

personal qualities and the scholarship of many of the translators and their motives for undertaking the work. Select bibliographies list the various versions (including those for which there is no room in the text) and a number of critical studies which will help the student to develop his interest in the subject.

James Sutherland's Clark Lectures for 1956 were published in 1958 under the title *English Satire*; they are now reprinted as a Cambridge paperback.[37] As they were fully noticed when they first appeared (see *YW* xxxix. 27), all that need be said here is that they are a very welcome addition to a series which will bring them within the reach of a wide circle of readers.

Literature as a Mode of Travel,[38] edited with an introduction by Warner G. Rice, contains six essays on English and American travel literature. W. T. Jewkes, whose field is travel books in the Renaissance, begins by questioning whether such books should not be associated rather with the sciences of history and geography than with literature; he concludes, however, that the 'element of strong personal coloring, the stamp of subjectivity', entitles them to be regarded as literature. He goes on to draw parallels between the authentic travel books—the collections of Hakluyt and Purchas and the travel-writings of Mandeville and Raleigh—and the romances of the period, such as *Arcadia*, *The Faerie Queene*, *Euphues*, *Menaphon*, and *Rosalynde*. In 'Travel Literature and the Rise of Neo-Hellenism in England' James M. Osborn's thesis is that the English

---

[36] *The English Bible*, by Donald Coggan, Archbishop of York. (Writers and their Work.) Longmans. pp. 43. 2s. 6d.

[37] *English Satire*, by James Sutherland. (The Clark Lectures, 1956.) C.U.P. pp. ix+ 174. 8s. 6d. $1.45.

[38] *Literature as a Mode of Travel*, ed. by Warner G. Rice. New York Public Library. pp. 119.

cult of Greece falls into clear phases: the 'bookish', neo-classical Hellenism of the late seventeenth century; the systematic description of antiquities which was fashionable through much of the eighteenth century; the romantic Philhellenism which characterizes the late eighteenth and the greater part of the nineteenth centuries; and finally, in the last seven or eight decades, a clear-eyed and objective view of Greece based on scholarship. In 'The Eighteenth-Century Traveler as Representative Man' Paul Fussell, Jr., offers an interesting study of Patrick Brydone, whose *Tour through Sicily and Malta* was published in 1773. Herbert Barrows discusses the experiences of Byron and Shelley in Italy and Greece and their attitudes towards these countries. Franklin R. Rogers's subject is Mark Twain's *Roughing It* as an example of burlesque travel literature. Finally, Philip L. Barbour makes a close study of Captain John Smith's *True Travels, Adventures, and Observations . . .* (1629). Smith's veracity has been called in question from an early time. Barbour decides that the *True Travels* is in the main a factual record, but that it is for the sake of vividness embroidered with a handful of invented or borrowed details.

John Freeman's *Literature and Locality*[39] is an agreeable guide, county by county, of places in Britain and Ireland which have associations with writers. Naturally London and Oxford and Cambridge, the last two of which are treated college by college, are the happiest hunting-grounds for Freeman's purpose, and these, together with a few favoured districts elsewhere, such as the Lake District, have the longest entries; but anyone who is interested in a particular county or locality will enjoy tracing its literary associations. Or if he is interested in, say, Dr. Johnson, or Thomas Fuller, or George Meredith, he can, with the help of the excellent index and the maps, follow him about as he changes his place of residence or pays memorable visits. The book is not as complete as is suggested by Freeman's claim that it is 'the first attempt at a comprehensive and systematic guide to the literary topography of the whole of Britain and Ireland'. Omissions that spring to mind with regard to Essex, for example, are that Gabriel Harvey was born at Saffron Walden and Thomas Tusser at Rivenhall, and that William Harrison was Rector of Radwinter when he wrote his admirable 'Description of England'. However, to include every even reasonably well-known writer would have required a very large volume indeed. The book has no particular academic value, but it would make a good present for anyone who is interested in English literature.

The three volumes of *English Literary Criticism*,[40] an anthology of critical texts issued in the Goldentree paperback series, will be of great value to students of English literature, particularly those who have a special interest in the historical development of English criticism. The first volume, edited by O. B. Hardison, Jr., covers the period between Caxton's Prefaces to *The Canterbury Tales* and to *Morte D'Arthur* (both 1484) and Cowley's Preface to his *Poems* (1656). Critical writings which are printed complete include Gascoigne's *Notes*

[39] *Literature and Locality: The Literary Topography of Britain and Ireland*, by John Freeman. Cassell. pp. xiii+402. 42*s*.

[40] *English Literary Criticism*. Three volumes. *The Renaissance*, ed. by O. B. Hardison, Jr. pp. xi+337. *Restoration and 18th Century*, ed. by Samuel Hynes. pp. ix+322. *Romantic and Victorian*, ed. by Daniel G. Hoffman and Samuel Hynes. pp. xi+322. New York: Appleton-Century-Crofts. (Goldentree Books.) Each vol. $2.95.

of Instruction, Sidney's *Apologie*, and prefaces by Spenser, Chapman, Harington, Whetstone, and Milton; and there are sizable extracts from Wilson, Ascham, Gosson, Puttenham, Heywood, Campion, Daniel, Bacon, Jonson, and others. In all there are twenty-six items, all except the Caxton, which is modernized, reprinted from the Renaissance editions; and, in addition to a prefatory survey, each author is introduced by a short biographical and critical note. The second volume, edited by Samuel Hynes, follows the same procedure, and reproduces about two dozen essays and extracts, from Dryden's *Essay of Dramatic Poesy* (1668) to Johnson's *Lives of the Poets* (1780). The third volume, edited by Daniel G. Hoffman and Samuel Hynes, covers the nineteenth century—from Blake's *Letter to Dr. Trusler* (1799) to Yeats's *The Symbolism of Poetry* (1900); among the works that are printed complete are Wordsworth's 1800 *Preface*, Peacock's *The Four Ages of Poetry*, Shelley's *Defence*, and Henry James's *The Art of Fiction*.

The volume of *English Critical Texts*[41] edited by D. J. Enright and Ernst de Chickera is not nearly as comprehensive a collection as that of the series just noticed, but it too will be found useful by students. Its dozen texts include several that appear in the larger work: Sidney's *Apologie*, Dryden's *Essay of Dramatic Poesy*, Wordsworth's *Preface*, and Shelley's *Defence*; but it adds, among others, Johnson's *Preface to Shakespeare* and four modern essays—D. H. Lawrence's *Why the Novel Matters*, T. S. Eliot's *Tradition and the Individual Talent* and *The Metaphysical Poets*,

and F. R. Leavis's *Keats*. Furthermore, it provides, in translation, a few significant passages from Aristotle's *Poetics*, Horace's *Ars Poetica*, and Longinus's treatise *On the Sublime*. Most of the works included are basic critical texts, and it is handy to have them brought together within a single volume.

Helen C. White's Presidential Address to the Modern Humanities Research Association surveys, under the title *Changing Styles in Literary Studies*,[42] the main trends in English literary criticism in the last four decades. Professor White discusses interestingly many critical works which have exerted a strong influence within this period, and some of which will remain important for some time. However, she questions whether the rapid increase of specialization that has characterized the criticism of recent times has been altogether salutary in its effects. While the young literary student has been furnished with 'valuable tools of analysis and exploration', he has often been allowed, and even led, to use these tools in a narrow way at the expense of a liberal approach to his studies; for 'critical reflection without wide reading can be a very sterile thing and even perverse'.

Theory of Literature,[43] by René Wellek and Austin Warren, was first published in 1949, and a revised edition appeared in 1956. Its third edition is now printed as a Peregrine Book. Apart from some small corrections and additions in the text and an amplified bibliography, this edition is the same as the second, which

---

[41] *English Critical Texts: 16th Century to 20th Century*, ed., with Notes and an Appendix of Classical Extracts, by D. J. Enright and Ernst de Chickera. O.U.P., 1962. pp. xvii+398. 18s.

[42] *Changing Styles in Literary Studies*, by Helen C. White. (Presidential Address of the Modern Humanities Research Association, 1963.) C.U.P. pp. 25. 3s. 6d.

[43] *Theory of Literature*, by René Wellek and Austin Warren. Penguin Books. pp. 375. 12s. 6d.

omitted the final chapter of the original work ('The Study of Literature in the Graduate School').

H. Coombes's *Literature and Criticism*,[44] which was first published in 1953, has been reprinted as a Pelican Book. This work might be described as a guide to practical criticism. Chapter by chapter, Coombes discusses such matters as rhythm, rhyme, imagery, poetic thought, feeling, and diction—in relation to both verse and prose; and at each stage he illustrates his comments with constant reference and analysis, which lend his work concreteness and clarity. To say that one does not always agree with his judgements is not to belittle the value of his book, which could be read with profit by sixth-formers and undergraduates.

5. BIBLIOGRAPHICAL STUDIES

Bibliographical studies relating to individual works are noticed under the relevant authors in other chapters. This section is devoted to works of general interest in the field of bibliography.

Studies in Bibliography[45] opens with a note in which J. C. T. Oates concludes, from a careful consideration of the surviving fragments of Pynson's edition of *The Little Gest of Robin Hood*, that the Lettersnijder edition is a reprint of Pynson's text. In 'The Composition of the Quarto of *Much Ado About Nothing*' John Hazel Smith sets out 'to prove that the *Much Ado* quarto must be added to the growing list of quartos known to have been cast off and composed

by formes'. Allan Pritchard prints and discusses an anonymous letter which was written in reply to George Wither's *The Schollers Purgatory*, and which throws some interesting light on Wither's quarrel with the Company of Stationers. L. A. Beaurline argues persuasively that at least two manuscripts of Suckling's *A Session of the Poets* 'probably stand closer to the author's papers than any of the printed editions, and consequently that a critical editor should base his text of this poem on a manuscript and treat the printed versions in the same way he would the other less authoritative manuscripts'. If Beaurline's reasoning is correct, the approach of editors to other seventeenth-century poets may need some rethinking. Richmond P. Bond gives an interesting account of the relations between the Company of Stationers and John Partridge, the famous astrologer and almanac-maker. Henry Fielding was an exacting critic of his own work, and in 'Fielding's Revisions of *Joseph Andrews*' Martin C. Battestin shows how, by means of constant revision through the first five editions of *Joseph Andrews*, he made significant changes both in the spirit and in the themes of the novel. Esther Rhoads Houghton draws attention to articles contributed by J. H. Newman and his friends to the old Church of England monthly journal *The British Critic*. Robert Scholes reproduces correspondence between Grant Richards and James Joyce relating to the publication by Richards of some of Joyce's early writings, including *Dubliners*. Rollo G. Silver discusses 'Government Printing in Massachusetts, 1751–1801'. In addition to these longer articles, the volume contains the following notes and observations: 'Privilege to Print', by James G. McManaway, a study of the patent granted by King James I

---

[44] *Literature and Criticism*, by H. Coombes. Penguin Books. pp. 160. 3s. 6d.

[45] *Studies in Bibliography: Papers of the Bibliographical Society of the University of Virginia*, ed. by Fredson Bowers. Vol. XVI. Charlottesville, Virginia: Bibliographical Soc. of the Univ. of Virginia. pp. iv+276. Non-members, $10.

to Sir William Woodhouse giving him sole right to print reports of the discussions in the Exchequer; '*The Hospitall of Incurable Fooles*', by William E. Miller, demonstrating that the translator of Garzoni's work was almost certainly not, as has been suggested, Thomas Nashe; an interesting reconsideration of 'The Text of "The Eve of St. Agnes"', by Jack Stillinger; an account, by Roger L. Brooks, of many projects which Matthew Arnold planned between 1846 and 1888, but never carried out; 'A "Mather" of Dates', by William R. Manierre, which relates to correspondence between Cotton Mather and August Hermann Francke; a note, by G. Thomas Tanselle, on an unrecorded early republication of Poe's 'The Raven' in the New York *Weekly News* for 8 February 1845; 'Evidence of Plate Damage as Applied to the First Impression of Ellen Glasgow's *The Wheel of Life* (1906)', by Oliver L. Steele; 'West's Revisions of *Miss Lonelyhearts*', by Carter A. Daniel; and 'A Further Note on the First Printing of *The Great Gatsby*', by Matthew J. Bruccoli. Rudolf Hirsch and Howell J. Heaney contribute a selective checklist of bibliographical scholarship for 1961.

Printing and the Mind of Man[46] is the extremely interesting descriptive catalogue of the impressive exhibitions assembled in 1963 at Earls Court and in the King's Library of the British Museum with the object of presenting 'a survey of the history of printing through five hundred years as one of the most important applied arts of the Western world, thus

demonstrating . . . the printing industry's debt to its historic past and the debt of civilization to typography'. The 660-odd exhibits displayed at Earls Court, and admirably described in the catalogue, range from the smallest tools of the printer's trade (from the fifteenth century onwards) to printing machines of every kind, representing all the processes of printing that have been used from the beginnings to the present day; also included are many specimens of the printer's craft in various stages of preparation. The British Museum exhibition is devoted to the finished product, the printed book, and the 200 examples of the printer's craft and art, also described in some detail, are again so arranged as to offer a clear history of printing from the Gutenberg Bible to an edition of the Gospels printed at Verona in 1962. The catalogue is generously illustrated, and should be of the greatest interest to everybody who is interested in the making of books.

The Cult of the Autograph Letter in England,[47] by A. N. L. Munby, is an important contribution to bibliographical studies. This is a subject on which little systematic work has hitherto been done. Munby covers a period extending approximately from the beginning of the eighteenth century to the First World War; it is to be hoped that he will find time in the not too distant future to write also about the activities of such early collectors as Parker, Cotton, Harley, Sloane, and Carte, to name only a few of the most famous. Information about some of the earlier figures with whom Munby deals in his book is scanty; however, he provides a clear survey of the endeavours, or inten-

[46] *Printing and the Mind of Man*. Catalogue of the Exhibitions at the British Museum and at Earls Court, London, 16–27 July 1963. F. W. Bridges & Sons Ltd. and the Assn. of British Manufacturers of Printers' Machinery (Proprietary) Ltd. Copies from the British Museum. pp. 187+ pp. 55 plates. 10s. 6d.

[47] *The Cult of the Autograph Letter in England*, by A. N. L. Munby. Athlone Press, 1962. pp. viii + 117. 21s.

tions, of eighteenth-century collectors, who include Humfrey Wanley (if indeed he formed a collection), Ralph Thoresby, Elizabeth Elstob, Thomas Tanner, Francis Henry Egerton, 8th Earl of Bridgewater, and John Thane. William Upcott and Dawson Turner demand much more extended treatment, and each is given a detailed chapter to himself. A further chapter is devoted to other notable collections of the nineteenth century, those, for example, of John L. Anderdon, Sir Thomas Phillipps, John Wild, Thomas Raffles, John Forster, and Sir William Tite. The volume closes with a valuable appendix, 'Sources of Information on Autograph Letters'.

Vinton A. Dearing opens his paper, *Methods of Textual Editing*,[48] with an account of modern methods used for the speedy collation of variant readings when a number of texts of an author have to be taken into account. The first method that was both efficient and comparatively rapid was the use of specially prepared cards by J. M. Manly and Edith Rickert in their edition of *The Canterbury Tales* in 1940. Where the relevant texts belong to the same edition of a particular book, like the surviving copies of the First Folio of Shakespeare, Charlton Hinman has been able to speed the work considerably by means of his photographic 'collating-machine'. In the preparation of the California *Dryden* Dearing himself and his colleagues have found their task of collating vastly reduced by the use of an IBM computer, and Dearing gives an extremely interesting account of the various processes that this involves. He goes on to describe the other editorial techniques that must be applied to the production of a modern edition: the collection and comparison of texts, the determination of the copy text, the rationale of emendation and normalization, the form of the textual notes, and things of that kind. Dearing's scholarly (and witty) paper should be of value to anyone who undertakes the task of editing an author of the past.

Two of the admirable Cambridge Authors' and Printers' Guides require notice. The first is G. V. Carey's *Making an Index*,[49] which now appears in a third edition. Anyone who thinks that the making of an index should be an easy and automatic business will almost certainly discover many pitfalls when he himself sets about making one, especially for a large-scale work of scholarship. To give an easy example, should the name de Lesseps be indexed under D or L, De Quincey under D or Q, de la Mare under D or L or M, and La Fontaine under L or F? There are, in fact, strict conventions which govern the placing of such entries, and Carey describes these, and a number of other conventions accepted in printing-houses, in very clear terms. He also gives advice about such matters as cross-referencing, and many hints that will reduce the work of the indexer. This edition, like the second, contains an index which has deliberately been made much more elaborate than is necessary for its purposes in order to illustrate the principles that are laid down in the text.

P. G. Burbidge's *Prelims and End-Pages*[50] is an admirably full and clear account, historical and descriptive,

---

[48] *Methods of Textual Editing*, by Vinton A. Dearing. Univ. of California, Los Angeles: William Andrews Clark Memorial Library. pp. iii + 35.

[49] *Making an Index*, by G. V. Carey. (Cambridge Authors' and Printers' Guides.) C.U.P. pp. 18. 3s. 6d.

[50] *Prelims and End-Pages*, by P. G. Burbidge. (Cambridge Authors' and Printers' Guides.) C.U.P. pp. 30. 3s. 6d.

C

of those parts of a book which precede and follow the text proper. For example, the reason for the half-title, or bastard title, the first printed page of a book containing only the title or a shortened version of the title, may not be generally known, but there is a sound historical and practical reason for its existence. In the early days of printing 'the top leaf of folded sheets which lay about for long periods waiting to be bound was apt to get soiled or damaged. If this leaf happened to be the title-page, the damage would mean shortage in the number of good sheets available for binding. As a protection, therefore, a blank leaf was imposed to cover the title, and then later, to assist identification, a false or bastard title was printed on the blank leaf.' Burbidge describes the conventions relating to all the other kinds of preliminary matter that may be required in a book: frontispiece, title-page, imprints, copyright notice, 'history', dedication, contents, preface, foreword, acknowledgements, introduction, and the rest; and he is equally thorough in his treatment of the end-pages, which contain such things as appendixes, notes, bibliographies, indexes, and the colophon. Throughout his pamphlet he gives examples of correct usage in these matters. Authors who study and observe the conventions here laid down would have the satisfaction of knowing that they are actively helping their printers in the production of their books.

6. ANTHOLOGIES AND COLLECTIONS

The fifth collection of *Poems of Today*,[51] assembled by Margaret Willy, stands up very well to comparison with its predecessors in this excellent

series of English Association anthologies. Its aim is to give some notion both of the diversity and of the accomplishment of poetry written in England between 1947 and the end of 1961. Within her allotted compass of 140 poems Miss Willy has had drastically to restrict the number of poems that she can allow to individual poets; of the eighty-odd poets represented, only W. H. Auden, Walter de la Mare, Robert Graves, and Edwin Muir are allowed as many as four poems, and several have only one. However, the interest and value of an anthology rest chiefly in the quality of the poetry chosen, and, much as the omission of this or that particular poem may be regretted, it would be difficult to find fault here with the choice as a whole. Among the numerous merits of the selection is the great variety of themes and techniques—and of generations— that it embraces. Robert Conquest's 'Guided Missiles Experimental Range' stands side by side with R. S. Thomas's farms and country rectories, and Patricia Beer's Juliet rubs shoulders with Stephen Spender's Judas Iscariot; and almost every imaginable combination of verse-rhythms and rhyme-patterns finds a place. One may compare the methods of the elder statesmen—de la Mare, born in 1873, and Frances Cornford, Edwin Muir, Dame Edith Sitwell, and Sir George Rostrevor Hamilton, all of them born in the 1880's—with those of young poets born in the 1930's, such as Edward Lucie-Smith and Peter Redgrove; one may trace recent developments in the work of the 'poets of the thirties', who are well represented; or one may watch the tireless experimenting with forms and sound-effects of the most recent poets. The anthology offers an endless variety of interest.

Of comparable interest is A. Al-

---

[51] *Poems of Today: Fifth Series*, selected by Margaret Willy. Macmillan, for the English Association. pp. xix+171. 13*s.* 6*d.*

varez's Penguin anthology entitled *The New Poetry*.[52] It covers much the same period of writing as *Poems of Today*, and indeed most of its poets are also represented in that volume— naturally enough, since both collectors have aimed at seeking out what is best in the poetry of very recent times. However, the principle of selection is different. In what he calls 'a personal anthology', Alvarez has deliberately omitted poets with long-standing reputations, and has included only what he thinks is 'the most significant work of the British poets who began to come into their own in the fifties', together with that of two American poets, John Berryman and Robert Lowell, 'who, although established before then, seem . . . to be concerned with problems that some of the new generation of poets over here are beginning to face'. Furthermore, where Miss Willy has spread her net not very wide, Alvarez has confined himself to twenty poets, allowing a minimum of five poems to each, and up to about twenty to such leading figures as Thom Gunn and Ted Hughes. This indeed is the great merit of the collection; it enables us to familiarize ourselves with the work of individual poets as well as with that of a 'period', and in this way it admirably complements Miss Willy's volume. Among the more striking poets included are Philip Larkin, R. S. Thomas, David Holbrook, Charles Tomlinson, Geoffrey Hill, and Peter Redgrove. In his introduction Alvarez gives an interesting survey of recent developments in English poetry, stressing, among other things, the influence of D. H. Lawrence and T. S. Eliot.

Two further Penguin anthologies have appeared during the year. The *Penguin Book of Religious Verse*[53] is introduced and edited by R. S. Thomas. The division into sections entitled 'God', 'Self', 'Nothing', 'It', and 'All' is not as strange as it might at first appear, for Thomas suggests that 'modern sensibility might wish to include more under the title "religious" than traditionalists could accept'. Many of the poems are not religious in the sense in which the word is normally understood, but in the wider sense that they show man brooding upon himself and his destiny. The first section, 'God', is fairly straightforward; it contains largely poems in which God is apostrophized or referred to as one of the Persons of the Holy Trinity—'The Wreck of the Deutschland', Herbert's 'Christmas', Skelton's 'Woefully Arrayed', Addison's 'The spacious firmament', and the like. Under 'Self' come many of the 'brooding' poems —some of Donne's Holy Sonnets, Coleridge's 'Dejection', Yeats's 'Vacillation', Wordsworth's Immortality Ode, passages from Shakespeare, Byron, and Marlowe, Dylan Thomas's 'Fern Hill', and other poems of doubt and question. The section entitled 'Nothing' contains 'terrible' sonnets by Hopkins, John Crowe Ransom's 'Eclogue' ('Jane Sneed began it . . .'), Dunbar's 'Of Man's Mortalitie', and similar poems; the general tone is that of a sense of insufficiency and at times of despair. The other two sections reflect moods predominantly of affirmation and triumphant acceptance. This is an unusual anthology which will commend itself to many readers.

George Macbeth's *Penguin Book of Sick Verse*[54] is a more serious and

[52] *The New Poetry*. An Anthology Selected and Introduced by A. Alvarez. Penguin Books. pp. 191. 5s.

[53] *The Penguin Book of Religious Verse*, introd. and ed. by R. S. Thomas. Penguin Books. pp. 192. 3s. 6d.

[54] *The Penguin Book of Sick Verse*, introd. and ed. by George Macbeth. Penguin Books. pp. 330. 5s.

more interesting anthology than its title might suggest. Little of the verse it contains is 'sick' in the recent acceptation of the word; indeed, the 'sickest' things about the volume are the headings of the various sections ('Mental Breakdown', 'Corpse-Love', 'Cruelty', 'Sick Jokes', and the like) and the end-page advertisements for such books as Muriel Spark's *Memento Mori* and Iris Murdoch's *A Severed Head*. When we examine the sections, we find that 'Visions of Doom', for example, contains such poems as Vaughan's 'The World', Southwell's 'The Burning Babe' and Crashaw's *'Dies Irae, Dies Illa'*; 'Lovesickness' includes Crashaw's 'Upon the Bleeding Crucifix', Wilfred Owen's 'Greater Love', and Keats's 'La Belle Dame'; 'Sick Jokes' includes Robert Graves's 'The Suicide in the Copse', and such ballads as 'Lord Randal' and 'Edward, Edward'; and other section-headings are similarly misleading. The emphasis of the anthology as a whole is on the 'horrid', but no squeamish reader need be deterred from embarking upon it by any apprehension that he will find it unpleasant or in bad taste.

Poetry in Perspective,[55] edited by E. L. and M. K. Flint, is an anthology intended for use in the middle forms of schools. It is a 'critical anthology' in the sense that each poem is accompanied by a critical commentary, and each of the nine periods within which the poems are grouped is introduced by a short background essay. Rightly believing that most school-children are likely to be attracted to poetry first by that which appeals to their own experience, the editors have reversed the usual chronological order, and, beginning with the moderns—Walter de la Mare, Robert

Frost, John Betjeman, Auden, Eliot, Day Lewis, MacNeice, and Dylan Thomas, among others—have travelled backwards through the centuries to *Everyman*, Chaucer, and even *Beowulf*, both in the original and in translation. Their choice of poems is, for the most part, more adventurous than that of most school anthologies; among the Victorians, for example, they have included Coventry Patmore, Mary Coleridge, and A. H. Clough. Both pupils and teachers should find this a stimulating book to work with.

In *An Anthology of Commonwealth Verse*[56] Margaret J. O'Donnell has aimed at bringing together within a single volume the best poetry written in the Commonwealth in the last century and a half. In successive sections she has assembled verse from England, Scotland, Wales, Ireland (can the poetry of Great Britain reasonably be divided in this way?), Canada, Australia, West Africa, India, Pakistan, and a number of other Commonwealth countries. The result, though it is not without interest, is not very impressive, for none of the countries is adequately represented. English poetry from Wordsworth to Ted Hughes and Geoffrey Hill is covered in three dozen poems, although the number rises when we add another fifty or so Scottish, Welsh, and Irish poems, almost all of them, however, belonging to this century. Of the Commonwealth countries Australia has perhaps produced the largest body of good poetry; it is represented by twenty-six poems, each by a different poet. And the choice from other countries is similarly meagre. The idea behind the volume is good, but the performance is unsatisfactory. It

---

[55] *Poetry in Perspective: A Critical Anthology*, ed. by E. L. Flint and M. K. Flint. Univ. of London Press. pp. 192. 9s.

[56] *An Anthology of Commonwealth Verse*, ed. by Margaret J. O'Donnell. Blackie. pp. xxxi+400. 17s. 6d.

is to be hoped that someone will take up the idea again, and, perhaps taking Great Britain for granted, will compile a sizeable anthology which does justice to the poetry of the Commonwealth.

There are two new-comers to the series of volumes of national short stories in the World's Classics. *Scottish Short Stories*[57] is edited and introduced by J. M. Reid. Almost inevitably it opens with Scott's *Wandering Willie's Tale*. Scotland does not seem to have produced many highly-gifted short-story writers in the nineteenth century, which, apart from Scott, is represented by only half a dozen authors (including Stevenson, S. R. Crockett, and Barrie), most of them from the very end of the century. Indeed, the last three decades provide almost as many of the stories in this collection as the century and a half before them. From these three decades come the stories of, among others, Neil M. Gunn, Naomi Mitchison, Eric Linklater, Ian Macpherson, George Scott-Moncrieff, Fred Urquhart, Morley Jamieson, and Dorothy K. Haynes; and it must be admitted that these are on the whole the liveliest contributors. Not that there is anything dull about the collection; it is well balanced in mood, and contains much good reading.

The World's Classics volume of *Australian Short Stories* which was compiled by Walter Murdoch and Henrietta Drake-Brockman and published in 1951 covered nearly a century of writing. A second volume,[58] edited by Brian James, has been added to the series. This covers the years

1930–60, although three-quarters of the twenty-eight contributors were born before the First World War, nine of them, indeed, before the turn of the century. These include that wonderful veteran Norman Lindsay who, born in 1879, never seems to grow old, and his near-contemporaries Katherine Susannah Prichard and Vance Palmer. Obviously writers of such distinction as these three possess could not be left out; nor could some of those of the next generation, like R. S. Porteous, Henrietta Drake-Brockman, and Xavier Herbert. However, it is a pity that the collection could not be extended to include more of the young writers who, as the *Coast to Coast* anthologies have shown, have been writing such admirable short stories in recent years. Perhaps they are being reserved for a third volume.

The Harrap Book of Humorous Prose,[59] edited by Michael Davis, is intended primarily for use in schools; it contains an appendix of 'talking-points', and an essay on humour in which Davis argues that the element common to all forms of true humour is its ability to induce in us a sense of superiority to the objects of our laughter. It is a well-balanced selection which includes almost every type of humour; its fourteen authors include A. P. Herbert, Dylan Thomas, George Orwell, Stephen Leacock, Evelyn Waugh, James Thurber, P. G. Wodehouse, 'Saki', and E. V. Knox. Humorous anthologies have a tendency to fall flat—even the best must be sipped, not gulped; this is one of the better examples of its kind.

Last year attention was drawn to the admirable spoken anthology, *The English Poets: From Chaucer to Yeats*, which is being issued by the

[57] *Scottish Short Stories*, sel. with an Introduction by J. M. Reid. O.U.P. (The World's Classics.) pp. xiii+328. 9s. 6d.

[58] *Australian Short Stories: Second Series*, sel. with an Introduction by Brian James. (The World's Classics.) pp. xvi+362. 8s. 6d.

[59] *The Harrap Book of Humorous Prose*, ed. by Michael Davis. Harrap. pp. 192. 6s. 6d.

Argo Record Company in association with the British Council and the O.U.P. (see *YW* xliii. 26–27). This anthology will eventually extend to more than sixty twelve-inch long-playing records, and will include a number of long poems as well as selections of shorter poems. Each record is accompanied by the complete text of its contents, and these texts will at a later stage be assembled and published in book form by the O.U.P. The records noticed last year contained selections from the poetry of Tennyson, Pope, Byron, Wordsworth (two records), and Browning; six further records are now available.[60] The first of these is *The Rape of the Lock*, which is presented complete. George Rylands and Peggy Ashcroft are the narrators, Margaret Field Hyde reads the part of Ariel, and other voices are supplied by Denis McCarthy, John Nettleton, Joan Hart, Prunella Scales, and Janette Richer. Many listeners will probably feel that Rylands, surprisingly, reads a little mechanically, at times even monotonously; he pays rather more attention to metre and rhyme than to the feel and texture of the couplets, and some of the effect of gauze and silver spangles of which Hazlitt speaks is lost. Nor is Margaret Field Hyde entirely successful in conveying the sheer beauty of Ariel's speeches. However, the other speakers lose nothing either of the wit or of the beauty of the poem, and if the record-

ing as a whole falls short of perfection, it is nevertheless extremely worth-while. The greatness, and attractiveness, of *Don Juan* depend to a large degree on its unpredictability, its sudden and unexpected transitions in subject-matter, tone, and technique; it is very much more than a mere narrative. For the next record the first two cantos of this poem have been abridged in order to provide a continuous narrative of Juan's adventures; the digressions, the reflections, and the incidental satire have been omitted. This is a great pity, but no doubt it was considered necessary in order that a reasonable amount of the story might be fitted into a single record. Once the mutilation is accepted, it is impossible to speak too highly of Richard Johnson's spirited reading, in which he is admirably supported by Peggy Ashcroft as Donna Julia. The only point in which Johnson perhaps fails to do justice to Byron's artistry is his apparently deliberate neglect of the rhyme-scheme; at times he seems rather to be reading passages of racy prose than ottava rima stanzas, except that the final couplets refuse to be entirely submerged. Otherwise both readers bring out to the full the humour, the wit, the innuendo, and the wonderful feeling for situation of the work. The Shelley record is also excellent. Gary Watson reads very movingly some passages from *Adonais*, and Richard Marquand and Patrick Garland are equally good in their extracts from *Prometheus Unbound*. All three give effective readings also of a number of the shorter poems. Chaucer's *Prologue* is read by Nevill Coghill, Norman Davis, and John Burrow. The only deficiency of this generally very fine recording is one which is perhaps inseparable from the nature of the task confronting the readers. In order to give perfect clarity to the

---

[60] The English Poets: From Chaucer to Yeats, recorded by Argo Record Co. Ltd., in association with the British Council and Oxford University Press. Directed by George Rylands. *Alexander Pope*, 'The Rape of the Lock', RG 373. *Lord Byron*, 'Don Juan', Cantos I and II (abridged), RG 374. *Percy Bysshe Shelley*, RG 380. *Geoffrey Chaucer*, 'Prologue to The Canterbury Tales', RG 401. *John Donne*, RG 403. *William Blake*, RG 428. Argo Record Co. Ltd., Each 12-inch record 37s. 6d.

Middle English pronunciation, they are compelled to read rather slowly, and, the variety of voices notwithstanding, before the end is reached the poem has begun to seem a little monotonous; a succession of set character-sketches of this kind probably needs a livelier presentation than has been possible here. However, the individual passages are most beautifully read, and this is a record to be grateful for. Twenty-six poems of Donne are read by Richard Johnson, Peter Orr, and William Squire. Once again Johnson shows how well he can identify himself with the mood of a poem; but indeed all three readers are first-rate, and this is another record that many people will wish to possess. Finally comes William Blake, who is represented by about forty-five poems and extracts, about half of them from *Songs of Innocence* and *Songs of Experience*. The readers are Alan Bates, Yvonne Bonnamy, William Devlin, Richard Johnson, Richard Marquand, and Peter Orr, and the voices have been so carefully balanced as to preclude any of the monotony that might have occurred in a reading of a great many short pieces. Devlin deserves special praise for his effective handling of 'difficult' passages from *Milton*. One of the numerous merits of these records is that the readers do not 'act', except where, as in certain episodes in *Don Juan*, some degree of dramatic interpretation is required; although of course they speak expressively, on the whole they allow the poems to bring out their own effects, and this is as it should be.

Another Argo collection entitled *What Passing Bell*[61] records a number

of poems and passages of prose (including letters) written during or shortly after the First World War. The readers are Jill Balcon, Hugh Burden, Michael Hordern, C. Day Lewis, John Stride, Gary Watson, and Patrick Wymark. The nature of this record is perhaps summed up by a quotation from the sleeve: 'This is not, by intention, merely an anthology of the best prose and poetry of the First World War. It is rather an attempt to use the anthology form in a dramatic way, in order to recreate some of the changing thoughts and attitudes of combatants and non-combatants. And because the anthology is concerned with men's minds as well as with their bodies, it almost inevitably traces the development of a new collective conscientious awareness.' The passages do not in fact trace a development, since they are not presented chronologically; it would have been interesting and helpful to have them dated on the sleeve. Nevertheless they illustrate a great many moods and attitudes that prevailed during the war—from Rupert Brooke's 'Blow out, you bugles, over the rich dead' and Julian Grenfell's 'I adore war . . . it's all the best fun' to Wilfred Owen's 'What passing bell for those who die as cattle?' and Siegfried Sassoon's 'War is a fiend who stopped our clocks'. Private Frank Richards's racy account of the unofficial 'armistice' of Christmas Day, 1914, stands in marked contrast to Field-Marshal Lord Haig's diary account of the same occurrence, the grimness of the anonymous 'The old battalion' to the silliness of Mrs. Jack May's fashion note on 'mourning modes' in the *Queen Magazine*. It is a well-chosen anthology the dominant emphasis of which falls on the horror and futility of war, as it is brought out especially in the writings of those who survived the early slaughter,

---

[61] *What Passing Bell.* A commemoration in poetry and prose of the fiftieth anniversary of the outbreak of the first world war, ed. and produced by Frederick Woods. RG 385. Argo Record Co. Ltd., 37s. 6d.

such as Owen, Sassoon, and Isaac Rosenberg.

7. TRANSLATIONS AND RELATED WORKS

Three further plays of Terence[62] have been published in the little paper-backed volumes of the Library of Liberal Arts series—*The Brothers* (*Adelphoe*), *The Mother-in-Law* (*Hecyra*), and *The Self-Tormentor* (*Heautontimorumenos*). As in his previous versions of Roman comedies, the translator, Frank O. Copley, has aimed rather at reproducing the spirit of the plays than at close verbal fidelity. His translations read quite well, and give the impression that they would also act well.

A welcome new-comer to the Penguin Classics is S. A. Handford's translation of *The Jugurthine War* and *The Conspiracy of Catiline* by Sallust.[63] This is translation at its best, 'scholar-proof', and at the same time in an idiom which is entirely appropriate to the subject-matter. Handford brings out well the vividness and the dramatic quality of Sallust's writing, but avoids his abruptness and his occasional affectations. He provides also a biographical account of Sallust, and excellent historical introductions to the two works he has translated.

For his translation of Virgil's *Eclogues*[64] C. Day Lewis uses the metre that he employed so effectively in his versions of the *Aeneid* and the *Georgics*, a loose six-stressed line without rhyme from which he departs only in the singing-matches and the songs; these he renders in the metrical patterns of certain English and Irish folk songs, such as 'Boolavogue' and 'The Lark in the Clear Air', for, he says, 'I like songs to have tunes.' Lewis's six-stressed line, while it seemed appropriate to his *Aeneid* and *Georgics*, misses some of the grace that Virgil imparts to his hexameters in the *Eclogues*; this is perhaps especially noticeable in the second and tenth eclogues. However, he captures extremely well the spirit of the individual poems, and the translation as a whole is one of the most satisfying renderings of Virgil that have appeared in recent times.

Horace on Poetry,[65] by C. O. Brink, is a thoroughgoing study of the *Ars Poetica*, with sections also on the shorter literary epistles, such as the *Epistle to Julius Florus* and the *Epistle to Augustus*. Brink is interested in the *Ars Poetica* both as a work of criticism and as a poem. He meets the attacks on its structure with a persuasive argument that the alleged disorder is in fact part of a plan; informal and discursive as the work is, it is carefully organized round a threefold scheme, preceded by a short introduction. Brink goes on to discuss Horace's debt to earlier critics, especially Neoptolemus of Parium and Aristotle, and shows how far Horace merely followed tradition, and how far he struck out for himself. After an examination of the other literary epistles and of the literary judgements expressed in the satires, Brink, in an extremely interesting chapter, analyses Horace's critical principles and sums up his achievement in

---

[2] Terence. '*The Brothers*'. '*The Mother-in-Law*'. '*The Self-Tormentor*', translated, with introductions, by Frank O. Copley. (The Library of Liberal Arts.) New York: Bobbs-Merrill. pp. viii+59; viii+46; ix+59. 50c; 50c; 65c.

[63] Sallust. '*The Jugurthine War*' and '*The Conspiracy of Catiline*', translated with an Introduction by S. A. Handford. Penguin Books. pp. 240. 4s.

[64] *The Eclogues of Virgil*, translated by C. Day Lewis. Cape. pp. 46. 16s.

[65] *Horace on Poetry: Prolegomena to the Literary Epistles*, by C. O. Brink. C.U.P. pp. xi+300. 45s.

this field. He ends with a consideration of the *Ars Poetica* from the point of view of its considerable poetic merits. This book will be of value to all students of literary theory, especially perhaps that of the Renaissance period, when the influence of Horace was particularly strong.

A volume of Paul Turner's excellent translations from Lucian was noticed a couple of years ago (*YW* xlii. 31). He has now republished his version of *The True History* together with a new translation of *Lucius or the Ass*,[66] which is sufficiently in the manner of Lucian to make it not unlikely that he wrote it. Although Lucian was something of a purist in style, Turner has rightly chosen to translate him in a racy and at times colloquial idiom, and occasionally even to alter him slightly in order to bring out, for example, the force of a pun, or to indicate a locality by its modern name. He has certainly succeeded extremely well in communicating Lucian's impudent humour and the 'mad fertility' of his invention, as well as his highly competent narrative technique. Of the two works *The True History*, so called because there is not a word of truth in it, is of the greater interest to readers of English literature for its influence on, among others, More and Swift, both of whom learned from it something of their method in recounting travels to strange lands, and both of whom owe much also to Lucian in their handling of irony and satire. *Lucius or the Ass* is delightfully funny, and is interesting also for a quality which is very rare in ancient literature, that is, a vein of sympathy for animal-life.

Since the discovery of the first of the Dead Sea Scrolls in 1947 quite a considerable literature has grown up round them, but their texts have not been available in English, and English readers have had to be content with merely reading about them. Such of them as have been published—some are too fragmentary for publication, or have not yet been published for other reasons—have now been translated by G. Vermes.[67] They consist largely of sets of rules for the guidance of the community by which they were originally produced, of hymns, many of them very similar to the Psalms, of liturgical fragments, and of Biblical commentaries, and they are of considerable interest even to the layman. Vermes provides a valuable long introduction in which he describes the community itself, its institutions and administration, its religious beliefs and practices, and many of the persons and events associated with it; and he also discusses problems relating to the decipherment and interpretation of the scrolls. The volume will be generally welcomed.

St. Augustine's *City of God* was first Englished by John Healey, whose version, published in 1610, is still very readable. The best-known modern version is probably R. V. G. Tasker's revision and modernization of Healey which appeared as two fairly stout Everyman volumes in 1945. However, the complete work is very long, and rather daunting for the average modern reader, and the Right Revd. J. W. C. Wand has performed a useful service in drastically abridging it and retranslating it in the language of today.[68] He has omitted nothing that could be considered of particular historical or devotional interest, and by preserving intact all the original chapter-headings he has made it

---

[66] Lucian. '*True History*' and '*Lucius or the Ass*', translated from the Greek by Paul Turner. John Calder. pp. xi+108. **10s. 6d.**

[67] *The Dead Sea Scrolls in English*, by G. Vermes. Penguin Books. pp. 255. **4s. 6d.**

[68] *St. Augustine's 'City of God'*, abridged and translated by J. W. C. Wand. O.U.P. pp. xxiv+428. **21s.**

possible for the reader to fill in at least in outline the content of the missing passages. The translation is easy, natural, and fluent, and it is to be hoped that it will draw many readers to the study of St. Augustine.

Apart from J. R. Hale's version, which was noticed in *YW* two years ago (xlii. 32), Machiavelli's comedy of manners, *Clizia*, appears not to have been previously translated into English, at any rate not in recent times, and it is therefore almost unknown in English-speaking countries. It now appears in a new translation by Oliver Evans.[69] It is a witty and rather bawdy comedy, and in Evans's lively translation it would probably revive very well, as did Machiavelli's other comedy of manners, *Mandragola*. In an interesting short introduction Evans relates *Clizia* to the tradition of comedy of manners, and in particular to its source, Plautus's *Casina*, to which, like Hale, he considers it to be in some respects superior.

Racine is often described as 'untranslatable', and indeed he must be one of the most difficult of authors to turn into English. Almost certainly prose will not do, and the majority of English translators have, with varying success, turned to blank verse. This is what John Cairncross has done for his renderings of *Iphigenia*, *Phaedra* and *Athaliah*.[70] It is a brave attempt, and compares well with other English translations, but it is not quite Racine, and, among other things, smacks rather of the study than of the stage. In French Racine transcends the con-

ventions within which he is writing; is it possible that in an English dress he will never go down well with audiences or readers? These reflections are prompted not so much by Cairncross's occasional archaisms and awkwardnesses—'With his new rank does he misprize his Queen?', 'I see you at this outrage blush', and the like —as by the general tenor of his translations. It must be added, however, that he provides an interesting biographical and critical account of Racine, and excellent introductions to the individual plays.

Edmond Cary's interesting little book *Les grands traducteurs français*[71] combines discussion with copious illustration. It is a study of the great French translators, from Étienne Dolet in the early sixteenth century and his slightly younger but much more long-lived contemporary Jacques Amyot down to Valery Larbaud, the translator of Butler's *Erewhon* and Joyce's *Ulysses*. Cary's methods may be exemplified from his treatment of a few of his translators. He devotes about a dozen pages to a consideration of Amyot's qualities as a translator, and then illustrates them by means of parallel passages of Plutarch, of Amyot's version, and of the version of B. Latzarus. For the translators of Homer he sets side by side some passages from the *Iliad* and the French versions of the passages by Paul Mazon, Mme. Dacier, Houdar de la Motte, Leconte de Lisle, E. Littré, and Charles Georgin. And he follows the same procedure with translators of Goethe's *Faust*, *The Thousand and One Nights*, and a variety of other works. This combined presentation of theory and practice gives the work a special interest and value.

[69] *Niccolo Machiavelli. 'Clizia'*. Introduction and translation by Oliver Evans. Great Neck, N.Y.: Barron's Educational Series. pp. v+85. $1.25.

[70] *Jean Racine. 'Iphigenia'*, *'Phaedra'*, *'Athaliah'*, translated and introduced by John Cairncross. Penguin Books. pp. 317. 6s.

[71] *Les grands traducteurs français*, par Edmond Cary. Geneva: Georg & Cie. pp. 132. Fr. 8.

R. Farquharson Sharp's translations of Ibsen have long been well known, and several of them, including the three under notice, *Ghosts*, *The Warriors at Helgeland*, and *An Enemy of the People*,[72] have been published in Everyman's Library. These three have now been issued in an Everyman Paperback, and will therefore be more easily within the compass of slender purses than before.

Small collections of Strindberg's plays have appeared in England from time to time. Elizabeth Sprigge has now translated and published a dozen plays,[73] a small proportion of the fifty-odd that he wrote, but enough perhaps to give some indication of his quality and range—hitherto he has been known in this country by little more than *The Father* and *Miss Julie*. These two plays of course appear in Miss Sprigge's volume; she includes

also the ironical and cynical *Creditors*, the curious little monologue *The Stronger*, some short plays which reflect the horror and futility of Strindberg's life, such as *The Bond*, the nightmarish *The Dance of Death*, *The Ghost Sonata*, and plays which represent other aspects of Strindberg's strange and warped genius. Strindberg is not to everyone's taste, but if he is to be acted in English, Miss Sprigge's versions are probably the best and the most actable that have appeared.

Finally, mention should be made of Donald Watson's translations of three of Ionesco's plays—*The Chairs*, *The Killer*, and *Maid to Marry*.[74] Watson appears to do justice to Ionesco's oddities, but probably the full effect of the plays can be brought out only on the stage. Even in the theatre, however, it is impossible to feel that Ionesco is so very great a playwright as he is often claimed to be.

[72] *Henrik Ibsen.* '*Ghosts*', '*The Warriors at Helgeland*', '*An Enemy of the People*', translated by R. Farquharson Sharp. Dent. (Everyman Paperback.) pp. xi+247. 4s.

[73] *Twelve Plays by August Strindberg*, translated from the Swedish by Elizabeth Sprigge. Constable. pp. xiv+689. 45s.

[74] *Eugène Ionesco. Three Plays:* '*The Chairs*'. '*The Killer*', '*Maid to Marry*', translated by Donald Watson. John Calder. (Jupiter Books.)pp. 189. 6s. 6d.

II

English Language

R. M. WILSON

A HISTORY of linguistic scholarship by J. T. Waterman[1] is particularly useful for its final chapter on the twentieth century, since it deals with the rise of structuralism and the work of Saussure, Troubetzkoy, Hjelmslev, Bloomfield, and others. The earlier part necessarily covers much the same ground as Pedersen's *Linguistic Science in the Nineteenth Century*, but there are revaluations of the work of some of the great scholars, notably Grimm, and modern structural linguistics is shown to be largely an extension and refinement of ideas that found their first expression in the works of nineteenth-century scholars.

M. Girsdansky,[2] in his general introduction to language, writes with enthusiasm and knowledge. He defines language, shows how ideas may be expressed in different ways in the various languages, discusses the different levels of language, semantic change, and the phonetic basis of language. The Indo-European languages are described, along with some of the other important languages of the world, and their particular characteristics indicated. A brief history of English includes some account of its merits and defects as an international language, while the final chapter gives an idea of the influence of communication theory on present-day concepts of language. The numerous examples are illuminating and instructive, and the book covers the ground well without evading difficulties, but the purple passages do not always come off, the humour is sometimes forced, and the proof reading has not been adequate. Grace Andrus de Laguna,[3] on the other hand, is essentially concerned with the social function of speech. It is compared in this respect with the animal cry, and a tentative theory is offered of the development of one from the other. Various aspects of the mental evolution of speech are discussed, while the remainder of the book deals with speech in the life of the individual, and in particular with its relation to the higher forms of intellectual life.

Ruth Hirsch Weir[4] analyses the monologues of a $2\frac{1}{2}$ year old child, lying in his cot and talking to himself. Phonology and grammar are dealt with in turn, and since the paragraph would appear to be the largest linguistic unit of discourse, this also is treated. In every case the linguistic structure is described with reference to what has been learned, to what is being learned, and to what is still absent in comparison with standard English. The result is a notable con-

[1] *Perspectives in Linguistics*, by J. T. Waterman. Chicago U.P. pp. 105. 30s.

[2] *The Adventure of Language*, by M. Girsdansky. Allen & Unwin. pp. xvi+347. 25s.

[3] *Speech: Its Function and Development*, by Grace Andrus de Laguna. Indiana U.P. pp. xii+363. $6.50.

[4] *Language in the Crib*, by Ruth Hirsch Weir. The Hague: Mouton & Co. pp. 216. 32 guilders.

tribution to a better understanding of linguistic development in children, while the presence or absence of certain elements in the language of a child may also give a clue to the identification of linguistic universals. In 'The Ontogeny of English Phrase Structure: The First Phase' (L) M. D. S. Braine examines the structural characteristics of the first word combinations uttered by three children from about the age of 18 months. Syntactically, it would seem that during the first four months the child learns the positions of pivot words, i.e. that each of a small number of words belongs in a particular position in an utterance. The word combinations that are uttered have a characteristic structure containing two parts of speech: the small number of words whose position has been learned, and the entire vocabulary except for some of the pivots. During the first phase the language grows structurally by the formation of new pivot words, and in vocabulary by additions to the other class. M. M. Lewis[5] describes systematically the growth of language from infancy through early to later childhood, making use of his own detailed observations as well as of other work on the subject. Of particular interest is the evidence derived from the study of children whose development has been retarded, since this is of importance in remedial work, and also in widening our knowledge of the linguistic development of normal children.

Language Standardization[6] is a fascinating collection of essays on an important subject. As Ray points out, standard languages are as much necessities as standard weights and measures, and a standard language is merely a preferred dialect among many, and one which has achieved its position by chance and not because of any superior efficiency or intrinsic merit. The first part is concerned with questions of linguistic efficiency, rationality, and policy, while in the second the most interesting and original chapters deal with the Roman numerals, and with the proposals for a uniform script for India. For the former Ray presents a scientific comparison between the two systems, and for the latter shows convincingly that a Roman script is the only possible choice. Other problems are discussed more briefly, while a final chapter deals with the value of a language and the formation of prose. At the present day, this is a particularly important book, more especially since it deals with problems which the descriptive linguist tends to ignore.

A general survey of modern structural linguistics by B. Malmberg[7] examines Saussure's theory of language, its influence on later linguists, and the developments from it. This is followed by a general theoretical description of the 'communication' process, a discussion of information theory, and an acoustico-phonetic analysis of the speech wave. Other chapters deal with the analysis of linguistic forms, the question of what is relevant in sound features, the concept of distinctive features, content analysis, the functions of language, and linguistic change. The book is essentially intended for the advanced student, but others will also find it useful, since the author manages to deal lucidly and intelligibly with a

[5] *Language, Thought and Personality in Infancy and Childhood*, by M. M. Lewis. Harrap. pp. 256. 18s.

[6] *Language Standardization*, by P. S. Ray. The Hague: Mouton & Co. pp. 159. 16 guilders.

[7] *Structural Linguistics and Human Communication*, by B. Malmberg. Heidelberg: Springer. pp. vii + 210. $9.75.

difficult subject. In 'Transformational Grammar: Form and Theory. A Contribution to the History of Linguistics' (*Lingua*) W. O. Dingwall presents a review of the formal and theoretical development of the transformational approach to the study of language. Unfortunately, only those already familiar with the theory are likely to get much benefit from the survey. Similarly, *Discourse Analysis Reprints*[8] makes no concessions to the reader. It first presents the theory, and then shows two stages of analysis of a scientific article; in the first the sentences are transformed to a 'normal' form, and in the second this is reduced to a summary. An appendix presents an earlier method of carrying out the analysis. E. M. Uhlenbeck, 'An Appraisal of Transformation Theory' (*Lingua*), objects that Chomsky tends to regard language as a self-contained system, and does not pay enough attention to the extralinguistic data which play such a crucial role in the interpretation of speech-utterance. This prevents him from getting the phenomena of ambiguity in a clear perspective, and this again leads him to posit distinctions foreign to the linguistic material. Moreover, he makes no attempt to analyse the semantic factors of language—although he recognizes the necessity for this—and he has adopted the traditional way of parsing without seeing clearly the basic shortcomings of this approach. In 'Generative Grammars without Transformation Rules: A Defense of Phrase Structure' (*L*) G. H. Harman argues that if Chomsky's definition of phrase-structure grammar is modified slightly, objections against it can be met; in that case there would be no need to introduce transformational rules into

<hr/>

[8] *Discourse Analysis Reprints*, by Z. S. Harris. The Hague: Mouton & Co. pp. 73. 10 guilders.

generative grammars of natural languages, and he suggests the necessary modifications of Chomsky's theory. C. J. Fillmore, 'The Position of Embedding Transformations in a Grammar' (*Word*), deals with the generative grammar which makes use of two types of transformational rules: the simple transformations which may be thought of pre-systematically as converting a sentence from one type to another; and the generalized transformations which combine two sentences to form a third. So far the position of the two types has been left unspecified, and Fillmore propounds a general solution to the problem of indicating the possible ways in which the result of a particular generalized transformation may be channelled back to a specific position in the sequence of simple transformations. P. Lackowski, 'Words as Grammatical Primes' (*L*), takes the general assumption that it is possible to write a generative grammar while adhering to three methodological restrictions: that neither semantics nor statistics enter into either the statement or the evaluation criteria of the grammar; that the grammar be finite; and that the grammar generate strings of morphemes. He attempts to show that it is not possible to write a grammar while keeping to these restrictions, and advances arguments in favour of eliminating the last. In ' "Meaning" and the Theory of the Morpheme' (*Lingua*) R. Fowler points out that in descriptive linguistics 'meaning' has entered the field of morphemics and morphology, both in 'definitions', and as a convenient but undesirable means to analysis. This brings with it various difficulties, but if lexis is rigidly separated from grammar, it would be easy to provide a theory of the morpheme and a practical morphemics which works with greater simplicity and consistency than the traditional morphemics. D. L. Bolinger, 'The Uniqueness of the Word' (*Lingua*), concludes that the word is the source not the result of phonemic contrasts, and that, despite attempts by linguists to show that words have no meaning, it is precisely the relative fixity of word meaning that makes it a viable unit of communication. Since linguistics is now often looked upon as a science, R. M. W. Dixon[9] first considers what is meant by 'science' in such a context, and compares it with other sciences. An examination of the interrelations between logic and linguistics is mainly devoted to the Chomsky school, and an investigation is made of the extent to which logical methods can be employed in linguistics. A paperback reprint of J. H. Greenberg's *Essays in Linguistics*[10] is now available. It contains eight essays on general linguistic subjects, the first two being concerned with the methodology of language description, the next two with historical linguistics, and the remainder with the relations between language and culture. In addition, E. R. Gammon, 'On Representing Syntactic Structure' (*L*), discusses some diagrammatic representations of it, and R. M. W. Dixon produces 'A Logical Statement of Grammatical Theory as Contained in Halliday's "Categories of the Theory of Grammar"' (*L*).

R. D. Stevick, 'The Biological Model and Historical Linguistics' (*L*), agrees that modern resistance to past analogies between historical linguistics and biology has been justified, but urges that the scientific model of organic evolution should now be given careful attention. Since linguistic change, like historical change, occurs as modification in persisting systems through selection combined with chance variation and the attendant factor of isolation, the whole conditioned by population structure, then linguistic and biological histories are closely similar particular examples of the general evolutionary model. In 'Lexicostatistics and Genetic Relationship' (*L*) K. V. Teeter examines some conclusions about the nature of linguistic change and genetic relationship implied in recent work, and concludes that lexical similarities are the only place at which to start, and preliminary hypotheses are based implicitly on the assumption that lexical and grammatical similarity are congruent. Since lexicostatistics provides no way of going beyond lexical similarity, it can be no more than a first step in studying genetic relationship, and its proper use is in the study of lexical and cultural change.

The main object of *The Meaning of Proper Names*[11] is the setting up of a meaning formula for them, and the introductory chapter therefore contains a brief account of the meaning of signs. The six following chapters examine various theories of proper names, and it would seem that the old Port-Royal theory that proper names are individual names 'has not been found untenable'. This is further elaborated, and made to lead up to a strictly linguistic formulation which applies only to English and to other structurally related languages, and may not be applicable to languages which have no article. The book is intended essentially for specialists,

[9] *Linguistic Science and Logic*, by R. M. W. Dixon. The Hague: Mouton & Co. pp. 108. 10 guilders.

[10] *Essays in Linguistics*, by J. H. Greenberg. Chicago U.P. pp. vii + 108. 8*s*. 6*d*.

[11] *The Meaning of Proper Names*, by H. S. Sørensen. Copenhagen: Gad. pp. 117. Kr. 21.50.

and is difficult though ultimately rewarding reading. B. Trnka, 'On the Problem of Proper Names' (*Philologica Pragensia*), discusses some previous theories, and suggests that the problem can be approached from the angle of structural linguistics. The proper name *Smith* and the common name *smith* are terms of the semantic opposition the mark of which consists in the use of the word for the purpose of pure and immediate identification. The proper name is a marked term of the opposition, the common name an unmarked one.

L. Hogben's *Essential World English*[12] derives in the main from Basic English, but in place of Ogden's 850-word list offers 1,300 items of what are called Essential Semantic Units. Each of these comprises a semantically unique word, together with information on its usage and on what arbitrary particles may accompany it. The need for an auxiliary language is stressed, and advice given on difficulties in spelling and grammar, along with various glossaries of essential world English equivalents for standard English terms.

M. W. Bloomfield and L. Newmark[13] introduce the student to sophisticated linguistic attitudes towards English by applying some of the new methods to the history of the language at various periods. Thus, a chapter on the phonemics and phonology of English describes one way of approaching language; an account of the comparative method shows how a family of languages is established; Old English morphology demonstrates one set of terms by which the grammatical structure of a language can be analysed; and the concept of dialect is illustrated by a study of the Middle English ones. Similarly, an exposition of Elizabethan English shows the principles used to describe the syntax of a language and gives a particularly clear presentation of the methods of generative grammar. The book thus gives a series of studies of English from selected perspectives; it is not intended as a complete history of the language, though in fact it can be used as such since excellent and up-to-date references in footnotes provide guides to those parts either omitted or passed over briefly. The method leads to a certain amount of repetition, but does give a good idea of the methods of modern linguistics by authors who can appreciate their value, and at the same time are not slow to criticise the exaggerated claims that have been made for them.

J. L. Sanderson and W. K. Gordon[14] reprint a series of articles and extracts from standard works on language dealing with many aspects of the subject, ranging from the origin of language to the doctrine of correctness, and including slang, the structure of English, dialects, semantics, and logic. Each selection is preceded by a brief introduction and followed by exercises and suggested essay subjects. A similar collection, now in a revised and enlarged edition, is that by L. F. Dean and K. G. Wilson.[15] In both cases some passages come from easily accessible books, side by side with others from

---

[12] *Essential World English*, by L. Hogben. Joseph. pp. 443. 35s.

[13] *A Linguistic Introduction to the History of English*, by M. W. Bloomfield and L. Newmark. New York: Knopf. pp. xvii+375. $8.95.

[14] *Exposition and the English Language*, by J. L. Sanderson and W. K. Gordon. New York: Appleton-Century-Crofts. pp. x+459. $3.95.

[15] *Essays on Language and Usage*, by L. F. Dean and K. G. Wilson. O.U.P. pp. viii+409. 26s.

books and articles less well known, and in general give a good idea of what language is about, and of the changes taking place in the subject today.

R. A. Peters lists the occurrences of the eleven words containing the elements 'Œ Ælf, -ælf, Ælfen, -ælfen' (*PQ*), and describes their phonology, etymology, and meaning. It would appear that *ælf* m. should be specifically described as 'malign or disease spirit' in contrast to the more gentle feminine counterparts, and a summary classification is given of the words according to their paradigms. In his examination of the 'Word Order of Noun Modifiers in Old English Prose' (*JEGP*) G. Carlton concludes that word order is a syntactic feature of noun modification in Old English, though it allowed some structures that are not used in modern English. There are six order classes for noun modifiers according to their position of occurrence before the noun, and the reverse order holds when the modifiers follow the noun.

G. K. W. Johnston has made an excellent translation of the fifth edition of Brunner's *Abriss der mittelenglischen Grammatik*[16] which shows only slight changes of presentation and notation from the German version. Brunner's work was easily the best introduction to the subject for students, and it is particularly useful to have this translation available.

A. McIntosh, in 'A New Approach to Middle English Dialectology' (*ES*), criticizes previous studies, especially by Moore, Meech, and Whitehall. Their weakness lies more in the methods of approach and in the absence of any ordered theoretical basis for these methods, than in the limitations of the material itself. Previous scholars have been unwilling to look at written texts without seeing them simply as a sort of encoded form of some variety of Middle English, whereas the proper way is to record the graphemic forms as such and to contrast them irrespective of their phonemic value. In this way a fuller use can be made of the literary material, and dialectally homogeneous texts, irrespective of their textual history, can provide useful material on Middle English dialects. But such material can only be used if we are fairly sure of our hypothesis about provenance, though every time we are fairly sure we gain new knowledge about the geographical distribution of dialectal features which, in turn, facilitates the task of further localizations. M. L. Samuels, 'Some Applications of Middle English Dialectology' (*ES*), attempts to forecast some of the questions that the survey envisaged by McIntosh will be competent to answer. It is the functional and systematic aspects of linguistic change that are most clearly illustrated, and this is exemplified by showing the spread of *they* and *though* forms. Moreover, the survey provides us with a frame of reference for isolating and classifying the less obviously dialectal types of language, and so throws light on the probable source of the written standard English that appears in the fifteenth century. J. C. McLaughlin[17] makes a graphemic-phonemic study of MS. Cotton Nero A x with the aim of presenting a

---

[16] *An Outline of Middle English Grammar*, by K. Brunner, translated by G. K. W. Johnston. Oxford: Blackwell. pp. vi+111. 15*s*.

[17] *A Graphemic-Phonemic Study of a Middle English Manuscript*, by J. C. McLaughlin. The Hague: Mouton & Co. pp. 162. 18 guilders.

D

complete description of the writing system employed in it, and of reconstructing a phonemic system of that language based on all the available evidence. In a general discussion of graphemic theory, he uses the term to denote both the identification of graphemes as distinct entities in an independent structure, and the description of the relationship which holds between the graphemes and the phonemes. It is argued that one of the most interesting features of an alphabetic writing is that, as a system of signs, it provides the basis for assumptions about the structure of the spoken system when that system is no longer available for direct observation, though precisely how one 'discovers' the phonological structure underlying a historical document is not too clear. The purpose of a graphemic analysis is to establish the written idiolect of a text, and this, when correlated with similar studies of other texts of approximately the same date, will enable the analyst to define the written dialect of a set of texts in terms of their common core and overall pattern. Consequently, a careful examination of the orthography of the manuscript is followed by chapters on the phonological significance, and a summary of the proposed graphonemic system. The value of such a survey must at present remain hypothetical, though McLaughlin certainly succeeds in providing a more accurate and detailed definition of a written dialect than has previously been presented for any Middle English text. B. Sundby[18] investigates the Middle English material found in official documents relating to Worcestershire. An intro-

ductory chapter deals with methods and sources, and then the vowels, diphthongs and consonants are taken in turn, with illustrative forms showing the developments, and followed by a discussion of the results. Various problems are considered: the loss or retention of final -*n* in weak positions; ME *lese*, *mede* as compared with *lesewe*, *medewe*; the Scandinavian element, &c. The data suggest a linguistic division between North and South Worcestershire, but by the mid-fourteenth century the two dialects have apparently fallen together, and later points of difference concern the incidence of phonemes and perhaps certain sections in grammar and phonology. The book contains a mass of material, well organized and analysed, which will be of the utmost value to all concerned with Middle or Modern English dialect studies.

Two further parts of the *Middle English Dictionary*[19] are open to much the same criticisms as before. The separation of the different senses of a word is sometimes questionable, as in the case of *gaderinge* 3(b) and (c), or the meaning given for *glodez* in *Sir Gawain* 2,181 as compared with that for *glode* in 2,266. The ascription of the quotations assembled under *God* and *god* is sometimes doubtful, e.g. *godisped*, *godelef*, *godwit* should presumably be under *God*. It is difficult to see how the meaning of *gaggen* (b) can be present in names; *galter*, appearing only as a surname, may well be for *Walter*; *garge*, with a single quotation, is an obvious mistake for *charge*; *gennowmbre* is presumably for *gouernowre*; in *gimber* it may be significant that, apart from the surnames, the spelling is always

---

[18] *Studies in the Middle English Dialect of Worcestershire Records*, by B. Sundby. Oslo: Norwegian Universities Press. pp. viii+280. Kr. 48.

[19] *Middle English Dictionary: Parts G 1, 2*, by S. M. Kuhn and J. Reidy. Michigan U.P. pp. 1–128, 129–256. $3 each part.

with medial *b*; *glaser* v. is presumably for *glasen* or *glaseren*; and *glinder* is rather 'one who makes' than 'one who lives by'. B. D. H. Miller makes a detailed examination of ' "Word in Hand": A Problem in "Dame Sirith" ' (*NQ*), and decides that the phrase should be rendered 'with your word in my hand, i.e. with your pledged word'. In 'Three Lexicographic Notes' (*EPS*) A. S. C. Ross gives a number of obscure and doubtful words found in the records of the Grocers' Company between 1345 and 1463, and notes an early occurrence of *kerbing* (1436) in the same records. A. D. Mills, 'Some Middle English Occupational Terms' (*NQ*), lists, with illustration and comment, over eighty such terms, most of which have not previously been recorded.

Johnson's Dictionary is one of those important books better known from the title than from the contents. A good selection[20] from the first edition includes the *Preface*, examples of his well-known biased definitions, others which illustrate Johnson's opinions on usage, literature, and science, some words in which a change of meaning has taken place, and the whole of the entries for Z. The introduction describes Johnson's methods of compilation, the characteristics of his dictionary and its particular excellencies for its time, while other necessary information is added in footnotes. N. E. Osselton, 'Formal and Informal Spelling in the 18th Century: *Errour, Honor*, and Related Words' (*ES*), deals with the present conventions for the spelling of such words, which are usually ascribed to the influence of Johnson. In his private correspondence Johnson has a marked preference for *-our*, but when it came to opting for one or the other in the *Dictionary*, he often chose a spelling in conflict with his own preferred practice. In such cases his choice was determined by the printers' usage of forty years before. Where Johnson's recommendations differ from the established practice of the current printers, they have apparently had little effect on later usage.

E. Partridge's *The Gentle Art of Lexicography*[21] is partly autobiographical, describing his early years and upbringing in New Zealand, and the development of his lexicographical interests. Its particular interest here is that it gives an excellent description of the problems and methods of lexicography, and from this point of view is all too short. The *Dictionary of Modern Pronunciation*[22] contains some 9,000 words likely to give difficulty, along with 306 categories dealing with prefixes, suffixes, combinations of letters, and letters pronounced differently in different words, most of the single-word entries containing cross-references to one or more of the categories. The aim of the dictionary is to record those pronunciations used today by most educated speakers in the States, though when there is a difference the British pronunciation is also given. Definitions appear only when a change in meaning causes a change in pronunciation, and the accented syllable is capitalized. A conventional spelling, clearly explained, is used to indicate the pronunciation; it works adequately enough, and within its self-imposed limitations the dictionary

---

[21] *The Gentle Art of Lexicography*, by E. Partridge. Deutsch. pp. 119. 17*s*. 6*d*.

[20] *Johnson's 'Dictionary': A Modern Selection*, by E. L. McAdam, Jr. and G. Milne. Gollancz. pp. xiv+465. 30*s*.

[22] *Dictionary of Modern Pronunciation*, by N. Lewis. New York: Harper & Row. pp. 309. $4.95.

does its work well. T. Ulving[23] gives a useful list of over 3,000 initial abbreviations of periodicals in philology and related subjects, including also some institutions, societies, dictionaries, and text editions. Whenever possible the place of publication is given, and abbreviations of publications written in other than the Latin alphabet are transcribed according to the system used in Swedish scientific libraries.

A. McIntosh, 'Language and Style' (*DUJ*), is concerned with some fairly widespread misconceptions about the nature of grammar, and with its relationship to our more normal spontaneous linguistic activities. The mere abstract grammatical rightness of a sentence does not necessarily make it even grammatically appropriate in a particular setting or context. The objective should be to relate all analysis to what in a vague way we call the purpose of the sentence, the reason for its having, of all things, this structure rather than many other possible ones. An example from *As You Like It* is analysed to show how some particular effect is often achieved by drawing upon the combined resources of a whole conglomeration of grammatical devices. A. Reszkiewicz[24] tries to establish objective criteria for isolating, determining, and defining basic syntactic units in present-day English. These are to be defined in terms of the internal and external syntactic relations, with the larger syntactic units established in terms of the formally defined basic units. Each element and unit is to be provided with symbols so as to facilitate the identification of,

and operation with, each of them, thus introducing what might be called 'syntactic transcription' on the clause level. Vivian Salmon, in 'Sentence Types in Modern English' (*Ang*), points out that structural grammar, although claiming to be formal, in fact describes the sentence according to notional categories. Some shortcomings in generative grammar are then indicated, and a tentative description of sentence types given, the classification depending on purely formal criteria. In general, it would appear that structural and generative grammar are equally useful in linguistics because they do different things, but both are susceptible of improvement, especially in their methods of dealing with sentence-types. I. Poldauf, 'The Third Syntactic Plan' (*Philologica Pragensia*), divides the sentence into structurally indispensable parts, the dispensable components of these parts, and others, not in themselves fundamental nor fully attached to the fundamental parts. These are classed as first, second, and third plans respectively, and English and Czech compared with respect to their use of the third plan. J. Šimko gives a general account of 'The Origin and Development of the Modern English Literary Language' (*Philologica Pragensia*), with some indication of the more important changes in vocabulary and grammar, while H. Spitzbardt examines and classifies various examples of 'Overstatement and Understatement in British and American English' (*Philologica Pragensia*). Although the usual assumption that the former is typical of American English, the latter of British English, is in general accurate enough, it must not be taken as absolutely so. P. D. Strevens[25] describes the nature of the

[23] *Periodica philologica abbreviata*, by T. Ulving. Stockholm: Almqvist & Wiksell. pp. 137. Kr. 15.

[24] *Internal Structure of Clauses in English*, by A. Reszkiewicz. Warsaw: Komitet Neofilologiczny Polskiej Akademii Nauk. pp. 63. zl. 10.

[25] *The Study of the Present-Day English Language*, by P. D. Strevens. Leeds U.P. pp. 27. 2s. 6d.

study of contemporary English, the methods appropriate to this, and its relationship with other subjects, especially with literature, but also with education and sociology. In 'Hypostasis' (*Lingua*) F. Hiorth considers two questions concerning linguistic signs occurring in hypostasis forms. In a sentence such as '"Happily" was spelt incorrectly', what is the subject, and to what word-class does it belong? He concludes that the hypostasis marks, the quotation marks, *and* that which is marked by them, are identical with the subject, and that hypostasis words are to be classified as nouns. L. M. Castelo, 'An Inquiry into Compounds and Syntactic Phrases' (*ZAA*), describes attempts to distinguish between the two, e.g. *blackbird* as compared with *black bird*. He finds that from the point of view of morphemics both are phrases whose difference of meaning is syntactic, but speaking unscientifically the term compound word can be used to describe certain phrases of common occurrence whose distribution is similar to that of words. 'On a Question of Contrary Analysis' (*ES*) by H. Marchand is concerned with the question of which, in such pairs as *judge* vb./*judge* sb., is to be considered the basis. It would appear that a substantive matched by a verb which falls under certain sense groups is a derivative of the verb, and all substantives which are not naturally analysed through the verb must be regarded as primary substantives.

Of the school grammars,[26] that by

W. H. Mittins claims to incorporate the findings of modern linguists. In fact there is little, apart from the terminology, to distinguish it from the usual type, except that it is perhaps more concise than most. L. S. Hall deals with the usual subjects, but intersperses passages from various writers to illustrate the different points made, and to throw light on other aspects of the subject. The whole book is skilfully organized, makes an effective use of diagrams, and contains in a lucid and agreeable form much more information than might have been expected. The book by R. L. Beckett and D. L. Garner includes a brief guide to usage which is sensible and undogmatic, while the general grammatical information is given clearly and effectively. M. W. Sullivan provides a programmed course in English which, in 1,783 frames, deals with the structure of the simple sentence and with the classes of words which it contains. It necessarily includes constant recapitulation and revision, but it is clear that the subject can be dealt with adequately enough in this way. *Grammar Self-Taught* is intended to enable the reader to teach himself the essentials of modern grammar, and begins with a test which will show the particular weaknesses that need improvement. T. E. Berry explains, briefly but clearly, various problems of everyday grammar and idiom, grouping the material according to subject, and giving rules which pay a proper regard to actual usage.

Some such books have particular

---

[26] *A Grammar of Modern English*, by W. H. Mittins. Methuen. pp. xii+162. 9s. 6d.

How Thinking is Written, by L. S. Hall. Boston: Heath & Co. pp. xi+312. $3.30.

Writing College English, by R. L. Beckett and D. L. Garner. San Francisco: Chandler Publishing Co. pp. xiii+306. $3.

Programmed English, by M. W. Sullivan.

New York: Macmillan; London: Collier-Macmillan. pp. iii+427. 60s.

Grammar Self-Taught, by G. A. Cevasco. New York: F. Fell Inc. pp. xvi+151. $4.95.

The Most Common Mistakes in English Usage, by T. E. Berry. Pitman. vii+151. 12s. 6d.

aspects of the subject in mind.[27] B. Blackstone claims that the complexities of indirect speech can more particularly serve as a link between language and literature, and he has produced a useful book on the subject. A chapter on general principles is followed by a discussion of the problems involved in turning various kinds of prose from direct into indirect speech in such a way as to express the particular shades of meaning. Ffrangcon Roberts takes her examples from medical writers, and gives good advice, applicable also to writing on other subjects, on the choice of words, grammar, syntax, etc. W. Gilman writes more especially for scientists, and includes numerous examples of both good and bad writing, usually on scientific subjects. Unlike many such writers, he assumes that his readers are reasonably intelligent, and capable of other than purely scientific interests, and the result is a sensible and unassuming book.

Of the books intended to help in composition,[28] that by L. D. Brennan

[27] *Indirect Speech*, by B. Blackstone. Longmans. pp. xiv+209. 8s.

Good English for Medical Writers, by Ffrangcon Roberts. Heinemann. pp. ix+179. 17s. 6d.

The Language of Science, by W. Gilman. English Universities Press. pp. 248. 21s.

[28] *Modern Communication Effectiveness*, by L. D. Brennan. Englewood Cliffs, New Jersey: Prentice-Hall. pp. x+501. $5.25.

English One, by R. Frazer and H. D. Kelling. Boston: Heath & Co. pp. x+854. $7.45.

English Composition, by C. H. Vivian and Bernetta M. Jackson. New York: Barnes & Noble. pp. xxxv+451. $2.50.

Logic, Rheotirc, and Style, by N. Friedman and C. A. McLaughlin. Boston: Little, Brown & Co. pp. xiv+274. $2.95.

Subject and Structure, by J. M. Wasson. Boston: Little, Brown & Co. pp. xi+442. $3.95.

A Basic Course in Modern English, by C. Laird, R. M. Gorrell, and R. J. Pflug. Englewood Cliffs, New Jersey: Prentice-Hall. pp. xi+244. $3.75.

deals with the general question of communication, with the difficulty of listening and assimilating information, the development of English, and the methods and instruments of research. *English One* contains an anthology of prose, poetry, and drama, followed by a complete reprint of the *College Handbook of Composition*. The result is a comprehensive collection of material which should prove useful. *English Composition* gives a full treatment of the subject, is well presented, and is in general a good representative of this kind of book. N. Friedman and C. A. McLaughlin use the traditional material of rhetoric and logic, but try to make it concrete and particular so that the student can see its relevance to his own particular problems. *Subject and Structure* consists of a series of passages illustrating the different types of writing. The hope is that students will find here something to imitate in their own work. The last of these books takes a selection of subjects which are likely to give trouble, and explains and comments on any special difficulties, taking as examples prose extracts from contemporary writers.

R. T. Nasr[29] provides a thoroughly professional approach to the problems of teaching English to nonnative speakers which makes use of the most recent techniques. The section on pronunciation includes also the suprasegmental features, and both here and when dealing with grammar particular attention is devoted to those features which are structurally significant in English and in Arabic. A section on the teaching of writing emphasizes practice in penmanship, while the final part deals with reading and vocabulary building, contextual

[29] *The Teaching of English to Arab Students*, by R. T. Nasr. Longmans. pp. xv+176. 21s.

and cultural orientation, and educational methods. *Style and Usage in Written English*[30] is intended for Japanese students, and treats more particularly the longer units of composition, the combination of sentences into paragraphs, and of paragraphs into longer units. Much of it consists of a glossary of usage and a list of common errors. The authors have had much experience of the teaching of English in Japan, and are particularly aware of the special difficulties likely to be met with. Two monographs from the Central Institute of English at Hyderabad[31] are intended to help in establishing a new methodology to raise the efficiency of teaching English. The first consists mainly of a list of 180 items representing an inventory and classification on a formal basis of all the verb forms in a corpus of unspecified size. Frequency numbers are added for each of the types of material investigated, and the list should help course designers to grade the introduction of verbal forms and groups in accordance with their frequency. In the second, H. V. George outlines a method of course design based on the list, and discusses some of the grammatical implications of the verb-form frequency count. Also to be mentioned is the reprint of an important book on the subject by C. C. and Agnes Fries.[32]

H. Mol[33] provides much of the technical information needed by phoneticians, beginning with the theory of sound and the microphonic properties of the ear, and continuing with the structure and function of the ear and of the auditory nerve. The possible importance of the cochlea is considered, and the final chapter discusses aural stimuli and their interpretation. Cynthia D. Buchanan[34] provides a programmed course in linguistics, expected to take about fourteen hours. It deals first with general information about the linguist and language, goes on to the production of speech sounds, the differences between phonetics and phonemics, and describes the consonant vowel, and suprasegmental phonemes of English. The subject is not particularly well suited to this method of teaching, but it is here presented clearly and in a consistent and comprehensible form, though the phonetics part of it will need to be accompanied by oral teaching as well. G. Scherer[35] has revised the work on English phonetics first published in the Sammlung Göschen series by H. Mutschmann, while M. Yasui[36] examines the occurrence, non-occurrence, or possibility of occurrence of consonants and consonant clusters in English, the general aim being the discovery of some principles on the subject. J. Vachek, 'The Phonematic Status of Modern Long Vowels and Diphthongs' (*Philologica Pragensia*), criticizes theories which

[30] *Style and Usage in Written English*, by T. Womack and Shin-ichi Miura. Tokyo: Kenyusha. pp. vi+201.

[31] *Report on a Verb-Form Frequency Count.* pp. 51. *A Verb-Form Frequency Count: Application to Course Design, Grammatical Implication*, by H. V. George. pp. 45. Monographs of the Central Institute of English, Hyderabad, Nos. 1 and 2.

[32] *Foundations for English Teaching*, by C. C. and Agnes Fries. Tokyo: Kenkyusha. pp. xiii+378. $7.

[33] *Fundamentals of Phonetics*, by H. Mol. The Hague: Mouton & Co. pp. 70. 19 guilders.

[34] *A Programmed Introduction to Linguistics: Phonetics and Phonemics*, by Cynthia D. Buchanan. Boston: Heath & Co. pp. xi+270. 39s.

[35] *Englische Phonetik*, by H. Mutschmann, revised by G. Scherer. Berlin: De Gruyter. pp. 127. DM.3.60.

[36] *Consonant Patterning in English*, by M. Yasui. Tokyo: Kenkyusha. pp. 124.

assume a biphonematic status of the modern English long vowels and diphthongs. The monophonematic interpretation of these sounds must be regarded as still valid, though forces detectable in the language may bring about the revaluation of the *i-/u*-diphthongs into biphonematic groups. F. G. Ryder, 'Off-Rhymes and Consonantal Confusion Groups. Some Hints from *Mother Goose* and the *Volkslied*' (*Lingua*), believes that in this kind of verse off-rhyme is by no means a casual approximation of sounds, but has rather discriminated among sounds as to degree of similarity, and that the consonantal rhymes tend to appear predominantly within the same auditory confusion groups.

A particularly important volume collects most of the phonological articles of R. Jakobson.[37] They are given in chronological order, but three of the early ones, along with a particularly interesting 'Retrospect', are in an appendix. They vary in length from two or three pages to over a hundred. The subjects dealt with fall into four main categories: phonemic theory, language typology, child language, and the phonology of specific languages. Jakobson's work has been decisive for the clarification of the notion of the phoneme; he has been responsible for a synthesis between phonemics and experimental phonetics, has brought American linguists into closer contact with the achievements of linguistics in pre-war Europe, and opened out the prospects of new advances in the subject. J. E. Conner, 'Old French Dissyllables and the Great Vowel Shift' (*ES*), gives fourteen 'beliefs' on the sound-change said to be so generally accepted by philogists that they do not

need documentation. He then produces evidence, sometimes of doubtful validity, to show that some must be modified and others completely rejected. But in fact few philologists would accept without a good deal of qualification the original fourteen points. In 'English-Welsh Loan-Words'[38] T. H. Parry-Williams shows that some of the loan-words reflect changes which were taking or had taken place in English at the time of borrowing, and so may provide evidence for the dating of these changes.

G. Scheurweghs[39] is compiling a bibliography of the writings on modern English morphology and syntax published between 1877 and 1960. In this first volume he excerpts the main philological and linguistic periodicals, listing and giving abstracts of all the articles which have any bearing on the subject. The material is arranged according to the country of origin of the periodical in question, then follow miscellanies, and collected papers. In each section the items are in chronological order, indexes of authors and subjects are provided, and there is an appendix by H. Yamaguchi on Japanese publications.

The first part of Emma Vorlat's *Progress in English Grammar*[40] deals with the general background from Bullokar to Jeremiah Wharton and from Wallis to Loughton. The influence of humanism, the Renaissance,

---

[37] *Selected Writings. 1. Phonological Studies*, by R. Jakobson. The Hague: Mouton & Co. pp. x + 678. 66 guilders.

[38] In *Angles and Britons. O'Donnell Lectures*. University of Wales Press. pp. iii + 168. 21s. Henceforth quoted as *AB*.

[39] *Analytical Bibliography of Writings on Modern English Morphology and Syntax 1877–1960, I*, by G. Scheurweghs. Louvain: Nauwelaerts. pp. xviii + 293. BF. 250.

[40] *Progress in English Grammar 1585–1735*, by Emma Vorlat. Luxembourg: Editions Armand Peiffer. 4 vols. xxv + 209, 1–266, 267–500, iv + 224.

the Reformation, and of the Latin grammars of Lily and Ramus is described, and seven grammarians of this period are treated in some detail. This is followed by a discussion of the general attitude towards Latin, of the influence of the Port-Royal grammar and of Wilkins's *Universal Grammar*, and a description of the work of seven of the later grammarians. Part II gives an analysis of grammatical theory in the early grammars, and then deals in turn with the different parts of speech, showing how the definitions of them and the opinions on their most characteristic accidents changed and developed. Part III is concerned to give a general picture of the progress of English grammar by determining the contribution to it of each grammarian, while Part IV takes the different parts of speech, gives the definitions by the different grammarians, and describes their treatments of the class. Much important material is included in this survey, and it is to be hoped that for the benefit of future scholars the author will sometime summarize her findings in a rather more accessible form.

F. Th. Visser's[41] impressive volume is the first of a proposed survey of the development from the earliest times to the present day of all the English syntactical constructions with a verbal form as their nucleus. This part deals with constructions with one verb, and is subdivided according to subject and complement. Numerous illustrative quotations are given, though since Visser is concerned essentially with the written language, he avoids sources which may approximate to the spoken language. The history of each structural pattern is traced from Old

English to the present day, including obsolete constructions which have not previously been dealt with, and which make it possible to solve a number of puzzles in the various periods of the language where previously emendation was thought necessary. Whenever possible, mention is made of the views of the early grammarians, so giving information on the development of linguistic theory. This very full treatment of the subject contains a mass of material, well arranged and clearly set out, which will be of the greatest value to future investigators. In 'The Chronological System of the English Verb' (*Word*) W. Diver finds unsatisfactory the answers suggested by Jespersen, Twaddell, and Hill to the question 'What are the meanings of the English verb-forms?'. He outlines a chronological system presented abstractly which, it is claimed, reveals two characteristics that appear to reflect fundamental theoretical principles concerning the nature of language: the economy with which a relatively limited number of elements is combined to produce a relatively large number of distinctive units, and the fact that the elements in the more highly structured section of the system have a much greater constraint in their range of dispersion than have the unmarked members.

T. Finkenstaedt[42] gives a comprehensive and well-documented account of the uses of the second person pronouns. In Old English the grammatical distinctions between singular and plural were usually observed, and it was only after the Conquest that the plural of address spread through courtly circles from Latin and French. Chaucer's usage is described in detail; the use and survival

[41] *An Historical Syntax of the English Language, Part I*, by F. Th. Visser. Leiden: Brill. pp. lxxxi + 657. 89 guilders.

[42] You *und* Thou: *Studien zur Anrede im Englischen*, by T. Finkenstaedt. Berlin: De Gruyter. pp. xi + 301. DM. 44.

of Biblical *thou* among Puritans and Quakers; the decay of the singular; and there is an excursus on the position in German. The changes in the use of the pronouns would appear to be due to sociological, religious, and legal factors, and structuralist theories on the subject are dismissed as irrelevant. R. B. Lees and E. S. Klima show that the 'Rules for English Pronominalization' (*L*) are grammatically very rigid. They examine the contrast between single personal pronouns, and the so-called reflexive pronouns in *-self* and the reciprocal *one another*, note certain peculiarities in their use, and formulate rules to account for them. N. E. Osselton, 'Anaphoric *this* Expressing Shared Experience' (*ES*), points out that the anaphoric use of *this* and *that* in English is usually accounted for in terms of the natural local distinctions between the two pronouns. He shows that *this* has now become common in contexts where *that* would seem to be traditional, and suggests that here *this* is used to suggest immediacy or introspection where *that* would imply detachment, objectivity. B. Jacobsson writes 'On the Use of *that* in non-restrictive Clauses' (*Moderna Språk*), and shows that the disagreement between grammarians arises partly from the difficulty of distinguishing clearly between restrictive and non-restrictive clauses.

S. Brorström[43] examines the comparative frequency of the prepositions *of* and *about* when used with the verbs *say, tell, talk, speak*. These are taken in turn, sub-divided according to the various constructions, and statistics and illustrative quotations given of the use of the prepositions. It seems clear that the use of *about* in such constructions is becoming more frequent, and Brorström considers that there is every reason to assume that it will continue to increase at the expense of other prepositions, especially *of* and *at*. In 'Again: The Stressing of Prepositions' (*ES*) Maria Schubiger comments on previous articles on the subject.

In an amusing and learned article on the 'Decline and Fall of Interjections' (*NM*) Beatrice M. I. White traces the different fashions in the use of them from the comparatively restricted examples in Old English, through the greatly increased number in Middle English, to their exuberance among the Elizabethans. But the Restoration dramatists have an even larger number to draw upon, and other references make it clear that in this they are only imitating contemporary life. From the beginning of the nineteenth century the language of abuse and disparagement loses its energy and creativeness, and the result is the comparative poverty of contemporary English in this respect.

Englische Idiomatik in Stillehre und Literatur[44] deals first with the teaching of idiomatic expressions of various kinds, and then surveys the stylistic use made of them by a number of authors ranging from Chaucer to Laurence Durrell. Sun Jai Kim[45] collects from seventeen contemporary novels some 3,000 examples of collocations of noun, adjective, adverb plus preposition or adverb. These are listed with illustrative quotations as Open or Close Class Collocations.

[43] *The Increasing Frequency of the Preposition 'about' during the Modern English Period*, by S. Brorström. Stockholm: Almqvist & Wiksell. pp. 335. Kr. 32.

[44] *Englische Idiomatik in Stillehre und Literatur*, by W. Schmidt-Hidding. München: Hueber. pp. 95. DM.6.80.

[45] *A Study of Concurrent Collocations of Noun, Adjective, Adverb plus Preposition-Adverb in Contemporary English*, by Sun Jai Kim. Yonsei U.P. pp. v+153.

Other lists contain high-frequency collocations and lexical variants, while a brief conclusion discusses the relationship between the elements of the different types and the lexical influences in their formation.

V. Fried, 'The Aftermath of George Bernard Shaw's Will' (*Philologica Pragensia*), describes the fate of Shaw's New English Alphabet, and summarizes the arguments of A. Wijk against the Augmented Roman Alphabet, comparing his detailed analysis of present-day English spelling with a similar one by J. Nosek.

In his very full account of the principles of punctuation H. Shaw[46] deals with the reasons for it, sketches its history, and comments on modern trends. The individual marks are then taken in alphabetical order and their use dealt with concisely but thoroughly, with numerous illustrative quotations. A glossary of terms and another of applied punctuation complete a description of the subject which is at once authoritative and easy to consult. D. Thomas perhaps hardly finds the answer to his question 'Whence the Semicolon?',[47] but in the course of the inquiry he manages to give an excellent brief account of the history and development of punctuation.

G. Faure[48] begins with a short chapter on the study of English intonation from Hart to the present day. He points out the importance and necessity of a phonological description of the intonation of a language, discusses the difficulties involved, and describes the general principles of his analysis. The differences between stress and intonation are indicated, and information given on the material used, the methods of analysis, and problems of terminology. The principles deduced are then applied to the description of intonation in modern English, dealing first with the fundamental tones, and then with the tones in the melodic line. M. A. K. Halliday, 'The Tones of English' (*A Ling*), argues that connected speech can be analysed into an unbroken succession of tone-groups each of which selects one or other of the five groups. He investigates these, and summarizes the set of phonological systems that are referred to collectively as 'intonation'. It would seem that no very precise statement can be made of the 'general meaning' of English intonation, since the meaning of a choice of tone is bound up with other grammatical choices in the utterance. But it is necessary to display the range of choices available, and Halliday shows how the study of texts in spoken English may help to throw light on the contrastive use of intonation resources, and how this in turn may contribute to the analysis of the resources themselves. In a second article, 'Intonation in English Grammar' (*TPS*), he attempts to organize some of the meaningful contrasts expounded by intonation in English into the framework of a grammatical statement, concentrating on those places where intonation can be shown to be independently systematic. In many cases the patterns can be systematized into a formal grammatical statement which enables us both to show what are the contrastive possibilities at specific places in the language and to link these with other

---

[46] *Punctuate it Right*, by H. Shaw. New York: Barnes & Noble. pp. xiii+176. $0.95.

[47] In *Early English and Norse Studies Presented to Hugh Smith in Honour of his Sixtieth Birthday*, edited by A. Brown and P. Foote. Methuen. pp. xii+225. 45s. Henceforth quoted as *EENS*.

[48] *Recherches sur les Caractères et le Rôle des éléments musicaux dans la Prononciation anglaise*, by G. Faure. Paris: Didier. pp. 380. Fr. 40.

grammatical choices. In fact, we cannot fully describe the grammar of spoken English without reference to contrasts expounded by intonation, since many important distinctions are made in this way, including some on which others not in themselves intonational can be shown to depend. These are important articles which would have been even more useful had an attempt been made to write them in language more easily comprehensible by the non-initiate.

L. Antal[49] argues that meaning is an objective not a psychic phenomenon, existing in a sphere outside and independent of the individual consciousness. Meaning is nothing more than a rule of word usage, and so can only be an abstract and fixed objective phenomenon. It is essentially and generally independent of context, and there are no meaningless words in languages. J. J. Katz and J. A. Fodor, 'The Structure of a Semantic Theory' (*L*), complain that semantics suffers from the lack of an adequate theory to organize, systematize, and generalize the known facts about meanings and meaning relations in natural languages. They proceed to formulate a theory which would accommodate in the most revealing way the facts about the semantic structure of that language supplied by descriptive research. D. C. Hildum proposes a form of statistical 'Semantic Analysis of Texts by Computer' (*L*), applicable to either a written or spoken body of material, while J. Nosek, 'Some Semantic Features of Modern Colloquial English' (*Philologica Pragensia*), defines colloquial speech and attempts to outline the stylistic features of its lexicon and phraseology as shown in some contemporary plays and novels.

J. C. Gray[50] reprints a number of articles, reviews, prefaces, etc., which move from general discussion of words and dictionaries to specific words from specific dictionaries. The various sections deal with the ways in which words change their meanings, and with the history and uses of dictionaries; they include essays on Webster's *Third New International Dictionary*, excerpts from Johnson's *Preface*, and two definitions of *irony* along with an essay on the term. Whether the book will really increase the reader's sensitivity to words is perhaps doubtful, but the selections are well chosen and interesting.

A useful survey of reduplicative words in English[51] describes the different types, the sources used, and the arrangement of the material. The words are listed under various headings according to the general sense, and under each appears a reference to the source, the date of the earliest appearance of the word, and its derivation. The different methods of formation are treated, the meaning and motivation of such words, and their origin. In general, reduplicatives do not constitute a uniform type; they are to a large extent products of rhythm and may be only vaguely connected with ordinary words. The assumed connexion with children's speech is mere speculation, and it would seem rather that the whole species is given to play, with language as well as with objects, and it is to this domain that reduplicatives belong. Two articles deal with blends: E. Standop, 'Strukturelle Überlagerungen im Englischen' (*Ang*), analyses

---

[49] *Questions of Meaning*, by L. Antal. The Hague: Mouton & Co. pp. 95. 10 guilders.

[50] *Words, Words, and Words about Dictionaries*, by J. C. Gray. San Francisco: Chandler Publishing Co. pp. xi+207. $2.25.

[51] *Reduplicative Words in English*, by N. Thun. Lund: Carl Blom. pp. xii+347. Kr.33. 46*s*.

the different types, and discusses juncture and the apparent intersection of phonemes, while K. Hansen, 'Wortverschmelzungen' (*ZAA*), investigates and classifies the different types of blends in contemporary English. In addition, Rosemarie Gläser writes on the different kinds of 'Neuwörter in politischen' (*ZAA*).

An important work deals with the entrance of Arabic, Persian, and similar words into Europe,[52] with the various ways in which they made their way into the different languages, via Spain or Sicily, through the Crusades, or by commerce and the caravan route. A good many etymologies are corrected, much is shown of the influence of the east on medieval and modern Europe, and though mainly concerned with loans into the romance languages, a number of words are included which have since been borrowed into English. 'Imparisyllabic Nouns in English' (*EPS*) by A. J. Bliss deals with those words borrowed from French of which the original Latin has more syllables in the oblique cases than in the nominative. When such nouns were borrowed into English it is usually the accusative which is taken over, but occasionally both were borrowed and remain distinct. In such cases there is a duplication of nouns, one form with final *-oun*, *-on*, the other without, the shorter forms being particularly liable to be used as other parts of speech. J. R. R. Tolkien (n. 38), 'English and Welsh' (*AB*), describes the possible effects of the two languages on each other, and notes some English forms on which a new light is thrown by Celtic evidence.

N. E. Enkvist lists with commentary those 'New Words in Roger

Barlow's *Brief Summe of Geographie* (1541)' (*EPS*) which do not appear in *O.E.D.*, as well as others which supply new meanings or earlier examples. In several instances *O.E.D.* suggests French or even Germanic sources for words which can be most directly traced back to Spanish. J. M. Steadman, 'Sylvester's "Bacchanalian Frowes" and *O.E.D.* "frow"' (*NQ*), provides additional support for the definition of *frow* in its obsolete sense 'applied to the Maenads or Bacchantes of classical paganism'. In 'A Note on the Etymology of *Argosy*' (*NQ*) R. Filipović brings forward evidence from Sir Richard Guylforde's *Pylgrymage* (1511) for the derivation of the word from *Ragusa*, and shows that Sir R. Torkington's *Pilgrimage* (1517) was in fact modelled on Guylforde.

The following corrections to *O.E.D* appear in *NQ*: J. C. Maxwell, ' "Bone-ache" '; Priscilla Bawcutt, 'Gavin Douglas: Some Additions to *O.E.D.* and *D.O.S.T.*'; J. S. Dean, Jr., 'Antedatings from Robert Greene'; G. Cross, 'Some Notes on the Vocabulary of John Marson'; J. Illo, '"Chiucha" and "Quica": An animal for the Dictionary'; L. R. Conisbee, 'More Animals for the Dictionary'; W. E. Morris, 'Donne's Early Use of the Word "Concoction"'; Elsie Leach, 'Some Commercial Terms in Seventeenth-Century Poetry'; D. B. Schneider, '*O.E.D.*: Additions and Antedatings'; St. Vincent Troubridge, '*O.E.D.* Antedatings from Play Titles, 1660–1900'; R. Hall, 'Some New Seventeenth-Century Words and Antedatings', and 'The Language of Logic: Some Unrecorded Uses'; D. B. Schneider, 'Words from Garth's "Dispensary" '; R. Hall, 'Cudworth: More New Words'; J. C. Maxwell, ' "Classic", and "Talk Dead": Pope and Johnson'; E. Tannenbaum, ' "Ballast" in Balloons: An Addition

---

[52] *Origin and Spread of Oriental Words in European Languages*, by A. Steiger. New York: Vanni. pp. 73. $3.

to *O.E.D.*'; C. B. L. Barr, ' "Rulley" ';
Bernice W. Kliman, 'Wordsworth's
Use of the Word "Reflex" '; R. Hall,
'Gleanings from Tennyson's "Idylls"
for *O.E.D.*', and '*O.E.D.* Antedatings
from William James'; J. C. Maxwell,
'The Swinburne Letters and *O.E.D.*';
R. Hall, 'Some Antedatings in Philo-
sophy and Psychology'.

Much of G. J. Copley's *Names and
Places*[53] is taken up with a dictionary
of common place-names, and a
glossary of elements. For the remainder, there are chapters on the
Celtic names, the river names, the
different types of Anglo-Saxon names,
and brief accounts of the Scandinavian and French elements. The
book is rather elementary, and though
what is included seems reasonably
accurate, there are a good many
omissions. It gives the impression of
having been compiled from standard
works by one who has himself had no
first-hand experience of place-name
study. K. I. Sandred[54] makes a
detailed survey of English place-
names in *-stead*, of which the first
part discusses the various problems,
and the second gives the material. In
names compounded with *-stead* two
large groups can be distinguished
according as they indicate a location
of activity or one of objects or people.
Such compounds cannot be used to
demonstrate any other meaning than
'place' for the word, and this type of
name is found all over England and
continued in use into the Middle
English period. The element seems
also to have had the meanings 'church
establishment, religious foundation'
and 'farmstead'. In addition, there is a
large number of such names in the

south-east of which the first elements
are the names of trees, plants, animals, topographical terms, adjectives,
and personal names. These are evidently of great antiquity, and appear
to have a non-habitative implication.
The sense 'pasture (probably en-
closed)' provides the best explanation
for the element, though other meanings like 'outlying area' are also
possible. The second part lists in
alphabetical order under the various
counties the place-names in *-stead*
recorded before 1500, with a full
selection of forms and a discussion
of the etymologies. Twenty-one selected papers by E. Ekwall,[55] most of
them dealing with place-names, have
been reprinted. Since some are not
easily accessible, it is useful to have
them available here. A. H. Smith[56]
completes his authoritative survey of
the place-names of the West Riding by
a comprehensive index of the names
dealt with in the first seven parts, and
incorporating also the place-names of
the East and North Ridings, thus
giving a complete index to the Yorkshire place-names dealt with in the
Society's surveys. In 'Place-Names
and the Geography of the Past'
(*EENS*, see n. 47) H. C. Darby
shows how the former throw light on
the latter, illustrating by maps showing the *chart* names of Sussex and
Kent, the early woodland in Warwick-
shire, and the *denn*, *falod*, and *hurst*
names of the Wealden area. G.
Barnes, 'Early English Settlement and
Society in Cheshire from the Evidence
of Place-Names' (*Trans. of the Lancs.
and Cheshire Antiquarian Society*),
shows that Anglo-Saxon settlement in

---

[53] *Names and Places*, by G. J. Copley.
Phoenix House. pp. xiv+226. 16s.

[54] *English Place-Names in -stead*, by K. I.
Sandred. Uppsala: Almqvist & Wiksell.
pp. 348. Kr. 40.

[55] *Selected Papers*, by E. Ekwall. Lund
Studies in English 33. Lund: Gleerup.
pp. 171. Kr.22.

[56] *The Place-Names of the West Riding of
Yorkshire, Part VIII*, by A. H. Smith.
English Place-Name Society, Vol. xxxvii.
C.U.P. pp. xiii+207. 35s.

the county took place comparatively late, and was probably from Mercia. K. Jackson, 'Angles and Britons in Northumbria and Cumbria' (*AB*, see n. 38), makes good use of place-names, as well as of other types of evidence, to show the survival of Britons in these areas, while B. G. Charles, 'The Welsh, their Language and Place-Names in Archenfield and Oswestry' (*AB*, see n. 38), demonstrates the results in place-names of the impact of one language on the other. In addition, R. S. Boumphrey shows how the 'Place-Names of the Falkland Islands' (*DUJ*) commemorate various people and events.

On personal names, A. Hillie, 'OE *Seoluini* and ON *Sjóli*' (*ES*), claims that the first element of the Old English name, found in the *Liber Vitae*, is unlikely to be OE *seolh* 'seal', and suggests connexion with ON *sjóli* 'king, chief', while O. von Feilitzen lists and comments on 'Some Continental Germanic Personal Names in England' (*EENS*, see n. 47).

E. Penttilä, in his description of the characteristics of 'Advertising English' (*Mémoires de la Société Néophilologique de Helsinki*), notes the comparative frequency in the use of the different parts of speech as compared with ordinary written English, and analyses their distinctive uses. He then deals with compounds, the use of technical terms, foreign words, and conversion, and describes the various stylistic devices. Numerous quotations illustrate the different characteristics, and help to give a good description of this particular type of English.

An excellent and badly needed book on English dialects comes from G. L. Brook.[57] He explains the relationship between dialect and language, and then deals briefly with the Old and Middle English dialects, but at some length with the modern ones. A chapter on English overseas is mainly concerned with American English, and though it also includes a good description of Australian English, more would have been welcome on some of the other varieties, especially on Irish, Canadian, and the African varieties. A history of dialect research is followed by a particularly interesting chapter on class and occupational dialects, while another on dialect and literature is especially good on Lancashire dialect verse. Useful bibliographies are included, and the book will obviously become the standard work on the subject, one that the general reader will find interesting and the student invaluable. Part II of the *Survey of English Dialects*[58] follows the plan described in *YW* xliii, 48–9, and contains answers from the northern counties to Books IV–VI, of the *Questionnaire*, while in Part III are those to the last three. Since these are concerned with more abstract matters than the preceding ones, they must have presented special difficulties to the field-workers, but if so they have solved them well. This completes the basic material for the six northern counties; altogether it presents a mass of material which will be of the greatest value in many fields of language study, and will provide numerous subjects for future investigation.

The fourth edition and the two supplements of Mencken's *The American Language* have been condensed into a single volume and brought up to date

---

[57] *English Dialects*, by G. L. Brook. Deutsch. pp 232. 30*s*.

[58] *Survey of English Dialects: Vol. I, The Six Northern Counties and the Isle of Man, Parts II and III*, edited by H. Orton and W. J. Halliday. Published for the University of Leeds by E. J. Arnold & Son, Leeds. pp. 342–732, 733–1,102. 90*s*. each part.

by R. I. McDavid.[59] The new material is placed in brackets, but transition sentences or summaries of Mencken have usually not been bracketed. Later editions of reference books have been used to check statements in the original, as also new ones which were not available to Mencken. In general, anecdotes and word-lists have been cut by at least a half, and the additions vary greatly in length, sometimes being comparatively short, at others including a good deal of new material. On the whole, the editor appears to have done his task reasonably well, though his additions are not always particularly relevant, and the bibliographical footnotes tend to be repetitive and to lack discrimination. Some of Mencken's misstatements about British English remain, and in fact have been added to. The flavour of the original is certainly preserved, and indeed its chauvinism is increased by the editor in some of his less happy additions. *Beginnings of American English*[60] is the reprint of a book first published in 1931. It consists in the main of long quotations on the subject from eighteenth- and early nineteenth-century writers, with comments by the author. Elizabeth M. Kerr and R. M. Aderman[61] have made a selection of articles and extracts from books on linguistic subjects by scholars such as C. C. Fries, R. A. Hall, A. A. Hill, etc.,

roughly arranged by subject. Some of the articles were previously difficult of access, but others come from standard works which are easily enough available, and in some cases more recent expositions of the particular subject might have been chosen. R. R. Leutenegger's[62] description of the speech sounds of American English, as well as the usual material and a chapter on the dynamics of speech sounds in context which deals with stress, intonation, assimilation, etc., includes also a number of phonetic crossword puzzles and word games. Each chapter is followed by a summary, and of particular value are the numerous exercises, usually followed by a discussion of the particular mistakes likely to have been made. R. Gunter divides 'Elliptical Sentences in American English' (*Lingua*) into telegraphic and contextual ellipses. The first represents the kind of shortening that appears in telegrams, newspaper headlines, etc.; the second depends directly upon some foregoing sentence or sentences for expansion to the underlying form. The former does not always permit agreement among informants who try to expand it to its underlying form, perhaps because it lacks a linguistic context to which it is related. The latter is always preceded by a sentence that holds the key to its expansion, the two being related in a formal grammatical way. The expansion of a contextual ellipsis is usually easy for an informant who has the context, but impossible for him without.

A good popular account of the modern dialects of the U.S.A.[63] deals

---

[59] *The American Language*, by H. L. Mencken. Abridged with annotations and new material by R. I. McDavid, Jr., with the assistance of D. W. Maurer. Routledge. pp. xxv + 777 + cxxiv. 90s.

[60] *Beginnings of American English*, by M. M. Mathews. Chicago U.P. pp. ix + 181. 10s. 6d.

[61] *Aspects of American English*, by Elizabeth M. Kerr and R. M. Aderman. New York: Harcourt, Brace, and World. pp. xii + 272. $2.45.

[62] *The Sounds of American English*, by R. R. Leutenegger. Chicago: Scott, Foresman & Co. pp. vi + 168. $2.50.

[63] *Dialects—U.S.A.*, by Jean Malmstrom and Annabel Ashley. Champion, Illinois: National Council of Teachers of English. pp. ix + 62. $1.

briefly with dialect differences and their causes, and indicates some of the main forces underlying the present distribution. The important dialect areas are described, with the influence of foreign-language settlements, and some indication is given of the use of dialect in literature. *Yankee Diction-ary*[64] contains definitions, ranging from a few lines to a page or more, of words or phrases peculiar in meaning or form to New England. Some are dialectal, others commemorate old customs, while still others have to do with folk-lore. R. W. Shuy[65] investigates the speech of native Illinois residents for the purpose of establishing the boundary separating the Northern from the Midland dialects. He describes the different problems to be solved and the techniques employed, and deals with pronunciation, vocabulary, morphology, and syntax. The survey is illustrated by numerous maps, the last of which gives the boundary as shown by the different types of evidence. G. R. Wood, 'Dialect Contours in the Southern States' (*AS*), demonstrates the way in which Midland words have made their entrance into those parts of the South settled after 1800, and correlates their spread with the various periods of expansion. 'The Social Motivation of a Sound Change' (*Word*) by W. Labov is concerned with the shift of the first elements of the /ai/ /au/ diphthongs to a central vowel in the island of Martha's Vineyard. A study of the frequency and distribution of the variants in the different regions, age levels, occupational and ethnic groups within the island makes it possible to isolate the

social factors bearing directly on the linguistic process.

A. W. Read, 'The First Stage in the History of "O.K." ', and 'The Second Stage in the History of "O.K." ' (*AS*), concludes that while *O.K.* had a certain currency from the spring of 1839, deriving from 'oll korreck' in a fad for misspelt initials, it received fresh impetus in the spring of 1840 from 'Old Kinderhook', a slogan adopted by a Tammany political club. W. B. Finnie lists a number of 'Ohio Valley Localisms: Topographical Terms, 1750–1800' (*AS*), as recorded by travellers of the period, while T. B. Haber, 'Canine Terms in Popular Names of Plants' (*AS*), collects and classifies the recorded plant names containing the terms *bitch, dog, hound, pup, puppy*. In addition, mention should be made of the following articles from *AS*: G. Monteiro, 'Truckers' Language in Rhode Island'; A. Dundes and M. R. Schonhorn, 'Kansas University Slang: A New Generation'; H. Jarka, 'The Language of Skiers'; A. Dundes and C. F. Porter, 'American Indian Student Slang'; B. H. Porter, 'A Newfoundland Vocabulary'.

P. Goetsch deals with the characteristics and problems of 'Das kanadische Englisch' (*Ang*), while C. Dean, 'Is There a Distinctive Literary Canadian English?' (*AS*), concludes that there is not one that would be recognized by everyone; Canadian writing impresses the British reader by its Americanisms, but the American reader by its Briticisms. J. Sharwood and S. Gerson, 'The Vocabulary of Australian English' (*Moderna Språk*), divide the distinctive words into ordinary English words used in a different sense, borrowings from aboriginal languages, English dialect words with a limited circulation in this country, and words and senses developed in Australian English

[64] *Yankee Dictionary*, by C. F. Haywood. Lynn, Mass.: Jackson & Phillips Inc. pp. iii+207. $2.95.

[65] *The Northern-Midland Dialect Boundary in Illinois*, by R. W. Shuy. Publication of the American Dialect Society, Number 38. Alabama U.P. pp. vii+79.

E

itself. A. S. C. Ross, 'On the Historical Study of Pidgins' (*EPS*), points out the particular problems concerned with the study of pidgin languages, while G. Cannon gives an interesting account of 'English and Other Languages in Afghanistan' (*MLJ*).

III

Old English Literature

R. M. WILSON

P. H. BLAIR begins his account of Roman Britain and early Anglo-Saxon England[1] with a critical description of the available sources, showing the different ways in which they supplement each other. The vicissitudes of the Roman occupation, and the social and religious life of the times are treated in detail, and, as we should expect, the author is particularly good on the early Anglo-Saxon settlements, a subject on which elsewhere he has himself thrown a good deal of light. The consolidation of Mercia and of Wessex, and the conversion, are then described, while the final chapter deals with the nature of Anglo-Saxon society. The result is an excellent introduction to the beginnings of English history which is at once clearly and interestingly written. Some excellent illustrations, including useful maps and diagrams, and a good list of suggestions for further reading, further increase the value of the book. Three articles by Nora K. Chadwick[2] are concerned with the early period. In 'The Celtic Background of Early Anglo-Saxon England' she traces briefly the origin and development of the Anglo-Saxon kingdoms, and the influence of the Celtic church in Northumbria and Mercia. To Celtic influence is ascribed the swift transition of the Anglo-Saxons from barbarism to civilization, and it is found also in the elegies, the Cynewulfian poems, and the tradition of glossing. In 'The Battle of Chester: A Study of Sources' a conflation is made of the Anglo-Saxon and Celtic accounts of the battle; whilst in 'The Conversion of Northumbria: A Comparison of Sources', particular attention is paid to those Celtic sources which tell of Edwin's baptism by Rhum. Also to be mentioned here is a reprint of H. M. Chadwick's *Studies on Anglo-Saxon Institutions*,[3] an important and influential work which has been too long out of print.

C. Green[4] gives a very full account of the Sutton Hoo excavation, with a valuable indication of the new light thrown by the finds on seventh-century Anglo-Saxon England. Particularly interesting is the description of the earlier excavation of three of the barrows, of the ship-barrow itself, and of the ship and the grave goods found there. Evidence is produced to show that the barrows were erected over members of the Wuffing dynasty, and it would seem that the ship-burial is likely to have been in honour of Æthelhere, killed at the battle of Winwed. The last four chapters deal with the origin and growth of the

---

[1] *Roman Britain and Early England, 55 B.C.-A.D. 871*, by P. H. Blair. Nelson. pp. xii + 292. 25s.

[2] All in *Celt and Saxon: Studies in the Early British Border*, ed. by Nora K. Chadwick. C.U.P. pp. viii + 365. 50s. Henceforth quoted as *C & S*.

[3] *Studies on Anglo-Saxon Institutions*, by H. M. Chadwick. New York: Russell & Russell. pp. xiii + 422. $8.50.

[4] *Sutton Hoo: The Excavation of a Royal Ship-Burial*, by C. Green. Merlin Press. pp. 168. Plates XXV. 35s.

East Anglian kingdom. There is some interesting material here, more particularly on the exact routes taken by the invaders across the North Sea, though the connexion of these chapters with the subject of the book is not particularly close. This is by far the fullest and most detailed account of Sutton Hoo that has so far appeared; the author is familiar with the literature that has grown up round the subject, and deals competently and critically with it, while the numerous and excellent plates and text-figures are particularly useful.

On the religious background, B. Colgrave describes 'The Earliest Life of St. Gregory the Great, written by a Whitby Monk' (*C & S*, see n. 2), comments on its differences from the usual saint's life, suggests reasons for this, and concludes that it was written earlier than the *Ecclesiastical History* and was unknown to Bede. In 'Egbert of York' (*DUJ*) J. Godfrey deals with the foundation of the province of York, and with the life of Archbishop Egbert whose chief claim to fame lies in his virtual foundation of the school at York. But he also maintained a connexion with the German mission, and his literary work, especially the *Dialogus Ecclesiasticus Institutionis* and the *Penitential*, are of some importance. A detailed history of the Church during the late Anglo-Saxon period comes from F. Barlow.[5] An introductory chapter describes its relations with the Western Church, and the author then gives short biographies of the various kings, nobles, bishops, etc., who figure in the history of the age. The part played by the Church in the government of the kingdom, its geographical organization and economy, the education of the clergy, ecclesiastical government

and jurisdiction, and the relations with the papacy, are all dealt with, while an appendix discusses Stigand's deposition. Of particular interest are the numerous brief biographies and the chapter on the education of the clergy, the latter including also a consideration of the vernacular prose writings. The author knows the various sources well, and places the English church in its European setting. The amount of detail in the book does not make for easy reading, and there is some repetition, but the sheer mass of information which it contains will make it the standard book on the subject. Joan and H. Taylor bring together information on the surviving 'Pre-Norman Churches of the Border' (*C & S*), (see n. 2), whether on the Scottish or Welsh border, and include useful lists of them. The Northumbrian crosses, Anglo-Saxon features in Northumberland churches, and tower churches, are all dealt with, whilst of particular interest on the Welsh border are the extensive use of herringbone technique in the masonry and the Herefordshire school of carving. The Devonshire border with the Britons is similarly treated, with a special note on Glastonbury and a description of recent excavations there.

Legal history is represented by an authoritative survey of the will in England down to the end of the thirteenth century.[6] The first three chapters deal with the Anglo-Saxon period, treating respectively the beginnings of the distribution of property at death, the legal nature and effect of Anglo-Saxon wills, and the limitations in the making of such wills, whether personal or material. In general, the last will of English common law derives from three

[5] *The English Church 1000–1066: A Constitutional History*, by F. Barlow. Longmans. pp. xii+324. 70s.

[6] *The Will in Medieval England*, by M. M. Sheehan. Toronto: Pontifical Institute of Mediaeval Studies. pp. xii+359.

sources: Roman law, the Christian practice of bequeathing part of the property in alms, and Germanic family custom and rules. It was introduced into England as an instrument for the giving of alms, but the Germanic customs survived, and, moulding the influence brought to bear on them, made their own contribution to the English will of the thirteenth century. C. H. Riggs makes a careful examination of those parts of Anglo-Saxon law dealing with asylum,[7] and comes to the conclusion that its origins are royal and ecclesiastical rather than popular. Changes in the law that led to the custom of regional abjuration in the later period are surveyed, and it is shown that current translations of the Anglo-Saxon laws are sometimes erroneous.

W. Bonser's book[8] contains a mass of material on Anglo-Saxon medicine and magic, whether pagan or Christian. Its thirty chapters, some very brief, deal with the sources for our knowledge of the subject, with the classical contribution, and with epidemics, hospitals, surgery, etc. Various kinds of magic are considered, the different diseases mentioned in the sources, and the remedies used against them whether herbal, animal, or mineral. One section deals with food and drink, and another with veterinary and agricultural magic. The book was apparently ready for publication in 1949, and later revision has not altogether removed a too great reliance on out-of-date editions and sources, while when more recent work is mentioned the result is not always happy. In general no attempt is made to assess the value of the different types of evidence, and if actual mistakes are perhaps few, the interpretations are often a good deal more dubious than the reader might suppose.

W. F. Bolton[9] has prepared an anthology of Old English prose and verse in which, so far as possible, complete works are given, and the texts, taken directly from the manuscripts, are treated conservatively. The arrangement seems to be roughly by subject, with the prose selections chosen to show the development of that medium. Each passage has a brief introduction, textual notes at the foot of the page deal with special difficulties, and a very full glossary is provided. Inevitably many of the passages appear also in similar anthologies and readers, but on the whole a good introduction is given to the different kinds of Old English literature, though the omission of anything from *Beowulf* is surprising, and rather more bibliographical references would have been welcome.

R. Quirk, 'Poetic Language and Old English Metre',[10] emphasizes that 'while formulaic utterances and habitual collocations are the necessary starting point in the study of the early alliterative poetry, they are *only* the starting point'. He points out some of the ways in which the Old English poets exploited the tendencies towards a relationship of at least lexical congruity between metrical units, but shows that for the very reason that there was a high expectation of congruity at specific points in metrical structure, the impact of the incongruous could be all the greater.

---

[7] *Criminal Aslyum in Anglo-Saxon Law*, by C. H. Riggs, Jr., Florida U.P. pp. 61. $2.

[8] *The Medical Background of Anglo-Saxon England*, by W. Bonser. The Wellcome Historical Medical Library & O.U.P. pp. xxv + 448. 50s.

[9] *An Old English Anthology*, by W. F. Bolton. Arnold. pp. x + 178. 20s.

[10] In *Early English and Norse Studies presented to Hugh Smith in Honour of his Sixtieth Birthday*, ed. by A. Brown and P. Foote. Methuen. pp. xii + 225. 45s. Henceforth quoted as *EENS*.

In an attempt to see exactly how formulaic verse is put together, R. E. Diamond[11] makes an analysis of an Anglo-Saxon poetic translation, choosing for the purpose *The Paris Psalter*, a close translation from Latin of which the sources are known. A sampling of about fifteen lines every fifteen pages of the text is taken, the Latin original given, every word of the Old English passage checked with the whole corpus of Old English verse, and the formulas in it indicated by underlining, while comments are added when necessary. The problems encountered by the poet are pointed out, as also the various ways in which he attempted to solve them. It seems clear that much of the choice of words depends more on mechanical considerations than on taste or inspiration, and it is not improbable that there is more of this element of mechanical compulsion in even the best of the poems than has previously been recognized. In 'Oral Techniques in the Composition of Expanded Anglo-Saxon Verses' (*PMLA*) L. E. Nicholson shows that in general such verse is formed by one or more words plus a normal verse formula, the latter usually being made up of an ordinary A or D verse. The various methods of forming the usual opening measure are indicated, as well as the more elaborate and complex type which seems to be an amalgam of two normal verses, and it is suggested that love of a complicated pattern by the Anglo-Saxon poets may be a sufficient reason for the use by them of such verses.

An excellent translation by the late B. J. Timmer of *Heroic Song and Heroic Legend*[12] is particularly wel-

come. The heroic poetry of the different Indo-European peoples is dealt with in some detail, with more general accounts of that in Babylonian, Finnish, Turkish, and Maori. The evidence for the reciting of such poetry is collected, and the author then goes on to the historical and mythical background of heroic legend, the character of the hero, and the pattern of heroic life, while the final chapter is concerned with the beginning and end of the heroic epic. According to de Vries the original heroic poetry must have consisted of short lays, the development of the epic showing the transition from oral recitation to written composition. Only when the author can make a rough draft and work it out in writing can a large epic arise. The particular importance of this work lies in the fact that it places the Old English heroic poetry against that of other nations, shows what in it is characteristic and what peculiar, and provides a necessary background for the reading of such poetry.

A facsimile of the *Beowulf* manuscript[13] contains a much longer introduction than is usual in this series. Most of it is taken up with a detailed examination and discussion of the various doubtful readings, but there is also a careful description of the hands of the two scribes and an account of the different foliations in the manuscript. On the whole, the plates appear to be good without being outstanding—the E.E.T.S. volume is much better value for the money—and there seems little point in yet another facsimile of this manuscript.

A competent prose translation of

[11] *The Diction of the Anglo-Saxon Metrical Psalms*, by R. E. Diamond. The Hague: Mouton & Co. pp. 59. 10 guilders.

[12] *Heroic Song and Heroic Legend*, by J. de Vries, translated by B. J. Timmer. O.U.P. pp. iii+278. 10s. 6d.

[13] *Early English Manuscripts in Facsimile. Vol. XII, The Nowell Codex*, edited by Kemp Malone. Copenhagen: Rosenkilde & Bagger. pp. 120. 222 plates. £42.

Beowulf by W. Alfred[14] is all the more useful for being accompanied by similar translations of *The Song of Roland* and *The Poem of the Cid* by W. S. Merwin, and of the *Nibelungenlied* by Helen M. Mustard. These are four of the major epics of the medieval period, and they show the heroic virtues as they appeared to different peoples at different times. Few will be able to read all of them in the originals, and these translations will allow useful comparisons between the four. In addition, a paperback edition has appeared of the verse translation of *Beowulf* by E. Morgan.[15] This is one of the best of such translations, and is particularly useful for its introductory essays on the problems of translating the poem, and on the art of *Beowulf*.

An *Anthology of 'Beowulf' Criticism*[16] contains seventeen essays and an extract from Chadwick's *The Heroic Age*. Some of the essays, including J. R. R. Tolkien's influential '*Beowulf*: The Monsters and the Critics', deal with the meaning and value of the poem as a whole; others concentrate on a single character, scene, or passage, while C. L. Wrenn discusses 'Sutton Hoo and *Beowulf*', and F. P. Magoun's important article on 'The Oral-Formulaic Character of Anglo-Saxon Narrative Poetry' is also included. The anthology brings together in a convenient form some of the most important articles that have appeared on *Beowulf* as a poem, and though most of them were reasonably accessible, it is useful to have them collected in an inexpensive volume.

In 'Narrative Technique in *Beowulf*' (*N*) T. Culbert examines the three fights, and concludes that the poet is most effective at precisely the wrong points. Greater narrative skill was employed in the depiction of the fight with Grendel than in that of either of the other combats. The fight with Grendel's dam loses some of its effectiveness because it is fundamentally the same kind of fight as the first, and although the poet did much to differentiate the two fights by varying the locales and the details of the fighting, the impression still remains that the second is to some extent an inartistic repetition of the first. Nor does the dragon fight impress the reader as forcibly as does the battle with Grendel. The fact that this is the third occasion on which Beowulf has performed in a difficult situation, the greater attention devoted to Wiglaf, the comitatus, and the ramifications of the combat—all these contribute to the comparatively ineffective picture of this fight. To make the reader feel, as well as understand, that the dragon fight is the real climax, the poet should have subordinated the earlier fights, and concentrated all his artistry and skill upon the last. An investigation of 'The Heroic Oath in *Beowulf*, the *Chanson de Roland*, and the *Nibelungenlied*'[17] leads A. Renoir to the conclusion that in *Beowulf* the hero himself triumphs over external evil when he kills the dragon with Wiglaf's help. In the *Chanson* the hero triumphs over internal evil when he becomes aware of his own *desmesure*, but only divine justice can vanquish external

[14] In *Medieval Epics*. New York: The Modern Library. pp. 590. $3.95.

[15] '*Beowulf*': A Verse Translation into Modern English, by E. Morgan. California U.P. & C.U.P. pp. xxxiv+94. 10s.

[16] An *Anthology of 'Beowulf' Criticism*, edited by L. E. Nicholson. Notre Dame U.P. pp. xii+386. $2.25.

[17] In *Studies in Old English Literature in Honor of Arthur G. Brodeur*, edited by S. B. Greenfield. Oregon U.P. pp. vii+272. $7.50. Henceforth quoted as *AGB*. Some of the articles included appeared in the Winter 1962 issue of *CL*, and have been dealt with in *YW* xliii.

evil. In the *Nibelungenlied* the hero had no internal evil to vanquish, and external evil is crushed through the purely human intervention of Dietrich and Hildebrand. The progression is not unexpected; as Western Europe changed its ideals, the poets followed suit by modifying their treatment of a common theme accordingly, and, as society grew larger and more complex, so the nature of the heroic oath grew more obscure and confusing. In *Beowulf* the hero never need think twice about what he must do to fulfil his oath; in the *Chanson* he belatedly learns what to do; and in the *Nibelungenlied* he knows even before setting out that the task is humanly impossible. Similarly, punishment and reward become more confused; *Beowulf* is immediately rewarded by being granted the kind of death most coveted by early Germanic heroes; Roland does not receive his reward until he is actually dead, and evil has to wait until the end of the poem to receive punishment; while in the *Nibelungenlied*, Ruedeger dies convinced that he has damned himself, and we have only our personal sense of justice to suggest that his unfailing adherence to the practices of courtly chivalry will receive its posthumous reward. S. Wallon, in 'The Christianity of *Beowulf*' (*MP*), dismisses as merely coincidental some of the elements which have been taken as distinctively Christian. The poem is the harmonious and consistent work of an imagination converted to a primitive form of Christianity; the poet's characters are Christian in the same sense that he was, and their perspective is the same as his, except that they do not see the monsters oppressing them as the descendants of Cain. Because the monsters and the hero appear to have been handed down from the past, it is hazardous to say that they are allegorical, or

invented to give point to the poet's philosophy of history. Rather the old tales were given a new meaning, not different from what they once had but fuller. *Beowulf* is an authentic document from a dark time just beginning to be enlightened by Christianity; it is an adventure, not a sermon, but by its religious orientation it has a coherence not to be found among its early predecessors as we have grounds for conceiving them. R. D. Stevick, 'Christian Elements and the Genesis of *Beowulf*' (*MP*), argues that the poet's conception of the hero and of Hrothgar as good men implies speech and action which would also be counted as good by the Christian poet and audience. The conception was not original with the poet, and the Christianizing modifications of heroic materials were not all of his making. His individual modifications in the proto-textual material were to a considerable degree determined by the Christianized *Beowulf* matter with which he worked; the materials of the poem though originally pagan were no longer so. The poet was a man who had rethought and revised his materials, but he did not introduce Christian elements into them for the first time. Within an oral tradition, and free from influence by an inflexible written text, *Beowulf* poems could become Christianized in some ways without uniformly taking on Christian signification or intention. The later poet no doubt extended, refined, and unified the elements, but not to the extent of transforming the theme into one that is exclusively Christian. B. Mitchell, ' "Until the Dragon Comes . . .". Some Thoughts on *Beowulf*' (*N*), considers the question of how Christian a poem it is, and more particularly whether it is to be regarded as merely for entertainment, for instruction, or as an elegy. He concludes that once the necessary basic assumptions are granted, each type of theory on the question is tenable, and has its special attraction. But in the end each reader will have to adopt the interpretation which appeals to him as an individual. The difficulties of interpretation clearly arise from our ignorance of the conventions within which the poem was written, so that we can never determine with any accuracy what the author took for granted in his audience. E. G. Stanley, '*Hæþenra Hyht* in *Beowulf*' (*AGB*, see n. 17), shows that the apparently Christian references to Danes and Geats are all in fact ambiguous. The poet evidently regarded both as pagan, and one of his chief aims was to present to his audience a heroic ideal, still attractive to his Christian audience, but fundamentally insufficient because it was pagan. The *hæþenra hyht* was in fact the absence of hope, and this is the tragedy of the poem. A. Metcalf concludes that although the 'Ten Natural Animals in *Beowulf*' (*NM*) have only secondary roles in the action, the use of them serves to heighten the effect of the poem. The three beasts of battle accentuate the sense of doom; the boar adds to the stature of the warriors who wear it as a totem; horses give some warriors nobility and, as gifts, add to the stature of Beowulf; the stag and the hounds illustrate the terror of Grendel's pond; the tame hawk indicates prosperity; the swan suggests the speed of Beowulf's ship; and the whale exemplifies the terrors of the deep. A. Bonjour, 'The *Beowulf* Poet and the Tragic Muse' (*AGB*, see n. 17), compares the poem with *Hamlet* to show that it is essentially tragic. It is clear that, in spite of the allusion to the possible salvation of Beowulf's soul, and of statements implying God's control over Fate, death is never looked upon in Christian terms as the happier land. The last time Beowulf's death is poetically referred to, it is called the laying aside of laughter, joy, and mirth, so that when death is spoken about in *Beowulf*, it is our apprehension of it that is referred to. In 'The Uses of Association: Hands and Feasts in *Beowulf*' (*PMLA*) J. L. Rosier claims that graphically the Heorot matter is characterized primarily by scenes of feasting and battle which alternate with and are posed against each other. This is shown by the use of the vocabulary of feasting in descriptions of battle, and the poet's references to the hand also show his gifts of association. In both cases the poet re-used similar scenes for different purposes, and re-stressed clusters of similar details in terms of new relationships. F. P. Magoun, Jr., in '*Beowulf B:* A Folk-Tale on Beowulf's Death' (*EENS*, see n. 10), argues for a multiple authorship of the poem on the ground that a cyclic poem is an unlikely creation in an oral tradition, and because of three details where a difference of treatment may suggest the work of two poets.

The 'Six *Beowulf* Cruces' (*JEGP*) discussed by N. D. Isaacs appear in lines 168–9, 303b–06a, 1,020b, 1,290b–91, 2,255–66, 2,570b–75a. In all these it is claimed that we are dealing with the Old English device of personification which goes far beyond the rhetorical device of the same name, since it is one of the terms of the oral-formulaic convention to understand that any person, animal, or inanimate thing may be spoken of in terms of any other person, animal, or inanimate thing. D. R. Evans, 'The Sequence of Events in *Beowulf*, 11. 207–16' (*MÆ*), argues that the Geatish ship was anchored off-shore, that the warriors sought their ship in dinghies, and having clambered aboard they proceeded to guide the vessel through the waters of the fjord back to shore. There the ship was loaded by means of a gang-plank, and the men, ready for the open sea, pushed the ship off the sand. If we assume that the Geats had dinghies in which they could seek their ships at anchor, it is not necessary to dismiss the passage as muddled narrative. A. D. Horgan, 'Beowulf, Lines 224–5' (EPS), compares OE eoletes with wætergelæt, found as a gloss for colimbus. The second element is almost certainly to be identified with the root of OE lǣtan, and the original sense of the word, 'outlet of water', may later have passed into the simple meaning 'stream, water-course'; alternatively -let may have the sense 'join' in which case the word would then mean 'confluence of waters'. On the other hand, P. H. Salus, 'OE eoletes' (Lingua), takes the second element to be related to OE. lǣtan in the sense 'to allow to remain, to leave behind', while the first is from eoh 'horse', and the translation would then be, 'then was the sea traversed, the horse abandoning was at an end'. N. E. Eliason, 'The þyle and Scop in Beowulf' (S), accepts Rosier's suggestion that as þyle Unferth was privileged to speak as he does and deserves no reprimand for it. Beowulf's reply would indicate that the poet, unwilling to give up a type of set-piece expected in a heroic poem, has nevertheless modified it and shifted the flyting accordingly. Neither speech is to be taken seriously, nor is there any real evidence that Unferth is allied to Hrothulf in treachery against the house of Hrothgar. Since there is no warrant for the supposed wickedness of Unferth, the difficulty of his later lending his sword to Beowulf disappears. R. E. Kaske argues that by the partial duplication of the names '"Hygelac" and "Hygd"' (AGB, see n. 17), a thematic contrast is intended between the wisdom of Hygd, tragically combined with a woman's lack of prowess, and the lack of wisdom of Hygelac, tragically combined with prowess. Perhaps the poet of Beowulf somehow inherited the name Hygelac as part of his historical information; he may have seen in the name a compound hyge-lāc, able to bear a meaning approximating to 'lack of thought', and this quasi-allegorical overtone, together with the contrast between Hygelac and his queen, provided the inspiration for the significantly named Hygd. G. Storms, 'The Subjectivity of the Style of Beowulf' (AGB see n. 17), examines in detail lines, 1,399–1,417 to show the literary craftmanship of the poet, and especially the emotional colouring, whether subjective or objective, of various of the words and phrases. The adjectives in -lēas scattered through the poem are used to show that the poet selected his words carefully and purposively, and that the exigencies of alliteration did not hamper his creative activity. In 'Geatish History: Poetic Art and Epic Quality in Beowulf' (N) S. B. Greenfield investigates the literary qualities of the passages in Part II conjoining Hygelac's Frisian raid and the Swedish–Geatish wars, and conclude's that they amply reveal the poet's artistry. In the first, Olympian detachment sustains a theme of survival; in the second, heroic purpose lingers on revenge; and in the third, vatic admonition sees beyond heroic presumption. The totality of such views may well lead to the universal quality which some critics have detected, and perhaps also contributes to the epic quality of the poem. It is precisely in the accretion of historical material that we are made epically aware. While the universal quality of other epics may reside in the assimilation of human motives and forces to suprahuman though basically anthropomorphic purposes, in *Beowulf* history subsumes the hero as an individual. P. B. Taylor, '*Heofon Riece Swealg*: A sign of Beowulf's State of Grace' (*PQ*), compares Snorri's description of Odin's funeral in *Ynglingasaga* to show that the use of this phrase is a subtle exploitation of an audience's expectation concerning funeral omens. The subsiding of the winds anticipates the omen of God's grace in the rising smoke, and the personification of Heaven nine lines later fulfils the expectation. The interpretation of the phrase as a sign of Beowulf's state of grace adds appreciably to the significance of the cremation scene, and implies that Beowulf has attained as high a place in heaven as any hero.

R. E. Kaske, in 'Weland and the *wurmas* in *Deor*' (*ES*), compares a passage in the thirteenth-century *Virginâl*, a Germanic epic of the Dietrich cycle, in which a silver adder, accompanied by a golden hammer and tongs, seems clearly introduced as a conventional device of the smith Weland. If so, the phrase *be wurman* can perhaps be understood as a synecdoche to be rendered 'among the (products of his craft, all marked with) serpents'. The same crux is dealt with by L. Whitbread, 'Four Notes on Old English Poems' (*ES*), who takes the phrase to be used in a figurative sense 'by means of sinews', and illustrates by a passage from the *Leechbook* in which earthworms are used as a cure for cut sinews. The other notes concern the *Rhyming Poem*, 27, where he proposes to read *sceaclas* for *scealcas*; *Judgment Day II*, 273, where he would emend *ealra* to *eallum*, so corresponding to L. *cunctis*; and *Seasons for Fasting*, 206–7, where a passage from *Ezechiel*, as expounded by Gregory, provides a more satisfactory source for this passage than any of those previously suggested.

S. B. Greenfield, 'Syntactic Analysis and Old English Poetry' (*NM*), makes a close analysis of a sentence in *The Wanderer*, lines 19–29, in order to show the contributions made by syntax and word order to the poetic effect. Many of the features may be only the result of the demands of metre, alliteration, and formula, but it is argued that the Old English poet, whether orally or in writing, did have some flexibility in these matters, and that he could and did use, consciously or unconsciously, these linguistic counters to contribute uniquely to his poetic effects. In 'Exile and Elegy in Anglo-Saxon Christian Epic Poetry' (*JEGP*) L. H. Frey points out that the verbal formulas at the disposal of the poets provided them with a wide and easy range for the statement of conditions governing exile. They could dramatize the condition by having some exile lament his lot, and in a broader sense the lot of all who have lost the good things of life. A favourite subject of reflection is the contrast between past joys and present sorrows, with the knowledge that sorrow follows joy in the nature of things. Another is the rhetorical *ubi sunt?* series of questions concerning what once was and is now dead and vanished. The whole pattern is well demonstrated in *The Wanderer*, and Frey shows how parts of it, separately or in combination, are to be found also in the Christian poetry. R. P. Fitzgerald, '*The Wife's Lament* and "The Search for the Lost Husband"' (*JEGP*), relates the poem to the famous folk-tale, of which *Cupid and Psyche* is an example. He analyses it from this point of view, reconstructs the story behind the poem, and claims that the comparison, though leaving many questions unanswered, nevertheless helps to resolve the chronology of events, the attitude of the wife towards the husband, and the motivation of the husband. 'Another View of the Old English *Wife's Lament*' (*JEGP*) is taken by R. C. Bambas, who tries to show that the speaker is a man. This would certainly solve some difficulties, but gives rise to others, more particularly the feminine inflexions in lines 1–2, for which his explanations are not convincing. S. A. Baker takes ' "Weal" in the Old English *Ruin*' (*NQ*) to be a variant of *wæl* 'a deep pool', and E. G. Stanley, ' "Weal" in the Old English *Ruin*: A Parallel?' (*NQ*), quotes *The Panther* 4–8 as a parallel which neither supports nor contradicts Baker, but perhaps indicates that associative habit rather than logic guided the poets of the two pieces.

In 'The Flood Narrative in the Junius Manuscript and in Baltic Literature' (*AGB*, see n. 17), F. L. Utley points out the ways in which a biblical narrative may be adapted and expanded in later sophisticated and folk literature; by the incorporation of the results of learned exegesis, by the elaboration with new apocryphal motifs, and by the alteration of the tone by new cultural elements. In Old English the transformation was that of Christian poets using liturgy, patristic exegesis, and a few touches from the apocrypha. By comparison the Lithuanian and Latvian narratives are less conservative, containing as they do a strange medley of authentic folk-legend, fairy-tale coloration, literary fancy, and didactic moralization. In the first of two articles on '*Genesis B* and its Background' (*RES*) J. M. Evans examines the possible sources of the poem, shows what was the standard teaching of the Church as available to a ninth-century Saxon, and points out peculiar features in the account of the Fall in *Genesis B*. He discusses possible explanations for the variations, and concludes that if the writer was indebted to any tradition it was to the literary and not to the theological one, to Avitus, Cyprian, Victor, and the *Vitæ Adæ et Evæ*. Since his task was the same as theirs, to provide a Christian alternative to the literature of paganism, this was natural enough, and his departure from orthodox patristic views in the Fall reveals him as less interested in doctrinal niceties than in telling a vivid and moving story. In the second article, Evans deals with the literary and theological implications of the changes introduced by the author, concluding that he has been influenced not only by the vocabulary and concepts of Germanic epic, but also by its characteristic narrative technique. He may have borrowed certain ideas from the works of the Christian–Latin poets, but his first concern seems to have been to write a poem which would be acceptable to an audience familiar with secular Germanic literature. As a result, *Genesis B* is not a piece of versified theology; it is a complex and often beautiful poem in its own right. Rosemary Woolf compares 'The Fall of Man in *Genesis B* and the *Mystère d'Adam*' (*AGB*, see n. 17), decides that the authors had a common source, and that this is responsible for the fact that both, contrary to the literary conventions of their respective periods, treat the Fall with psychological realism. Moreover, the *Mystère d'Adam* can be used to help in the correct interpretation of *Genesis B*, since the same plot occurs in it but without the elements, such as the poet's sympathetic interventions, which have led to misunderstandings.

'The Edged Teeth' (*AGB*, see n. 17), by F. G. Cassidy deals with lines

402–9 of *The Phoenix* where are combined the two themes, of the fruit which brings punishment to the eaters, and that of the punishment which descends from parents to offspring. He traces the development of the themes in English, and discusses *idge* in line 407, taking it to be a phonetically valid form connected with OE *ecgede*, though the reason for it, and its dialectal status, are uncertain. L. Whitbread, 'Old English and Old High German: A Note on *Judgment Day II*, 292–293' (*SP*), accepts *drut* and *frowe* as feminine substantives derived, with little or no change, from a dialect of Old High German, and used in the poem more or less with their German meanings. It would appear that there was in circulation in later tenth-century England, or at any rate there was known to the author, one or more Old High German poems or prayers akin to the *Mariendichtung*, in which these terms were applied to the Virgin, and the author echoed these as familiar terms when he came upon a description of Mary in his source.

For obvious reasons the *Riddles* are perhaps the most difficult of the Old English poems to translate, and only the best of them had previously been rendered into modern English. P. F. Baum[18] now provides a good translation of all of them, using a loose line, generally of four stresses, and as much alliteration as comes without forcing. The arrangement is by subject, the number of the Riddle in the Krapp-Dobbie edition of the *Exeter Book* is given, and the solution commented on when necessary. An introduction discusses riddles in general and the Anglo-Saxon ones in particular, and points out the difficulties involved in translating them. One of A. S. C. Ross's 'Three Lexico-

graphic Notes' (*EPS*) deals with Old English. In this he suggests the meaning 'pig-meat' for *flǣsc* in the *Runic Poem*, line 78.

N. D. Isaacs finds a submerged metaphor in '"The Battle of Brunanburh" 13b–17a' (*NQ*). In the whole passage the comparison is between God and the sun on the one hand, and a lord and his loyal retainer on the other. W. A. Samouce, 'General Byrhtnoth' (*JEGP*), examines the generalship shown at Maldon. In the circumstances Byrhtnoth had no choice but to accept battle; his evaluation of factors affecting the fight was accurate and complete, his choice of terrain good, and the tactical formation adopted was the strongest known to the military science of the time. His failure to fall upon the Vikings whilst they were crossing the bridge precipitated the disaster, but for this the ethics of the age were responsible, and not necessarily the leadership. Samouce makes out a reasonable case, but he reads too much into the poem, and does not always distinguish between what is there and the remarks of the various commentators.

T. H. Towers, 'Thematic Unity in the Story of Cynewulf and Cyneheard' (*JEGP*), notes that the narrative breaks into two more or less distinct major sections: the deposition and eventual murder of Sigebyrht, and the two battles at Merton. He rejects attempts to find a uniting theme in *comitatus* loyalty or in personal loyalty, and instead believes that background and theme are political. The basic interest is the personal ambition of Cyneheard seeking to disrupt a sound and orderly national system represented by Cynewulf, and the issue becomes ultimately the disposition of the realm. B. Mitchell's 'Old English Syntactical Notes' (*NQ*) deal with

---

[18] *Anglo-Saxon Riddles of the Exeter Book*, by P. F. Baum. Duke U.P. pp. xx+70. $3.

three passages from the *Cura Pastoralis*, and with *Daniel* 598.

On the later prose, J. E. Cross[19] shows, as against Smetana, that Ælfric does in fact in one of his homilies echo or translate parts of Maximus of Turin's second sermon. Consequently, Smetana is wrong in deducing that Ælfric used a variant of Paul's *Homiliary* which omitted the sermons of Maximus, and Cross goes on to point out some of the sources for others of Ælfric's homilies. W. Braekman, 'Ælfric's Old English Homily "De Doctrina Apostolica": An Edition' (*Studia Germanica Gandensia* V), prints with variants the text from MS. Hatton 115, while the introduction deals with the manuscripts, their relationships, Ælfric's style, sources, and methods of translation. In '"Archbishop Wulfstan's Commonplace-Book" and the *Canons of Edgar*' (*MÆ*) R. G. Fowler tests the theory that C.C.C.C. MS. 265 is a commonplace-book of the archbishop. Since the *Canons* offer definite proof of Wulfstan's use of a collection such as that found in the manuscript, it would seem that Wulfstan was responsible for having the collection made, and there is good reason to believe that it was made with the *Canons* in mind. Dorothy Bethurum, 'Episcopal Magnificence in the Eleventh Century' (*AGB*, see n. 17,) examines the *Rectitudines Singularum Personarum* and the *Gerefa* which describe in detail the services due to the owner of a fief from his tenants. She produces evidence to show that both, the second to a greater degree than the first, represent Wulfstan's re-writing of an older document. In addition, A. Taylor notes two Old English versions and various Middle English ones of the proverb '"He that

will not when he may; when he will shall have nay"'(*AGB*, see n. 17), but shows that there was no continuing tradition of the proverb from Old to Middle English, nor did the Middle English poets follow exactly the continental tradition. It owes its currency to its use by such church fathers as St. Basil the Great, Augustine, and Gregory.

On the glosses, note should be made of an important review by F. Henry of the Urs Graf facsimile of '*The Lindisfarne Gospels*' (*Antiquity*) which more particularly criticizes some of the conclusions on its affiliations appearing in the introduction. Henry suggests that the type of ornament found in the manuscript is simply a rather desiccated reflexion of the live and creative schools of book decoration which probably existed in Ireland at the time when it is likely to have been decorated, i.e. *c*.710–20. In 1941 Holthausen printed a group of Latin prayers with Old English glosses from MS. Arundel 155, but broke off leaving a dozen of them still unpublished. These 'Prayers from Ms Arundel 155' (*Ang*) are now printed by J. J. Campbell who ascribes the manuscript to the mid-eleventh century, notes that the phonology of the glosses is normal late West Saxon, and points out a dozen or so words not listed in the dictionaries. 'A Reexamination of the Old English Glosses in the *Blickling Psalter*' (*Ang*) by R. L. Collins corrects some disputed readings, adds three glosses not previously printed, and also some examples of alternative Latin words for the Old English word, while H. Kökeritz, 'The Anglo-Saxon Unicorn' (*EENS*, see n. 10), lists and comments on the Old English glosses to *unicornus* to be found in the glosses of *Psalters*. In 'Strange Sauce from Worcester' (*AGB* see n. 17), H. D. Meritt comments on

---

[19] *Ælfric and the Mediæval Homiliary—Objection and Contribution*, by J. E. Cross. Lund: Gleerup. pp. 34. Kr.6.50.

sweorsaga, supposed to gloss *allec* in a copy of Bede's *De arte metrica* in the Worcester Cathedral Library. He takes it to be for *swe orsaga*, the second word, otherwise unrecorded, being cognate with OHG *ursage* used to gloss L. *ratio*, *occasio*, the latter word also used as a gloss for *facultas*. Consequently, the Old English gloss has been misplaced in the manuscript and really belongs to the preceding *ut facultas*. '*Ætnes* and *Ytend*: Two Rare Old English Glossary Words (*PQ*) are known only from single occurrences in Latin-Old English glossaries. R. Oliphant brings forward evidence from other Latin glossaries and from sources of glossary material to show that *ætnes* is rather 'food' than 'edibility', and *ytend* 'one who expels' rather than 'devastator'.

IV

Middle English: excluding Chaucer

A. MACDONALD and BETTY HILL

THE year 1963 was perhaps more notable for what was omitted than what appeared—there was, for instance, no book on *Piers Plowman*, and little on the medieval lyric. Yet the year did produce, mainly through the medium of the Early English Text Society, a number of most useful texts. Outstanding among these was the first volume of Laȝamon's *Brut*,[1] edited from the two famous MSS in the British Museum. This volume represents approximately half of the text of the *Brut*, and is the first to give the complete text since Madden's edition of 1847 (which incidentally printed it in half-lines). The work will be completed in two further volumes, one containing the remainder of the text, the other with the critical apparatus. It is obviously better to defer comment on the edition until the rest of the edition is published; meanwhile one must compliment the editors on what is a most welcome addition to the ever-increasing list of Middle English texts, and one especially valuable in view of the number of scholars who have no immediate access to Madden.

It has now become almost terrifying to contemplate the fact that editions of the various texts of the *Ancrene Riwle* have been appearing for more than twenty years, and still

the toll is not complete. The latest is that from MS Cotton Titus D. XVIII[2] along with the Lanhydrock Fragment, which gives us a version of the text where an attempt has been made to address the teaching of the work to men as well as to women recluses, thus causing, among other things, a certain uncertainty in the use of pronouns. But one must admit that it is, though perfunctory and rather careless, nevertheless an important version, and very near to the Nero version.

The third Early English Text Society's publication to be noticed is the facsimile edition of the *Owl and the Nightingale*,[3] the second of the Society's series of reproductions of Early English manuscripts, which gives us the two surviving texts of *The Owl and the Nightingale*, J on the verso sides and C on the recto. Ker's Introduction packs in a great deal of palaeographical material, including descriptions of the two MSS, number of leaves and foliation, quiring, size of leaf and written space, ruling and the like, and ending with brief notes

---

[1] Laȝamon: *Brut*, edited from British Museum MS Cotton Caligula A. IX and British Museum MS Cotton Otho C. XIII by G. L. Brook and R. F. Leslie. Volume I. Text (Lines 1–8,020). E.E.T.S. No. 250. O.U.P. pp. xvi+416. 80s.

[2] The English Text of the *Ancrene Riwle*, edited from MS Cotton Titus D. XVIII by Frances M. Mack. Together with the Lanhydrock Fragment Bodleian MS. Eng. th. *c.* 70 edited by A. Zettersten. E.E.T.S. No. 252. O.U.P. pp. xviii+172. 40s.

[3] *The Owl and the Nightingale*, reproduced in Facsimile from the Surviving Manuscripts Jesus College Oxford 29 and British Museum Cotton Caligula A. IX. With an Introduction by N. R. Ker. E.E.T.S. No. 251. O.U.P. pp. xxii+55 plates. 42s.

on the binding and history of the MSS. Ker refuses to date one MS earlier than the other, declaring that 'The difference between the hands is a difference of kind, not of date,' and asserting that the *J* MS is 'amateur', *C* 'professional'.

In 'The Couplet System in *Havelok the Dane*' (*NQ*), Bruce Mitchell suggests that acceptance of the authority of the late and corrupt Cambridge fragment can indicate a solution to the hiatus between lines 546–7. The line between these in the Cambridge fragment should be inserted, for the couplet system in *Havelok* and *Kyng Alisaunder* in the Laud MS is not as inviolate as has been supposed. From there he makes two further suggestions, one with reference to the reading of the Cambridge fragment. He rejects any case for the existence of triplets where the couplet system breaks down at 428–32, 313–16, while after 1,414 it is better to postulate a gap of 179 lines.

R. S. Loomis, in *The Development of Arthurian Romance*,[4] attempts, within the obvious limitations of his space, to interpret 'a significant and perplexing body of literature', in other words to trace the development of the Arthurian legend from its shadowy beginnings in Welsh hero-legend and mythology to its full flowerings in *Sir Galvain and the Green Knight* and Malory. Not unnaturally he makes full use of the symposium *Arthurian Literature in the Middle Ages* (*YW*. xl.66) which he edited, and which may be taken to represent, on the whole, the findings of the latest research on the subject. But the greater part of this book is confined to developments in England, though there are chapters on Chrétien de Troyes and Wolfram von Eschenbach. This is really for the amateur, not the professional Arthurian, and unfortunately some of Loomis's judgements seem questionable, and some of the statements of fact (e.g. on Chaucer) quite wrong.

The *topos* of *descriptio loci* is not usually associated with oral heroic poetry. In 'Rhetorical *Descriptio* of Place in the Alliterative *Morte Arthure*' (*MP*), John Finlayson first discusses three examples of *descriptio veri* (920–32, 2,501–12, 2,670–77), notable for a mingling of concrete detail and impressionism, which reinforce the atmosphere of the following *aventures* and place them 'in a different scheme of values from those which dominate the larger pattern of the poem'. His fourth passage (3,230–49) belongs to the *genus* of dream landscapes in which wild scenery is combined with the *locus amoenus*. The description of wild beasts is paralleled in a religious lyric, while the *locus amoenus* is a type of Earthly Paradise, but their combination is remarkable. The motif of the Dreamer fleeing from wild beasts in a wilderness and arriving at an Earthly Paradise is paralleled in courtly love allegory, but in elaboration and function the passage is unique in Middle English poetry. None of the four descriptions occur in the poem's sources. In 'A Mediaeval Reviser at Work' (*MÆ*), M. Mills discusses the 'rationalizations' in the Ashmole, Naples and Percy Folio MSS (*ANP*) of *Libeaus Desconus*, of incongruous elements in Chestre's account of the story in the Caligula and Lambeth MSS. The most significant revisions in *ANP* involve the rationalization of the characters of Maugis and Lambard and the loose end in the fight between Irain and Libeaus by adding fresh commonplace material, sometimes from another part of the romance.

---

[4] *The Development of Arthurian Romance*, by Roger Sherman Loomis. Hutchinson. pp. 200. 15*s*.

F

Mills briefly indicates how the incongruities have entered the story of Libeaus. Other revisions in *ANP* arise from unconscious reminiscences of other romances. Neither kind of revision integrates with the other parts of the story or is stylistically admirable. They are the work of a *disour*, and Mills finally discusses what light this throws on the problems of editorial method. The view of medieval romance as hardly worth our close consideration as serious literature is challenged by D. M. Hill in 'Romance as Epic' (*ES*). His first section is devoted to quoting and replying to the view, of which W. P. Ker is the influential though not the only spokesman, that romance is approachable through epic to which it is inferior, being only a 'mystery and fantasy' indifferently achieved. In his second section he seeks to prove the continuity between *Beowulf*, *Roland* and various romances in structure, conventions and narrative technique, taking the view that romance is not one element in epic, but that epic broadens out into romance. He takes no account of the effects of oral circulation on composition and the cumulative effects of convention and technique on the finished work of art. The difference between epic and romance is illustrated from *Paradise Lost* where a clash between the two is involved.

Only one book has been noted dealing with the *Gawain*-poet, but that is a decidedly unusual one. *A Graphemic-Phonemic Study of a Middle English Manuscript*[5] is in fact a study of Cotton Nero A. X from an unusual point of view—that of linguistics. McLaughlin attempts, in effect, to provide 'at least some preliminary codification' of a system of

[5] *A Graphemic-Phonemic Study of a Middle English Manuscript*, by John C. McLaughlin. The Hague: Mouton. pp. 162. 18 guilders.

alphabetic writing, which he then applies to this manuscript, giving as an example of its use a short passage from *Perle*. An examination of this method would necessarily have to be too detailed to permit its discussion here; perhaps it will be enough to say that the use of this new method to examine an older literary work will surely depend upon the nature of the language of that work—e.g. whether it is written in an unmixed dialect or not.

In 'What *Sir Gawain and the Green Knight* is About' (*MÆ*), G. V. Smithers asks why the Green Knight is associated with a chapel, why he of all people should hear Gawain's confession, and why Gawain should make one at that point. The answers to the first two questions are first sought in *Perlesvaus*, where hermits provided wandering knights with shelter, were sources of information for people on quests and received confessions from errant knights. The name of the Green Chapel implies that the Green Knight, Bercilak de Hautdesert, 'of the high hermitage', had a hermitage and was therefore fit to hear Gawain's confession. That the Green Knight is given the function and, by his name, the abode of a hermit is explained from *La Queste del Sainte Graal*, where the closeness of the ruined chapel, sought by Gawain and Hector, to a hermitage on high ground, and especially the hermitage and its approach, suggested the conception of the Green Chapel and its approach. The Green Chapel is a sinister inversion of the Arthurian chapel in the wilds because it expresses the demonic part of the Green Knight's two-fold origins. Smithers discusses the precise significance of the confession and its function as giving Gawain the chance to realize and acknowledge his fault in accepting the girdle. He finally considers at some length chivalric and Christian ideals in the poem, pointing out 'the dichotomy of secular and spiritual knighthood, and the primacy of the latter', which can be paralleled in the *Queste*. Mother Angela Carson, O.S.U., in 'The Green Chapel: Its Meaning and Its Function' (*SP*), suggests that, although the chapels at the castles of Arthur and Bercilak must be understood in the current fourteenth-century sense of the word, the (Green) Chapel is a twelfth-century word meaning 'the place where heavy blows are given and where slaying is accomplished'. The Green Knight uses the word in this sense in *chapayle vpon grounde* (1,069–70), and Gawain should have known it was a place of slaughter from his guide's words (2,103–9). The irony lies in the fact that Gawain is only aware of the equivocation when faced with a burial mound (*a lawe as it were* is quoted), and there is no inconsistency between what he looked for and what he found. She presents no evidence that the twelfth-century *chapel* was ever used in England and known in the fourteenth century. In *ELN*, Mother Angela Carson considers 'The Green Knight's Name', Bercilak de Hautdesert, as a double compound name of pure invention, which has a causal relationship with Morgne la Faye's magical powers, and can be 'significantly equated' with Bercilak's role in the plot as challenger, host and antagonist. In 'A New Approach to Middle English Dialectology' (*ES*), Angus McIntosh notes that on linguistic examination the *extant* text of *Sir Gawain and the Green Knight* fits into a very small area of S. E. Cheshire or just over the border in N. E. Staffs. This finding agrees with R. W. V. Elliot's suggestion about the provenance of the *original* ('Sir Gawain in Staffordshire', The *London Times*, 21st May

1958) from the localization of Bercilak's castle and the Green Chapel in the poem. R. H. Bowers, in '*Gawain and the Green Knight* as Entertainment' (*MLQ*), reviews the interpretations of Markman (*YW* xxxviii. 85), Moorman (*YW* xxxvii. 80) and Burrow (*YW* xl. 69), and argues that the good-natured laughter in the poem should be given its proper place in setting the poem's tone and meaning. David Farly Hills considers that the apparent contradiction between 'Gawain's Fault in *Sir Gawain and the Green Knight*' (*RES*) as confessed by him and as understood by Bercilak and the poet can be resolved by examining the medieval sin of covetousness. The *couetyse* to which Gawain confesses he was led by *cowardyse* (2,374–83) is to be equated with *cupiditas* in its Augustinian and general sense of inordinate love for oneself by seeking consolation in transitory things, and is antithetical to *caritas* 'love of God'. (It may be objected that in the poem *couetyse* is apparently equivalent to *vyse* and antithetical to *larges* which befits knights.) Gawain shows inordinate love for himself by accepting the girdle to save his life. Bercilak's assertion that Gawain was at fault because he wished to save his life and the poet's reference to the girdle (2,040) define Gawain's covetousness more exactly. Gawain's attitude to his fault differs from that of others in the poem because they were aware of mitigating circumstances, as is shown by medieval attitudes towards the nature of fear. Smithers (above) considers the mitigation to lie in the fact that Gawain kept the tryst for the return blow, and suggests that *couetyse* may merely mean 'a desire for something owned by someone else'.

V. E. Watts indicates some literary parallels in fourth-century Latin works, available in fourteenth-century England, to '*Pearl* as a *Consolatio*' (*MÆ*). Christian authors modified the classified traditional *solacia* of the Roman Empire by including the promise of eternal life after death (just as in *Pearl* the father's consolation is his vision of his daughter's life in Heaven), and by using them to instruct the faithful. St. Paulinus of Nola's *carmen* xxxi, which is more like a theological treatise than a *consolatio*, which deals briefly with the dead son in Heaven among the *virgines* following the Lamb, and which ends with an exhortation to repentance, affords a close parallel in form and purpose to *Pearl*. Isabel E. Rathborne, in 'New Light on *Pearl* 690' (*T*), points out that in liturgical use in the fourteenth century, *Wisdom* 10, 10a, the source of 690–2, appears as 'Justum deduxit Dominus per vias rectas et ostendit illum regnum Dei'. In this may be recognized the immediate source of the defective line 690 which should read, as in Gollancz's text of 1891, 'How kyntly oure [lord hym] con aquyle'. There is then no need to emend MS. *he* in 691. In 'The Role of the Narrator in *Patience*' (*MP*), Charles Moorman finds the use of a moralistic narrator-preacher structurally and thematically essential to the poem. He discusses the prologue, 'a reasoned statement of faith', and its relationship to the *exemplum* of Jonah who lacks poverty of spirit and patience, and brings worse on himself by resisting the tasks given, as the preacher has forewarned. The narrative repeats this point made in the prologue by developing scenes suggested by the Vulgate, and by the constant intrusion of the narrator-preacher. The purple passages in the poem are not digressions, but a necessary part of the *exemplum*. A. C. Spearing, in 'Verbal Repetition in *Piers Plowman* B and C' (*JEGP*),

demonstrates from a comparison of passages in B and C how the rhetorical device of verbal repetition is intensified in C. Langland repeats single words and phrases, beyond the requirements of sense, to bring home the power of the theme, and employs elaborate interlocked repetition to bring certain concepts into closer association and act out his meaning. Spearing examines C XXI in some detail, pointing out the different repetitive clusters. He concludes that Langland's practice is related to the *ars praedicandi*, but it goes beyond preaching, producing 'large theologically undefined ideas' which will arouse emotion and stir to action. R. E. Kaske gives a 'relentless exegesis' of '*Ex Vi Transicionis* and Its Passage in *Piers Plowman*' (*JEGP*), a study complementary in part to that of Ben H. Smith (*YW* xlii. 69). By taking line 151 as the first line of Patience's resumed speech, he paraphrases B XIII, 151–6. Taking line 151 as the final line of Love's speech, Kaske gives another paraphrase of 150–1, and finally briefly considers the revision of the passage in C XVI. 138 ff. In 'Some Applications of Middle English Dialectology' (*ES*), M. L. Samuels mentions that the C-texts of *Piers Plowman* circulated in the Malvern Hills, the B-texts had a more cosmopolitan circulation, especially in the Worcester and London areas. The extant A-texts belong to South Sussex, Essex, Norfolk and Durham, but not to the more central areas of the others. These distributions may be related to Langland's travels or to the suitability of the three versions to the area and milieu in which they were written. In 'A *Piers Plowman* Manuscript in the Huntington Library' (*HLQ*), G. H. Russell and Venetia Nathan demonstrate that the text in HM 114, though basically a B-text, has been subjected to a thorough editorial process based on a close knowledge of all three texts. Readings from A and C have been substantially incorporated to produce a conflated text. The editorial thoroughness is most evident in Passus IV-VIII. The authors set out the insertions in detail, Passus by Passus, and finally illustrate the editor's handling of his material from Passus VI. 160–186. In the Critical Forum in *EC*, Jasodhara sen Gupta in '*Piers Plowman*' and Ojars Kratins '*Piers Plowman* and Arthurian Romance' add brief comments to Rosemary Woolf's article (*YW* xliii. 71–2). Kratins suggests that the 'romantic uncertainty' in the figure of Piers can be paralleled in Arthurian romance, allegory and romance being literary forms conceived by the same kind of intellect. Piers's role is symbolic rather than allegorical and as a symbol he does not provide the key to the poem.

In *Three Middle English Religious Poems*[6] R. H. Bowers publishes for the first time three religious poems, two from MSS. in the British Museum, and the third in the Cambridge University Library. All three texts are of the first half of the fifteenth century, palaeographically speaking, two of the poems dealing with the Passion and the third with the Resurrection. Bowers gives the poems 'the full treatment', lavishing on them a wealth of notes and critical apparatus, perhaps more really than they deserve, for they can hardly be called great literature, their metre is indifferent, and their dialects mixed. It is, however, perhaps worth pointing out that they do reflect the same kind

of taste as is to be found in contemporary art.

R. T. Davies, in his anthology of medieval English lyrics[7], claims that it is 'the first critical anthology of medieval English lyrics to be published', and the first comprehensive anthology since Chambers and Sidgwick. Comprising 187 of the best and most interesting shorter medieval English poems, it is intended for the non-specialist reader without any linguistic knowledge who wants to enjoy English poetry between St. Godric and Thomas Wyatt. One could claim the first 97 poems as falling within the scope of this chapter, and as giving a more than adequate idea of the sweep of the whole. Secular love poems, aristocratic and otherwise, religious love poems, roundels, carols, ballades, historical poems, poems *de contemptu mundi* and on the *Ubi sunt* theme, complaints, and the rest, they are all here. The poems are followed by notes, succinct and informative, and by an Appendix which is a sort of concordance. The spelling of the poems has been 'adjusted' (according to the 'blurb') or made consistent with modern usage; each poem is followed by a translation complete or in note form. The introduction deals *inter alia* with some of the themes found in lyric and with the various influences on them, as well as explaining the editor's aims in his selection.

In 'Good Gossips Reunited' (*BMQ*), Rossell Hope Robbins prints the first stanzas of the Ale-wives poem (*Index of M.E. Verse* No. *32) missing from Cotton MS Titus A. xxvi, and now found on a single leaf, f. 43, of Cotton MS Vitellius D. xii. The poem, probably in its original

[6] *Three Middle English Religious Poems*, edited with an Introduction and Commentary by R. H. Bowers. (University of Florida Monographs Humanities No. 12, Winter 1963). Gainesville, Fla.: Florida U.P. pp. vi+66. $2.00.

[7] *Medieval English Lyrics*. A critical Anthology edited with an introduction and notes by R. T. Davies. Faber. pp. 384. 45s.

version here, does not have the carol burden as heading and some of the stanzas differ from those of the carol variant. The verso of the leaf has, in the same hand, the end of the *Siege of Rhodes*, the rubric of which appears on f. 160 v of the Titus MS. If the Vitellius MS had the complete text some thirty folios must be missing.

Robbins also discusses and reprints, from the early fifteenth-century Bodleian MS. 315, copies of five inscriptions of moralizing proverbs found as 'Wall Paintings at Launceston Priory' (*Archiv*). Johannes Steuenys, an Exeter canon, who gave the manuscript to Exeter *c.* 1475, probably accompanied an episcopal visitation to Launceston in the early fifteenth century, and copied them from the dining-room wall into his manuscript. In *NQ* Barbara M. H. Strang notes that, although the subject of 'O certe necessarium Ade peccatum. O felix culpa' is not treated in an extant lyric until the fifteenth century where it contains inversions motivated by the character of related clauses, it is mentioned in '*Piers Plowman*, B Text, Passus V, 491–2'. The fact that the inversion there is not grammatically motivated, is untypical of Langland and suggests quotation syntax, implies the existence of a lyric on the *felix culpa* theme, with motivated inversion, by the late 1370's. Merle Fifield in 'Thirteenth-Century Lyrics and the Alliterative Tradition' (*JEGP*), presents statistical results from her unpublished list of alliterative phrases in thirteenth-century lyrics, and seeks to establish their relationship to the alliterative tradition. The lyrics preserve the Old English alliterative tradition of religious poetry and prose, and some phrases were in common use, but more than half are not part of Old and Early Middle

English alliterative usage, and some, from their French element, are thirteenth-century formations. Certain phrases (some recorded only in the lyrics) reappear in the alliterative revival and romances, the fact that some occur only in one or the other suggesting that the lyrics were independent preservers of the alliterative tradition. The lyric phrases, including new formulas, were also kept alive in fourteenth-century lyrics (and particularly, though not in such variety, in MS Harley 2253) and in fifteenth-century lyrics. The religious lyrics employed a tradition separate from that of the secular lyrics and alliterative revival. In his four-part discussion of 'The Five Wounds of Our Lord' (*NQ*), Douglas Gray prints the text, with mention of the illustrations, from Bodleian MS Douce 1, including textual variants from the sixteenth-century printed version. He then gives an account of the origin and development of the cult with its iconographical connexions. He continues with literary and iconographical illustrations of the themes of the Five Wounds as remedies, as a refuge, and as wells or fountains, themes which are prominent in the poem in MS Douce 1 (a tiny book for private devotion), where an invocation is addressed to each of the wounds in turn. The naming of the wounds as wells and the illustrations are repeated in William Billyng's early fifteenth-century *The Five Wounds of Christ*. Billyng's poem, however, differs in details and was intended for public display, while his naming of the wells is paralleled in fifteenth-century finger-rings and stained-glass windows. Gray finally discusses other medieval illustrated poems, concluding that the illustrations in MS Douce 1 have most in common with the popular image of piety in the fifteenth century.

A continuing, and perhaps increasing interest in Mandeville, marked by the reprinting by the E.E.T.S., in 1960 and 1961, of the two volumes edited by Hamelius as long ago as 1916, is now clearly shown by the publication of the shorter Mandeville,[8] in which the details of the itinerary are pruned and attention is focused upon the marvels. Seymour's introduction, commentary and glossary are severely compressed, perhaps over-much so; it does not perhaps matter so much with the glossary, which does not contain many difficult words, but one would have liked notes at times more informative than merely mentioning details omitted in the shorter version, and most of all, it is tantalizing to find that the most important finding, that the scribe of MS E Musaeo 116 also wrote C.U.L. MS Gg. iv. 27, Part I, and may have been the amanuensis of Margery Kempe, 'will appear elsewhere'.

Seymour discusses 'The Irish Version of Mandeville's *Travels*' (*NQ*) extant in an incomplete state in two main manuscripts. This deliberate redaction, close in design to the Bodley version, was carefully made by Fingin O'Mahony in 1475 from an English defective version which is no longer extant. Also in *NQ*, Seymour and R. A. Waldron write on 'The Danish Version of Mandeville's *Travels*', extant in three MSS of the fifteenth and sixteenth centuries deriving independently from a lost archetype, which was probably translated in 1444 from an unidentified text of the Latin Vulgate Version.

William Matthews's anthology of Later Medieval English Prose[9] is an odd mixture; it has an excellent introduction, which has packed a great deal of information into comparatively small compass; in the main its bibliography is good (except perhaps for Wyclif), and its selections cover pretty well all aspects of medieval life. But the trouble is that the anthology is intended for the non-specialist reader, and the editor has modernized the spelling (which does not always matter), has replaced some forms by their modern equivalents, and has glossed obsolete words. It is always a hard task to judge how much (if at all) one should modernize; in this case—as in the passage from John Arderne—one wishes he had left well alone, as it seems to be more difficult to understand than the original.

Miss M. D. Anderson's book, *Drama and Imagery in English Medieval Churches*[10] breaks much new ground in an attempt to examine the relationship—if any—between church iconography and the medieval drama, especially the mystery plays. It is a fascinating study, if one in which it is too often impossible to come to a definite conclusion. Granted that certain scenes are shown in stained glass, on wall paintings and in sculpture, which figure also in medieval drama, if this material is aimed at the same popular audience then is it not likely that one influenced the other? Miss Anderson has certainly convinced the present writer that at the very least she has a case.

In 'A Suggested Location for the Digby *Mary Magdalene* (*TS*), Harry

[8] *The Bodley Version of Mandeville's Travels*. From Bodleian MS E Musaeo 116 with Parallel Extracts from the Latin Text of British Museum MS Royal 13 E. IX, edited by M. C. Seymour. E.E.T.S. No. 253. O.U.P. pp. xx + 188. 40s.

[9] *Later Medieval English Prose*, ed. by William Matthews. (Golden-tree Books Series.) New York: Appleton-Century-Crofts. pp. xii + 336.

[10] *Drama and Imagery in English Medieval Churches*, by M. D. Anderson. C.U.P. pp. xii + 248. 45s.

M. Ritchie points out the complex stage requirements of the play and suggests as a location Lincoln, which has a considerable religious dramatic tradition in the fourteenth and fifteenth centuries. A strong link between Lincoln Cathedral and the play lies in the presence at the Cathedral of the relics of Mary Magdalene, whose validity depended on the Magdalene in Gaul legend, which is extant in English only in the Digby play. In 'Shepherds and Prophets: Religious Unity in the Towneley *Secunda Pastorum*' (*PMLA*), William M. Manly raises again the question of whether the play functions as a secular farce with a Nativity scene or as 'a unified religious statement' in a traditional cycle. He finds the latter true, but not only because of parallel episodes. Following on E. Catherine Dunn (*YW* xlii. 72), Manly finds a 'prophetic principle' in the forward-linking undercurrent of Christian expletive in the language of the Shepherds who await Christ's birth. The insistent quality of their piety suggests more than unconscious anachronism or realism and reminds the audience that the play is an oft-told tale. The shepherds unconsciously function as a dramatically-integrated *Processus prophetarum*. The shepherds' speeches and especially Daw's have other suggestions of prophecy in their vision of world harshness appropriate to the play's dramatic purpose. Finally Manly sees echoes of Antichrist in the structural function and characterization of Mak, echoes which swell the religious-prophetic current of the play. John E. Bernbrock in 'Notes on the Towneley Cycle *Slaying of Abel*' (*JEGP*), points out how various unique features of plot and character in the play, such as Abel urging Cain to sacrifice, Cain's innate dislike of Abel, and the characterization of Cain in the first

part, could have been suggested by St. Ambrose's fourth-century treatise *De Cain et Abel*. The detailed parallels, for which no other source has been found, suggest that the Wakefield Master drew heavily on St. Ambrose.

D. S. Bland, in 'The Chester Nativity: One Play or Two' (*NQ*), notes that in this play the first 176 lines of an Annunciation plot, complete in itself, is followed by a *Nuntius* announcing Octavian and the Sybil in a scene which, in the Towneley Cycle, occupies its correct position as a prophecy of the birth of Christ before the Annunciation. In the Chester play after the prophecy, the plot moves on to the nativity and Octavian and the Sybil reappear to witness the fulfilment of the prophecy. The Annunciation-Nativity play was originally two, and the stitching is visible in the words of *Nuntius* which are in order at the beginning of a play but not a third of the way through it. The amalgamation may result from the failure of a guild or group of them to carry on their play. The York cycle includes a group of eight alliterative and realistic Passion plays (XXVI, XXVIII–XXXIII, XXXVI), which technically resemble each other and may be regarded as the rewriting (apart from change in basic subject matter) of one dramatist working after 1415. In 'The Art of the York Realist' (*MP*), J. W. Robinson measures the dramatist's success against other mystery plays and vernacular narratives which influenced the York cycle. He first briefly discusses the conventional aspects of the author's dramatic art and finds the openings of the plays distinguished by their variety, vigour and dramatic function. He then examines at greater length the unique quality of his realism, which is seen to advantage in the emphasis on (1) processes of behaviour, by according in detail dramatic speech with dramatic action, (2) mental processes, by showing action to be the result of genuine decision, in its turn the result of genuine persuasion, and (3) the realistic elaboration of character and situation in the various scenes. None of his special kind of realism is evident in the other four non-alliterative plays, except XL, XLVI, and none in the four non-alliterative plays associated with the Passion. The York reviser is a naturalistic dramatist, and each of his plays is self-contained, displaying variety in treatment, detail and stanzaic form.

V

Middle English: Chaucer

By JOYCE BAZIRE

1. GENERAL

Wolfgang Clemen's *Der Junge Chaucer*, which appeared in 1938 (*YW* xix, 64–66), has in the main been rewritten and enlarged, taking into account the research of the intervening years. As *Chaucer's Early Poetry*,[1] it is now readily available in an English translation by C. A. M. Sym, and covers those poems written during the first ten to twelve years of Chaucer's literary career. It is a valuable and straight-forward book, which should commend itself particularly to the student. It gives due emphasis to these early poems, treating them in their own right, not as experimental for the *Tales*, and showing Chaucer's achievement in transforming well-known frames and models and making them serve a new purpose. In the case of each of the three major poems, there is a careful examination to show how the effects are obtained through structure, verse, allusion, etc., and the chapter is conveniently divided into sections; but the 'allegory' of the poems is not discussed. Further points of interest discussed are Chaucer's reflection of his age and his position among his contemporaries.

The chapters on the *Book of the Duchess* and the *Parliament* are interesting to compare with *Fruyt and Chaf* (*ut inf.*) in view of the differing interpretations of the same elements, since Clemen provides a thorough commentary from the more conventional angle, in the first poem showing particularly in what ways Chaucer has gone beyond his French models. The *House of Fame* of course differs radically from the earlier poem, and conforms even less to existing genres. No one should demand from it unity or a central theme.

As the author acknowledges, the chapter on the *Parliament* owes much to the work of Bennett and Brewer, but the result is none the less essentially his own. Considerable emphasis is laid on the way in which Chaucer's art developed in the course of writing these poems, and shows in the *Parliament* the achievement of much of what he was striving after earlier.

In the minor poems too Clemen notes how Chaucer develops by experimenting from a more formal reliance on his models. Though his later poems may show the fulfilment of some of his earlier strivings, many new aspects emerge to make of them very different poems. [Reviews: S. S. Hussey, *NQ* xi, N.S. (1946), 348–9; Dorothy Bethurum, *S* xxxix (1964), 510–13; an article in *TLS* (1964, p. 510), 'Chaucer Grim and Genial', reviews Robertson (*A Preface to Chaucer YW* xliii, 78–9) Huppé and Robertson, Payne, Clemen, Craik, Brewer and Baugh.]

Fruyt and Chaf[2], which approaches

[1] *Chaucer's Early Poetry*, by Wolfgang Clemen. London and New York: Methuen, and Barnes & Noble. pp. x+214. 25s. & $5.

[2] *Fruyt and Chaf*, by Bernard F. Huppè and D. W. Robertson, Jr. Princeton U.P. and O.U.P. pp. viii+157. $4.50 and 36s.

two of Chaucer's poems along the lines proposed by Robertson in *A Preface to Chaucer* (*ut sup.*), suggests the main outline of what Chaucer wished to convey to the reader of the *Book of the Duchess* and the *Parliament of Foules*, though the authors do not believe in a single or absolute interpretation for either poem. Starting with Augustine, they establish the background for a hypothetical reconstruction of Chaucer's view of poetry, and show how through the ages the meaning was the essential, the kernel, and the fable or poetry the rind; they distinguish between *sense* and *sentence*. The burden was placed on the reader of discovering the real meaning, not only of the whole work, but also of the individual images.

The application of this theory is seen in the detailed and interesting commentary on the *Book of the Duchess*, which fits all parts of the poem into the interpretation that the authors place on it, though at some points the meaning of the images seems to be pressed too far. It is the death of Blanche that has deprived the dreamer of sleep, and Seys's message to Alcyone—one that she cannot accept—has a significance for the dreamer which he finally appreciates. The authors do not believe that the Black Knight is John of Gaunt (cf. *A Preface to Chaucer*, p. 465), but rather the sorrowing *alter ego* of the speaker in the poem, who is Alcyone-like in his grief. Through the questioning of the Knight, in order to reveal the true nature of his grief, the character of Blanche is also revealed and thus eulogized. Also by means of this dialogue, in the course of which it is shown that in his despair and desire the Black Knight is wrong, the dreamer himself is turned to the true Physician. In conclusion, the authors remark that the poem 'exists only partly in what it says'; its implications are left to develop in the reader's mind.

In similar fashion a careful commentary and interpretation are provided for the *Parliament*, and the emphasis is laid throughout on the two kinds of love, particularly in the case of the eagles whose self-centredness shows no conception of true love in accordance with God's order. The two levels in the poem are concerned with the earthly interpretation on the one hand and the heavenly on the other. Because of 'the great intellectual distance' between the original reader and the modern, a certain amount of the humour of the poem may be lost or seem different to us.

Whether or not one agrees with the authors in their theses, this book is very readable. It provides food for much thought and induces a careful re-reading of the poems. [Reviews: Rosemary Woolf, *EC* xiv (1964), 301–7; Donald R. Howard, *S* xxxix (1964), 537–41.]

While in his review article, 'Chaucer and Medieval Allegory' (*ELH*), appraising D. W. Robertson, Jr.'s *A Preface to Chaucer*, R. E. Kaske shows that he agrees in general with Robertson's views, he considers that one of the major values of the book is the fact that it suggests so many new starting points for reassessment of Chaucer. Kaske discusses fairly fully certain matters on which he differs from Robertson, some being points of detail, though others are rather wider issues, but he gives due praise to 'the richness of learning and the complexity of suggestion' in the book.

Albert C. Baugh's edition, *Chaucer's Major Poetry*,[3] omits *Anelida*,

[3] *Chaucer's Major Poetry*, ed. by Albert C. Baugh. New York and London: Appleton-Century-Crofts and Routledge & Kegan Paul. pp. xlvii + 615. $7.95 and £3.

the *Romaunt*, most of the *Legends* and over half the short poems. After a useful introduction covering Chaucer's life, language (here the section on syntax is particularly valuable) and versification, there follows a fairly comprehensive bibliography.

The most striking feature of the edition is the annotation of the texts at the foot of the page. The majority of the notes gloss words rather than explain allusions; those of the latter type are partly for the better understanding of the text, partly to indicate the extent of Chaucer's reading. Only very occasionally are references made to manuscript readings or suggested emendations. Baugh admits that the explanations may be repeated under different texts and gives his reasons for this, but there is repetition even in the same poem, where cross-references could have been used. The meanings of the majority of the words and phrases are to be found in addition in the Glossary, where again more cross-references would have made forms easier to find in certain cases.

In the space allowed at the beginning of each poem it is not possible for Baugh to do much more than indicate the main features of the works and the relevant trends in scholarship.

There is no doubt that by this edition most difficulties in translation will be removed for the student, but it is to be questioned whether, apart from sections of the introduction, it answers any other need. [Review: J. Burrow, *EC* xiv (1964), 307–10.]

The first chapter of Robert O. Payne's *The Key of Remembrance*[4] is devoted to 'The Rhetorical Tradition', a compilation of observations of other writers on the subject, with

a study of rhetoric and poetic and the merging of the two in rhetorical poetic.

From this he proceeds to Chaucer on the art of poetry and provides, with commentary, extracts in which Chaucer gives indications of his own attitude, though these are not viewed in chronological order. In the more individual survey of Chaucer's poems, much attention is paid to the *Prologue* to the *Legend of Good Women*, which seems to Payne 'more immediately concerned with the subject of poetry than any other single work' of Chaucer, and 'to reflect in a number of ways the uncertainty and searching of the transition from the *Troilus* kind of narrative to the *Canterbury Tales* kind'.

The three early poems all show some version of a formula 'book-experience-dream', and have several common features. In the *Hous of Fame* earlier problems, such as those found in the *Book of the Duchess*, are made the central motif, in so far as there is one, whilst the *Parliament* produces a much more finished statement, 'making of the whole an essay in poetics as well as a poem about its subject'.

Problems are again touched on in both the frame and the stories of the *Canterbury Tales*, and the tales Payne divides into three blocks, pointing out the use Chaucer made of the various types; and among the tales of 'sentimental experiment' he examines the *Prioress's Tale* more particularly.

Different from the other poems in that Chaucer has here remade 'a single, extensive, unframed narrative', *Troilus* can be analysed more satisfactorily than the others by the kind of criticism practised in the rhetorical manuals; and the analysis comes under four headings—action, characterization, lyric interpolation and

---

[4] *The Key of Remembrance*, by Robert O. Payne. London and New Haven: Yale U.P. p.p. xii+246. 37s 6d and $5.

authorial commentary—and emphasizes how much the poem stands apart from its predecessors. In it what Chaucer has been striving after earlier, comes closer to perfection. It is a highly rhetorical poem, but so much more than rhetoric.

Payne's book contains a good deal that is debatable, suggesting that Chaucer's work is much more contrived than it appears, and it is doubtful how far the later chapters really develop from the earlier. [Reviews: Gardiner Stillwell, *JEGP* lxiii (1964), 332–6; Elizabeth Salter, *NQ* xi, N.S. (1964), 109; R. T. Davies, *MLR* lix (1964), 625–7.]

Derek Brewer's *Chaucer in his Time*[5] provides an account, readable and interesting, though sometimes too colloquial, of the background against which Chaucer wrote. Although references are made to the poet's life and works where relevant, they are not directly discussed. The book is well illustrated by both quotation and photograph. [Review: R. M. Wilson, *English* xv (1964), 107.]

Brewer's approach contrasts with that of G. G. Coulton, who hung his account of the background on the pegs of Chaucer's life and works in *Chaucer and his England*.[6] This is a paperback edition of Coulton's well-known book, first published in 1908. In order to bring it somewhat up to date in the light of more recent criticism of Chaucer's works, a new bibliography, fairly general in character, has been supplied by T. W. Craik.

A new edition has appeared of

Tatlock and Kennedy's *Concordance*.[7]

Unlike Manly ('Chaucer and the Rhetoricians' [*Proceedings of the British Academy* xii (1926), 97]), William J. Farrell does not believe that Chaucer gradually abandoned rhetorical devices. Indeed the purpose of Farrell's article, 'Chaucer's Use of the Catalogue' (*TSLL*), is to demonstrate Chaucer's changing use of them by examining his practice in the use of the catalogue. In the *Book of the Duchess*, where the device appears frequently, it lacks originality. The *Parliament* shows the beginnings of its use for a real artistic purpose, and in Sir Thopas it is used for satirical purpose. By the period of *Troilus* 'it had become an integral part of the poetic context in which it appeared'.

To gain a proper understanding of Chaucer's use of the Dido-Aeneas story, Louis B. Hall evaluates this in the light of the tradition of Virgilian adaptation in 'Chaucer and the Dido-and-Aeneas Story' (*MS*). He examines five selected examples of the tradition, and finds that the techniques are similar. After comparing these with Chaucer's practices, he concludes that Chaucer alone in the *Hous of Fame* used the story as an exemplum, and in the *Legend of Dido* has presented a 'thoroughly integrated narrative'.

What was Chaucer's own view of the role of the poet? Some possible answers to this question are suggested by Alain Renoir in 'Tradition and Moral Realism: Chaucer's Conception of the Poet' (*SN*), which he summarizes as: 'a moral realist writing within the framework of his craft and his cultural tradition'.

In 'Chaucer and the Unnatural History of Animals' (*MS*) Beryl

---

[5] *Chaucer in his Time*, by Derek Brewer. London and New York: Nelson. pp. x+243. 25s. and $5.

[6] *Chaucer and his England*, by G. G. Coulton. London and New York: Methuen, and Barnes & Noble. pp. xvii+283. 25s. and $2.25.

[7] *A Concordance to the complete works of Geoffrey Chaucer and to the 'Romaunt of the Rose'*, by J. S. P. Tatlock and A. G. Kennedy. Peter Smith. $30.

Rowland examines the use Chaucer makes for comparative purposes of animals and their attributes.

2. CANTERBURY TALES

Students should benefit from T. W. Craik's exposition of *The Comic Tales of Chaucer*[8] as his detailed analysis leads to a greater understanding of them. Only those whose 'direct and distinct purpose . . . is to raise merriment' are included, and Craik defends his choice of some, for example the *Merchant's Tale*, which might not at first sight be classed as such. The tales are fitted into their dramatic context, though the *Shipman's Tale* at least seems almost independent of this, and here the interest lies in what Chaucer has been able to make of his source-material in which he was less fortunate. Naturally Craik does not dwell at length on problems in the tales, such as whether or not the Shipman's was originally intended for the Wife, but his account provides a good introduction to Chaucer's great poem and his work in general.

'Two Chaucer Notes' (*NM*) by Beatrice White deal first with proper names in the *Canterbury Tales*, with reference to their position in the line and the number of times they occur, and then with Sir Thopas's swearing 'on ale and bread'.

R. J. Beck's article, 'Educational Expectation and Rhetorical Result in *The Canterbury Tales*' (*ES*), first compares Chaucer's use of rhetoric in his earliest and his later works (where it was no longer external, but integral), and then groups the tales according to the part played by rhetoric in connexion with the relationship of tale and teller.

Alan A. Stambusky describes in

'Chaucer and Moliére: Kindred Patterns of the Dramatic Impulse in Human Comedy' (*Lock Haven Review*) the resemblances which he believes can be seen between certain of the *Canterbury Tales* and some of Moliére's works, in respect of the way the two authors set about their task of creating comic art. Despite the difference in time between them, in this sphere their abilities followed a common line.

It is the pilgrims' attitude to money that governs the order in which they appear in the *Prologue*. So Ruth Nevo maintains in 'Chaucer: Motive and Mask in the "General Prologue"' (*MLR*), and she explains how certain pilgrims—such as the Clerk—who may seem misplaced, can be fitted into her proposed order. As most are completely taken up with the world, the framework of the pilgrimage adds irony to their descriptions.

The several similarities between the tales of the Miller and the Merchant lead Janet Boothman to study particularly the two old husbands in '"Who hath no wyf, he is no cokewold": A Study of John and January in Chaucer's *Miller's* and *Merchant's Tales*' (*Thoth*). Both seem to suffer a moral chastisement, but they differ in that John, unlike January, does not appear as an 'exceptionally lewd old fellow'; and although Chaucer is regarding courtly love cynically, yet Nicholas and Alison are presented more favourably than their counterparts. Since the husbands are vehicles for the purposes of both Chaucer and the individual narrators, they are the victims of double irony. This parallelism raises the question of whether or not there is an underlying philosophical purpose in the relationship of all the tales.

James A. Hart refutes the idea that *the droghte of March* reflects Mediterranean rather than English climatic

---

[8] *The Comic Tales of Chaucer*, by T. W. Craik. London and New York: Methuen, and Barnes & Noble. pp. xv+156. 21s. and $4.50.

conditions. In '"The Droghte of March"': A Common Misunderstanding' (*TSLL*) he asserts that the description would fit the season in south-eastern England.

Stoddard Malarkey argues in 'Chaucer's Yeoman Again' (*CE*) that, in view of the rules of chivalry by which the Knight obviously lives, the Yeoman is much more likely to be his servant than the Squire's.

John M. Steadman, writing on 'The Prioress' Brooch and St. Leonard' (*ES*), indicates comments which may be made on the liberation associated with the saint and the suggestion of bondage in *vincit*, if the Prioress really belonged to St. Leonard's, Bromley.

Edmund Reiss argues in 'Chaucer's Friar and the Man in the Moon' (*JEGP*) that, by naming his Friar Huberd, Chaucer may have been playing on a popular association of friars and the Man in the Moon (and also Cain), and that the penultimate lines of the portrait may emphasize this.

In '*Double-Entendre* and the Doctour of Phisik' (*ANQ*) Joseph E. Grennen suggests other meanings which may lie behind *esy of dispence*.

Dennis Biggins, '"Pulling Finches and Woodcocks": A Comment' (*ES*), refers to Ericson's earlier remarks on this line in the description of the Summoner (*YW* xlii, 77).

Beryl Rowland comments on the reading *a cokkow or* (var. *of*) *an hare* in 'Chaucer's The Knight's Tale', A. 1810' (*Ex*).

Before the main action is reached in the *Miller's Tale*, Chaucer has established his characters by set portraits and preliminary action, so that the eventual punishments of the men are seen to be just. Paul A. Olson continues his article, 'Poetic Justice in the "Miller's Tale"' (*MLQ*), by considering the 'more intellectual logic' that the medieval reader may

have discerned. First he examines the imagery, and then the vices that the male characters illustrate, and notes the appropriateness of the tale for the Miller. Finally he remarks on the tale's effect on its two audiences, the fictive and the real.

Ruth H. Cline's 'Three Notes on The Miller's Tale' (*HLQ*) are concerned with three local (Oxford) saints, Oseney Abbey and the question of Absolon's lack of the tonsure.

James T. Bratcher comments on 'A Chaucer Analogue in Spanish-American Tradition' (*NQ*) with reference to the *Miller's Tale*.

'Chaucer's Custance' (*NM*), by Claude E. Jones, contains a brief résumé of Custance's persecutions, with references to source-material and Chaucer's additions, the most important of which Jones considers to be 'his revitalization of the principal character'.

Arthur Huseboe's article, 'Chaucerian Puns on "Brotel"' (*North Dakota Quarterly*), refers specifically to three passages in the *Merchant's Tale*, where a meaning connected with lechery as well as with fickleness or insecurity is to be understood.

'The Man of Law's Merchant-Source' (*ANQ*) by Neil D. Isaacs suggests two reasons for ascribing the source of the tale to a merchant.

The Wife of Bath's Prologue and *Tale* is the first of the masterpieces selected by Willene van Loenen Pursell for the essay, 'Love and Marriage in three English Authors: Chaucer, Milton, and Eliot' (*Stanford Honors Essays in Humanities*, vii) 'in which appear significant expressions of love's influence upon the woman's role in marriage'. Despite all she says, it is the Wife's desire for love, not her demand for mastery, that is supreme, and her tale is an illustration attached to the message of the prologue. Just as the important result of her fight with Jankyn was not the apparent mastery for her, but the knowledge that he loved her, so again in the story it is the heroine's quest for love which is important, with the characters really Alice and Jankyn in disguise.

As Robert A. Pratt indicates in 'Saint Jerome in Jankyn's Book of Wikked Wyves' (*Criticism*), only excerpts from *Jerome against Jovinian* were contained in Jankyn's book. Alice quotes the stories to enhance her own position, and Chaucer uses the accounts of good wives among the excerpts—neglected by Jankyn and Alice—in Dorigen's complaint, as a counterblow.

Richard L. Hoffman supports his interpretation of 1. 418 of the Wife's *Prologue* as a reference to the Dunmow flitch by mentioning an explicit allusion to it earlier in her *Prologue* ('The Wife of Bath and the Dunmow Bacon' [*NQ*]).

Beverly Boyd notes for the benefit of American readers the meaning 'spring' to be applied to 'The Wife of Bath's Gay Lente' (*ANQ*).

Beryl Rowland explains the significance of '"Wood . . . as an Hare" (The Friar's Tale, 1327)' (*NQ*).

To the defence of the *Clerk's Tale* comes Donald H. Reiman in 'The Real *Clerk's Tale*; or, Patient Griselda Exposed' (*TSLL*). The dramatic context suggests that the Clerk is resorting to irony, and all is directed to deciding 'the proper object of man's primary allegiance, the glories and the pleasures of this world, or God and the life hereafter'. Just as Walter's values were distorted, so were Griselda's in vowing perfect obedience to an earthly lord, which brought her into conflict with Divine Law, and it is the question of sovereignty and order, not patience, which links all parts of the tale. Reiman meets in advance objections which may be

made to his reading, one being that the pilgrims did not realize that Griselda was being satirized.

Far from being an 'organically unified characterization of a vicious and demented personality', the *Merchant's Tale* is 'an extraordinarily *un*-unified tale' and one not without humour. So maintains Robert M. Jordan in 'The Non-Dramatic Disunity of the *Merchant's Tale*' (*PMLA*). In the marriage encomium the husband is replaced by Chaucer the innocent, and a similar lack of unity is shown elsewhere in the tale; for example, the first half has little action, the second is courtly romance; January plays different roles in the two parts. Jordan concludes that the tale is of a composite nature containing many contradictions which, in their several ways, answer the demands of the particular situation of the moment, but throughout all the moral viewpoint remains firm.

Paul E. Beichner compares the Pardoner's achievement in his tale with that of the Wife of Bath in hers, namely an account of what each knows best—in the Pardoner's case fund-raising—for the entertainment of the pilgrims. In 'Chaucer's Pardoner as Entertainer' (*MS*) he shows how the Pardoner first describes his tricks, methods and props in the *Prologue*, then gives an example of his 'money-raising-sermon stuff', followed by a burlesque demonstration, but the Host, instead of responding in like manner, is angry and retaliates.

'Bihoold the Murye Wordes of the Hoost to Chaucer' (*NM*) by Beryl Rowland deals specifically with *elvyssh* and *fynde an hare* which, she suggests, may refer to a popular superstition.

'The "Greyn" in the "Prioress's Tale"' (*NQ*) is explained by James T. Bratcher as a breath-sweetener.

'Adam's Hell', by George B. Pace

(*PMLA*), singles out for comment the Monk's two opening tragedies, to be taken as a pair. They raise the question of Chaucer's concept of Hell, with the significance of its mention in the last line of the stanza, and this involves the study, particularly in English literature, of 'the matrix of medieval theology and legend' which gave rise to the tragedies. Apart from one, examples in English do not suggest that Adam was eternally damned, though some (which mention *limbus* or *limbo*) regard his stay as physically painless, whilst the others (which refer to bonds) indicate physical suffering. Pace concludes that it is the latter tradition that lies behind the Monk's version, though he believes that Chaucer himself was not unaware of the other tradition.

An interesting article by Arthur T. Broes, 'Chaucer's Disgruntled Cleric: *The Nun's Priest's Tale*' (*PMLA*), supports even here the theory that the story exists for the sake of the teller, although there is no portrait of the Nun's Priest in the *Prologue*. Differences are found from the French version of the tale, which enables the Priest to criticize the Prioress and show the cock, with whom the Priest is equated, in a more favourable light. The Prioress is to be identified with Pertelote, and she is also satirized by the implied comparison with the poor widow of the introduction, and her tale is ridiculed through Chauntecleer's discussion of dreams. The digressions have their place in establishing the Priest's intellectual supremacy over the Prioress. Through the satiric purpose, Broes maintains, a unity and added dimension are provided for this version of the beast-fable.

The problem discussed in R. T. Lenaghan's 'The Nun's Priest's Fable' (*PMLA*) is to define the quality of the combination of the two tones dis-cernible in the tale. To achieve this Lenaghan turns to the medieval history of the fable and establishes three reference points which he then proceeds to elaborate.

In 'Chauntecleer's "Venymous" Cathartics' (*NQ*) Joseph Grennen discusses the meaning of *venymous* in the *Nun's Priest's Tale*.

Grennen also writes on 'Chaucer's "Secree of Secrees": An Alchemical "Topic"' (*PQ*), and is concerned with the meaning of Chaucer's phrase in the *Canon's Yeoman's Tale* against the background induced by the *topos*.

A new attitude to the tale is proposed by Richard Hazelton in 'The *Manciple's Tale*: Parody and Critique' (*JEGP*). He asserts that the apparent incongruity is really carefully worked out for parodical effect. For true appreciation of this a study of the sources is essential, and superficially Chaucer's version is in the tradition of the moral fable, but Chaucer has realized the perverted moral of the tale. In his treatment of it in fabliau fashion he employs comic inversion for his characterization, and, as illustration of this, Hazelton reviews in detail Chaucer's conception of Phebus and shows how fabliau triumphs over romance. The excessive moralizing of the work also plays a part in the parody.

Hazelton, who is convinced that Chaucer's version is a later one than that of Gower, notes clues that point to Gower as the butt of Chaucer's parody, and also to the matter that was at the root of their disagreement, if there really was one. Hazelton also discusses Chaucer's relationship with his audience in this poem, and the Manciple's apparent identification of himself with the crow, and, through this, the crow's connexion with the author.

D. Biggins concludes in 'Chaucer:

G

CT (X) I 42–46' (*PQ*) that there is much significance behind the Parson's use of *rum, ram, ruf.*

3. TROILUS AND CRISEYDE

By way of some consideration of other examples from the *Canterbury Tales* of Chaucer's pose—that his poetic mission was 'the reporting of facts in tolerable verse'—E. Talbot Donaldson comes to discuss its literary value particularly in 'The Ending of Chaucer's *Troilus*'[9]. Modesty, he maintains, is endemic with Chaucer, the narrator, and his dramatic creations, and this modesty can lead to a complexity in meaning particularly in the end of *Triolus*. It is not that Chaucer himself was bewildered by his poem, as some have thought, but that tension has developed in the narrator's mind between what should be and what actually was. In a detailed examination of the last eighteen stanzas of the poem Donaldson demonstrates this, and also the meaning that Chaucer achieves thereby.

In the opinion of S. Nagarajan ('The Conclusion to Chaucer's *Troilus and Criseyde*' [*EC*]) the Christian conclusion is generally justified at the expense of the emotional response to the rest of the story. Nagarajan believes that the seeds of impermanence were shown in the love which was dependent on Fortune, and that it is still the narrator and not Chaucer who is speaking in the conclusion.

After commenting on the various dilemmas with which the three main characters of *Troilus* are confronted, and the ways in which they try to resolve them, Katherine Lever turns finally in 'The Christian Classicist's

[9] In *Early English and Norse Studies*, ed. Arthur Brown and Peter Foote. Methuen. pp. xii+225. 45*s*.

Dilemma' (*Classical Journal*) to the dilemma presented by the opposition of classicism and Christianity.

John F. Adams suggests in his article, 'Irony in Troilus' Apostrophe to the Vacant House of Criseyde' (*MLQ*), that the relevant passage contains astrological associations, and he sees sexual implications in it which throw a different light on Troilus's attitude to love.

Saralyn Daly's article, 'Criseyde's Blasphemous Aube' (*NQ*), is concerned with the implications of Criseyde's criticism, after her night with Troilus, of God's arrangement of night and day.

S. R. T. O. d'Ardenne points out in '*Troilus and Criseyde* and *The Tragic Comedians*' (*ES*) the indications that Meredith had Chaucer's poem in mind when he wrote his own work.

4. THE BOOK OF THE DUCHESS

A more unusual direction is given to the examination of the poem in 'Transitions and Meaning in *The Book of the Duchess*' (*JEGP*) by Georgia R. Crampton, a direction 'toward the hard statements Chaucer makes about deprivation, consolation, the hazards of fortune and the consequences of decision', which is achieved by 'the management of the transitions'. The author discusses the transitions of the narrative before the meeting with the Black Knight, which show three ways of meeting loss. In the next section Chaucer's inquiries about the nature of the loss act as refrain to the different stages—'shifts in attitude and progression in the narrative'. The final message is that, despite all happenings, life must go on.

After citing opinions of several writers on the *Book of the Duchess*, Rebecca L. Moreton, in 'Literary Convention in *The Book of the*

Duchess' (*UMSE*), concludes that, despite resemblances shown to exist between Chaucer's poem and this and that French love-vision, no incontrovertible model has yet been found for Chaucer.

Beryl Rowland, in '"A Round Tour of Yvoyre" ("The Book of the Duchess", 946)' (*NQ*) suspects there is a further reference to a chess piece here. She also suggests, pursuing the subject of 'The Chess Problem in Chaucer's *Book of the Duchess*' (*Ang*), that Chaucer's reference to *ferses twelve* indicates that he had in mind a different kind of chess-board, such as that used in the Courier game, on which twelve *ferses* could be made, and also that an astrological significance is implied.

'The Sources of "The Book of the Duchess"' (*MS*) by J. Burke Severs, concentrates mainly on the resemblances, which are more than just verbal, between the *Book of the Duchess* and *Le Songe Vert*, though resemblances to other French poems are also noted.

5. OTHER WORKS

J. Norton-Smith's 'Chaucer's *Etas Prima*' (*MÆ*) contains a detailed study of that poem, its connexion or otherwise with Boethius, its mood and probable date.

A consideration of whether or not a daisy has a smell is made by Beryl Rowland in 'Chaucer's Daisy (Prol. LGW, F. 120–3; G. 109–11)' (*NQ*).

Under the title, 'Structure of Three Minor Poems by Chaucer' (*UMSE*), A. Wigfall Green discusses these poems with abstract themes in respect of such matters as rhyme, vocabulary, tone and philosophy.

VI

The Renaissance

B. E. C. DAVIS

ADVENTURE and discovery are prime motives directing the course of the Renaissance, and in default of any comprehensive study wider in scope this chapter may suitably open with tribute to *The Age of Reconnaissance*,[1] by J. H. Parry, which tells the story of exploration, trade, and settlement beyond Europe during the fifteenth, sixteenth, and seventeenth centuries. Individuality, curiosity, and political consciousness were common to both Renaissance and Reconnaissance, but the Renaissance 'was primarily a Mediterranean achievement, the Reconnaissance primarily an Atlantic one'. The Iberian Peninsula, a starting point for most of the earlier voyagers, provided a rendezvous 'where Mediterranean knowledge, curiosity, and inventiveness met and inspired Atlantic courage and skill', but the earliest Atlantic voyagers were sailing long before the Italian Renaissance had seriously affected Iberian culture. Until the close of the fifteenth century knowledge of the world was confined within narrow limits, explorers having to rely largely on archaic maps, half-fictitious records, and guess-work. The three parts of Parry's work are entitled 'The Conditions for Discovery', 'The Story of Discovery', and 'The Fruits of Discovery'. His main concern is not so much with the tales of voyagers as with the factors and instincts which made the voyages possible and facilitated their expansion. The sphere of Reconnaissance surveyed embraces shipbuilding, seamanship, pilotage, navigation, cartography, armour, and fighting capacity. The political, economic, and moral forces directing the course and conduct of discovery resolve themselves into the crude formula 'Serve God, and grow rich', fulfilled in conquest, colonization, and the slave-trade. This is a handsome volume, generously illustrated, and supplying a wealth of information pertinent to different aspects of the Renaissance.

The Arensburg Lectures, first published under the title *Facets of the Renaissance*,[2] have been reprinted in the Academy Library of Harper Torchbooks. Wallace K. Ferguson examines 'The Reinterpretation of the Renaissance' through a survey of Renaissance historiography. Burckhardt's synthetic picture of Renaissance civilization he regards as derivative from a traditional anti-scholastic bias first encouraged by Petrarch, other humanists, and Protestant reformers. The reaction against Burckhardt may be attributed to revaluation of medieval scholarship and national self-consciousness. More recent writers, such as Panofsky and Cassirer, suggest a counter-reaction, perceiving new forces of the Renaissance reflected in social organization, philosophy, and art. Garrett Mattingly

---

[1] *The Age of Reconnaissance*, by J. H. Parry. Weidenfeld & Nicolson. pp. xv + 365. 50s.

[2] *Facets of the Renaissance*, ed. by William K. Werkmeister. New York: Harper & Row. Harper Torchbooks. pp. vi + 130. $1.25.

discusses 'Changing attitudes towards the State during the Renaissance' from the pioneer work of Marsiglio of Padua, who anticipates the modern notion of the sovereign state as a means of securing domestic peace. Imitation of Greece and Rome in Italian city-states 'meant a long step in the direction of substituting the religion of patriotism for the religion of Christ'. The resulting conflict is manifest in Machiavelli, 'a man mad about the state', who realized, none the less, that politics cannot be divorced from ethics, and, despairing of men left to their own resources, wistfully extolled the virtues of Lycurgan Sparta, and the early Roman republic. E. Harris Harbison compares Machiavelli's *Prince* and More's *Utopia* as two contemporary pictures of an ideal sovereign state, each of which has given a word to the vocabulary, and which together 'have come to personify the beginnings of modern political thinking'. Both More and Machiavelli were saved from the dilettantism of many other humanists through strong practical interests reflected in their common awareness of a changing society and in simplicity of style. The contrast between them was conditioned by differences of status and temperament. Machiavelli, reacting against the traditional 'Mirror of Princes', missed the 'moral dimension' of power. More, on the other hand, viewed the key sins of English society with the eyes of a city-dweller or a clergyman, finding unexploited resources in a Christian humanism compounded of classical and Christian ethic. Yet there are passages in *Utopia* which read like a commentary on *The Prince* and suggest a certain self-righteousness 'not unrelated to the later More, who conscientiously defended the burning of heretics'. Myron P. Gilmore, reviewing 'The Renaissance Conception of the Lessons of History', finds evidence of a new attitude in Petrarch's preoccupation with time, represented, on the one hand in the *Triumphs*, and, on the other, in his letters to Livy and Cicero, revealing his sense of association with the classical past. The growing importance attached to the humanistic study of history is shown at successive stages in the works of Salutati, Vergerio, Bruni, da Feltre, Machiavelli, and Bodin, the last of whom illustrates the sixteenth-century tendency to associate historical with legal studies. Paul Oskar Kristeller, writing on Renaissance Platonism, pleads for closer attention to the significance and influence of Renaissance philosophy, which, in his opinion, derives both from medieval Augustinian sources, and from direct study of Greek authors through contact with Byzantine scholars. The resulting theory of knowledge prefigured the Cartesian notion of innate ideas, and made a distinctive contribution to the natural, social and political science of the age.

A revised and much enlarged version of Gilmore's essay is included in *Humanists and Jurists*,[3] a collection of studies on different aspects of Renaissance historiography, the others bearing the titles 'Individualism in Renaissance Historians', 'Lawyers and the Church in the Italian Renaissance', 'Fides et Eruditio: Erasmus and the Study of History', 'Erasmus and the Cause of Christian Humanism', and 'Boniface Amerbach'. Of these the first, third, and fourth are pertinent to this chapter. Allowing that Burckhardt exaggerates the Renaissance cult of individualism, Gilmore finds some support for such a theory in the humanists' emphasis on the exemplary value of history,

[3] *Humanists and Jurists*, by Myron P. Gilmore. New York: Harper & Row. Harper Torchbooks. pp. xiv+184. $4.25.

noting, however, the other factors, more especially divine rule and destiny, taken into account by historians and political theorists. The writings of Erasmus, as a whole, are little concerned with history or historiography, as might be expected of a scholar whose proclivities were international rather than national; but the first of his works to appear in print was a letter in praise of Gaguin's *Compendium* of French history, with comments on the nature of history and the character of the historian, while his lifelong devotion to accurate scholarship, and the wealth of historical analogues embodied in his *New Testament* bear witness to a deep sense of historical values.

In a chronological survey of works specifically related to English history priority must be given to Eric Simons's *Lord of London*,[4] which tells the story of Jack Cade, 'a man of mystery', 'a gentleman in learning, whatever he may have been by birth', to judge from his proclamations, which show education and verbal skill, and from the fact that his forces were well trained, drilled, and equipped. Viewed on the surface, Cade's early successes, which brought him within near reach of becoming veritably 'Lord of London', are as unaccountable as his sudden collapse, precipitated through irresponsibility and successive blunders. His story, as here recounted, makes good reading. The author has fulfilled his object, which was 'to infuse into it some of the excitement it aroused in me', and in the process he has presented a vivid picture of turbulent London in the mid-fifteenth century. A new

selection of the *Paston Letters*[5] is designed by the editor, Norman Davis, 'to present an outline of as many of the principal concerns of the Paston family as can be made intelligible within its scope', a record the more memorable since what they write 'is perhaps of smaller consequence than their ability to write it'. The letters are abridged, technical passages being excluded, and the language has been modernized, though not to the extent of losing the essential character of the original. Many readers will be glad to have available this classic document of English social history, enriched with ample annotation, in a compact form and at a moderate price.

The domestic papers of another family contemporary with the later Pastons, the Celys of Aveley, Essex, provide the subject of an article by Alison Hanham entitled 'A Fifteenth-Century Merchant Family' (*History To-Day*). Lacking the humour and sophistication of the Paston letters, those of the Celys, none the less, furnish a full and realistic record of the everyday concerns of a wool-merchant family subject to the capricious fortunes of the rising *bourgeoisie*. There are the usual details of household expenses, rural affairs and pastimes, marriage arrangements, and the like. Of particular interest is the correspondence between Robert Cely the elder and his son George, conducted while the latter was combining business with education in Calais. Though some of the Cely papers were published by the Camden Society, many still remain in manuscript.

The contribution of English sailors and merchants to geographical exploit and discovery during the reign of Henry VII supplies material for a volume of the Hakluyt Society publications, edited by James A. William-

---

[4] *Lord of London*, by Eric Simons. Muller. pp. 243. 21s.

[5] *The Paston Letters*. A Selection in Modern Spelling, ed. with Introduction, Notes, and Glossary by Norman Davis. O.U.P. pp. xx+288. 8s. 6d.

son.[6] Its contents comprise an introductory survey of geographical knowledge and theory during the Middle Ages, documents relating to the Cabot voyages, Bristol and the New Found Land, and a Cartography of voyages, by R. A. Skelton. The documentary evidence cited indicates the rapid expansion of geographical project and discovery, showing that, by the end of the fifteenth century, Bristol sailors shared with the Portuguese knowledge of the Atlantic islands. Incidental items of special interest are John Dee's dating of the discovery of North America, the statement that John Cabot was of English origin, and excerpts from the *London Chronicle* concerning the voyages of 1498. This volume well deserves its place in the series to which it has been added, but a compilation embodying so much varied material should have included something more in the nature of a selective bibliography than the scanty list of references provided.

G. R. Elton's *England under the Tudors*[7] has been reprinted with an enlarged bibliography. Throughout this work the author's main concern is 'the condition, reconstruction, and gradual moulding of a state, the history of a nation and its leaders in political action, and therefore the history of government in the widest sense'. The Tudor form of government, in Elton's view, was not, as often stated, a new monarchy, but a return to an older one established by Edward I, which had steadily declined, Henry VII succeeding to a much depleted inheritance as ruler of a depressed people, whose mentality found expression in 'Timor mortis

conturbat me'. His achievement was to consolidate the monarchy, increase the revenue, and establish law and order. Throughout the reign of Henry VIII the political scene was dominated by the personality and self-interest of the King, supported, at successive critical phases, by Wolsey and Cromwell. 'The Tudor Revolution', brought about through the breach with Rome, the Act of Supremacy, and Cromwell's diplomacy, meant the establishment of 'national sovereignty,' i.e. government by a supreme head in matters spiritual and temporal, co-operating with a 'body politic' authorized to administer justice under the king. The policy of Wolsey, apart from his judicial activities, Elton considers to have been ineffective and misguided. Cromwell, on the other hand, he regards as an administrator of genius, who 'displayed to the full a constructive statesmanship the like of which is seldom found'. The later chapters of Elton's history deal with changing relations between Church and State under the later Tudors, the growth of sea-power, the conflict with Spain, and the Elizabethan Renaissance in literature and the other arts. This is an authoritative work and is likely to remain so, notwithstanding the criticisms of some of the author's conclusions made by other historians. His objection to the commonly accepted idea of Tudor despotism supplies a basis for discussion in 'A Revolution in Tudor History' (*Past and Present*), two sub-sections of which, by Penry Williams, concern 'Dr. Elton's Interpretation of the Age', and 'The Tudor State'. To these J. P. Cooper replies in a later note. In another article of the same periodical W. T. MacCaffrey, surveying 'Elizabethan Politics 1558–1568', finds government within this period, as opposed to the radical forces of the

---

[6] *The Cabot Voyages and Bristol Discovery under Henry VII*, ed. by James A. Williamson, with Cartography of the Voyages by R. A. Skelton. Hakluyt Soc. Publ. C.U.P. pp. xvi+332. 40s.

[7] *England under the Tudors*, by G. R. Elton. Methuen. pp. xi+504. 25s.

two previous reigns, deeply and consistently conservative. Lacking her father's 'naked ambitions', Elizabeth was conservative in her regard for the prerogative of royalty, her abhorrence of rebels, and a 'royal obstinacy' in maintaining her will against those of anxious and importunate advisers. Politics opened the way to both personal and family success for politicians of widely different types, ranging from Cecil, 'the first English statesman, with the exception of Cromwell, who could separate his own and his mistress's personal interests for the needs of the English state', and 'the joker in the pack', Robert Dudley.

The Reformation in England,[8] by Philip Hughes, first published in three successive volumes between 1950 and 1954, has been reissued in a new one-volume edition. Though the text as a whole has not been reset, the author has made some changes and corrections, and has added a book-list of important relevant works which have appeared since 1954. His book is already well established as an up-to-date authority of distinction by an expert historian and theologian. On the historical side motifs of special interest are the social and political consequences of changing religious organization and practice, the status and attitudes of the clergy, and relations between Elizabeth and her recusant subjects, on all of which topics new light is thrown. Concurrently the basic antitheses in dogma underlying these changes are treated at length. Embodying a vast store of erudition, theoretical and factual, this is at the same time a work of high literary quality, in which the author has sifted and ordered his material in such a manner as to impart

an Aristotelian dramatic interest to each of its three phases, 'The King's Proceedings', 'Religio Depopulata', 'True Religion Now Established'. While avowedly partisan, he presents his argument as a whole fairly and judiciously, and if, in this respect, exception may be taken to his treatment of Tyndale or special pleading in connexion with the Marian persecution, one has only to recall the spate of traditional polemic that has proceeded from the other side. In its new compact form this volume will make a handsome addition to any library. Another welcome reprint is Cape's paperback issue of Garrett Mattingly's *Catherine of Aragon*,[9] a full-scale biography of the ill-starred queen, whose personality and decisions, in the author's view, provide the key to much of the activity of the Spanish embassy for a third of a century, and constitute 'the story of a life which shaped history by not moving with its flow'. As Spanish princess and as England's queen, successively graced and disgraced, Catherine figures as the pawn of wrangling powers and intriguing politicians, in public life loved and respected, in private lonely, frustrated, and impoverished. On the other side of the picture is her versatile activity in promoting the new learning, furthering Henry's foreign policy, and saving the lives of London 'prentices after the ill May Day of 1517. True to the political faith in which she had been nurtured, she never preferred her own interests to those of her dynasty. The value and interest of this book exceed the limits of pure biography, extending to the European scene and its protagonists throughout a vital era of English history. An episode of the drama preceding Henry's divorce, when the King suddenly, in 1525,

---

[8] *The Reformation in England*, by Philip Hughes. Revised Edition. Burns & Oates. pp. xxv+408, xxiii+366, xxvii+460. 90s.

[9] *Catherine of Aragon*, by Garrett Mattingly Cape. pp. 343. 10s 6d.

exalted his natural son, Henry Fitzroy, as potential heir is the theme of a short article by J. Duncan Derrett (*RN*), who discusses the legal aspects of Henry's position and the consequent dilemma that confronted him, in view of the incompatibility between incestuous marriage and the testamentary recognition of a bastard as heir.

English Catholic education from the beginning of the Reformation to the end of the seventeenth century is the theme of an original study by A. C. F. Beales.[10] Three basic elements in this 'education under penalty' are distinguished as person-to-person relationship, modelled on the person of Christ, character training of the militant Christian, and Tridentine educational reform. The first is typified in William Allen, the second in Robert Parsons, and the third in Reginald Pole. The concept of *intellectus agens*, deriving from Augustine and Aquinas, presupposes a solemn partnership between parent, teacher, Church, and State, which was the bedrock of resistance, and still remains a central assertion in the Catholic educational creed. The roots of Elizabethan educational policy were laid during the reign of Edward VI. 'The educational policy of the later Tudors was quite clearly determined by their religious policy.' The reign of Queen Mary witnessed the installation of Cardinal Pole as Chancellor of both universities, removal of many heads of colleges, and provision for training Catholic clergy. The suppression of Catholic education under Elizabeth inspired Allen and Parsons, 'the inaugurators of modern Catholic education', to found colleges abroad. Allen's endeavours to keep clear of politics failed to prevent trouble between the secular

[10] *Education under Penalty*, by A. C. F. Beales. Athlone P. pp. xii+306. 50s.

clergy and Jesuits. Parsons returned to England in company with Campion, entrusted with the dual mission of spiritual ministration and the distribution of books. Beales's work throws new light upon many of the activities and achievements of the English mission, including the spread of the Catholic printing industry, the persecution and escape of recusant schoolboys, and clandestine teaching both by private teachers and in schools, as at Scarisbreak, Lancs, where 'Catholics to-day can claim a tradition of schooling hardly broken since the Elizabethan settlement'.

The use of computers in textual research, with special reference to the work of S. M. Parrish and E. G. Fogel, is described in 'The Year's Contribution to English Renaissance Textual Study' (*Manuscripta*), by William C. McAvoy, who suggests 'that we are entering into the most exciting and potentially rewarding period of textual criticism that not only Elizabethan, but textual scholars of all periods have ever known'. This, clearly, at present remains an open question. In the meantime the year has brought an average harvest of bibliographical work on traditional lines. 'The Books and Patronage of Learning of a Fifteenth-Century Prince' (*BC*), i.e. of John, Duke of Bedford, brother of Henry V, are discussed by M. J. Barber from the evidence of Bedford's surviving books and records of his contacts with English and French universities. His library included, besides devotional works, treatises on natural science and astrology, some of which he commissioned. He encouraged a vigorous reconstruction of studies at Paris, appears to have possessed a library at Rouen, and bestowed patronage on the universities of Caen and Oxford. Allowing for genuine piety and a taste for the magnificent, 'the necessity of playing patron to learned men and to the world of learning illustrates how essential a part such matters played in the climate of political opinion as well as in the everyday routine of the household of a great prince'. Two contributions to *Gutenberg Jahrbuch* call for notice. 'Caxton through the Looking Glass', by George D. Painter, is an examination of offsets of a fragment of Caxton's *Fifteen Oes* preserved in the British Museum as a pastedown within a copy of the second edition of *The Mirrour of the Worlde*. The fragment was described by Henry Bradshaw, whose inference that this copy of the *Mirrour* was bound by Caxton's binders is confirmed by later investigation. Painter produces evidence suggesting that the offset derives from an edition of the *Horae*, and weighs the claims of Caxton and De Worde as its printer. Frederic C. Avis contributes an account of 'St. Paul's Churchyard as a Sixteenth-Century Printing Centre', based upon records dating from 1509, which show that in the course of the century about one quarter of London printers were established in this area. The names recorded include those of the royal printer to Edward VI, the earliest printer of copperplate in England, and others prominent in the affairs of Church and State. Their publications can be classified as religious, polemical, legal, educational, and literary. Appended to the article is a reconstructed plan of printing-houses, and a list of printers' signs.

In *The Script of Humanism*,[11] based on lectures given at King's College, London, James Wardrop examines the origin and development of humanistic cursive, the antiquarian and scholarly influences that affected its character, and its extension from study to curia. Such a line of research he justifies on the ground that 'we may confidently expect the personalities and the scripts of the humanists mutually to illustrate and explain one another'. Script was first the servant of scholarship; thus, 'informality is the keynote of italic; rapidity its virtue; utility its aim'. Appended to the lectures are a bibliography, critical apparatus, and plates. *The Italic Hand in Tudor Cambridge*,[12] by Alfred Fairbank and Bruce Dickins, consists of a collection, with comment, of forty-one specimen plates designed to illustrate 'the skill, taste, and charm of Tudor Cambridge calligraphy'. The illustrations are drawn from letters addressed to state officials by dignitaries of the University, where skill in penmanship was considered a necessary qualification for the office of Orator. The calligraphical material, compiled by Fairbank, is amplified with historical, biographical, and bibliographical commentary by Bruce Dickins. Close examination shows that 'Personality is expressed even in the most disciplined handwriting', which justifies reference to 'the Cambridge style' and even 'the Cheke style', the latter being endorsed in Strype's assertion that Cheke 'brought in fair and graceful writing by his Pen, as he wrote an excellent hand himself'. The influence of Cheke's penmanship was more widely disseminated through the secretarial activities of his pupil Ascham both at Cambridge and at the courts of four monarchs, which, in Fairbank's view, would account for the subsequent trend in the style of Italic writing. *The Cambridge Bibliographical Society*

[11] *The Script of Humanism*. Some aspects of Humanist Script 1460–1560, by James Wardrop. Clarendon P. pp. xiv+60. 63s.

[12] *The Italic Hand in Tudor Cambridge*, by Alfred Fairbank and Bruce Dickins. Camb. Bibliog. Soc., Monog. No. 5. Bowes & Bowes. pp. viii+32. 21s.

Transactions include articles on 'A Sixteenth-Century Inventory of the Library of Corpus Christi College, Cambridge', by John M. Fletcher and James K. McConica, 'English Bokes concernyng James Morice', by J. C. T. Oates, and 'The First Book printed in Anglo-Saxon Types', by John Bromwich. The Corpus Christi inventory is written in a sixteenth-century hand by a well-informed scholar, and was possibly designed to serve as a catalogue of books housed in a new room over the kitchen. The writers of the article suggest that the list may have been compiled during the reign of Queen Mary, when Cardinal Pole appointed a commission to visit the University and report on the contents of its libraries, a situation which would account for the lack of reference to any modern or controversial works. The 'Kalender' of Morice's books is entered on a leaf in a Cambridge University Library copy of the English *De Senectute* printed by Caxton in 1481. Morice has been identified by Sears Jayne with the Clerk of Works to Margaret Beaufort, and further details concerning his life and family are here added by Oates, who dates the 'Kalender' about 1508. The books listed represent a typical cross-section of early printed texts, including the *Kalender of Shepherdes*, the *Seven Wise Masters*, the *Canterbury Tales*, 'Gower', and 'Lydgate'. The earliest text printed in Anglo-Saxon was one of Ælfric's Easter homilies, prepared by Archbishop Parker, and published in 1567 under the title *A testimonie of antiquitie* with the immediate object of defending Communion in both kinds by appealing to ancient precedent and to the authority of an English divine, whose ruling had been deliberately neglected. 'Money, time, and learning were lavishly expended on it, because it was politically, as well as doctrinally

important.' Of the five extant manuscripts, two in Cambridge University Library, two in that of Corpus Christi, Cambridge, and one in the British Museum, four apparently were known to Parker and his assistants, whose combined efforts produced a book representing a triumph over great technical difficulties. This is sufficiently evident from the specimens reproduced in the article, and from the marked manuscripts upon which they are based.

Walter F. Schirmer's *Der Englische Frühhumanismus*, first published in 1931, has been reissued by another publisher with minor additions and revisions.[13] This was a pioneer study of a neglected phase of the English Renaissance, covering the development of humanism in England from book-collecting by Richard of Bury to systematic study in Italy by Linacre and his contemporaries, and taking into account Poggio's sojourn in England, the scholarly patronage of Duke Humphrey, and the Italianate contact of fifteenth-century English scholars. Inevitably further attention has been given to this subject in the course of the last thirty years, but Schirmer's work still holds its place as a basic authority, and the new edition, rendered more attractive by much improved type and lay-out, is welcome. 'Work in Progress II: Renaissance Literature' (*EC*), by F. W. Bateson, is an extract from a forthcoming guide-book to English and American literature, containing lists, with comments, of editions, biographies, etc., 'with inter-chapters on the proper approach to each of the principal periods'. Contrasting his own view of the Renaissance with that of some earlier writers, for instance Pater and Eliot, Bateson stresses first

---

[13] *Der Englische Frühhumanismus*, by Walter F. Schirmer. Tübingen: Max Niemeyer. pp. vii+183. DM. 26.

the impact of the economic factor. 'Shakespeare's plays *were* the product of inflation, because at bottom they are the objective correlatives of a morality that had been developed in the process of his society's adjustment to inflation.' The necessity of getting more money was met by the alternative solutions of unadventurous hard work and adventurous fortune-hunting, particularly at Court, the former typified in the middle-class Puritan, the latter in the upstart courtier. Hence the dichotomy between the 'bravery' and 'affectate curiosity' figured by Fraunce in the *Arcadian Rhetorike* and the ambiguity of speech between Court, City, and Country. Thus far, with reservations, one can follow Bateson's argument, but not necessarily to the point of accepting his distinction between the 'literary bravery' of the court poet, and the neo-classic patterns of the middle-class Puritan typified in *Lycidas*. The second section of the article illustrates the predominance in Renaissance literature of dramatic speech, exemplified in the forcefulness, immediacy, and resonance of short passages and poems, even of single lines from Wyatt to Webster, where the literary unit is a speech-unit expressive of a situation, and compounding past, present, and future. The theme of the last section is 'The Ego and Fortune', figuring the Stoic fatalism predominant in much Renaissance literature, particularly in tragedy. While some of Bateson's conclusions seem overstrained, his article, read as a whole, suggests some interesting revaluations. A different way of approach to the Elizabethan age is indicated by John Buxton in *Elizabethan Taste*,[14] in which literature is surveyed in juxtaposition with architecture, painting, sculpture, and music. The pre-

vailing confidence of the Elizabethans Buxton attributes to the fusion of native and classical traditions, which characterized much of Elizabethan literature and culminated in *The Faerie Queene*. The same tendency reveals itself in the spirit of compromise directing the work of judicious Hooker, and in the sense of balance, a detached, critical view reflected in the Elizabethan concept of the courtier, as contrasted with the uncompromising fanaticism of the seventeenth century. This thesis, if over-simplified, is plausibly argued. Other features noted as common to literature and the other arts are love of ceremony, elaboration, and gaiety in reaction against the sombreness of the later Middle Ages. In architecture homes took precedence over castles, and the Elizabethan mansion, typified in the work of Bess of Hardwick, shows the eclecticism characteristic of Elizabethan art. Literary description is clearly influenced by visual art, though little seems to have been known at first-hand of the Italian painters. Changing taste in music is indicated in the contrasting views of Ascham expressed in *Toxophilus* and *The Schoolmaster*. It is disappointing that Buxton should have virtually ignored taste in literary criticism, apart from some comment on the Elizabethan attitude to Chaucer, but this may be attributed to the plan of his book as a comprehensive general survey, lacking space for close analysis.

Margaret Schlauch's *Antecedents of the English Novel, 1400–1600*[15] covers a wide range of topics, including the heritage of medieval fiction, different types of romance, the rise of popular fiction, *novelle* of the early Renaissance, Elizabethan courtly

[14] *Elizabethan Taste*, by John Buxton. Macmillan. pp. xiv+370. 35s.

[15] *Antecedents of the English Novel, 1400–1600*, by Margaret Schlauch. Warszawa PWN and O.U.P. pp. 264. 25s.

tales, and the immediate precursors of the modern novel. Throughout her survey the author preserves an even balance of interest between the contents and form of the works discussed against their social and domestic background, as exemplified in her comments on the contributory techniques of romance, the survival of earlier fictional types in the later Middle Ages, and the use of allegory, debate, fabliaux, and *exempla*. The importance of romances as documents of social history is shown in sections on the place of women in the chivalric code and on *Sir Gawain* as 'society romance', prefiguring developments in later fiction, even 'to an exceptional degree that unity of point of view which was to become a cardinal matter of technique for later writers like Henry James'. The fictional works of Caxton reflect the influence of printing, the contact of the printer with his patrons, the revival of interest in anti-Saracen romance following the capture of Constantinople, and the impress of a new military society. Advance towards realism appears in the jesting heroes of anti-romantic *novelle*, and distinctive common patterns can be traced between late medieval romance and the well-mannered fiction of Lyly, Sidney, and other Elizabethans, who fused chivalry with Hellenism, Arcadianism, and Euphuism. In an article contributed to *Philologica Pragensia* Miss Schlauch examines an unfamiliar English prose version of the tale of Mary of Nijmeghen, 'the female Faust'. Printed at Antwerp by Jan Doesborgh, this tale was derived, directly or indirectly, from a Netherlandish miracle-play of the later fifteenth century. The author has perfunctorily followed the stage directions, speeches, and dialogue from his original, only occasionally adding vivid touches of his own. He has been identified with Lawrence Andrews, who worked for Doesborgh, and Miss Schlauch notes some parallels between the tale and other ones in English of Netherlandish origin belonging to the same period.

Specimens of an important antecedent to realistic fiction are provided in *A Hundred Merry Tales and Other Jest-Books of the Fifteenth and Sixteenth Centuries*,[16] edited by P. M. Zall and designed 'to show milestones in the development of jest-books printed between 1484 and 1584'. The collection comprises Caxton's *Fables of Alfonce and Page*, *A Hundred Merry Tales*, *Howleglas*, *Tales and Quick Answers*, *Merry Tales Made by Master Skelton*, and a selection from Deloney's *Mirrour of Mirth*. The spelling, punctuation, and typography of the original texts have been modernized, but with the minimum of tampering with the language itself. An introduction sketches the background to jest-books in classical and medieval sources, the effect of which appears in the blending of classical, oriental, and humanistic features. The stories are shown to have served diverse functions, the provision of *exempla* for preachers, quick answers like those of Howleglas, 'a rounded figure, consistently inconsistent', lessons in theology or civility. All alike are meant to be spoken, not merely read, being 'sometimes seemingly taken down from actual speech'. In style, setting, and characterization they foreshadow *The Mirrour of Mirth*, which employs techniques of dramatic realism and portraiture similar to those of the jest-books, but with a more acute sense of artistic form.

Vinaver's theories concerning the

---

[16] *A Hundred Merry Tales and Other Jest-Books of the Fifteenth and Sixteenth Centuries*, ed. by P. M. Zall. Lincoln: Nebraska U.P. pp. 394. $6.00.

composition of Malory's *Morte Darthur*, deduced from analysis of the Winchester manuscript, provide a point of departure for each of the contributors to *Essays on Malory*,[17] edited by J. A. W. Bennett. The collection opens, appropriately, with Walter Oakeshott's exciting story of his discovery of the manuscript, 'the result of a fortunate series of accidents', in the course of research work unconnected with Malory, whom he had never read. C. S. Lewis confronts us with five paradoxes which struck him in reading Malory, the contrast between the shady record of the author and the ethic of his work, his seeming effort 'in telling marvels to eliminate the marvellous', his incongruous treatment of 'interwoven or polyphonic narrative', his handling of the Graal motif, inconsistency between individual stories and their assemblage in one book, and, in sum, the grand paradox that the work 'should succeed by its failure to realize every single intention he had when he made it'. In an epistolary reply, 'On nature and art', Vinaver relates such paradoxes to the discrepancy between intention and achievement perceptible in every art, and defends his views on the structure of Malory's work as those of the editor rather than of the critic. The unity of 'the hoole book', according to D. S. Brewer, depends not upon structure, like that of ancient epic, but upon tone, atmosphere, and the society which it depicts. Combining elements of *fabula* and *historia* derived from its originals, it is lacking alike in abstract thought and conscious artistry. P. E. Tucker, discussing 'Chivalry in the *Morte Darthur*', argues that Malory has rejected the ideal of courtly love presented in French romance, and discovered for himself

a new ideal of high moral character, presented at large in Lancelot, Tristan, and the Graal story, 'the highest type of excellence in man, his worship'. A different interpretation of Lancelot is offered by F. Whitehead, who finds in 'Lancelot's Penance' the prevailing themes of thwarted affection and lamentation for former friends. Sally Shaw, in a closing essay on 'Caxton and Malory', compares the collected works in the Winchester manuscript and Caxton's *Morte Darthur* with respect to text, structure, language, and style, noting the greater predominance in Caxton's version of moral and Christian motifs, and concluding that this is the later text. A chapter in R. S. Loomis's *Development of Arthurian Romance*[18] is devoted to *Morte Darthur*, with special reference to Malory's treatment of his sources, which, Loomis considers, showed sound judgement and steadily progressive artistry. While Malory may not at first have conceived of the work as a single grandiose project, long before he completed it 'he surely recognized that the units could be worked into a larger, somewhat more coherent whole, and so took measures to achieve this coherence'. Malory's uneven style is attributable partly to his use of different types of material, though sometimes his apparent faults may be counted as merits, and it is paradoxical that from the mediocre stanzaic *Morte Darthur* he should have derived some of his most memorable phrases, particularly in the last episode of Arthur and Bedivere.

A copy of Ficino's *Epistolae* in the library of All Souls' College, Oxford, with extensive additions in the handwriting of Colet, supplies data for Sears Jayne's *John Colet and Marsilio*

---

[17] *Essays on Malory*, ed. by J. A. W. Bennett. Clarendon P. pp. x + 147. 21s.

[18] *The Development of Arthurian Romance*, by Roger Sherman Loomis. Hutchinson. University Library. pp. 199. 15s.

Ficino,[19] comprising introduction, text and translation, and appendixes. The additions include two letters from Ficino to Colet, one from Colet to Ficino, and some 5,000 words of marginal comment, which 'thus presents us with one of the few extant detailed commentaries by a Tudor scholar on the work of an Italian humanist, and adds a good deal to the available primary material about Colet'. It suggests that Colet never met Ficino, that his primary interest was theological and practical rather than philosophical and theoretical, and his mentality Aristotelian rather than Platonic, Platonism being only a tributary to the main stream of his thought, 'colouring its waters for a short distance, and then disappearing'. From internal and external evidence Jayne deduces the chronological order of Colet's commentaries, suggesting that some of these were designed to serve as qualification for the D.D. The *Enchiridion Militis Christiani* of Erasmus, first published in 1503, ran to more than thirty editions in five different languages during the next twenty years. A new translation,[20] by Raymond Himelick, is designed to make good the scarcity of English versions of a work which 'reveals the influence of Colet's advocacy of faith and self-sacrificing loyalty to Christ rather than to dogma or the performance of rites', and reflects 'the deep impression Colet's preaching on St. Paul had made on Erasmus'. The *Enchiridion* presents Erasmus's concept of 'an inward religion, a Christianity based upon the ethical implications of the "philosophy of Christ"', and a return to Christian primitivism to the exclusion of ceremonial accessories; at the same time, the vision is that of a humanist, a 'classical Christianity', inspired partly by generous admiration of pagan authors. Here, as in many of his writings, Erasmus is on common ground with Colet and other English humanists. The new translation is supported and clarified by brief notes supplying references and analogues from other Erasmian works. The letters of Erasmus relating to Cambridge have been published in a translation by D. F. S. Thomson, with commentary and notes by H. C. Porter.[21] They are of particular interest since it was at Cambridge that Erasmus began to lecture on the Greek language and began systematic work on his translation of the New Testament. The collection contains sixty-four letters, the two earliest being dated August, 1511, and addressed from Queen's College, with which Erasmus appears to have had some special association. It includes six letters to Colet, and throws light on the writer's opinions, reading, and impressions of Cambridge, 'this silly, dirty place', characterized by a 'spirit of laziness', and 'quiet ugliness'.

The History of King Richard III has appeared as Volume II of the Yale edition of More's complete works.[22] It comprises both the English (1557) and Latin (1565) texts, printed in parallel, a full textual apparatus, including variant readings from the Chronicles of Hardyng and Hall, a collation of extant manuscript versions, and the draft of the Latin text preserved in MS Arundel 43 at the College of Arms. The relation between

[19] *John Colet and Marsilio Ficino*, by Sears Jayne. New York and O.U.P. pp. 172. 45s.

[20] *The 'Enchiridion' of Erasmus*, tr. with an introduction by Raymond Himelick. Bloomington: Indiana U.P. pp. 224. $2.45.

[21] *The Cambridge Letters of Erasmus*, tr. by D. F. S. Thomson, with Introduction, Commentary, and Notes by H. C. Porter. Toronto U.P., and O.U.P. 52s.

[22] *The History of King Richard III*, ed. by Richard S. Sylvester. The Yale Edition of the Complete Works of St. Thomas More, Vol. 2. Yale U.P. pp. cvi+312. $12.50. 90s.

the texts is examined in the Introduction. Comparison of the five English printed versions with the four Latin ones, three of which are extant only in manuscript, points to the conclusion that More wrote the *History* in both languages for the benefit of both English and European readers, leaving both unfinished, and, further, that each text has been affected by redactions. The problem of textual variants is related to More's treatment of his theme, his object in shaping 'the Richard legend', and his habit of composition *per occasionem* shown in this and other works, including *Utopia*. On the purely historical side, the editor makes no claim to have plucked out the heart of the mystery, leaving 'both white and red rose to flourish in the arbors of those who know best how to tend them'. The Introduction incorporates useful comments on variant readings in the Latin versions, More's use of his sources, his literary methods, and his notion of history as *exemplum*, reflected in the contrast he draws between 'the good king that was' and 'the bad king to be', which connects *Richard III* with the nearly contemporary *Utopia*. This is an authoritative work of scholarship, well produced, and illuminated by excellent illustrations. It promises well for the edition which it inaugurates. This does not exhaust the editor's contribution to the year's work on More, which includes two articles on panegyric poems by More's admirers. 'The "Man for all Seasons" Again' (*HLQ*) concerns two poems addressed to More by Robert Whittington, the author of the descriptive cognomen recently popularized, which echoes a phrase in *The Praise of Folly*. The first extols More's poetic gift, his knowledge of ancient languages, law, and history, and the power of his oratory, controlled by

wisdom, and tempered by humour. The second is less ostentatiously poetic, its interest stemming mainly from an early reference to *Utopia*. Both imply personal knowledge of More, and seem to be products of the 'grammarians' war'. In another article, contributed to *PQ*, Sylvester discusses two poems to More by John Constable included by the latter in a collection of his Latin poems. These closely resemble the two poems of Whittington, published in the previous year (1519), which they may have been intended to rival or attack, in view of Constable's violent abuse of Whittington in another of his poems.

The scope of *L'Univers de Thomas More*, by Germain Marc'hadour, is defined in a sub-title as 'A critical chronology of More, Erasmus, and their epoch (1477–1536)'.[23] In a lively prologue the author describes his object and way of approach to the 'universe' of the statesman, humanist, and Christian martyr, 'without fear and without reproach', whose whole achievement affords a rare example of the fusion of literature and life. The chronological compilation constituting the main body of the work falls into three phases, from 1477, accepted as the date of More's birth, to 1500, from 1500 to 1536, and, as epilogue, from 1537 to 1559. Included with the date heading each yearly division in the central part is the date of Easter Day, in consideration of the influence of Easter and Lent on the general pattern of life at this time. The first part consists of a detailed inventory of events in 'Theatrum Mundi' and in the biography of More, running continuously in chronological order. In the central part, constituting about

[23] *L' Univers de Thomas More*. Chronologie critique de More, Erasme, et leur époque (1477–1536), by Germain Marc'hadour. Paris: Vrin. pp. 588. 60 NF.

four-fifths of the whole work, the items under 'Theatrum Mundi' and 'Erasmus and More' appear side by side on opposite pages. The 'Epilogue' is a single chronological list of outstanding events in 'Theatrum Mundi' and in the circle of More up to 1559. An immense amount of research and careful sifting has been devoted to this compilation, which the author describes as 'only a chapter, though a gigantic one', in a more ambitious study of More. It should prove an invaluable book of reference to other workers in the same field.

The function of the prefatory letters and verses in *Utopia*, is the theme of an article in *S Ren*, by Peter R. Allen, who considers this somewhat complicated machinery to be not merely a blurb, but specifically designed to ensure interpretation of the ensuing work as a document of northern European humanism. He supports this view by sketching the careers and activities of the principal contributors and persons mentioned, noting the contacts of each with the broad humanistic movement, to which More himself became attached during his visit to Flanders in 1515. Turning from the contributors to their contributions, we enter a world of scholarly discussion. 'The letters thus foreshorten space, and, in their one language, create the sense of a small, friendly group of humanists, whose conversation revolves around the central subject of *Utopia*.' The speakers consciously take part in a literary game, thereby adding to the ambiguity of *Utopia* in its blend of fact and fiction. The subjects of their discussion are the commonplaces of humanism, the value of scholarship, the ideal state, the man of many-sided talent, Christian ethic. Thus their letters and verses 'share in both the fictional aspect of *Utopia*, and in its serious intent, and commend it both

as a delightful literary game, and an important philosophical work.' A. R. Heiserman, discussing 'Satire in the *Utopia*' (*PMLA*), argues that More has his own concept of satire, distinct from that of Erasmus, and that this may be deduced from the preface to his translations from Lucian and from the letter to Giles concerning the nature of fiction in *Utopia*. In practice, as shown throughout *Utopia*, he pays close attention to satiric objects and techniques as means of inducing satiric verisimilitude and of creating a *via diversa* after the manner of the *Republic*; but the fusion of elements in his satire is organic, not mechanical. 'All of More's ideas and inventions were determined by a formal principle, to teach virtue by an attack on vice.' The satiric element in *Utopia* is discussed, though from a different aspect, by Robert C. Elliott, in 'The Shape of *Utopia*' (*ELH*), where it is related to More's apparent inconsistencies and heterodox views on communism, toleration, euthanasia, and other topics of disputation. In Elliott's view *Utopia* can be considered a prose variation on the types of satire represented in Horace, Juvenal, and Persius, as well as that in Lucian and Augustine. The satiric intention is both positive and negative, realistic and idealistic. '*Utopia*, like many formal verse satires, is "framed" by an encounter between a satirist and an adversary.' Both More and Hythloday are expert in their roles, and the former does not necessarily speak in his own person, but rather as a mercurial character after the manner of traditional satire. Hythloday, likewise, 'can use the technique lightly, . . . or with bitter, driving, daring intensity', with the result that 'the shape of *Utopia* is finished off, enigmatically but firmly, in the terms Hythloday provides'. In a note on More's mention of the

'Syrians' in *Utopia* (*NQ*), Mahmoud Manzaloui supports Lupton's suggestion that this may refer to the Mamelukes on the additional ground that it may be a topical allusion to the defeat of the Mameluke troops by the Ottoman army in August, 1516, in which case *Utopia*, Book 1, at least in its final form, should be dated somewhat later than is generally supposed.

Rainer Pineas pursues his examination of More's polemic duel with Tyndale in 'More versus Tyndale: A Study of Controversial Technique' (*MLQ*), and 'William Tyndale: Controversialist' (*SP*). Having dealt in an earlier article with More's use of dialogue, he now particularizes more closely the polemic devices which More habitually uses as appeal to the authority of the Church and the Fathers, the testimony of miracles wrought by God through the Church, the appeal to custom and to Holy Scripture, the use of Colet's method of Biblical exegesis, logical reasoning, changing his terms within an argument, and innuendo at his opponent's expense. In Tyndale Pineas notes the frequent use of irony, with a humorous by-play distinct from the straight humour of More, quotation from the Bible, and the reduction to absurdity of his opponent's arguments. Tyndale's method of argumentation tends to be pragmatic rather than theoretical, reflecting his preference of dogma to theory, and showing a predilection for fallacies, sophism, and question-begging. His use of 'modified dialogue form' is 'a major example of the economy of treatment which is the outstanding characteristic of all his polemical works, and which gives him the advantage, as a popular writer, over More, who admits that the length of his own works creates a barrier to his readers'. To conclude the survey of work on More and his circle, attention is called to the reprint of E. V. Hitchcock's edition of Harpsfield's *Life* for the Early English Text Society[24] and the issue of the two Lives, by Roper and Harpsfield, in Everyman's Library.[25]

Discussing 'Sir Thomas Eliot's Intention in the opening chapters of the *Governour*' (*SP*), Pearl Hogrefe dissents from Lehmberg's conclusion that Elyot wrote the opening chapters in order to please the King by supporting unlimited royal power. She dismisses two of Lehmberg's arguments, the imprint of Berthelet, the King's printer, and the use of the perfect tense, suggesting revision, on the grounds that Berthelet printed every book by Elyot, while 'the tenses in the first three chapters usually indicate that Elyot was looking forward, not inserting chapters after the remainder of Book 1 had been written'. In the opening chapters Elyot limits the King's power by the same kind of regulation as in the rest of the book, 'by emphasizing his duty to rule for the welfare of his inferiors, and stating that his rewards should be in proportion to these standards'. The analogy of the sun, in Chapter 2, gives no sanction for despotism. In brief, even throughout the opening chapters 'Elyot was laying a firm foundation for a complete structure of limitations on the king's power, limitations which a king should set up by his own virtue, wisdom, and concern for the public weal.'

Lawrence V. Ryan's *Roger*

---

[24] *The Life and Death of Sr. Thomas More*, by Nicholas Harpsfield, ed. by E. V. Hitchcock. O.U.P. for the E.E.T.S. pp. ccxxxi +400. 45*s*.

[25] *Lives of Saint Thomas More*, by William Roper, and Nicholas Harpsfield, ed. with an introduction by E. E. Reynolds. New York: Dutton, and London: Dent. pp. 175. $1.95. 15*s*.

Ascham,[26] justly described by its publishers as the first full-length study of Ascham, makes good a serious lacuna in English Renaissance scholarship. The author has drawn extensively upon Giles's edition of Ascham's writings, making his own translations from the correspondence, and has produced a full, well-balanced, and readable biography of the humanist don, who was also a courtier, traveller, and diplomat. The story now fully told brings into the foreground 'one of those lesser but surprisingly influential men who, more by their typicalness and their frank revelations about themselves than by the remarkableness of their writings or lives, afford posterity an intimate view of their times'. It illuminates incidental allusions in Ascham's better-known works, and serves to modify some commonly accepted notions concerning his tastes and mode of life. The encounter with Lady Jane Grey, of which much is made in the opening of *The Scholemaster*, was brief and casual. On the other hand, the tribute to the scholarly zeal and capacity of Queen Elizabeth was not mere flattery, but the genuine praise of a tutor, who had directed her education daily during her youth, and had studied with her intermittently for many years. The detachment and tranquillity of *Toxophilus* and *The Scholemaster* seem incompatible with a career harassed by ill-health, lack of means, and frustration in a continual struggle for preferment. The ten-day stay in Italy, recorded as giving first-hand evidence of Italianate iniquity, appears to have been a flying visit from Innsbruck, to which there is no other reference. The lighter side of Ascham, which finds expression in the urbane, though

pedantic *Toxophilus*, is revealed in many of the letters, particularly during his travels abroad in company with 'merry Morison'. His alleged 'puritanism' may have been overstressed. Like many of his contemporaries he was willing to sail with the wind, retaining his status and keeping on good terms with the ruling Catholic prelates throughout the reign of Queen Mary, when many of his former colleagues, including his revered master Cheke, suffered exile or imprisonment. The historical and biographical material assembled in Ryan's study entails some re-assessment of Ascham and his work. Over and above this we are given extensive comment on his English writings, including the neglected *Report of Germany*, 'the earliest essay at pragmatic political history by a Tudor Englishman'. Ascham's assimilative scholarship, illustrated in parallelism between his works and those of Elyot and Machiavelli, is shown not to impair either the freshness or the vigour of his vernacular prose. Ryan's biography can be recommended both to the specialist and to the general reader. The provision of full notes to each chapter precludes the necessity of an extensive bibliography, but room might have been found for a brief list of editions and major authorities cited.

Ascham's 'ready way to the Latin tongue' and its historical perspective are surveyed by William E. Miller in an article on 'Double Translation in English Education' (*SRen*). The novelty of Ascham's suggestion 'lay not so much in the principles, or even the details of the proposal, as in the fact that his was the first widely published description of the system in England'. In framing his argument Ascham refers to the *De Oratore* of Cicero, who merely mentions the possibility of using one language to

---

[26] *Roger Ascham*, by Lawrence V. Ryan. Stanford U.P. and O.U.P. pp. viii+352. $7.50. 45s.

improve another. More direct and more recent precedents noted by Miller are Vives, Cheke, and Bishop James Pilkington, who prescribes the method of double translation in his statute for Rivington Grammar School. The popularity of *The Schole-master*, more particularly, perhaps, Ascham's reference to 'his greatest triumph in the use of double translation: the training of the Princess Elizabeth' appears to have borne effect, and Miller refers to several later writers and teachers who advocate the same method, including John Brinsley the elder, Charles Hoole, and Edward Gibbon, the last of whom records that he used this method for improving his Latin and French.

An abridgement of William Thomas's *History of Italy*, edited by George B. Parks, has been published in the series 'Folger Documents of Tudor and Stuart Civilization'.[27] The text, printed in modernized spelling, runs to about one-third of the original, omitting Thomas's summaries from chronicles. An introduction sketches Thomas's life and traces evidence of the Italianate cult in England resulting from acquaintance with Italy and the Italian language. In view of the dearth of English books about Italy at the time when Thomas was writing and of the intensive study of the country and the language which he must have undertaken during his three-years' stay, the editor suggests that he may have written both the *History* and the Italian Grammar, published in the following year, to inform himself. The *History* reads as, primarily, the record of a particular traveller's observations, without ulterior motive. 'Thomas may best be viewed as approaching that Renaiss-

ance ideal of Ulysses, who, in Homer's phrase, "knew many men's manners, and saw many cities"', the social observer recording what Italy was like as a country to live in. This is a timely reissue of a pioneer work, which inaugurated the long and remarkable tradition of books on Italy by resident or visiting Englishmen.

A new edition of William Bourne's *A Regiment for the Sea*, published for the Hakluyt Society,[28] restores to notice an outstanding Elizabethan work on navigational science, inspired throughout with the enthusiasm for invention and experiment that characterized this age of discovery. This Gravesend innkeeper, an eye-witness of the constant passage of river and sea traffic, designed his books for the benefit of 'meaner men', in other words for skilled artisans and master craftsmen. He sought to instruct folk removed from the literary world by means of mathematical rules rather than the rule of thumb, and so to offer them the benefit of his own learning, 'couched in homely style, to correct or supplement their traditional lore'. The *Regiment* provided a complete seaman's manual, improving upon the 'Rules' of earlier almanacks in style, format, and scientific accuracy. Re-edited and reprinted at least ten times, even translated into Dutch, it secured for its author a more than local reputation, and gained patrons for his other treatises, which deal with mensuration, ordnance, and strategy. The present edition is fully documented and contains a wealth of interesting material relating to Bourne's life and work, his knowledge of earlier writers, classical, Italian, and English, which he seems to have acquired on his own

---

[27] *The History of Italy, 1549*, by William Thomas, ed. by George B. Parks. Folger Documents by Tudor and Stuart Civilization. Cornell U.P. pp. 145. $4.25.

[28] *A Regiment for the Sea and other Writings on Navigation*, by William Bourne, ed. by E. G. R. Taylor. Hakluyt Soc. Publ. C.U.P. xxxv+464. 50s.

initiative, and his independent study of applied mathematics, to which he made a notable contribution. Reading him, one may well endorse the view of his editor: 'These self-educated men had, indeed, an advantage over those schooled in the classics in that they enjoyed a freshness of outlook, and a readiness to speculate unchecked by an inculcated reverence for authority.'

The diverse writings included under the title *Tudor Books of Saints and Martyrs*,[29] by Helen C. White, are given an added meaning through being grouped as a distinctive literary genre, set against the historical background of Christian hagiology. An introductory chapter, tracing the development of the Saint's Legend from the first to the fourteenth century, is followed by eight others, which deal with *The Golden Legend*, the Protestant attack on the Saint's Legend, the Catholic martyrs under Henry VIII, Foxe's *Book of Martyrs*, the Catholic recusants, and the new interest in Church history emerging towards the close of the sixteenth century. Treated in this way the heterogeneous literature of religious controversy, much of which was designed for a particular occasion, is seen in broader perspective and parallel with other literary forms. *The Golden Legend*, in Caxton's version, commemorates for English readers the glory of martyrdom, and may anticipate, at some distance, the forthcoming translations of the Bible, even 'the mingling of many elements in the subtle complexity of baroque art'. In the development of the More legend it is possible to recapitulate 'the development of the whole of the preceding martyrological traditions'. Foxe's *Actes and Monuments* is at once a martyrology, an ecclesiastical history in the tradition of Eusebius and an encyclopedia of the English Reformation, revealing its author as a master of horror, 'a storyteller of quite remarkable power, one of the greatest of a great age', endowed with 'the authentic Elizabethan genius for the unforgettable detail, especially of the homely, dramatic order'. The later martyrologies, compared with *The Golden Legend*, reveal shifts of emphasis, reflecting the circumstances of their authors, most of whom were priests, and the change of religious climate, represented, for instance, in the attitude towards monasticism. This book will satisfy the expectations of readers familiar with Miss White's other works. It is a distinguished example of wide and sound scholarship put to constructive use, embodying much material interesting both historically and as literature. The author's comments on writers, both familiar and unfamiliar, are cogent and illuminating, quickened by good judgement and a sense of humour.

A selection of essays by Robert Barnes, edited by Neelak S. Tjernagel,[30] brings to general notice the literary work of a prominent early reformer in the service of Henry VIII from 1534 until 1540, when he was burnt as a heretic. The essays, which are abridged and modernized in style and vocabulary 'have been chosen with the purpose of exhibiting the theology of the foremost English Lutheran of the sixteenth century'. The subjects treated are justification, the Church, free will and election, Holy Scripture, and religious authority. An appendix gives notes on three of Barnes's principal works, the *Sentences*, the *Supplication*, and *Lives of the Popes*. Barnes figures, though

---

[29] *Tudor Books of Saints and Martyrs*, by Helen C. White. Wisconsin U.P. pp. x+381. $6.75.

[30] *The Reformation Essays of Dr. Robert Barnes*, ed. by Neelak S. Tjernagel. Concordia Publishing House. pp. 112. 5s.

not very conspicuously, among the martyr throng whose heroic ends are recorded in Foxe's *Actes and Monumentes*. The significance of this remarkable work not merely as a martyrology but as a political and theological manifesto of Protestants on behalf of Elizabethan nationalism is the theme of William Haller's *Foxe's Book of Martyrs and the Elect Nation*,[31] a study of Foxe's book within the context of its time, and in relation to other Protestant literature of edification. Viewed from this aspect, the publication of the book, following soon after the accession of Elizabeth, was an emergency measure designed to safeguard the cause of Protestantism when its future was still uncertain. The first part of Haller's study deals with Foxe's earlier career, his association with Grindal and Bale, and their influence upon the project and scheme of his major work. In the light of these associations *Actes and Monumentes* appears as essentially, if not primarily, an historical compilation comparable with the works of Bale in eulogizing English nationalism against Popish pretensions and usurpation. The plan 'seems to have been that Foxe should bring his already published history of the Church down to the end of the reign of Henry VIII', and continue the story from that point, making use of the materials supplied by Grindal, the account of the Marian martyrdoms being added later, and greatly elaborated in the enlarged edition of 1570. The influence both of Bale and of the compilers of the Geneva Bible is reflected in Foxe's concept of an elect nation, maintaining the religion of the Word against the heresies of a Popish Antichrist, all alike 'appropriating and adapting to their own

purpose and occasion the conception of history and the legend of the Church which had been fixed by Eusebius and Augustine'. In short, *Actes and Monumentes* is a propagandist document, a plea for the advancement of Protestantism against Popery within the Established Church. Its political implications appear in the special pleading which exonerates King Henry and Queen Mary from blame at the expense of their corrupt ministers, and which misrepresents the young Princess Elizabeth, during her sister's reign, as a long-suffering prisoner in danger of martyrdom. In his dedication to the Queen, Foxe covertly hints at her responsibility by associating with 'the voice of Christ's gospel' knowledge of Church history and of God's mighty working in His Church. What would otherwise appear to be a disparate mass of details is focused upon a single objective, the Elect Nation, under the sovereign, holding fast the religion of the Word. The book was at once accepted as an authoritative history of Church and Nation, and the order for provision of copies for use in churches was perfectly logical. In the concluding chapter and appendix to his work Haller surveys changing attitudes to Foxe's book after 1600, with the increasing corruption and vulgarization of *Actes and Monumentes* into *The Book of Martyrs*.

In pursuance of a recent study of *John Jewel as Apologist of the Church of England*, John E. Booty has edited a new issue of Lady Ann Bacon's translation of Jewel's *Apologia*.[32] Included with the text is Parker's letter to the translator, and a tract on the government of the Church of England, both of which were appended

[31] *Foxe's Book of Martyrs and the Elect Nation*, by William Haller. Cape. pp. 259. 30s.

[32] *An Apology of the Church of England*, by John Jewel, ed. by J. E. Booty. Folger Documents of Tudor and Stuart Civilization. Cornell U.P. pp. xlvii + 157. $4.

to the original translation. An extensive introduction deals with Jewel's life and work, particularly with the part he played in religious controversy and in formulating the principles of the Elizabethan Established Church. Footnotes expand and clarify Jewel's marginal references, and, where possible, identify names and titles. In an age with a flair for literary polemic Jewel was a skilled and forceful debater, and readers will welcome this reissue of a major work by a distinguished English divine acclaimed by Hooker as 'the worthiest that Christendom has bred for some hundreds of years'.

Proceeding to work on poetry and drama, priority may suitably be given to the newly revised edition of Douglas Bush's *Mythology and the Renaissance Tradition in English Poetry*.[33] The focus of the original text has not been enlarged or blurred by the addition of references to the modern conception of archetypal myth, since the book deals strictly with classical myths and stories, and with the poetical practice of Renaissance writers 'who had their own equivalent and no less valid conception'. Parts of the history, however, have been rewritten, and small changes have been made throughout in deference to altered opinions or advances in scholarly knowledge. Footnotes reduced in bulk and number, and a revised bibliography take account of work published since 1932. For over thirty years this book has held its place as a fine specimen of scholarship and imaginative criticism, presented in a form and style which should hold readers' attention and add greatly to understanding of a basic element in Renaissance poetry. The earlier chapters, most pertinent

to notice here, deal with classical themes in the Middle Ages, the background of classical mythology as treated in the sixteenth century, myths in earlier Elizabethan poetry, and the change from allegorical to pagan treatment of Ovid. The publishers are offering generous value in issuing this large, authoritative study at so moderate a price.

The Scottish poets, during this year, have attracted comparatively little attention. The Clarendon Press has published a selection of Henryson's poems, edited with introduction, notes, and glossary by Charles Elliott.[34] Douglas J. McMillan, under the title 'Classical Tale plus Folk Tale', traces in Henryson's 'Traitie of Orpheus Kyng' the fusion of elements from *Sir Orfeo* and from classical versions of the Orpheus story (*ANQ*). Tatyana Moran, discussing 'The Meeting of the Lovers in "The Testament of Cresseid"' (*NQ*), suggests that Cresseid fails to recognize Troilus since she is on her way to purgation, living in her own world, which is totally incompatible with the world in which she loved and betrayed Troilus. As a preliminary to an edition of the shorter poems of Gavin Douglas, Priscilla Bennett, in *NQ*, contributes, from Douglas's work, some additions to the O.E.D. and the Dictionary of the Older Scottish Tongue, concluding that these early usages reveal his interest in linguistic matters, his admiration for the copiousness of Latin, and his desire to enrich the native vocabulary. A. G. Rigg, discussing Dunbar's 'Fenyeit Freir' (*RES*), connects it with 'How Dunbar wes Desyrd to be Ane Freir', concluding that both are fictional, and not autobiographical.

[33] *Mythology and the Renaissance Tradition in English Poetry*, by Douglas Bush. New York: Norton. pp. xiii+372. $1.85.

[34] *Poems of Robert Henryson*, selected and ed. with an Introduction, Notes, and Glossary by Charles Elliott. Clarendon P. pp. 184. 18s.

'The convention of the "fenyeit freir", if such it was, would be useful to satirists for two reasons; not only would it enable a writer to represent as eye-witness accounts the otherwise hearsay charges against friars, but also it carried connotations of its own.'

La Poesia di John Skelton,[35] by Edvige Schulte, reveals a certain reaction against the general trend of recent criticism in stressing Skelton's knowledge of Italian humanistic writers, and the resulting humanistic features in his poetry. Surveying his literary career in three chronological phases, Miss Schulte notes in the first phase works compounded of erudition and realism typically medieval, in the second the influence of Latin poets, particularly those of the Silver Age, within poetry focused more directly on life, and in the third 'the fusion of medieval elements with ideas obtained from the current aesthetics of Renaissance humanism'. Thus, the early elegies, lyrics, and religious pieces are reminiscent of Chaucer, Boccaccio, and other poets of courtly love. The poems of invective and 'flyting' show the blend of medieval allegory with the type of macaronic satire exploited by Poggio, Folengo, Valla, and Politian. Parallels in motif and phrasing are traced between *The Garland of Laurel* and the *Rime* and *Trionfi* of Petrarch, more particularly in the poets' expression of assurance in the promise of fame secured through their art. *A Replication* voices the Neoplatonic notion of divine inspiration in poetry, a commonplace of Renaissance aesthetics. The possibility of Skelton's contact with English humanists is strengthened by Erasmus's tribute to his achievement as a vernacular poet and by parallels between *Colin Clout* and Colet's Convocation Sermon of

February, 1512. While pursuing an independent line of argument, Miss Schulte has made ample use of both early and very recent work on Skelton. If, as some may feel, her evidence at times is far-fetched, her study, as a whole, is well balanced and informative. It includes a useful chapter on Skelton's language, versification, and influence. Robert S. Kinsman's article, 'Voices of Dissonance: Pattern in Skelton's *Colyn Cloute*' (*HLQ*), is designed 'to show that in *Colyn Cloute* Skelton does achieve a structure and enliven medieval convention through the deliberate and controlled use of "dissonant voices", first the heroic voice of the poet, then the "documentary drone" of Colin Clout', who signifies the jangling voices of laity, heretics, nobles, and, at the end, the 'testy, haughty tones of Wolsey'. While the poem, with its biblical epigraph, follows the pulpit tradition of homily and complaint, it has also a fierce fictive quality which deepens its literary value. The voice of the poet as hero and prophet is distinguished from that of Colin Clout, the mask of the poet, and the success of the poem depends upon the interplay of these voices in concord or discord, Colin representing the ethos of the poem heard against the pathos of the poet. A. D. Deyermond, in *NQ*, calls attention to parallelism between Skelton's *Garlande of Laurell* and the Epilogue to *Doctor Faustus*, suggesting that Marlowe may have been familiar with the work of Skelton, which, by his time, had become unfashionable, and that, in this case, 'we are able to trace the workings of his creative processes at one of the key points of the play'.

Kenneth Muir's *Life and Letters of Sir Thomas Wyatt*[36] is the logical

[35] *La Poesia di John Skelton*, by Edvige Schulte. Napoli: Liguori. pp. 264. L 3000.

[36] *Life and Letters of Sir Thomas Wyatt*, by Kenneth Muir. Liverpool. U.P. pp. xiii+282. 45s.

sequel to his recent editions of Wyatt's poems, including those in the Blage manuscript, previously unpublished. The publication of these letters throws new light upon Wyatt's personality and diplomatic activities, at the same time revealing him as an accomplished writer of fine prose. In the first two chapters Muir gives an account of Wyatt's early years and his associations with Anne Boleyn. In the four which follow the biographical record of Wyatt's career as ambassador successively in Spain, France, and Flanders, his dealings with Thomas Cromwell, and his trial supply the context to the letters, all of which date from the last five years of his life. The stylistic forcefulness and individuality of the letters is comparable to that of Wyatt's best poetry, as illustrated most poignantly in those addressed to the King and to Cromwell, and in his impassioned Defence after the indictment of 1541. In a concluding reassessment of Wyatt's poetry Muir modifies some of his earlier published views, particularly with respect to the translations of 'Penitential Psalms'. Leland's *Funeral Songs*, extracts from David Lloyd's *State-Worthies*, and a poem by Sir George Blage are reprinted in Appendixes. This is a serviceable study, the more so in view of the sporadic and inchoate character of much recent work on Wyatt. An article on 'Meter of Some Poems of Wyatt' (*SP*), by Elias Schwartz, re-opens an already well-worked subject of debate. Dissatisfied with both alternative scansions of Wyatt's 'irregular' verses suggested by C. S. Lewis and D. W. Harding, Schwartz suggests one which would appear to be a compromise between them, applying it to 'Whoso list to hunt' and 'They fle from me'. This is as a four-beat line with an irregular number of syllables, which 'makes good rhythmic "sense" precisely at those points where violence is done by an iambic norm'. It dispenses with the rigid caesura and heavy alliteration required by Lewis's scansions, achieving something of the flexibility of Harding's, while 'its marked isochronism allows a principle of metrical variation unavailable in most free verse'. In 'The Falconer's Dream of Trust: Wyatt's "They Fle from Me"' (*Sew*) Ann Berthoff offers a new interpretation of this poem, which, she considers, has been misconstrued through the distortion of its imagery and rhetorical structure. 'The manners and intrigue, expectations and degradations of which Wyatt writes are those of the court of Henry VIII, not of the Cour d'Amour,' the relation of Fortune and Love is political. Admonishing the courtier to play the game of hypocrisy, throughout the poem Wyatt 'turns to the lexicon of falconry', representing himself as the falconer. In 'A Note on Wyatt and Ovid' (*MLR*), C. E. Nelson calls attention to analogues in Ovid's *Amores* to Wyatt's 'What menythe thys' and 'They fle from me', finding the latter, under Ovidian influence, erotic, to an unusual degree for Wyatt, and the only one of his poems with erotic, as opposed to amatory content. In both pieces Wyatt appears to be adapting themes and imagery from Ovid to the courtly-Petrarchan tradition and the Tudor context. William M. Tydeman (*NQ*), supplies some corrections to Muir's notes on Wyatt's poems in the Blage manuscript, and lists parallels between other poems in the manuscript and poems in Wyatt's collected works.

Two timely reissues of early Tudor texts have been added to the University of California English Studies. Florence H. Ridley's edition of

Surrey's *Aeneid*,[37] based on Tottel's text, with a few modernizations, is designed 'to make as clear as possible the evidence of his borrowing from Douglas, and to control as effectively as possible any influence that might tend to negate that evidence, including the effect of literal translation of the *Aeneid*, or its commentaries'. Surrey's apparent borrowings from Douglas are italicized, and the sources given in footnotes, the text of Virgil being quoted where necessary. The introduction deals with the date and text of the translation, its relation to Douglas's version, and its prosody, style, and literary relations. The editor regards this as a mature work, dating it from between the summer of 1539 and the autumn of 1540, and tracing within it the reflection of recent Italian poetry. Standing at the beginning of the English Renaissance in poetry it is 'the product of all that had gone before'. John Heywood's *A Dialogue of Proverbs*[38] has been issued in the same series, edited with introduction, commentary, and notes by Rudolph E. Habenicht. The edition includes both the original text of 1546 and the expanded version of 1550. The commentary provides explanations of hard words and phrases, and illustrations to the critical apparatus. A full account is given of the tradition of proverb and dialogue in earlier literature and the uses of both by writers of the sixteenth century. There are three indexes, the first of which lists proverbs and epithets, the second figurative expressions, and the third idiomatic phrases and oaths. This reissue is useful both in making accessible a distinctive text of the early English Renaissance, and as a book of reference to proverb literature.

In *SP* Stanley R. Maveety writes on 'Versification in *The Steele Glas*', which he relates, surprisingly, to the four-beat alliterative line of *Piers Plowman*. In support of this he notes the predominance of alliteration and of end-stopped lines, which, in fact, proves little, in view of the frequency of both in all types of poetry belonging to this period; and his conclusion that Gascoigne, failing to understand the metre both of *Piers Plowman* and of contemporary Elizabethan verse, attempted a compromise between them, conflicts both with Gascoigne's practice as a poet and with the principles which he enunciated in his *Notes of Instruction* on the making of English verse.

'Notes on the Towneley Cycle *Slaying of Abel*' (*JEGP*), by John E. Bernbrock, demonstrate the playwright's use of a homily of St. Ambrose, particularly in his presentation of the characters and callings of the two brothers. At the same time comparison of the play with its analogue goes further to prove his skill and dexterity in adapting his material for dramatic effect, particularly through the introduction of comedy. Donald C. Baker dates the play *Mankind* about 1466 on the evidence of reference to contemporary coinage (*PQ*). Jean Robertson suggests that the Chester 'Nativity' may have been originally divided into two plays, and was made into one through failure on the part of one guild or group of guilds to produce one part alone (*NQ*). Thomas F. Van Laan, examining the structure of *Everyman* (*PMLA*) finds in this a key to much of the play's theatrical popularity and critical esteem. The structural pattern is indicated by the Prologue and Epilogue, which together present the play

[37] *The 'Aeneid' of Henry Howard. Earl of Surrey*, ed. by Florence H. Ridley. California U.P. pp. 158. $4.

[38] *John Heywood's 'A Dialogue of Proverbs'* ed. with introduction, commentary, and indexes by Rudolph E. Habenicht. California U.P. pp. xi+300. $6.

as a continuous process of successive descent and ascent, in which the medieval notion of the wheel of fortune assists the theological and cosmological scheme. The play differs from the average morality in its narrow focus, excluding the objective presentation of Vice and the Seven Deadly Sins, all of which, however, covertly participate in Everyman's downfall. 'The structure of *Everyman* thus constitutes a complete and continuous pattern, both movements of which receive visual summation at the end of the play, when Everyman enters his grave to attain Heaven.' The style of the play is an image of its structural artistry.

'Satirical Parody in *Roister Doister*: A Reinterpretation', by A. W. Plumstead (*SP*), is focused on an overlooked dimension of the play, namely the parody of chivalric virtues, humility, courtesy, and 'gentilesse', 'which lends more humour and meaning to the play, making it a better comedy in its own right, and one which adds further commentary on the tones and directions that English comedy was to take'. Viewed against the chivalric code of love ethic, the principal characters are much funnier than as mere imitations of the stock *miles gloriosus*, parasite, and mistress of Roman comedy, and Udall's juxtaposing of braggart and knight in one motley character begins a long line of braggarts in love which include Sir Andrew Aguecheek and Sir Epicure Mammon. Ralph's pretence at chivalry, his letter to his mistress, and his love-despair all show a reversal of the knightly code, and look forward to Falstaff on the field at Worcester. The conclusions drawn are that the play is more sophisticated than is commonly supposed, grounded in native and not merely classical characters, and including a dimension of irony which looks forward to

Jonson. Discussing 'Who Pointed Roister's Letter?' (*NQ*), Plumstead argues that Custance has read the letter before Merygreeke reads aloud what he has before him, and that Roister had mispointed it when copying the original, a further example of Udall's originality in the use of comic irony.

R. Marienstras has contributed to *Ea* an article entitled '*Jack Juggler*. Aspects de la conscience individuelle dans une farce de 16e siècle'. Granting the author's indebtedness to the *Amphitryon* of Plautus, even to the extent of translating passages from his original, Marienstras stresses the independence of the play as a transitional English farce, in which he has adapted his material by simplifying the plot, reducing the number of characters, and eliminating erotic and pagan references. Careaway is an English type, amiable, clownish, astute, with a taste for nature and vagabondage. Jack Juggler derives from the morality. The other characters are Chaucerian rather than Plautan. Though the play is lacking in homiletic content, the author follows the morality tradition in expressing the hope that it 'may sygnifye sum further meaning', and this is effected through his treatment of character, representing the knowledge of 'myself', and the awakening of the individual conscience. R. S. Varma, discussing 'Act and Scene Divisions in "The Marriage of Wit and Science"' (*NQ*), suggests that these divisions were an afterthought, not envisaged by the author. In support of this he notes as a pecularity in the play frequent reference towards the end of a scene to the place of action following the scene, which would appear to be designed to create the semblance of continuity. O. A. W. Dilke traces in Thomas Hughes's *Misfortunes of Arthur* extensive borrowings from Lucan and

Seneca, and suggests that Hughes may have been helped in his translations from these authors by William Fulbeck, an authority on ancient history and Roman Law (*NQ*). Robert Y. Turner, examining 'The Causal Induction in Some Elizabethan Plays' (*SP*), argues that the Induction supplied dramatists with the means of dramatizing the causes of their central stories by embodying them as characters in an introductory episode or framework. From this aspect, the Induction, as distinct from the choric prologue, epilogue, or dumb-show, represents 'a hang-over from the allegorical habit of mind', reflecting the transition from allegorical to regular drama, as shown distinctively in the Inductions to *Appius and Virginia* and *The Conflict of Conscience*.

VII

Shakespeare

T. S. DORSCH

1. EDITIONS

Pericles is one of the most difficult of Shakespeare's plays to edit. Quite apart from the problem of its authorship (with which is bound up the question of its very uneven literary quality), its text bristles with difficulties; much of its verse is presented as prose or as extremely irregular verse, many stage-directions and speech-headings are omitted, speeches are misattributed, and there are numerous gross errors of other kinds, some of which remain as unsolved cruces. In his Arden edition of *Pericles*[1] F. D. Hoeniger has faced all these problems squarely and with good sense. The basis of his text is the 1609 Quarto, which he has rightly treated as conservatively as possible, although as an Arden editor he has had to make substantial corrections— more substantial, one feels, than he would have wished. He rejects the theory that the Quarto text was set up from foul papers, accepting instead the main conclusion of Philip Edward's fine bibliographical study of the play (*Sh S*, 1952), 'that Q was set up from corrupt reported copy'; however, he does not agree with Edwards's views on the nature of the reporting, but attributes many of the irregularities to hasty and careless printing. He discusses admirably the relationship of the play to its main

sources in Gower and Lawrence Twine, and to George Wilkins's *Painefull Adventures*, which, contrary to the opinion of several other scholars, he regards as 'a very inferior and thus undependable report of the play', although it can give useful help to an editor. Hoeniger breaks new ground in the matter of the authorship of *Pericles*. No one seriously questions that Shakespeare wrote most or all of Acts III–V, but the authorship of the first two acts has long been a matter for dispute. Hoeniger rejects Rowley and Heywood out of hand; like many others, he accepts Wilkins as a likely candidate, but he argues an interesting case for John Day as at least part-author of these two acts. He dates the composition of the play in late 1607 or early 1608. His annotations are full and helpful, and his introduction contains much interesting criticism, especially in the sections on the spectacular elements in the play and on the influence exerted on it by medieval drama.

J. H. P. Pafford's Arden *Winter's Tale*[2] is also an extremely interesting edition. Pafford was faced by none of the textual complexities with which Hoeniger had to deal, for *The Winter's Tale* is a comparatively clean text, probably printed from a transcript made by Ralph Crane from a manuscript of good authority, the nature of which, however, is unknown. Nor is

---

[1] *Pericles*, ed. by F. D. Hoeniger. (The Arden Shakespeare.) Methuen and Harvard U.P. pp. xci+188. 21s.

[2] *The Winter's Tale*, ed. by J. H. P. Pafford. (The Arden Shakespeare.) Methuen and Harvard U.P. pp. lxxxix+225. 25s.

the play as difficult to date as most of Shakespeare's plays; it was almost certainly written within a few months before it was seen by Simon Forman on 15 May 1611. Pafford demonstrates by a careful analysis how closely Shakespeare followed his primary source, Green's *Pandosto*, and shows also the extent of his indebtedness to other works. However, the edition is of special value for the critical sections of its introduction. Here Pafford gives an excellent survey of recent criticism of the last plays, and discusses the relationship between them. He writes well also about the dramatic structure of *The Winter's Tale*, arguing, in the face of contrary opinions, that 'it is a whole, and its unity has the rhythm and variety of a great work of art'. In his appendixes he provides some notes for which there would not have been room at the foot of the pages, discusses the music and the songs, gives an interesting stage history, and prints the text of *Pandosto* complete.

The volumes of the Cambridge Pocket Shakespeare have been noticed in *YW* as they have appeared during the past six or seven years. This year *Titus Andronicus* and *All's Well*[3] have been added to the series. Like the previous volumes, these are reprints of John Dover Wilson's texts and the glossaries in the New Shakespeare edition.

The Furness *New Variorum Shakespeare* is much too well known to need description here. With its vast store of critical commentary and of textual and interpretative notes, it remains an essential work of reference in spite of the proliferation of Shakespearian texts edited in the light of more recent scholarship. It is to be found as

[3] *Titus Andronicus*, ed. by John Dover Wilson. pp. iv+104. *All's Well that Ends Well*, ed. by John Dover Wilson. pp. iv+113. (The Cambridge Pocket Shakespeare.) C.U.P. Each vol. 6s.

a matter of course in every academic library, but the cost of its volumes has hitherto been too high for most private pockets. Its republication in a very reasonably priced paperback form must be warmly welcomed. The seven plays issued in 1963[4] are *A Midsummer Night's Dream*, *As You Like It*, *Hamlet* (two volumes), *King Lear*, *Macbeth*, *Othello*, and *Romeo and Juliet*. Other volumes are to follow.

Individual volumes of the Folger Library General Reader's Shakespeare, edited by Louis B. Wright and Virginia A. LaMar, have been noticed in *YW* as they have appeared during the past six or seven years. Seventeen of the plays are now published together in a single stout volume.[5] As the title of the original series indicates, this is Shakespeare for the 'general reader'; accordingly the pages are not cluttered with elaborate annotations, but footnotes have been kept to 'the minimum consistent with an adequate explanation of essential meanings and essential facts'. The plays are presented in sound texts based on a fresh study of the authoritative early texts, and are prefaced by short but sensible critical commentaries. Appendixes cover such matters as the life of Shakespeare, the theatres and dramatic conventions of his age, and early criticism of his works—from Ben Jonson to Samuel Johnson; and the volume closes with some useful bibliographies.

The first fifteen plays in a new

[4] A New Variorum Edition of Shakespeare, ed. by Horace Howard Furness. *A Midsummer Night's Dream*, pp. xxxv+357. *As You Like It*, pp. ix+452. *Hamlet*, 2 vols. pp. xx+473, ii+432. *King Lear*, pp. vi+503. *Macbeth*, pp. xiv+565. *Othello*, pp. viii +471. *Romeo and Juliet*, pp. xxiii+480. New York: Dover Publications. Each vol. $2.25. 18s.

[5] *The Play's the Thing: Seventeen of Shakespeare's Greatest Dramas*, ed. by Louis B. Wright and Virginia A. LaMar. New York: Harper & Row. pp. viii+781.

paperback edition of Shakespeare have been published in the course of the year.[6] This is the Signet Classic Shakespeare, the general editor of which is Sylvan Barnet. American, English, and German scholars have so far participated in the production of the series. Each play is freshly edited from the relevant substantive text, and its editor provides a critical introduction, a bibliographical note, and an apparatus criticus. The general editor provides a prefatory chapter which is common to all the volumes, and which deals with such topics as Shakespeare's life, the Elizabethan theatre, and the chronology of the plays. There are substantial extracts from the sources for each play, and admirably full reading lists. Finally each play is accompanied by a series of critical essays or excerpts from well-known critical writings. Thus, for example, the *Lear* volume contains passages by Johnson, Bradley, Granville-Barker, and Harry Levin; the *Midsummer Night's Dream* has passages by Hazlitt, Dowden, Enid Welsford, H. A. Myers, and J. R. Brown. The names of the editors (see footnote) will give some indication of

the quality of the scholarship that has gone into the editing. This series may be commended to anyone who wishes to have a handy and cheap pocket edition of Shakespeare.

The editorial methods of the Laurel Shakespeare were fully described in *YW* two years ago (xlii. 103). The text is that of C. J. Sisson. The general editor, Francis Fergusson, provides an introduction to each play, a note on its text, suggestions for further reading, and an essay on Shakespeare and his theatre; a 'modern commentary' is contributed by a writer who has a theatrical or otherwise non-academic approach to Shakespeare; and the glosses are compiled by H. H. Smith. The latest additions to this admirable series[7] are the three parts of *Henry VI*, with a commentary by James Sandoe, and *Timon of Athens*, with a commentary by Kenneth Burke.

Under the title *Shakespeare's Comedies of Romance*[8] Francis Fergusson has republished as a Delta paperback four of the comedies that have already appeared in the Laurel Shakespeare— *A Midsummer Night's Dream, Much Ado, As You Like It,* and *Twelfth Night.* In this edition the 'modern commentaries' of the Laurel series are omitted, and there is a new glossary based on Hilda Hulme's glossary in C. J. Sisson's edition of Shakespeare. Fergusson has added a general introduction on 'Shakespeare's World of Romance', and a preface outlining his plans to produce further groups of

[6] The Signet Classic Shakespeare. General editor, Sylvan Barnet. *King Lear,* ed. by Russell Fraser, pp. 287. *Macbeth,* ed. by Sylvan Barnet, pp. 247. *Othello,* ed. by Alvin Kernan, pp. 270. *Richard II,* ed. by Kenneth Muir, pp. 255. *The Winter's Tale,* ed. by Frank Kermode, pp. 223. *As You Like It,* ed. by Albert Gilman, pp. 237. *Hamlet,* ed. by Edward Hubler, pp. 271. *Julius Caesar,* ed. by William and Barbara Rosen, pp. 240. *A Midsummer Night's Dream,* ed. by Wolfgang Clemen, pp. 186. *Troilus and Cressida,* ed. by Daniel Seltzer, pp. 288. *Much Ado about Nothing,* ed. by David L. Stevenson, pp. 160. *The Tempest,* ed. by Robert Langbaum, pp. 224. *Titus Andronicus,* ed. by Sylvan Barnet, pp. 181. *Antony and Cleopatra,* ed. by Barbara Everett, pp. 276. *The Two Gentlemen of Verona,* ed. by Bertrand Evans, pp. 200. New York: The New American Library, and London: The New English Library, Ltd. Each vol. 50c, 3s. 6d.

[7] The Laurel Shakespeare. General editor, Francis Fergusson. *Henry VI, Parts One, Two and Three,* commentary by James Sandoe. pp. 512, 95c. *Timon of Athens,* commentary by Kenneth Burke. pp. 191. 35c. New York: Dell.

[8] *Shakespeare's Comedies of Romance: 'A Midsummer Night's Dream', 'Much Ado About Nothing', 'As You Like It', 'Twelfth Night',* ed., with Introductions, by Francis Fergusson. New York: Dell (Delta Books). pp. 415. $2.25.

plays in the present series, and has reprinted the original introductions to the individual plays.

This year's Folio Society play is *All's Well that Ends Well*.[9] The volume is as beautifully printed and bound as its predecessors in the series. The text is that of the New Temple Shakespeare, edited by M. R. Ridley, and Jean Rook has again compiled the glossary. In his introduction Osbert Lancaster can find little good to say about the plot and the characters, apart from Parolles, 'the wide boy so sharp that he must always cut himself'. The play is redeemed, in his view, very largely by 'the contrast of the two main settings. On the one hand Rossillion and the Court of France, medieval, old-fashioned, hierarchic; on the other Renaissance Florence, tough, realistic, modern'. The volume is embellished by eight of the designs which Lancaster created for the 1953 production at the Old Vic.

Martin Seymour-Smith's edition of *Shakespeare's Sonnets*[10] is an extremely useful contribution to the study of the Sonnets. Apart from facsimiles and Hyder Edward Rollins's *New Variorum* edition, this is the first modern reprint which reproduces Thomas Thorpe's 1609 Quarto verbatim, except that it eliminates the long *s* and conforms with modern usage in respect of *u* and *v*, *i* and *j*. 'Obvious misprints' have also been corrected, but never without notification, so that the reader may judge for himself whether the change is justified. In an interesting introduction Seymour-Smith outlines the bibliographical history of the Son-

nets, summarizes the many controversies that have grown up round them, and indicates what he regards as the most likely conclusions. It may be felt that, in spite of his generally cautious approach, he is too ready to accept Wordsworth's view that 'with this key Shakespeare unlocked his heart', that he sees in the Sonnets more of a personal spiritual autobiography than an Elizabethan poet would have been likely to provide in a sonnet-sequence; however, his arguments are never silly, and are always presented in a stimulating way. At the end of the volume the individual sonnets are liberally and sensibly annotated, and, where necessary, helpfully interpreted in relation to their context in the sequence or to the controversies discussed in the introduction.

Mention should also be made of an edition of the Sonnets edited by Levi Fox.[11] It is a pleasantly produced little volume which would fit easily into a pocket, and even into a handbag. Well printed and chastely bound, it would make an agreeable present.

Many school editions of various of the plays have appeared in the course of the year. These are listed in the annotated bibliography for 1963 which is published in the Summer 1964 issue of *Sh. Q.*

The translators remain as busy as ever. More than a hundred translations, whether of the complete works or of individual plays, are listed in the *Sh. Q* bibliography. Languages represented this year include Albanian, Serbo-Croatian, Uzbeck, Malayalam, Russian-Chuvash, Chilean, and Vietnamese.

2. GENERAL STUDIES

In a third World's Classics volume of *Shakespeare Criticism*[12] Anne Ridler brings us up to date with

[9] *All's Well That Ends Well*. Introduction and Designs by Osbert Lancaster. The Folio Society. pp. 94.

[10] *Shakespeare's Sonnets*, ed. with an Introduction and Commentary by Martin Seymour-Smith. Heinemann. pp. vi+194. 10*s*. 6*d*.

[11] *The Sonnets of William Shakespeare*, ed. by Levi Fox. Cotman House. pp. vi+154.

[12] *Shakespeare Criticism: 1935–60*, selected

eighteen essays or extracts from the years 1935–60. In a period in which so many millions of words have been written about Shakespeare, her task of selection must have been very difficult; but it must be said at once that she has brought together an interesting and representative collection from the best Shakespearian criticism of the quarter-century that she covers. The volume opens with R. W. Chambers's pioneer rehabilitation of *Measure for Measure* and Hardin Craig's 'Motivation in Shakespeare's Choice of Materials', which was first published in *Sh S*, and closes with M. C. Bradbrook's 'The Fashioning of a Courtier', from *Shakespeare and Elizabethan Poetry*, and Clifford Leech's 'The Unity of *2 Henry IV*', from *Sh. S*. It also contains F. P. Wilson's 'Shakespeare and the Diction of Common Life', Peter Alexander's 'Restoring Shakespeare', J. I. M. Stewart's 'Shakespeare's Men and their Morals', and Helen Gardner's 'The Noble Moor'; and other critics represented include J. Dover Wilson, E. M. W. Tillyard, G. Wilson Knight, Cleanth Brooks, L. C. Knights, and Kenneth Muir.

The four volumes of Harley Granville-Barker's *Prefaces to Shakespeare* have long been a standard work of criticism for all who, whether from the academic or from the theatrical point of view, are interested in Shakespeare. They have now been reprinted in four very reasonably priced paperbacked volumes.[13] *Hamlet* retains a

volume to itself, but the other nine plays have been regrouped, as will be seen by reference to the footnote. Together with other introductory material and notes, M. St. Clare Byrne has provided an extremely interesting introduction on Granville-Barker's work as a Shakespearian producer, actor, and scholar; and she has also been responsible for the selection and description of nearly 200 excellent illustrations, most of them photographs of productions. This is one of the most welcome reprints of recent years.

Alfred Harbage's aim, in his *William Shakespeare: A Reader's Guide*,[14] is 'to induce a noticing mood, to encourage attentive reading, and to save the fundamental, the conspicuous, the important, from being dismissed as elementary'. To this end he prefaces the main body of the book with a ninety-page introductory section which is designed to teach the reader just how to read noticingly. This is admirable. Harbage discusses in some detail, and with plenty of analysis, Shakespeare's immensely varied use of language and of the arts of language, his ability to achieve almost any effect by the use of alliteration, or metaphor, or wordplay, or a hundred other devices. He could perhaps have said more about common words whose meanings have changed since Shakespeare's day, since these so frequently lead inexperienced readers astray; however, his treatment of diction is for the most part very helpful. He is similarly thorough in his discussion of Shakespeare's verse and prose rhythms and patterns and his dramatic structures. When he turns to the plays, of which he singles out fourteen for detailed consideration, his method is a scene-

with an Introduction by Anne Ridler (The World's Classics.) O.U.P. pp. xiii+401. 9s. 6d.

[13] *Prefaces to Shakespeare*, by Harley Granville-Barker. Four volumes, with Introductions and Notes by M. St. Clare Byrne. Vol. I, *Hamlet*. pp. xlii+310. Vol. II, *King Lear*, *Cymbeline*, *Julius Caesar*. pp. xlv+274. Vol. III, *Antony and Cleopatra*, *Coriolanus*. pp. x+310. Vol. IV, *Love's Labour's Lost*, *Romeo and Juliet*, *Merchant of Venice*, *Othello*. pp. x+333. Batsford. Each vol. 6s.

[14] *William Shakespeare: A Reader's Guide*, by Alfred Harbage. New York: Noonday Press. pp. xiii+498. $2.75.

I

by-scene analysis in which, on the whole, he explains but does not interpret—his wish is 'to guide the reader but not direct him'. This sometimes leads to too much summary, but the result is as a rule a very clear picture of the play—of its action, its design, and its characters. From here the reader may go on to read more elaborate or more specialized criticism. Like all of Harbage's work, the book is clearly and vigorously written, and it fulfils excellently the function of a guide.

Stopford A. Brooke's *Ten More Plays of Shakespeare*, first published in 1913, has been reissued.[15] It offers studies of *Much Ado, Twelfth Night, Caesar, Hamlet, Measure for Measure, Othello, Lear, King John*, the two parts of *Henry IV*, and *Henry V*. Brooke's criticism belongs to the days, half a century ago, before highly specialized approaches to the plays of Shakespeare had become the fashion, and is none the worse for that. The reappearance of his book will be generally welcomed.

In the view of Bernard Beckerman, the building of the Globe theatre in 1599 had a significant effect on Shakespeare's development as a playwright. The ten years during which the Chamberlain's—King's Men played at this theatre saw the production of his major comedies and tragedies, and the character of the theatre and of its audience to some degree influenced the style, the structure, and the methods of production of these plays. The leasing in 1608–9 of the more intimate indoor Blackfriars theatre, with its smaller and more sophisticated audience, necessitated new styles and techniques, and this is one of the reasons why Shakespeare's last plays differ so markedly

from those that came before them. In *Shakespeare at the Globe, 1599–1609*[16] Beckerman makes a thorough-going study of the Globe period. After a survey of the types of play that shared the Globe stage with those of Shakespeare, he turns to the dramaturgy, and finds in all of Shakespeare's Globe plays certain common features: 'a means for bringing about justice or of winning love', 'a judge-figure who pronounces judgment', 'a ranking figure who reasserts order', and normally 'a public resolution'. He goes on to consider the stage, and the variety of location which its different acting areas and levels made possible; and in a long and interesting chapter he discusses the acting, which was necessarily more rhetorical in an outdoor than in a closed theatre. He closes with a section on special aspects of staging, such as stage illusion, actors' entries, recurrent patterns in staging, and the staging of the finales. This book should be of particular value to stage historians who have a special interest in Shakespeare and the Elizabethan period generally.

John Russell Brown's *Shakespeare and his Comedies* was fully noticed when it appeared in 1957 (*YW* xxxviii. 133). It now appears in a new edition with an additional chapter covering the late comedies, or romances.[17] While he accepts what might be called the standard view of these plays, that they are much concerned with themes of 'birth, separation, tempest, remorse, penitence or patience, reconciliation and peace', Brown believes that not sufficient attention has been paid to the relationships of love and friendship that

[15] *Ten More Plays of Shakespeare*, by Stopford A. Brooke. New York: Barnes & Noble. pp. v+313. $5.

[16] *Shakespeare at the Globe, 1599–1609*, by Bernard Beckerman. New York: The Macmillan Company, 1962. pp. xvi+254.

[17] *Shakespeare and his Comedies*, by John Russell Brown. Second edition, with a new chapter on the later comedies. Methuen, 1962. pp. 253. 21s.

are developed in them, and he analyses them by methods similar to those that he applied to the earlier comedies. In *The Winter's Tale* Shakespeare has 'created a picture of a man who learns by dispossession and begins to respond in true love after he has given up all hope and fear, of young people who have to risk everything for their "affections" (IV. iv. 490–1), and of sophisticated and simple societies seen in relation to individual men and women and to the holy and just gods'. In *Pericles*, too, characters come at last to understand something of the will of the gods, and *Cymbeline* closes with 'men and women at peace with each other, a stable relationship which has been given eloquence through a persistent and minute judgement on divided minds throughout the play'. *The Tempest* cannot be seen in quite the same terms as the other plays. Prospero cannot enforce repentance or true love and service, but he can at least 'draw men to the place where such responses are possible and then act with mercy, rather than justice'.

In 'Comic Truth in Shakespeare and Jonson' (*SAQ*) Peter G. Phialas brings out differences in the comic spirit of the two playwrights. Jonson 'rejects romance and instead invents plots which dramatize human imperfection'. Shakespeare, on the other hand, depicts 'imperfect man's reaching toward perfection'. Jonson's comic vision suggests a human Hell; Shakespeare's promises a human Eden. In 'The Function of Satire in Shakespeare's Romantic Comedies' (*Univ. of Colorado Stud., Series in Lang. and Lit.*) Rufus Putney suggests that critics too often seek a moral purpose in Shakespeare's comedies. The satirical aspects of these plays are designed to provide complications in plot, suspense, and diversity of interest; they have no moral purpose.

Laurence Lerner's collection of critical essays and extracts relating to Shakespeare's tragedies[18] is both useful and interesting. For each of the tragedies Lerner has printed from two to half a dozen passages which throw light on various aspects of the play, except that *Timon of Athens* is represented only by a single passage, an excerpt from J. C. Maxwell's introduction to his New Shakespeare edition. Lerner's method may be illustrated by examples. *Othello* is covered by A. C. Bradley's analysis of Iago, Maud Bodkin's study of 'The Hero and the Devil' from *Archetypal Patterns in Poetry*, William Empson's 'Honest in *Othello*' from *The Structure of Complex Words*, and R. B. Heilman's 'Modes of Irony in *Othello*' from *Magic in the Web*. For *Romeo and Juliet* there are extracts from M. M. Mahood's *Shakespeare's Wordplay* and Charles Williams's *The English Poetic Mind*. The three dozen passages which make up the volume are sufficiently well known not to require individual notice here. It should perhaps be mentioned that the last half-dozen are general approaches to tragedy or to Shakespearian tragedy. Lerner provides helpful suggestions for further reading, and an introduction in which he discusses modern trends in the criticism of the tragedies.

From experience in the theatre F. W. Sternfeld has, like other scholars and producers, been confirmed in his belief that the right music historically is the right music for Shakespearian audiences. He has written many articles on Shakespeare's music, and now, in *Music in Shakespearean Tragedy*,[19] he publishes the results of

[18] *Shakespeare's Tragedies: A Selection of Modern Criticism*, ed. by Laurence Lerner. Penguin Books. pp. 317. 4s. 6d.

[19] *Music in Shakespearean Tragedy*, by F. W. Sternfeld. Routledge & Kegan Paul. pp. xxii+334. 45s.

his research on one side of this subject. There is less music in Elizabethan tragedy than in any other dramatic genre, yet songs occur, and there is a good deal of instrumental music. Sternfeld begins with an excellent survey of the incidence of both songs and instrumental music in tragedy from *Gorboduc* to Shakespeare, concentrating on tragic drama, but at the same time illuminating his commentary by illustration from the comedies of the period. As might be expected, he discovers that Shakespeare integrates his songs more closely with the dialogue and the dramatic structure of his plays than any other dramatist, and this is an important part of his thesis. He illustrates his findings most effectively in chapters on the willow song in *Othello* and on Ophelia's songs, and, after an interlude on Robert Armin's role as a singer and his probable influence in increasing the number of songs in Shakespeare's plays, he discusses the other songs in the tragedies, devoting a separate chapter to the interplay of blank verse, prose, and songs in *King Lear*. Two further chapters deal with the instrumental music. The final chapter is a retrospect of scholarship on Shakespeare's music. The volume closes with a long bibliography of sources and an index of all the lyrics in Shakespeare's plays, together with some by other playwrights, and it is lavishly illustrated with musical scores and with illustrations relevant to the subject of Elizabethan music. All lovers of Shakespeare will be grateful to Sternfeld for this valuable and extremely interesting book.

Elmer Edgar Stoll's *Art and Artifice in Shakespeare*[20] was first published in 1933, and has long been out of

print. It is one of the most stimulating of the many books that have been written about Shakespeare's tragedies, especially in what it says about the structural design of *Othello*, *Macbeth*, *Hamlet*, and *King Lear*, and about the artistic devices by which the finest effects of these plays are achieved, and its reappearance as a University Paperback will be generally welcomed.

Charles Norton Coe's *Demi-Devils*: *The Character of Shakespeare's Villains*[21] is little more than an enlarged version of his *Shakespeare's Villains*, which was fully noticed when it appeared in 1958 (*YW* xxxix. 114). The same eleven villains are discussed, grouped in the same way: Aaron and Iago; Richard III, Macbeth, and Lady Macbeth; Angelo and Shylock; Regan, Goneril, Edmund, and Claudius. Coe has treated them in a rather more detailed way than before, and has at times slightly modified his views about them in the light of his reading of such recent books as Bernard Spivack's *Shakespeare and the Allegory of Evil* and Bernard Grebanier's *The Heart of Hamlet*. However, his conclusions remain substantially the same, and are open to the same criticism as was expressed in the previous notice. It is difficult not to feel that he might have employed himself more profitably in developing an entirely new approach to his subject.

In *The Problem Plays of Shakespeare*[22] Ernest Schanzer rejects the now traditional grouping together as problem plays of *Measure for Measure*, *All's Well*, *Troilus and Cressida*, and sometimes *Hamlet*. Except in

---

[20] *Art and Artifice in Shakespeare: A Study in Dramatic Contrast and Illusion*, by Elmer Edgar Stoll. (University Paperbacks.) Methuen. pp. xiii + 178. 10s. 6d.

[21] *Demi-Devils: The Character of Shakespeare's Villains*, by Charles Norton Coe. New York: Bookman Associates. pp. 122.

[22] *The Problem Plays of Shakespeare: A Study of 'Julius Caesar', 'Measure for Measure', 'Antony and Cleopatra'*, by Ernest Schanzer. Routledge & Kegan Paul. pp. x + 196. 25s.

Measure for Measure, he sees in these no dominant moral problems; he believes that such problems exist to a much more significant degree in *Julius Caesar* and *Antony and Cleopatra*, and his book is a close and interesting study of these two plays and of *Measure for Measure*. He illustrates the divided Renaissance response to the assassination of Caesar, and after a careful analysis of the play *Julius Caesar*, and especially of the presentation of Caesar and Brutus, he concludes 'that in this play Shakespeare put a twofold problem before his audience: the psychological problem of the nature of the "real" Caesar; and, hinging upon this, the moral problem of the justifiability of the murder'. He believes that 'by the orientation of his material Shakespeare deliberately avoided giving a plain and clear-cut answer to either of these problems'. *Measure for Measure*, says Schanzer, 'has two main concerns: in the field of public ethics it is with the nature of Justice and Good Rule; in the field of private ethics it is with the choice of Isabel. The two concerns are united by a common reprobation of legalism in favour of a more humane, more truly just interpretation of the Law, whether man-made or divine. And whereas the private moral issue is treated problematically, the public moral issue is not.' Schanzer discusses *Antony and Cleopatra* largely in terms of the conflicts it dramatizes between love and honour, and between the life of pleasure and the life of power-politics.

Derek Traversi's *Shakespeare: The Roman Plays*[23] is a full-scale study of *Julius Caesar*, *Antony and Cleopatra*, and *Coriolanus*. Traversi has laid aside his former preoccupation with symbols, and his method here is straightforward analysis of the plays, almost scene by scene, in which he makes many illuminating comments on the characters and the conduct of the action. He brings out particularly well the interplay of contrasted personalities in *Julius Caesar*, and the way in which almost every thought and action 'is concentrated upon Caesar's assumption of unique and unlimited power and upon the doom to which this leads'. The thesis of the long essay on *Antony and Cleopatra* can perhaps best be summed up by its final sentence: 'The emotions of Antony and Cleopatra have been built upon "dungy earth", upon "Nilus' slime", and so upon the impermanence which the nature of these elements implies; but, just as earth and slime can be quickened into life, briefly and elusively indeed, but none the less truly, by the action upon them of fire and air, so the very elements of waste and vanity which nurtured this tragedy have become, by the time it reaches its necessary conclusion, constituent ingredients in the creation of an intuition of immortality'—an ugly sentence, it is true, but a perspicacious comment. Traversi writes sensibly also about *Coriolanus*, especially when he is discussing its irony.

T. J. B. Spencer's *The Roman Plays*[24] in the Writers and Their Work series is necessarily very much shorter, but Spencer has compressed into it much excellent criticism. He begins with a survey of 'the widespread literary use of subjects from Roman history' in Elizabethan times, showing that the general familiarity with such subjects enabled Shakespeare 'to achieve an extra dimension, as it were, in retelling the stories', and

[23] *Shakespeare: The Roman Plays*, by Derek Traversi. Hollis & Carter. pp. 288. 30s.

[24] *William Shakespeare: The Roman Plays*, by T. J. B. Spencer. (Writers and Their Work.) Longmans. pp. 56. 2s. 6d.

drawing attention to his concern with grave and provocative problems of political morality. Spencer notes the fine use of suspense in *Titus Andronicus*, a play which is much more effective in performance than on the printed page. With the reading of Plutarch Shakespeare gained a much deeper insight into the Roman mind and the Roman background, and Spencer brings out well the clash of personalities and of personal and political motives in *Julius Caesar*, *Antony and Cleopatra*, and *Coriolanus*. He emphasizes in *Julius Caesar* the greatness of Caesar and the growth in stature of Brutus and Cassius; in *Antony and Cleopatra* the conflict in Antony, 'who is repeatedly confronted with a choice between his love for Cleopatra and his loyalty to the political and moral dignity of Rome'; and in *Coriolanus* the careful balance maintained between the virtues and vices of the different political forces.

In the same series Frank Kermode writes on *The Final Plays*.[25] Kermode begins with a survey of recent criticism of these plays, and goes on to speculate on the reasons why Shakespeare at this period concerned himself with the types of theme that they share—those of the recovery of lost royal children, of acute suffering, of repentance, healing, and reconciliation. The most profitable explanation, he believes, is 'that which postulates a revival of theatrical interest in romance, and seeks the reason for it not so much in the older drama as in the great heroic romances of the period, Sidney's *Arcadia* and Spenser's *Faerie Queene*'. He relates each of the five plays—for he includes *The Two Noble Kinsmen*—to sources of this character, and shows how in each, though in different ways, Shakespeare develops

the themes that have been referred to. Kermode's approach is fresh, and his criticism is balanced and sensible.

His Exits and His Entrances,[26] by Louis Marder, is, as its sub-title indicates, 'The Story of Shakespeare's Reputation'. Each of the twelve chapters follows one particular type of Shakespearian activity through its ups and downs in the course of the last three and a half centuries. Thus the chapter entitled 'The Remarkable Paradox' describes the fortunes of Shakespeare in the theatre, the paradox being that the most widely acclaimed playwright that has ever lived should have ruined so many directors and managers. Of the acclaim he has received from almost every generation since his career began, there can be no doubt. In the eighteenth century, for example, more than 7,000 performances of his plays are recorded in the London theatres alone, and unrecorded thousands must have taken place elsewhere. Another chapter, 'Un-Willingly to School', gives an account of the role that Shakespeare has assumed in education; it is interesting to learn that his plays first became 'prescribed texts' in England with the establishment of the Oxford and Cambridge Local Examinations in 1858. Other chapters deal with the growth of 'Bardolatry', the publication of Shakespeare's works from the Quartos and the Folios to the present day, the proliferation of Shakespearian scholarship in its many forms, the various 'anti-Stratfordian' theories, the Shakespearian forgeries and hoaxes, the likenesses of Shakespeare, genuine and spurious, the Shakespeare festivals, from Garrick's to those of today, Shakespeare in

[25] *William Shakespeare: The Final Plays*, by Frank Kermode. (Writers and Their Work.) Longmans. pp. 59. 2*s*. 6*d*.

[26] *His Exits and His Entrances: The Story of Shakespeare's Reputation*, by Louis Marder. New York: Lippincott, and London: John Murray. pp. 386. 30*s*.

America, and Shakespeare in the non-English-speaking world—he has been translated into about a hundred languages. Marder has compressed a great deal of interesting information into his book, and it makes very good reading.

Gabriele Baldini's *Le Fonti per la Biografia di William Shakespeare*[27] is an excellent survey of the sources from which it has been possible to reconstruct the biography of Shakespeare. It covers both the public records from which so many facts have been culled, and the literary documents which have enabled us to build at least something of a personality round the facts.

A. L. Rowse's *William Shakespeare: A Biography*[28] would have been a better book than it is if it had been written with a little more scholarly humility, and with fewer sneers at literary scholars, who, in Rowse's view, are less likely to be able to know Shakespeare than a historian like himself. Much of the book is good. Rowse writes interestingly about the background against which Shakespeare lived his life in Stratford and London, and indeed, as long as he keeps to biography, he can be listened to with respect. He is less sound in his interpretation of some of Shakespeare's writings. His most controversial chapter relates to the Sonnets, although it is here that he is at his most arrogant. 'Now, for the first time,' he writes, 'certainty as to dating has been achieved . . . all the main problems of the sonnets receive their solution.' The sonnets were written, we are told, in the years 1592–5, 'as is clear for all to see'; 'we now know' that the young friend

was Southampton; the rival poet could not possibly be anyone but Marlowe; Mr. W. H. 'the onlie begetter', was Sir William Harvey, third husband to Southampton's mother. As scholarly reviewers have been quick to point out, Rowse stands on very slippery ground in these confident conclusions. Nor can his opinions about the backgrounds of some of the plays be accepted without reservations. He contributes usefully to Shakespearian biography, but not to Shakespearian literary criticism.

John Dover Wilson's *Introduction to the Sonnets of Shakespeare*[29] may perhaps more appropriately be noticed here than in the later section on the Sonnets, since it is to some extent concerned with the problems that Rowse claims to have solved. Wilson's approach is broader and more literary than Rowse's, as might be expected in what is to be the introduction to his forthcoming N.S. edition of the Sonnets; as he says of the sequence, 'Begin by . . . recognizing the whole as the greatest love-poem in the language, and the mystery of the detail becomes so unimportant as to fade away.' This is what he himself does, and he also discusses the themes that are developed, and the sources. Turning to the 'problems', Wilson convincingly disposes of the commonly expressed view that Shakespeare was a 'conscious paederast'; there is nothing reprehensible in the relationship between him and his young friend. Wilson's case for identifying the friend with William Herbert, third Earl of Pembroke, is more persuasive than Rowse's for the Earl of Southampton, as are his arguments for Chapman as the rival poet; but he is

---

[27] *Le Fonti per la Biografia di William Shakespeare*, di Gabriele Baldini. Firenze: Le Monnier. pp. 42. L.600.

[28] *William Shakespeare: A Biography*, by A. L. Rowse. Macmillan. pp. xiv+485. 45s.

[29] *An Introduction to the Sonnets of Shakespeare: For the Use of Historians and Others*, by John Dover Wilson. C.U.P. pp. v+88. 5s. 95c.

too good a scholar to claim certainty where no certainty exists. Herbert is also the 'onlie begetter', and Wilson believes that Shakespeare was writing his sonnets to Herbert between about 1593 and 1606. However, the more scholars argue about the story behind the sonnets, the more obvious it becomes that the most profitable approach to them is literary rather than biographical; it is encouraging to find this emphasized by a scholar of Wilson's stature.

Peter Quennell also touches on the problems of the sonnets. For him, as for Rowse, the friend is Southampton, and the 'onlie begetter' Sir William Harvey; he believes that the sequence was begun in 1594 or 1595, but makes no suggestion about the number of years over which its composition was spread. The best parts of Quennell's *Shakespeare: the poet and his background*[30] are those which relate to the background. The chapters on Shakespeare's early years in Stratford and those in which he was making his mark in London contain much interesting detail about the life of the age which enables us to see him and his associates in their Elizabethan setting. In the later chapters, too, Quennell continually enriches his narrative with pictures of what was going on while Shakespeare was writing his plays, and he brings out well the way in which the climate of thought and feeling changed in the last years of Queen Elizabeth's reign and the early years of James I. His book is an interesting contribution to Shakespearian biography, and contains some good criticism.

How Shakespeare Spent the Day,[31] by Ivor Brown, is an interesting attempt to show 'the man at his job or rather his variety of jobs', to build up a picture of 'this Shakespeare, actor, manager and investor, as well as author, Shakespeare the man going down to rehearsal and back to his desk, working with a team, counting his money, and fitting all into the hurrying day'. The Elizabethan actor was probably a much busier man than his counterpart today, especially if he was a 'sharer' in his company and was otherwise concerned with its running and with the writing and production of its plays, as Shakespeare was. Brown gives a lively account of 'the daily round' of such a man, referring not only to Shakespeare, but to a number of the other great theatrical figures of the day. He describes the functions and responsibilities of the sharers, and tells us a great deal about Shakespeare's associates, both in their professional and their private capacities. He describes also the theatres in which they worked, and in some interesting chapters reconstructs, of necessity to some degree conjecturally, the ways in which they rehearsed and mounted their productions. He also has to use his imagination in writing about Shakespeare at work on the composition of his plays, but on the whole he is convincing in these sections, and this is no place to argue with him over details. Shakespeare was also a busy man of affairs, and Brown tells us something of this side of him. None of the factual information that Brown presents is new, but he weaves it all together into a vivid and credible account of Shakespeare's day-to-day life, and his book makes good reading.

Reference has been made previously to Charlton Hinman's work on the collation of copies of the First Folio in the Folger Library (see *YW* xxxiv. 114, xlii. 114). With the help of his photographic 'collating-

---

[30] *Shakespeare: the poet and his background*, by Peter Quennell. Weidenfeld & Nicolson. pp. 352. 36s.

[31] *How Shakespeare Spent the Day*, by Ivor Brown. Bodley Head. pp. 237. 25s.

machine' Hinman has now collated the complete text of more than fifty copies, and in the two solid but absorbingly interesting volumes of *The Printing and Proof-Reading of the First Folio of Shakespeare*[32] he gives a detailed account of what he has discovered. In a short notice it is possible to touch on only a few of the points that he makes. By tracing all the occurrences of some 600 pieces of damaged type he has been able to establish the order in which most of the pages of the Folio were set up. This was not the order of the pages as they appear in the complete volume. In the main two compositors (the now famous Compositors A and B) worked simultaneously on pairs of pages; but there is evidence also of the hands of three further compositors, the last of whom appears to have worked only on the tragedies. Hinman adds a good deal to our knowledge of the habits of the various compositors, and shows that their work on the Folio was interrupted several times, presumably for the setting-up of other volumes. Proof-reading was sporadic and casual, and printed pages seem rarely to have been checked by reference to copy. The uncorrected pages, as well as the corrected, were used in the assembling and binding of complete copies. It is clear, indeed, that the printers cared much more for the appearance of their work than for verbal accuracy. It is scarcely necessary to say that Hinman's book will be of very great value to textual critics and editors.

In 'Bibliographical Problems in Shakespearean Scholarship' (*Stechert-Hafner Book News*), Louis Marder outlines some of the difficulties confronting the student who is con-fined to the resources of the average academic library for his Shakespearian research. A completely exhaustive Shakespeare collection, he estimates, would today have to contain at least 75,000 items 'without counting the peripheral materials'. No library is as complete as this, and the vast majority contain only a small fraction of the necessary works. Marder goes on to suggest that there is 'a need for a fully exhaustive compendium and augmentation of all existing bibliographies into an author and subject compilation'.

Shakespeare and His Rivals[33] is, as its sub-title describes it, 'A Casebook on the Authorship Controversy'. It might be felt that no further books were needed to prove that William Shakespeare, the actor who was born at Stratford-upon-Avon in 1564, wrote the plays that bear his name; but as the *Sh Q* bibliography annually bears witness, there are still plenty of cranks ready to argue the claims of other authors—disciples of Looney and Batty and other less appropriately named but equally moronic 'anti-Stratfordians'. The compilers of the present volume, George McMichael and Edgar M. Glenn, do not themselves take sides; they merely present evidence, giving a fair hearing all round. They begin by assembling the many contemporary and near-contemporary allusions to Shakespeare the playwright and poet. Then in successive chapters they present, in the advocates' own words, the cases that have been argued for some of the chief rival claimants to the authorship of the plays, together with a number of rejoinders. They concentrate on the claims of Bacon, Marlowe, Anne Whateley, Oxford, and

---

[32] *The Printing and Proof-Reading of the First Folio of Shakespeare*, by Charlton Hinman. O.U.P. Two volumes: pp. 507, 560. £7.7.0.

[33] *Shakespeare and His Rivals: A Casebook on the Authorship Controversy*, by George McMichael and Edgar M. Glenn. New York: Odyssey Press, 1962. pp. x+262. $1.95.

the Bacon-Oxford-Shakespeare syndicate, and waste no time on the numerous even more impossible candates (Batty, it will be remembered, supported Defoe). It is perhaps hardly necessary to say that, on the evidence presented, and fairly presented, the 'anti-Stratfordian' cases are shown up —to express it in the mildest possible terms—as arrant nonsense.

After these comments it will scarcely be expected that George Elliott Sweet's *Shake-speare—The Mystery*[34] should be given very serious consideration. Sweet is a geophysicist— he is, indeed, President of the Sweet Geophysical Company. By processes of careful scientific reasoning, which involve, among other things, some new theories about the personages of the Sonnets, and the dating of *Timon* and *Pericles* in 1580, and of *Cymbeline* and *The Tempest* in 1582, he reaches the conclusion (in which, however, he has been forestalled) 'that Queen Elizabeth, as a literary bequest to her beloved kingdom, created the plays and poems of Shake-speare'. His views are supported, with only 0.1 per cent of doubt, by Erle Stanley Gardner, who writes: 'I am 99.9 per cent convinced of the correctness of Sweet's theory.'

From Ernest William Talbert come two useful books on certain Elizabethan conceptions and outlooks which, as commonplaces of the age, are constantly reflected in its literature, including the plays of Shakespeare. In *The Problem of Order*[35] Talbert examines a number of books and pamphlets which are concerned with the nature of states, sometimes

specifically the English state, and with problems of political order. He devotes particular attention to Sir Thomas Smith's *De Republica Anglorum* (posthumously published in 1583), Hooker's *Laws of Ecclesiastical Polity*, Sidney's *Arcadia*, and such pamphlets as John Ponet's *Shorte Treatise of Politike Power* (1556). From such works as these he extracts what might be called an Elizabethan theory of political order, embodying such concepts as the chain of being, the analogy inherent in the phrase 'body politic', and other relevant commonplaces of the day. He goes on to show how the influence of this theory may be seen in Daniel's *Philotas* and Shakespeare's *Richard II*, analysing in particular detail the Flint Castle episode and the scene of Richard's deposition in order to show how, 'through the use of equivocal contexts, Shakespeare was able to interpret an important aspect of the political thought of the day and still escape censorship', for it was necessary to walk warily in representing such episodes as these. Talbert's book should be of interest to all students of Elizabethan literature.

In *Elizabethan Drama and Shakespeare's Early Plays*[36] Talbert discusses Shakespeare's artistry in his early plays 'in the light of the probable expectations of contemporary theater-goers and their possible familiarity with current concepts, current representational methods, and current features of the Elizabethan scene'. An Elizabethan theatre audience would, he suggests, expect certain elements in a comedy—song and dance, for example, or tavern revelry, or the aping by a comic actor of the ways of his betters; certain types of

[34] *Shake-speare—The Mystery*, by George Eliott Sweet. Neville Spearman. pp. 200. 21*s*.

[35] *The Problem of Order: Elizabethan Political Commonplaces and an Example of Shakespeare's Art*, by Ernest William Talbert. North Carolina U.P. and O.U.P., 1962. pp. xi+244. $6. 48*s*.

[36] *Elizabethan Drama and Shakespeare's Early Plays: An Essay in Historical Criticism*, by Ernest William Talbert. North Carolina U.P. and O.U.P. pp. viii+410. $8. 64*s*.

situation, too, would be expected, such as comic wooing, or parodies of wooing and marriage which 'usually emphasized shrewish wives and the noisy bawdry of brawling females'. Talbert analyses the recurrent situations of Elizabethan comedy and the characters associated with them, and then turns to the serious drama, where again he finds recurrent character-types, such as the suffering hero, the vicious antagonist, the tyrant, and the like; where, too, he finds certain recurrent forms of dramatic structure. He applies his findings to the study of individual plays. He shows, for example, that there is much that would be 'comically familiar' to Elizabethan theatre-goers in *Love's Labour's Lost*, and such characters as Thurio, and Faulconbridge in some of his aspects, would also to some degree fulfil their expectations. To say that Shakespeare gave his audiences what they wanted is not to deny, however, that his 'use of conventionally comic motifs and representational methods demonstrates a true originality'. Talbert's analyses of the serious plays down to *Richard II* also aim at showing how Shakespeare used, but at the same time transformed, 'concepts and methods thoroughly conventional to his theater and his age'.

Although all available evidence indicates that Shakespeare was a conforming member of the Church of England, the nature of his personal religious beliefs is not known. However, he makes much use of Christian doctrine and of Biblical imagery in his plays, and in *Shakespeare and Christian Doctrine*[37] Roland Mushat Frye sets out to determine whether he does so in order to propagate Christian theology, as some critics have claimed, or whether, as others believe, he

used material of this kind merely to serve his dramatic purposes. In Part I of the book Frye considers in some detail both the 'theologizing analyses' of such critics as G. Wilson Knight, who finds references to Christ and to the Christian doctrines of redemption even where the words and contexts point to other meanings, and the 'secular analyses' of those who consider Christian theology entirely irrelevant to Shakespeare's writing. He himself steers a midway course between the two extremes. He demonstrates convincingly that Shakespeare's 'citation of theological doctrines . . . shows an easy and intimate familiarity with Christian theology. Always, however, the theology he knew and used is contributory to the drama, and not vice versa.' In Part II Frye supports this conclusion with an interesting study of the theological background against which a mature and intelligent Elizabethan like Shakespeare moved; he pays special attention to the writings of such figures as Luther, Calvin, and Hooker, and their attitudes towards literature. The long third part discusses the theological terms and concepts of which Shakespeare makes extensive use—atonement, freedom, guilt justice and judgement, mercy, pride, repentance, and the like. This is a wise book which contributes valuably to the understanding of Shakespeare.

First published in 1946, Edward A. Armstrong's *Shakespeare's Imagination*,[38] which is perhaps best known for its pioneer study of Shakespearian image-clusters, has now been republished as a paperback, with slight modifications to the text and the addition of two interesting appendixes. In the first of these, 'Submerged

---

[37] *Shakespeare and Christian Doctrine*, by Roland Mushat Frye. Princeton U.P. and O.U.P. pp. ix+314. $6. 48s.

[38] *Shakespeare's Imagination: A Study of the Psychology of Association and Inspiration*, by Edward A. Armstrong. Nebraska U.P. pp. v+230. $1.60.

Themes', Armstrong, extending the method of the book as a whole, aims at showing that Shakespeare's mind may be 'subconsciously influenced or dominated by a theme to the extent of using words and images obtained from it in contexts irrelevant to the theme'. To give an obvious example, a series of images derived from the Bible may appear in speeches which are not concerned with religion. In the second appendix Armstrong applies the test of image-clusters to the 'Shakespearian' scenes of *The Two Noble Kinsmen*. He does so more rigorously than Kenneth Muir in *Shakespeare as Collaborator* (1961), but reaches the same conclusion, 'that cluster analysis has supplied definitive proof that Shakespeare wrote the scenes scrutinized'. He adds, however, that 'peculiarities in style and imagery indicate that here we are dealing with the poet's work when his creative imagination had passed its prime'.

Shakespeare's Use of Off-Stage Sounds,[39] by Frances Ann Shirley, goes much further than W. J. Lawrence's work on this subject. Miss Shirley begins with an interesting chapter on the mechanical devices which were used in the Elizabethan theatre to produce a variety of off-stage sound-effects: musical instruments, the blank charge fired in a short-mouthed cannon, the 'roul'd bullet' which made thunder as it moved down an unevenly-stepped trough, the possible use of bellows to excite hounds which were required to bay, and the like. She goes on to discuss the dramatic purposes of off-stage sounds—in reproducing the noises of battle, in heightening the effects of scenes of pageantry, in adding realism to crowd scenes, and in increasing the eeriness of the

supernatural. Finally, she makes a close analysis of the sound-effects in *Julius Caesar, Hamlet,* and *Macbeth*. Miss Shirley's book should be of special value to producers; it will also contribute to the understanding of readers of Shakespeare.

In two articles in *Tulane Drama Review* John Russell Brown discusses 'Shakespeare's Subtext'—Stanislavsky's term for 'the manifest, the inwardly felt expression of a human being in a part, which flows uninterruptedly beneath the words of the text'. Brown sees Julius Caesar as, among other things, 'an outward show which covers an inner reality'. For example, Caesar has all the outward show of an emperor, but the 'subtextual reality' of his fear is revealed in 'nervous tensions, movements of sudden ease or power, unexplained transitions or contradictions. . .'. In his second article Brown, with reference to *Hamlet*, extends the sense of 'subtext' to include unanticipated silences, tones of voice, peculiar emphases or hesitations, and apparently meaningless mannerisms.

In 'Shakespeare's Use of Children' (*ETJ*), Arlin J. Hiken describes some of the dramatic functions of Shakespeare's child characters: among others, they create pathetic effects, give reality to domestic situations, and serve as foils to other characters. A careful study of these child characters might help producers to increase the effectiveness of their productions.

Hilda M. Hulme's *Exploration in Shakespeare's Language*[40] is a work of some importance both for the principles it lays down (or reformulates) and for its elucidation of many linguistic difficulties in Shakespeare. Innumerable words and phrases in the

[39] *Shakespeare's Use of Off-Stage Sounds*, by Frances Ann Shirley. Nebraska U.P. pp. xvii+258. $5.

[40] *Explorations in Shakespeare's Language: Some Problems of Lexical Meaning in the Dramatic Text*, by Hilda M. Hulme. Longmans, 1962. pp. xii+351. 30s.

plays have seemed meaningless to readers and editors of the last two centuries, and a great many of these have been given some show of meaning only by emendation. In recent times, however, it has become increasingly obvious that our difficulties with Shakespeare's language are less often due to textual corruption than to ignorance of Elizabethan language and usage. Miss Hulme is less willing than most scholars to be defeated by these difficulties. Observing Johnson's theory, if not his practice, she works according to the following principle: 'In any passage which appears to have normal Elizabethan or Shakespearean structure . . . words or phrases which are at present considered as unintelligible (and perhaps as textual corruptions) are accepted by the linguist as if they are genuine forms which may perhaps be shown as meaningful (*a*) somewhere within the wide range of Elizabethan spoken English patterns and (*b*) within the tightly controlled unity of the Shakespearean play.' By reading very widely in 'the recesses of obscure and obsolete papers' of Shakespeare's day, many of them colloquial in character, many of them bristling with forgotten dialect or cant terms, by delving into folk-lore and proverb-lore, and by intensive and intelligent study of comparatively neglected reference works of the period, she has been able to cast light on many obscurities, and to bring out many meanings, often indecent meanings, which have not been apparent since the plays were first performed. To give a few examples, Othello's 'defunct, and proper satisfaction' is satisfaction that is 'free—of danger, punishment, penalty incurred'; the hearts that 'pannelled' Antony at—heels are both prostituted hearts and spaniel hearts; Hamlet's 'grounds More Relative then this' are grounds 'able to be related, having

some chance of being believed'. However, examples cannot do justice to Miss Hulme's substantial and well-ordered book, almost every page of which increases our understanding of what Shakespeare wrote.

Martin Lehnert also concerns himself with Shakespeare's language, but he describes rather than elucidates. In his lecture *Shakespeares Sprache und Wir*[41] he illustrates many of the differences between Shakespeare's language and the language of today, and shows some of the ways in which Shakespeare modified, or distorted, language to suit his dramatic purposes—in, for instance, changing the grammatical function of words in such expressions as 'I'll . . . foot her home again', or 'Three great ones . . . off-capp'd to him'. He gives examples of the comic use that Shakespeare makes of the misunderstanding of learned terms, as in Dull's ''Twas not a hand credo; 'twas a pricket', and demonstrates his adventurousness in the invention of new words and usages. Finally, he brings out his boldness in imagery and in all the figures of rhetoric.

The reappearance, with slight modifications and additions, of F. P. Wilson's *The Plague in Shakespeare's London*,[42] which was first published in 1927, will be welcomed. The interest provided by this book is of many kinds. It is, of course, an important contribution to the social history of England in the time of Shakespeare. However, Wilson's approach is literarary as well as historical, and he has much to say about plague literature, and about the impact of the plague on

[41] *Shakespeares Sprache und Wir*, von Martin Lehnert. Berlin: Akademie-Verlag. pp. 67.

[42] *The Plague in Shakespeare's London*, by F. P. Wilson. (Oxford Paperbacks.) O.U.P. pp. xii+228. 6s.

Elizabethan authors and theatrical companies. Much of his information is, indeed, derived from such writers as Nashe and Dekker, who lived through various visitations of the plague. Two further items[43] have been added to the series of Folger Booklets on Tudor and Stuart Civilization—a series which is invaluable for what it fills in of the Shakespearian background. In *The 'Invicible' Armada and Elizabethan England* Garrett Mattingly gives a lively reconstruction of the events which led to the equipping and launching of the Spanish Armada, and of its destruction. He questions whether, as is so often asserted, 'the event produced in England a mood of buoyant optimism, which somehow stimulated the flowering of Elizabethan literature, and particularly of the Elizabethan drama'. He finds no convincing evidence that anything in the events of 1588 or of the fifteen years' war which followed them encouraged these productions, 'and it is surprising how little the theme of the defeat of the Armada itself contributed to them'. His sixteen plates include seven illustrations of the fleets and their engagements from John Pine's *The Tapestry Hangings* (1739); the remainder are mostly portraits of the principal personages concerned on both sides. Ellen C. Eyler's *Early English Gardens and Garden Books* is an extremely interesting account, with special reference to Elizabethan and Jacobean literature, of the development of the Englishman's delight in gardens, particularly pleasure gardens, and of the gardening books that were read with avid interest in this period, such as Sir Hugh Plat's *Floraes Paradise* (1608), John Barkinson's *Paradisi in sole, Paradisus terrestris*, and the works of Thomas Tusser and Gervase Markham. The twenty excellent plates, drawn from contemporary works, represent personalities, garden plans, and a variety of popular plants.

The annual publications remain to be noticed. The central theme of *Shakespeare Survey 16*[44] is Shakespeare in the modern world, and several of its contributions are versions of papers which were read at the tenth International Shakespeare Conference held at Stratford-upon-Avon in 1961. In 'An Obligation to Shakespeare and the Public' Louis B. Wright speaks of the functions of the Shakespearian critic, and surveys some notable criticism of recent years. However, not all scholars have the capacity to winnow the chaff from the wheat, and Wright believes that 'Shakespearian studies would benefit from a cool and detached scepticism that would seek to evaluate every instrument of learning and utilize each for what it is worth.' R. M. Samarin's thesis, which in 'Our Closeness to Shakespeare' he develops with special reference to Russian literature, is that 'the whole of European and American literature in the nineteenth and twentieth centuries may be regarded as having sprung out of the heritage bequeathed by Shakespeare'. Norman Sanders considers 'The Popularity of Shakespeare' particularly in relation to the Royal Shakespeare Theatre's repertory since the Second World War. In 'Shakespeare and the Fashion of these

[43] *The 'Invincible' Armada and Elizabethan England*, by Garrett Mattingly. pp. iii+54. *Early English Gardens and Garden Books*, by Ellen C. Eyler. pp. iii+70. (Folger Booklets on Tudor and Stuart Civilization.) Cornell U.P. for the Folger Shakespeare Library.

[44] *Shakespeare Survey 16; An Annual Survey of Shakespearian Study and Production*, ed. by Allardyce Nicoll. C.U.P. pp. ix+189. 30s.

Times' J. P. Brockbank shows how Shakespeare criticism of the past has reflected the literary climate of the age in which it was written, as indeed it to some extent does today. However, 'the plays keep alive many modes of understanding and delight that are alien to current life and belief, and the miracle is that the art can stay quick when our understanding of it is virtually dead. In such cases it is better to consult more thoroughly the fashion of Shakespeare's times and let our own go momentarily unregarded.' In 'An Approach to Shakespearian Tragedy' V. Y. Kantak discusses characterization primarily by means of a study of the actor image in *Macbeth*. A. José Axelrad sums up 'Shakespeare's Impact Today in France'; on the whole 'England's Shakespeare is now also France's Shakespeare. We have travelled a long way since the days of M. de Voltaire.' Wolfgang Clemen's title is 'Shakespeare and the Modern World'. Clemen brings out many aspects of Shakespeare's 'dramatic presentation of fundamental issues which may be said to appeal strongly to a modern audience'. Rudolf Stamm speaks of 'Modern "Theatrical" Translations of Shakespeare', especially those of the German translators. In 'Shakespeare as a "Corrupter of Words"', Michel Grivelet considers some of the difficulties that French translators encounter in trying to find an acceptable idiom for their versions of Shakespeare. D. S. Baker gives an account of the impact of Shakespeare in Ghana. In the general section of the volume David Cook offers a study of *Timon of Athens*; he suggests, among other things, that the reason why Shakespeare failed to finish, or at any rate polish, *Timon* was 'that, in the event, the hero proved too negative a vehicle for his thinking, and the whole fabric of the play too destruc-

tive at a time when his thoughts were slowly gestating the new positive ideas of the final group of plays'. In 'Who Strutted and Bellowed?' A. J. Gurr contrasts the acting styles of Alleyn and Burbage. Stanley Wells discusses 'Shakespeare in Planché's Extravaganzas'. Planché's parodies and burlesques provide general evidence on his attitude and that of his early nineteenth-century audiences to Shakespeare; they also 'yield interesting information on specific points of the staging of Shakespeare's plays over a wide period of time'. Paul Morgan draws attention to a copy of the third edition of Lope de Vega's *Rimas* (1613) which contains, in Leonard Digges's hand, a joint tribute to de Vega and Shakespeare. Philip Parsons writes on Shakespeare's use of masks in *Love's Labour's Lost* and *Romeo and Juliet*. John Russell Brown reviews the performances at the Royal Shakespeare Theatre in August 1962, and Arnold Edinborough surveys the achievement, over its first ten years, of the Shakespeare Festival at Stratford, Ontario. The volume contains also International Notes, a list of Shakespeare productions in the United Kingdom in 1961, and a number of interesting illustrations. It closes with the usual conspectus of the year's contribution to Shakespearian studies in which critical studies are reviewed by Philip Edwards, textual studies by J. G. McManaway, and works relating to Shakespeare's life, times, and stage by Norman Sanders.

The articles in *Shakespeare Quarterly*[45] are, as usual, noticed under relevant headings elsewhere in this chapter. Only one requires attention in this general section. In 'The Grants

[45] *Shakespeare Quarterly*. The Journal of The Shakespeare Assn. of America, Inc. Vol. XIV. Four numbers, pp. 489. Annual subscription $8.

of Arms to Shakespeare's Father' Raymond Carter Sutherland establishes that the still common assertion that Shakespeare 'secured arms to show the fact that he had "arrived" is pure assumption with no basis in fact'. We must not forget that it was John Shakespeare who got the arms, and it is probable that they 'were expected to descend to anticipated sons of the poet's brothers'. As usual, *Sh Q* contains articles on almost every aspect of Shakespearian scholarship and production, and is embellished with a number of admirable plates. The summer number contains an invaluable annotated bibliography for for 1962, compiled by Robert W. Dent with the assistance of a committee of twenty-six foreign correspondents. No Shakespearian scholar today can do without the wonderfully complete *Sh Q* bibliographies.

The dozen articles in *Shakespeare Jahrbuch*[46] are also noticed in later sections. In addition to these the volume contains reviews of German productions by Karl Brinkmann and of Swiss productions by Lydia Benz-Burger; a sixty-page section of reviews of books and articles contributed by Hermann Heuer; Association notes; and a Shakespeare bibliography for 1962.

Ashland Studies for Shakespeare, 1962,[47] following the procedure of previous volumes in the series, was prepared to be read in short academic courses which accompanied the production, at the 1962 Oregon Shakespeare Festival, of *Coriolanus, As*

You Like It, The Comedy of Errors, and *2 Henry IV.* It opens with a reprint of H. H. Child's 'Shakespearean Productions of John Philip Kemble', which reviews nineteenth-century cuts and interpolations in performances of Shakespeare, especially those adopted by Kemble, and which has a special relevance to the study of *Coriolanus.* This is followed by a short guide for pilgrims to the Holy Land printed in 1498 by Wynkyn de Worde; had Henry IV carried out his intention to make such a pilgrimage, he might have profited from reading such a guide. From John T. Marvin comes an article entitled 'Causation of Tragedy in the History Plays'; this illustrates the change from belief in external influences to self-determination in the history plays from *King John* to *2 Henry IV.* Next come notes on 'Armorial Ensigns of Westminster' by Sir John Hawkins, the biographer of Dr. Johnson. In 'The "Age & Body" of Music in Shakespearean Drama' Stanley R. Plummer gives an interesting survey of the dramatic use of music in plays of the Elizabethan and Jacobean period. Each of these items is accompanied by appendixes and by a number of reproductions of early prints. The volume closes with 'The Courteous Carman and the Amorous Maid', a popular Elizabethan ballad. *Ashland Studies* always reprints unusual early material which throws light on the plays with which it is concerned.

3. STUDIES OF INDIVIDUAL PLAYS AND POEMS

Apart from the first entry in this section, the plays are, as usual, treated in the order of the First Folio, and are followed by the poems.

It seems convenient to notice at this point a series of 'guides' to plays of

[46] *Shakespeare Jahrbuch*, Bd. 99. Herausgegeben im Auftrage der deutschen Shakespeare-Gesellschaft von Hermann Heuer, unter Mitwirkung von Ernst Theodor Sehrt und Rudolf Stamm. pp. 370. Heidelberg: Quelle & Meyer.

[47] *Ashland Studies for Shakespeare, 1962,* ed. by Margery Bailey. Published for the Oregon Shakespeare Festival (Box 27, Ashland, Oregon). pp. 117+appendixes. $2.

Shakespeare[48] which have appeared in the Guides to English Literature series. Ten plays have so far been included (see footnote). The guides are intended for the use of G.C.E. candidates, and they should prove useful at this level. Each play is, in an introductory section, placed in its setting among the plays of Shakespeare, and any background material that is necessary for its understanding is sketched in; this is particularly helpful with the history plays. Then comes a section on the characters—nothing elaborate, merely sufficient to indicate their significance in the action. The main body of the guide is a critical scene-by-scene analysis of the play; read in conjunction with the play itself, this should enable the student to draw together all that it is necessary for him to know about either the action or the characters.

The Tempest

Rose Abdelnour Zimbardo joins issue with those critics—and they are in a large majority—who link *The Tempest* with the other romances as a play concerned with the theme of regeneration. To see the play in this way is to ignore its key speech, 'Our revels now are ended . . .'. In 'Form and Disorder in *The Tempest*' (*Sh Q*), Dr. Zimbardo argues that the theme of the play is 'not regeneration through suffering, but the eternal conflict between order and chaos, the

attempt of art to impose form upon the formless and chaotic, and the limitations of art in this endeavor'. Prospero is the agent of order, as is Gonzalo at a different level; all the other characters have in some sense and in differing degrees to be manipulated into accepting this order by means of Prospero's art. However, it is only on the enchanted island, in a world of art, that order controls disorder; when art must at last be abandoned, 'nothing is left mankind but to sue for grace'.

In 'The Transfer of Power in "King Lear" and "The Tempest"' (*REL*), Eleanor N. Hutchens develops the view that in many of Shakespeare's plays a 'transfer of power from right to wrong' is brought about by the failure of good 'to function adequately'. 'When right, either moral or legal, fails to carry out all its proper functions, there occurs a power vacuum into which wrong moves with a force thus generated by the negative behaviour of right itself.' This is particularly well exemplified in *Lear* and *The Tempest*. In both plays, however, 'the idea of power is linked with another idea which, as it is worked out in the play, casts light on the proper use of power. This other idea is love in *King Lear*, labour in *The Tempest*.' Miss Hutchens shows how 'the power-love theme' is worked through to a quiet end in *Lear*, and in *The Tempest* to the conception of 'absolute freedom gained through achievement'.

In 'The Tempest: An Interpretation' (*JEGP*), Frank Davidson undertakes an analysis, 'based on philosophical and psychological thinking of the Tudor era', which leads him to the view that Prospero, by subduing within himself elements to some degree represented by Ariel and Caliban, achieves the balance that makes of him the Tudor ideal of the prince.

---

[48] Guides to English Literature. General Editor, S. H. Atkins. Shakespeare: *Macbeth*, by S. Farrar, pp. iv+57. *Henry IV, Part One*, by S. H. Atkins, pp. iv+59. *Henry V*, by K. M. Lobb, pp. iv+59. *As You Like It*, by G. G. Urwin, pp. iv+57. *The Merchant of Venice*, by S. H. Atkins, pp. iv+54. *Twelfth Night*, by H. M. Burton, pp. iv+59. *The Tempest*, by S. H. Atkins, pp. iv+47. *A Midsummer Night's Dream*, by J. Atherton, pp. iv+60. *Julius Caesar*, by S. H. Atkins, pp. iv+53. *Romeo and Juliet*, by H. M. Burton, pp. iv+59. Hulton Educational Publications. Each vol. 3s. 6d.

K

A possible source for 'mountaineers Dew-lapp'd like bulls, whose throats had hanging at 'em Wallets of flesh' is suggested (*Sh Q*), by Paul F. Cranefield and Walter Federn. This is the account of the Styrians in Boemus's *The Manner, Lawes, and Customs of All Nations*, which, written in Latin in 1520, appeared in an English translation in 1611. Since this passage was borrowed almost verbatim by the geographer Ortelius, Shakespeare could also have read the description of the Styrians whose throats were 'like a sacke or wallet' in the English translation of Ortelius which appeared in 1606.

The Two Gentlemen of Verona

Many critics have felt that the comic figures have no organic part in the structure of *The Two Gentlemen*. Harold F. Brooks counters this view in 'Two Clowns in a Comedy (to say nothing of the Dog): Speed, Launce (and Crab) in "The Two Gentlemen of Verona"' (*E & S*). Brooks argues that, 'side by side with the causal sequence that carries forward his romantic plot, Shakespeare, in the parts he has given to Speed and Launce, is developing his play by means of comic parallels that illustrate and extend its themes. The parallels, as well as the causal sequence, are part of the organic structure.' In 'The Failure of *The Two Gentlemen of Verona*' (*Sh S*), Stanley Wells considers what he sees as the 'peculiarities, limitations, and plain faults' of the play—weakness in much of the dialogue, the inability to handle more than two characters at the same time, and the failure to integrate plot and characterization. However, these deficiencies are to some degree offset by the skilful use of recurrent imagery and puns, by the figure of Launce, and by some excellent individual scenes.

The Merry Wives of Windsor

It has been noted before that, in causing Falstaff to impersonate Herne the Hunter in the last of *The Merry Wives*, Shakespeare is burlesquing the myth of Actaeon. In 'Falstaff as Actaeon: A Dramatic Emblem' (*Sh Q*), John M. Steadman claims that 'Shakespeare's treatment of the Falstaff-Actaeon parallel also displays several marked affinities with the representation of this myth in Renaissance iconography and mythography.' Falstaff's disguise is virtually identical with conventional illustrations of Actaeon in Renaissance emblem literature and in editions of the *Metamorphoses*. 'Moreover, the moral significance of Falstaff's ordeal —the punishment the "unclean knight" receives for his "corrupted heart" and "lecheries"—closely resembles a familiar Renaissance interpretation of Actaeon's fate.'

Measure for Measure

D. R. C. Marsh finds the key to 'The Mood of *Measure for Measure*' (*Sh Q*) in the character and activities of the Duke. No one in the play wins our unqualified admiration, and the Duke, who controls so much of the action, is, no less than Isabella and Angelo, 'man, proud man, Drest in a little briefe authoritie'. 'It is a mood of wry clear-sightedness that seems to characterize this play. One might call it pessimistic, except that pessimism and optimism are terms that label rather than illuminate. It is in many ways a funny play, for the exposure of human vanity is often comic, but the comic scenes always have a profoundly serious intention, and always reflect the central theme.'

Two further articles in *Sh Q* relate to *Measure for Measure*. Eileen Mackay points out, in '*Measure for Measure*', that the play manifests a cynical attitude towards the Roman Catholic Church. 'We have been repeatedly told that Isabella's white figure shines out against a carefully drawn background of unscrupulous lust and sex at its most mercenary and evil; but surely it may well have been the author's intention that Isabella's white figure should also shine out against a carefully drawn background of ecclesiastical corruption and degradation.' Isabella is an idealist, outstanding in her integrity and humility; but she is no prig, and much should not be made of her as a novice of St. Clare, a role which she early abandons. 'She is young, warm, human, and hot-tempered, and should not be played as an ascetic, a stained-glass window figure, a "thing enskied and sainted".' In '*Measure for Measure* and Elizabethan Betrothals' S. Nagarajan, countering the views of previous commentators on this subject, argues that Angelo, though tyrannical, was legally correct in his treatment of Claudio because Claudio's betrothal was a *de futuro* betrothal; Mariana's, on the other hand, was a *de praesenti* betrothal, although her deceit of Angelo needed to be justified by marriage. Isabella agreed to the 'bed-trick' 'as much at least for the sake of Mariana as of her brother'.

Love's Labour's Lost

In 'A Show of the Nine Worthies' (*Sh Q*) John L. Nevinson describes two large and copiously illustrated commonplace books completed, in 1608 and 1616, by Thomas Trevelyon, a London scrivener; in each nine pages are devoted to the Nine Worthies, who are both pictured and described. Nevinson relates these volumes to earlier pictorial and literary representations of the Worthies, and points out that in *Love's Labour's Lost* Shakespeare is making

fun of pageants very similar to that which Trevelyon illustrates. Also in *Sh Q*, Gustav Ungerer discusses 'Two Items of Spanish Pronunciation in *Love's Labour's Lost*'. Armado signs a letter as 'Don Adriano de Armatho', and Costard adresses him as 'Armatho'. Ungerer suggests that, like *renegatho* in *Twelfth Night* and *Bermoothes* in *The Tempest*, this form is intended to represent a Spanish pronunciation. This seems also to be the case with Armado's *Chirra*, for 'Sirrah', as may be guessed from such forms as *chivil*, *chitty*, and *chickness* in *Blurt, Master Constable*. Shakespeare may have picked up such pronunciations from Spaniards whom he met, or from one of the Spanish textbooks written for English readers shortly after the defeat of the Spanish Armada. Tinsley Helton, in 'Shakespeare's *Love's Labour's Lost*, V. ii. 940–941' (*Ex*), interprets the last two lines of the play as meaning that the words of the messenger who brings news of the King's death ('The words of Mercury') are harsh because they end the Apollonian festival ('the songs of Apollo') which the play has hitherto been.

A Midsummer Night's Dream

In a note in *Sh Q*, 'The Fierce Vexation of a (Midsummer Night's) Dreame', John P. Cutts discusses 'Shakespeare's symbolical use of the flower "Love in idlenesse" to induce the romantic "vexation of a dreame" and "Dians bud" to dispel it'.

The Merchant of Venice

The Truth About Shylock,[49] by Bernard Grebanier, is an attempt to answer the question, 'What did Shakespeare mean by Shylock?' Grebanier begins by trying to find out

[49] *The Truth about Shylock*, by Bernard Grebanier. New York: Random House. pp. ix + 369.

what Jews meant to the Elizabethans. Marlowe was no hater of the Jews, and his Barabas is, in spite of as well as because of his excesses, 'the kind of superman his author admired'. However, more in tune with the attitude of their age, Nashe in *The Unfortunate Traveller* and Thomas Coryate in his *Crudities* portray their Jews as comic or grotesque figures, and with an entire lack of sympathy. Usury is frequently referred to in Elizabethan literature, almost invariably in terms of abhorrence, and almost invariably the usurer comes to a bad end. Grebanier goes on to consider the treatment of the pound-of-flesh story in literature earlier than Shakespeare and in *The Merchant of Venice*. When he comes to consider Shylock's part in this story, and indeed Shakespeare's presentation of him in general, he can find few signs of the sympathy towards Jews that many critics see in Shakespeare. He suggests, indeed, that Shakespeare makes little of Shylock as a Jew; rather he shows him as he might have shown a cruel and false usurer of any race. He is, however, a very able and intelligent man, though utterly perverted, and the outcome of his trial can never be in doubt. At the end of the play we may feel sorry for him, but 'only because he manages to maintain dignity in the midst of savage cruelty'; he has been granted more leniency than he was entitled to. 'As he leaves the play, we are glad to have him go. But we cannot avoid a sense of tremendous waste that a man of such gifts should have perverted them all in the wretched service of greed.' There is much that is irritating in Grebanier's manner of writing; but his earlier chapters on the social and literary background of *The Merchant of Venice* contribute something to our understanding of Shakespeare's portrayal of Shylock.

Among the reasons for Shylock's rage at Jessica's elopement is her theft of the 'Turkies' which Leah had given to him when he was a bachelor. In 'Shylock's Turquoise Ring' (*Sh Q*), Jackson Campbell Boswell, assuming Shakespeare's knowledge of gemlore, declares that it was appropriate that Leah should have given Shylock a turquoise ring as a betrothal gift, 'for she would have been familiar with the Eastern folklore of safety, prosperity, and love associated with the stone'; on the other hand, Jessica very readily parted with it for a monkey 'because of the European superstition that it would cause sterility'. Louis Marder, writing 'In Defence of Shakespeare and Shylock' (*SNL*), takes the view that Shakespeare, though not anti-Semitic, is 'anti-Shylock', but nevertheless humanizes him.

As You Like It

In 'Form and Attitude in Comedy' (*Drama Survey*) William G. McCollom defines comedy as that which depicts 'the natural desires of man as a social being', and represents life as 'a product of natural law and erratic fortune'; it ends by favouring the average at the expense of the exceptional. McCollom illustrates his definition with an analysis of *As You Like It*. In' "As You Like It": A Grammatical Clue to Character' (*REL*), Angus McIntosh suggests that the incidence of such 'alternative' forms as *thou* and *you* in Shakespeare's plays may provide clues to characterization, as may be exemplified by the use of the forms in the relationship of Rosalind and Celia. This, McIntosh claims, reveals 'a steady toning down of their friendship' in the second half of the play; 'we are being prepared for . . . honouring of high wedlock, and the old relationship has had its day'.

The Taming of the Shrew

It is generally accepted that in *The Taming of the Shrew* 'the three plot strands of shrew-taming, love intrigue or "supposes", and induction' are skilfully interwoven and unified, and most critics agree that it is the shrew plot which draws a less vital sub-plot into this unity. In '"Supposes" as the Unifying Theme in *The Taming of the Shrew (Sh Q)* Cecil C. Seronsy argues that it is rather the sub-plot, 'with its theme of "supposes" which enters substantially into both the shrew action and the induction', that accounts for Shakespeare's fine handling of all three elements of the play.

All's Well that Ends Well.

Eric La Guardia examines the concepts of 'Chastity, Regeneration, and World Order in *All's Well that Ends Well' (Myth and Symbol)*. He characterizes the play as 'a symbolic drama with the objective of reconciling the extremities of the laws of nature, represented . . . by the romantic problem of passion vs. purity'. The ending represents metaphorically 'the condition of *concordia mundi*'.

The Winter's Tale

Jerry H. Bryant considers the relationship between 'The Winter's Tale and the Pastoral Tradition' *(Sh Q)*. He traces the growth of the tradition in both verse and prose, and shows how Shakespeare turned its conventional subjects—chastity, fidelity, and the obstacles to love—to his own purposes in exploring the nature of truth. The jealousy of Leontes represents a distortion or misapprehension of reality, and this contrasts with the misapprehensions in the pastoral scenes arising from the pastoral devices of disguise and mistaken identity. Shakespeare 'converts the stereotyped conventions of the pastoral drama into highly original instruments', and through them effects 'the means of restoring a civic body to health'. In the same issue of *Sh Q* William O. Scott discusses the symbolism of 'Seasons and Flowers in *The Winter's Tale'*, showing how Shakespeare develops the analogy between the life of man and the four seasons of the year, and bringing out the appropriateness of the flowers that Perdita offers to the various personages in the sheep-shearing scene. In a note later in the volume, 'Hermione, a Dangerous Ornament', Stanley R. Maveety argues that the 'dagger muzzled' which Leontes refers to (I. i. 156), 'emphasizes the contrast between the innocent boyhood of Leontes and Polixenes and the adult world of sordid possibilities which is about to close in on them'. He goes on to suggest that it is a conscious echo, ironically used, of a proverb which Chaucer also uses ironically in *The Merchant's Tale*, 'A man may do no sinne with his wyfe Ne hurte hymselven with his owene knyfe'. All editors have had difficulty in interpreting the passage at I. ii. 138–46 ('Affection? thy Intention stabs the Center . . . And hardning of my Browes.'). In 'Leontes' *Affectio'* *(Sh Q)*, Hallett Smith suggests that much of the difficulty vanishes if *Affection* is interpreted in the Ciceronian sense of the word *affectio*, glossed by Cooper as 'Affection: a disposition or mutation happening to bodie or minde: trouble of minde'.

Richard II

In 'Richard II and Shakespeare's Tragic Mode' *(TSLL)*, Peter G. Phialas differentiates *Richard II* from earlier tragedies of the 'falls of illustrious men' type. The play is a milepost in Shakespeare's career in being his first tragedy with 'human causality the chief tragic force'. In

Sh Q, Robert Hapgood discusses what he sees as 'Three Eras in *Richard II*'. The play looks both back and forward. In the earlier scenes the era of Edward III is reflected in 'the reminiscences and old-fashioned ways of thinking and acting of its survivors'. The greater part of the play naturally reflects the era of Richard. But by the end we have also been given glimpses of the era of Henry IV.

Arthur Freeman suggests (*Sh Q*), that, although it has hitherto been overlooked, the most obvious source of the lines, 'O, who can hold a fire in his hand By thinking on the frosty Caucasus' (I. i. 294–5), is the Prometheus legend. In classical legend the Caucasus is best known as the region where Prometheus was chained to a mountain by Zeus. 'Prometheus, of course, was an archetypal exile, and the analogy becomes quite neat when we remember that it was he of all the gods who distinguished himself by carrying, from heaven to earth, "a fire in his hand".' Another possible source for passages in *Richard II* is noted by Harold F. Brooks in 'Shakespeare and *The Gouernour*, Bk. II, ch. xiii. Parallels with *Richard II* and the *More* Addition' (*Sh Q*). Brooks finds parallels, though somewhat tenuous ones, between this chapter of Sir Thomas Elyot's *Gouernour* and two passages in Shakespeare's play: first, when the deposed king moralizes upon the defection of roan Barbary, and secondly, in the political allegory of the garden scene. There is also a parallel in line 121 of the Hand D Addition to *Sir Thomas More*, 'and leade the ma(ies)tie of law in liom'. Brooks's article adds to the mounting evidence that Shakespeare was well acquainted with *The Gouernour*.

Henry IV, Parts 1 and 2

The two parts of *Henry IV*, says Maggie Tomlinson in 'Henry IV' (*MCR*), are not to be regarded as being partially tragic. They are a comedy centred upon Falstaff, who, though he is not the whole play, is 'the embodiment of a comic spirit to which all are subservient', and a 'supreme illusionist'. The rejection of Falstaff is inevitable, even though it means the extinction of so much life and force. U. C. Knoepflmacher, in 'The Humors as Symbolic Nucleus in *Henry IV*' (*CE*), analyses Shakespeare's use in *1 Henry IV* of the concept of the humours. The metaphorical use of this concept, he contends, 'binds the play's abundant references to blood, sickness and the four elements to those related to heavenly bodies and to time, and stresses the Christian import of Prince Hal's transcendence'.

In 'Falstaff and the Succession' (*CE*), Eben Bass brings out what, in the context of the history plays as a whole, is a striking contrast between Prince Hal and Richard II. In his dealings with Falstaff, the Prince shows that he is capable of rejecting vanity, unlike Richard, and is thus safe from deposition. In 'Hotspur: The Integration of Character and Theme' (*RP*, 1962), Raymond H. Reno argues, in the face of a good deal of criticism to the opposite effect, that Hotspur's internal chaos is not merely a reflection of the theme of disorder that is developed in the play; he is himself partly responsible for the disorder.

In 'Shakespeare's Delayed Reactions' (*EC*), Robert Hapgood observes how successfully Shakespeare reverses the attitude of the audience towards central figures in his plays. He does this in his presentation of the deposition of Richard II, of the assassination of Julius Caesar, and of the rejection of Falstaff. He is least successful with Falstaff, since he has from the beginning made him too appealing a character.

In representing the encounter between Prince John and the rebel army just after the beginning of Act IV of *2 Henry IV*, the 1600 Quarto and the Folio give different positions to the entry stage-direction for Prince John. In '"Enter Prince John", Quarto or Folio?' (*Sh Q*), Robert J. Fusillo suggests, in the face of editorial emendation, that the Folio version may stand, and that in the Quarto the stage-direction is misplaced. Perhaps, however, the Quarto version is that of Shakespeare's foul papers, and the Folio stems from a theatrical manuscript in which the position of the stage-direction has been made to conform with stage practice.

Henry V

In 'The Renewal of the King's Symbolic Role: From *Richard II* to *Henry V*' (*TSSL*, 1962), Joan Webber discusses Shakespeare's presentation of his monarchs in the Lancastrian tetralogy. In his years of apprenticeship as a prince, she argues, Henry V learns how to restore and renew the traditional role of king, and he expresses 'a world-view more meaningful' than Richard II's, 'in a language more inspiring' than Henry IV's.

Richard III

In 'Shakespeare's Richard III and St. Paul' (*Sh Q*), Geoffrey Carnall reminds us that Richard habitually swears by St. Paul. Carnall cites a number of Elizabethan opinions of St. Paul in support of his contention that 'Richard's invocation of St. Paul, in fact, is more than mock-piety, more than a clothing of his naked villainy "with odd old ends stol'n forth of holy writ", so that he may seem a saint when most he plays the devil. He is positively impersonating, with mischievous exhilaration, the unscrupulous Apostle of the Gentiles.' In '"Determined" in *Richard III*, I. i. 30' (*Sh Q*), David S. Berkeley glosses *determined* with the double sense of 'am resolved' and 'am decreed, or fore-ordained, by God'.

Henry VIII

In 'Shakespeare's Song and Masque Hand in *Henry VIII*' (*Sh J*), John P. Cutts argues, from parallels, that it was Shakespeare and not Fletcher who wrote the shepherd's masque (I. iv), the song 'Orpheus with his lute . . .' (III. i.), and the masque-vision (IV. ii).

Coriolanus

In 'Reflections upon Shakespeare's *Coriolanus*' (*Philological Pragnesia*) Anselm Schlösser makes a thorough study of the play in terms of class conflict. Neither of the contending parties, plebeians and patricians, is shown in a favourable light, and it is not possible to judge where Shakespeare's sympathies lie. 'The interplay of social forces and ideologies in a period of transition has in all its intricacies been fully realized and transformed into dramatic action by Shakespeare.' Schlösser also discusses Bertolt Brecht's version of *Coriolanus*, about two-thirds of which are 'a free yet faithfull rendering' of Shakespeare's play, with passages taken from other plays by Shakespeare. However, Brecht has given to the conflict 'such a twist that the tribunes no longer appear as demagogues but as the responsible leaders of the plebeians who finally succeed in uniting the Roman citizenry'.

In 'Shakespeare's *Coriolanus* and Plutarch's Life of Cato' (*RP*, 1962), Fred Chappel conjectures that the life of Cato 'is operating in the play *Coriolanus* certainly as an ideological source', and perhaps too as a source for some of the imagery.

Titus Andronicus

In the face of much adverse criticism of the play, A. C. Hamilton maintains, in 'Titus Andronicus: The Form of Shakespearian Tragedy' (Sh Q), that Titus Andronicus 'may have been carefully conceived and deliberately planned'. It is characterized by excesses of many kinds, and it is largely these that, have antagonized the critics. However, 'the mark of excess characterizes all of Shakespeare's early work. It is a sign of strength, not of weakness.' After a careful analysis of the play, Hamilton reminds us that it foreshadows several of Shakespeare's mature tragedies. 'The reason is, I believe, that his first tragedy is their archetype.'

Also in Sh Q, Judith M. Karr draws attention to six pleas in Titus Andronicus which, since they 'echo and mirror one another', help to give unity to a play sometimes charged with a lack of unity. In I. i. 103–20 Tamora begs Titus to spare her son; the second plea (I. i. 370–83), is directed to Titus by Marcus, Lucius, Quintus, and Martius; at I. i. 428 ff. Tamora begs Saturninus to pardon Titus; at II. iii. 136 ff. Lavinia pleads with Tamora for mercy; then there is Titus's plea to the Judges and Senators (III. i. 1–26); and finally (III. i. 205–6), Titus prays to heaven for mercy, and gets none. The pattern of these pleas, with their echoes and parallels, draws together several motives in the play.

Siegfried Korninger, in 'Shakespeare's Titus Andronicus' (Moderne Sprachen), finds many parallels between Titus Andronicus and other revenge tragedies of the sixteenth and seventeenth centuries.

Shakespeare gives Aaron no obvious motives for his crimes. Certainly his ebullience and panache would not suggest that he is a typical melancholy villain in Elizabethan tragedy. And yet, as Eldred D. Jones points out in 'Aaron and Melancholy in Titus Andronicus' (Sh Q), in rejecting Tamora's advances (II. iii. 30–39), Aaron makes himself out to be a melancholic. 'In temporarily assuming the pose of melancholy, Aaron thus chooses a plausible disguise. His blackness and his race make this easy. He uses these to excuse another of the traits of melancholy—the pursuit of vengeance.'

Romeo and Juliet

In 'Romeo and Juliet, II. i. 13: Further Commentary' (N M), Robert O. Evans argues for the reading 'Young Adam: Cupid', with its 'oxymoron-like effect', suggesting love that is both ancient and young. Arthur Freeman's 'Shakespeare and "Solyman and Perseda"' (MLR), also has relevance to Romeo and Juliet. Freeman brings forward evidence that Solyman and Perseda was probably written in 1591–2, later than The Spanish Tragedy, but earlier than King John and Romeo and Juliet, both of which it influenced.

Julius Caesar

W. A. Cook notes, in 'Shakespeare's Cinna—Tribune not Poet' (Sh Q), that Shakespeare was misled by North's Plutarch into describing the Cinna who was murdered by the mob as a poet. Historically this Cinna was not the poet Gaius Helvius Cinna, but a certain Helvius Cinna who was a tribune friendly to Caesar.

Macbeth

Dolora G. Cunningham's thesis, in 'Macbeth: The Tragedy of the Hardened Heart' (Sh Q), is that 'Macbeth, shown in the beginning as having a genuine sense of human kindness, gradually so hardens himself in the custom of evil that he becomes eventually incapable of altering the pattern in which his very being and, for a while, the total action of the play are fixed.' Dr. Cunningham believes that 'the hardening of the heart against itself that covers Macbeth with irrevocable loss' is a formative element in Shakespearian tragedy generally.

J. P. Dyson considers 'The Structural Function of the Banquet Scene in *Macbeth*' (*Sh Q*). Shakespeare tends to focus the meaning of his major plays in key scenes, and Dyson believes that the banquet scene (III. iv), is such a key scene in relation to the structure of *Macbeth*. It is in this scene that Macbeth first clearly perceives the consequences of the assassination: he has rejected the world of the martlet, which represents sleep, fertility, and harmony, and has allied himself with the world of the raven, which represents evil, sterility, and damnation. 'The raven-martlet tension underlies the play . . . on all levels.' In 'The Pattern of Behaviour Culminating in *Macbeth*' (*SEL*), Ruth L. Anderson discusses some of the ideas associated by Renaissance writers with ambition, usurpation, and tyranny. She finds the patterns of behaviour described by these writers strikingly exemplified by Shakespeare in *Richard III* and *Macbeth*.

In 'Reversal of Values in *Macbeth*' (*ESA*), D. J. Brindley distinguishes and analyses four kinds of values which are temporarily reversed in *Macbeth*—natural, sexual, moral, and spiritual. Jay L. Halio, in 'Bird Imagery in *Macbeth*' (*SNL*), isolates a strain of imagery which reflects Macbeth's degeneration into 'a vicious, swift, and detestable bird'.

Hamlet

A complete volume of the series of *Stratford-upon-Avon Studies*, the general editors of which are John Russell Brown and Bernard Harris, is devoted to *Hamlet*.[50] In the opening paper, 'Character and Role from Richard III to Hamlet', Peter Ure links together Shakespeare's early tragic heroes—the two Richards, Brutus, and Hamlet—as men who find themselves, or are placed, in the position of having to fill roles that are expected of them; as they nerve themselves to complete their roles as kings or avengers, we see them wrenching and redefining these roles to make them match their own conceptions of what is due to them. Hamlet differs from the earlier heroes in that 'he glimpses a freedom which is beyond rule', and 'as he liberates himself gradually from Claudius's dark monarchy, this freedom grows more absolute'. In 'Hamlet in the Theatre' David William writes interestingly about the interpretation of the part of Hamlet in production, suggesting that for the actor who plays this part the 'supreme test of imaginative courage comes in the scenes with the ghost. Only by rising to that challenge can the actor work that magic on an audience which bends them where he wills.' J. K. Walton discusses 'The Structure of *Hamlet*', bringing out the supreme skill with which Shakespeare develops the relationship of the hero with the forces with which he is in conflict. G. K. Hunter examines 'The Heroism of Hamlet' in relation to three qualities traditionally associated with the hero: the power to command and control human affairs, goodness, and force of personality. The title of Patrick Cruttwell's paper is 'The Morality of Hamlet—"Sweet Prince" or "Arrant Knave"?' Cruttwell answers the question he has set himself by likening Hamlet to a conscript in a

---

[50] *Stratford-upon-Avon Studies 5: 'Hamlet'*, ed. by John Russell Brown and Bernard Harris. Arnold. pp. 212. 25*s*.

war. 'He has done things, as we all do in wars, he would rather not have done; but he believes it to be a just war, and all in all, he has borne himself well.' In 'The Politics in *Hamlet* and "The World of the Play"' E. A. J. Honigmann discusses the constitutions of Denmark and Norway as they are sketched in by Shakespeare, and argues that it is of some importance to realize that the monarchy of Denmark was an elective monarchy; the failure to accept this has led to misrepresentation of some of the motives and actions both of Hamlet and of Claudius. R. A. Foakes's subject is 'Character and Speech in *Hamlet*'. Attention has often been drawn to the images of corruption in the play, and to Hamlet's riddles and wordplay. Foakes shows that both the images and the wordplay emphasize the contrast between appearance and reality, and in particular they 'relate to Hamlet's perception of his world'. He goes on to show how well the speech of the other characters reflects their outlooks and personalities. Following the lead of Gordon Craig, John Russell Brown, in 'The Setting for Hamlet', discusses the setting, movements, and tempo of *Hamlet* in performance. In 'The Decline of Hamlet' T. J. B. Spencer surveys the *Hamlet* criticism of the last two and a half centuries, and notes that critics of the twentieth century have on the whole 'tried to convince us that we should abandon the long theatrical tradition of Hamlet as "the Darling of the English Audience"'; he cites, among others, G. Wilson Knight, L. C. Knights, and Rebecca West as adverse critics of the Prince. Finally, in 'A Reader's Guide to *Hamlet*' Stanley Wells reviews the most important criticism of *Hamlet* of the last few decades.

The theme that Herbert R. Coursen, Jr., develops in 'That Within: Hamlet and Revenge' (*Bu R*), is that, as soon as Hamlet has made up his mind that his father's ghost is a true ghost, it 'becomes the devil', and 'accepts completely the revenge thesis'. From now on Hamlet's course is towards damnation. In 'Discerning the Ghost in *Hamlet*' (*PMLA*), Paul N. Siegel joins issue with Sister Miriam Joseph, C.S.C., who in an article bearing the same title (*PMLA*, 1961), interpreted Shakespeare's presentation of the Ghost in terms of scholastic philosophy. Siegel considers this interpretation too narrow. The Ghost is compounded of many elements, and is too complex a figure to be explained in the light of scholastic texts.

Charles R. Forker's paper, 'Shakespeare's Theatrical Symbolism and Its Function in *Hamlet*' (*Sh Q*), is a careful study of the imagery of the theatre and acting that permeates the play. Forker aims at showing that an analysis of this imagery, or symbolism, can throw light on some of the central issues, such as Hamlet's delay, his disillusion and madness, his intrigue against Claudius, his relations with his mother, and his knowledge of himself. In 'Ophelia: Shakespeare's Pathetic Plot Device' (*Sh Q*), Linda Welshimer Wagner contends that Ophelia has grown 'to assume greater importance to the audience of *Hamlet* than she ever held for Hamlet himself, or for Shakespeare'. Shakespeare developed the role of Ophelia as little more than 'a condescension to the audience, who were expecting some romance and pathos'.

King Lear

M. J. C. Echeruo, in 'Dramatic Intensity and Shakespeare's *King Lear*' (*ESA*), draws a distinction between the lyrical early tragedies of Shakespeare, in which the imagery arises from the poet, and the later, in which the imagery has its source in the characters. In *Lear* the King's defects are obscured by the intensity and the functional character of the imagery. Under the title 'Agony on the Way to the Sacred Grove', *The Times* (29 Aug.), summarizes a lecture at Stratford-upon-Avon by George Steiner in which *King Lear* is characterized as 'a terrible prophetic allegory of the world of Belsen'. L. C. Knights, in '*King Lear* as Metaphor' (*Myth and Symbol*), discusses the use of the 'key-word' *justice* in *Lear*. The play is 'a moving image of life', he says, and, partly through the conceptions of justice that it represents, it 'sets in motion those powers of apprehension through which we simultaneously become aware of, and make, our world'.

In '"Our Means Secure Us" (*King Lear*, IV. i. 20)' (*N*), William Elton notes that in Shakespeare's time the word 'means' had theological connotations—'outward occasions', or the opposite of 'defects', 'good works', or the opposite of 'inward grace'. Gloucester 'attributes the error of false complacency to those who rest securely with good works, or means'; he believes that '"our mere defects", our deficiency of works, may prove ironically less disadvantageous or harmful'. In a note in *Sh Q*, 'Lear's "Learned Theban"', John P. Cutts questions whether Lear's reference to Poor Tom as 'learned Theban' should be taken as an indication that Lear is mad. Lear may be thinking of Oedipus, whom Lydgate describes as 'passing prudent', and the reference may be intended to show that Lear 'sees in Tom the source of his bewildering enlightenment at the recognition of his own newly, more fully realized being'. Following the method that he describes elsewhere in an article on *As You Like It*, Angus

McIntosh, in '*King Lear*, Act I, Scene i: A Stylistic Note' (*RES*), demonstrates how Lear's varying use of *thou* and *you* in this scene reflects the variations in his mood. In the same journal Colin Williamson extends McIntosh's study to include Lear's changes from *we, our, us* to *I, my, me*. In 'Lear's Fool: A Boy, not a Man' (*EC*), Huntington Brown claims that Shakespeare intended the Fool's role for a boy, and not for a man.

Othello

No one would deny that Desdemona is both virtuous and innocent, but did her behaviour perhaps make it fairly easy for Iago to taint her credit with the Moor? In 'The Indiscretions of Desdemona' (*Sh Q*), Margaret Loftus Ranald shows, by reference to a number of Elizabethan courtesy books and to canonical literature, that Desdemona did not always act very discreetly. She disobeyed both her father and the conventions of matrimonial choice. She conversed a great deal with Othello alone before their marriage. She met Cassio privately, and without her husband's consent. Although such actions arose from her impulsive and sympathetic nature, they unhappily gave some colour to Iago's insinuations against her virtue. 'On the basis of scenic context and general characterization,' David S. Berkeley, in 'A Vulgarization of Desdemona' (*SEL*), argues for the reading *rights*, rather than *rites*, at I. iii. 258. This 'makes Desdemona a more consistent character, and at the same time deepens the tragedy'.

Karina Williamson offers a study of '"Honest" and "False" in *Othello*' (*SN*). A key-passage in this connexion is Othello's question, 'But why should honour outlive honesty?' (V. ii. 243). Here Othello has 'a momentary glimpse of a truth which lies behind the whole tragedy'; he apprehends the self-destructiveness of an 'unquestioning acceptance of simple moral categories'. In 'Three Readings in the Text of *Othello*' (*Sh Q*), Lawrence J. Ross argues that at IV. iii. 23 the Folio reading 'good Father' is to be preferred to the Quarto 'good faith'. At V. ii. 253, he believes, the Folio 'It was a Sword of Spaine, the Ice brookes temper' should be rejected in favour of the Quarto 'It is a sword of Spaine, the Isebrookes temper'— a Spanish blade of the best Innsbruck temper. And at III. iii. 468–9 he justifies the Folio 'And to obey shall be in me remorse, What bloody businesse ever'. In 'The Staging of Desdemona's Bed' (*Sh Q*), Richard Hosley argues, with parallels from a number of other early seventeenth-century plays, that the beginning of V. ii Desdemona's bed is not revealed to the audience in a curtained recess or a 'fit-up booth', but is brought on stage. In a short note, also in *Sh Q*, Stephen J. Herben observes that the first recorded example of the limerick stanza-form is Iago's song, 'And let me the Canakin clink, clink' (II. iii).

Antony and Cleopatra

In 'Death Imagery in *Antony and Cleopatra*' (*Sh Q*) Katherine Vance MacMullen observes that this is 'the last Shakespearian play in which the theme of love and death is employed as an integral part of the dramatic situation'. Together with the love imagery, the death imagery helps to establish the character of Cleopatra, and it also looks forward to the death of Antony. After Antony's death the love and death images in Cleopatra's speeches recall Antony to the minds of the audience. Dr. MacMullen analyses the relevant image-clusters in the play—those relating to 'sleep-death' and to 'light-darkness-death'. In 'Cleopatra and the "Mortal

Wretch"' (*Sh J*), Mary Olive Thomas claims that Cleopatra sees in her death the source of life for the asp which kills her, and thus 'even in the moment of her death she shows the extent of her involvement in life'. The symbol of the serpent at the breast is 'a possible reminder of the classical Nourishing Earth, the mediaeval Lust, and the Renaissance Charity'.

Pericles

In 'Themes and Variations in Shakespeare's *Pericles*' (*ES*) Gerard A. Barker suggests that Shakespeare's play and George Wilkins's *Painful Adventures* both probably derive from an 'Ur-Pericles' based on the Apollonius story which can be hypothetically reconstructed. By comparing the two later works with this hypothetical version and with each other, we may deduce that Shakespeare converted 'the old play of kingship into a drama of faith and transformed the traditional hero of the legend into a Job-like figure of patience'.

Venus and Adonis

In recent years several critics have drawn attention to comic elements in *Venus and Adonis*. In 'An Iconographical Interpretation of *Venus and Adonis*, Shakespeare's Ovidian Comedy' (*Sh Q*), Eugene B. Cantelupe describes Shakespeare's presentation of the story as 'outrageously comic'. 'Adonis laughs at and scorns love, and Venus dwells upon it *ad nauseam*. Either form of behavior was considered excessive and unreasonable by the Elizabethans, and for the dramatists it was a subject for comedy.' Cantelupe develops the comic aspects of the poem in some detail. He points out, however, that 'the lust motif enables Shakespeare to make of his poem something not only delightful but also didactic, those dual aims which all Elizabethans, poets and readers, believed poetry must realize.' Cantelupe rather overstates his case, but the article contains some persuasive arguments. R. H. Bowers, in 'Anagnorisis, or the Shock of Recognition, in Shakespeare's *Venus and Adonis*' (*RP*, 1962), describes Venus as the protagonist of the story, in that 'she seizes the initiative'; Adonis 'merely serves as a foil'. In her highly-coloured description of how the boar killed Adonis, Venus comes to the sudden ironic recognition, 'Had I been tooth'd like him, I must confess, With kissing him I should have kill'd him first.'

The Sonnets

The most interesting general work on the Sonnets is John Dover Wilson's *An Introduction to the Sonnets of Shakespeare, For the Use of Historians and Others*, which for special reasons has been noticed in an earlier section of this chapter (see note 29).

The Introduction to Hilton Landry's *Interpretations in Shakespeare's Sonnets*[51] contains much sound sense. Like Wilson, Landry insists that the most important and fruitful approach to the Sonnets is to regard them as poetry, and he wisely refuses to embroil himself in speculations on the identity of persons in them or connected with them. Indeed, he regards such speculations as 'the greatest obstacle to reading these poems for themselves', although he naturally accepts that the poet's personal experience underlies the collection. He is especially impatient of those who tamper with the order of the Sonnets in the 1609 Quarto, and regroup them in order to bolster up

theories about their background. As he points out, 'the average Elizabethan sonnet sequence cannot be called a sequence in any strict sense of the word, and . . . is not organized upon any discernible internal principle'. 'Like the famous and seminal sonnet collection of Petrarch, which he appropriately called "fragments" and "scattered rimes", the Elizabethan sequence is essentially a collection of separate poems which tend to form small groups organized upon various principles.' It is in these terms that Shakespeare's sonnets must be viewed; nor does Landry believe that there is any more 'narrative' in them than in Petrarch's collection. Turning to the sonnets themselves, Landry treats them in small groups of consecutive poems—not, however, without cross-reference to other groups—and singles out for close analysis particular sonnets which, within their group, have a special significance in establishing a theme or a tone. Thus, for example, in the group comprising Sonnets 87–96, Sonnet 94, 'They that have pow'r to hurt . . .', has a special importance as a bridge between the first seven and the last two components of the group, and may best be interpreted with reference to its Biblical echoes and its parallels with passages in *Measure for Measure*. Sonnets 33–35, 40–42, and 57–58 are discussed together as being linked by the theme stated in the first line of Sonnet 35, 'Such civil war is in my love and hate . . .'. Landry similarly analyses other groups, and individual sonnets within them, without, however, finding a single unifying theme that binds the whole sequence together. His discussion is always practical and helpful, and contributes something of real value to the criticism of the Sonnets.

G. Wilson Knight joins the controversy fanned into flame by A. L.

Rowse's book (see note 28). In 'Shakespeare's Sonnets' (*TLS*, 26 Dec.) Knight, supplementing the views he expressed in *The Mutual Flame*, rejects Southampton as the young man to whom the Sonnets are addressed, supports Chapman as the rival poet, and describes the first series of the Sonnets as being marked by 'homosexual idealism'.

In 'A Note on Shakespeare's Sonnet 30' (*Sh Q*), Ralph Aiken points out that the famous phrase 'remembrance of things past' appears in exactly the same form in North's translation of the essay which Jacques Amyot prefixed to his French version of Plutarch's *Lives*. In 'Shakespeare's Sonnet 97' (*RES*) E. C. Evans claims that the incoherence with which this sonnet has been charged disappears if *summer's time* in line 5 is read as meaning, not 'summer-time', but 'summer's end or death'. In '"A Pretty Pleasing Pricket"—on the Use of Alliteration in Shakespeare's Sonnets' (*Sh Q*), Anton M. Pirkhofer makes a careful statistical analysis of the incidence of alliteration in the Sonnets, and reaches the conclusion that Shakespeare's alliterative habits 'move between the extremes of deliberate harshness and a subtly refined grace while shirking monotony which is only admitted for special effects'.

4. SHAKESPEARIAN PRODUCTION

Three years ago the first of a series of seventeenth-century Shakespearian prompt-books and acting editions to be issued under the sponsorship of the Bibliographical Society of the University of Virginia was noticed in the Shakespeare chapter of *YW* (xli. 113). This was the *Macbeth* which, together with *Measure for Measure* and *The Winter's Tale*, is marked for prompt purposes in a copy of the First Folio at Padua. Its editor, G.

Blakemore Evans, described this copy of the Folio and the circumstances in which it may have been marked. Evans has now edited the marked texts of *Measure for Measure* and *The Winter's Tale*.[52] In the first of his two slim volumes he discusses the marks and provides collations. Like *Macbeth*, *Measure for Measure* has been drastically cut, chiefly in order to reduce the length of the principal parts, but no attempt has been made to reduce the number of characters, nor are any changes made in the assignment of speeches. The prompter tends to bring characters on a little earlier than the Folio stage-directions indicate, and the prompt-warnings suggest a pre-Restoration date for the work. The marks in *The Winter's Tale* are in a different hand from those in *Macbeth* and *Measure for Measure*, and the cutting seems not to have been completed for production. In his second volume Evans prints facsimiles of the whole of the Padua text of *Measure for Measure*, and of a specimen leaf of *The Winter's Tale*.

Another extremely interesting prompt-book facsimile is *Mr. Macready Produces 'As You Like It': A Prompt-Book Study*,[53] by Charles H. Shattuck, a companion to Shattuck's edition of Macready's prompt-copy of *King John* (see *YW* xliii. 110). Macready's 1842–3 production of *As You Like It* at Drury Lane 'was a significant event in the stage history of the play. Macready "restored the true

---

[52] *Shakespearean Prompt-Books of the Seventeenth Century*, ed. by G. Blakemore Evans. Vol. II: Part i: Introductions to the Padua *Measure for Measure* and *The Winter's Tale*. Collations. pp. iii+29. Vol. II: Part ii: Text of the Padua *Measure for Measure* and *The Winter's Tale*. pp. ii+29. Bibliographical Soc. of the Univ. of Virginia. $20.

[53] *Mr. Macready Produces 'As You Like It': A Prompt-Book Study*, by Charles H. Shattuck. Urbana: Beta Phi Mu, Univ. of Illinois, 1962. pp. 225 with illustrations. $10.

text" (as far as time and public morality permitted) in what then seemed a revolutionary manner;' it was, as Macready himself said, an 'endeavour to give to Shakespeare all his attributes, to enrich his poetry with scenes worthy of its interpretation', and it was very well received. In the words of George Ellis, the stage-manager whose transcription of the prompt-book Shattuck reproduces in facsimile, it was 'the most wonderfully perfect representation of court, and pastoral life, ever witnessed on the English stage'. Macready's cuts, some demanded by time, some by propriety, amount to 387 lines out of a total of 2,845; they are fewer than were traditional in his day, for he was anxious to be as true to Shakespeare as possible. His prompt-book (or Ellis's) is an interleaved text of *As You Like It*, but the edition is not specified. The blank leaves contain numerous prompter's directions, notes relating to 'business', rewritten lines and passages, and sketches—the cuts are of course indicated in the text —and it is possible to reconstruct the production in some detail. On these leaves, too, Shattuck has printed his explanatory notes and comments. Eight of Charles Hamilton Smith's costume designs have recently been discovered by Macready's grand-daughter, Mrs. Lisa Puckle, and these are reproduced in the volume.

The central theme of the 1963 *Shakespeare Jahrbuch* (see note 46) is the interpretation of Shakespeare in the theatre. In 'Rohmaterial' Allardyce Nicoll deplores the tendency to regard Shakespearian texts as 'raw material' for translators and producers. There is plenty of evidence that Elizabethan playwrights were interested in the accurate printing of their works, even though the responsibility for having them printed may have lain with their companies.

Shakespeare was an important member of the Chamberlain's company, and it is not unlikely that he took some personal responsibility for the printing of the 'good' Quartos as correctives to the 'bad' Quartos. Nahum Tate's 'improvement' of *King Lear* is the subject of Margareta Braun's 'This is not Lear'. In trying to impose the dramatic unities on the play and to bring about 'poetic justice', Tate diminishes Lear's greatness, and makes him too senile; Cordelia becomes in effect the central character, and too much prominence is given to the machinations of Edmund. Tate also fails to do justice to Shakespeare's careful deployment of his imagery. In 'From Farce to Romance: *All's Well that Ends Well* 1756-1811' Joseph G. Price discusses productions of the play by Garrick (with adaptations) in the 1750's, by Frederick Pilon in 1785, and by J. P. Kemble, again with adaptations, in 1793 and 1811. Price shows that within this period audiences had come to prefer sentimental comedy to farce, and this accounts for significant differences in these productions. In '*Der Kaufmann von Venedig* auf der Illusionsbühne der Meininger' Wolfgang Iser considers the 1886 production of *The Merchant of Venice* by the famous Saxe-Meiningen Court Theatre group. Aiming at historical realism, the group distorted the play by cutting out or playing down many of the fairy-tale qualities that are an important element in it. Edmund Stadler writes on 'Reinhardt und Shakespeare, 1904-1914', defending Reinhardt against charges of injudicious cutting, and pointing out that his productions moved towards greater stylization and simplification in his settings. Hanns Braun, in 'Das Niemandsland des Spielleiters, ein Problem von heute: Zu Shakespeare-Inscenierungen Fritz Kortners', analyses some of Kortner's recent productions of Shakespeare in Munich, and suggests that they belong to a sort of 'No Man's Land' between theatre and literature. In 'Barrault's *Hamlet*' Elisabeth Brock-Sulzer expresses the view that the different French versions in which Jean-Louis Barrault has played the part of Hamlet—those of Marcel Schwob, Eugène Morand, Jules Laforgue, Guy de Pourtalès, and André Gide—reflect developments in Barrault's style of acting. In 'Probleme der Aufführung Shakespeares in Japan' Kenji Izume gives reasons for the comparative lack of success of Shakespeare productions in Japan. Good translations are, from the nature of the language, two or three times as long as the originals, and performances are therefore protracted beyond the endurance of normal audiences. Also, while the Japanese drama is diversified with much song and dance, Shakespeare conveys his meaning almost solely with words. In 'Offender und geschlossener Dramenstil in Shakespeare's *Tempest*' Erika Flamm recalls Volker Klotz's classification of drama into the 'open' play, which presents reality as a 'whole in segments', and the 'closed' play, which presents it as 'a segment of the whole'. She argues that *The Tempest*, while fundamentally an open play, has elements of both types of drama.

In 'Adaptations of Shakespeare and His Critics, 1660–1790' (*Indian Journ. of Eng. Studies*) Sailendra Kumar Sen outlines the history of Restoration and eighteenth-century adaptations, or 'improvements', of Shakespeare. At first the changes were made, on the whole, in accordance with clear critical principles, but later adapters tended to be more irresponsible, or alternatively they turned the plays into operas. When, in the course of the eighteenth century, criticism concerned itself more seriously with the purity of Shakespearian texts, large-scale adaptation ceased, and modern scholars and producers have come to realize that, the less the plays are tampered with, the more effective they are in the theatre.

Christopher Spencer's 'A Word for Tate's *King Lear*' (*SEL*), shows a different attitude towards Tate's adaptation from that of Margareta Braun's *Sh J* article which is noticed above. If we accept Tate's *Lear* as a play in its own right, and not as a perversion of Shakespeare, we shall find it 'both coherent and entertaining'. In 'The Chronicles in Cibber's *Richard III*', also in *SEL*, Albert E. Kalson demonstrates that Colley Cibber drew the new material for his *Richard III* from the Elizabethan chronicle histories of Holinshed, Stow, Speed, and Baker.

As actor-manager of the Smock Alley Theatre, Dublin, Thomas Sheridan worked as tirelessly as his rival Garrick to popularize Shakespeare; he produced him very frequently, and he 'equalled Garrick in the number of Shakespearian roles he played', his favourite being Hamlet. In 'Sheridan's *Coriolanus*: An 18th-Century Compromise' (*Sh Q*), from which these facts are taken, Esther K. Sheldon makes a special study of Sheridan's adaptation of *Coriolanus*, which he altered very freely in order to bring it in line with mid-eighteenth-century taste. Although the result shocks us today, it popularized a play which in its original form would not have been acceptable to audiences of the period.

Nineteenth-century audiences seem to have had little desire to see Shakespeare presented in the Elizabethan manner. 'They were confident in the belief that their new staging methods were a vast improvement over the old.' In 'Shakespeare and Nineteenth-Century Realism' (*Theatre Survey*)

Theodore J. Shank describes the attempts of J. P. Kemble, Macready, and Charles Kean in England, and of William Burton, Edwin Booth, and other producers in America, to stage Shakespeare as realistically as possible, to make their productions 'as authentic as diligent historical and archaeological research will permit'. Shank's article is illustrated with sixteen excellent plates which demonstrate the lengths to which producers would go in their attempts to provide realistic settings.

Two articles in *ETJ* may be noticed here. In 'Shakespeare as a Character in Drama: 1679–1899' James W. Nichols notes that within this period Shakespeare is used as a character more than 200 times, and is nearly always portrayed as a romantic superman or an untutored genius. Often he serves as the mouthpiece of a playwright who wishes to express his dissatisfaction with contemporary drama. In 'The Secret of Shakespeare's Power in Germany' Lawrence F. McNamee points out that great men of letters in Germany have always encouraged the study and appreciation of Shakespeare, and that the Germans have been fortunate in their translators. Germany has more productions of Shakespeare than all the rest of the world.

In *Sh Q* notable Shakespearian productions in England in 1963, particularly at Stratford-upon-Avon and at the Old Vic, are reviewed by Robert Speaight. The 1963 Festival at Stratford, Ontario, is reviewed by Arnold Edinborough; the Season at Stratford, Connecticut, by Dunbar H. Ogden; the New York Shakespeare Festival by Alice Griffin; the Seasons at Ashland, Oregon, and at San Diego by Eleanor Prosser; the Great Lakes Festival by Robert G. Shedd; and the Colorado Festival by Robert L. Perkin. F. W. Sternfeld takes exception to Peter Brook's production of *Lear* at the Royal Shakespeare Theatre on two grounds: first, the omission of the Fool's songs deprived the audience of 'some of the most poignant lines which this strange but eloquent philosopher-chorus is allotted by Shakespeare'; secondly, the dissonant music provided in IV. vii was 'the wrong music to restore a Shakespearian hero to mental equilibrium'.

In 'Colley Cibber at San Diego', in an earlier issue of *Sh Q*, Eleanor Prosser describes a performance of *2 Henry IV* which she saw at San Diego in 1962. Its director, William Ball, who also acted Prince Hal, had taken 'outrageous' liberties with the text, rewriting and rearranging much of it. Nevertheless, so lively was the production, and so successfully did it present the play to its modern audience in terms that they could understand, that she almost, if not quite, became a 'defecting purist'. In the same journal Isabel Roome Mann gives an interesting account of 'The Royal Gala of 1830', the festival at Stratford-upon-Avon which first introduced plays of Shakespeare as a feature of the birthday celebrations. Also in *Sh Q*, George H. Quinby surveys the first fifty Shakespeare seasons at Bowdoin College.

In *Sh J* German and Swiss productions of Shakespeare in 1962 are reviewed by Karl Brinkmann and Lydia Benz-Burger respectively.

A great many articles and reviews relating to 1963 productions of Shakespeare in the theatre and cinema, and on television and radio, are listed in the *Sh Q* bibliography (Summer 1964).

5. SHAKESPEARIAN SCHOLARSHIP. ECHOES AND ALLUSIONS

Oswald LeWinter's *Shakespeare in*

Europe[54] is a collection of twenty-five essays, or extracts, on Shakespeare by European writers from Voltaire to Jean-Louis Barrault. The passage from Voltaire (from the Preface to his *Brutus*) is more laudatory than some of his pronouncements on Shakespeare, although it speaks of the 'barbaric irregularities' of *Julius Caesar*. Barrault has done perhaps more than anyone else to make Shakespeare acceptable, even popular, in France with his insistence that 'Shakespeare is for us a vital need', and he always writes interestingly about him. Other French authors represented include Chateaubriand, Stendhal, and Victor Hugo. Stendhal's support of Shakespeare against the upholders of strict classical correctness is of particular interest. The Germans, from Goethe to Hugo von Hofmannsthal, are well represented; and there are extracts from Pushkin, Turgenev, and Tolstoy. Sensible essays on Shylock by Ortega y Gasset, and on Hamlet by Salvador de Madariaga, show what Shakespeare has come to mean in Spain, and there are some perceptive comments on the Sonnets by Giuseppe Ungaretti. The anthology makes good reading, and provides a useful survey of Continental criticism of Shakespeare over the last two centuries.

In 'Milton's "On Shakespeare" and Henry Lawes' (*Sh Q*), Morris Freedman asks how it came about that commendatory verses by a then unknown poet found their way into the Second Folio. Freedman develops a probable connexion, through William Herbert, Earl of Pembroke, between Henry Lawes and the publisher of F2, and suggests that Lawes

was instrumental in having Milton's poem included in the volume.

A. E. Dyson suggests in an editorial in *CQ* that a major reappraisal of Shakespeare is at present taking place. This is reflected in the work of such critics as Barbara Everett, John Russell Brown, and John Holloway. In his series of brief biographies of Shakespearian critics and interpreters, John J. McAleer in successive issues of *SNL* outlines the careers of Harley Granville-Barker, Isaac Reed, Malone and Ritson, Mary Cowden Clarke, Samuel Tannenbaum, and Sir Henry Irving.

In 'Shakespeare Echoed' (*Sh Q*), John Crow notes in John Day's prologue to *The Ile of Guls* the lines 'the idle buzzing of a flie, Heard, not regarded', which echo from *1 Henry IV* the lines 'but as the Cuckoe is in June, Heard, not regarded'. In 'An Early *Hamlet* Echo?' (*Sh Q*) Robert W. Dent draws attention to what appear to be echoes of the 'To be or not to be' soliloquy in its *Q1* version in Samuel Garey's *A Short and necessary Treatise, entituled: Deaths welcome* of 1605 (*S.T.C.* 11600). Dent thinks it possible that Garey saw at Cambridge a performance of *Hamlet* 'where the relevant soliloquy approximated that in Q1', although it is not impossible that he had read the Quarto itself. In 'Macbeth on Sleep: Two Parallels' (*Sh Q*), C. J. Rawson records an unnoted parallel with Macbeth's lines on sleep (II. ii. 37–40) in the opening lines of a sonnet in Bartholomew Griffin's *Fidessa* (1596). He also points out that a parallel in '*Saint Peter's Complaint. Poems*' to which Capell drew attention should be attributed to the author of the poems, Robert Southwell, not to John Wolfe, who was the printer.

James G. McManaway draws attention (*Sh Q*), to some lines written

---

[54] *Shakespeare in Europe*, ed. by Oswald LeWinter. (Meridian Books.) Cleveland and New York: World Publishing Co. pp. 382. $2.45.

in 1650 by one Richard Washington in his copy of Massinger's *The Picture*. The lines, written in praise of Massinger, refer to 'sterne Johnson and our smoth tongued Shakespeares Layes'.

6. GRAMOPHONE RECORDINGS

With *Titus Andronicus*, the three parts of *Henry VI*, and *Pericles*, the recording by the Marlowe Society of the works of Shakespeare is brought to completion.[55] These are not among the 'popular' plays of Shakespeare, but the same loving care has gone into their production as has hitherto marked the series. The quality of the recordings may be guessed from the names of the players who take part in them. These include William Devlin, Patrick Wymark, William Squire, Miles Malleson, Peter Orr, Tony Church, Margaretta Scott, Prunella Scales, and Mary Morris; although no cast-lists are provided, theatre-goers will be able to put the right names to many of the voices. The general excellence of the series has been commented on at some length in past issues of *YW* (see, e.g. xliii. 127–9); all that is necessary here is to draw attention to some of the special merits of these last five recordings. Nothing is lost of the violence and horror of *Titus Andronicus*, nor of the flashes of beauty and the occasional passages of true pathos. All the moods of Titus, noble, arrogant, self-

willed, torn by pity, driven mad by suffering, are admirably conveyed, and he is well supported by a Tamora and an Aaron who impart to their roles all the remorselessness and evil that are required of them. Scenes which remain in the mind are that in which the ravished and mutilated Lavinia tries to communicate the names of her ravishers, and the great final scene; even slightly mishandled, either scene might topple into bathos, but there is no faltering in this production, and both are triumphant successes. It may be that the gramophone is the best medium for scenes of this description—*ne pueros coram populo Medea trucidet*. A potential danger in recording the *Henry VI* plays is that the multiplicity of characters might lead to confusion; this danger has been obviated by the very careful selection of voices, and the plays are reasonably easy to follow without the help of an open text. In these records especially fine performances are given of the parts of Talbot, Henry VI, Joan of Arc, Warwick, and Richard of Gloucester; but most of the minor parts are well played, certainly never less than adequately, and there are many memorable scenes, including those in which Joan appears and the Jack Cade scenes. The *Pericles* is another well-balanced production. In this play much depends on those who play the parts of Pericles and Marina; here both are entirely convincing, and they are on the whole very well supported by the less important characters. Fault could be found with all five recordings, as indeed with all five plays, but their merits so far outweigh their deficiencies that only the most captious critic would wish to pick holes in them. Above all, as has been constantly remarked in previous notices in *YW*, it is the very high quality of the verse-speaking that lends a

[55] *The Works of William Shakespeare*, recorded by the Marlowe Society of the University of Cambridge and professional players, under the direction of George Rylands. Musical Director, Thurston Dart. *Titus Andronicus*, RG 357–359. *Henry VI, Part 1*, RG 386–388. *Henry VI, Part 2*, RG 389–392. *Henry VI, Part 3*, RG 393–396. *Pericles, Prince of Tyre*, RG 411–413. Issued, in association with C.U.P., and under the auspices of the British Council, by Argo Record Co., Ltd. Each 12-inch record 37s. 6d.

special distinction to the Marlowe Society productions; for this, it may be guessed, most of the credit should be given to the director, George Rylands.

ADDENDUM

Two books have been received for notice since this chapter was completed.

As has been amply demonstrated by M. P. Tilley and a number of other scholars, Elizabethan authors generally, and perhaps particularly Shakespeare, very freely incorporated and adapted proverbs and *sententiae* in their writings. In *Shakespeare's Proverb Lore*[56] Charles G. Smith makes a special study of two collections of Latin *sententiae* whose influence on Shakespeare has not been sufficiently explored—those of the German Leonhardus Culmannus (1497-8–1952) and of the first-century Roman Publilius Styrus. There is evidence which suggests that Culman's *Sententiae Pueriles* was 'a universal textbook', and that every Elizabethan schoolboy was required to memorize most or all of its maxims. The *Sententiae* of Styrus, usually with accretions, were also readily available—for example, Erasmus published them together with his *Disticha Catonis* in 1514—and appear also to have been much used in Elizabethan schools. There can be no doubt that Shakespeare was thoroughly familiar with both collections. Smith prints 346 proverbs or maxims from these two sources, arranged alphabetically under key-words, together with passages in which Shakespeare seems to be making use of them; 166 show parallels with Culmann, 137 with Styrus, and forty-three with both, though it is fair to add that many of them are commonplaces which Shakespeare may have derived from other sources, or even at times struck out for himself. However, the evidence that he was well acquainted with both authors (or collectors) is overwhelming. As would be expected, he often adapted the *sententiae*, and usually placed them in settings which gave them freshness or new force. Smith's three analytical indexes make his book easy to use, and, apart from its general interest, it will, like Tilley's volumes, be useful to future editors.

In the late Renaissance a proposition not infrequently advanced was that one of the higher forms of wisdom is a kind of ignorance, or folly, and the fool became a prominent figure in European literature. In *Praisers of Folly*[57] Walter Kaiser examines three such 'fools' in sixteenth-century literature—Erasmus's Stultitia in *The Praise of Folly*, Rabelais's Panurge, and Shakespeare's Falstaff; in a short final chapter he adds Cervantes's Don Quixote to their company, because Don Quixote in some senses brings this literary tradition of the fool as hero to a close. Although his studies of Stultitia and Panurge are extremely interesting, it is his treatment of Falstaff that entitles his book to consideration in this chapter. Falstaff, as Kaiser points out, is not in the direct line of descent from Stultitia and Panurge; his progenitor is rather the vice of the moral interludes. Yet he has affinities with the other two. He is 'the fattest, the oldest, the funniest, the most natural fool of the three. One might say that in his huge girth he embodies both Stultitia and Panurge. Like Erasmus' fool, he is a stultiloquent jester who overturns all the accepted

---

[56] *Shakespeare's Proverb Lore: His Use of the 'Sententiae' of Leonard Culman and Publilius Styrus*, by Charles G. Smith. Harvard U.P. pp. ix+181. $4.

[57] *Praisers of Folly: Erasmus, Rabelais, Shakespeare*, by Walter Kaiser. Harvard U.P. pp. xiii+318. $7.75.

values; like Rabelais', he is the incorrigible rogue who serves as a companion to the youthful prince.' These are the aspects of Falstaff that Kaiser emphasizes in his detailed study of the two parts of *Henry IV*, and he shows, too, that because Falstaff cannot be cured, he must be killed. Kaiser's book is lively and sensible, and is of special interest for what it contributes to our understanding of Shakespeare's Renaissance background.

(The annual production of books and articles on Shakespeare is nowadays so vast that this chapter must of necessity be to some extent selective. A certain number of articles, and even at times books, are disregarded because they do not seem to contribute significantly to the understanding of Shakespeare. Others, however, are missed, often with much regret, because they are not available in this country. *YW* has no correspondents abroad, and its editors would be grateful if scholars whose work is printed outside England would arrange for relevant books and offprints, or copies of journals with a limited circulation, to be sent to the English Association for notice.)

VIII

Later Elizabethan
and Early Stuart Drama

ARTHUR BROWN

THE most substantial contribution to the scholarly literature of the period this year was the second volume of Glynne Wickham's *Early English Stages*,[1] the first volume of which was noted four years ago (*YW* xl. 96). Wickham's earlier concern was to trace the indebtedness of the Elizabethan Court and public theatres to their antecedents in the Middle Ages, to create a fuller understanding of the conditions under which medieval plays were produced, and to link Elizabethan theatrical traditions more closely with those of early Tudor drama. He is now concerned with the effect on drama of revolutionary changes, characteristic of the sixteenth century in England, in religious and political thought on the one hand, and in social behaviour on the other. Religious changes, for example, characterized by the Reformation and by the sovereign's assumption of ultimate authority in doctrinal matters, 'automatically translated the subject matter of a predominantly religious drama into a political issue', leading inevitably to state censorship and to the threatening of 'the very concept of drama as a means by which to mirror the cosmos in art'. By 1660, Wickham suggests, this concept is virtually dead. The notion of independent nationhood, as opposed to internationalism,

'is reflected most acutely in the formation of dramatic theory differing widely from country to country, but common to all in one respect: a gradual exposure of divergence between the characteristics of life as lived in a country and the traditional stage conventions employed to depict it in the theatre'. The changes in social behaviour, in particular the 'increasing distinction of classes in society brought about by the power of money to work changes in the hierarchy of feudal degree', result in the theatre in 'the splitting of the audience into broad social strata governed by conditions of admission (prices and entrée) and with it a divorce between sophisticated and popular taste'. Book I of the present volume is devoted to an assessment of the sixteenth century's dramatic inheritance from the medieval past and to an account of the way in which this inheritance stood up to these various changes and assaults. Book II is concerned with the theatre buildings and the performances given in them, and this theme will be continued in the forthcoming third volume. Eight appendixes include such material as the Midsummer Shows and Lord Mayors' Shows from 1504 to 1603, a list of Jacobean and Caroline Lord Mayors' Shows, the Chamberlains' Accounts at Norwich from 1534 to 1550, the text of the City Proclamation (in London) of 6 February 1545,

---

[1] *Early English Stages 1300 to 1660*, Vol. 2, 1576 to 1660, Part 1, by Glynne Wickham. Routledge & Kegan Paul. pp. xxiv+408. 60s.

details of professional acting companies and the plays and scenic units prepared for them by the Revels Office from 1564 to 1576, and a number of other similar documents. The volume is profusely illustrated and altogether a worthy successor to the first.

The late Karl J. Holzknecht's *Outlines of Tudor and Stuart Plays 1497–1642*, which first appeared in 1947, has been re-issued in paperback form.[2] The book contains the complete story of over eighty plays, describes each major figure in the *dramatis personae* by quoting from the play itself, gives biographical information about thirty-four playwrights and critical comments about their work, and includes bibliographical information and sources and indexes to authors, plays, and characters. The author has had three main purposes in mind: to demonstrate that, far from being mean and insignificant, Elizabethan drama-plots on the whole are not impossibly or purposely intricate or poorly constructed; to make clear that an ability to follow the plot is essential to an understanding of the play; and to point out that with the plot clearly in mind the reader is better able to appreciate 'that understanding of the great constants of human nature in both joy and sorrow which has made the best Elizabethan drama a lastingly relevant commentary on human life'.

'Probably no major author in English has suffered such a catastrophic decline in popularity since his own day as has Ben Jonson. Certainly none has been so punished for the crime of not being Shakespeare.' So writes Jonas A. Barish in the intro-duction to a collection of twentieth-century critical essays on Jonson which attempt, from various points of view, to redress the balance.[3] The twelve contributions are as follows: 'Ben Jonson', by T. S. Eliot; 'Tradition and Ben Jonson', by L. C. Knights; 'An Introduction to Ben Jonson' by Harry Levin; 'Morose Ben Jonson' by Edmund Wilson; 'Introduction to *Every Man In His Humour*', by Arthur Sale; 'Introduction to *Every Man Out of His Humour*', by C. H. Herford; 'The Double Plot in *Volpone*', by Jonas A. Barish; 'Comic Plots: *The Alchemist*', by Paul Goodman; '*Epicene*', by Edward B. Partridge; 'Unifying Symbols in the Comedy of Ben Jonson', by Ray L. Heffner, Jr.; '*Catiline* and the Nature of Jonson's Tragic Fable', by Joseph Allen Byrant, Jr.; and 'The Jonsonian Masque as a Literary Form', by Dolora Cunningham. The volume also includes a chronology of important dates and a selected bibliography.

The purpose of the new Regents Renaissance Drama Series, we are told, is 'to provide soundly edited texts, in modern spelling, of the more significant plays of the Elizabethan, Jacobean, and Caroline theatre', and a good start has been made with the publication of Greene's *Friar Bacon and Friar Bungay* and Beaumont's and Fletcher's *A King and No King*.[4] A fresh collation of the sixteenth- and seventeenth-century editions has been made in each case, and the textual

[2] *Outlines of Tudor and Stuart Plays 1497–1642*, by Karl J. Holzknecht. Methuen (University Paperbacks No. 64). pp. xiv + 442. 18s.

[3] *Ben Jonson: A Collection of Critical Essays*, ed. by Jonas A. Barish. Englewood Cliffs, N.J., Prentice-Hall, Inc. pp. v + 180. $1.95.

[4] *Friar Bacon and Friar Bungay*, by Robert Greene, ed. by Daniel Seltzer. Nebraska U.P. pp. xxi + 106. $1.30. *A King and No King*, by Francis Beaumont and John Fletcher, ed. by Robert K. Turner, Jr. Nebraska U.P. pp. xxx + 154. $1.00.

notes, at the bottom of each page, record all substantive departures from the edition used as the copy-text. Every effort has been made to make the volumes readable as well as scholarly; the introductions give concisely and clearly all the information needed for a proper appreciation of the plays, and there is a useful chronology at the end. The General Editor, Cyrus Hoy, and the Advisory Editor, G. E. Bentley, are to be congratulated on their initiative and on the attractive appearance of the volumes.

The Malone Society published two volumes this year, George Wilkins's *The Miseries of Enforced Marriage*, based on a collation of the eight known copies of the quarto of 1607, and the anonymous *A Knack to Know a Knave*, based on a collation of the four known copies of the quarto of 1594.[5]

For some years now Professor S. Schoenbaum, of Northwestern University, has been editing and circulating an informal but very valuable publication of the Modern Language Association Conference on Opportunities for Research in Renaissance Drama. The appearance this year of the sixth instalment marks one or two developments in the form and content of the publication.[6] Mimeograph reproduction has been replaced by multilith duplication, the quality of the paper has been improved, and a printed cover has been provided. In

addition to the usual reports on research in progress from scholars in a variety of countries, a number of papers of great interest to students in this field are also included. R. A. Foakes writes on 'Henslowe and the Theatre of the 1590's', defending Henslowe against some of the opinions about him circulated by Greg and Fleay, and calling for a new study of the theatre and the relevant documents during these formative years. He asks in particular for a study of Henslowe's language, vocabulary, and spellings, for a reconsideration of the theatrical accounts, for a new analysis of the relations of actors with the company, and of actors and authors with the theatre-owner, for a revision of Greg's commentary in his edition of Henslowe's *Diary*, taking into account the evidence that has accumulated since that edition was published, and for a study of the unpublished documents at Dulwich relating to Henslowe, Alleyn, and their associates. In 'Criticism of Elizabethan and Jacobean Drama', Irving Ribner suggests that 'while criticism of Shakespeare has reached a virtual saturation point, that of his contemporaries is in its infancy'. He surveys the major contributions in this field during the twentieth century, and draws attention to the deficiencies and lacunae. 'Finally,' he remarks, 'as critics we need to stop being apologetic for our dramatists, reading them always in the light of Shakespeare and explaining them as lesser offspring of an age and a drama overshadowed by one commanding figure. We need to determine what value our plays would still have even if Shakespeare had never lived.' Louis A. Schuster and Leicester Bradner both deal with the problems of Neo-Latin Drama, the former in 'Pioneering in Neo-Latin Drama', and the latter in 'Desiderata for the Study of Neo-Latin Drama',

[5] *The Miseries of Enforced Marriage*, by George Wilkins, ed. by Glenn H. Blayney. O.U.P. for the Malone Society. pp. xv+70. Issued to members only. *A Knack to Know a Knave*, ed. by G. R. Proudfoot. O.U.P. for the Malone Society. pp. xvii+56. Issued to members only.

[6] *Renaissance Drama: A Report on Research Opportunities*, ed. by S. Schoenbaum. Evanston, Ill.; Northwestern Univ., for the Modern Language Association Conference on Opportunities for Research in Renaissance Drama. pp. 79. Copies available free of charge from the Editor.

while Marvin T. Herrick considers 'Opportunities for Research in the Italian Drama of the Renaissance'; these three articles will be particularly useful for would-be research workers in the Renaissance field. Charles S. Felver, writing on 'The *Commedia dell'Arte* and English Drama in the Sixteenth and Early Seventeenth Centuries', lists a number of what he calls 'scholarly vices' which, in one degree or another, have affected much of the work in this area. 'The vices of unified-field theories, moralism, and too-zealous source-hunting are those of special pleading, and serve to remind us how important it is to get back to the primary sources,' says Felver, but he goes on to remind us that there are many difficulties in the way of this—lack of specialized collections, linguistic difficulties, baffling topicalities, differences in acting styles, to mention only a few. This is a thought-provoking essay and deserves serious attention. Lawrence J. Ross writes on 'Art and the Study of Early English Drama', and although his paper suffers a little from the fact that the circumstances of publication prevented the inclusion of the illustrations which originally accompanied its delivery, there is still much of importance to be gained from it. Finally Richard Hosley writes on 'An Approach to the Elizabethan Stage', and presents the ideas which are to be extended and documented in his forthcoming book, *Elizabethan Playhouse Stages: A Study of Theatrical Form in the Age of Shakespeare.*

In 'Who pointed Roister's letter?' (*NQ*), A. W. Plumstead discusses two points in *Roister Doister* concerning the letter sent by Roister to Dame Custance, which is read aloud by Merygreeke, and found insulting, in III. iv. The first, a minor one, is whether Custance had read and understood the mispointed letter before this scene, and Plumstead is of the opinion that the text suggests that she had. If this interpretation is correct, then the Dame 'is fully aware of the letter's monstrosities, and she delights in subtly kidding Merygreeke about Roister's stupidity in front of him. And because both Merygreeke and the audience know nothing yet of the letter's contents, she has a private laugh, and adds to the audience's anticipation . . . of the letter. To anyone playing the part, here is room for sophisticated dalliance, not just detached ignorance.' The second point, more important, is: who originally pointed the letter carelessly? Plumstead rejects an earlier suggestion that it was Merygreeke who pointed the letter on the spot, 'turning it into an insult for the pure fun of it'; he feels that Merygreeke was merely reading what was in front of him, and that Roister mispointed the letter when he copied the Scrivener's original. In this way Udall has introduced dramatic irony—an important step forward 'in the development of sophisticated satire'—and the audience's and reader's realization that Roister mispointed his love-letter adds further to their enjoyment of his misguided pretence.

Leonard H. Frey writes on 'Antithetical Balance in the Opening and Close of *Doctor Faustus*' (*MLQ*). These scenes, he suggests, 'set forth the essential Faust-theme with an urgency that transcends the dubious and scattered middle sections' of the tragedy, and their effectiveness 'depends upon an elaborate antithetical balance in structure, content, and imagery of Faustus's opening and closing soliloquies'. To an Elizabethan audience a soliloquy meant a certain moment of truth, 'an unqualified and direct revelation of character'; the first of the two under discussion allows Faustus to pursue a series of unaccepted career possibilities through to a final commitment, while in the second, again a series of alternatives followed by a certainty, Faustus desperately casts about for avenues of escape from damnation. In the first soliloquy he is the epitome of Renaissance man, exultant, enthusiastic, assertive, aggressive; in the second his rejoicing in intellectual consciousness has turned to despair, and its pattern is a grim parody of the first.

Paul H. Kocher, writing on 'English Legal History in Marlowe's *Jew of Malta*' (*HLQ*), draws attention to the case of Richard Rose or Rouse who, in 1529 or 1530, for reasons unknown, 'contrived to put poison into the porridge being cooked in the kitchen of the Bishop of Rochester. This food was eaten by a number of people in the bishop's entourage and, when put outside his gate as alms for the poor, was eaten also by a number of them. An unspecified number of persons died as a result.' In 1530 murder by poison was considered so horrible and dangerous to the State that it was declared high treason by Parliament, and the punishment of boiling to death in water was imposed for it; Rouse underwent this form of execution. The case was long remembered, and Kocher thinks that Marlowe may well have had it in mind, either picked up through gossip in Canterbury, where he lived until 1580, only thirty miles from Rochester, or later in London, when he wrote the scenes in which Barabas poisoned the nuns in order to avenge himself upon his own daughter, and later died in his own boiling cauldron.

Following up a suggestion by Robert Turner (*YW* xli. 132) that the emendation of 'Blacke-door'd Italian' to 'Back-door'd Italian' (*1 Honest Whore*, II. i. 355) should be allowed to stand, Richard Levin, in 'Dekker's Back-Door'd Italian and Middleton's Hebrew Pen' (*NQ*), produces further examples from Jacobean plays 'which indicate that Englishmen of the time did believe that the Italians were especially given to this particular perversion'.

In 'Anthony Mundy and *Sir Thomas More*' (*NQ*), McD. P. Jackson thinks that the erroneous form 'fashis' for 'fashiõ' at line, 1847 of this play was not consciously intended at all, but was the result of a mere slip of the pen, the writer's mind and hand inadvertently moving forward to the succeeding 'sits'. If this is so, then it disposes of Sir Walter Greg's point that 'it is a mistake of which it is almost impossible to suppose that an author would be guilty in copying his own work'.

'Although the importance of the code of honour in sixteenth- and seventeenth-century England has long been recognized,' says Elizabeth Brennan, 'the extent to which its influence was reflected in the drama has only recently been studied.' In 'The Relationship between Brother and Sister in the Plays of John Webster' (*MLR*), she considers this subject with particular reference to *The Duchess of Malfi*. She shows, first of all, how it was as a result of the dramatists' interest 'in a code which governed the behaviour of a large proportion of their audience that the theme of revenge tragedy changed from revenge for murder to revenge for honour'. In the case of Webster, who, like Ford, was interested in the dramatic possibilities of a variation in the normal relationship between brother and sister (including both the abnegation of brotherly consideration and protection, and hints of or the realization of incestuous feelings), we find that his major works 'show how the real or imagined dishonour of his heroines affects their brothers at least as much as it affects the men who love them'. In the attitudes and behaviour of Flamineo, Vittoria, Brachiano, Romelio, and Leonora, Miss Brennan finds evidence that Webster was interested 'not so much in honour or revenge for honour as in their use as disguises for other passions'. As far as *The Duchess of Malfi* is concerned, which Miss Brennan goes on to consider in some detail, 'revenge for honour was only a cloak to cover a passion which was, in Ferdinand at least, more horrible and unnatural'.

This play is also the subject of P. F. Vernon's 'The Duchess of Malfi's Guilt' (*NQ*). He finds that one of the main difficulties involved in the interpretation of the play concerns the dramatist's moral attitude towards his central character: are we to regard the Duchess as wholly innocent, or is her downfall related to some moral error or flaw? Vernon considers the opposing views of Clifford Leech (who finds that the Duchess committed a double offence against the contemporary social code) and F. W. Wadsworth (who claims that the disapproval of the remarriage of a widow and of marriage to a person of lower rank was by no means unanimous at this period). He finds that the play is mainly concerned with 'how good and noble people ought to behave in a society dominated by the values of "Machiavellian" policy, as the early seventeenth century understood it'; they should 'nere stagger in distrust / To suffer death, or shame, for what is just' (V. v. 127–8). The tragic error of the Duchess and Antonio is to ignore this dictum; they consider the ends without considering the means, but they both gain stature as they learn from their mistakes.

In 'Homer and the Fallen World: Focus of Satire in George Chapman's *The Widow's Tears*' (*JEGP*), Henry M. Weidner feels that the full energy and scope of this play have not been realized. Chapman, he suggests, is principally concerned with more important affairs than the silliness of Lysander and Cynthia. The chief object of the satire lies elsewhere, in the figure of Tharsalio, the intriguer, whose view of the world, far from being proved 'correct' by what happens in the play (as some commentators have argued), in fact represents everything that Chapman denounces. Weidner draws attention to certain 'norms of idealism' which are crucial to this part of the dramatist's career, but which have not been fully explored. 'Permeating all of Chapman's later comedies (and some of his tragedies) is the ideal of a Homeric "golden age". *The Widow's Tears* (*ca.* 1605), then, may best be viewed as part of a tapestry which is begun in the idyllic world of formal romance in *The Gentleman Usher* (*ca.* 1603); continued in the purely ironic, but tolerantly comic world of *Monsieur D'Olive* (*ca.* 1604); and brought to a fitting logical conclusion both in the latest of these three plays and in Chapman's tragedies.' He finds, in short, that the play is 'a horrendous climactic statement in Chapman's increasingly embittered dialectic between Homeric virtue and modern corruption'.

G. A. Wilkes has a short article on 'Chapman's "Lost" Play, *The Fount of New Fashions*' (*JEGP*), and produces evidence, admittedly limited, to show that the *Sir Gyles Goosecappe* performed at the Blackfriars may be a later version of *The Fount of New Fashions*, written in 1598 for Henslowe, and transferred from the one company (The Admiral's Men) to the other (the Children at Blackfriars) in the manner of *Al Fooles*.

P. H. Davison, writing on '*Volpone*

and the Old Comedy' (*MLQ*), reviews the various critical opinions about the nature of this play, and suggests that it is a comedy, 'but a special kind of comedy, the ultimate source of which is to be found in the Old Comedy of Greece'. Jonson's familiarity with the comedy of Aristophanes has often been noted, but Davison feels that not enough attention has been paid to his adaptation in *Volpone* of such Aristophanic characters as the Impostor and the Ironical Buffoon.

In 'The Sources of Marston's *The Wonder of Women or the Tragedie of Sophonisba*' (*NQ*), John Orrell suggests that although Harvey Wood was right in thinking that Marston's chief source for this play was Appian's *Roman History*, it is also possible that he used Livy's *History of Rome* as a supplementary source. In addition to certain verbal echoes already noted by Wood, there are two important elements in the fifth act of the play, Masinissa's vow to Sophonisba and his 'distraction' when the injunction comes from Scipio, which appear only in Livy's account of the story. The chief objection to accepting Appian as Marston's source has been in the basic contradiction between the historian's conception of Sophonisba's character and the playwright's. Orrell thinks, however, that it is just possible that Marston was prompted to remould the whole story in Sophonisba's failure by a marginal gloss in the English translation of Appian, that 'she dyeth like a noble harted Ladye'. Similarly he thinks that another marginal gloss on the battle between Syphax and Masinissa may have suggested to Marston the dramatic idea of a single combat between them.

Richard Levin, in 'The Lady and her Horsekeeper Middleton or Rowley?' (*NQ*), takes up a point in an earlier article by Stanley Wells (*YW*

xli. 132). He does not feel that the various references to the lady and her stable groom are particularly characteristic of any one author, or that they necessarily refer to any topical scandal which might help in the dating of the plays in which they occur. He thinks, rather, that what we have here 'is an item of basic folk-lore which continually reappears at various times and places, presumably because it satisfies some need deeply rooted in our human nature', and he goes on to cite parallels from earlier folk-tales and legends, and from more modern writers—Williams, Lawrence, Maugham—where the motif usually appears in a more sophisticated form.

'It has for long been said that the plays of Beaumont and Fletcher served to do no more than provide a variety of skilful theatrical thrills designed specifically for sophisticated audiences,' says Peter Davison, but in his 'The Serious Concerns of *Philaster*' (*ELH*), he tries to show that in this play the authors 'gave much deeper and more serious consideration to the political affairs of their time than has so far been admitted'. He draws a number of interesting parallels between the play and the *Works* of King James, some concerned with the nature of kings, some with the precise nature of the contract between God and King, and some with the right of subjects to question the king and demand reasons of him. Davison does not claim that the quotations in the play have their source in the *Works*, but only that the play closely mirrored aspects of contemporary political thought; furthermore he feels that in their handling of this political material Beaumont and Fletcher made effective and dramatic comments on it, and he draws attention to the possible significance of the two different end-ings which appeared in the quartos of 1620 and 1622. The authors, he suggests, 'show themselves aware of the alarming division between King and Parliament. We now know that the eventual outcome was the Civil War: the two were not to be reconciled. But to Beaumont and Fletcher it must have seemed reasonable, civilized, and natural, that some such reconciliation should—indeed, must—be effected. That which they effect in *Philaster* gives that blending, that "balance of all the elements", which the urge for order in Elizabethan society demanded.'

In 'The Authorship of *The Tell-Tale*' (*JEGP*), Arthur Freeman is prepared on the basis of internal evidence to attribute the play chiefly, if not entirely, to Dekker. He claims that it is very close, both thematically and stylistically, to Dekker's surviving late plays, and although Dekker is not a self-plagiarist, he does have recourse again and again to the same or very similar themes and devices. The same kind of 'French Doctor' appears in *The Tell-Tale* as in *The Wonder of a Kingdom* and *Old Fortunatus*; Dekker's fondness for ill-used soldiers and scholars, apparent in almost all his plays in one form or another, also appears in *The Tell-Tale*; the very theme of tale-telling is a popular one with him—he is very fond of parables and of illustrations from natural history, and it may be significant that 'the emblematic description of the Pelican feeding its young with blood from its own breast' (*Tell-Tale*, 11. 63–69) is duplicated in *II Honest Whore*, I. ii. 174 ff. Other important parallels are cited in plot, characters, style, and imagery.

'Hamartia' and 'De casibus virorum illustrium' have long been recognized as patterns or shaping motifs for Elizabethan tragedy. To these Irving Ribner (*Patterns in Shakespearean Tragedy*, 1960) added the tragedy of the virtuous man's fall through deception, the tragedy of the deliberately evil man's rise and fall, and the tragedy of 'the ordinary man's growth to maturity'. Thomas B. Stroup, in 'The Testing Pattern in Elizabethan Tragedy' (*SEL*), adds one which he thinks is even more basic to tragedy, and in comedy more obviously apparent; this he calls the 'testing pattern', or the proving of a man. 'The play takes its shape, I believe, from the testing force of Providence. As the protagonist moves across the stage of the world he is proved, like Job, and in his proving he undergoes as trial a series of pretty well defined Christian tests. Now, in some cases, he meets the tests, proves himself, and is saved; in others he fails and is destroyed, to the terror of the spectator.' Stroup derives this notion ultimately from 'the concept of the world as stage, mankind as actors, and God as director of the play'. He traces it in Democritus, in Lucian (from where Erasmus quotes it), in St. Chrysostom, in Plotinus, and in Vives. By the Elizabethan period 'it had come to be a more widespread metaphor for the expression of the Elizabethan World Picture than the Great Chain of Being or the bee hive.' Having established the origins and descent of this pattern, Stroup then discusses its appearance in some of the better-known plays of the period.

The following short contributions are noted only briefly. In 'Act and Scene Divisions in *The Marriage of Wit and Science*' (*NQ*), R. S. Varma takes previous editors to task for their failure to divide this play satisfactorily and presents his own solution. H. D. S. Mithal, in 'The Variants in Robert Wilson's *The Three Lords of London*' (*Lib*), is also concerned with the shortcomings of his predecessors, and produces further press-variants in this play. MacD. P. Jackson, in 'An Emendation to *Arden of Feversham*' (*NQ*), proposes to alter 'there' (in 1. 83 of the Malone Society Reprint) to 'then', the normal Elizabethan spelling for 'than'. In 'Skelton and the Epilogue to Marlowe's *Doctor Faustus*' (*NQ*), A. D. Deyermond suggests that Marlowe's first line may contain a reminiscence of some lines from Skelton's *Garland of Laurel*. Allusions to Marlowe's translation of Ovid's *Amores* in *The Insatiate Countess* are discussed by R. W. Dent in 'Ovid, Marlowe, and *The Insatiate Countess*' (*NQ*). In '*The White Devil*, I. ii. 295: An Emendation' (*NQ*), Arthur Freeman suggests that at this point a comma and a question-mark have been reversed. A further emendation is proposed by Eugene M. Waith in 'A Misprint in *Bartholomew Fair*' (*NQ*), who argues that at V. v. 50–51 (Herford-Simpson edition) the lines at present attributed to Quarlous should be given to Grace Wellborn. Gustav Cross completes his long series of articles on Marston's language with 'Some Notes on the Vocabulary of John Marston—XXIV' (*NQ*). In 'A Note on Thomas Heywood's *A Woman Killed with Kindness*' (*MLR*), Lloyd E. Berry suggests that the first and second scenes of the play have a closer structural relationship than has been realized, that the second is a burlesque of the first and acts as a bridge between the first and the third. F. P. Wilson gently chides E. K. Chambers, in 'Lambarde, the Bel Savage, and the Theatre' (*NQ*), for overlooking a reference to the Bel Savage and its use as a playhouse in the first edition of Lambarde's *Perambulation of Kent* (1576). In 'Thomas Hughes, Plagiarist' (*NQ*), O. A. W. Dilke lists a considerable number of Hughes's borrowings, in *The Misfortunes of Arthur*, from Seneca and, more particularly, from Lucan. In 'Captain Thomas Stukeley' (*NQ*), John M. Yoklavich discusses the dependence of this play on a tract entitled *The Explanation. Of the True and Lawfull Right and Tytle, of the Moste Excellent Prince, Anthonie* . . . (1585).

IX

The Later Tudor Period
Excluding Drama

PATRICIA THOMSON

INSIGHT into this period, and particularly into its political life, is provided by Amos C. Miller's biography[1] of Sir Henry Killigrew which he describes as 'an attempt to assess Killigrew as a diplomat, a Puritan sympathizer and forward Protestant, as a courtier, office holder, man of property, and, above all, as a human being'. Killigrew, whom Elizabeth had learned to trust even before her accession, died only a few weeks before her. His career, one of the longest of his day, covers major episodes in her reign, and his character precisely fits his role as a Tudor servant of state. He was devoted, cautious, and discreet (in this respect presenting a marked contrast to his outspoken and tactless colleague, Sir Nicholas Throckmorton). Miller describes him as primarily the craftsman, the skilled negotiator, not so much the royal adviser. He lacked Burleigh's political genius no less than Leicester's flamboyant independence. Typically, he remained on good terms with both. Though he was not dashing enough to appeal strongly to the Queen, he was obviously an excellent servant. His biography is not the less interesting for his limitations. Such men were the indispensable Horatios of the Elizabethan scene, and, in many ways, they

illuminate it more steadily than do their dazzling superiors.

A picture of Elizabethan Winchester, based on contemporary documents and especially on the city archives, is provided by the city archivist himself. Tom Atkinson[2] arranges his material not chronologically but under selected heads. Important topics are given a chapter apiece. There is an account of the topography of Elizabethan Winchester, based on the tarrage roll, and an account of local government, based on the charters and on the records of the Burgh-mote as a legislative body. Four chapters are given to local administration, and others to such matters as the city courts, health, trade, and religion. Since Roman and medieval Winchester are comparatively well known to us, it is interesting to learn of its less spectacular life under Elizabeth. Atkinson does not give the impression that the city lacked vigour at this time, but certainly it had shrunk. Whereas in Norman times the population was about 8,000, on the accession of Elizabeth it was less than half that total. Moreover, its wool trade had declined. Winchester did not keep 'in step with any general advance'. National events, such as the defeat of the Armada, made little impact on it. It was a self-contained community.

[1] *Sir Henry Killigrew: Elizabethan Soldier and Diplomat*, by Amos C. Miller. Leicester U.P. pp. xi+279. 35s.

[2] *Elizabethan Winchester*, by Tom Atkinson. Faber & Faber. pp. 268. 30s.

'For most of its inhabitants the city walls or the suburbs were the limits of their world.' Its officers were mainly conservative in outlook, and medieval customs were to a large extent maintained.

A short but comprehensive account of *Tudor Economic Problems*,[3] a contribution to 'The Men and Ideas Series', is given by Peter Ramsey. Some of the problems (enclosures, inflation, the 'rise of the middle class', and the expansion of trade) have been subjects of controversy, and here his hope is 'only to state the present "state of the question"'. Ramsey's own opinions are not meant to obtrude, but he makes some suggestions: for example, that government intervention in economic and social life was not a completely random affair, and, again, that the effect of the rise of prices on social structure has probably been exaggerated. Agrarian problems, the subject of the first chapter, are rightly given pride of place, for farming was the chief occupation of sixteenth-century Englishmen. Ramsey then goes on to chapters on overseas trade, industry and the towns, prices and social change, and the role of government.

Garrett Mattingly has undertaken with outstanding success the difficult task of presenting to the non-specialist and in concentrated form a subject in which he is deeply versed. His pamphlet[4] on the Armada is largely given over to the destruction of the 'compulsive national fantasies' connected with the nine days of fighting in the Channel in the summer of 1588. And in dealing with its aftermath he dispels the illusion that their victory induced in the English 'a mood of buoyant optimism, which somehow stimulated the flowering of Elizabethan literature'.

Catholic education from 1547 to 1689 is the subject of A. C. F. Beales's book,[5] Chapters III, IV, and V of which deal, in some detail, with the Elizabethan period. When Elizabeth, early in her reign, required of all teachers the oaths of supremacy and conformity, the English schools and universities were virtually lost to Catholics. In the first place, this beginning of State control of education seems to have caused a 'brain drain', for its immediate result was an exodus from Oxford and Cambridge, followed by the foundation of English colleges abroad. With the arrival in England of a dozen Catholic missionaries, including the intrepid Campion and Parsons, in 1580, began a period of resistance, and consequently one of renewed persecution.

The Catholic exodus from England forms the subject of A. J. Loomie's book[6] focusing on five 'Spaniolized' Elizabethans, each of whom spent over twenty-five years abroad: Sir Francis Englefield, who had much to do with the Hapsburgs' pension system for Catholic refugees and who became the spokesman for his fellows; Hugh Owen, the notable 'intelligencer' who gathered information on England at the court of the Archdukes in Brussels; Lady Jane Dormer, Duchess of Feria, who so nearly rallied the exiles under her leadership; Sir William Stanley, whose military prowess, once enlisted on the Protestant side, was turned to Catholic advantage; and Joseph Creswell,

---

[3] *Tudor Economic Problems*, by Peter Ramsey. Gollancz. pp. 192. 13s. 6d.

[4] *The 'Invincible' Armada and Elizabethan England*, by Garrett Mattingly. Folger Booklets on Tudor and Stuart Civilization. Cornell U.P. pp. 54. $1.

[5] *Education under Penalty: English Catholic Education from the Reformation to the Fall of James II, 1547–1689*, by A. C. F. Beales. Athlone Press. pp. xii+306. £2. 10s.

[6] *The Spanish Elizabethans: The Exiles at the Court of Philip II*, by Albert J. Loomie, S. J. Fordham U.P. pp. xii+280. $6.

the Jesuit priest, who devoted himself to the essential drudgery of maintaining the new English colleges in Spain. This is a learned work drawing on new material from Spanish as well as from English archives.

Loomie also gives, in *Recusant History*, a description of a Folger manuscript containing a Catholic petition, of 1601, to the Earl of Essex. A number of other short articles, also in *Recusant History*, deal with aspects of Elizabethan Catholicism. P. R. Harris writes on William Fleetwood, who was active in hunting down Catholics in London. Anthony Petti provided, in 1962, an account of the recusant poet and Cambridge tutor, Stephen Vallenger, and this included a list of the books he had with him in the Fleet prison at the time of his death. This year Petti adds a bibliography of Vallenger's published works. In 1962, John Bossy examined Henry Constable's *Examen pacifique de la Doctrine des Huguenots*, a relatively moderate statement of the Catholic position. And Anthony Kenny supplied some new evidence to show that Anthony Munday was at the English College in Rome and to authenticate Munday's own account, in *The English Romayne Life*, of the college and of the mutiny of the English scholars against the rector, Morus Clynnog.

A contribution to knowledge of the Anglican side of Elizabethan religious controversy is provided in John S. Marshall's book[7] on Richard Hooker. Concerned to relate this greatest of Anglican theologians to the appropriate tradition, he devotes the first part to such matters as the Erasmian Catholicism of Henry VIII's Church, the Catholic and Protestant Biblical reformers, the Marian exiles, Jewel,

Whitgift, and the controversies with the Puritans Cartwright and Travers. Proceeding to Hooker himself, Marshall is at pains to connect his theology with the revived Thomism of the Renaissance, especially as exemplified in the work of the Roman Catholic Cardinal Cajetan. In the *Laws of Ecclesiastical Polity* Hooker is not only answering seven main Puritan theses, but presenting a basically Catholic theology, and one congenial with the *Book of Common Prayer*. Yet, for Marshall, he is not merely a man of the establishment, much less a belated medievalist. He is himself the author of a *summa*, and a great synthesizing genius comparable with his masters Aristotle and St. Thomas. Hooker is also the subject of a number of articles. Arthur S. McGrade (*JHI*), launches a sharp attack on the current scholarly opinion that the *Laws of Ecclesiastical Polity* is a 'tragically incoherent' work: the last three books, he attempts to show, are consistent with the earlier ones and do not reveal a decline into secularism and 'excessive rationalism'. J. R. Parris (*Scottish Journal of Theology*) describes Hooker's Eucharistic theology, which laid the foundation of a distinctively Anglican doctrine. Egil Grislis discusses 'Hooker's Image of Man' (*RP*), as a being dependent on both grace and human reason, and, in 'Richard Hooker's Method of Theological Inquiry' (*ATR*), shows how he distrusted undue subjectivity in the search for truth, promoting instead an objective method based on revelation, reason, and the *consensus gentium*. Differences among Anglicans are brought out in Robert Orr's 'Chillingworth versus Hooker' (*Journal of Religious History*, 1962); in spite of their common purpose, the defence of the Church of England, Chillingworth became a critic of the traditional

---

[7] *Hooker and the Anglican Tradition*, by John S. Marshall. Adam & Charles Black. pp. x + 180. 25s.

M

theory of natural law held by Hooker.

Some of Hooker's fellow bishops are studied by Edward O. Smith, Jr., in *ATR*; his concern is with the manner in which episcopal sermons preached before Elizabeth promoted the doctrine of the 'godly prince', and he provides illustrations from the utterances of Whitgift, Jewel, Sandys, and others. The cleric's son Edwin Sandys's *Relation of the State of Religion* is of interest 'mainly for the unusual tolerance it displayed toward Roman Catholics'; Theodore K. Rabb (*HLQ*), gives an account of the early publishing history of this work, which, though completed in 1599, was not in print till 1605, and which was burned by order of the high commission in the same year.

Relevant to both Catholic and Protestant religious history and literature is Helen C. White's book[8] tracing the saint's legend as a literary type through the sixteenth century and some way into the seventeenth. The *Legenda Aurea*, published as *The Golden Legend* by Caxton in 1483, set the original pattern, though it was, for obvious reasons, repudiated by such Protestant martyrologists as John Foxe. Yet for all the Protestants' attack on the cult of saints, they created their own, and Foxe's 'Book of Martyrs' provides a substitute for *The Golden Legend*, while also serving the functions of an ecclesiastical history (Foxe saw himself as a new Eusebius) and of a propagandist encyclopedia of the Reformation in England. With the accession of Elizabeth it was now again the Catholic turn to glorify the martyrs, and there result, for example, Thomas Alfield's and William Allen's accounts of Campion and the other members of

the English mission who were put to death. With Campion's successor, Robert Southwell, a new phase starts and a new literary impulse is released. Where the Campion group was militant, Southwell was upon a mission of comfort to the afflicted. He was, furthermore, himself an outstanding religious writer. It was largely under his influence, and particularly under that of his *Saint Peter's Complaint*, that the 'literature of lamentation', with the figure of the repentant and weeping sinner, came into its own as a Renaissance poetic type in England. The chapter dealing with this phase is amongst the most relevant to this chapter of *YW*. So also is its successor on 'Continuing Classics and Emergent Types', with its account of the recasting of the old saint's legend into the fashionable forms of Elizabeth's reign, as in George Pettie's euphuistic version of the story of Alexius, and Richard Johnson's chivalric romance *The Seaven Champions of Christendome*. The establishment did not fail to contribute to the genre, and Drayton's poem on Moses and the biographies of such churchmen as Jewel and Parker stand squarely in the hagiographical tradition.

The Latin letters[9] of the two Scottish scholars John Johnston and Robert Howie have been carefully transcribed, edited, annotated, and introduced by James Kerr Cameron. Following a medieval Scottish custom, they wandered, as young graduates, from one European university to another, returning at last to fill academic posts in their native land. Their letters, which cover the years 1586–1611, concern, besides personal matters, contemporary political and religious history, and their corres-

---

[8] *Tudor Books of Saints and Martyrs*, by Helen C. White. Wisconsin U.P. pp. vi+381. $6.75.

[9] *Letters of John Johnston c. 1565–1611 and Robert Howie c. 1565–c. 1645*, ed. by James Kerr Cameron. Oliver and Boyd. pp. lxxxiv+392. £3. 3s.

pondents include such eminent European scholars as Isaac Casaubon, Jakob Grynaeus, Francis Junius, John Piscator, Theodore Beza, and William Camden. For all the similarity in background and experience, it is interesting to notice the point at which Johnston and Howie diverge: Johnston was against, Howie for, the episcopacy.

The great English scholar and educationalist, Sir Henry Savile, Warden of Merton from 1585 to 1622, is the subject of a hitherto unpublished essay in a collection[10] by H. W. Garrod. Though evidently not enamoured of Savile's character, which was quarrelsome, severe, even tyrannical, he does him justice as scholar, mathematician, and book-lover. Savile is to be remembered for his edition of Chrysostom, for his foundation of the Oxford chairs of Astronomy and Geometry, and for his generosity to the Oxford libraries, as well as for that crabby distrust of 'wits' which is suggested in his 'give me the plodding student'. Savile's autograph commonplace book, acquired by Merton College Library in 1960, is described by J. R. L. Highfield in *Bodleian Library Record*.

The second volume of *The Pelican History of Music*[11] contains a section on the early Renaissance by Brian Trowell, one on the late Renaissance by Anthony Milner, and three on the 'Baroque' period (one apiece by Henry Raynor, Alec Harman and Denis Stevens). Though written by specialists, this history 'has been designed to satisfy the needs of intelligent and open-minded readers who know something about the history of

art and literature yet lack the opportunity to link their knowledge with the more detailed aspects of musical art-forms'. There is a consistent attempt to relate music to various aspects of history, for example, to the history of the Reformation; the churches varied in their attitudes to music and to the musical style appropriate to religious services. Sixteenth-century English music naturally forms only a part of this survey of European music from the fifteenth to the early eighteenth century, but it is useful to see it against a large canvas, and to notice its slowness to absorb the newer European styles in the years preceding the brilliant outburst of the last two decades of Elizabeth's reign.

An authoritative account of *Portraits of Queen Elizabeth I*[12] accompanies Roy C. Strong's catalogue of all those which can fairly claim authenticity. He classifies them according to the various set facial patterns. In the Darnley and Ditchley portraits her face is long and angular, in the Armada and Buccleuch portraits round and full. We shall never know what she really looked like, only how she wished to look. Her public images are fixed. Early in her reign a proclamation against the debased and unofficial portraits then in circulation was issued. The official portraits of Elizabeth, like those of her peers, were not intended to reveal individuality. They are, one and all, 'ceremonial' portraits, representing queenly majesty and virtue. They took their part in the universal cult of the Virgin Queen. Noblemen liked to possess her portrait, and the habit of wearing cameos depicting the royal image was widespread. Strong, whose sense of the period as a whole is powerful, points out that 'The sacred images of Christ, the Virgin and

[10] *The Study of Good Letters*, by H. W. Garrod. Ed. by John Jones. O.U.P. pp. vii +211. 30s.

[11] *The Pelican History of Music, Vol. II. Renaissance and Baroque*, ed. by Alec Robertson and Denis Stevens. Penguin Books. pp. 335. 7s. 6d.

[12] *Portraits of Queen Elizabeth I*, by Roy C. Strong. O.U.P. pp. xiv+173+plates. 42s.

saints had been cast out of the churches as so much rubbish, while in their place we see the meteoric rise of the sacred images of the *Diva Elizabetha*'. His specialized study implies much that is of general interest and importance to the understanding of Elizabeth and her times.

In an Elizabethan portrait the richly embroidered costume of the sitter will often catch and hold the attention more than his or her mask-like face and beady eyes. The period was, in fact, a great age in English embroidery, rivalled only by the age of *Opus Anglicanum* in the thirteenth and fourteenth centuries. George Wingfield Digby, Keeper of Textiles in the Victoria and Albert Museum, conveys its full glory in a handsomely illustrated book,[13] equipped with a readable text and efficient bibliographies. Embroidery was, he points out, no mere pastime, but an important craft, practised by all ranks and by men as well as women. The professionals were in considerable demand, and were well appreciated by such gifted amateurs as Mary Queen of Scots and Bess of Hardwick, to whose labours as needlewomen a section of this book is devoted. (The noteworthy collection at Hardwick Hall also provides some of the finest of its plates.) Embroidered garments and furnishings surviving from the Ezliabethan period give considerable insight into its taste, bearing out what is learned from other sources: it is no shock to find, in abundance, flower designs, and emblematic or mythological scenes, nor gold and silver thread in constant use. This minor art is worth more than a glance.

John Buxton's *Elizabethan Taste*[14]

is a capacious study of its subject, rich in description and quotation from Elizabethan sources, though underburdened with scholarly references. The idea of 'good taste', taken in its modern sense as a personal gift, was, of course, alien to the Elizabethans themselves. The complete gentleman had, however, been educated through the study and practice of the arts to acquire discrimination. Reason, nature, decorum, the 'love of the ceremonious', the belief that 'perfection was within man's reach': these are amongst the aesthetic inclinations or standards noticed by Buxton in his survey of major art forms. Throughout he is concerned to distinguish Elizabethan from modern taste, and his book is, in fact, primarily a plea, polite but pressing, that we should bring to Elizabethan art and literature, not our own irrelevant tastes, but a willingness to identify ourselves with the tastes of those who were catered for by Bess of Hardwick's architects, by Epiphanius Evesham (the best Elizabethan sculptor), by Nicholas Hilliard, by William Byrd, and by Sidney, Spenser, and Shakespeare. Buxton gives chapters to Architecture, Painting, Sculpture, and Music, before coming to Literature, the subject in which he is best qualified to pass judgement and to which he gives most space. Wisely, he does not survey the whole field, selecting examples of literary works which were of high repute in their day and which are alike in being difficult for the modern reader to enjoy unless he has cultivated a close sympathy with Elizabethan taste. And if the modern reader does enjoy, say, *Venus and Adonis*, he is likely to do so in a non-Elizabethan spirit; he will praise its naturalistic touches, where Shakespeare's first readers would have praised its artificialities. Again, it is unhistorical to read *Astrophel and*

[13] *Elizabethan Embroidery*, by George Wingfield Digby. Faber & Faber. pp. 151 +plates. 52s. 6d.

[14] *Elizabethan Taste*, by John Buxton. Macmillan. pp. xiv+370. 35s.

Stella as 'mere self-revelation', that is, in a Romantic spirit; Sidney's first readers would have delighted in its rhetoric, both formal and colloquial. Besides these works, Buxton also handles *The Shepheardes Calender, Arcadia, Hamlet,* and Donne's poems. His best section is, perhaps, the one on *Arcadia* and the reasons for its original success.

The remaining contributions to this year's general and background work on Elizabethan literature are as follows. Anthony Petti (*E & S*), shows how the Elizabethans 'saw in the animal kingdom a valuable commentary on the nature and state of man'. Beasts provide analogies to human behaviour in general and political behaviour in particular. Elizabeth's self-sacrifice is represented through the phoenix and pelican, her chastity through the unicorn. The fox and lion also denote chracteristics of rulers. In satire, as, for example, Spenser's *Mother Hubberds Tale* and Nashe's *Pierce Penilesse*, animal symbols disguise the well-known personalities of the 1590's. S. M. Pratt (*MLQ*) studies the impact of the successive sackings of Antwerp on the Elizabethan mind. George Gascoigne's *The Spoyle of Antwerpe*, an eye-witness account, supplied materials for the 'balladers'. Nashe's *Christ's Tears over Jerusalem* is in different vein, for, while alluding to Antwerp, he actually draws on material concerning the destruction of Jerusalem. This leads Pratt to a discussion of what he calls the 'literature of alarm' and the 'genre of alarm'. C. A. Patrides provides a 'bibliographical note' on 'The Renaissance View of Time' (*NQ*), and points out that, in general, this period 'adhered to the Augustinian formulation'. William E. Miller (*S Ren*) deals with the teaching method called 'double translation', specially favoured by Ascham but also used by

later educationalists of the sixteenth and seventeenth centuries.

A number of important Elizabethan items are included in O. B. Hardison Jr.'s anthology[15] of literary criticism produced between 1484 and 1671: George Gascoigne's *Certayne Notes of Instruction* (1575), an extract from Stephen Gosson's *School of Abuse* (1579), Sidney's *Apologie* (1583?), several chapters of George Puttenham's *Arte of English Poesie* (1589), the Preface to Spenser's *Shepheardes Calender* (1579), his 'October Eclogue' with E. K.'s 'Glosse' (1579), and his 'Letter to Raleigh' (1590), Sir John Harington's Preface to his translation of *Orlando Furioso* (1591), George Whetstone's Preface to *Promos and Cassandra* (1578), and extracts from Thomas Campion's *Observations in the Art of English Poesie* (1602) and from Samuel Daniel's refutation of it, *A Defence of Ryme* (1603). Most of this material is divided between two sections, 'The Defense of Poetry' and 'Practical Criticism' (this term is not to be understood in its modern sense, but applies to criticism having relevance to, or attached to, a particular work). Each item is briefly introduced, and short bibliographies are provided. The volume does not cover so much ground as G. Gregory Smith's *Elizabethan Critical Essays*, but it should, in its way, prove equally useful.

The bulkiest and best of this year's studies of Spenser's poetry is William Nelson's.[16] It is up to date. Nelson has assimilated a great deal of recent criticism. But he is far from critic-ridden and his primary sources are Spenser's text and the relevant work

[15] *English Literary Criticism: The Renaissance*, ed. by O. B. Hardison, Jr. (Goldentree Books.) Appleton-Century-Crofts. pp. ix +337. $2.95.
[16] *The Poetry of Edmund Spenser*, by William Nelson. Columbia U.P. pp. xi+350. $6. 45s.

of Spenser's predecessors and contemporaries. He contrives to be modern, without being merely fashionable. His point of view is, in fact, one increasingly held by informed Spenserians: that Spenser is an 'eloquent, highly sophisticated artist'. His aim is to direct attention to 'the intellectual core of the poems and then to the techniques by which their meanings are given shape, precision, and power'. His first task therefore is to find Spenser's central theme in each poem, for 'theme', in his view, is the central structural element. All this is worked out in detail in successive chapters on the pastoral poems (*The Shepheardes Calender* and *Colin Clouts Come Home Againe*), on the complaints and elegies (a group including *Mother Hubberds Tale*), on the love poems (the *Hymnes*, wedding songs, and *Amoretti*), and on each book of *The Faerie Queene* (including the Mutability Cantos). Those who want to be taken through the text could do worse than choose Nelson as guide, though there is more to his book than this implies. The study of themes, and of themes in relation to poetic structures, reveals a Spenser in many ways the opposite of the 'simple, sensuous, passionate' poet seen by the critics of an older school. Remarking of *Colin Clout* that, for Spenser, 'the poet's task is to grapple with error, not escape from it', Nelson both dispels the illusion of an escapist, idealizing Spenser, and points to a major theme of his. He never entertains illusions of a sin-free world. Calidore succeeds in his quest, to capture the Blatant Beast, but the last we hear of this representative of sinful slander is that he is at large again. 'The world contrasted with a state of excellence' is, from the early complaints to the later books of *The Faerie Queene*, a recurrent theme. But if the complaints, like all their

kind, tend to gloom, Spenser's optimism in his mature work is equally evident. The recognition of sin means no yielding to despair. 'The necessarily imperfect can imitate the necessarily perfect', and Artegall's justice imitates that of Astraea. It is impossible to summarize here all the ideas suggested by Nelson's book. It contains numerous things of value. Amongst them are the challenges to the interpretations of *The Faerie Queene* Book I as a *Bildungsroman* and of *Mother Hubberds Tale* as primarily a topical comment; the discussions of the literary models appropriate to Spenser's poems (*e.g.* of *Metamorphoses* in connexion with the Mutability Cantos); and the analysis of Spenser's equation of birth and worth in *The Faerie Queene* Book VI.

In discussing Spenser's verse forms, early and late, Robert Beum (*NM*), seeks to show that they were devised to suit his vision and, where appropriate, his narrative, and that, accordingly, they are not to be regarded primarily as the product of his indulgence in technical virtuosity.

Two of Charles Grosvenor Osgood's published addresses[17] are on Spenser, and make very light reading. 'The New Poet' is a survey of Spenser's career and an attempt to connect his life, particularly its hardships, with his poetry. As for the title, the preface to *The Shepheardes Calender* in which he is hailed as 'the new poet' is, in Osgood's opinion, quite likely to be by Spenser himself. The claim itself he considers valid in view of the fact that England had produced no great poet since Chaucer, and felt culturally inferior to continental Europe. 'Spenser and Shakespeare' is largely an account of the common

[17] *Creed of a Humanist*, by Charles Grosvenor Osgood. Washington U.P. pp. xi + 143. $4.50.

ground shared by these two poets. Osgood considers Shakespeare's reading of Spenser, Spenser's importing of numerous sophisticated continental forms and ideas also found in Shakespeare's pages, and that relationship which depends upon 'a far more important bond: the figure of their Queen'. This book also includes a select bibliography of Osgood's writings, with a number on Spenser, including, most notably, his contributions to the Variorum edition.

In a new periodical, *English Language Notes*,[18] Hugh Maclean makes a vigorous and detailed attack on Paul McLane's identification of the 'E.K.' of *The Shepheardes Calender* with Fulke Greville (see *YW* xlii. 146). McLane himself writes, also in *English Language Notes*, on Spenser's attitude to the Primitive Church especially as shown in the *Calender*: here he is frequently following his Catholic source, Mantuan, and, in general, he looks through conservative eyes.

The title of Thomas Greene's *The Descent from Heaven*,[19] which contains a chapter on Spenser, refers to an epic convention, originating in Homer and Virgil and recurrent down to Milton: 'the descent of an emissary god or angel from heaven bearing a message to earth'. As the subject of a book, this turns out to be by no means as narrow as might at first be expected. Greene is well able to use it as a critical springboard, and, in any case, the celestial messenger's descent is often a crucial episode in epic narrative: 'it represents the intersection of time and the timeless; it points to the human realm of paramount concern to the gods; and it

[18] First published September 1963. Address: 1200 University Avenue, Boulder, Colorado 80304.

[19] *The Descent from Heaven: A Study in Epic Continuity*, by Thomas Greene. Yale U.P. pp. 434. $7.50.

brings divine authority to the unfolding heroic action'. Greene's two chief examples from Spenser occur in *Mother Hubberds Tale* and the Mutability Cantos of *The Faerie Queene*. In the first, Mercury acts as rather more than the *deus ex machina*, for his intervention in the fable 'exposes the impostor and his philosophy, demonstrates continuity by the lion's restoration, and offers a victorious alternative to the principle of flux'. The principle of flux occurs again, and in the typically Spenserian conflict with the principle of constancy, in *The Faerie Queene*. The Mutability Cantos, where Mercury again figures, provide the palmary Elizabethan example of the meeting of terrestrial and celestial in epic writing.

Following in the footsteps of A. K. Hieatt, whose book on *Epithalamion* was reviewed in *YW* xli. 149–50, Alastair Fowler has noticed and closely investigated the numerological patterns in *The Faerie Queene*. His article (*JWCI*, 1962), gives a foretaste of an important book to be published next year.

Madeleine Pelner Cosman has made a painstaking analysis of image groups in *The Faerie Queene*, and in *SEL* discusses the largest, that constituted by 230 animal images. She considers the animals used, the handling and the effect, and claims that Spenser was genuinely interested in animal life, though much in his imagery is to be referred to his literary sources.

J. F. Kermode's Warton lecture, delivered in 1962, is now available in *PBA* and as a booklet.[20] He deals with *The Faerie Queene* Book I in the same manner as he formerly dealt with Book II (see *YW* xli. 151), studying its esoteric meaning, and unveiling

[20] *Spenser and the Allegorists*, by J. F. Kermode. From *PBA*, Vol. xlviii. O.U.P. pp. 19. 5s.

the myths that hide behind Spenser's allegorical stories. He is not the first to notice that many images in Book I derive from *Revelation*, but he differs from several predecessors in his endeavour not to isolate Spenser's apocalyptic myths from their historical context in Elizabethan England. Spenser, he believes, is unlike the modern apocalyptic writer, D. H. Lawrence, in that he does not reject actuality in favour of archetypes. *The Faerie Queene*, if reduced to a primitive myth, its importance as a national heroic poem forgotten, gains a dubious prestige but is, in the end, impoverished.

In a lively, chatty article in *University of Kansas City Review*, John W. Major, Jr., pleads that in *The Faerie Queene* Book I Spenser still has something to say to us about the human soul, holiness, and the education of the young.

Robert L. Kellogg and Oliver L. Steele (*PMLA*) discuss the punctuation, and hence the meaning, of *The Faerie Queene* I. ii. 13, lines 4–5, and III. x. 57, lines 2–6.

B. Nellish (*ELH*) offers an interpretation of the allegory of Guyon's voyage to the Bower of Bliss in *The Faerie Queene* Book II. He refers to other literary and allegorical voyages, with the object of throwing Spenser's greatness, as allegorist, into relief. This greatness is seen in the fact that he reaches out 'from the allegory of nouns to full adverbial allegory'. (For example, the boatman does not represent steadfastness in the abstract, but simply acts steadfastly.)

James McAuley's inaugural lecture[21] at the University of Tasmania, now in print, offers a 'critical excursion' into the work of Spenser and George Eliot. Based on a comparison

between the Malbecco episode in *The Faerie Queene* (III. 9–10) and *Middlemarch* (each contains a story of a woman married to a rich, but jealous and repellent, old man), the paper gives valuable insights into the complexity of Spenser's construction and the skill with which he brings together different themes and styles. Thus 'high-romance figures . . . drawn from the highest stratum of the epic' are found in conjunction with a 'fabliaustyle comedy'. 'The shifts of level from "base" to "high" styles, and the composite effects, are tricky and require skilful adjustment by the poet, as he first insinuates a comic tale into the romantic-heroic framework, and then inserts within it such materials as the unhelmeting of Britomart and the "Trojan" political myth, thereafter again transforming the mode to accommodate the satyrscene, and ending in pure allegory.'

Richard N. Ringler (*SP*) draws attention to the hitherto unnoticed debt of *The Faerie Queene* II. iv. 29–44 (the adventures of Marinell and Cymoent) to the *Achilleid* of Statius. Rudolf Gottfried (*RN*) makes a 'spurious composite' of III. ix. 19, lines 1–6, and III. ix. 25, lines 7–9. Since they fit together perfectly, he concludes that Spenser actually did write the 'composite' stanza, and then divided it, inserting the intervening lines. If so, these lines, mainly devoted to the discovery of Britomart's sex, were written later than the rest of canto ix.

A complete edition of the translations of the Psalms by Sir Philip Sidney and his sister Mary, Countess of Pembroke, has long been needed. The first and, till this year, the last was S. W. Singer's of 1823. Various editors have, of course, handled Sidney's translations, the most recent being William A. Ringler (see *YW* xliii. 155). But Sidney broke off after

---

[21] *Edmund Spenser and George Eliot*, by James McAuley. University of Tasmania. pp. 21. 4s. 6d.

Psalm 43, and it was left to his sister both to edit his versions and to add her own of the remaining 128 Psalms. J. C. A. Rathmell's edition[22] is accordingly most welcome. From the fourteen known manuscripts he has chosen as his copy text the transcription by John Davies of Hereford in the Penshurst collection. His aim has been to present the Countess's final version of the joint work. Ringler restored, as far as possible, Sidney's own text. Rathmell gives the Countess's emended version of his work. She was a respectful editor, revising her brother's work with due caution. Her corrections to her own work are naturally more drastic, and here is the clue to her importance as a translator of the Psalms. She was a careful, conscientious artist. The results she achieved in this case are superior to Sidney's obviously more hasty work. Rathmell's edition rightly gives her pride of place in terms of quality as well as of quantity. This is no mere historical curiosity, but a volume of English religious lyrics as good as any before George Herbert's *Temple*. The opening of Psalm 130, the 'De Profundis', provides evidence:

From depth of grief
Where droun'd I ly,
Lord for relief
To thee I cry:
My earnest, vehement, cryeng, prayeng,
Graunt quick, attentive, hearing, waighing.

Again, a vigorous description of the wicked in their pride (Psalm 73) is moulded into a complex stanza. The variety of metrical forms used is the subject of comment in Rathmell's informative introduction, and he convincingly argues for the Countess's advance upon the unvaried, over-simple, unsubtle versions, such as the long-lived 'Sternhold and Hopkins', used for public worship in her day. By contrast, her purpose was literary, her emphasis on private devotion. And though neither she nor her brother knew Hebrew, they seem to have made a scholarly study of various early translations of the Psalms and their commentaries. This book is well produced, except that pages xvii and xxvii have been accidentally transposed. An appendix provides, for the purposes of comparison, the text of Psalm 58 in four sources used by the Sidneys and in six English verse translations ranging from the sixteenth century to the nineteenth. Another describes the textual sources, and there is a bibliography of works referring to the 'Sidneian Psalms'.

George W. Hallam (*RP*) considers the appearance of Ramist logic in Sidney's work, especially in his *Apologie*, questioning how far he accepted it. His conclusion is that 'Sidney may have believed Peter Ramus to be the best writer on the art of logic, but so long as he had any of the poet in him, he parted company with the Ramists themselves'.

Sidney's comparatively unnoticed pastoral masque *The Lady of May* is taken up by S. K. Orgel (*JWCI*). Particularly valuable is his examination of the use of a basic convention of pastoral, 'the assumption that the contemplative life is intrinsically more virtuous than the active life'. There follows some comment on the inclusion of Elizabeth in the masque, and on Sidney's debate structure and its rhetoric.

Another useful article on Sidney's pastoral writing is David Kalstone's 'The Transformation of Arcadia: Sannazaro and Sir Philip Sidney' (*CL*). He shows first how Sannazaro adapted Virgil's 'Arcadia' to suit

[22] *The Psalms of Sir Philip Sidney and the Countess of Pembroke*, ed. by J. C. A. Rathmell. (The Stuart Editions.) New York U.P. pp. xxxviii+362. $6.50.

early sixteenth-century Italian tastes. Then he moves on to Sidney, showing how Sannazaro provided a framework for that most successful pastoral poem, the double sestina 'You Goteheard Gods' in *Arcadia*. The contrasts are as interesting as the similarities, for Sidney's vein is comparatively dark and melancholy, and, Kalstone concludes, his poem 'must be taken . . . as a criticism of the uncomplicated happiness of Sannazaro's *Arcadia*'.

Bent Juel-Jensen (*BC*) provides a promised addition to last year's bibliographical work on Sidney (see *YW* xliii. 156). There is little work on *Astrophel and Stella* to report; John Buxton's book, reviewed above (see note 14), deals with it, and also with Sidney's *Arcadia*.

A collection of Ovidian narrative poems, appearing under the (rather odd) title *Elizabethan Minor Epics*,[23] is ably edited and introduced by Elizabeth Story Donno, covers the period 1589–1646, and includes contributions by Lodge, Marlowe, Chapman, Thomas Heywood, Thomas Edwards, Drayton, Marston, John Weever, Beaumont, Phineas Fletcher and James Shirley. Ovid, in the Middle Ages and early Renaissance, had been one of the most popular of classical poets, and Golding's translation of the *Metamorphoses* (1565–7), bringing his riches to those with 'small Latin', made him even more so. His 'delectable histories', for all the attempts to moralize and allegorize them, must always have provided more 'delight' than 'profit'. And with the emergence of the Ovidian epyllion as a distinct Elizabethan genre, profitable moralizing is cast to the winds: 'My wanton lines doe treate of amorous love' is the opening of

[23] *Elizabethan Minor Epics*, ed. by Elizabeth Story Donno. Routledge & Kegan Paul. pp. vii+351. 40s.

Beaumont's *Salmacis and Hermaphroditus*. First in the field and first in the collection under review stands Lodge's *Scillaes Metamorphosis* (1589), which set the pattern for the new genre. Based on a classical myth, it is 'passionate with painings', richly descriptive, and, like many poems in this kind, allows the heroine to take the initiative in ardent wooing. The conventional elements recur. Heywood's Oenone woos the infatuated and unfaithful Paris and 'plains' for many a stanza amidst glorious scenery. Shirley's Echo woos Narcissus, who is so alluring that even the twigs above his woodland pillow are love-sick. Love is overmastering desire, a 'passion' which 'hotly holds its course', a 'strong fit', a 'sweet Fever', as Drayton terms it. The atmosphere is always heady, and the scenic detail often corresponds: Aurora can hardly appear without 'her blushing face'. This is clearly a genre the Elizabethans revelled in, even excelled in. For Marlowe's *Hero and Leander*, though outstanding, is not alone in being memorable, and the verse narratives printed here are all, at the very least, readable and zestful.

Hero and Leander has also received attention elsewhere. Erich Segal (*CL*) analyses and compares the handling of the ancient myth by Marlowe and Góngora, contemporaries and, alike, iconoclasts. Where the classical poets had treated it with romantic reverence, these two poets 'could not forbear cynical comment'. Marlowe sees the love story as a case of sensuality, Góngora as one of folly. Eugene B. Cantelupe, on the other hand, imputes to Marlowe a more serious purpose than he has usually been allowed to have. His article in *CE* comprises an analysis of *Hero and Leander* as a tragi-comedy of love in the Ovidian genre: the stress on the tragic makes for a certain seriousness. In a note on

Hero and Leander I, 45–50, T. N. Marsh (*Ex*) advances the view that Marlowe alludes to night and not (as some authorities have supposed) to negroes. R. W. Dent (*NQ*) cites a hitherto unnoticed allusion to Marlowe's translation of Ovid's *Amores* in *The Insatiate Countess* (the play attributed to Marston or, alternatively, to William Barksted). S. K. Heninger, Jr., (*RP*, 1962) relates Marlowe's well-known shepherd's song, 'Come live with me and be my love', to the nymph's reply, 'If all the world and love were young'; he believes that its meaning is hereby enhanced.

The selections from Sir John Harington's translation (1591) of Ariosto's *Orlando Furioso*[24] edited by Rudolf Gottfried, authority on Italian Renaissance literature, make delightful and easy reading. He was the wittiest and one of the most fluent of Elizabeth's courtiers. He loved jokes, especially wanton ones. According to tradition, he at first translated the vulgar and misogynistic fabliau of Iocondo from Canto 38 of *Orlando Furioso*, then allowed it to circulate among the ladies at court, and, as a result, was banished until he had turned the whole work into English verse. Yet, whatever the appearances to the contrary, Harington was, as Gottfried points out, not a mere dilettante but a learned man, and, in the free style of his time, a competent translator. His verse, if often flat, is good for passages of action:

Sometimes they proffer; then they
   pause a while;
Sometime strike out, like masters of
   the play;
Now stand upright; now stoop
   another while &c. (Canto 2, p. 50).

[24] *Ariosto's 'Orlando Furioso': Selections from the Translation of Sir John Harington*, ed. by Rudolf Gottfried. Indiana U.P. pp. 351. $2.95.

He is less delicate than Ariosto, but Ariosto's ironic humour does come across in the translation. In the first canto, Rinaldo and Ferraú, rivals for Angelica, fight fast and furious until it dawns on them that meanwhile she has slipped away; whereupon they suddenly make 'a sound and friendly league', and after Ariosto has extolled the 'gran bontà de cavallieri antiqui', a trot on amicably together. There is a wide gap between this episode, with its accompanying tone of irony, and that of comparable episodes in *The Faerie Queene*. Spenser takes chivalric activities seriously. Ariosto has seen through them. Yet he has not lost all faith in chivalric ideals. He is like Shakespeare's Rosalind in that his disillusion with the ways of men and of love has left virtually intact his capacity for romantic feeling. The enchantment is still there, as it is with Spenser. And so Gottfried's wish to provide not only a big sample of Ariosto's poem but suitable background reading for students of Spenser is reasonable. *Orlando Furioso*, as the chief and most influential Italian chivalric romance of the sixteenth century, is important to the understanding of *The Faerie Queene*. Harington, very much in harmony with the reading habits of his time, was inclined to take it as allegory. Hence Ariosto's allegory, real or supposed, as well as his structure, that of the episodic romance, probably influenced Spenser. Ariosto's 'noble Bradamant' is not unlike Spenser's Britomart. And his poetry, even in Harington's translation, is often reminiscent of Spenser's: knights 'As lions meet or bulls in pastures green', and 'Like as two mastiff dogs with hungry maws' they get to grips with each other. This is an attractive book, well introduced and presented, with useful, unobtrusive annotation.

Michael Drayton figures in Elizabeth Donno's anthology reviewed above (see note 23), and is the subject of two valuable articles by Anthony LaBranche. 'Drayton's *The Barons Warres* and the Rhetoric of Historical Poetry' (*JEGP*) surveys his historical poems, showing that his 'progress is, first, toward a conscientious and factual handling of historical material and, second, toward a discovery of the kind of rhetoric which will present this material most cogently'. The comments on Lucan's rhetorical influence in the passages where Drayton wishes to convey 'martial excitement' are particularly illuminating. In 'The "Twofold Vitality" of Drayton's Odes' (*CL*), LaBranche focuses on the balance of native and classical elements. He affords the odes a careful analysis, comparing them with those of Horace, Ronsard, and others, and concludes that Drayton is no pedantic imitator of the ancient form, but a vigorous and original contributor to the ode tradition.

Warren R. Maurer (*CL*) discerns a 'curious similarity' between the lives and works of Robert Southwell and the German Jesuit missionary Friedrich von Spee. Spee was thirty years Southwell's junior, but the similarities are not explicable in terms of Southwell's influence, being rather the 'product of a very similar religious and literary environment'. Thus both write 'patently didactic' poems, influenced by the art of meditation, dealing with the same religious themes, and alike enriched with nature images. Southwell is one of the three religious poets (the others are Constable and Alabaster) studied by Toshihiko Kawasaki (*Studies in English Literature:* Tokyo). These poets all have claims to be considered forerunners of Donne and the metaphysical school. Southwell's religious 'parodies' (i.e. religious poems using secular conceits) do,

Kawasaki thinks, inaugurate a new kind of devotional verse. Alabaster, not the comparatively naïve Constable, represents the intermediate stage between Southwell and Donne. Helen White's book reviewed above (see note 8) also contains a useful investigation of Southwell's importance as a religious poet.

There have been several editions of Richard Barnfield's poems within the last century, but never, till this year, a book on his life and work. Indeed, Grosart's introduction to his edition (1876) has provided the only account of any length, and, valuable though it is, it needs correction. Harry Morris's book[25] now makes certain corrections, and, in general, fills a literary gap. He deals at length with *The Affectionate Shepheard* (1594), *Cynthia* (1595), and *The Encomion of Lady Pecunia* (1598), all three certainly Barnfield's work, before turning to *Greenes Funeralls* (*c.* 1594), which he claims tentatively for Barnfield, and then to other 'doubtful' works, most of which he dismisses from the canon. He tackles many other problems. He would support Abraham Fraunce's claim to be Barnfield's 'Amyntas' in place of the usual candidate Thomas Watson, and elaborates the theory that Fraunce introduced the young Barnfield to the Countess of Pembroke's literary circle. But perhaps his most useful work is in elucidating Barnfield's sources. There is scarcely an Elizabethan pastoralist on whom he does not draw, but the chief debt is to Spenser. In fact Morris's main thesis is that Barnfield is 'Colin's child', Spenser's first and chief imitator, rivalled, as such, only by Drayton. On the other hand, he defends him on the charge of derivativeness. 'Still his own unique talent

[25] *Richard Barnfield, Colin's Child*, by Harry Morris. Florida State University Studies: No. 38. pp. xiii+203. $5.

made all his volumes uniquely his own.' This is perhaps best shown in *Lady Pecunia*, a mock encomium in the tradition of *Virgil's Gnat*, and yet 'novel' and 'sprightly' in its way. Again, there is the perfectly controlled lyric 'Nights were short' to convince us of Barnfield's powers. Still, Morris does not hesitate to criticize elsewhere, finding that Barnfield, though ready enough to embark on a literary project, often flags. He is a minor poet, worth scholarly attention at not too frequent intervals. Morris's book, considered as literary criticism, is not very stimulating, but it contains valuable literary history, and material which would prove essential to a future editor of Barnfield's poems.

The remaining contributions to the year's work on minor poets and poetry are as follows. Stanley R. Maveety (*SP*) describes Gascoigne's versification in *The Steele Glas* (1576), which, though providing the first example of original non-dramatic blank verse in English, is not in other respects of the metrical *avant garde*. P. J. Finkelpearl (*NQ*) finds a possible cause for Sir John Davies's notorious attack on Richard Martin in the Middle Temple Hall: the Christmas revels of 1597, in which Martin took part, contain mockery of one who, like Davies, had a 'straddling' gait. Richard E. Quaintance, Jr., (*NQ*) suggests that Greene's lyric 'What thing is Loue' in *Menaphon* derives from Saint-Gelais's 'Description d'Amour'. Walter F. Staton, Jr., (*NQ*) supports Thomas Watson's claim to the authorship of the lyric 'Aurora now' in *The Phoenix Nest*. Continuing his researches into manuscript material at the Rosenbach Foundation Museum, James L. Sanderson provides a note in *MLR* on three unpublished wedding poems written for the wedding of Elizabeth Vere and the sixth Earl of Derby in

1595; and in *NQ* he reports on an unprinted and unique text of 'A libell against some Grayes Inn gentlemen and Reuellers'. John Durkan (*Bibliotheck*) lists and describes the Latin verses of the Scot Andrew Leech, considering also the possibility that they provided a source for Milton's *Lycidas*. A careful, detailed account of what is known of the portraits of a more famous Scottish author, George Buchanan, is supplied by J. K. Cameron (*Scottish Historical Review*). Gustav Cross's notes (*NQ*) on Marston's vocabulary draw to a close this year. John J. McAleer's 'Ballads of the Spanish Armada' (*TSLL*) appeared in 1962, and provided a discussion of the four which have survived of the twenty-eight listed in the Stationer's Register.

Familiar and unfamiliar names figure in this year's work on Elizabethan prose translation. The Centaur Press edition, by Paul Turner, of sixteen of Plutarch's *Lives*[26] in the translation by Sir Thomas North is an object of great beauty and high price. It is, indeed, a pity that the publishers did not undertake all fifty lives while they were about it, though this would doubtless have proved too formidable for the general reader, for whom, primarily, the present publication caters. Plutarch is certainly worth the attention of readers all and sundry. The editor's claim that he should appeal as strongly to the twentieth as he did to the sixteenth century contains truth. North's English gives an added delight. For, for all his misunderstandings of Amyot's French version (which was his source), and for all his failures in logic, North was, as Turner points out, 'imaginatively

---

[26] *Selected Lives from the Lives of the Noble Grecians and Romans*, ed. by Paul Turner. Centaur Press. 2 vols. Vol. I: pp. xxxii+338. Vol. II: pp. xlix+231. £8. 8s.

aware of narrative content'. Though its selectiveness will inevitably limit the academic uses of this book, Turner's editorial work offers compensation. He includes the lives which provided sources for Shakespeare's Roman plays and *Timon of Athens*, a glossary of Elizabethan terms, and notes explaining historical and mythological allusions, the relation of North's phrasing to Plutarch's and Amyot's, etc. Students of Shakespeare's sources and of Elizabethan translation will find some material here.

Thomas Blundeville, though less famous and less colourful than North, was nevertheless a very competent and far from dull translator. His translation of Furió Ceriol's *El concejo i consejeros del principe*, an important Spanish political treatise of the sixteenth century, was done from an Italian version, and published, with a dedication to the Earl of Leicester, in 1570. This work is now republished under the title *Of Councils and Counselors*[27] in the Scholars' Facsimiles and Reprints series, already known for the excellence and clarity of its reproductions of old and inaccessible texts. It is of interest both as a translation and as a sample of Renaissance political thinking. Blundeville handles his original freely, making what appear to be purposeful cuts. Thus, evidently disliking repetition, he 'thinks good to reduce' nine of Ceriol's points to six. His prose likewise is economical, and for that and other reasons more readable than the prose of some of his contemporaries. Presumably Blundeville believed that his patron, a man pre-eminent among Elizabeth's coun-

sellors, would find a practical use for this treatise on the art of government. It tells how 'the Prince that wil gouerne well, ought to haue seauen counsels, differing one from another in offices, officers, and in authoritie' (e.g., one group deals with finance, another with defence, another with the law, and so on). It also gives advice on the choice of counsellors, the qualities to look for; this section, though it contains some trifling comment on the importance of good looks, a 'playne and smooth' nose etc., is sensible enough and historically interesting.

Thomas Lodge's translation of Seneca's *De beneficiis* and other moral essays, and of Justus Lipsius's *Life of Seneca*, receive a comment from Karl Sørensen (*Archiv*, 1962).

Dale B. J. Randall[28] surveys non-chivalric Spanish fiction in English translation during the period 1543–1657, and amongst the forty-odd works he discusses are a number of important Elizabethan ones, such as David Rowland's version (1576) of the anonymous picaresque story *Lazarillo de Tormes* and Bartholomew Yong's (1598) of Montemayor's pastoral romance *Diana*. Randall agrees up to a point with J. G. Underhill's opinion that the dissemination of Spanish books in England was dependent on the course of politics. But he would qualify it: a *Lazarillo* could find readers even when interest in Spain was at a low ebb. Certainly knowledge of the Spanish language was regarded as important by the end of the sixteenth century, and at that time 'England's concern with Spain was both courtly and literary, though

---

[27] *Of Councils and Counselors*, by Thomas Blundeville. A facsimile reproduction with an introduction by Karl-Ludwig Selig. Scholars' Facsimiles and Reprints. pp. xi+140. $6.

[28] *The Golden Tapestry: A Critical Survey of Non-chivalric Spanish Fiction in English Translation (1543–1657)*, by Dale B. J. Randall. Duke U.P. and C.U.P. pp. viii +262. 70s.

it was also practical, political, commercial and religious'. This carefully documented book is mainly for specialists. It serves as a useful introduction to the work on original English prose fiction.

Margaret Schlauch's *Antecedents of the English Novel 1400–1600*[29] covers a great deal of English fiction (mainly prose), as well as the classical and continental influences upon it, from Chaucer to Deloney. Ernest Baker, who devoted the first volume of his *History of the English Novel* (1924) to roughly the same period, saw it primarily as the 'Age of Romance', overlooking much work which had to do with ordinary life and which, because of that, points forward to the age, starting with Defoe, of the novel proper. This gap is filled, and the old ground resurveyed, in the new book under discussion. *Gawaine*, *Troilus and Criseyde*, the medieval *exempla* and fabliaux, the *Morte d'Arthur*, Caxton's publications, and other early fictions are given due weight. Then, with the sixteenth century, come the jest-books, the 'miniature stories' embedded in the social pamphlets of Awdelay, Harman, and Greene, the picaresque *Long Meg*, and a whole crop of romances deriving from Boccaccio, Bandello, and Belleforest; William Painter's *Palace of Pleasure* (1566), Geoffrey Fenton's *Certaine Tragicall Discourses* (1567), and Barnaby Rich's *Farewell to Military Profession* (1581) are notable collections. The 'framed' *novelle* approximate more closely to the later novel: a hitherto unnoticed example is *A Courtlie Controversie of Cupids Cautels* (1578), while *The Cobler of Canterburie* (1590), embodying the

tales of a group aboard a Thames barge, earns attention as a 'minor masterpiece'. Turning to the later romances, Miss Schlauch notes, as a rather curious phenomenon, the popularity of these archaic, aristocratic tales with the rising mercantile classes: Anthony Munday was an author who met this reactionary demand. The neo-Hellenic romances of both the Arcadian and the Euphuistic schools are naturally given full treatment. Sidney's *Arcadia*, 'the pioneer English experiment in combining pastoral with chivalric adventure in a complicated plot', is 'a consummate work of its kind', but it has 'less kinship with the modern novel than some of the late French prose romances which Caxton had put into robust English back in the 15th century'. Lyly's and Greene's purely euphuistic novels are perhaps less interesting than those by Lodge and Chettle which 'alternated euphuistic mannerism with a certain kind of social satire'. In the penultimate chapter, called 'Towards the Forms of Modern Fiction', there is, besides accounts of the picaresque style of Nashe's *Unfortunate Traveller* and Breton's *Mavillia*, and of Deloney's pseudo-historical tales of tradesmen and craftsmen, an interesting section on Gabriel Harvey's *A Nobleman's Suit to a Country Maid* (a *Pamela*-type of story), and George Gascoigne's *The Adventures of Master F. J.* (not unlike a Jamesian house-party story). Though these two fictions stand apart from the main Elizabethan lines of development, they 'show marks of genius far beyond the ordinary' and 'clearly anticipate certain aspects of the modern novel'.

An edition of Anthony Munday's incomplete novel *Zelauto* (1580) is, in any event, welcome, for the original is a great rarity and has inevitably

[29] *Antecedents of the English Novel, 1400–1600*, by Margaret Schlauch. Warsawa PWN and O.U.P. pp. viii+264. 25s.

suffered neglect from literary historians. Jack Stillinger's edition,[30] based on the unique copy in the Bodleian, and equipped with a useful introduction, is doubly welcome because it is a good job. The book, which is well printed, will adorn the shelves of university libraries. There is no call, of course, to regard *Zelauto* as an unrecognized classic. But for many reasons it was worth resurrecting. It is an early example of Elizabethan prose fiction, and at least as good as its four or five predecessors. The chief of these was *Euphues*. Munday, like Lyly, was a protégé of the Earl of Oxford, and it seems likely that he attempted to cash in on the success of Lyly's novel. Yet the label euphuistic does not account for everything in *Zelauto*, which, as Stillinger points out, is also indebted to chivalric romance, the *novella*, and the jest-book. Its prose is less artful and more racy than that of *Euphues*. It has more action: the lively version of the flesh-bond story in Part III may have influenced *The Merchant of Venice*. Again, the plan of *Zelauto* is more ambitious than that of any work of English prose fiction before *Arcadia*. It is distinctly Elizabethan, and hence bears but little resemblance to the modern novel. Thus the characterization is minimal, the dialogues are elaborately phrased and formal, the opportunities to include lyrics or eulogies (of England and Elizabeth) are not missed. Munday says that it was 'delightfull to me in the writing', but, perhaps because *Zelauto* was not an immediate success in 1580, he did not turn to the task of finishing it, or to a similar work. Celeste Turner Wright (*PQ*) continues her researches into Munday's life, and, amongst other things, identifies him with 'Lazarus Pyott'.

Jaroslav Hornát is providing an account of the development in Greene's narrative art within the euphuistic framework which, as early as *Mamillia*, he had adopted. His '*Mamillia*: Robert Greene's Controversy with *Euphues*' (*Philologica Pragensia*) appeared in 1962. This year's article (*Philologica Pragensia*) is on *The Carde of Fancie* and *Pandosto*, which followed *Mamillia*. In the *Carde* euphuism is still found in the love confessions, the conversations, the letters, the theme of education, and the symmetrical structure. The influence of Greek romances has, however, cut across the euphuistic influence, and Greene likewise shows signs of opposing Lyly's misogyny. With *Pandosto* he breaks yet a little more with euphuism, no longer planning his story on a symmetrical scheme, working out his narrative on a much broader scale, and again drawing on the Greek romances as well as (possibly) on certain actual historical events of fourteenth-century Poland and Bohemia. In spite of all this, Hornát's closely reasoned statement concludes that '*Pandosto* still remains an "euphuistic novel" with all its essential artistic limitations'. Greene's vocabulary is briefly handled by James S. Dean, Jr., in a note (*NQ*) antedating words recorded in *O.E.D.* from *Euphues his Censure to Philautus* and *Philomela*.

The important work on Nashe this year has been biographical. In a substantial article in *RES*, C. G. Harlow first makes a slight alteration to McKerrow's dating of Nashe's visit to the Isle of Wight. He shifts it about a year forward, to December–February 1593–4, and this enables him to revise the chronology of Nashe's life and works, as well as to show him in an 'almost respectable' light. (During

---

[30] *Zelauto: The Fountaine of Fame*, by Anthony Munday. Ed. by Jack Stillinger. Southern Illinois U.P. pp. xxix+204. $10.

the period 1592–4 he was only once in trouble, instead of three times, as has been supposed). Harlow also provides a note (*NQ*) on the identity of Richard Clarke, 'the Counsel Table Asse', to whom Nashe compares his opponent Gabriel Harvey in *Strange News*; he was probably a 'servant' of the Privy Council. *The Hospitall of Incurable Fooles*, a translation from Italian published by Edward Blount in 1600, has been doubtfully attributed to Nashe; William E. Miller (*SB*) thinks there is no case and prefers the possibility, suggested by Sidney Lee, that Blount himself was the author. This opportunity may be taken to correct the misleading slip by which Nashe's prose pamphlet *Christ's Tears over Jerusalem* was referred to as a poem in last year's *YW* (xliii. 160).

The anonymous treatise *The Sceptic*, attributed to Raleigh, is considered by S. E. Sprott (*PQ*). He first studies and compares the various manuscripts, of which there appear to be at least two 'families'. Then he assembles evidence to show that this work was written with reference to an Elizabethan translation of Sextus Empiricus, a translation evidently also known to Nashe and Samuel Rowlands. Raleigh as geographer is dealt with by R. A. Skelton (*The Virginia Magazine of History and Biography*). He discusses, among other things, the *Discoverie of Guiana*, Raleigh's 'major attempt at descriptive or regional geography', a work which 'reveals his sensitivity to climate and natural conditions and his ability to characterize landscape'.

Hakluyt's editing of Giles Fletcher's *Of the Russe Common Wealth*, which he used for the *Principal Navigations*, is described by Robert O. Lindsay (*PBSA*). Evidently he expurgated references to Russian tyranny and cruelty, perhaps in order to avoid prejudicing amicable Anglo-Russian relations. But he was not consistent in doing so, and the study of his method here does nothing to enhance his 'much-praised reputation as a competent and objective editor'.

Some of the first technical writings for English sailors are edited by E. G. R. Taylor.[31] They are the work of William Bourne (*c*. 1535–82), an innkeeper of Gravesend, a self-educated man, with a fresh, empirical, and unbookish approach to navigation. In his day, Spanish and Portuguese pilots were already making use of mathematics and astronomy, of charts and instruments for measuring the height of sun or star. Meanwhile the English still felt their way around the seas with the aid of lead, line, compass, and such landmarks as were in sight. Bourne perceived the need for professional instruction in the 'new navigation' for simple men, those to whom astronomy and mathematics, the preserve of gentlemen and scholars, remained a closed book. He therefore produced a series of useful technical manuals, of which *A Regiment for the Sea* (1574) was the most important, and, earning many reprintings, the most successful: 'I haue written this base and simple Regiment for the Sea, and Rules of Nauigation, for that I knowe it to be so needefull and necessarie for all sortes of Sea men.' Its practical bias is at once apparent. For example, Bourne tells the seaman not only how to measure the height of the sun with a cross staff but how to avoid hurting his eyes in the process. His style is in accordance with his character and purpose, plain, even blunt.

Florio's borrowings from Anton Francesco Doni, the sixteenth-century

[31] *A Regiment for the Sea and other Writings on Navigation*, by William Bourne. Ed. by E. G. R. Taylor. C.U.P. for the Hakluyt Society. pp. xxxv + 464. £2. 10*s*.

Italian author, are noted for the first time and illustrated in detail by D. G. Rees (*CL*). His 'lexical idiom' receives close attention from James L. Rosier (*ES*).

F. P. Wilson (*NQ*) comments on the passage in William Lambarde's *Perambulation of Kent* (1576) in which he refers to the 'Bell Sauage' Inn as a place for 'Fence playe'. E. K.

Chambers said that this did not appear in the first edition. But it does, and this must be one of the first references to the use of the inn for the purpose described.

Arthur E. Barker reviews recent books and articles on Renaissance literature in *SEL*, while F. W. Bateson's 'Work in Progress' (*EC*) surveys present attitudes to the period.

X

The Earlier Stuart and the Commonwealth Period, excluding Drama

AGNES M. C. LATHAM

A GOOD introduction to the period is A. G. H. Bachrach's account of the experiences of Constantine Huygens in the England of King James.[1] It is based on original documents in Dutch, English, French, and Latin, with the intention of illuminating Anglo-Dutch cultural relations. Bachrach is both widely and deeply read in the period. He has a lively historical imagination and is quick to grasp analogies with modern times. His picture of the Court of King James, into which the democratic young Dutchman was plunged, can hardly be bettered. It ends with the dry comment that 'to guide and control the English Court . . . required more strength and patience than was the common share of man. James's share of these qualities was rather less.'

Robert Donington has written, in a lucid and sensitive style, a very solid, learned, and technical work on baroque music from Monteverdi to J. S. Bach.[2] His aim is to help modern performers to understand and do justice to it. He quotes from the writings of early authorities, which he describes as unsystematic but faithful to the human situation. It is possible to deduce, from the diversity of opinion, certain tacit assumptions and habitual attitudes. English music, he contends, was markedly individual and strong throughout the seventeenth century, down to the time of Purcell. In the earlier periods much embellishment was left to the discretion of the performer. The fact that ornamental passages were not written out in full and that there were not many marks of expression does not mean that ornament and expression were lacking, but that a high value was placed on spontaneity. Ornament so excessive as to obscure the words was recognized as a fault, especially in a religious service. The solo songs of the English lutanists were embellished freely in performance, the singer 'reconciling the complementary requirements of passion and of serenity'.

A selection of musical settings of the period has been recently transcribed, for the most part from manuscripts, and adapted by André Souris.[3]

William R. Keast's collection of modern essays on metaphysical poetry and on particular poets from Donne to Dryden, reprints twenty-

---

[1] *Sir Constantine Huygens and Britain 1596–1687*, by A. G. H. Bachrach. Volume I, 1596–1619. O.U.P. and Leiden: Sir Thomas Browne Institute, 1962. pp. xii+238.

[2] *The Interpretation of Early Music*, by Robert Donington. Faber & Faber. pp. 605. £6 6s.

[3] *Poèmes de Donne, Herbert et Crashaw, mis en musique par leurs contemporains.* Transcription et Realisation par André Souris, d'après des recherches effectués sur les sources par John Cutts. Introduction par Jean Jacquot. Editions du Centre National de la Recherche Scientifique. Paris, 1961. pp. xix+26. 12 NF.

seven pieces.[4] They cover forty years of criticism, from Grierson in 1921 to Gardner in 1961. Inevitably the ungrateful reader asks for more and other names. Where are Rosemond Tuve and A. J. Smith? Something on Vaughan and surely something on Cowley? But it is a rich sheaf, and the constituent essays are chosen with discretion to illustrate different possible approaches. Milton is missing because he is later to have a volume to himself.

K. G. Hamilton has written a book on Renaissance poetics[5] to explain how Dryden, at the end of the seventeenth century, could hesitate whether to use poetry or prose, as though these were alternative ways of setting out the same matter. No major change came in with Donne, however fresh he may seem, or with Milton. Poetry was still thought of as a branch of rhetoric. But it could not be so classed much longer, since the scientists were turning prose to strictly utilitarian ends. Poetry began to be dismissed as no more than ornamental language, a valuation from which it was rescued by the Romantic poets with a new stress upon the primacy of the imagination. It seems unlikely that it will ever again have the same relation to prose that it has as a matter of course throughout the seventeenth century. This makes it hard for a present-day student to see what the earlier poets were at. Hamilton is a very intelligent writer, widely acquainted with poetic theory from Aristotle onwards, and he supplies much cud for chewing.

Maren-Sofie Røstvig traces the influence upon the poetry of the seventeenth century of Horace and Virgil and the classical ideal of the happy countryman.[6] A mass of translation, imitation, and original verse was devoted to this subject, succeeding generations adapting it to their own needs and fantasies. She distinguishes four main periods. The stoic ideal of the contemplative man, reflected in such poets as Milton, was followed by the introduction of neo-platonic, hermetic, and religious ideas, which in poets like Marvell and Vaughan led to a special value set upon *res creatae* as divine hieroglyphs, and to ecstatic descriptions of an earthly paradise with a profoundly spiritual significance. At the Restoration, good sense and less rigorous moral standards provoked a veering alike from the ascetic and the esoteric to an epicurean pleasure in country life, conceived of as a state of gentlemanly ease, which lets the world go by. The end of the century, however, saw the ideal of retirement beginning to take on a moral significance again. Particular attention is paid to Marvell and to Cowley, while at the same time a host of minor poets are called to give evidence. There is a valuable account of the admired neo-Latin verse of Casimire Sarbiewski, which strongly influenced English writers. Seventeenth-century poets drew much of their inspiration from the books they read. That is one reason why it is possible to trace in detail the combinations and transmutations of a literary and philosophical theme. At the same time the turmoil of the Civil War gave an often pressingly personal meaning to poems about security and repose. The classical *beatus vir* became for the royalists an antithesis to

[4] *Seventeenth-Century English Poetry. Modern Essays in Criticism*, ed. by William R. Keast. O.U.P., 1962. (A Galaxy Book.) pp. 434. Paperback 15s. $2.25.

[5] *The Two Harmonies: Poetry and Prose in the Seventeenth Century*, by K. G. Hamilton. O.U.P. pp. 218. 32s. 6d.

[6] *The Happy Man: Studies in the Metamorphosis of a Classical Ideal*, by Maren-Sofie Røstvig. Volume I 1600–1700. Norwegian U.P. Oslo Studies in English. (2nd. ed. 1962). pp. 346. 35s. Kr.35.

the Puritan archetype of the wayfaring and warfaring Christian.

J. C. Arens, in 'Sarbiewski's Ode against Tears imitated by Lovelace, Yalden and Watts' (N), quotes the Latin original, which he thinks had a particular appeal to the English, in that it bids the mourner suppress indulgent tears. He prints beside it translations by Lovelace, Yalden, and Watts.

Edmund Blunden and Bernard Mellor have made a collection of unfamiliar poems by minor poets, and by ladies and gentlemen who wrote for their private pleasure.[7] Sources in early nineteenth-century collections, such as Clifford's *Tixall Poetry* and Brydges's *Restituta*, suggest that there was a lively appreciation at that time of the charm and interest inherent in such verses.

The Stuart Editions, a new series under the general editorship of J. Max Patrick, will make several appearances in this chapter. Patrick has based a text of Herrick mainly upon the first edition of *Hesperides*, very slightly modernized and emended, with explanatory footnotes, more needful than one might at first think for Herrick.[8] Poems from manuscript have received more editing, and some fresh manuscript readings are recorded. The introduction calls attention to Herrick's extremely wide range and the multiple sensibility he demands from his readers. William O. Harris, in 'Herrick's "Upon Julia's Clothes"' (*Ex*), thinks we are too ready to assume that Herrick is concerned

entirely with a visual experience. He begins by *hearing* the flow of Julia's clothes before he sees their glittering.

William B. Hunter, Jr., edits Ben Jonson's poems for the Stuart Editions.[9] He includes all Jonson's known verse (except his plays), together with some of the original music to which the songs were set. He follows the earliest editions, and prints variants from manuscripts and texts before 1700. Paul M. Cubeta writes on 'A Jonsonian Ideal: *To Penshurst*' (*PQ*), showing how even outside his plays Jonson was a moralist and social reformer, whose manner was to establish an ideal in sharp contrast to the reality of the world he lived in. Unlike Martial, who contrasts a trim, unproductive town garden with a real farm, untidy and flourishing, Jonson makes everything about Penshurst fertile, and orderly, too, and the very fruit hangs 'where every child may reach'. In 'Ben Jonson's Religious Lyrics' (*JEGP*), Cubeta traces the influence of the conventional Catholic devotional exercise on Jonson's moderately pitched, quietly confident religious lyrics. Peter Steese, in 'Jonson's *A Song*' (*Ex*), sees this 'inhumanly frigid lyric' as based on the Aristotelian doctrine of the mean. In 'The *Epitaph on Elizabeth, L.H.* and Ben Jonson's Style' (*JEGP*), Howard S. Babb calls attention to the enigmatic ending of the poem, and praises the 'spareness' and 'stark gravity' of Jonson.

L. A. Beaurline describes 'An Editorial Experiment: Suckling's *A Sessions of the Poets*' (*SB*). He thinks that editors of seventeenth-century poetry have had too much faith in early printed texts and too little in

---

[7] *Wayside Poems of the Seventeenth Century*. An Anthology gathered by Edmund Blunden and Bernard Mellor. O.U.P. and Hong Kong U.P. pp. xiv+138. 21s. $3.

[8] *The Complete Poetry of Robert Herrick*, ed. with an Introduction and Notes by J. Max Patrick. New York U.P. The Stuart Editions. Published first in paperback in the Doubleday-Anchor Seventeenth Century Series. pp. xvi+579. $7.50.

[9] *The Complete Poetry of Ben Jonson*, ed. with an Introduction, Notes, and Variants by William B. Hunter, Jr. New York U.P. The Stuart Editions. Published first in paperback in the Doubleday-Anchor Seventeenth Century Series. pp. 494. $7.50.

manuscripts. In '"Why So Pale and Wan"': An Essay in Critical Method' (*TSLL*), Beaurline seeks a 'language to discuss simplicity'.

Paul Grant Stanwood's 'St. Teresa and Joseph Beaumont's *Psyche*' (*JEGP*), is an account of what is probably the longest poem in English. Though St. Teresa is never mentioned in it, it is devoted, amongst other things, to understanding her mystical experiences.

Pauline Palmer, in 'Carew: An Unnoticed Allusion to Davenant's Illegitimacy' (*NQ*), reads the final couplet of Carew's commendatory poem upon Davenant's *Madagascar* as a reference to his supposed descent from Shakespeare, in which he was known to take pride.

Allan Pritchard has a good deal to say about Wither. In *MP* he prints from a Bodleian manuscript 'An Unpublished Poem by George Wither', addressed by Wither to Charles I as Prince of Wales, in the belief that the Prince had interceded for him with the King when he was imprisoned in 1621. As a Puritan and a Parliamentarian Wither preferred not to print it. In '*Abuses Stript and Whipt* and Wither's Imprisonment' (*RES*), Pritchard suggests that Wither's satire hid an attack on the Roman Catholic Henry Howard, Earl of Northampton, and his pro-Spanish policy. In 'A Manuscript of George Wither's Psalms' (*HLQ*), he gives an account of the care Wither took with his metrical psalms, and surmises that he laid them aside because he found King James was similarly employed upon versions to replace Sternhold and Hopkins. Ultimately Wither had a patent from King James whereby his *Hymns and Songs of the Church* were to be inserted in all bound metrical psalters, but it availed him little against the opposition of the Stationers' Company. In 'George Wither's Quarrel with the Stationers: An Anonymous Reply to *The Schollers Purgatory*' (*SB*), Pritchard prints a transcript of a letter giving the Stationers' point of view and making it clear that they expected a lion's share of any profits. Authors are 'too Mercenary' if they write for money. Wither has one's sympathy.

Discussions of John Donne, edited by Frank Kermode,[10] brings together a stimulating collection of critical opinions on Donne, beginning with Jonson, and including a number of comments by nineteenth-century critics, some as well known as Coleridge and De Quincey, others anonymous contributors to reviews of the period, and one not hitherto noticed at all, writing in *The Working Man's Friend* (1851). We have not the monopoly we may think we have in Donne. Valuable modern essays come from Edgar H. Duncan on 'Donne's Alchemical Figures', S. L. Bethell on 'The Nature of Metaphysical Wit', and A. J. Smith on 'The Metaphysic of Love'. These are not necessarily better than others better known, but they have not till now been easily available.

Kay Davis supplies to *NQ* 'Unpublished Coleridge Marginalia in a Volume of John Donne's Poetry'. F. M. Kuna, in 'T. S. Eliot's Dissociation of Sensibility and the Critics of Metaphysical Poetry' (*EC*), warns against the application of modern poetic theory to the seventeenth century. Thomas O. Sloan, in 'The Rhetoric in the Poetry of John Donne' (*SEL*), shows the value of analysing Donne's poems by means of a specific Renaissance rhetorical theory. His choice of Ramism for his demonstration does not mean that he

---

[10] *Discussions of John Donne*, ed. with an Introduction by Frank Kermode. Boston: D. C. Heath. pp. ix+160.

thinks Donne was preponderantly a Ramist.

In 'Donne's Conceit and Petrarchan Wit' (*PMLA*), Donald L. Guss claims that Donne's wit derives from the *presecentisti*, Serafino, Tasso, and Guarini, who 'adapt Petrarchanism to a world like that of Restoration drama'. Donne is thus both Petrarchan and anti-Petrarchan. He comes at the end of three centuries of progressive secularizing of the *dolce stil nuovo*. In 'Donne and the Greek Anthology' (*NQ*), Guss notes some parallel conceits, which probably came to Donne indirectly, after being absorbed into Renaissance literature. In 'Elizabethan Wit in Metaphor and Conceit: Sidney, Shakespeare, Donne' (*EM*), T. N. Marsh finds a resemblance between Sidney's ironic verses on Mopsa and Donne's Second Elegy, and between a prose image from *Arcadia* of blood filling the 'wrinkles of the sea's visage' and one of Donne's *Holy Sonnets*.

N. J. C. Andreasen considers 'Theme and Structure in Donne's *Satyres*' (*SEL*), claiming for them 'considerable intrinsic literary merit'. They are inter-related. The speaker is always the same person, a retiring, idealistic scholar, shocked at what he meets when he walks abroad, a skilled debater using ridicule rather than anger against worldlings. Some readers are repelled by ugly descriptions of vice, but these are accompanied by an affirmation of true values, and the lessons are driven home by 'a rollicking *jeu d'esprit* which the reader can hardly fail to find delightful'. Niall Rudd writes to *TLS*, 22 March, comparing Donne's *Fourth Satire* with Horace, Juvenal, and Cicero. P. J. Finkelpearl, in 'Donne and Everard Gilpin: Additions, Corrections, and Conjectures' (*RES*), denies that there are grounds for identifying some figures in Gilpin's satires with Donne,

but thinks Gilpin had Donne in mind when he wrote, 'folles doe sit/More honored then the *Prester John* of wit'.

Albert Gérard, in a paper contributed to *Publications de l'Université de l'Etat à Elisabethville* (1961), tussles with 'The Extasie'. He sees a deadlock resolved in the common form of a scholastic argument, but where many critics assume that Donne is content with his conclusion that man is a complex of soul and body, Gérard believes that he would have preferred it otherwise. The body is an *alloy* and the soul *descends* to sense. Donne must regretfully acquiesce in 'the unescapable conditions of human passion'. The emphasis at the end upon 'see . . . small change' is in contradistinction to the immense invisible change, the growth in self-awareness. M. K. Paffard, in 'Donne's *The Extasie*, 57–60, 68' (*Ex*), thinks there is a reference to the incarnation in the demand that love take a body, with a pun on air/heir. The 'great Prince in prison' is a child to be born to the lovers, and also a continuation of the incarnation idea.

John Freccero, in 'Donne's "Valediction: Forbidding Mourning"' (*ELH*), supplies an elaborate analysis of the poem. Donne, he says, set about 'rescuing human love from both the angelic mysticism and the erotic formalism of the Italian tradition and restoring it to its proper domain: humanity'. He examines the compass image at great length and with curious learning. The compass executes two movements, along a radius and back to the centre, and round the circumference. This ultimately implies a spiral, an accepted Platonic symbol for humanity as distinguished from angel and beast, and also the path of the planets as distinguished from the fixed stars and sublunary matter.

Arthur K. Moore sees a possible connexion between 'Donne's "Love's

Deitie" and *De Planctu Naturae*
(*PQ*). Laurence Perrine, in 'Donne's
Lecture Upon the Shadow' (*Ex*),
rejects the interpretation of the poem
as an address to a wife in middle age.
The morning shadows are not decep-
tions which the lovers practise upon
one another, but are intended to con-
ceal their love, which may be licit or
illicit, from outsiders.

John E. Parish supplies comments
upon Donne's *Holy Sonnets*. In *Ex* he
calls attention to the blatantly falla-
cious argument of Sonnet XIII, that
Christ must be pitiful because He is
beautiful, and thinks Donne is deliberately offering an example of a
meditation inadequately devout. In
CE, Parish emphasizes the unity of
Sonnet XIV, in which Donne invokes
'three-person'd God' because he
wants Him to use all His strength, and
not with the intention of analysing
the separate functions of the three
Persons. The poem effectively combines two traditional metaphors, the
moral concept of the body as a be-
leaguered city and the love-conceit of
laying siege to a lady's heart.

Frank Manley has produced an
edition of Donne's *Anniversaries*,
based on the first editions of 1611 and
1612, with an excellent critical apparatus.[11] Fifty introductory pages give
the facts about the poems, clearing
Donne of the imputation of flattering
a girl unknown to him for the sake of
her father's money, and thereafter
attempting to illuminate their meaning by examining the tradition of
Wisdom in the Renaissance. Manley
handles Plato's Aphrodite Urania,
the Hebrew Shekinah, the Christian
sapientia creata, Boehme's 'Virgin
Sophia', and Dante's Beatrice. The
First Anniversary is described as

exploring the limits of reason or
scientia. It is a purgative process,
preparing for the *Second Anniversary*
in which the soul has regained lost
Wisdom, or 'the right valuation of
this world, and of the next'. Not
every one will care for the word
'vague' used so often of Donne.
Manley claims that 'the only way to
understand the *Anniversaries* is in-
tuitively, through symbolic understanding'. George Williamson, considering 'The Design of Donne's
Anniversaries' (*MP*), thinks that any
resemblance to Jesuit meditative
techniques must be coincidental.
Donne was not at the time according
to Loyola and the Jesuits much reverence.

Louis L. Martz has edited an
anthology of meditative poetry.[12] To
such familiar names as Herbert,
Vaughan, Quarles, Milton, Crashaw,
Marvell, and Traherne, he has added
Southwell, Alabaster, and Edward
Taylor. Dawson's *Practical Methode
of Meditation* (1614) acts as preface.
A fresh principle of selection, an
explanatory introduction, and the
very generous number of poems by
which contributors are represented
(Herbert tops the list with sixty-eight)
give the book its distinction.

In a brief and admirable introduction to the anonymous *Select Hymns
taken out of Mr. Herbert's Temple*
(*1697*),[13] William E. Stephenson considers the changes which came over
dissenting sentiment and practice in

[11] *John Donne: The Anniversaries*, ed. with
Introduction and Commentary by Frank
Manley. O.U.P. and Johns Hopkins U.P.
pp. vii+209. 40s. $4.95.

[12] *The Meditative Poem.* An Anthology of
Seventeenth-Century Verse, ed. with an
Introduction and Notes by Louis L. Martz.
New York U.P. The Stuart Editions. Pub-
lished first in paperback in the Doubleday-
Anchor Seventeenth Century Series. pp.
xxxii+566. $7.50.

[13] *Select Hymns Taken Out of Mr. Her-
bert's Temple* (*1697*). Introduction by
William E. Stephenson. California U.P.
Augustan Reprint Society (98). William
Andrews Clark Memorial Library. (1962).
pp. vii+48.

the late seventeenth century; first the allowing of hymns at all, then the selection of those which expressed the soul's yearning for heaven, and finally the fashion in 'sublime language', which spread from sermons to hymns, and was the reason why Mason, Watts, and Wesley displaced Herbert. The booklet is reprinted from the only surviving copy, in Dr. Williams' Library.

George Watson discusses 'The Fabric of Herbert's *Temple*' (*JWCI*), in the belief that a poet so 'professionally erudite and technique-conscious' must have arranged his poems in a significant order. R. L. Colie, in '*Logos* in *The Temple*: George Herbert and the Shape of Content' (ibid.), examines the literary complexity behind Herbert's apparent simplicity, with reference to the creating Logos. 'In Herbert's poetry verse and rhyme are notably persistent metaphors for divine creation, for bringing order from chaos, for fitting, for balancing, for satisfying and making content.'

Mary Ellen Rickey, in 'Herbert's Technical Development' (*JEGP*), notes an increased concentration and incisiveness in Herbert's later verse. In 'Parody as a Literary Form: George Herbert and Wilfred Owen' (*EC*), Rosemary Freeman observes that the techniques of parody can be used to evoke other than comic responses. A new attitude can be defined and emphasized by placing old forms in new contexts, thereby revealing some shallowness or inadequacy in older usages. Both Herbert and Owen do this with the formulae of love poetry.

L. C. Martin's splendid edition of Vaughan has been reprinted in the series of Oxford English Texts.[14] This is the second edition of 1957. It includes *The Chymists Key*, which is not in the first edition of 1914.

James D. Simmonds, in 'Henry Vaughan's Amoret and Etesia' (*PQ*), cannot believe that two distinct names were used by the poet for the same woman. He suggests that because Etesia was in fact another woman Vaughan witheld the poems about her until after his wife's death, though they were composed before the poems to Amoret. They complain of 'lingring tortures' and end with a parting, whereas the poems to Amoret are balanced, assured and disinterested, suggesting a spiritual affinity.

A. W. Rudrum's 'Henry Vaughan and the Theme of Transfiguration' (*SR*) claims Vaughan's view of nature, part hermetic and part Christian, as truly mystical. The poem 'Regeneration' is an account of a mystical experience of conversion, which includes a new way of looking at nature. It can be paralleled in Thomas Vaughan's *Lumen de Lumine*. In 'Vaughan's "The Book": Hermetic or Meditative?' (*N*), James D. Simmonds emends the interpretation Rudrum gave in *AUMLA*, 1961. He sees the poem as meditative, and hence subjective and moral, without metaphysical flights. Vaughan's prayer to be allowed a personal part in the transfiguration of the world on the Last Day could be made by any Christian oppressed by mortality, without reference to hermetic 'restitution', and though the poem undoubtedly uses this idea it is not the poet's chief concern.

An intensive examination of Crashaw's poetic technique is almost always rewarding. George Walton Williams[15] has concentrated upon the system of repetitive and interrelated

---

[14] *The Works of Henry Vaughan*, ed. by L. C. Martin. O.U.P. Second ed. 1957, reprinted. pp. xxviii+771. 65s.

[15] *Image and Symbol in the Sacred Poetry of Richard Crashaw*, by George Walton Williams. South Carolina U.P. pp. 151. $5.00.

images which Crashaw used almost as a private language. He reduces them to three main categories: images of quantity, expressive of God's greatness and love and of human littleness, images of colour and light, the red of love and the white of purity, and images of fluidity, varying from floods to water drops. 'The examination of these symbolic significances,' he says, 'will tend to clarify the interweaving of poetry and saintliness and to demonstrate Crashaw's ability to marry a poetic image and a powerful sacred connotation and to make the two live together peaceably, congenially, and in a manner mutually co-operative.'

Cleanth Brooks, in a brilliant essay,[16] offers an explication of Marvell's 'Horatian Ode', in which he demonstrates the fallacy of applying to poetry what are purely historical judgements and of expecting a poem to *say* things, as prose does. Marvell's poem is dramatic. It is 'diagnostic rather than remedial, and eventuates, not in a course of action, but in contemplation'. Its main subject is Cromwell. In a close analysis of his character, it reveals what was great about him, and even what was tragic in his situation as the 'Wars and Fortunes Son'. This does not necessarily mean that Marvell thought Cromwell's actions just or the King's cause indefensible. John M. Wallace's 'Andrew Marvell and Cromwell's Kingship: "The First Anniversary"' (*ELH*), claims the poem as deliberative, an argument that Cromwell should accept the crown and found a new dynasty. Marvell was not indulging in servile flattery but was concerned for his country's future.

In 'Pastoral Form and Idea in Some Poems of Marvell's' (*TSLL*), Harold E. Toliver makes an interesting distinction between poems of 'pastoral success' and of 'pastoral failure'. He shows Marvell using both, sometimes finding himself unable to stay inside the dream, from which he awakens to harsh reality, sometimes using a 'pattern of retreat, discovery of creative capacity, and resurgent control of nature'. Patrick G. Hogan, Jr., offers a reading of 'To His Coy Mistress' based on 'Marvell's "Vegetable Love"' (*SP*). He will not have it considered a *carpe diem* poem. It is a progress from 'vegetable Love' to contact with Oneness. E. E. Phare (*TLS*, 12 April) refers to gardening books of 1629 and 1653 to prove the actual existence of a variety of striped tulip called the Swiss or the Switzer.

L. N. Wall, in 'Marvell and the Skinners' (*NQ*), finds no trace of Edward Skinner travelling abroad when Marvell was on the Continent.

Robert Beum examines 'The Scientific Affinities of English Baroque Prose' (*EM*). He contrasts the orderly, balanced, assured periods of the Elizabethans with the restless, asymmetrical prose which matched a new universe of doubt and uncertainty. Tentativeness had become a virtue. Oratory gave place to the essay and the report. Writers wanted to record data and communicate clearly and quickly, persuading through logic and the abundance and accuracy of detailed observation, rather than through sentiment or imagination. This was an early effect of science, which had much to do with creating the kind of prose it was later called upon to rectify.

Catherine Drinker Bowen, in *Francis Bacon. The Temper of the Man*,[17] gives an account of Bacon's

---

[16] In *Explication as Criticism: Selected Papers from the English Institute 1941–1952*. Ed. W. K. Wimsatt, Jr. Columbia U.P. pp. xv+202. 33s. 6d.

[17] *Sir Francis Bacon: The Temper of the Man*, by Catherine Drinker Bowen. Hamish Hamilton. pp. 195. 25s.

upbringing, of his struggle for office and his rivalry with Coke, and probes the discrepancy between his great gifts and large vision and his humiliating fall. He was vulnerable through a kind of magnanimity, which made him careless of what went on in his own household. The charges which brought him down were not levelled against him personally or as Chancellor, but were a means of discrediting a corrupt government, whose great ones, the King and Buckingham, were untouchable.

Marie Boas Hall writes in *The Personalist* 'In Defense of Bacon's Views on the Reform of Science'. She shows Bacon's interest in the examples he uses in the *Novum Organum* driving him to develop them further than was required to show his logical method, but not fully enough for them to stand alone. A fruitful cause of misunderstanding is his use of conventional terms, the only ones available to him, with unconventional meanings. It is important to know what he meant by 'forms' and why he lays such stress on them. In 'Bacon and the Renaissance Ideal of Self-Knowledge' (ibid.), Sidney Warhaft shows that Bacon deprecated introspection. His aspirations were not towards the old wisdom but the new plenty, and he neglected 'things as they ought to be'.

Bacon, however, created a utopia, upon which Judah Bierman comments, in 'Science and Society in the *New Atlantis* and other Renaissance Utopias' (*PMLA*). The striking thing about Bacon's is the isolation of his College from the rest of his utopian state, which is politically and socially conservative and religiously orthodox. More does without any scientific powerhouse. Campanella and Andreae both allot structures and space to science. Andreae makes practical science serve social progress

and includes it in education. But what Bacon loved was creative discovery. He rightly wished to keep science free of politics, but so complete an isolation calls for further explanation.

R. L. Eagle, in 'The Manuscripts of the Authorized Version' (*TLS*, 28 Nov.), calls attention to the astonishing disappearance of the mass of manuscripts relating to the translation of the Authorized Version. R. Ellrodt, in 'William Drummond's *Cypresse Grove* and the *Somnium Scipionis*' (*NQ*), traces some notable parallels. James G. McManaway's 'Privilege to Print' (*SB*) concerns a royal patent giving Sir William Woodhouse sole right to print reports of important discussions concerning the Post Nati. The following year, 1609, James rendered it otiose by asking Lord Chancellor Ellesmere to publish his speech on the subject.

All students will be grateful for a small selection of Donne's sermons in the Potter-Simpson text.[18] Evelyn Simpson has made a representative choice, designed to show something of the range of Donne's style and sympathy, and something, too, of his finest prose and the subjects that were his most constant concern. The ten sermons do not include 'Death's Duell', easily available elsewhere and in some respects not characteristic. The introduction is all it should be. Thomas F. Van Laan, in 'John Donne's *Devotions* and the Jesuit Spiritual Exercises' (*SP*), examines the unusual structure of the work, which suggests to him that Donne was practising something like the schematic spiritual exercise.

James Winny has edited a neat little *Religio Medici*, basing it on Denonain's

---

[18] *John Donne's Sermons on the Psalms and Gospels. With a Selection of Prayers and Meditations*, ed., with an Introduction, by Evelyn M. Simpson. C.U.P. and California U.P. pp. 244. 40*s*. Paperback 17*s*.

text (1955) with help from V. Sanna's (1958).[19] It is modernized, glossed and annotated. The introduction departs notably from current ideas of Browne as the 'true amphibium', poised significantly between the old world and the new. Browne took a look at the new, Winny surmises, when he studied abroad, disliked what he saw, and thereafter entrenched himself firmly and serenely in the old. He had not enough of the modern spirit even to be able to paint a lifelike self-portrait. He displays himself in the stereotyped attitudes he thinks proper to Renaissance man. No psychological explanation can effectively account for the inconsistencies in the picture, which is constructed from contemporary commonplaces. The axioms he propounds with such an air of deep personal consideration are none of his. He thinks they become him or that he can coax a paradox out of them. Browne has charmed the world by his rhetoric rather than by his philosophy. How much the charm of rhetoric suffices to account for his contemporary reputation Winny does not say.

Charles Mish has edited a selection of short fiction of the seventeenth century.[20] He finds it easy enough to offer something in this field that has never been offered before, namely *The Famous History of Morindos* (1609), *Moriomachia* (1613), *Long Meg of Westminster* (1620), *The Tinker of Turvey* (1630), *Don Juan and Marsillia* (1635), *The Man in the Moon* (1638), *Eurialus and Lucretia* (1639), *Cawood the Rook* (1640),

Alexis and Angelica (1640), and *Fortunatus* (c. 1700). Spelling and punctuation have been discreetly modernized.

A well-documented study of Prynne, by William M. Lamont,[21] illuminates the rather muddled but always well-meant attempts of 'the most prolific writer of the seventeenth century' to raise the moral standard of English life and keep popery at bay. Prynne did not write well and he wrote at great length, with a peculiarly irritating kind of badness, which impressed ignorant people. He lends himself to misinterpretation. Even contemporaries misunderstood him, and it has required considerable industry and insight to unravel his tangled thinking. In the process a good deal of the thought of the time and the pressures to which he was responding are clarified and defined. Prynne had an ideal, nourished on Foxe and Jewel, of a godly, sober England under a godly, sober monarch. He attacked Laud because he saw, in his claim to derive authority from God, the elevation of bishop above king and the infiltration of popish principles. Though his later position has been described as Erastian, in the worser sense of the term, he would never have championed any secular power which did not seem to him to serve the best interests of religion. He was in many ways an unattractive person, wanting in the graces of self-knowledge and self-criticism, grotesque even in his misfortunes, but his biographer does not fail to demand for him the respect due to his high aspirations and earnest endeavour.

Not so a review in *TLS*, 9 August, which equates Prynne with 'those obsessed characters with minds that

---

[19] *Sir Thomas Browne. Religio Medici.* Ed. by James Winny. C.U.P. pp. xxxiv+154. 8s. 6d.

[20] *Short Fiction of the Seventeenth Century.* Selected and edited by Charles C. Mish. New York U.P. The Stuart Editions. Published first in paperback in the Doubleday-Anchor Seventeenth Century Series. pp. xvii+485. $6.50.

[21] *Marginal Prynne 1600–1669*, by William M. Lamont. Routledge & Kegan Paul. pp. ix+250. 35s.

teeter on the borders of lunacy but whose writings, fortunately, do not get into print unless they themselves pay for their publication'. Promptly, on 16 August, two correspondents leap to his defence. Michael Prynne (disclaiming kinship) objects to the description of some of his massive tomes as 'pamphlets', praises his concern for ancient manuscripts, and denies that everybody found him unattractive. E. K. Timings also has high praise for his work as Keeper of the Records, and notes that Anthony à Wood pictures him as generous and helpful. He is an important figure in the history of the seventeenth century because he was 'in the true conservative tradition', and it was his cause, without his violence and fanaticism, which triumphed in 1660.

Another great Puritan scholar and preacher, whose contemporary reputation needs some justification in a world no longer subject to the problems with which he wrestled, has been interpreted by Larzer Ziff.[22] Ziff has concentrated upon the wider aspects of John Cotton's career and his place in Puritan thought, rather than on details of personal biography. The early chapters recreate the position of a reformer within the Church of England, accustomed to certain kinds of compromise. Later chapters describe the effect upon him of the large freedoms of the churches in New England, which shocked Old England by the extremes to which they would go and the rigour with which they imposed their doctrine. After twenty years in Boston, Lincolnshire, Cotton spent nearly twenty more in Boston, Massachusetts, attempting with one hand to prevent the new congregations from losing all continuity and stability in a flood of private inspira-

[22] *The Career of John Cotton: Puritanism and the American Experience*, by Larzer Ziff. Princeton U.P. pp. x+280. $6.00.

tion and perfectionist polity, and with the other to consolidate and preserve a working model of what, if not perfect, was at least the godliest commonwealth on earth. These early days have implanted certain attitudes in the American consciousness which Cotton would hardly recognize as his work. Even in his lifetime they tended to emerge in forms he had not foreseen. There is great interest in Ziff's contention that Puritan writing was intended to have 'a future in its human consequences rather than in its form'. That is why Milton could not write like Hooker. 'The Puritan prose work was powered by history. It was a bark confidently tossed on the swift-flowing stream of time, moved and sustained not by its own structure but by the waters which were carrying it to the ocean of the Millennium. As such, it was, as often as not, ill constructed even in fundamentals.' He goes on to observe that many a great American work since has been 'propelled more by a sense of the American experience as one of changes hastening along to one millennium or another, than by an inner principle of aesthetic form'.

In 'The Literary Consequences of Puritanism' (*ELH*), Ziff calls upon the puritan preacher's conviction that 'reality is secondary to the absolute message behind it' to explain two contradictory aspects of pulpit-style, extreme plainness and passionate allegorizing. A puritan, however profound his scholarship and however sophisticated his audience, felt bound to speak God's word plainly, without learned or literary embellishments. On the other hand, God's word might come to him in a supernatural transport or in biblical typology. This 'characteristic combination of plainness, passion, and allegory crystallized in the century 1560–1660 and has ever since been a strong feature if not a separate tradition in our literature'.

In 'Jonathan Edwards: The Theory behind his Use of Figurative Language' (*PMLA*), Paul R. Baumgartner attacks the notion that the puritan preacher 'accommodated' himself reluctantly to the sensual nature of man when he fell back upon images to express spiritual truths. Jonathan Edwards provides a theoretical justification for analogical usage. Truth is in God, is in the created universe as an emanation of God, and in man's mind in so far as he comprehends and consents to the universe as God created it. Through figurative language we understand the truth of things.

No one can complain that it is hard to lay hands on Hobbes these days. An edited text of *Leviathan* and a book of selections including his *Little Treatise, Elements of Law, De Corpore, Of Liberty and Necessity*, and part of his *Dialogue between a Philosopher and a Student of the Common Laws*, appeared in 1962 in paper-back.[23] Brief introductions by Richard S. Peters place Hobbes in the history of thought, commending 'his attempt to establish psychology and political science as objective studies, untrammelled by theological assumptions and moralizing, to preserve a detached an uninvolved attitude towards man and society as well as towards nature'. The kind of 'editing' the works have undergone is nowhere described.

In 'Dryden, Hobbes, and the Nimble Spaniel' (*NQ*), George Watson quotes an early source for the metaphor, employed by Hobbes and Dryden, of the poet's imagination as a ranging spaniel. The sixteenth-century Spanish physician, Juan Huarle, used it in his *Examen de ingenios*, translated by Richard Carew in 1594. H. Neville Davies (ibid.) distinguishes between Hobbes's spaniel, doggedly and assiduously hunting rhymes, and Dryden's much livelier and wider ranging animal, in search of ideas.

MILTON

Work on Milton is treated in four sections. The first deals with some miscellaneous and general material, the second and third with the minor and major poems, and the fourth with the prose, very scantily represented this year.

(*i*) *General*

There is one new edition of Milton's poems, edited by J. T. Shawcross.[24] It substitutes literal prose translations for the text of the Greek, Latin, and Italian pieces. The poems are carefully dated, and printed in what the editor conceives to be their chronological order, in which *Samson Agonistes* precedes both *Paradise Lost* and *Paradise Regained*. Unobtrusive footnotes help the modern reader to understand the text. Thirteen illustrations from Tonson's edition of 1688 are offered as 'significant contemporary commentary'.

William B. Hunter, Jr., in *The Journal of the History of Medicine* (1962), offers 'Some Speculations on the Nature of Milton's Blindness'. Accepting a diagnosis of glaucoma, he successfully relates what is known of Milton's personality to that observed in glaucomatous patients, whose disease is often a response to

[23] *Thomas Hobbes. Leviathan*, selected and with an Introduction by Richard S. Peters. Ed. by Michael Oakeshott. pp. 511. *Body, Man and Citizen: Selections from Hobbes's Writings*. Ed. and with an Introduction by Richard S. Peters. pp. 414. New York: Collier Books. (1962). 95c. 7s. 6d.

[24] *The Complete Poetry of John Milton*. Arranged in Chronological Order with an Introduction, Notes, and Variants by John T. Shawcross. New York U.P. The Stuart Editions. Published first in paperback in the Doubleday-Anchor Seventeenth Century Series. pp. xv + 574. $7.50.

frustrating life-situations. It is obviously difficult to name any one trouble as more pressing on Milton than another. Hunter suggests that the first serious onset may have been provoked by the bad reception of the divorce pamphlets. Milton suddenly, and to his great bewilderment, found himself an alien in what he had thought was his own party. His move away from the Presbyterians towards the Independents can have been accomplished only with great emotional disturbance. The second eye was probably affected by the well-meant advice of his physicians who, by warning him of the risk he ran when he insisted upon finishing his answer to Salmasius, focused his anxiety upon his eyesight and only succeeded in making bad worse. Since glaucoma is often associated with hypermetropia, it seems likely that Milton's schoolboy headaches were caused by longsightedness. How, in any case, can the theory that he was shortsighted be made to agree with his pride in his swordsmanship?

Douglas Bush, in 'John Milton',[25] argues that a critic does not need biographical evidence in order to understand a poem, and is liable, when he has it, to make bad use of it. He deplores the stress on Milton the rebel, and Milton the misogynist. Even Milton the egoist can blind critics to the supremely classical and impersonal nature of this poet's art.

John T. Shawcross, in 'Milton's Decision to Become a Poet' (*MLQ*), suggests that Milton's intention crystallized in the early autumn of 1637, shortly before he wrote of it to Diodati, very secretly, rather shamefacedly, and as something not previously known. Before that he had

written only occasional verse. He felt himself 'church-outed' by Laud's visitations of 1633–7. In the spring of 1638 he wrote *Ad Patrem* to explain his decision to his father.

C. A. Patrides handles a number of Milton's ideas. In 'The Renaissance View of Time: A Bibliographical Note' (*NQ*), he observes that where the usual conception was the Augustinian one of a world made with time, not in time, Milton preferred to fuse Aristotelian and Platonic notions and to deny that eternity was timeless before the creation, though he allows that after the Last Judgement time will 'stand fixt'. In 'The "Protevangelium" in Renaissance Theology and *Paradise Lost*' (*SEL*), Patrides discusses contemporary interpretations of God's promise to Adam that the Woman's seed shall bruise the Serpent's head. Because Adam was told this, it was possible to claim him as the first Protestant, thereby answering the taunt of 'Where was your church before Luther?' Calvin raised a dissentient voice, reading 'seed' as 'a Nowne collective'. In 'Psychopannychism in Renaissance Europe' (*SP*), Patrides deals with Milton's mortalist heresy. This was so much denounced that it is clear it was widely held, especially by the Anabaptists and even by some Catholics.

William O. Scott's 'Ramism and Milton's Concept of Poetic Fancy' (*PQ*) examines Adam's explanation of Eve's dream with reference to Milton's Ramistic *Art of Logic*, and considers the place of logic in his poetic theory. Carl W. Cobb, in 'Milton and Blank Verse in Spain' (ibid.), seeks those 'Spanish poets of prime note' who according to Milton 'have rejected rime', and fails to find them. Poets before Milton's time never really did reject rhyme. Milton may have been struck by Ascham's reference to the translation of the *Odyssey*

[25] In *Explication as Criticism: Selected Papers from the English Institute 1941–1952*, ed. by W. K. Wimsatt, Jr. Columbia U.P. pp. xv+202. 33s. 6d.

which Gonzalvo Perez published in 1550, or by Juan de Jauregui's translation of Tasso's *Aminta* in 1607. Thomas Kranidas opens new possibilities when, in 'Milton's "Grand Master Peece"' (*ANQ*), he shows Milton and some contemporaries using 'masterpiece' in a pejorative sense.

John T. Shawcross has been working on Milton's spelling. In 'What We Can Learn from Milton's Spelling' (*HLQ*), he indicates places where it shows pronunciation and thus affects prosody. It can also be a means of dating a work, and even a proof of authorship. On spelling evidence Milton was the author of 'A Postscript' in *An Answer to. . . An Humble Remonstrance* (1641), and wrote it in January or February. *A Briefe History of Muscovia* was probably written before 1651. His spelling was not systematic or rigid, nor does he seem to have cared very much himself about preserving it, but it is sufficiently characteristic to have left some traces in printed texts and in the practice of amanuenses whom he had taught. In *PLMA* Shawcross confines himself to 'One Aspect of Milton's Spelling: Idle Final "E"', bringing evidence from a complete concordance of all English spellings in holograph material, with corroboration from early printed texts. It appears from this that Milton began to abandon final 'e', in certain categories, around 1640, and that his practice in this respect was nearly consistent by early 1642. Shawcross does not believe that Milton developed a stressed-unstressed principle of spelling 'be', personal pronouns, etc.

William Elton, in 'New Light on Milton's Amanuensis' (*HLQ*), finds that a Jeremie Picard was an inmate of Bedlam in 1678, which may explain the absence of much bio-graphical material about this rather mysterious personage.

Marjorie Hope Nicolson's *John Milton: A Reader's Guide*[26] is a book in every way admirable for its purpose, which is to present Milton's life and work to the modern reader. The author is equally at home with Milton and with his critics, sympathetic and level-headed, learned but easy. She declares Milton no Arian, but a 'subordinationist', basing her conclusions on a doctoral thesis published on microfilm in 1960 by Ruth M. Kivette. An interesting sidelight is a reported tribute from a veteran of World War II to the truth and effectiveness of Milton's much criticized account of the War in Heaven.

Roy Daniells is convinced that literature can be fruitfully related to prevalent styles in architecture, sculpture, and painting, and he is well equipped to make this fascinating marriage. *Milton, Mannerism and Baroque* shows a genuinely new approach to Milton.[27] Daniells treats him as a superlative artist, whose work reflects both a personal passion and 'the great controlling ideas of form which imbued the collective mind of the period'. He delights in indicating contradictions, stresses, near-failures, startling incongruities, and illogicalities, not with the intention of dismissing Milton's poems as failures, but to underline their success and the virtuosity and daring of the poet. This is reflected in points both large and small. It is omnipresent. *Paradise Lost* appears as a wonderfully, not a reprehensibly, artificial

---

[26] *John Milton: A Reader's Guide to His Poetry*, by Marjorie Hope Nicolson. New York: Farrar, Strauss & Co. pp. xv+385. $5.95.

[27] *Milton, Mannerism and Baroque*, by Roy Daniells. Toronto U.P. pp. 229.

construction, and typically baroque in the way it contorts normal expression in order to express what is almost inexpressible, 'things unattempted yet'. Central to Milton's epic and to the spirit of baroque is the desire for power and the predominance of the will. There is no rational explanation offered of why Satan and mankind should rebel against God. 'Milton's reluctance to move outward from the simple axis of man's rebellious will thrusting up against the will of God keeps him from doing more than suggest the existence of the complexities of moral degeneracy or the ramifications of spiritual wickedness. This,' Daniells insists, 'is a deeply revealing and endlessly significant fact.' Admittedly England, too poor and harried for vast undertakings, has no great baroque architecture. It is paradoxical that in a congeries of Puritans, shot through with iconoclasm and deeply suspicious of contrived aesthetic effects, the supreme verbal embodiment of baroque was achieved.

Harry F. Robins writes on Milton's theology,[28] which he sees as a complete and logical system, equally available in *Christian Doctrine* and in *Paradise Lost*. He even suggests that *Christian Doctrine* may have been written 'in part as a kind of preliminary exercise to the composition of *Paradise Lost*'. However, 'the subtleties of dogma tend to get lost in the pleasant labyrinth of poetic ornamentation'. Both treatise and poem were in many places out of line with the accepted tenets of the churches in Milton's day. His foremost authority was Scripture. His way of interpreting it and the conclusions he came to are strikingly like the methods and beliefs of the church in its earlier days before the Council of Nicea, that is, in Milton's view, before human corruption had crept in. A comparison of Milton's system with Origen's shows that the two thinkers had much in common. Robins treats Origen less as a formal 'source' than as an illuminating parallel. He challenges commentators to 'produce a resemblance equally complete', and justly complains of the innumerable minor identifications which have been used to link Milton momentarily with this and that writer or creed. Milton's mind did not work in a jackdaw way. Of major importance is Milton's view of matter as God's substance from which He has withdrawn His goodness (not, as Saurat has it, His will), thus leaving it absolutely free. It is a freedom shared by all the 'forms' which creation, in Milton's sense of the term, can draw from lifeless and neutral matter. The creator is the Logos, mysteriously self-created; not of God's essence, since there cannot be two Gods, both infinite, but in every way in accord with God. The invisible Logos creates heaven, the angels, and hell. Then comes the moment when He is manifested in heaven, declared the Son of God and the anointed Christ, and offers Himself as the Redeemer. (Kelley is wrong in thinking that He is, at this point, the incarnate Christ.) It is now that Satan feels himself 'impaired', not because an angel of surpassing but hitherto unrecognized merit has been raised above him, but because an entirely new and superior Being has suddenly appeared in the heavenly hierarchy. As Son and anointed Christ the Logos creates the world. Later He takes on flesh as man's Redeemer. It is the Logos whom Milton invokes as his Muse—not God Himself, not the Holy Spirit, and not a sublimated earthly muse.

[28] *If This Be Heresy: A Study of Milton and Origen*, by Harry F. Robins. Illinois U.P. Illinois Studies in Language and Literature (51). pp. 196. Cloth $4.50. Paper $3.50.

(ii) Minor Poems

John Carey, discussing 'The Date of Milton's Italian Poems' (*RES*), suggests that the pastoral works, to which Milton alludes at the end of *Elegy VI* (pressa . . . patriis meditata cicutis), were in fact his Italian poems, which Diodati was to judge and possibly to correct because they were in his native tongue. They may therefore be dated some time shortly before Christmas 1629, the date of the *Elegy*. John T. Shawcross writes 'Of Chronology and the Dates of Milton's Translations from Horace and the *New Forcers of Conscience*' (*SEL*). He speculates upon the copy for the 1673 edition of Milton's poems and the order in which they appear there, which is partly the chronological order of composition and partly arrangement by kinds. He concentrates finally upon the date of the Fifth Ode of Horace and of the sonnet on *The New Forcers of Conscience*, dating the former 1646 and suggesting that, though *The New Forcers* should properly follow the sonnets, the printer probably displaced it so that the Latin text of Horace and the English translation could be read side by side without turning a page. Dated by the events to which it refers, it seems to belong to the first two months of 1647. Morris Freedman, in 'Milton's *On Shakespeare* and Henry Lawes' (*ShQ*), proposes Lawes as the intermediary through whom the verses of Milton, then unknown as a poet, came to be printed in the Second Folio. He indicates possible, if shadowy, links between Lawes and the printers.

V. B. Halpert gives four reasons for supposing it is the lark that comes to the window, and not the poet, in 'On Coming to the Window in *L'Allegro*' (*Ang*).

A letter from J. A. W. Bennett, headed 'Milton's "Cato"' (*TLS*, 5 April), derives the final couplet of Milton's sonnet to Lawrence from *Disticha Catonis*, a familiar school text. This supports the mock-serious tone of the whole sonnet. The text reads, 'Interpone tuis interdum gaudia curis / Ut possis animo quemvis suffere laborem'. On 26 April, J. C. Maxwell hails the new source as settling once and for all that Milton's 'spare to interpose' does not mean 'refrain from interposing'. On 10 May V. Scholderer retorts that on the contrary Horace's *interdum* makes it plain that Milton was using 'spare' in a restrictive sense. On 17 May, Maxwell repeats his conviction that the tenor of the whole passage supports the less severe interpretation.

To judge by the amount of commentary it has provoked, *Lycidas* is both a very great and a very difficult poem. C. A. Patrides has made it the subject of a collection of critical appreciations, recommended in a preface by M. H. Abrams as a valuable teaching book.[29] An opening section consists of the text, together with the most significant corrections from the Trinity College manuscript. This is followed by *Epitaphium Damonis* and Helen Waddell's translation, which the editor says 'captures the emotional intensity of the original to such an extent that it deserves greater attention than it has hitherto received'. J. H. Hanford is allowed to expound the tradition of the pastoral elegy in a revised version of an article previously published in *PMLA*, 1910. Dr. Johnson alone speaks for an earlier period, which seems fair enough, since he started this ball rolling. It would have been helpful for students had there been some

[29] *Milton's Lycidas: The Tradition and the Poem*, ed. by C. A. Patrides. New York: Holt, Rinehart & Winston, 1961. pp. x+246.

explanation of what he meant by 'harsh diction' and 'unpleasing numbers', not to mention 'easy, vulgar and therefore disgusting'. Modern contributors are Tillyard, Ransom, More, Miles, Daiches, Adams, Shumaker, Brooks and Hardy, Prince, Tuve, Frye, and Abrams. An annotated reading list indicates other places where the poem and the tradition have been elucidated. To the regret of the present writer, the book has walked the town since 1961 without a notice in *YW*.

William M. Jones considers 'Immortality in two of Milton's Elegies'.[30] He notes how at the end of *On the Death of a Fair Infant* Milton returns firmly to reality, offering as the best consolation he can think of that his sister will bear another child. At the end of *Lycidas* and even more strikingly at the end of *Epitaphium Damonis* the promise of fertility is what is opposed to the pain of loss. William G. Madsen, in 'The Voice of Michael in *Lycidas*' (*SEL*), says it is important to recognize that the poem is not organized like a picture or a piece of music, but is a speech by an 'Uncouth swain'. The speaker remains obstinately pastoral, pagan, and uncomforted until the Angel does indeed 'melt with ruth'. It is the voice of Michael which offers the consolation, an account of 'other groves and other streams' where Lycidas is still alive. Thus there is a dramatic irony in that the reader knows more than the swain, and there is a reason for the mingled paganism and Christianity. The pagan motifs are typological foreshadowings. In the last eight lines Milton himself takes over the narration, commenting upon the fresh experience which has come to the shepherd.

John S. Coolidge, in 'Boethius and "That Last Infirmity of Noble Mind"' (*PQ*), finds that the treatment Boethius gives to the desire for fame is nearer Milton's thought than the more commonly quoted passages from Tacitus. Tacitus would reject it entirely as a mere worldly good. Dame Philosophy tells Boethius that a good man naturally desires a good name, but that he is in error in supposing that such a desire can be adequately fulfilled on earth. Edgar F. Daniels, in 'Milton's *Lycidas*, 29' (*Ex*), has an explanation of 'batt'ning our flocks with the fresh dews of night'. Since wet grass is bad for sheep, and Milton knew that 'rank mist' would swell and rot them, he has his shepherds fold them out of harm's way when the dew begins to fall. 'Batt'ning' must be taken as blocking up an entrance. The actual operation would be brief, and cannot be described as extending till nightfall, but the shepherd's toil in general can fairly be said to be from dawn till dusk.

(iii) Major Poems

A notable contribution to the understanding of *Paradise Lost* comes from the increased attention paid nowadays to poetical *personae*. Anne Davidson Ferry, by defining the role of the narrator, clears up misinterpretations which arise when Milton's poem is treated as effective only when it is dramatic.[31] She shows that the voice of the narrator is not in conflict with the voices of the characters, and does not say things Milton knew should be said but did not really feel. The whole epic is presented by a speaker who is 'Milton' only in a very specialized sense. He is the blind

[30] In *Myth and Symbol: Critical Approaches and Applications*, ed. by Bernice Slote. Nebraska U.P. pp. viii+196. $1.95.

[31] *Milton's Epic Voice: The Narrator in Paradise Lost*, by Anne Davidson Ferry. Harvard U.P. pp. xv+187. $4.25.

bard, with the compensating gift of spiritual insight, or a bird singing in darkness and soaring upwards into unearthly realms. Since he is an inhabitant of a fallen world, he is not too remote. He can speak feelingly of 'all our woe', but at the same time he can tell of 'things unattempted yet', of heaven and hell and the world before the Fall. The severity of the moral commentary is his, but so is the tender understanding with which the story is told. The elaborate epic similes are essentially his, as he speaks from the fallen world of time and place and seasonal change. There is a reason for the rolls of proper names, over and above their sonority and their evocative power. They are a strong contrast to the timeless abstractions of heaven. God's language has not these figures, and the angels speak in the simple pastoral terms of the prelapsarian world. One after another Milton's habits of language are given a purposeful propriety. He requires double meanings to express the narrator's double viewpoint, 'his fallen knowledge and his inspired vision'. Pat to his hand come the Latin terms. And so pat to the author's hand come the illustrations of her thesis that it is hard not to see it as largely proven.

A. B. Chambers elucidates 'Chaos in *Paradise Lost*' (*JHI*). In *Christian Doctrine* Milton states that matter is good. But Chaos, which plays so large a part in *Paradise Lost*, is plainly opposed to God. In a long and interesting investigation of its nature, source, and meaning, Chambers suggests that Milton's Chaos owes much to Plato's concept of space. It is not mere emptiness, but is full of warring material elements. It is evil only in so far as it is ruled by chance, the inversion of God's providence. When God puts out His active goodness it can be reduced to order, as at the creation.

When Satan struggles through Chaos on his dark journey all remains contrary, repeating the contraries in his own breast. In Milton's poem Chaos is the opposite of the created world as hell is the opposite of heaven.

Donald R. Pearce considers 'The Style of Milton's Epic' (*YR*). He sees no profit in denying its Latinisms, its artifice, and even a kind of pedantry, from which its virtues derive. It is not the artifice of poetry so much as of formal, rhetorical, classical prose. Milton uses many words not common in poetry. The way they are used sets them apart from ordinary speech and from the Italianate mood of the minor poems. For years he had been writing prose notable for 'clarity, passion and strength'. The stylistic model for *Paradise Lost* is Milton's own state papers. He achieves an extreme precision of utterance, 'a relentless, nuclear certainty, penetrating from the philosophical to the rhetorical to the grammatical details of the text'. Eighteenth- and nineteenth-century miltonics are bad because they lack this quality and rely too much on chance verbal resonance, which is by no means Milton's only or major resource.

John M. Steadman considers 'Allegory and Verisimilitude in *Paradise Lost*: the Problem of the "Impossible Credible"' (*PMLA*). Viewed as Milton viewed them, through the eyes of the Italian critics of the epic, the figures of Sin and Death, the Limbo of Vanity, etc., can be defended. Impossibilities are permissible as a way of telling a truth allegorically and of supplying the epic with the desirable elements of the marvellous. Milton, however, uses his allegorical marvels with restraint, lest they should appear to derogate from the true marvels of God's performing. Steadman has several articles investigating Milton's Muse. In 'Spirit and

Muse: A Reconsideration of Milton's Urania (*Paradise Lost* I, 1–26)' (*Archiv*), he distinguishes between Milton's pleas to a conventional Muse for 'answerable style' and his prayer to the Spirit of God for instruction and illumination. In 'Urania, Wisdom, and Scriptural Exegesis (*Paradise Lost*, VII, 1–12)' (*N*), Steadman examines Milton's authority for making Urania sister to 'Eternal Wisdom', like her antedating the creation, and with her 'playing' in the presence of God. In 'Chaste Muse and "Casta Juventus": Milton, Minturno, and Scaliger on Inspiration and the Poet's Character' (*Italica*), he finds support in Renaissance theory for Milton's distinction between the heavenly and the earthly Muse, and his insistence upon the poet's chaste life.

Peter L. Thorsley, Jr., in 'The Romantic Mind Its Own Place' (*CL*), considers Milton's Satan as a potent influence upon 'the egotistical sublime' of the nineteenth century, and studies 'the mind is its own place' as a key passage in the romantic misreading of Milton. A. B. Chambers, in 'The Mind is its Own Place, *Paradise Lost*, I. 253–255' (*RN*), examines the philosophical implication of Satan's claim, and finds it up to a point justifiable. 'What Satan cannot escape is the ultimate placing of himself by God.' In 'Wisdom at one entrance quite shut out: *Paradise Lost*, III. 1–55' (*PQ*), Chambers shows that what Milton regrets is not that blindness cuts him off from the charm of nature, but that it denies him the opportunity to 'read in Nature's book'. The progress of the poem from the darkness of hell, through the sunlit world, to the light of heaven parallels the growth of spiritual vision. In 'Milton's Proteus and Satan's Visit to the Sun' (*JEGP*), Chambers inquires what Milton

meant by claiming that earthly chemists have called up 'In various shapes olde Proteus from the Sea', and decides in favour of 'prime matter', an allegorical myth and not an alchemical term. Many other values of the myth are relevant, as Chambers goes on to show. In '"Sin" and "Sign" in *Paradise Lost*' (*HLQ*), Chambers relates Milton's naming of Sin, 'a Sign Portentous', to Latin *portentosus* and *portentum*, and to the Latin translation of Aristotle's *Physics*, where the 'mistakes' of nature are called *peccata*. Robert C. Fox, in 'Milton's "Sin": Addenda' (*PQ*), has some new instances of the human serpent figure in Vida, Rabelais, and Erasmus.

Nat V. Daniel looks at 'Some have I chosen of peculiar grace/Elect above the rest; so is my will'. In 'The Theology of *Paradise Lost*, III, 183–4, Re-examined' (*RP*), he suggests that Milton may reproduce the words of the Bible deliberately, in all their ambiguity, thus laying his work open to as many contradictory interpretations as the Bible itself has provoked. George W. Whiting's 'Abdiel and the Prophet Abdias' (*SP*) calls attention to the prophetic strain in Abdiel's denunciation of Satan, and suggests Milton perhaps adapted the name of the prophet Abdias (Obadiah) and his prophecy against Edom. Mother M. Christopher Pecheux, O.S.U., in 'The Conclusion of Book VI of *Paradise Lost*' (*SEL*), interprets the 'timerous flock' which the Son drives before him as a reference to the Gadarene swine. C. A. Patrides, in '*Paradise Lost* and the Theory of Accommodation' (*TSLL*), defends Milton's account of the War in Heaven and his anthropomorphic Deity by reference to the constant use in Christian teaching of terms fitted to the human understanding which are not to be taken literally. There is no need to deride Milton for doing what is still done. Irene Samuel has a note on the closeness of Dante's transformed thieves and Milton's transformed devils, in 'The Valley of Serpents: *Inferno* XXIV–XXV and *Paradise Lost* X. 504–577' (*PMLA*). Simon Trefman's 'A Note on the Bridge of Chaos in *Paradise Lost* and Matthew xvi. 18–19' (*SCN*) points to the way Milton's account of the 'Art Pontifical' parallels Matthew's account of the founding of Christ's Church, but with an opposite meaning.

The conclusion of Milton's epic receives special notice. Berta Moritz-Siebeck has undertaken the fullest possible analysis and defence of the last two books.[32] Since she sees them as an integral part of the whole work, she begins by a consideration of its structure, making an important distinction between theme, the glory of God, and subject, the fall of man. It is not, she insists, a pessimistic poem. Stress is not laid upon the origin of evil, which remains a mystery to be accepted as within the will of God, but upon the final outcome whereby God will turn all to good. The fall of the angels is followed by a new beginning, the creation of the world. Adam is as important as Satan because it is Adam who is to be redeemed. Book XI shows the process of purification and enlightenment, and Book XII is the book of consolation and promise. It is in some ways less explicit than any other book, since Milton felt himself personally and privately involved in the hope of redemption. He is very daring when he undertakes to show God's guiding hand in the events of human history, and his critics have too often been depressed by his stern picture of sin

and suffering, and have overlooked his profound belief that good must come out of evil. The consolation he offers is real, and more than a vague hope of heaven.

In 'Structure and the Symbolism of Vision in Michael's Prophecy, *Paradise Lost*, Books XI and XII' (*PQ*), Barbara Kiefer Lewalski offers an interpretation of the last books, in which she sees the consequences of moral blindness displayed to Adam's purged sight, while more secret and inward things are revealed to him by the angel's narration. In the end he is returned to his place in time, having seen with heightened spiritual vision the way to the Promised Land. 'The Education of Adam,' as George Williamson points out (*MP*), is an important theme in a poem where the main interest necessarily lies elsewhere than in suspense as to the outcome. A brief note by C. A. Patrides, in *Franciscan Studies*, 'Adam's "Happy Fault" and XVIIth-Century Apologetics', shows Milton using the theological commonplaces of the Fortunate Fall, redemption a greater work than creation, and evil an instrument of good.

One of the most interesting comments made by Willene van Loenen Pursell, in 'Love's Place in the Orderly System of Marriage in *Paradise Lost*',[33] is that Milton borrows something important from the courtly love tradition, while appearing wholly to reject it. The pure and uplifting passion in his picture of unfallen love is far more than innocent sensuality and is recognizably 'romantic'. The passion he condemns is mere animal appetite. The new love between Adam and Eve, when they

[32] *Untersuchungen zu Milton's 'Paradise Lost': Interpretation der Beiden Schluss-bücher*, von Berta Moritz-Siebeck. Berlin: Walter de Gruyter & Co. pp. 274. DM36.

[33] In *Love and Marriage in Three English Authors: Chaucer, Milton and Eliot*, by Willene van Loenen Pursell. Stanford, California. Stanford Honors Essays in Humanities (VII).

are repentant, is part of their hope of a new paradise.

G. A. Wilkes, in 'The Interpretation of *Samson Agonistes*' (*HLQ*), declares the master-pattern of the play psychologically inexplicable. We do not see two wills interacting in harmony, but God's will imposed. Six times Samson refuses to go to the Games, then he receives divine grace and guidance and—blindly—he goes. The intention of the poem is to 'assert Eternal Providence', and not, as we are so often told, to show the stages of Samson's regeneration. William O. Harris, in 'Despair and "Patience as the Truest Fortitude" in *Samson Agonistes*' (*ELH*), claims that the doctrinal concept informing the play is of patience as the highest manifestation of fortitude, which is the virtue traditionally opposed to despair. The sudden influx of divine grace comes because Samson has at last learnt this kind of fortitude. Two choral passages reflect on patience. The first arraigns God's justice and shows little belief in the patience it preaches. In the second magnanimity is praised with more fervour. But the speakers make merely human judgements, and the play teaches a wisdom surpassing theirs. Patience does most for Samson. A. B. Chambers, in 'Wisdom and Fortitude in *Samson Agonistes*' (*PMLA*), emphasizes the importance of 'magnanimity of mind' to Milton's hero. When he refuses to submit to the officer's imperious commands he is showing fortitude, and also wisdom, in that he fears God more than man. Paul R. Baumgartner's 'Milton and Patience' (*SP*) is relevant here. Milton met the setbacks of his later career with what Macaulay described as 'sedate and majestic patience', but his early temper was self-sufficient, active and intransigent. We do wrong to dismiss the hard-won submission of the last poems as

due to pessimism or fatigue. It comes of an active endeavour to know God's will and do it. Christ in *Paradise Regained* does not refuse to act simply because 'his time is not yet come'. Samson acts, but his action is entirely in accordance with God's will, and even against his own, which prompts him to stay away from the Dagonalia. Satan, in his proud stoicism, lacks patience. Adam learns it. The heroes of all Milton's last poems are 'lowly wise'.

Robert A. van Kluyve, in '"Out, out Hyaena!"' (*ANQ*), investigates some of the traditional lore about the hyena which is particularly appropriate to Dalila.

It is a considerable tribute to William Riley Parker's work on Milton's debt to the Greeks in *Samson Agonistes* that it should be reprinted, unaltered and unabridged, from the first edition of 1937.[34] Scholars still turn to Parker for an extended statement on this subject.

G. A. Wilkes discusses '*Paradise Regained* and the Conventions of the Sacred Epic' (*ES*). The minor epic was a familiar kind, seen in the *Judith* of Du Bartas and Drayton's *Moses*. It was characterized by speeches in which a personage, often the exemplary hero, draws moral edification from some incident in the story. The speeches of Milton's Christ, delivered from set moral positions, must be seen in this light and not interpreted in terms of character.

(iv) Prose

'Milton, Salmasius, and the Natural Law' (*JHI*) is a consideration by William J. Grace of Milton's confident assertion of the law of nature.

[34] *Milton's Debt to Greek Tragedy in 'Samson Agonistes'*, by William Riley Parker. Hamden, Conn: The Shoe String Press. Archon Books. pp. xiii+260. $6.50. Reprint.

In this he was more classical and even more scholastic than he himself realized. Because he held the Thomist position that man's understanding was not corrupted by the Fall, he could support Parliament against the King in the belief that there are discernible laws of nature which are superior to the mere law of the land. When Salmasius asked by what (written) law the King was beheaded, Milton infuriatingly replied that it was by the (unwritten) law of nature. Another source of misunderstanding, this time of Puritan origin, was Milton's use of 'the people' for a wise and virtuous minority with the right to take the law into their own hands. 'The people' to Salmasius meant either all the King's subjects or the lower classes. Milton never explains how his godly *élite* are in fact to be recognized.

J. Milton French's 'A Royalist Gibe at Milton's Antagonist Salmasius' (*PQ*) confirms that Salmasius was openly rebuked, in a coronation sermon before King Charles II, for the pernicious doctrine that kings can do no wrong.

XI

The Restoration Period

B. D. GREENSLADE

1. GENERAL:

(a) *Poetry* (b) *Criticism and Prose* (c) *Drama*

(a) The year under review has brought the first volume of the Yale Edition of *Poems on Affairs of State*: *Augustan Satirical Verse, 1660–1714.*[1] The title follows that of the series of collections published 1689–1716. The edition is planned to run to seven volumes, the last a register of all known verse of this kind, published or not, for the period of fifty-four years, estimated at about 3,000 printed poems, with another 2,500 surviving in manuscript. George de F. Lord, the general editor, is responsible for the first volume. The next three will cover only the ten years from the Popish Plot to the Revolution. Where so much of the material first circulated anonymously and surreptitiously, the choice of texts presents obvious difficulties. Priority has been given in general to manuscripts or early editions of single poems, rather than collections. (Of forty-six manuscript copy-texts used, twenty are in the Bodleian, seven in the B.M.) Texts have been modernized, justifiably. 'Affairs of State' has been interpreted generously to include literary affairs, bringing in poems by Rochester, Mulgrave, and Dryden, amongst others, where literary and political satire are hard to

distinguish. Head notes and annotation are full and reliable, and embody much research on disputed points. An introduction of thirty-two pages describes the historical context, and discusses authorship, methods of circulation, and satiric modes—crude invective and personal lampoon, ballad and song, dialogue and mock encomium, advice to the painter, vision poems, and mock epic. Such, in brief, are the scale and plan of this major assault on the 'suburbian Muse'. Sixty-five poems appear in the first volume. The editor has much to say on authorship and dating, and his challenges will be taken up. *Mac-Flecknoe*, for instance, is put as early as 1676–7. Among the Painter poems Margoliouth found only one, *Last Instructions*, which he would take as Marvell's, where Lord credits him with four. The full arguments have to be looked for in *BNYPL* (1958–9). In general the editor might have been freer with question marks, against Rochester as well as Marvell. The poems are outstandingly useful to the historian, especially if read for the experience they embody as well as for their facts and allusions. Scurrilous savaging of Clarendon, and anguished, noble prophecy, committed to 'forsaken Virtue's cause', issue from the same poet. From the literary point of view, if an ungenerous critic finds an intolerable deal of scrap (or perhaps chamber-pots instead of well-wrought urns), the editor can point to many poems (e.g. *On the Prorogation*,

[1] *Poems on Affairs of State: Augustan Satirical Verse, 1660–1714. Vol. I: 1660–1678*, ed. by George de F. Lord. Yale U.P. pp. lvi+506. $10.00. 72s.

anticipating Zimri), which justify his claim that the great Augustans profited by the example of these 'excrements of wit'. All concerned in this handsome, well-illustrated volume are to be congratulated on giving a great scholarly enterprise so promising a start.

Our knowledge of seventeenth-century political verse is growing fast. Eleanor Withington has done outstanding work on the canon of Cleveland's poetry (*BNYPL*): and Ruth Nevo's critical study[2] is claimed to be the first to attempt to cover the whole field, both 'panegyric and phillipic' (Marvell's phrase). Her title is taken from Davenant's praise of the King as a kind of moral chronometer for his subjects, who 'by his Diall set their motion right'. The first half of the book, on the early Waller, *Cooper's Hill*, Cleveland, and poems on Cromwell, is outside the scope of this chapter. The remainder deals with Restoration panegyric; the Advice to a Painter poems, and Oldham; Burlesque and Raillery; *Hudibras*; and finally a chapter on *Absalom and Achitophel*, seen as the climax of a movement towards raising satire to a heroic level, or alternatively, towards bending the heroic to the purposes of satire. Against this background, explored through Cowley, Marvell's *Last Instructions*, Butler, Oldham, and much obscurer verse (not all of it in the Lord collection), Dryden's poem may be read as the last, rather than as the first, of its kind. There is interesting discussion of the 'grandiloquent heroic' in poems praising the restored Charles, of the relations between raillery and scepticism, and of the use of ironic Biblical allegory before Dryden. This is a pioneering book

which can profitably be read alongside the Yale edition.

W. J. Cameron has made a detailed bibliographical study of 'The Princeton Copies of *Poems on Affairs of State*, Vol. II, 1703' (*PULC*), showing that other copies of this edition are reprints, and that only the Princeton copies are of real textual value, thus correcting Case and *C.B.E.L.* Cameron also describes 'A Late Seventeenth-Century Scriptorium' (*RMS*), the source of various manuscript volumes of post-Revolution political verse-satire, including some in the Nottingham Portland collection.

Edmund Blunden and Bernard Mellor have gathered *Wayside Poems of the Seventeenth Century*,[3] in the tradition of minor-verse collections by G. Thorn Drury, Massingham, Ault, and L. Birkett Marshall. About half the poems belong to the Restoration period, among them poems by Ayres, Aphra Behn, Tom Brown, Cotton, Evelyn, Flecknoe, Katherine Philips, and Temple. Spelling and punctuation have been modernized, and there are a commentary and a glossary. The chief sources are *Tixall Poetry*, Brydges's *Restituta*, articles by Mitford in *The Gentleman's Magazine*, and the collections of John Nichols. There are no sensational discoveries, but the whole makes a modestly elegant collection. *Loose and Humorous Songs*[4] is an anthology of a very different complexion. Most of the poems are pre-1660, but represent a continuing taste. Bishop Percy withheld them from publication, but they

[3] *Wayside Poems of the Seventeenth Century: An Anthology*, gathered by Edmund Blunden and Bernard Mellor. Hong Kong U.P. and O.U.P. pp. xiv+138. $3. 21s.

[4] *Loose and Humorous Songs: From Bishop Percy's Folio Manuscript*, ed. by Frederick J. Furnivall, with an Introduction by John Greenway. Folklore Associates Inc. and Herbert Jenkins. pp. ix+127. $8.50. 42s.

[2] *The Dial of Virtue: A Study of Poems on Affairs of State in the Seventeenth Century*, by Ruth Nevo. Princeton U.P. and O.U.P. pp. x+284. $6.00. 48s.

were later published by Furnivall. John Greenway has added a useful preface to this facsimile edition of a scarce book. It contains some vigorous and skilful songs which deserve a wider currency.

(b) K. G. Hamilton's *The Two Harmonies*[5] is, in effect, a contribution to the discussion of 'what happened' to the seventeenth-century literary consciousness. Hamilton recognizes the limitations of considering 'what men *thought* they were doing when they chose to write in poetry rather than in prose, . . . rather than what they were actually doing', but he believes there may be advantages in his approach. The book is controlled by the assumption that modern criticism stresses the unique function of poetry and the 'autonomy of the poet's imaginative activity'. What, he asks, would the modern contrast between 'utilitarian' discourse and 'creative' writing have meant in the seventeenth century? In four chapters he surveys the history of stylistic distinctions between poetry and prose, the nature of the rhetorical tradition, the rise of new criteria of 'utility', brought about by profound changes in man's experience of the external world, and finally, the concept of the imagination, where he finds little evidence of new developments. Imagination was still restricted to the purposes of reason. Yet, as the rediscovery of Longinus suggests, poets were not for long to be 'satisfied with retailing goods of someone else's manufacture'. 'Poetry . . . will always insist on being a mode of thought as well as a means of communication.' The 'thing said' cannot be separated from the 'way of saying'. But with the decline of the role assigned to the poet by the best of Renaissance rhetoric, poetry in the age of Dryden 'at most . . . was seen as a specially effective or persuasive way of saying things', until a new *rationale* for poetry could be found. The width of Hamilton's reference to the works of other scholars amply justifies his hope that the book may be a useful reference work for Renaissance literary theory, but also lays it open to criticism from those expert enough to find the patient survey of familiar ground heavy going. At the same time there is some novelty in so lucid and closely argued a presentation of the familiar, and still more in Hamilton's many original insights, e.g. his reasoned disagreements with the arguments of R. F. Jones and George Williamson, or his acute discussions of 'strong lines' and Biblical criticism. The student will find the book invaluable for its masterly summaries, e.g. the fifty pages on rhetoric; and he will get much help if he has trouble with Dryden. A cheaper edition would be welcome, with an index of topics and some corrections in the list of modern authorities. An earlier work in the same field, S. L. Bethell's *The Cultural Revolution of the Seventeenth Century*,[6] first published in 1951, has been reprinted.

The Royal Society programme for prose style, discussed by Hamilton, is examined by Richard Foster Jones in 'The Rhetoric of Science in England of the Mid-Seventeenth Century', the opening essay in a splendid collection honouring Alan Dugald McKillop.[7] Jones has taken the trouble to work

[5] *The Two Harmonies: Poetry and Prose in the Seventeenth Century*, by K. G. Hamilton. O.U.P. pp. vii+218. 32s. 6d.

[6] *The Cultural Revolution of the Seventeenth Century*, by S. L. Bethell. Dobson Books Ltd. pp. 162. 21s.

[7] *Restoration and Eighteenth-Century Literature: Essays in Honor of Alan Dugald McKillop*, ed. by Carroll Camden. Chicago U.P., for William Marsh Rice University pp. xi+435. $8.50. 63s.

out what he believes to be the precise context of Sprat's attack on 'amplifications, digressions and swellings of style', and of the stylistic creed announced in the Statutes. The polemic and warnings were directed at certain writers notorious for their metaphoric excesses, identified by Jones as, in particular, Walter Charleton and Kenelm Digby. The argument was philosophic as well as stylistic. Mechanical philosphers such as Charleton were speculative atomists, indifferent to the needs of artisans and farmers. Charleton believed that Nature's mysterious activity of minute particles could be explored and represented only by vivid analogy, humanizing the motion of atoms and communicating the exhilaration of visualizing Nature's 'inward Recesses and Latent motions' in the 'laboratory' of the imagination. Jones quotes extensively from Charleton's extraordinary prose, especially the *Physiologia* (1654). He was a Royal Society member, but found it difficult to conform, and is not mentioned in the records after 1667.

For some, Charles II was a 'Diall of virtue', for others, a tyrant 'red hot with wine and whore', as one poet in *Poems on Affairs of State* saw him. But 'The Impact of Charles II on Restoration Literature', examined by James Sutherland in *McKillop Essays* (See note 7), extended beyond the panegyric and philippic which he provoked. His friendship with writers as various as Hobbes and Durfey was only fitfully expressed in practical support; a tale of fair words and broken promises. But even fair words, from a King, counted for much. His influence on the drama, especially on comedy, was unmistakable. Above all, his personal style and preferences, which put a premium on both plainness and wit, 'radiated outwards . . . to the writer in his study', and to

the preacher in his pulpit. His impact on literature, illustrated from many sources in this lively essay, was greater than that of any other English monarch, Elizabeth I excepted. Another aspect of the literary taste of the time is displayed in David Foxon's long three-part article in *BC*, 'Libertine literature in England, 1660–1745', also issued separately.[8] Written from a learned vantage-point in the British Museum, this is an account of the present state of knowledge about the publication of prose pornography in England during the period. There are ten pages of plates. Much of it is detective work exercised on suppressed writings, which survive only in transcripts included in legal proceedings. The earliest specific reference to a pornographic book in England is of Pepys ('the first great middle-class civil servant') buying *L'École des Filles* in 1668, but nothing survives complete in English before 1740. Foxon suggests that it will not do to attribute the English emergence of pornography simply to a reaction against Puritanism, since it was a European phenomenon. On the assumption that it has been 'the apparently respectable (and often scholarly) professional man who has provided the bulk of the demand for pornography', Foxon offers his own hypothesis: that pornography was associated with the pressures of a new individualism in personal life and religion, and with the rising complexity of government. Roland Hall contributes three notes to *NQ*: 'Some New Seventeenth-Century Words and Antedatings'; 'The Language of Logic: Some Unrecorded Uses' (both concerned with the Port-Royal *Logic*, translated into English in 1685); and 'Cudworth: More New Words'.

[8] *Libertine Literature in England, 1660–1745*, by David Foxon. Shenval Press. pp. 63. 21s.

(c) Irène Simon surveys 'Restoration Comedy and the Critics' (RLV), from Collier to the present day, suggesting that some modern critics, in vindicating the serious content of the plays, may 'run the risk of talking solemn nonsense'. She uses a book which she admires, Norman Hollan's *The First Modern Comedies* (1959: YW xl. 180), as debating ground for her own criticism of *The Man of Mode*, *The Country Wife*, and *The Way of the World*. The tendency of these plays is to expose rather than to instruct. In different ways they also dramatize conceptions of naturalness: animal or sub-animal nature, nature formalized out of existence, 'nature made more natural by the skilful use of forms'. Congreve, who 'deals with the right relation between art and nature', is more sympathetically engaged with his material than the others, and more complex and constructive. The article is distinguished by close criticism and balanced judgement.

The remaining general material on the drama is wholly concerned with theatrical history. 'From Forestage to Proscenium: A Study of Restoration Staging Techniques' (TS), by Lee J. Martin, traces the increasingly sophisticated management of movable scenery in the Restoration theatre and the consequent extension of the acting area behind the proscenium opening. Roughly similar accounts of the physical properties of the stage may be found elsewhere, e.g. in the section on staging in the California *Dryden* Vol. VIII, but Martin's original contribution is a detailed analysis of the staging of plays by Sedley, Crowne, and Aphra Behn, identifying the scenes which must have been acted behind the forestage. Kenneth M. Cameron contributes two articles to *TN*: 'The Edinburgh Theatre, 1668–1682', and 'The Mon-

mouth and Portsmouth Troupes', in which he considers the evidence for the existence and activity of these obscure companies. Using some of the same data, John Harold Wilson argues in *NQ* that 'The Duchess of Portsmouth's Players' are an invention of scholars, and that the evidence refers simply to one private performance in the Portsmouth household. Wilson also has two notes in *TN*: 'Players' lists in the Lord Chamberlain's *Registers*' prints lists of players and others in the Royal Companies, 1660–98, from the P.R.O; 'Biographical Notes on Some Restoration Actresses' corrects and supplements material in his book *All The King's Ladies* (1958). Standing out from the minutiae is a quotation from some memorable doggerel by the comedian Jo Haynes, mourning his dead mistress, the actress Mrs. Knepp, 'that delicate Compound of Spiritt & Rump'. A. Langhans presents a detailed and ingenious analysis of 'New Restoration Theatre Accounts 1682–1692' (TN), based on P.R.O. documents. From Loyola University, Chicago, comes the second issue of the journal *Restoration and 18th Century Theatre Research*, edited by David G. Spencer and Carl J. Stratman, in two parts and improved format. This is already a most useful publication in its field. Items to note are: 'The Restoration Stage: Suggestions for Future Work'; an annotated Bibliography for 1962; and 'Theses and Dissertations in Restoration and 18th Century Theatre', with 352 entries for the period 1897–1962.

Finally, there are ten authoritative pages on the acting of Restoration comedy in *The Live Theatre*[9] by Hugh Hunt, who from his experience

[9] *The Live Theatre: An Introduction to the History and Practice of the Stage*, by Hugh Hunt. O.U.P. pp. viii+200. 25s.

as a former Director of the Old Vic Company (he is now Professor of Drama at Manchester) insists that the acting of these plays demands a serious study by the actors of the attitudes of the age.

2. DRYDEN:

(a) Books (b) Articles and chapters in the order: Poetry, Criticism, Drama

(a) James Kinsley and Roger Sharrock have each edited a selection of Dryden's poems.[10] There is surprisingly little duplication, although the volumes are published at the same price, and prepared, most efficiently, for the same readership. Only six of the complete poems chosen appear in each volume. Kinsley's text follows that of his Oxford *Dryden*, and where possible the same annotation is used. He includes a strong section on Translation, and in general the emphasis of selection and commentary is on Dryden's mastery of a wide range of verse-kinds. Sharrock's text is modernized; the introduction and notes explain Dryden's intellectual and literary milieu and his importance as a great representative of his age.

John M. Aden has compiled a *Dictionary*[11] of Dryden's criticism. He has drawn on the whole of the prose works, including letters, biography, and dedications, so that many opinions absent from the standard collections of criticism can be found here, although the exclusion of critical statements in verse is to be regretted. It was also unfortunate that Watson's Everyman edition of the criticism came too late for Aden to refer to it. A chronological list of the sources conveys at a glance the range of Dryden's prose. Items are arranged alphabetically by subject, and the development of Dryden's opinions on major topics is suggested by the chronological ordering of material under the main heading. The largest topic is Dryden himself—Life, Character, Literary Life, Works. Other long sections are: Critics, English *v.* French, Epic, Prosody, Rhyme, Satire, Shakespeare, Tragedy, Translation, Unities, Virgil. There is an elaborate system of cross-references which works well, after a run-through. A Selective Index provides a sample of familiar phrases, quotations, and allusions. This is an indispensable reference work, and also an absorbing anthology.

Sir Walter Scott's *Life of Dryden*,[12] published in 1808 as the first volume of his *Works* of Dryden, has been reissued by Bernard Kreissman in a photographic reproduction. He uses the 1834 edition by Lockhart, whose notes accompany Scott's. There is an introduction, and ten pages of notes are 'restricted to points of classification and to essential corrections'. Another reprint from amongst the pioneers of Dryden criticism is *Lectures on Dryden*[13] by A. W. Verrall, first published in 1914. A selection from the work on Dryden since Verrall has been made by

---

[10] *Dryden: Selected Poems*, chosen and ed. by James Kinsley. O.U.P. (New Oxford English Series.) pp. 188. 9s. 6d.
Selected Poems of John Dryden, ed. with an Introduction and Notes by Roger Sharrock. Heinemann. (The Poetry Bookshelf.) pp. vi+148. 9s. 6d.

[11] *The Critical Opinions of John Dryden: A Dictionary*, compiled and ed. by John M. Aden. Vanderbilt U.P. and Blackwell's. pp. xxviii+292. $7.50. 54s.

[12] *The Life of John Dryden*, by Sir Walter Scott. Ed. with an Introduction by Bernard Kreissman. Nebraska U.P. pp. xix+471. Cloth $5.00, paper $1.70. 14s.

[13] *Lectures on Dryden*, delivered by A. W. Verrall, and ed. by Margaret De G. Verrall. New York: Russell & Russell Inc. pp. viii+271. $6.50. 52s.

Bernard N. Schilling,[14] ranging from Eliot's 1921 review of Van Doren to three items of 1962. Most of the essays are chapters (some revised) from books by Bredvold, Osborn, Brower, Wasserman, Kaufmann, Prior, Tillyard, Hollander, and Hoffman. There are three articles from journals, by Edwin Morgan, Earl Miner, and E. N. Hooker. Schilling credits modern Dryden criticism with having done Dryden the justice of 'seeing him as a poet, not of "striking passages or of noble fragments", but of large design'. British critics do not show up in much force; of two well-known essays by D. W. Jefferson (1940 and 1954), the first, at least, should have been included.

In *The Nobler Pleasure*,[15] Frank Harper Moore explores chronologically the connexion between Dryden's thirteen comedies or tragicomedies and the corresponding criticism. He finds that the criticism falls into two major phases, the first relating to the period ending with *Marriage à la Mode* and *The Assignation* (1671–2). Influenced by his admiration for the style of the Court and by his study of Jonson and Fletcher, Dryden developed a conception of high comedy, in which the comic and the heroic were combined, and where, as he explained in his *Preface* to *An Evening's Love* (1668), wit 'moves you, if not always to laughter, yet to a pleasure that is more noble', through the elaboration of repartee and rhetorical art. Later, a somewhat disillusioned Dryden

attempted a more natural and satirical style, of which the best example is *Amphitryon* (1690). Moore believes that the preference for high comedy was 'in part a rationalization of his desire to escape from an uncongenial genre', and that the example his theory and practice set to his friend Congreve may in the end have been the most productive result of his labours.

J. A. Van der Welle's *Dryden and Holland*[16] is concerned with the treatment of the Dutch in Dryden's work, the impact of his writing on Dutch writers (very small), and Dryden's knowledge of Dutch scholarship, shown mostly in his translating period. The most profitable part of this dissertation is the commentary on *Annus Mirabilis* and *Amboyna*; the notes on the latter, by a scholar familiar with the Dutch pamphlets, prints, and medals of the period, should be useful to a future editor.

James Sutherland's W. P. Ker Memorial Lecture, *John Dryden: The Poet as Orator*,[17] might be read as a pithier, and wittier, counterpart to Hamilton's *The Two Harmonies* (see note 5). Like Hamilton, he describes Dryden as a Public Orator (a more enlightening title than Laureate), who devoted his talents and rhetorical training to the celebration and dignifying of occasions and persons; a poet whose life was largely spent in the practice of many kinds of public utterance—panegyric, debate, and the arts of the playhouse. He believed 'in the ability of words to move and

[14] *Dryden: A Collection of Critical Essays*, ed. by Bernard N. Schilling. Prentice-Hall Inc. (Twentieth Century Views.) pp. vi+186. Cloth 32s. Paper $1.95. 16s.

[15] *The Nobler Pleasure: Dryden's Comedy in Theory and Practice*, by Frank Harper Moore. North Carolina U.P. and O.U.P. pp. viii+264. $6.00. 48s.

[16] *Dryden and Holland*, by J. A. Van der Welle. Groningen: J. B. Wolters, 1962. pp. iv+154. fl.9.50.

[17] *John Dryden: The Poet as Orator*, by James Sutherland. The twentieth W. P. Ker Memorial Lecture delivered in the University of Glasgow, 21 February 1962. Jackson, Son & Company, Publishers to the University. pp. 30. 6s.

control the reader'. It was 'the energy a poet brought to bear on his material' which mattered: *materiam superabat opus*. Sutherland is not concerned with what Dryden *thought* he was doing, although he quotes a little of that, too, but with his poetic achievement, from this point of view, as seen in various levels of prologue and epilogue, *Threnodia Augustalis*, *Eleonora*, and other poems.

(*b*) A very different aspect of Dryden is the subject of Reuben A. Brower's essay, 'Dryden and the "Invention" of Pope', in *McKillop Essays* (see note 7). Like some other great poets, Dryden went on exploring and experimenting into old age. From 1685 until his death, the poet-orator turned more and more to descriptive and pastoral verse, and to the theme of retirement, 'free from Business and Debate'. Comparison between early and late verse-epistles emphasizes the extent to which (as in those to Congreve and his kinsman Driden) he had achieved a relaxed and familiar 'accent of private conversation'. Retirement from Court, renewed acquaintance with rural life, and the stimulus of the poets whom he was translating, all encouraged the anticipation of much that has been regarded as due to the 'invention' of Pope. Brower's article is a persuasive invitation to a re-reading of late Dryden.

To turn to satire: Bruce King writes on '*Absalom and Achitophel*: Machiavelli and the False Messiah' (*Ea*). He suggests that imagery in Achitophel's speeches associates Absalom with the numerous Messianic figures of the period, such as John Nayler; and in lines 230–61 he finds echoes of Machiavelli's *Il Principe*, Books 25–6. King also has a note on 'Dryden's *Absalom and Achitophel*, 150–166' in *Ex*, offering a Hobbesian

interpretation of Shaftesbury's 'madness' (*Leviathan* I, 8). The 'working out' of the 'fiery Soul' refers literally to Shaftesbury's drainage tube; the diseased body was the origin of the unbalanced mind. 'Amnon's Murther' (*NQ*), Edward S. Le Comte believes to refer not to Monmouth's attack on Coventry, but to his part in the murder of a watchman. Tom H. Towers offers an interesting interpretation in 'The Lineage of Shadwell: An Approach to *MacFlecknoe*' (*SEL*). He argues that the poem must be read in a context of theatrical quarrels. Dryden objected on both critical and financial grounds to the visually spectacular productions with which Shadwell and Davenant had been successful. He therefore provided Shadwell with a set of theatrical ancestors (Dekker, Heywood, etc.) who were all associated with despised pageantry and show, as was Flecknoe himself. Shadwell's lineage was correctly traced, in that Davenant had taken over from Beeston, who had been responsible for the noisy spectacles at the Red Bull. 'Dryden's *MacFlecknoe*, 48' (*Ex*), by David P. French, considers the various Restoration figures who might be alluded to in 'Aston Hall', which has so far baffled editors. If there is a solution, it probably lies in Chapter 10 of Vieth's *Attribution in Restoration Poetry* (see Note 20.) A stimulating general essay on satire, by Philip Pinkus, 'Satire and St. George' (*QQ*), makes a few perceptive comments on *MacFlecknoe*.

Earl Miner's 'The Wolf's Progress in *The Hind and the Panther*' (*BNYPL*) is an admirably clear exposition of a difficult passage. What, he asks, are references to Jewish, Saxon, and Medieval history doing in an attack on Restoration Presbyterianism? Miner's answer is that here, as elsewhere in the poem, Dryden is writing a progress-piece. Calvinism, politically and theologically, was a particular case of a persistent Whiggish-fanatical trait in human nature that showed itself in the Sanhedrin, in the Saxon church, and in Medieval dissent. The Calvinistic Exclusionist, the Wolf's latest manifestation, had earlier existences as a Jewish rebel or one of '*Wickliff's* brood'. But Miner's learned interpretation does not acquit Dryden's verse of obscurity.

John Barnard's 'Dryden, Tonson, and Subscriptions for the 1697 *Virgil*' (*PBSA*) presents evidence which shows that Ward's *Life of Dryden* underestimates Dryden's earnings from copy-money and subscriptions. There are some interesting pages on the place of the *Virgil* in the history of subscription publication. In 'The Dates of Six Dryden Letters' (*PQ*), Barnard disagrees with dates proposed by Margaret Boddy in her rather obscure article entitled 'Dryden-Lauderdale Relationships, Some Bibliographical Notes and a Suggestion' (*PQ*). Barnard can accept only one of the revised dates; the rest must stay as they are. A scholarly Norwegian collection[18] contains a chapter by Arvid Løsnes, 'Dryden's *Aeneis* and The Delphin *Virgil*', proving by detailed analysis of editions that the Latin Text on which Dryden mostly worked was the second edition of the Delphin Virgil.

Some important studies of various aspects of Dryden's criticism have appeared. George Watson's 'Dryden's First Answer to Rymer' (*RES*), develops the notes and commentary on the 'Heads of an Answer to Rymer' included in his Everyman edition of the criticism. The reasons for using Tonson's version of the

'Heads' are given in full, and Watson goes on to sum up the importance of the 'Heads' as 'the one critical document in English between the Restoration and Johnson's Shakespeare in which the *Poetics* of Aristotle are attacked frontally and without qualification'. But they remained 'a brilliant curiosity'. They led nowhere, either for Dryden himself, who retired into a more cautious position, or for his immediate successors, who did not know of them.

Irène Simon examines 'Dryden's Revision of the *Essay of Dramatic Poesy*' (*RES*). His alterations were 'far more than a matter of removing terminal prepositions'. The earlier version was too close to the spoken word to satisfy Dryden's standards in 1684. The removal of colloquialisms and dated expressions, and many grammatical and syntactical changes, resulted in greater clarity, ease, and smoothness, but there was some 'loss of vigour and of idiomatic flavour'. Dryden aimed at a polite conversational mean between 'vulgarity' and scholarly stiffness. Irène Simon discusses and develops Brown's earlier treatment of Dryden's debt to Tillotson (1961: *YW* xlii. 179). Nial Rudd, a classical scholar, gives a severely corrective account of 'Dryden on Horace and Juvenal' (*UTQ*), an attack on the *Discourse on Satire*. There is no denying the verdict that both on literary and historical grounds, 'as far as Horace and Juvenal are concerned Dryden's essay is wrong or misleading on almost every point'. The judgement is weightily and elegantly supported. Rudd writes to protect those readers for whom Dryden 'is probably their only source of information about Horace and Juvenal'. Not surprisingly, however, Dryden's essay somehow survives. If the critic is kicked out of the front door, the poet comes

[18] *The Hidden Sense, and other Essays*, by Maren-Sofie Røstvig *et al.* (Norwegian Studies in English, No. 9.) Oslo U.P. pp. vi+226. N.Kr. 35.00.

P

in from the back. The extent to which Dryden was using his subject as part of his personal debate about the practice of satire is now clearer than ever. The article may usefully be compared with Ruth Nevo's discussion of the *Discourse* (see note 2). In a footnote Rudd suggests a likely contributory source in Horace for Zimri (*Sat*. I. 3. 9–19: 'nil aequale homini fuit . . .'). 'The Voice of Mr. Bayes', by Eugene M. Waith (*SEL*), is primarily concerned with interpreting Dryden's neglected dedications. The voice that sounds through most of them was parodied in *The Rehearsal*, but Waith believes that Dryden intended more than obsequious compliment of his patrons. Apart from their straight critical content, the dedications of the heroic plays sought to create an ideal situation for the reception of the plays. Waith illustrates this well from the dedication of *Troilus and Cressida* to Sunderland, and of *The Indian Emperor* to the Duchess of Monmouth. The rhetoric creates an image of nobility for patrons and audience to live up to; the voice 'aims at transforming an audience of fops and lechers into an audience of heroes'. James Sutherland contributes a brief, pointed account of 'John Dryden' to a series 'Critics Who Have Influenced Taste' (*The Times*, 11 April). In an ill-natured age Dryden's honourable contribution was 'to be at once seriously concerned about good writing and good literature, and yet to maintain an equable and lively temper'.

All but one of the articles on Dryden's drama deal with *All for Love*. In 'Dryden's Intent in *All for Love*' (*CE*), Bruce King argues that the play and the preface represent different stages of Dryden's thinking about tragedy. In the play his indifference to poetic justice and his striving for emotional sympathy correspond approximately to the critical ideas of the 'Heads of an Answer to Rymer', which must have been written at about the same time as the play. Shortly afterwards he came under the moralizing and strictly neo-classical influence of Le Bossu, and wrote the *Preface*, calling attention to the 'excellency of the moral'. The fault of *All for Love* may be that it narrows tragedy to emotional heightening of pity; but within those limits it is consistently written. Contributing a chapter on 'Passion and Pity in *All for Love*' to *The Hidden Sense* (see Note 18), Otto Reinert agrees with King about the *Preface*, but is concerned with the larger subject of the play's coherence. He sets out to show that when all comparisons with Shakespeare have been made, *All for Love* achieves unity 'in its sustained mode of pathos and in its theme of a world of cold reason well lost for passion', and that, to a larger extent than has been conceded, the theme is inherent in the plot and imagery. Reason cannot endorse the conduct of the lovers as admirable; but reason, cold and sexless, is also suspect as a 'guide to the conduct—not of the safe, but of the fulfilled, life'. This is a well-documented essay. Two notes on *All for Love* are S. Klima, 'Some Unrecorded Borrowings from Shakespeare in Dryden's "All for Love"' (*NQ*); and Carl J. Stratman, 'John Dryden's "All for Love": Unrecorded Editions' (*PBSA*). Richard N. Ringler discusses 'Two Sources for Dryden's *The Indian Emperor*' (*PQ*): Donne's *First Anniversary*, and *The Faerie Queene*, I and II.

3. OTHER AUTHORS

(*a*) *Poets and Dramatists* (*b*) *Prose Authors.*

(*a*) H. J. Oliver's critical biography

of Sir Robert Howard[19] attempts the difficult biographical task of rehabilitating a faded and stereotyped reputation. His success is due to a thorough mastery of the material, including Howard's long political and administrative career, but perhaps still more to his avoidance of conjecture, and the scrupulous moderation of his claims for Howard. The result is striking enough; at least, the old picture of the Dryden-Howard relationship seems displaced for good, though perhaps not beyond further argument. The editors of the California *Dryden* Vol. VIII strongly suspect that 'virtually all' *The Indian Queen* was by Dryden. Oliver has come to the opposite conclusion, 'that on the external evidence alone, no strong case could be made out for a large share by Dryden'. He has the advantage over other scholars in having closely studied Howard's versification before 1664, and so can assert that 'all theories which divide the authors' shares . . . on the supposition that Dryden could write regular verse but Howard could not, are simply wrong.' A judicious chapter on Howard's argument with Dryden about dramatic verse, and the conduct of the two towards each other (which Johnson cautiously described as 'not now easily to be explained'), makes Howard's part appear more honourable and intelligent, and Dryden's accomplished sarcasm in the *Defence of an Essay* more gratuitous, than traditional accounts suggest. On the central point at issue, 'Howard was, after all, right'. Apart from this, Howard 'wrote one of the best comedies of his time in *The Committee* (and this before Dryden or Etherege had contributed significantly to Restoration drama); and he had some share (at least) in one of the best tragi-comedies of the age, *The Duke of Lerma*.' Without claiming much more than this, Oliver establishes Howard as rather more significant than simply Dryden's brother-in-law and a pompous butt. He has not attempted 'to psychoanalyze' him; but perhaps a Character would not have come amiss in the first full biography.

As the title of David M. Vieth's exhaustive and argumentative book[20] indicates, his inquiries extend some way beyond his essential subject, which is the canon and text of Rochester's *Poems* (1680). On the primary sources for the whole group which Rochester represents, there is little that he does not touch. His analyses are offered as 'prolegomena to a future critical edition of Rochester's works', so that a certain mingling of textual theory, tabulation, bibliographical detection, literary criticism, polemic, and drum-beating is not unexpected, and makes a long book. Textual criticism can be a pugnacious calling. Developing Thorpe's pioneer work on *Poems*, Vieth's main and notable achievement is to establish the status and collateral relationship of the printed text, as found in the Huntington edition, and a manuscript miscellany which he is the first to study thoroughly, described as Yale MS. In a brief notice it is hard to do justice to Vieth's industry and skill. He shows the primary importance of the Yale MS ascriptions, with the result that of the sixty-one poems in the 1680 text, he can establish that thirty-four are certainly or probably Rochester's, and can offer authoritative evidence for the authorship of most of the remainder — Buckhurst, Scroope,

[19] *Sir Robert Howard (1626–1698): A Critical Biography*, by H. J. Oliver. Duke U.P. and C.U.P. pp. xiv+346. $9.25. 74s.

[20] *Attribution in Restoration Poetry: A Study of Rochester's 'Poems' of 1680*, by David M. Vieth. Yale U.P. (Yale Studies in English No. 153.) pp. xx+538. $12.50. 90s.

Etherege, Behn, Oldham, and others; only two in fact are utterly 'unknown'. These conclusions are set out in an impressive 124-page list in Part III. They are not all new—Thorpe, Pinto, and others have prepared the way; but the difference between Thorpe's findings that there were thirty-seven poems which could not be shown *not* to be Rochester's, and the more positive conclusions of Vieth about most of his thirty-four, is considerable. Part II of *Attribution* consists of a series of essays on specific problems, where, in some cases resorting to literary history and criticism in the absence of bibliographical evidence, and sometimes criticism alone, Vieth is more vulnerable. There is good use of internal evidence on *Timon* and *Tunbridge Wells*, the attribution of 'I cannot change' to Scroope is acceptable, though a pity, and there are interesting discussions of the Buckhurst–Etherege *Epistles* and of satires on Rochester. On the other hand, there is the question of *An Epistolary Essay* and the *Heroical Epistle*. V. de Sola Pinto is very much a party to this debate, and in his long review of Vieth in *PQ* (1964), pp. 381–4, has some damaging criticisms to make. If Pinto was wrong, as he admits, about the nature of the *Heroical Epistle* (along with other scholars), until corrected by Wilson, he may well still be right about the *Epistolary Essay*, on an ironic interpretation of which Vieth constructs a new date and much else. It is regrettable that in this and other matters, what is still far from settled has been taken over as established fact by the editor of the Yale *Poems on Affairs of State*. This is a field in which such imprimaturs ought only to be grudgingly given.

James Thorpe has had to work

over some of the same ground as Vieth in order to establish the canon and text of Etherege's *Poems*,[21] and has been able to refer to Vieth's researches in his Notes. With the *Plays and Letterbook* properly edited, Etherege's writings have now received their due of scholarly attention. Modestly, Thorpe expects more poems to turn up; however, including songs from plays, his total of thirty-one poems almost doubles the number of poems which can be attributed to Etherege, by comparison with Verity's edition of 1888. Thorpe has included two verse-letters by Buckhurst, and one by Dryden, ghosted for the unpoetic Secretary of State, Middleton; this diplomatic-bag, mannerly-obscene correspondence has had a thorough airing this year. The collection reminds us that Etherege could be tender and grave as well as lewd. Thorpe's admirable edition, and Etherege, are the subject of a full-page article in *TLS*, 18 October.

Richard E. Quaintance's researches into 'The French Sources of the Restoration "Imperfect Enjoyment" Poem' (*PQ*), are referred to by Thorpe, with regard to Etherege's poem on that theme. Amongst other poems, Etherege's 'imitation' is examined in the light of its French source, a poem by Charles Beys, quoted in full. Quaintance concludes that the English poets developed further than the French the idea that 'our flames are punished by their own excess'; they expressed distrust of 'the interference of rational or imaginative faculties in a situation properly physical'.

David Rawlinson writes on 'Cowley and the Current Status of Metaphysical Poetry' (*EC*). He believes that Cowley's poetic status should be judged not by *The Mistress* but by the mature elegies on Hervey and Crashaw, and that the moral insight

---

[21] *The Poems of Sir George Etherege*, ed. by James Thorpe. Princeton U.P. and O.U.P. pp. xvi+150. $4.50. 36s.

and poise of his *Essays in Prose and Verse* have been underrated. W. J. Cameron considers 'The Authorship of "Commendatory Verses" 1700' (*NQ*), written to Blackmore. A Sydney copy provides authoritative ascriptions.

Forty years after first editing Congreve, Bonamy Dobrée writes a brief account of him and his work,[22] in the series of which Dobrée is general editor. The tone and 'position' of the essay, by a master of the familiar-polite, are in keeping with the temperate scepticism of Congreve's lines to Cobham, to which Dobrée's last sentence refers: 'All may not agree with that philosophy; some will combat it fiercely; yet it is wisdom of a kind . . . and might be expected of a man who had a good deal pondered, and experienced, the way of the world.' He does not claim too much, simply that what Congreve as dramatist did well, he did better than anyone. Dull? Trivial? He has a courteous but unyielding reply. Anthony Gosse identifies 'The Omitted Scene in Congreve's *Love for Love*' (*MP*), using Dobrée's scene numbering, as the eleventh scene of Act III. It was not acted in the first production. Congreve's achievement as librettist is discussed in two articles by Stoddard Lincoln: 'Eccles and Congreve: Music and Drama on the Restoration Stage' (*TN*); and 'The First Setting of Congreve's "Semele"' (*Music and Letters*), with correspondence and a reply. P. F. Vernon, on 'Social Satire in Shadwell's *Timon*' (*SN*), finds that it is 'one of the few Restoration tragedies which may be profitably considered as a play of ideas'. Shadwell's Timon, more of a victim than Shakespeare's, was a vehicle for satire on the corruptions of society, including the mercenary exploitation of marriage. Shadwell made a serious attempt to deal with the social issues of his day within the medium of tragedy.

(*b*) In an important contribution to *McKillop Essays*, 'Roger North and the Art of Biography' (see note 7), James L. Clifford calls attention to the manuscripts of the biographer Roger North, which survive in neglected profusion in the B.M. and other libraries, including St. John's College, Cambridge. North published almost nothing in his lifetime, but wrote assiduously, from his retirement in the 1690's until his death in 1734. Clifford has sampled the collections, and emphasizes two main aspects of their interest: first, the light which the many manuscript versions of the Lives throw on North's biographical methods; and second, North's remarkable and, in its time, unique, discussion of the problems of biography, in the drafts of a 'General Preface' to the St. John's College manuscript of the Life of Lord Keeper North. Clifford has quoted from the Preface in his study, *Biography as an Art* (1962: *YW* xliii. 22). Both in his biographical experiments and in his discussions of principle, North was far in advance of his time, and anticipated later developments by Johnson and Boswell. Clifford expresses the hope that scholars will one day get to work on the mass of North material. A specimen of the kind of biographical compilation which North condemned is Winstanley's *Lives of the Poets*[23] (1687), now reproduced in facsimile. In a brief introduction the editor does his best

22 *William Congreve*, by Bonamy Dobrée. (Writers and their Work.) Longmans, for the British Council and the National Book League. pp. 35. 2*s.* 6*d.*

23 *The Lives of the Most Famous English Poets (1687)*, by William Winstanley. A Facsimile Reproduction with an Introduction by William Riley Parker. Gainesville, Florida: Scholars' Facsimiles & Reprints. pp. viii+248. £3.

for Winstanley, showing to what extent he improved on his main authority, Edward Phillips. But as literary historians have squeezed Winstanley dry, his work was hardly worth reprinting.

C. S. Emden has gone over familiar ground in examining *Pepys Himself*.[24] This is a character-study based on the Diary, not a biography. Emden's reflections on the tensions between Pepys's public and private character may be compared with Foxon's hypothesis (see note 8). J. P. Kenyon edits a selection, *Pepys's Diary*,[25] choosing to emphasize Pepys's career as administrator rather than his pleasures and domestic life. He has included some appropriate illustrations. Margaret Willy contributes a useful essay on Evelyn and Pepys[26] to 'Writers and their Work', divided equally between them. Anthony Powell's *John Aubrey and his Friends*,[27] first published in 1948, appears in a revised edition.

The outstanding work in the sphere of diaries and memoirs is *The Journal of James Yonge (1647–1721): Plymouth Surgeon*,[28] edited by F. N. L. Poynter from a manuscript owned by the Plymouth Athenaeum. Yonge began as a surgeon-apprentice in Cromwell's navy at the age of eleven; he became a prosperous surgeon, Mayor of Plymouth, and an F.R.S. He kept notes and a diary,

and at various stages of his life wrote them out retrospectively as a journal. There is some good terse narrative, including an expert account of his months as a sick prisoner-of-war in Holland. Yonge was tough, ambitious, intelligent, fairly well-read, skilful and respected in his profession, and, fortunately for us, persistently curious about the notabilities of his time. He was often in London pressing for government jobs with which to supplement his Plymouth practice, and recorded his leisurely journeys through the southern counties, and the London sights he enjoyed after the lobbying was over; the long visit of 1681 is especially interesting. At various times he saw the 'old paralytick claret drinker' Samuel Butler, Oates in prison in 1687, 'as fat, brisk and sportive as ever, only less superbous', Queen Catherine (whom he had convoyed from Portugal) 'waddling like a duck' at Windsor, and many famous scientists, some of whom he knew. The aged Walter Charleton examined him for his L.R.C.P. He heard the shepherds whistling on the Plain, as they had done for Aubrey, and was moved by the noble prospect of city and river from Richmond Hill. Comparisons with Evelyn or Pepys would be fruitless; the scale and potentialities are obviously quite different, and there is much that is perfunctory, or of interest only to naval historians. But judged on its own merits, the Journal is a valuable and fascinating record. The editing is just adequate, although we are told almost nothing about the manuscript; and where a man's holograph is available, there seems no case for modernizing.

Among the 'sights', for Yonge, were Sir William Temple ('a black, sour fac't man'), and his 'delicate' garden at Sheen, which Yonge 'got into'. Temple's fame was in part

[24] *Pepys Himself*, by Cecil S. Emden. O.U.P. pp. xii + 148. 21s.

[25] *Pepys's Diary*, ed. by J. P. Kenyon. Batsford. pp. x + 246. Cloth 18s. paper 12s. 6d.

[26] *English Diarists: Evelyn & Pepys*, by Margaret Willy. (Writers and their Work.) Longmans, for the British Council and the National Book League. pp. 47. 2s. 6d.

[27] *John Aubrey and his Friends*, by Anthony Powell. New and revised Edition. Heinemann. pp. 342. 42s.

[28] *The Journal of James Yonge (1647–1721): Plymouth Surgeon*, ed. by F. N. L. Poynter. Hamden, Conn.: Archon Books. London: Longmans. pp. 247. $6.00. 35s.

derived from his Essays, a selection[29] from which has been made by Samuel Holt Monk. He has chosen those on the Gardens of Epicurus, Heroic Virtue, Poetry, and the two on Ancient and Modern Learning. Monk has refrained from annotation and has modernized the text of 1692 and 1701. A long introductory essay gives an extremely useful account of Temple's career and the intellectual context of the Essays (although there is a mistake on p. xiii: in 1667 Temple was negotiating the Triple Alliance, not the marriage of William and Mary). William Roberts reproduces the title page and text (58 lines) of Temple's poem *Upon the Death of Mrs. Catherine Philips*, in 'Sir William Temple on Orinda: Neglected Publications' (*PBSA*). This probably unique Yale copy, printed 1664, is a version earlier than that in the B.M.

T. A. Birrell introduces a reprint of *A Brief Account of the New Sect of Latitude-Men* (*1662*),[30] and argues the case for Simon Patrick's authorship. This seems to have been the first appearance in print of the term as applied to the moderate Cambridge group, later to be described at length by Burnet. Patrick defends their position and tells a fable about a Clockmender, 'a talkative fellow', which vividly suggests the impatience of the new philosophers with scholastic philosophy. Birrell discusses some interesting features of Patrick's vocabulary. Corinne Comstock Weston, examining '"The King's Prerogative", 1680' (*NQ*), attributed by

S.T.C. to John Nalson, has found that in fact it is identical with *Lex Terrae* (1647) by the Royalist David Jenkins.

Chief among the very few items on Bunyan is a dissertation from the University of Mainz, *Bunyan als Künstler*,[31] by Berta Haferkamp. The most original sections of the book are very usefully devoted to a detailed stylistic analysis of *The Pilgrim's Progress*. The major stylistic influences are examined in turn—Biblical; popular sources (vocabulary, grammar, and idioms); fairy-tale and romance. This is followed by analyses of the main characteristics of Bunyan's handling of the language, e.g. in word-order, parallelism, antithesis, figures, and of his narrative technique. There are seven pages of summary in English. James F. Forrest contributes two articles on Bunyan. 'Mercy with her Mirror' (*PQ*) considers an episode in *The Pilgrim's Progress*, Part II. Forrest relates Bunyan's use of the mirror-emblem to iconographic tradition and to its place in some other Puritan writings. The longing for the glass represents a desire for a revelation of the soul's inner state, through the 'glass' of the Word of God. In this and some other respects Mercy is a type of the Virgin Mary. Forrest's second article, 'Bunyan's Ignorance and the Flatterer: A Study in the Literary Art of Damnation' (*SP*), emphasizes Bunyan's deliberate art in placing the 'Character' of Ignorance functionally in the narrative structure. Ignorance's choice of the wrong kind of certainty embodies the complacency and pride by which the pilgrims are tempted. He is kept on the margin of the narrative; the shock of his condemnation has been carefully contrived.

---

[29] *Five Miscellaneous Essays*, by Sir William Temple. Ed. with an Introduction by Samuel Holt Monk. Michigan U.P. and Cresset Press. pp. xlvi+203. $5.00. 30s.

[30] *A Brief Account of the New Sect of Latitude–Men* (*1662*), by Simon Patrick. Ed. with an Introduction by T. A. Birrell. (Augustan Reprint Society, No. 100.) Los Angeles: Clark Memorial Library, Univ. of California. pp. vi+24. For members.

[31] *Bunyan als Künstler: Stilkritische Studien zu seinem Hauptwerk 'The Pilgrim's Progress'*, by Berta Haferkamp. Tübingen: Max Niemeyer Verlag. pp. viii+224. DM.28.

J. M. Cohen has edited a reprint[32] of one of L'Estrange's best works, his 'translation' of Quevedo's *Visions*. Unfortunately this edition, although admirably printed and bound, is of little use to the reader who wants an accurate reproduction of L'Estrange's text. Cohen appears to have used an eighteenth-century version, different at many points from L'Estrange's text of 1667 or 1673. He has omitted the Preface 'To the Readers Gentle and Simple'. Modern scholarly editions of L'Estrange are virtually non-existent (there are some accurate extracts in Peter Ure's Pelican anthology, *Seventeenth-Century Prose*); an obvious opportunity has been missed.

The last item in this section concerns some verses which belong to an essentially prose group. William Morrell was a confidence-trickster, a later Volpone whose career reached a climax in 1692 when he took lodgings with a London baker, and gave out that he was a rich country squire in retreat from his family. He fell ill, his dupe the watchful baker sent for physicians, a will was made with large bequests to baker and neighbours, a handsome funeral was ordered, and so the 'squire' died. The will, Morrell's last and most sensational fraud, was published, on the day of his pauper's funeral, as *Diego Redivivus* (recently reprinted by the Augustan Reprint Society). Spiro Peterson has discovered a previously unknown broadside ballad, 'The Pretended Country Squire', in Chetham's Library, Manchester, and prints it, together with a verse epitaph from *The Gentleman's Journal*, in 'William Morrell and Late Seventeenth-Century Fiction' (*PQ*). The fullest of contemporary accounts

was Settle's *Compleat Memoirs* (1694). The relationship between the verses and the prose pieces is described.

4. HISTORY, PAINTING AND MUSIC

David Ogg's *England in the Reign of Charles II*[33] has appeared in paperback, with some minor corrections and additions. This very welcome reprint coincides with the publication of a *Festschrift*[34] in his honour. All students of the later seventeenth century are greatly in his debt. In this collection, an essay by Maurice Ashley, 'King James II and the Revolution of 1688: Some Reflections on the Historiography', examines the disagreements amongst historians over the last 250 years on the subject of James II, with particular reference to the debate about James's attitude to the Dissenters. James and the Revolution attract considerable attention. In *History Today* Ashley attempts to answer the question 'Is There a Case for James II?'. J. P. Kenyon's Inaugural Lecture at Hull discussed *The Nobility in the Revolution of 1688*.[35] Fewer than 10 per cent were active; their resentments showed, not in opposition, 'but in something very like a paralysis of will'. Kenyon also gives in *History Today* an entertaining account of 'The Birth of the Old Pretender', and the extraordinary inquiry which followed it. Gerald M. Straka[36] has collected

---

[32] *Visions*, by Francisco de Quevedo. As Translated by Sir Roger L'Estrange, and now introduced by J. M. Cohen. (Centaur Classics.) Southern Illinois U.P. and Centaur Press. pp. 146. $12.00. £3. 3s.

[33] *England in the Reign of Charles II*, by David Ogg. Second edition, corrected. (Oxford Paperbacks.) O.U.P. 2 vols. pp. xiv+390; viii+392. $1.95. 15s.

[34] *Historical Essays 1600–1750 Presented to David Ogg*, ed. by H. E. Bell and R. L. Ollard. Bell. pp. xi+274. 35s.

[35] *The Nobility in the Revolution of 1688*, by J. P. Kenyon. University of Hull Publications. pp. 22. 4s.

[36] *The Revolution of 1688: Whig Triumph or Palace Revolution?* Ed. with an Introduction by Gerald M. Straka. (Problems in European Civilization.) D. C. Heath & Co. and Harrap. pp. xiv+98. 11s. 6d.

contemporary narratives of the Revolution and extracts from the historians. The emphasis is on the debate between Whig or neo-Whig historians and their critics. This is a serviceable volume, provided it does not replace the reading of original works. From the literary point of view, D. C. Coleman's biography, *Sir John Banks, Baronet and Businessman*,[37] may be compared in usefulness with A. Upton's *Sir Arthur Ingram* (1961), where the career of a Jacobean financier was highly suggestive of themes in the drama. Appropriately, Coleman has chosen an epigraph from *The Country Wife*. Banks, from the lower Kentish gentry, made his first pile by victualling the Cromwellian navy. He died in 1699, in modern terms a multi-millionaire, one of the Crown's largest creditors; his fortune set up two peerages. But he was also the familiar friend of Pepys, an employer of Locke as travelling tutor to his son, an F.R.S., and a moderate Tory, despised by aristocratic Exclusionists. While correcting some of the slacker generalizations about connexions between Whiggism and finance, Coleman takes Banks to be representative of his generation (Boyle, Locke, Hooke, Halifax, Dryden), with 'its cooling temper, its rationalistic interests, its tendency to toleration'; they had all learned that 'adaptation was the condition of survival'. Coleman has constructed an interesting book out of ledgers and business papers. Maurice Ashley's *The Stuarts in Love*[38] is based on much study of primary sources. While most of the book is concerned with Royal marriages and love-affairs (avoiding the usual backstairs knowingness), the most original pages are on love and marriage among the classes of Stuart society.

The following deal with religious life and thought: W. C. de Pauley, 'Richard Baxter Surveyed' (*Church Quarterly Review*), an essay on Baxter's theology; A. Harold Wood, *Church Unity Without Uniformity*,[39] largely concerned with Baxter, the Savoy Conference and the events leading to the exodus of 1662; and 'The Religion of Protestants' by the late Norman Sykes, a chapter in *The Cambridge History of the Bible*.[40] Sykes makes unexpected use of Dryden, in expounding the Authority of the Bible, Puritan Preaching, and Biblical Criticism.

A. R. Hall has written a masterly history of scientific thought and discovery, *From Galileo to Newton*.[41] He takes Milton as a representative figure, who 'having gone to school with Aristotle and Ptolemy . . . could have seen "at Mr. Crosse's house at Oxford" the very beginning of the long road that led to Rutherford'. The mathematical sciences dominate the book, but there are also excellent chapters on the descriptive sciences. With full notes, bibliographies, and well-chosen illustrations, this is an indispensable book for any student of the period.

A trade-fair catalogue may not often figure in these pages, but the

---

[37] *Sir John Banks, Baronet and Businessman: A Study of Business, Politics and Society in Later Stuart England*, by D. C. Coleman. O.U.P. pp. xi+215. 40s.

[38] *The Stuarts in Love: With some reflections on Love and Marriage in the Sixteenth and Seventeenth Centuries*, by Maurice Ashley. Hodder & Stoughton. pp. 256. 30s.

[39] *Church Unity Without Uniformity: A Study of Seventeenth-century English Church Movements and of Richard Baxter's Proposals for a Comprehensive Church*, by A. Harold Wood. Epworth Press. pp. 324. 35s.

[40] *The Cambridge History of the Bible: The West from the Reformation to the Present Day*, ed. by S. L. Greenslade. C.U.P. pp. x+590. 45s.

[41] *From Galileo to Newton: 1630–1720*, by A. R. Hall. (The Rise of Modern Science, Vol. III. General Editor, A. R. Hall.) Collins. pp. 380. 30s.

catalogue[42] of the Printing Exhibition of 1963 (IPEX) at Earls Court, London, and the B.M., deserves some mention. Historical annexes to the exhibition displayed the history of printing processes, a collection of printing since Gutenberg, and a range of works demonstrating the impact of printing, with the stress on the propagation of ideas. As far as this period is concerned, the printing specimens include e.g. Hill's *Aesop's Fables* (1687) with the Barlow etchings and Mrs. Behn's verses beneath them, the Dryden-Tonson *Virgil*, and Clarendon's *History*. Illustrating the spread of ideas through print are some thirty late seventeenth-century works, from *Leviathan* to Tyson's *Orang-Outang* (1699). This is an invaluable record of five centuries of intellectual history, annotated and illustrated.

Our knowledge of seventeenth-century painting has been greatly advanced by three works likely to be definitive in the subject, each the product of authoritative scholarship. To include first a publication of 1962: the first volume[43] of Edward Croft-Murray's *Decorative Painting in England 1537–1837*, covers the Tudor and Stuart periods. There are seven chapters of text, 139 plates, and seven chapters of Catalogue, arranged alphabetically under artists. The bibliography runs to fifteen large pages. This is the book in which to

check on what Pope referred to in 'painted Cielings. . . . Where sprawl the Saints of Verrio or Laguerre'. David Piper's *Catalogue of Seventeenth-Century Portraits in the National Portrait Gallery, 1625–1714*,[44] is scholarly, immensely detailed, and scrupulous in its inspection of traditional linkings of portraits and names. The arrangement is alphabetical under sitters. Oliver Millar is engaged on the first complete catalogue of Royal Pictures, to be completed in five volumes. The first two-part volume[45] (part one, text; part two, plates), carries the record down to the early Georges. Court beauties of the Restoration are here in force. Daphne Foskett's *British Portrait Miniatures*[46] has three chapters on the later seventeenth century, with illustrations.

F. B. Zimmerman's *Catalogue*[47] of the works of Purcell, the first of its kind on a major English composer, is a great work of scholarship. The extent of its researches in manuscripts on both sides of the Atlantic inspires admiration. The Catalogue's relevance to the study of the drama hardly needs to be stated: there was no dramatist of any note, from the 1670's to Purcell's death, who did not at some time turn to him for incidental music or song settings. The main sections or movements of every work, from catches to operas, are illustrated with musical incipits.

[42] *Printing and the Mind of Man: A Catalogue of a Display of Printing Mechanisms and Printed Materials Arranged to Illustrate the History of Western Civilization and the Means of the Multiplication of Literary Texts Since the XV Century . . . Assembled at The British Museum and at Earls Court London 16–27 July 1963*. F. W. Bridges & Sons Ltd. and the Association of Printers' Machinery (Proprietary) Ltd. pp. 166. Copies obtainable from the British Museum. 10s. 6d.

[43] *Decorative Painting in England 1537–1837. Vol. I: Early Tudor to Sir James Thornhill*, by Edward Croft-Murray. Country Life, 1962. pp. 326. £12. 12s.

[44] *A Catalogue of Seventeenth-Century Portraits in the National Portrait Gallery, 1625–1714*, compiled by David Piper. C.U.P. for the Trustees of the National Portrait Gallery. pp. xxxviii+410. £5.

[45] *The Pictures in the Collection of Her Majesty the Queen: I. Tudor, Stuart and Early Georgian Pictures*, by Oliver Millar. Phaidon Press, 2 vols. pp. 227+11+226 plates. £5.

[46] *British Portrait Miniatures*, by Daphne Foskett. Methuen. pp. 199. £5. 5s.

[47] *Henry Purcell, 1659–1695: An Analytical Catalogue of his Music*, ed. by F. B. Zimmerman. New York: St. Martin's Press. London: Macmillan. pp. xxiv+576. £8. 8s.

XII

The Eighteenth Century

C. H. PEAKE and J. CHALKER

THE chapter proceeds as follows: (*a*) general studies of the century or of the first half of it; (*b*) Swift, Addison and Steele, Pope, and Johnson; (*c*) miscellaneous poetry, prose (excluding the novel), and drama to 1725 [these sections are contributed by C. H. Peake]; (*d*) the novel; (*e*) poetry after Pope; (*f*) later prose; (*g*) drama after 1725 [these sections are contributed by J. Chalker].

(*a*) The accumulation of articles with no other principle of coherence than that their authors wished jointly to honour a colleague can produce a very mixed and sometimes unrewarding bag. But occasionally a *Festschrift* includes work of such distinction that it overcomes the weaknesses of its nature and establishes itself as one of the indispensable books on its period. In eighteenth-century studies the collections presented to George Sherburn and David Nichol Smith are examples; and now to them must be added *Restoration and Eighteenth-Century Literature: Essays in Honor of Alan Dugald McKillop*.[1] The bibliography of McKillop's writings which concludes the volume reminds us of the variety of his literary activities, and the essays included are appropriately varied while maintain-

ing a consistently high standard of scholarship and critical penetration. Most of them concern an individual author and are referred to in other sections of this and the preceding chapters (with the general reference *McKillop Essays*), but two have a more general reference to the eighteenth century. Irvin Ehrenpreis considers the current critical fondness for identifying and analysing authors' *personae*, and has no difficulty in showing that, although this procedure has often been useful, it has also often been carried to absurd extremes. He goes on to distinguish between useful and misleading approaches to *personae* with particular reference to the *Epistle to Arbuthnot*, *Gulliver's Travels*, and *A Modest Proposal*, and, although these more specific discussions are more challengeable, they serve to illustrate the dangers of uncritical acceptance of critical fashions. The other general essay concerning this period is Geoffrey Tillotson's 'The Methods of Description in Eighteenth- and Nineteenth-Century Poetry', which is concerned exclusively with syntax, and distinguishes between a descriptive method derived from Milton which employs a single extended sentence and a method initiated in the first quatrain of Gray's *Elegy* where each line forms a complete grammatical statement.

In an article entitled 'Newton further demands the Muse' (*SEL*),

[1] *Restoration and Eighteenth-Century Literature: Essays in Honor of Alan Dugald McKillop*, ed. by Carroll Camden. University of Chicago Press for William Marsh Rice University. pp. xi+435. $8.50. 63s.

William Powell Jones adds to Marjorie Hope Nicolson's account of the influence of Newton's *Optics* on eighteenth-century poetry evidence to show that the *Principia* controlled even more powerfully the poets' visions of an universal order. A different kind of influence is the subject of Lee Andrew Elioseff's 'Pastorals, Politics, and the Idea of Nature in the Reign of Queen Anne' (*Journal of Aesthetics and Art Criticism*) which relates differing views on the pastoral and opposing political allegiances to two fundamental ideas about Nature, the ideal and the empirical. A more obvious link between literature and society is investigated by David Foxon, whose 'Libertine Literature in England, 1660–1745' (*BC*), is a general survey of what is known about the publication of prose pornography and of proceedings taken against such writings. In 'Scottish Popular Ballads and Lyrics of the Eighteenth and Early Nineteenth Centuries: Some Preliminary Conclusions' (*Studies in Scottish Literature*) Thomas Crawford supplies an introductory analysis of the available materials on the subject; G. A. Cranfield has outlined *The Development of the Provincial Newspaper, 1700–1760*[2]; Nancy Lee Riffe's 'Contributions to a Finding List of Eighteenth-Century Periodicals' (*BNYPL*), consist of details of twenty-five British periodicals prior to 1789 not listed in Crane and Kaye's *Census of British Newspapers and Periodicals, 1620–1800* (1927); Paul Kaufman, in 'Reading Vogues at English Cathedral Libraries of the Eighteenth Century' (*BNYPL*), lists titles of books borrowed from eight such libraries by borrowers who include Warton, Percy, Sterne, and

Coleridge; and J. D. Fleeman records the discovery of seven '18th-Century Printing Ledgers' (*TLS*) belonging to the important publishing firm of the two Bowyers.

The materials included in Samuel Hynes's anthology of *English Literary Criticism: Restoration and 18th Century*[3] are for the most part the obvious choices since the edition is designed for use in schools and colleges, but the texts are good and there are brief introductory notes on the critics. Those who know Paul Hazard's *La crise de la conscience européenne* (1934), will welcome the appearance in paperback form of J. Lewis May's translation, *The European Mind, 1680–1715*,[4] first published in 1953. Inevitably such a wide-ranging subject leads to simplifications, and occasionally observations on particular works seem superficial (see, for instance, the remarks on Swift's *Argument against Abolishing Christianity*), but such faults are pardonable in a bold and sweeping survey of a critical period in European culture. The nature of the didactic poetry of the period is discussed by Ulrich Broich in 'Das Lehrgedicht als Teil der epischen Tradition des englischen Klassizismus' (*Germanisch-romanische Monatsschrift*); and Robert Halsband surveys 'Recent Studies in the Restoration and Eighteenth Century' (*SEL*).

(*b*) Uncertainty about the precise meaning to be attached to the word 'satire' has bedevilled many discussions of Swift's writings, and Edward

---

[2] *The Development of the Provincial Newspaper, 1700–1760*, by G. A. Cranfield. O.U.P. 1962. pp. xiv+287. $6.10. 38s.

[3] *English Literary Criticism: Restoration and 18th Century*, ed. by Samuel Hynes. New York: Appleton-Century-Crofts. pp. viii+322. $2.95.

[4] *The European Mind, 1680–1715*, by Paul Hazard. (Translated by J. Lewis May.) Penguin Books. pp. 512. 8s. 6d.

W. Rosenheim, Jr., consequently devotes the first of the four chapters of his *Swift and the Satirist's Art*[5] to the search for an adequate definition, concluding that 'satire consists of an attack by means of a manifest fiction upon discernible historic particulars'. Despite its plausible appearance this definition contains assertions which are difficult to accept; for instance, the insistence on 'discernible historic particulars' implies a refusal to regard human nature in its most general sense as a target for the satirist, or, rather, asserts that the label 'satire' must not be applied to generalized attacks on human follies and vices. But Rosenheim fails to perceive that he is merely arguing for a narrower definition of a word; in fact, he explicitly denies this, and claims that he is concerned with defining the nature of a specific literary mode. Yet most English practitioners of this mode have regarded the satirizing of vices and follies as their highest function and the local and transient applications as secondary; Rosenheim's definition undermines the conception of the permanence of true satire which made Pope imitate Horace and Johnson Juvenal, and denies the name of satire to much of *Gulliver's Travels*. Similarly the distinction drawn between 'punitive' and 'persuasive' satire will not bear too close a scrutiny. But the argument is well conducted and concerns matters usually overlooked, so that whether the reader agrees or disagrees he is likely to finish the chapter with his own ideas more precisely defined. Certainly this opening chapter gives rise to some interesting analyses of Swift's writings. There is an attempt to fix the ironic position of the

Argument against Abolishing Christianity, though here Rosenheim seems to allow too little for the flexibility of Swift's mind and his characteristic delight in achieving several disparate satirical ends at once; the emphasis on the historical particularity of the satirist's targets leads to a greater awareness of the ridicule of such writers as L'Estrange in *A Tale of a Tub*; and the fourth voyage of Gulliver is treated as philosophical vision rather than satire. The terms 'stimulating' and 'challenging' are worn, reviewer's counters, but this book is one to which they could fairly be applied.

A much-needed and careful revision of Teerink's *Bibliography of the Writings of Jonathan Swift*[6] has been carried out by Arthur H. Scouten; Mackie L. Jarrell plausibly identifies as 'A New Swift Attribution: The Preface to Sheridan's Sermon on St. Cecilia's Day' (*PMLA*); and, in a discussion of Swift's 'obscene' poems, Herbert Davis attributes to Swift himself 'A Modest Defence of "The Lady's Dressing Room"' (*McKillop Essays*—see note 1), a pamphlet first published by George Faulkner in 1732.

In contrast to recent attempts to trace a thematic unity in *A Tale of a Tub*, Philip Pinkus emphasizes the general inversion of values in 'The Upside-down World of *A Tale of a Tub*' (*ES*), which culminates in the equation of madness and greatness; N. J. C. Andreasen explores 'Swift's Satire on the Occult in *A Tale of a Tub*' (*TSLL*); David P. French, in 'Swift, Temple, and "A Digression on Madness"' (*TSLL*), argues that Swift's irony in the 'Digression'

[5] *Swift and the Satirist's Art*, by Edward W. Rosenheim, Jr. Chicago U.P. pp. xiii+243. $5.95. 44s. 6d.

[6] *A Bibliography of the Writings of Jonathan Swift*, by H. Teerink. Second edition, revised and corrected. Edited by Arthur H. Scouten. Pennsylvania U.P. pp. xviii+453. $25. £10.

enabled him to avoid committing himself to a judgement of Temple's Neo-Epicureanism; and Robert C. Steensma's 'Swift on Standing Armies: A Possible Source' (*NQ*) offers new arguments for supposing that Swift's ideas on this subject had been influenced by Temple.

Richmond P. Bond describes the career of 'Isaac Bickerstaff, Esq.' (*McKillop Essays*—see note 1), and tells how Swift's invention 'caught the whim of the Town, how other authors adopted his signature for their own use, how he was transformed by Steele and Addison and their associates into the celebrated Censor of the *Tatler*'. The same author records a legal dispute, in which Bickerstaff's most famous victim was involved, in 'John Partridge and the Company of Stationers' (*SB*). Richard I. Cook follows up his recent studies of the political writings (see *YW* xliii. 202) with an account of 'The Audience of Swift's Tory Tracts, 1710–14' (*MLQ*), and also examines 'Swift's Polemical Characters' (*Discourse*), paying particular attention to the use of irony for the purpose of praise and to the pretence of detachment in the histories.

Three articles are concerned with the origins of the materials of the third voyage of Gulliver. S. Klima wonders whether de Longueville's *Histoire des personnes qui ont vécu plusieurs siècles* may be 'A Possible Source for Swift's Struldbrugs?' (*PQ*); Cecil C. Seronsy thinks that some of the fantasies suggest the Jonsonian presence of 'Sir Politic Would-Be in Laputa' (*ELN*); and Kathleen Williams notes an interesting resemblance between the appearance of 'Swift's Laputians and "Mathematica"' (*NQ*), the latter being an emblematic figure in the Italian *Icones symbolicae* (1626). As usual, the critical attention has centred upon the fourth voyage. In 'The Complexity of Swift: Gulliver's Fourth Voyage' (*SP*), W. B. Carnochan makes an interesting approach to some of the difficulties by suggesting that 'Swift's commentary on the satirist Gulliver is partly an Horatian revenge on the Juvenalian side of his own character', and partly a kind of self-depreciation which implies that 'the world is ugly indeed that so prevails on the satirist to respond against his own inclinations'. Less persuasively, Benjamin C. Harlow, in 'Houyhnhnmland: A Utopian Satire' (*McNeese Review*), argues that Swift was ridiculing the idea of an earthly Utopia because he believed that a society governed exclusively by reason was impossible; and John Traugott makes a rather strained case for reading 'Swift's Allegory: The Yahoo and the Man-of-Mode' (*UTQ*), as a representation of the way in which the pursuit of what is modish and fashionable in behaviour leads to a Yahoo-like degeneracy. Other articles on *Gulliver's Travels* include a summary by Barry Slepian of 'The Publication History of Faulkner's Edition of *Gulliver's Travels*' (*PBSA*), a general discussion of some of the book's complexities in James A. Preu's 'The Case of the Mysterious Manuscript' (*EJ*), and Patricia Bruckmann's consideration of the significance of food, especially salt, in 'Gulliver, Cum Grano Salis' (*Satire Newsletter*). In *Jonathan Swift avoue . . . I. Le Secret de Gulliver*,[7] Pierre Henrion adds one more to the heap of ingenious but implausible attempts to decipher Swift's invented proper names.

The difficulty of providing an adequate edition of *Polite Conversation* arises partly because, although the task demands highly specialized learn-

---

[7] *Jonathan Swift avoue . . . I. Le Secret de Gulliver*, by Pierre Henrion. Lycée Hoche, Versailles: by the author. pp. 110.

ing, anything like sober scholarship tends to look comically pedantic. Eric Partridge is perhaps the ideal editor; he has the expert knowledge of the colloquial and slangy, but has never allowed his expertise to extinguish his sense of the comic. Consequently, although one may find a few explanations which seem a little off the mark or rather prudish, his edition[8] is both learned and delightful, and should make this neglected *jeu d'esprit* familiar to a much wider circle of readers. Almost equally neglected is Swift's verse, although this year two critics have examined particular poems: T. Henry Smith demonstrates how the reader is 'bit' in 'Swift's "The Day of Judgement"' (*Ex*), and Barry Slepian, in a thoughtful assessment of 'The Ironic Intention of Swift's Verses on His Own Death' (*RES*), considers the total significance of the poem, and in the light of this argues that critics have overlooked the irony in the conclusion where Swift appears to praise himself and his own satire.

In 'Swift and Dry Religion' (*QQ*), Paul West contends that Swift's religious views were over-rational and lacking in emotion, joy, and spirituality; Richard I. Cook's 'Defoe and Swift: Contrasts in Satire' (*DR*), investigates the differences in purpose, method, and general effect between the *Shortest Way with Dissenters* and the *Modest Proposal*: Donald T. Torchiana relates and compares the attitudes towards political and intellectual freedom of two great Irishmen in 'W. B. Yeats, Jonathan Swift, and Liberty' (*MP*): Sybil Le Brocquy offers a modicum of factual information and a mass of loose biographical fantasy in *Cade-*

nus: A Reassessment in the Light of New Evidence of the Relationship Between Swift, Stella and Vanessa:[9] and Jack G. Gilbert makes an unsupported guess that 'The Drapier's Initials' (*NQ*) stand for Marcus Brutus.

Although the importance of the cultural influence of *The Tatler* and *The Spectator* has long been a commonplace, there has been no thorough attempt to relate Addison's individual position to its sources and to contemporary influences and notions, a situation which Lee Andrew Elioseff sets out to remedy in his study of *The Cultural Milieu of Addison's Literary Criticism*.[10] He considers the critical assumptions that were reflected in or offended by such papers as the essay on *Chevy Chase*, assesses the relative importance of more general cultural factors, and shows how Addison, prompted by Locke, introduced, in the *Pleasures of the Imagination* essays, what was in effect a new kind of psychological criticism. The emphasis is on Addison's theoretical and fundamental position as a critic rather than on his specific judgements, although these are, of course, called on for evidence. In places the reader may be irritated by quite unnecessary quotation of 'authorities' to justify some minor or obvious point, by occasional over-simplifications, and by a tendency to retreat into critical jargon, but the book does succeed, as a whole, in drawing attention to the fact that although Addison may have been a 'popularizer' he extended the range of criticism in many important

---

[8] *Jonathan Swift: Polite Conversation*, with Introduction, Notes, and Extensive Commentary by Eric Partridge. O.U.P. pp. 182. $4.50. 18*s*.

[9] *Cadenus: A Reassessment in the Light of New Evidence of the Relationship Between Swift, Stella and Vanessa*, by Sybil Le Brocquy. Dublin: Dolmen Press. London: O.U.P. pp. 160. $5. 18*s*. 6*d*.

[10] *The Cultural Milieu of Addison's Literary Criticism*, by Lee Andrew Elioseff. Texas U.P. pp. xiii+252. $5.75.

ways. Some of the same ground is touched on in Helmut Papajewski's 'Addison, Virgil und die *Chevy Chase* Ballade' (*Ang*), which examines the implications of Addison's praise of the ballad's simplicity as opposed to Gothic complexity. A brief general view of Addison and Steele in the cultural context of their time is supplied by Calhoun Winton in 'Addison and Steele in the English Enlightenment'.[11]

The *McKillop Essays* (see note 1) include two contributions referring to Steele, one directly, one indirectly. Rae Blanchard quotes some newly-discovered draft-letters from Henry Newman which throw a curious and interesting light on the friendship between 'Richard Steele and the Secretary of the SPCK', and Donald F. Bond gives a lively account of 'Armand de la Chapelle and the First French Version of the *Tatler*', a translation by a man who was 'admirably suited to reproducing in another language the peculiar tone and spirit of Steele's periodical essay', but who was not above introducing an essay of his own composition in furtherance of his dispute with the Huguenot preacher, Jacques Saurin. Another sidelight on Steele is provided by Calhoun Winton's 'Steele, Mrs. Manley, and John Lacy' (*PQ*), which denies that Lacy was responsible for the attack on Steele entitled *The Ecclesiastical and Political History of Whig-Land of Late Years*, and suggests that the author was Mrs. Manley.

Few authors are as consistent in their ideas or their development as critics would like them to be, and yet critics are inevitably and rightly drawn to the search for an adequate formulation of the whole course of a writer's work. One such attempt is made by Thomas R. Edwards, Jr., in *This Dark Estate: A Reading of Pope*,[12] where Pope's characteristic mood is traced from an early Augustanism in which the universe is seen as controlled by a permanent and providential moral law (though this view is coloured by gloomier apprehensions of death and transience) to a more complex state of mind where the sense of order, though not abandoned, is infected with intuitions of universal chaos to which all things tend to return. This development is traced through all Pope's poetry with some plausibility and with some perceptive comments on individual passages, but occasionally a quotation is mis-applied or misconstrued (as when the lines 'Fix'd like a plant on his peculiar spot / To draw nutrition, propagate, and rot' are taken as referring to man instead of to a hypothetical creature with reason but without self-love). But although poems are sometimes pulled out of shape by an excessive insistence on certain elements or themes, the thesis does at least draw attention to some aspects of Pope's poetry which are easily overlooked.

A number of articles concern particular poems. Harold F. DeLisle relates the 'Structure in Part I of Pope's *Essay on Criticism*' (*ELN*) to the divisions of the classical oration; David Ridgley Clark demonstrates the ways in which such painters as Claude influenced the 'Landscape Painting Effects in Pope's Homer' (*Journal of Aesthetics and Art Criticism*); P. Dixon traces 'The Theme of Friendship in

[11] In *Transactions of the First International Congress on the Enlightenment*, ed. by Theodore Besterman. (Studies on Voltaire and the Eighteenth Century, Vols. XXIV–XXVII.) Geneva: Institut et Musée Voltaire. pp. 1,918.

[12] *This Dark Estate: A Reading of Pope*, by Thomas R. Edwards, Jr. (Perspectives in Criticism, No. 11.) California U.P. pp. xi+142. $3.95. 32s.

the *Epistle to Dr. Arbuthnot'* (*ES*), and notes the propriety with which a poem of this kind was addressed to the amiable doctor; and Aubrey Williams, in 'Pope and Horace: *The Second Epistle of the Second Book'* (*McKillop Essays*—see note I), observes how Pope deviates from his model and introduces the controlling metaphor of 'thievery' to place original emphasis on the central themes of the poem—'first, the decays and losses to which men are subjected by the inexorable passage of time, and, second, the proper attitude with which these decays and losses are to be faced'. Some points of detail are noted by Samuel A. Golden, who suggests that the reference to Queen Anne's 'tea' in 'Pope's *The Rape of the Lock*, III, 8' (*Ex*) might be understood as an allusion to her intemperance; by James M. Osborn, who identifies the Walter Carey who was 'Addison's Tavern Companion and Pope's "Umbra"' (*PQ*); and by Hans-Joachim Zimmermann, who observes that the expression '. . . *as* Brault *translated it'* (*Archiv*), in a letter from Fenton to Broome concerning the translation of Homer, should read 'as Perault translated it'. Various sources and influences are discussed: Reuben A. Brower's 'Dryden and the "Invention" of Pope' (*McKillop Essays*—see note 1) shows how some of Dryden's later poetry anticipated Pope's easy Horatian treatment of rural themes; in 'Pope and Boileau: A Supplementary Note' (*NM*) G. Thomas Fairclough argues that too little attention has been paid to similarities between the two poets' views on moral and religious matters; Richard I. Cook points out that, while resemblances have been often noticed between 'Garth's *Dispensary* and Pope's *Rape of the Lock*' (*CLA*), it is equally important to recognize the differences between Garth's didactic treatment of a contemporary issue and Pope's perception of universal truths in a social triviality; and Arthur Johnston shows that the expression '"The Purple Year" in Pope and Gray' (*RES*), echoed earlier uses by Milton and Dryden and came originally from the Latin poets, in particular Ovid and the author of *Pervigilium Veneris*.

Benjamin Boyce describes, in 'Mr. Pope, in Bath, Improves the Design of his Grotto' (*McKillop Essays*—see note 1), how Pope in consultation with some friends brought the conception of his grotto closer to that of a natural cave displaying all the mineral wonders of the earth, and, in the same collection, Maynard Mack's essay, '"The Shadowy Cave": Some Speculations on a Twickenham Grotto', shows that in many ways the nature of the grotto reflected aspects of Pope's life and poetic imagination, especially his fondness for rural retirement and for the beauties of nature, which are not sufficiently taken account of in the usual image of the urban poet. In 'Pope and God at Twickenham' (*Personalist*) Edwin Nierenberg tries to sum up the poet's religious position as that of one who, if not 'a religious deist', was 'a deistical religious'.

Other studies less immediately concerned with Pope are 'La Caverne Aux Vapeurs' (*PQ*), by L. P. Goggin, which compares Desfontaine's translation of the Cave of Spleen passage from *The Rape of the Lock* with Voltaire's version; Emerson Robert Loomis's report of a political quarrel of the 1790's which dragged Pope's name into a dispute concerning Grattan—in an article exaggeratedly entitled 'The Turning Point in Pope's Reputation: A Dispute which Preceded the Bowles-Byron Controversy' (*PQ*); a laboured attempt by Jae Ho Lee to find 'Alexander Pope in Eliot's

"East Coker"' (NQ); and W. K. Wimsatt, Jr.'s ' "Amicitiae Causa" : A Birthday Present from Curll to Pope' (*McKillop Essays*—see note 1), which includes two portraits of the poet, one engraved by Jonathan Richardson for the title-page of Pope's *Letters* of May 1737, and the other a careful replica commissioned by Curll for his *New Letters of Mr. Alexander Pope*, and relates them to the intrigues and hostilities surrounding the publication of the poet's correspondence.

The second volume of the Yale edition of Johnson's works contains *The Idler* and *The Adventurer*[13], the former edited by W. J. Bate in collaboration with John M. Bullitt, and the latter by L. F. Powell with whom Bate has collaborated in the critical annotation. One might quibble about the inclusion of an unnecessary note or the omission of a desirable one, or object to the obscuring of certain emphases through the removal of capitals in the modernized text, without significantly qualifying the merited praise of this well-presented, accurately edited, and fully annotated edition : one wishes only that it could be cheaper and so come into the hands of many readers who would find it an antidote to the out-dated notions about Johnson which unfortunately still survive. *The Idler* papers would be particularly valuable in this respect, since in them Johnson, without altogether abandoning the majestic moralities of *The Rambler*, relaxed more frequently and displayed the lighter side of his talents, as in the Minim essays, the analogy between punch and conversation, and the 'Proposal for a Female Army'. *The Adventurer* was nearer in character to *The Rambler*, though not so fre-

quently and richly sombre. Both contain magnificent writing which will more than compensate for the cost of this worthy edition.

Two books of selections from Johnson's writings and sayings appeared during 1963. There is something a little old-fashioned about the method (as about the title) of Henry Darcy Curwen's *A Johnson Sampler*,[14] which arranges brief extracts from the writings and the recorded conversations under subject-headings, but although 'gems' suffer when plucked out of their setting in any writer's work, Curwen's arrangement creates interesting new relationships and juxtapositions. It is difficult to imagine for whom *Johnson's Dictionary: A Modern Selection*,[15] edited by E. L. McAdam, Jr., and George Milne, is designed. The ordinary reader may find pleasure in a collection of aphorisms but is hardly likely to enjoy reading a series of definitions, while the literary student will find that this selection tends to display what is amusing, eccentric, or wrong-headed in the dictionary rather than to illustrate in abridged form the essential character and solid achievement of Johnson as a lexicographer.

There have been so many new attributions to Johnson in recent years that Donald J. Greene's account of 'The Development of the Johnson Canon' (*McKillop Essays*—see note 1) is likely to prove an invaluable guide to all students. Greene deplores the critical neglect of Johnson's minor writings and the reliance on Boswell's incomplete list of the works, and, most importantly, supplies a preliminary listing of 'the

---

[13] *Samuel Johnson: 'The Idler' and 'The Adventurer'*, ed. by W. J. Bate, John M. Bullitt, and L. F. Powell. (The Yale Edition of the Works of Samuel Johnson, Vol. II.) Yale U.P. pp. xxix+516. $12.50. 90s.

[14] *A Johnson Sampler*, by Henry Darcy Curwen. Harvard U.P. pp. xi+320. $5.95.

[15] *Johnson's Dictionary: A Modern Selection*, ed. by E. L. McAdam, Jr., and George Milne. New York: Pantheon Books. London: Gollancz. pp. xiv+465. $6.50. 30s.

earliest published attributions to Johnson of most of his known and presumed writings'. One addition to the Johnson canon briefly reported last year is amplified in J. A. V. Chapple's account of a recently discovered copy of 'Samuel Johnson's *Proposals for Printing the History of the Council of Trent*' (*BJRL*); and in 'Johnson's "Little Pompadour": A Textual Crux and a Hypothesis' (*McKillop Essays*—see note 1) Gwin J. Kolb uses a letter from Johnson to his publisher to suggest tentatively that it was Johnson who wrote the English version of *The History of the Marchioness de Pompadour* (1758). In another essay in the same collection, William R. Keast's 'Johnson and "Cibber's" *Lives of the Poets*, 1753', Keast shows how this book (written by Robert Shiels, not Theophilus Cibber) acknowledged its indebtedness to Johnson's lives of Savage and Roscommon (published in *The Gentleman's Magazine*), and was probably supplied by him with other materials, so that when Johnson made use of Shiels's book for his own *Lives of the Poets* he was probably reclaiming his own. Other articles relating to Johnson's criticism are Robert J. Griffen's brief discussion of 'Dr. Johnson and the Drama' (*Discourse*); Max F. Schulz's observation of 'Coleridge's "Debt" to Dryden and Johnson' (*NQ*) in his remarks on the metaphysical poets; and J. D. Fleeman's scrutiny of 'Some Proofs of Johnson's *Prefaces to the Poets*' (*Lib*), leading to some conclusions about the care with which Johnson corrected his proofs.

In 'Samuel Johnson and "Natural Law"' (*Journal of British Studies*), Donald J. Greene maintains that, far from accepting the concept of a 'natural law' which would be valid even in a Godless universe and which even God himself could not contra-

vene, Johnson would have rejected 'any suggestion that ethical values have any other foundation but the will of God'. In the same journal, Peter J. Stanlis has a 'Comment on Samuel Johnson and "Natural Law"' which argues that Greene has confused 'nature' and 'reason' and ignored passages in Johnson's writings where his belief in the 'natural law' is evident; Greene has the last word in a 'Response to Mr. Stanlis's Comment'. Another article concerned with Johnson's general position is Arieh Sachs's 'Samuel Johnson on the "Vacuity of Life"'(*SEL*), which emphasizes the centrality in Johnson's thought of the notion that life was a kind of emptiness which man was always vainly trying to fill, and suggests an origin in Johnson's personal experience of mental stagnation. M. G. Irwin blames 'Doctor Johnson's Troubled Mind' (*Literature and Psychology*) on his mother's unsatisfactory behaviour to him as a child. More general observations are supplied by Louis I. Bredvold in 'Dr. Johnson for Our Time' (*Ball State Teachers College Forum*), which praises chiefly Johnson's intellectual powers and moral responsibility, and by H. A. Morgan in 'Samuel Johnson: Address Given at the Annual Commemoration of the Johnson Society of London' (*New Rambler*).

In '"The Fourth Son of the Mighty Emperor": The Ethiopian Background of Johnson's *Rasselas*' (*PMLA*), Donald M. Lockhart lists 'original European works containing information on Ethiopia published before 1759', and demonstrates the indebtedness of *Rasselas* and *Rambler* essays 204 and 205 to certain of these forgotten works; R. K. Kaul suggests that 'The Philosopher of Nature in *Rasselas* XXII' (*Indian Journal of English Studies*) was a composite figure, embodying various philosophical views, and more like Shaftesbury than anyone else; and L. F. Powell notes 'For Johnsonian Collectors' (*TLS*) some information concerning the first Dutch translation of *Rasselas*.

Other articles on Johnson include: J. C. Maxwell's '"Talk Dead": Pope and Johnson' (*NQ*), which suggests that the expression in *London* was probably borrowed from Pope's *Essay on Criticism*; R. K. Kaul's '*A Journey to the Western Isles* Reconsidered' (*EC*), which points out that the journey confirmed Johnson in his opinion that, without centralized government, a social hierarchy, law, and commerce, human life was isolated and wretched; Michael L. Lasser's account of 'Johnson in Scotland: New Life Amid the "Ruins of Iona"' (*Midwest Quarterly*); Donald Greene's 'Reflections on a Literary Anniversary' (*QQ*), which makes the anniversary of the first meeting between Johnson and Boswell the occasion for recommending Sir John Hawkins as the more accurate portrayer of Johnson; Josip Torbarina's note on 'The Meeting of Bošković with Dr. Johnson' (*Studia romanica et anglica Zagrabiensia*); and F. W. M. Draper's account of the life of 'Topham Beauclerk at The Grove, Muswell Hill' (*New Rambler*). The book by Lewis P. Curtis and Herman W. Liebert entitled *Esto Perpetua: The Club of Dr. Johnson and His Friends, 1764–1784*[16] was not available.

(*c*) Favourable or unfavourable prejudices dating from childhood are perhaps responsible for the scarcity of balanced critical estimates of the literary quality of hymns. In 1962 Frank Baker attempted some judgement of the hymns of Charles Wesley, and now Harry Escott looks with a critical but not irreverent eye at another writer of hymns in *Isaac Watts, Hymnographer: A Study of the Beginnings, Development, and Philosophy of the English Hymn*.[17] The result is an enthusiastic but not undiscriminating celebration of Watts's religious verse, stressing his skill as a prosodist and the structural sense shown in the collections of hymns, and relating his work to earlier hymnodists and religious thinkers.

A number of articles deal with minor poets and poetry: Peter B. Steese discusses 'Dennis's influence on Watts's Preface to *Horae Lyricae*' (*PQ*); Frank H. Ellis and David Foxon record a broadside edition of 'Prior's *Simile*' (*PBSA*); C. F. Burgess finds 'Scriblerian Influence in *The Shepherd's Week*' (*NQ*) in the pedantic pseudo-index; C. J. Rawson, in 'Parnell on Whiston' (*PBSA*), notes a contemporary letter attributing the *Ode to Musick*, usually attributed to Gay, to Parnell; J. C. Arens explains the popularity of 'Sarbiewski's Ode Against Tears Imitated by Lovelace, Yalden and Watts' (*N*); Catharine K. Firman has an interesting discussion of *An Epistle to the Lord Bolingbroke* (1714) in 'An Unrecorded Poem by Edward Young' (*NQ*); H. B. Forster fixes the dates of 'The Ordination of Edward Young' (*ELN*); and John Street writes on 'The Poets and the English Garden' (*Listener*), naming Pope, Addison, Thomson, and Shenstone among the poets who helped create the English Garden.

---

[16] *Esto Perpetua: The Club of Dr. Johnson and His Friends, 1764–1784*, by Lewis P. Curtis and Herman W. Liebert. Hamden, Connecticut: Archon Books. pp. 108. $4.

[17] *Isaac Watts, Hymnographer: A Study of the Beginnings, Development, and Philosophy of the English Hymn*, by Harry Escott. Independent Press. pp. 302. 28*s*. 6*d*.

The *Proceedings of the Leeds Philosophical and Literary Society, Literary and Historical Section* for 1963 contain three *Bentley Commemorative Lectures*, delivered the year before—W. S. Maguinness's 'Bentley as Man and Scholar', D. R. Shackleton Bailey's 'Bentley and Horace', and J. A. Davidson's 'Bentley and the Greeks'. C. B. Hunt quotes 'Contemporary References to the Work of Richard Bentley' (*Bodleian Library Record*), to show how great was his reputation among the scholars of Europe.

James L. Clifford, in 'Roger North and the Art of Biography' (*McKillop Essays*—see note 1), makes a strong plea for recognition of North's achievement as a biographer and as a thinker about the art of biography far in advance of his time; James A. Preu outlines Mandeville's position on the question of 'Private Vices—Public Benefits' (*EJ*); and Nathan Rosenberg, in an article entitled 'Mandeville and Laissez-faire' (*JHI*), observes that Mandeville has been claimed as a supporter both of *laissez-faire* and of government intervention, while his true position was that a skilful politician would so manipulate affairs that direct intervention would be unnecessary. Interesting minor figures are the subjects of three articles: John Lawson outlines the career of 'An Early Disciple of Locke: John Clarke (1686–1734), Educational Reformer and Moralist' (*Durham Research Review*, 1962); C. E. L. Sclater, in 'William Sclater and John Slater: A Question of Authorship' (*NQ*), suggests that *An Original Draught of the Primitive Church* (1717), often attributed to the former, was in fact the work of the latter; and Leonard Forster throws light on eighteenth-century cultural relations with Germany in 'John Disney and the Study of German in Early Eighteenth-Century England' (*German Life and Letters*).

Much the most important study of the eighteenth-century drama this year is John Loftis's *The Politics of Drama in Augustan England*,[18] which traces the relationship between the theatre and the political world in the reign of Queen Anne, and describes the various uses made of the stage for political purposes and the resultant governmental pressures. Paul E. Parnell, examining 'The Sentimental Mask' (*PMLA*) with particular reference to Steele's *Conscious Lovers*, Cibber's *Careless Husband*, and Lillo's *London Merchant*, concludes that 'the first trait of sentimentality . . . is self-esteem raised to the presumptuous level of self-adoration, self-worship; and since love is a basic Christian attribute, the sentimentalist drenches all his relationships with professions of charity and altruism.' Steele's and Lillo's plays are among the *Six Eighteenth-Century Plays*[19] edited in a convenient paperback, which also includes *The Fair Penitent, The Beggar's Opera, She Stoops to Conquer*, and *The School for Scandal*. Lindley A. Wyman, in 'The Tradition of the Formal Meditation in Rowe's *The Fair Penitent*' (*PQ*), interprets the last act as a dramatic adaptation of the traditional meditation on death, used by Rowe 'to illustrate the central experience of his heroine'. Albert E. Kalson's 'The Chronicles in Cibber's *Richard III*' (*SEL*), shows that Cibber referred to the old sources, especially Speed and Holinshed. An interesting aspect of the theatre is discussed in Stoddard Lincoln's 'Eccles and

---

[18] *The Politics of Drama in Augustan England*, by John Loftis. O.U.P. pp. 173. $4.80. 30s.

[19] *Six Eighteenth-Century Plays*, ed. by John Harold Wilson. (Riverside Editions.) Boston: Houghton Mifflin. pp. x+374. $1.50.

Congreve: Music and Drama on the Restoration Stage' (*Theatre Notebook*), which praises both the librettos written by Congreve and Eccles's settings; the same author describes in more detail 'The First Setting of Congreve's "Semele"' (*Music and Letters*), a setting by Eccles which was finished in 1707 but was never produced. Ifan Kyrle Fletcher lists and illustrates seventeen 'British Playbills before 1718' (*Theatre Notebook*).

(*d*) As usual there has been a great deal of work on the novel. Maximillian E. Novak has followed his study of Defoe's economic theories (see *YW* xliii. 200) with a book which deals with his ideas on nature and human behaviour. In *Defoe and the Nature of Man*[20] Novak's starting-point is Defoe's long poem *Jure Divino*; finding in it references to Hugo Grotius and Samuel Pufendorf, he uses these as the starting-point for a study which suggests that 'Defoe formulated his own scheme of natural law, and by borrowing, combining and emphasizing various concepts in the writings of Grotius, Hobbes, Locke and many other philosophers, he was able to achieve a certain eclectic originality'. The behaviour and motivation of some of the major characters, and Defoe's attitude to their actions, is then examined from this 'ideological basis'. The book does not so much attempt a critical examination of the novels as provide a framework of ideas which will need to be taken into account in future critical studies.

Novak also discusses, in '*Robinson Crusoe* and Economic Utopia' (*KR*), the extent to which *Robinson Crusoe* embodies Defoe's economic ideas, especially the Lockean position 'that

[20] *Defoe and the Nature of Man*, by Maximillian E. Novak. (Oxford English Monographs.) O.U.P. pp. viii+176. 25*s*.

labour and invention create things of use and that the value of things depends on their utility'. Crusoe is consistently Defoe's spokesman for the idea of use-value in spite of his inability to rid himself of his partiality for gold. This partiality shows that Defoe never reduced Crusoe to an economic abstraction; he knew that Crusoe was fallible and full of contradictions, and that an economic system must take account of human inconsistency. J. Paul Hunter writes usefully on 'Friday as a Convert: Defoe and the Accounts of Indian Missionaries' (*RES*). Friday's conversion is often regarded as unrealistic because of the quickness with which he asks awkward philosophical questions, but Hunter is able to show that Defoe's presentation of Friday was validated by the accounts of missionaries, and he suggests that this is important because Defoe 'uses Friday's conversion to give us a dramatic insight into Crusoe's spiritual accomplishment'.

Moll Flanders continues to attract attention. 'Moll's Muddle: Defoe's Use of Irony in *Moll Flanders*' (*ELH*), by Howard L. Koonce, discusses Ian Watt's views on Defoe's irony. The essence of the book is seen as a conflict of values, but 'though Defoe perceived Moll's attitude towards her conflicting sets of values ironically, his conception of the conflict she is caught in was only partially worked out. The book fails to sustain the ironic mode in its more profound possibilities.' Denis Donoghue is also critical of Defoe in 'The Values of *Moll Flanders*' (*Sew*). He analyses the way in which trading terms and analogies dominate both *Robinson Crusoe* and *Moll Flanders*, and argues that Defoe's commitment to a single, unified view of life accounts for the excitement of *Moll* and its significance in literary history, but also for its limitations. The terms of the work assume 'that whatever cannot be measured cannot exist. As a result, the book cannot even conceive of human action as genial, charitable, or selfless; hence it cannot survive comparison with a novel like *Portrait of a Lady* in which the enabling vision of life is wide, generous, answerable to human possibility.' Writing from a technical point of view Robert R. Columbus is more enthusiastic. In 'Conscious Artistry in *Moll Flanders*' (*SEL*), his analysis is conducted in three ways: 'through the technique of the point of view, through Defoe's dramatization of the influence upon Moll of the values of security, love and money, and through Defoe's own moral perception of his heroine, for he appraises the conflict in her of a natural moral code with her equally natural inclination to gain advantage'.

'The Problem of Realism in Defoe's *Captain Singleton*' (*HLQ*), by Gary J. Scrimgeour, argues that Defoe had available much more information about Africa than is commonly supposed. The novel is discussed in comparison with seven sources, and it is suggested that Defoe was little interested in realism as such. 'It is simply a device, almost a trick, used spasmodically and not in any sense created by an artistic or ethical ideal —the real Defoe trademark appears not in the necessary though meretricious authenticity of his narrative, but in the way in which he uses it, the way in which both aesthetics and reality bow their heads before commerce.' Manuel R. Schonhorn's 'Defoe's Pirates: A New Source' (*RES*), notes an origin for the section of *Captain Singleton* which deals with the theft of a merchant vessel at the Groyne.

'Daniel Defoe: Precursor of Samuel Richardson',[21] by John Robert

Moore, is concerned with Defoe's use of the letter form both in journalism and in the novels, where, although 'there are often special reasons why there should be few or no letters', they do nevertheless sometimes occur 'to express strong emotion or to provide a climax for a situation'.

Two articles deal with non-literary aspects of Defoe. In 'Defoe, Thomas Burnet and the "Deistical" Passages of *Robert Drury's Journal*' (*PQ*), Maximillian E. Novak plots the gradual development of Defoe's approval for Burnet's views, and argues that the supposedly deistical passages in the *Journal*, 'far from being grounds for rejecting Defoe's authorship, actually provide us with information about both Defoe's religious beliefs and the manner in which he used religious doctrines in his fiction'. It is important, Novak suggests, not to use the word 'deistic' as a blanket term, but to distinguish between writers like Collins and Toland, who believed that reason alone was sufficient, and Defoe and Burnet, who were willing to apply reason to religion.

Lawrence Poston III's 'Defoe and the Peace Campaign, 1710–13: A Reconsideration' (*HLQ*) is a predominantly historical study. 'Defoe and Swift: Contrasts in Satire' (*DR*), by Richard I. Cook, is an unspecialized article which discusses some differences in technique between *The Shortest Way With Dissenters* and *A Modest Proposal*.

Two re-issues of Everyman editions of works by Defoe are to be welcomed. *A Tour Through the Whole Island of Great Britain*[22] now includes

---

[21] In *Restoration and Eighteenth-Century Literature*. See note 1.

[22] *A Tour Through the Whole Island of Great Britain*, by Daniel Defoe. With Introductions by G. D. H. Cole and D. C. Browning. (Everyman's Library.) Dent, 1962. Vol. 1: pp. xxv+376; Vol. 2: pp. v+437. 30s.

the section on Scotland with a new introduction by D. C. Browning. *Captain Singleton*[23] is a reprint of the 1720 text (not generally available elsewhere) with a new introduction by James Sutherland.

As a transition from Defoe to Richardson a useful reprint of some inaccessible examples of early eighteenth-century fiction may be noted. *Four Before Richardson*,[24] edited by W. H. McBurney, is an attempt to combat a general tendency to treat the great eighteenth-century novelists as though each had somehow 'developed autonomously', by reprinting four short works that 'each in various ways and to varying degrees anticipates the work of' Richardson, Fielding, and Smollett. The novels included are *Luck at Last; or, The Happy Unfortunate*, by Arthur Blackmore; *The Jamaica Lady; or, The Life of Bavia*, by W. P.; *Philidore and Placentia; or, L'Amour trop délicat*, by Eliza Haywood; and *The Accomplished Rake; or, Modern Fine Gentleman*, by Mary Davys. There is an Introduction which places the novels in their context.

The most substantial contribution on Richardson himself is Morris Golden's *Richardson's Characters*.[25] Rather unexpectedly Golden argues that the women are often seen from the outside, but that certain types of men are viewed from within. Particularly with the men there is a pervasiveness of fantasy in the creation of character, fantasy mainly of dominance and subordination, which seems to have been that of Richardson himself, and this is accompanied in the main characters by acute feelings of guilt. In the novels the ideal man is one with powerful urges towards dominance which he is trained to restrain in conformity with the practices of society, and which he exercises for the good of all around him. The central conflict is between reason and the passions, and between 'good emotions' and fear of their social effects. In the women characters the dominance-urge is still strong and is apparent when suffering is used as a means of self-exaltation. There is some danger here of the novels being pressed into the service of a thesis, but Golden's psychological approach gives many insights into the books, and it is especially valuable in the discussion of Lovelace's character.

In an interesting article on 'The Problem of Pamela, or, Virtue Unrewarded' (*SEL*), Robert A. Donovan argues that too much attention has been paid to the moral and too little to the social aspects of Richardson's first novel. Pamela's real problem is not whether she should submit to Mr. B (since the answer to this question is obvious), but how she should act towards him without violating the code of behaviour imposed by their servant-master relationship, and after the marriage this problem shifts to the wider social context of Pamela's encounter with Lady Davers. *Pamela* should be seen as a comedy of manners—'a tale of the social success of a flesh and blood heroine armed, not with abstract "Good Deeds", but with the world's own weapons'.

William J. Farrell considers some formal aspects of Richardson's prose in 'The Style and the Action in *Clarissa*' (*SEL*), and shows that Richardson uses elaborately rhetorical speech patterns more often than is commonly supposed. Lovelace uses courtly rhetoric at his most

[23] *The Life, Adventures and Piracies of the Famous Captain Singleton*, by Daniel Defoe. With an Introduction by James Sutherland. Everyman Library. pp. xvi+335. 12*s*. 6*d*.

[24] *Four Before Richardson: Selected English Novels, 1720–1727*, ed. by W. H. McBurney. Nebraska U.P. pp. xxxv+373. $5.50.

[25] *Richardson's Characters*, by Morris Golden. Michigan U.P. pp. xi+202. $5.

triumphant moments (the moments when he is most completely the stage villain), and Clarissa's style becomes most elevated when she appears clearly as 'the pathetic but noble victim'. Here we find Richardson adapting the conventions of literary prose to the artistic needs of his work.

There are two more general articles, both dealing with Richardson's use of gesture. In 'Theatrical Convention in Richardson: Some Observations on a Novelist's Technique',[26] Leo Hughes discusses Richardson's use of theatrical gesture and dress, and considers the sources for some of his most frequently recurring motifs. George Sherburn's 'Writing to the Moment: One Aspect'[27] is concerned with the novelist's use and sharp visualization of conventional gestures and bodily movements to express emotion.

Finally John Carroll's 'Richardson on Pope and Swift' (*UTQ*), prints letters in which Richardson attacks the two satirists because, it is suggested, 'neither author healed with morals what he hurt with wit'. Pope and Swift did not embody Richardson's exalted idea of the moral utility of literature.

There is less to report on Fielding than for some years past, but Martin C. Battestin contributes two articles. In 'Fielding's Revisions of *Joseph Andrews*' (*SB*), he shows that Fielding revised the text of his first novel significantly not only in the second but also in the third and fourth editions. Many revisions are minor, but there are many which affect the style, the characterization, and the narrative, and these offer 'much useful information about Fielding's habits of composition, and his techniques and intentions as a writer'. The article ends with a large sample from more

than six hundred variants that occur amongst the editions of *Joseph Andrews* published during Fielding's lifetime. 'Lord Hervey's Role in *Joseph Andrews*' (*PQ*) shows how Hervey's known characteristics, and episodes in his life, were used in the creation of Beau Didapper. 'Under the artist's hands the local, the topical, the private, are shaped into the timeless and symbolic, and are adapted to the requirements of the story.' Andrew Wright gives a more general account of the book in 'Work in Progress III: *Joseph Andrews*, Mask and Feast' (*EC*). Fielding's intrusive author technique is seen as pointing to the essentially artificial nature of the book: 'by directing our attention to the apparatus of his fiction, [Fielding] reminds us of its fictive quality.' The function of the book is not directly imitative or satirical: it is to provide a kind of ideal delight. 'Art has the wonderfully beneficial motive of idealizing morality by making the actions of men into arrangements that are amusing and sometimes even beautiful.'

'Fielding's Bill of Fare in *Tom Jones*' (*ELH*), by Michael Bliss, is a discussion of the relationship between the introductory chapters and the narrative. Surprisingly this is the only item concerned exclusively with *Tom Jones*; but Dietrich Rolle's systematic discussion of the function of the narrator and his relations with the reader in Fielding and Sterne should also be mentioned here.[28]

William B. Coley's 'Fielding, Hogarth, and Three Italian Masters' (*MLQ*), is an explication of the reference to Hogarth and three Italian painters in Book III, Chapter 6, of

[26] In *Restoration and Eighteenth-Century Literature.* See note 1.
[27] *Ibid.*

[28] *Fielding und Sterne: Untersuchungen über die Funktion des Erzählers*, by Dietrich Rolle. (Neue Beiträge zur Englischen Philologie, Band 2.) Münster: Verlag Aschendorff. pp. x+196.

Joseph Andrews, while Claude E. Jones's 'Satire and Certain English Satirists of the Enlightenment'[29] touches upon parallels between Hogarth's work and Fielding's.

One is glad to see that H. K. Banerji's general study of *Henry Fielding*, first published in 1929 but long out of print, has now been re-issued as part of Russell & Russell's very useful list.[30]

Also to be noted, although no copy has been available, is an edition of *The Journal of a Voyage to Lisbon*, edited by Harold E. Pagliaro.[31]

William Bowman Piper's 'The Large Diffused Picture of Life in Smollett's Early Novels' (*SP*) distinguishes between different types of grotesque in Smollett's work, and shows how the 'blank' and flexible heroes interact with the grotesques to produce a special view of life. In a more specialized article, 'The Briton and *Humphry Clinker*' (*SEL*), Byron Gassman discusses the relationship between Smollett's political views in the journals and in the letters of Matthew Bramble and his fellow-travellers. *Humphry Clinker* does not embody a consistent political system, but passages of political comment in the novel 'cohere as segments of a definable framework of attitudes and beliefs'. Smollett was convinced that the Whig ascendancy had led to a decline in public morals, and he therefore believed in encouraging a strong monarchy and a more rigid social hierarchy. These ideas are manifest in the *Briton*, and form 'a strong undercurrent in the thought of *Humphry Clinker*'. Robert Hunting provides a 'Footnote to a Comparative Study: Smollett and Ibsen' (*NQ*): Smollett's *An Essay on the External Waters* (1752) is found to anticipate the action and theme of Ibsen's *An Enemy of the People*. Also to be listed are Robert C. Alberts's 'The Fantastic Adventures of Captain Stobo' (*American Heritage*), and 'Smollett, MacKercher, and the Annesley Claimant' (*ELN*), by Lewis M. Knapp and Lillian de la Torre.

The most generally useful article on Sterne this year is William J. Farrell's 'Nature Versus Art as a Comic Pattern in *Tristram Shandy*' (*ELH*). This analyses Sterne's use of rhetorical devices both of style and gesture to show how he 'creates a comic clash between art and nature', and suggests that the structure of the book is also intended to underline this opposition. Tristram constantly attempts to impose art on nature, but the collapse of his attempt is 'a devastating parody of the shapeless "true-account" that served for fiction in the eighteenth century'. Joan Joffe Hall's 'The Hobbyhorsical World of *Tristram Shandy*' (*MLQ*), is a study of the theme of impotence in the novel. Sterne's emphasis on sexual impotence is seen as a reflection of the failure to communicate: 'all kinds of human intercourse prove imperfect.' In a surprising article, '*Tristram Shandy* and *Oedipus Rex*: Reflections on Comedy and Tragedy' (*CE*), Stanley G. Eskin insists that the two works of his title are similar in that they show man confronting destiny, and he suggests that the tensions engendered 'may be resolved either as comedy or as tragedy, depending, among other things, on the amount of pain and terror involved and on the way in which our sympathies are directed'. Louis A. Landa's 'The Shandean Homunculus: The Background of

[29] In *Transactions of the First International Congress on the Enlightenment*. (See note 11.)

[30] *Henry Fielding, Playwright, Journalist and Master of the Art of Fiction: His Life and Works*, by H. K. Banerji. New York: Russell & Russell, 1962. pp. vii + 342. $7.50.

[31] *The Journal of a Voyage to Lisbon*, ed. by Harold E. Pagliaro. New York: Nardon Press. pp. 159. $2.50.

Sterne's "Little Gentleman"[32] deals with scientific controversies (between ovists and animalculists) on the nature of generation, and shows that Sterne's discussion of conception in Book I of *Tristram Shandy* is firmly based on a knowledge of the scientific controversies of the day. In 'Yorick's *Sentimental Journey*: A Comic "Pilgrim's Progress" for the Man of Feeling' (*ELH*), Gardner Dominick Stout, Jr., argues that, in narrating the journey, Yorick consistently plays a double role, that of a 'man of feeling' and that of a jester who observes his impulsively benevolent counterpart with sympathetic amusement and ironic detachment. The story is a 'fable' intended to illustrate the comic perplexities of an attempt to fulfil the eighteenth-century moral imperative to *Know Thyself*. Finally, on Sterne, there is 'Sterne's Use of Catachresis in *Tristram Shandy*' (*Iowa English Yearbook*), by John B. Shackford.

The publication of Cleland's *Memoirs of a Woman of Pleasure*[33] has not passed unremarked, but his *Memoirs of a Coxcomb*[34] is also of interest. There is a learned article on the bibliographical history of the *Memoirs*, 'John Cleland and the Publication of the *Memoirs of a Woman of Pleasure*' (*BC*), by David Foxon which chronicles the history of the publication and includes a letter from Cleland to Lovel Stanhope in defence of his work. John Hollander's 'The Old Last Act: Some Observations on *Fanny Hill*' (*Encounter*) is a long review article.

MacDonald Emslie's *Goldsmith: The Vicar of Wakefield*[35] subjects the novel to an intensive critical examination. This may seem a dangerous approach to a work which has for so long relied on a largely unanalysed charm for its reputation. Yet the detailed study of technique, themes, and style, while it may leave us convinced that *The Vicar of Wakefield* is not a novel of the first rank, had become necessary if the book was not to be permanently regarded simply as an exhibit in a museum of popular taste. This rigorous yet sympathetic study establishes the extent as well as the limitations of Goldsmith's achievement. Arthur Friedman writes on 'The Time of Composition of Goldsmith's *Edwin and Angelina*',[36] which is included in *The Vicar of Wakefield* and which was first privately printed in 1765.

The most substantial work on the Gothic novel is Malcolm Ware's *Sublimity in the Novels of Ann Radcliffe*,[37] which assembles the evidence that Mrs. Radcliffe consciously adopted Burke's theory of the sublime and shows how central Burkean categories are to the terror produced by the descriptive passages of her novels. The *Journey* is used to show how Mrs. Radcliffe responded to actual scenery, and there is a concluding section in which her descriptions are compared with those by Charlotte Dacre in

---

[32] In *Restoration and Eighteenth-Century Literature*. See note 1.

[33] *John Cleland's Memoirs of a Woman of Pleasure*, with an Introduction for Modern Readers by Peter Quennell. New York: G. Putnam's Sons. pp. 319. $6.

[34] *Memoirs of a Coxcomb*, by John Cleland. New York: Lancer Books. pp. 192.

[35] *Goldsmith: The Vicar of Wakefield*, by MacDonald Emslie. Studies in English Literature, ed. by David Daiches, No. 9 Edward Arnold. pp. 79. 6s.

[36] In *Restoration and Eighteenth-Century Literature*. See note 1.

[37] *Sublimity in the Novels of Ann Radcliffe: A Study of the Influence Upon Her Craft of Emund Burke's 'Enquiry . . .*', by Malcolm Ware. (Upsala University English Institute: Essays and Studies on English Language and Literature, 25.) Upsala: AB Lundequistka Bokhandeln. pp. 62. Sw. Kr.15. 15s.

Zofloya and Mary Shelley in *Franken-stein*. Frederick L. Beaty, in 'Mrs. Radcliffe's Fading Gleam' (*PQ*), suggests that Coleridge in *The Mad Monk* and Wordsworth in *Ode: Intimations of Immortality* were influenced by descriptive passages in *The Mysteries of Udolpho*. 'An Early Copy of *The Monk*' (*PBSA*), by Louis F. Peck, describes a hitherto unreported form of Lewis's romance to serve as an addendum to Todd's work on the early editions of the book.

Two general articles on the eighteenth-century novel may be noted here: Vivienne Mylne's 'Changing Attitudes towards Truth in Fiction' (*RMS*), which has some useful comparisons between French and English writers, and Sheridan Baker's 'The Idea of Romance in the Eighteenth-Century Novel' (*Studies in English Literature*, Tokyo).

Finally, there is a reprint of William Godwin's *Imogen* (*BNYPL*), which has been issued also as a separate publication.[38] The plot of this short novel is based on *Comus*, but the story is modified and set in Druidical times. It is complementary in its ideas to *Political Justice* and *Caleb Williams*. The critical articles which accompany the reprint discuss the novel's primitivism, its literary antecedents, and its Preface (which contains an extended parody of the contemporary Ossianic tradition).

(*e*) In this section the central figures will be dealt with first, and criticism of minor poets reserved until the end. 'Thomson's *Seasons* and Virgil's *Georgics*: the Problem of Primitivism

[38] *Imogen: A Pastoral Romance from the Ancient British*, by William Godwin. Reprinted from the 1784 Edition with an Introduction by Jack W. Marken and Critical Discussions by Martha Winburn England, Burton R. Pollin and Irwin Primer. New York: New York Public Library. pp. 121. $2.50.

and Progress' (*SN*), by John Chalker, is concerned to place Thomson's passages of patriotism and overt moralizing in a literary tradition. It is suggested that the interpretation of life that Thomson offers is essentially that of Virgil's *Georgics*, the poem which formed his chief model. In 'Thomson's *The Castle of Indolence*' (*Ex*), Robert J. Griffin suggests that, 'in the light of certain Biblical references and overtones of the poem, and parallels between its characters and events and their counterparts in Christian tradition, we can see that Thomson provided his two-part poem with more thematic unity than is generally acknowledged'.

F. Doherty's 'The Two Voices of Gray' (*EC*) distinguishes between Gray's public voice, where 'he devises a sort of language proper to his sense of exaltation' and the demands of his Bardic role, and his personal voice, where he writes as a social poet who relies on the reader's ear to register tone and to respond to the 'extra charge of emotion' which is conveyed by 'a distinct and human voice'. Two articles deal with Gray's influence. Geoffrey Tillotson notes, in 'The Methods of Description in Eighteenth and Nineteenth Century Poetry,[39] that Gray's technique, in the opening of the *Elegy*, of making each line of description an independent grammatical unit was frequently followed by nineteenth-century poets. William Powell Jones's 'Imitations of Gray's *Elegy*, 1751–1800' (*Bulletin of Bibliography*) is a check-list supplementary to Northup and Starr's bibliographies. In 'Gray's "Spring of Tears"' (*RES*) John Sparrow notes that the Alcaic stanza *O lacrymarum fons* is paralleled by some lines in the poet's paraphrase of Psalm lxxxiv. Finally, students of Gray have been

[39] In *Restoration and Eighteenth-Century Literature*. See note 1.

well served this year by the reprinting of a critical work that has been long out of print, Amy Louise Reed's *The Background of Gray's 'Elegy'*.[40]

Ricardo Quintana writes on 'The Scheme of Collins' *Odes on Several . . . Subjects'*.[41] He distinguishes between two groups of odes in the 1746 volume: six are concerned with the poetic kinds and five with patriotism, while the *Ode to Evening* appears to stand midway between the two groups, at once defining the mood of the pastoral and bringing pastoralism and patriotism close to one another. In an article on 'Structure and Effect in Collins' Progress Poems' (*SP*), John R. Crider provides a detailed discussion of the odes to *Pity*, *Fear*, *Simplicity*, and *Liberty*. He is concerned not only with the form, but also with the meaning of the poems.

The year saw the publication of a major work on Cowper. *A Bibliography of William Cowper to 1837*[42] by Norma Russell will be an essential tool for the serious student. Not only does it provide a complete bibliographical description of the editions of Cowper up to the publication of Southey's edition of the *Works*, but it also deals with such ancillary material as biographical and critical notices in periodicals, and with poetical tributes to Cowper. The presentation of the material is beautifully lucid, and the volume (which includes many illustrations) is most handsomely produced. The only other Cowper item to record is a facsimile of the original manuscript of *The Cast-away*, edited by Charles Ryskamp.[43]

There is rather less criticism than usual devoted to Christopher Smart. However, Albert J. Kuhn contributes an interesting paper on 'Christopher Smart: The Poet as Patriot of the Lord' (*ELH*). Smart thought that England was especially blessed and dedicated to a divine mission, and that his own role was to be a patriot of the Lord. This idea is discussed in relation to *Jubilate Agno*, a poem which is 'prophetic . . . in both style and purpose'. Max Keith Sutton's 'Smart's "Compleat Cat"' (*CE*) recapitulates the things that Smart says about his cat Jeoffry. Charles Parish presents a new interpretation of the Greek letters which head stanzas 31–37 of the *Song to David* in 'Christopher Smart's "Pillars of the Lord"' (*MLQ*). Cecil Price provides a brief note on two 'Books Owned by Smart and Cowper' (*NQ*).

As will be expected there has been a great deal of discussion of Blake, and it will be well to begin with the two books that have appeared during the year. *William Blake: A Reading of the Shorter Poems*[44] by Hazard Adams is a work both for the specialist and the general reader. Adams consciously follows Northrop Frye's archetypal criticism, and believes that, within the bounds of that approach, a more penetrating look at the shorter poems is now possible by paying attention 'to detail, to perspective, to related images in Blake's other works, and to symbolic conventions in literature'. The opening section provides a discussion of 'The Problem'; after a

---

[40] *The Background of Gray's 'Elegy'*, by Amy Louise Reed. New York: Russell & Russell, 1962. pp. ix+270. $6.50.

[41] In *Restoration and Eighteenth-Century Literature*. See note 1.

[42] *A Bibliography of William Cowper to 1837*, by Norma Russell. O.U.P. pp. xxvi +339. 50s. or $8.

[43] *The Cast-away*. The Text of the Original Manuscript and the First Printing of Cowper's Latin Translation, ed. by Charles Ryskamp. Princeton University Library. pp. 20+8 of facsimile and illustration. $2.

[44] *William Blake: A Reading of the Shorter Poems*, by Hazard Adams. Washington U.P. pp. xiii+337. $10.

survey of different ways of interpreting the poetry there is a valuable chapter on 'Blake's Archetypes' (containing also an analysis of his theory of perception), while Chapter III has a full analysis of *The Tyger* to demonstrate the importance of reading this poem—so frequently detached and anthologized—in the whole context of Blake's work. Adams next deals, at greater length than has been common, with the Pickering poems, and ends with a study of *Songs of Innocence and Experience*. The book is full of detailed analysis linked to overall interpretations which are clear and forthright, and it deserves to be widely read. Its essential approach is summed up not so much in the slightly disappointing last chapter as in a comment on *Auguries of Innocence*: 'The unity of Blake's thought makes one idea evoke another. What has seemed to be disorganization in the poet's structure is actually the result of Blake's effort to illustrate in the form the idea that all of his themes are essentially one theme, interchangeable because the existence of one idea implies logically and analogically the existence of the others.'

Harold Bloom's *Blake's Apocalypse*[45] is concerned with Blake's total literary achievement. There is a penetrating section on the Minor Poems (with some excellent pages on *The Marriage of Heaven and Hell*), but the book will be particularly useful to those readers who want a clear guide to *The Four Zoas*, *Milton*, and *Jerusalem*. Bloom is interested not only in the spiritual and intellectual framework of the major works, but also in 'evidencing how a masterful design is carried through into the

minute articulations of each poem'. The treatment is chronoiogical, and detailed explication is well combined with a general framework of interpretation to make this one of the most generally useful of recent works on Blake.

First place amongst articles should go to Kathleen Raine's long contribution, 'Blake's Debt to Antiquity' (*Sew*), a concentrated study of the poet's debt to Platonic and alchemical thought. In 'William Blake Rejects the Enlightenment'[46] Jean H. Hagstrum is concerned with the obverse of Kathleen Raine's thesis. It is shown how the early influence of Macpherson and Chatterton soon gave way to a rejection of the 'neoclassical' establishment which was deeper than mere 'pre-romanticism'. Blake's rejection of Locke, Bacon, and Newton is traced and his eventual dethronement of Voltaire and Rousseau. But the article goes on to argue that, 'though Blake's rejection of the Enlightenment is conceptually firm and consistent, it is his artistic embodiment of meaning that ought to command the attention of the twentieth century'.

Several articles explicate particular poems. John E. Grant's 'Interpreting Blake's *The Fly*' (*BNYPL*) is an elaborate refutation of Kirschbaum (see *YW* xlii. 221) which discusses both text and illustration. Whereas Kirschbaum gave us a Urizenic reading of the poem that attempts to justify the twofold vision of the speaker, Grant believes that the speaker is in error. The Bard 'must deplore both the thoughtless indifference that leads to the extermination of flies (as well as of men) and rationalizations that justify the inhumanity of all creatures to one another'. In 'William Blake's *The Clod and the*

[45] *Blake's Apocalypse: A Study in Poetic Argument*, by Harold Bloom. Victor Gollancz and Garden City, New York: Doubleday. pp. 454. 42*s*. and $5.95.

[46] In *Transactions of the First International Congress on the Enlightenment*. See note 11.

Pebble[47]   Jean   H.   Hagstrum argues that this poem should be read in the context of the poems printed close to it in the *Songs of Experience* and of *Urizen*, and that it is the Pebble which embodies Blake's viewpoint: 'value resides with the Pebble who makes a revolutionary hell out of heaven, not with the Urizenic Clod, who makes a conventional heaven out of hell'. Edward J. Rose contributes an account of 'The Structure of Blake's *Jerusalem*' (*Bu R*); and John Adlard suggests, in 'Blake and Thomas Taylor' (*ES*), that Blake's use of the clod in *The Book of Thel* may derive from a passage in Thomas Taylor's *A Vindication of the Rights of Brutes*.

The most important of the articles on Blake as an artist is Paul Miner's 'The Apprentice of Great Queen Street' (*BNYPL*). This discusses, with illustrations, the possible attribution to Blake of drawings in the topographical collection which Richard Gough bequeathed to the Bodleian, and in material which Sir Joseph Ayloffe presented to the Society of Antiquaries. Geoffrey Keynes points to 'A Blake Engraving in Bonnycastle's *Mensuration*, 1782' (*BC*). John Ingamells, in 'An Image Shared by Blake and Henri Rousseau' (*British Journal of Aesthetics*), discusses the lion and girl image found both in Blake's *The Little Girl Lost* and in Rousseau's *La Bohémienne Endormie*.

'John Flaxman and the Matthew Clan' (*BNYPL*), by G. E. Bentley, Jr., is an attempt to sort out the extremely complicated evidence concerning the identity of Blake's first patron, Mr. Matthew, who was minister of the proprietary chapel in Percy Street, London.

Two articles touch on Blake and

the Continent. In 'Amédée Pichot's Discovery of Blake' (*Ea*), C. H. Moore contributes to our knowledge of Blake's reputation in France, while Albert Maillet studies parallels between 'Blake et Nietzsche' (*Revue des Lettres Modernes*).

Of editions published during the year the most ambitious and the most important is *William Blake: Vala or the Four Zoas*,[48] edited by G. E. Bentley, Jr., a facsimile text with a complete critical apparatus which will now be the standard one for all serious students. Two other works should be listed, although they have not yet been available for examination: *The Marriage of Heaven and Hell*,[49] edited by Clark Emery, and *Blake's Grave . . .*,[50] with a commentary by S. Foster Damon.

There is little on Burns this year, but one excellent article can be reported. 'The Identity of Burns',[51] by David Daiches, combines a survey of Burns's achievement with a critical and detailed examination of individual works. It considers the main facts of the poet's education and life, discusses the 'native' and 'English' elements in his work, the effect of environment on his writing, and some fallacies in the Burns cult. The main emphasis is on the affirmative side of his writing. One would like to see this

[47] In *Restoration and Eighteenth-Century Literature*. See note 1.

[48] *William Blake: Vala or the Four Zoas*, ed. by G. E. Bentley, Jr. A Facsimile of the Manuscript, a Transcript of the Poem, and a Study of Its Growth and Significance. O.U.P. pp. xviii + 220. £8. 8s. $26.90.

[49] *Blake's 'The Marriage of Heaven and Hell'*, ed. by Clark Emery. (University of Miami Critical Studies, 1.) Miami U.P. pp. 104. $2.

[50] *Blake's Grave: A Prophetic Book, being William Blake's Illustrations for Robert Blair's 'The Grave'*. Arranged as Blake directed. With a commentary by S. Foster Damon. Brown U.P. pp. 45. $6.

[51] In *Restoration and Eighteenth-Century Literature*. See note 1.

article reprinted. G. Ross Roy contributes a long article on 'French Translations of Robert Burns (to 1893)' (*RLC*), and Basil Skinner has produced a pleasant booklet, *Burns: Authentic Likenesses*,[52] which reproduces eight portraits of Burns, gives a full account of their history, and discusses the problems involved in establishing what his true likeness was.

The Scottish Text Society edition of *The Works of Allan Ramsay* has now been completed (as far as the text itself is concerned) with a volume devoted to 'Poems: Miscellaneous and Uncollected'.[53] A final volume will contain the apparatus, and further comment will be held over until this is available.

One or two articles dealing with minor figures in the earlier part of the century may be grouped together. In 'John Byrom, 1692–1763' (*Manchester Review*), N. K. Firby notes copies of works by and about Byrom in the Manchester Central Library. J. C. Arens reprints a poem by Watts in 'Sarbiewski's *Ode Against Tears* Imitated by Lovelace, Yalden and Watts' (*N*), and Peter B. Steese demonstrates 'Dennis's Influence on Watts's Preface to *Horae Lyricae*' (*PQ*). Clarence Tracy provides an illustrated check-list of Savage's separate printed works in 'Some Uncollected Authors: XXXVI: Richard Savage d. 1743' (*BC*).

Two small items have to do with Shenstone, especially as a gardener: John Street's 'The Poets and the English Garden' (*Listener*), and Marjorie Williams's 'A Man of Taste' (*Listener*).

In his inaugural lecture, 'A Man of Genius, and a Welch Man',[54] Cecil J. L. Price considers the work of Evan Lloyd, a satirist with a considerable reputation in his own day, but now completely neglected. Lloyd is shown to be 'a man with a natural talent for writing, a gift of phrase, and an ability to communicate his opinions, whether they were comic or satiric'.

Thomas Arne's translation of a libretto by Metastasio—*Artaxerxes*[55] —has been edited by William Gillis; the opera was a successful adaptation of the Italian style and was performed until the 1830's.

'"Ossian" Macpherson and the Gaelic World of the Eighteenth Century' (*Aberdeen University Review*), by Derrick Thomson, was a public lecture given to mark the two-hundredth anniversary of the publication of *Fingal*. It gives an account of Macpherson's manner of proceeding in creating the work and of the ensuing controversy, and discusses contemporary English notions about the Highlands and the actual state of Celtic culture at the time.

Two items deal with Chatterton. Basil Cottle's *Thomas Chatterton*[56] is a brief general survey which gives the main facts of the life and comments briefly on the verse. 'It is the purpose

---

[52] *Burns: Authentic Likenesses*, by Basil C. Skinner. Oliver & Boyd. pp. 15. 5s.

[53] *The Works of Allan Ramsay*, ed. by Alexander M. Kinghorn and Alexander Law. Vol. 3 (*Poems: Miscellaneous and Uncollected*). Scottish Text Society Publications, 3rd ser., 29. Old Manse, Pilmuir (Haddington): Scottish Text Society. pp. xviii+347 +10. Subscription only.

[54] 'A Man of Genius, and a Welch Man' (Inaugural Lecture of the Professor of English Language and Literature delivered at the College on 5 February 1963), by Cecil J. L. Price. University College of Swansea. pp. 27.

[55] *Artaxerxes* (1761), ed. with an Introduction by William Gillis. (Augustan Reprint Society, No. 99.) Los Angeles: Clark Memorial Library, University of California. pp. vii+47.

[56] *Thomas Chatterton*, by Basil Cottle. (Historical Association. Bristol Branch. Local History Pamphlets, No. 6.) Bristol University. pp. 15. 2s.

of this study to show Chatterton as England's youngest writer of sustained adult verse, but more vitally as her loudest herald of the Gothic revival, late in the eighteenth century, of an interest in medieval buildings and writings.' 'Thomas Chatterton: the Marvellous Boy' (*RLC*), by Hans Wolpe, is concerned with the treatment of Chatterton on the Continent. Paul Kaufman writes on 'Chatterton's Brother-Poet, William Roberts' (*PBSA*). Roberts died in 1811, aged 19, and his poems were published by Southey. Among them is a tribute to Chatterton written in his own manner.

In 'Robert Merry, Political Romanticist' (*SIR*) M. Ray Adams argues that the leader of the Della Cruscan school should not be remembered simply as a writer of sentimental bombast. In verse inspired with a zeal for liberty he sometimes sloughs off artificiality and writes with direct feeling, and in satire he showed that there was 'iron in his blood after all'.

Two general articles may be noted here. William Powell Jones's 'Newton Further Demands the Muse' (*SEL*) supplements Marjorie Nicolson's work on the *Optics* by tracing the influence of the *Principia* on poetry from 1715 to 1800. Thomas Crawford's 'Scottish Popular Ballads and Lyrics of the Eighteenth and Early Nineteenth Centuries: Some Preliminary Conclusions' (*Studies in Scottish Literature*) analyses and considers various categorizations for source material in manuscripts, printed broadsides, and song-books. It concludes that the term 'people' (*das Volk*) might be replaced by a series of terms emphasizing the possibility of different societies and social groups producing different types of song. Secondly, it is stressed that the 'pure' folk songs cannot survive an age of general literacy. Once songs are com-

mitted to paper 'they acquire all the authority of the written word and are less liable to spontaneous variation in future'.

Also to be noted is 'Some Notes on the Bibliography of William Hayley: III' (*TCBS*, 1962), by N. J. Barker.

Finally, in this section, there is Desmond King-Hele's book on *Erasmus Darwin*.[57] The author is a mathematician who works as a scientific officer, and he is particularly interested in the range of Darwin's scientific interests and the extent to which he anticipated later developments, not only in his formulation of the theory of evolution, but also in his medical practice and his lively interest in technology. King-Hele also considers Darwin's literary achievement, stressing the vein of humour which is so often ignored, and discussing the decline in his reputation (brought about by the general atmosphere of conformism and suspicion which followed the French Revolution) and his influence on the Romantic poets. This is an informative account of a minor poet, but a very interesting man.

(*f*) The most recent volume of the general edition of the Boswell papers, *Boswell: The Ominous Years, 1774–1776*,[58] includes four months when Boswell was away from Edinburgh. During this time he was often in Johnson's company, and it is his account of this period that will be of most general interest. The volume shows Boswell's well-known contradictoriness of character very clearly,

[57] *Erasmus Darwin*, by Desmond King-Hele. Macmillan, and New York: St. Martin's Press. pp. viii + 183. 30s.

[58] *Boswell: The Ominous Years, 1774–1776*, ed. by Charles Ryskamp and Frederick A. Pottle. Yale Edition of the Works of James Boswell. New York: McGraw Hill, and London: Heinemann. pp. xxiv + 427. $8.50. 42s.

R

the oscillation between piety and sensuality, ambition and the pursuit of trivia. 'If no man,' as the editors put it, 'ever entered upon life with a more overweening ambition, none ever left it with a more complete realization of failure.'

Donald Greene's 'Reflections on a Literary Anniversary' (*QQ*) is an attack on Boswell's *Life of Johnson* which, it is suggested, presents a Johnson of 'the Toby mugs, the church-warden pipes, and the Cheshire Cheese', and thereby prevents him from being taken seriously as a literary figure. 'Boswell's Account of the Johnson-Wilkes Meeting' (*SEL*), by Sven Eric Molin, analyses Boswell's skill in presenting the drama of that famous dinner-party. In an extremely well-documented account of 'Jemmie Boswell and the London Daily Press, 1785–1795' (*BNYPL*)— which is also reprinted as a booklet[59]— Lucyle Werkmeister shows that Boswell was subjected to a great deal of journalistic abuse, often political in origin, and that the *Life* was attacked and parodied with vehemence and some wit. However, he thrived on abuse, and even welcomed it for its advertising value. This is an article which is of considerable interest to those who are concerned with the interaction between political and literary events in the period. Finally, two more Boswell items may be briefly listed: 'Boswell's *Life of Johnson*, 1791' (*ANQ*), by Herman W. Liebert, is a bibliographical note on variants in different copies of this edition; Frederick A. Pottle's 'Boswell as Icarus'[60] discusses Boswell's election to the College of Arcadia in Rome.

The most substantial contribution to Burke studies this year is the appearance of the fourth volume of *The Correspondence*.[61] This contains 227 letters written either wholly or in part by Burke. His relations with his constituents in Bristol and with Lord Rockingham are major themes in the volume. The student of English, on the other hand, may be more concerned with letters from Burke to Boswell and William Jones, the orientalist, and with those from Crabbe to Burke. John C. Weston, Jr., considers 'Edmund Burke's Wit' (*REL*). He recalls Johnson's repeated denials that Burke had wit, and, following the examination of many examples, concludes that Burke probably did lack the social wit that depends upon humour, but that he undeniably possessed that 'brilliance of intellectual faculty which produces laughter in order to accomplish some serious purpose'. In 'Edmund Burke's Friends and *The Annual Register*' (*Lib*), Thomas W. Copeland shows that, although Burke probably retired from the editorship of *The Annual Register* in 1765, he was friendly with many of those who were afterwards most closely engaged in the project (notably Thomas English and Walker King), and it can reasonably be maintained that he 'did not lose interest in the magazine or his power of influencing its activities'. C. P. Courtney is concerned with aesthetic ideas in 'Edmund Burke and Petrus Camper' (*ES*).

An item on political matters which should be listed here is James Maclean's *Reward is Secondary*,[62]

[59] *Jemmie Boswell and the London Daily Press, 1785–1795*, by Lucyle Werkmeister. New York: New York Public Library. pp. 59. $1.50.

[60] In *Restoration and Eighteenth-Century Literature*. See note 1.

[61] *The Correspondence of Edmund Burke. Volume IV: July 1778–June 1782*, ed. by John A. Woods. C.U.P. and Chicago U.P. pp. xxiv+475. 84s. $12.

[62] *Reward is Secondary: The Life of a Political Adventurer and an Enquiry into the Mystery of 'Junius'*, by James Maclean. Hodder & Stoughton. pp. xix+558. 63s.

which argues the case for seeing Laughlin Macleane in the role of Junius. However, it seems likely that this controversy has been settled by Ellegård's work which was reviewed here last year.

There are two Gibbon items: Nicholas Barker provides a 'Note on the Bibliography of Gibbon, 1776–1802' (*Lib*), and James Hamilton Doggart writes on 'Gibbon's Eyesight' (*TCBS*), with some comments on other aspects of his medical history.

On Walpole the only contribution this year is Bonamy Dobrée's 'Horace Walpole'.[63] Dobrée is particularly concerned with what he sees as a struggle in Walpole's make-up between the reasonable and the incipiently romantic. The character, 'the ideal social self', often oppressed the personality.

There is a spate of activity on the Scottish critics this year. Attention may first be drawn to a chapter of *David Hume: A Symposium*,[64] edited by David Francis Pears. The book is mainly concerned with philosophic matters, but P. L. Gardiner discusses 'Hume's Theory of the Passions'. There is a reprint of Alexander Gerard's *An Essay on Taste*.[65] Gerard was one of the group of theorists who were concerned with systematizing aesthetics and with the explanation of beauty, and who laid stress upon distinctions such as those between the beautiful and the sublime, the picturesque and the ridiculous. The

introduction places Gerard's book in its philosophic context.

Unexpectedly recovered from the past are extensive notes of *Lectures on Rhetoric and Belles Lettres . . . by Adam Smith*.[66] The chief importance of these lectures is that they show Adam Smith to have been a prime mover in stimulating the transition from a study of formal rhetoric to 'that of Belles Lettres or polite literature'. In the lectures directly concerned with style Smith recommended a concise and direct expression of thought and emotion, and in his survey of past writing 'he ranges at ease in the world of scholarship, of literature and of literary principles.' His course was attended by such eminent figures as Hugh Blair and Lord Kames, and it is probable that its success led to the creation of the Regius Chair of Rhetoric and Belles Lettres at Edinburgh.

In 'Literary Aesthetics and the Sympathetic Emotions—A Main Trend in Eighteenth Century Scottish Criticism' (*Studies in Scottish Literature*), A. M. Kinghorn shows that Scottish critics (Hume, Kames, Beattie, Blair) stressed the generation of sympathetic feeling as a criterion in artistic judgement. He also examines attitudes to tragedy, comedy, and the ballad, and discusses the problem of the relationship between artistic pleasure and morality. Ernest Campbell Mossner gives a detailed account of an unpublished work which has some affinity with both Johnson's *Journey to the Western Isles* and Boswell's *Journal of a Tour to the Hebrides*, and which contains a discussion of aesthetic and moral questions: 'Adam Ferguson's *Dialogue on*

---

[63] In *Restoration and Eighteenth-Century Literature*. See note 1.

[64] *David Hume: A Symposium*, by Stuart Hampshire (and others), ed. by David Francis Pears. Macmillan, and New York: St. Martin's Press. pp. vi+100. 16*s*. $2.75.

[65] *An Essay on Taste* (*1759*), *together with Observations Concerning the Imitative Nature of Poetry*. Facsimile Reproduction of the 3rd Edition (1780). Introduction by Walter J. Hipple, Jr. Gainesville: Scholars' Facsimiles and Reprints. pp. xxviii+284. $7.50.

[66] *Lectures on Rhetoric and Belles Lettres Delivered in the University of Glasgow by Adam Smith: Reported by a Student in 1762–63*, ed. by John M. Lothian. Nelson. pp. xl+205. 42*s*. $9.25.

a Highland Jaunt with Robert Adam, William Cleghorn, David Hume, and William Wilkie.'[67]

Douglas McDermott suggests, in 'George Campbell and the Classical Tradition' (*QJS*), that a new view should be taken of Campbell's originality. It is true that he discarded the classical terminology of rhetoric, but his real importance lies in his 'attempt to link rhetoric with the psychological principles of the human mind'. Also to be noted is Douglas Ehninger's 'Campbell, Blair, and Whately: Old Friends Revisited' (*Southern Speech Journal*). An edition of Campbell's *The Philosophy of Rhetoric*[68] can be listed, although it has not been available for examination. Also to be listed is Vincent M. Bevilacqua's 'Lord Kames's Theory of Rhetoric' (*Speech Monographs*).

A volume which bears mainly upon eighteenth-century oratory is *Essays from 'Select British Eloquence'*[69] by Chauncey Allen Goodrich. These introductions to such figures as Burke, Sheridan, Fox, and Pitt were published by the former Professor of Rhetoric at Yale in 1852, and they have an interest both in relation to the subjects themselves and for the light they throw on nineteenth-century attitudes to the study of rhetoric.

The Augustan Reprint Society has continued its most useful work by making available, sixty years after the last edition, Richard Hurd's *Letters on Chivalry and Romance*,[70] a defence of the romance element in Renaissance literature as being 'conducive to the sublime'. Hoyt Trowbridge's Introduction stresses the traditional elements in Hurd's ideas, and the extent to which he is a representative figure of his time rather than the romantic precursor that he has often been made out to be.

An account of Warton's attitude to the Middle English writers that he deals with can be found in A. M. Kinghorn's 'Warton's *History* and Early English Poetry' (*ES*), while William Powell Jones writes about 'John Aikin on the Use of Natural History in Poetry' (*Journal of Aesthetics and Art Criticism*).

A book which is particularly concerned with visual art, but which is of interest also to literary students, is Carl Paul Barbier's well-illustrated *William Gilpin: His Drawings, Teaching, and Theory of the Picturesque*.[71]

Two books on the press should be noted. As its title implies, Robert R. Rea's *The English Press in Politics, 1760–1774*[72] is mainly concerned with historical matters. In *The London Daily Press, 1772–1792*[73] Lucyle Werkmeister studies the development of the Press as a medium of popular entertainment and scandal. She deals with

---

[67] In *Restoration and Eighteenth-Century Literature*. See note 1.

[68] *The Philosophy of Rhetoric*, by George Campbell, ed by Lloyd F. Bitzer. Foreword by David Potter. (Landmarks in Rhetoric and Public Address.) Southern Illinois U.P. pp. lii + 415 + liii–lxi. $7.

[69] *Essays from 'Select British Eloquence'*, by Chauncey Allen Goodrich, ed. by A. Craig Baird and David Potter. (Landmarks in Rhetoric and Public Address). Southern Illinois U.P. pp. xlviii + 359. $7.50. 60s.

[70] *Letters on Chivalry and Romance* (1762), by Richard Hurd, ed. with an Introduction by Hoyt Trowbridge. (Augustan Reprint Society, Nos. 101, 102.) Los Angeles: Clark Memorial Library, University of California. pp. xi + 120.

[71] *William Gilpin: His Drawings, Teaching, and Theory of the Picturesque*, by Carl Paul Barbier. O.U.P. pp. xiv + 196. 63s. $10.10.

[72] *The English Press in Politics, 1760–1774*, by Robert R. Rea. Nebraska U.P. pp. ix + 272. $5.50.

[73] *The London Daily Press, 1772–1792*, by Lucyle Werkmeister. Nebraska U.P. pp. ix + 470. $7.50.

six papers, the *Morning Post*, the *London Courant*, the *General Advertiser*, the *World*, the *Star* (the first evening newspaper), and the 'spurious' *Star*, and studies the relationship between the Government and the papers, especially from 1789 to 1792. Appendixes provide extracts from the papers themselves.

Two articles deal with problems of attribution in journals. In 'A New Fielding Essay from the *Champion*' (*PQ*), John B. Shipley suggests that a leader on essay writing, which he reprints from the *Dublin Evening Advertiser*, may have been taken from an issue of the *Champion* now lost. Philip Mahone Griffith writes on 'The Authorship of the Papers Signed "A" in Hawkesworth's *Adventurer*: A Stronger Case for Dr. Richard Bathurst' (*TSE*, 1962).

The first of two articles by Roger Lonsdale on 'Dr. Burney and the *Monthly Review*' (*RES*) discusses Ralph Griffith's editorial principles in his organization of reviewing, and concludes that, although claims for the editorial impartiality of the *Monthly Review* are basically justified, there was none the less 'considerable scope for his reviewers to indulge in self-advertisement and personal animosity on a lesser scale', which the editor could do little to prevent. Examples from Burney's reviews are then adduced to show how personal quarrels and an understandable concern for his own reputation could colour his approach.

Randolph Hudson writes on 'Henry Mackenzie, James Beattie, *et al.* and the Edinburgh *Mirror*' (*ELN*), and there is an article by Alan D. McKillop on the Newberry Library copy of 'Lintot's *Monthly Catalogue*' (*Newberry Library Bulletin*).

To be listed here, although no copy has been available for examination, is a volume of *New Essays by Arthur Murphy*.[74]

A. J. Sambrook discusses the manoeuvres that underlay 'Fanny Burney's First Letter to Dr. Johnson' (*RES*). The episode illustrates the arch and confident way in which the 'saucy spirited little puss' (in Mrs. Thrale's phrase) handled Johnson.

'Travel Literature and the Rise of Neo-Hellenism in England' (*BNYPL*), by James M. Osborn, covers the period from 1675, when Sir George Wheeler went to Greece, until the nineteenth century.

Finally, a note on Shakespearian editing should be listed here. Hilton Landry's 'Malone as Editor of Shakespeare's Sonnets' (*BNYPL*) argues that, although Malone was 'incomparable in his own day . . . his day has long since passed. However much we may admire his accomplishments, we must also face squarely his obvious limitations.'

(*g*) The most important study of drama in the period is Jean Dulck's *Les Comédies de R. B. Sheridan*,[75] surprisingly the first book to deal entirely with Sheridan's work as a dramatist. As is common with French studies of this kind, this book has a comprehensiveness of approach that is seldom attempted now by English critics. The historical situation of the drama when Sheridan came to write is surveyed, together with the dramatist's life and personality; there is a detailed examination of the production and literary history of each play, followed by chapters on such topics as the style, the characters, and the structure of Sheridan's work. This is a volume which will be indispensable to

[74] *New Essays by Arthur Murphy*, ed. with an Introduction by Arthur Sherbo. Michigan State U.P. pp. x+217.
[75] *Les Comédies de R. B. Sheridan: Etude Littéraire*, by Jean Dulck. Etudes anglaises 12. Didier, 1962. pp. 611. 90 F.

future students of the subject. Also to be noted on Sheridan is Cecil Price's 'Another Crewe MS. of *The School for Scandal*' (*PBSA*), which adduces evidence to suggest that there may have been not merely one Crewe MS (as has always been assumed), but two.

A long-projected publication has been brought to completion with the appearance of *The Letters of David Garrick*[76] in three beautifully produced volumes. Some 1,360 letters are printed (of which over half were hitherto unpublished), together with a comparatively limited selection of material from the letters of Garrick's correspondents, a long biographical introduction which discusses the relationships that gave rise to the letters, and copious annotations.

This section must end with a rather miscellaneous collection of items. Edgar V. Roberts's 'Fielding's Ballad Opera *The Lottery* (1732) and the English State Lottery of 1731' (*HLQ*) gives an account of the way in which lotteries were conducted and the various types of speculation that they encouraged. 'The Play That Would Not Die: George Lillo's *The London Merchant*' (*QJS*), by Herbert L. Carson, is a straightforward account of the play, its reception, and its subsequent reputation. An interesting sidelight on eighteenth-century attitudes to Shakespeare is provided by Esther K. Sheldon's 'Sheridan's *Coriolanus*: An Eighteenth Century Compromise' (*ShQ*). In 1752, at his Smock Alley Theatre, Dublin, Thomas Sheridan produced a version of *Coriolanus* which was taken partly from Shakespeare and partly from a quite different play by Thomson. Sheridan elaborated the spectacle, and in general tried to keep Thomson's regular 'classical' plot and Shakespeare's characterization. His textual changes sometimes reflect contemporary taste and his own sense of propriety. The play was a success both in Dublin and London.

'Olympus at Billingsgate: The Burlettas of Kane O'Hara' (*ETJ*), by Margaret F. Maxwell, gives an account of two burlettas, *Midas* (1764) and *The Golden Pippin* (1777), and suggests that they are 'two of the best examples of burlesque of classical myth which the century affords'. Laetitia Kennedy-Skipton provides 'Notes on a Copy of William Capon's Plan of Goodman's Fields Theatre, 1786 and 1802, and on a Copy of One of the Ceiling Paintings in the Folger Shakespeare Library' (*TN*). 'F. L. Schröder, J. F. Regnard, and M. G. Lewis' (*HLQ*), by Karl S. Guthke, provides new evidence to support the view that in writing *The Twins* (cf. *YW* xliii. 215) Lewis was influenced by Schröder's *Zwillingsbrüder*.

Finally, Dougald Macmillan writes on 'George Steevens's Contributions to *Biographica Dramatica*'.[77] With the help of MS notes by John Payne Collier in a Huntington Library copy of the *Biographica Dramatica* Steevens's contributions to this still authoritative reference book are identified and discussed. Steevens's critical comments are often original and forthright and, although he was prejudiced against the Scots and against medieval work, many of his judgements are discriminating and still acceptable.

---

[76] *The Letters of David Garrick*, ed. by David M. Little and George M. Kahrl; Associate Editor Phoebe de K. Wilson. Belknap Press of Harvard U.P., and Oxford U.P. 3 vols. pp. lxxiv+1,418. $35. £9. 9s.

[77] In *Restoration and Eighteenth-Century Literature*. See note 1.

XIII

The Nineteenth Century

P. M. YARKER and BRIAN LEE

THIS chapter comprises the following sections: (a) Social and Intellectual Background; (b) Poetry and Drama; (c) Novels and Novelists; (d) Selected Prose Writers. Of these the first two are by P. M. Yarker, and the last two by Brian Lee.

(A) SOCIAL AND INTELLECTUAL BACKGROUND

Social history occupies the most prominent position among the background studies, with pride of place going to E. P. Thompson's close and exhaustive scrutiny of the years between 1792 and 1832.[1] The first of these dates is significant to Thompson for the founding of the London Correspondence Society, a branch of the subversive network of artisan groups which, with their post-war successors, the Hampden Clubs, were the means of disseminating Radical opinion throughout the country. The informed minority thus produced was able to give organized support to the many popular movements for which the period was notable, and which have sometimes been regarded as sporadic. Luddism, for example, was not a mere 'blind opposition to machinery' breaking into violence here and there, but was the considered reaction of those who saw in the factory system the final destruction of their status as independent men. But although he

gives a full account of these movements, the historical factors that brought them about, and the measures taken by the authorities to suppress them, their chronicling is not Thompson's main concern. These events are seen by him as 'the raw material of experience' from which the working class was made. Thompson stresses that there was no spontaneous emergence of this class; 'it was present at its own making.' It is not a 'thing' but a 'relationship'; 'an historical phenomenon, unifying a number of disparate and seemingly unconnected events'. His book therefore deals with a complex of ideas and events far too vast to be epitomized here. Briefly, it presents views on the historical inheritance from which the factory system developed, the reactions of the independent artisans, conscious and unconscious, to the establishment of industrialism, and finally 'the working-class presence', and an examination of the popular culture that emerged, seen through the eyes of commentators such as Hazlitt, and in the writings of agitators like Thelwall, Cobbett, Richard Carlile, and many others.

Thompson speaks of 'the Tory-Radical strain which runs through Cobbett to Oastler', and Richard Oastler is among the principal figures in a study of the Factory Movement by J. T. Ward,[2] which thus carries on

[1] *The Making of the English Working Class*, by E. P. Thompson. Gollancz. pp. 848. 73s. 6d.

[2] *The Factory Movement: 1830–1855*, by J. T. Ward. Macmillan. pp. xi+515. 50s.

the story, to some extent, until the middle of the century. A third book, by K. S. Inglis,[3] although it stands somewhat apart from the other two, has a bearing on both and deals mainly with the later part of the century. Its subject is the alienation of the working class from the Churches. E. P. Thompson considers the place of Methodism as a factor in the social complex, and concludes that its influence was negative. He acknowledges Hazlitt's remark that Methodists were 'a collection of religious invalids', but claims that the war years saw a great expansion of Methodism, notably among the working class. Inglis, however, writing, it is true, of a few years later, finds 'little evidence that . . . it was extending its ministry far into the great body of working-class people who attended no religious worship'. Ward's study is mainly concerned with the efforts of Oastler, with G. S. Bull and other clergy, to promote the Ten Hour Bill, but Inglis does not mention this side of the Church's activity. His concern is with the extent to which the Church and the working class had parted company, and with the efforts made late in the century to remedy this by the establishment of 'Settlements' and other means. Philip N. Backstrom, Jr., argues (VS) that 'The Practical Side of Christian Socialism in Victorian England' was the work, not of F. D. Maurice (who was concerned with much more theoretical aspects), but of such men as J. M. Ludlow, E. V. Neale, and Thomas Hughes.

It is possibly something of a relief to turn from the troubled progress of the Industrial Revolution to a study of the relatively tranquil affairs of the landed aristocracy.[4] The author, F. M. L. Thompson, considers the subject in three main ways. The first part of the book deals with the institutions of the aristocracy; the second part deals with their part in the economy during the first three-quarters of the century; and the last part deals with their decline. In a review of the book in *VS* H. L. Beales says that 'the third section of the McGregor Introduction to Lord Ernle's *English Farming Past and Present* should be obligatory reading' to those who are attracted to this 'useful preliminary aid to the historical assessment of the Victorian landed interest'. In 'Aristocracy, Social Structure, and Religion in the Early Victorian Period' (*VS*) David Spring presents a pleasing picture of the steady growth of virtue among the upper classes.

A collection of critical essays of the nineteenth century[5] is based on a distinction between 'visionary' and 'moral' criticism. Such categories, however plausibly advocated, are bound to be misleading, for a place must, after all, be found for purely literary considerations, and here there is none. Of the seventeen writers represented, Wordsworth, Ruskin, George Eliot, Arnold, and Meredith are regarded as moralists, and all the rest are visionaries, with the exception of Peacock and Hopkins. Peacock's *Four Ages of Poetry* is included apparently as a companion to Shelley's *Defence of Poetry*, but Hopkins appears to be unrelated. Arnold's Preface of 1853 is regarded as a moralizing tract, unconnected with

[3] *Churches and the Working Classes in Victorian England*, by K. S. Inglis. Routledge & Kegan Paul. pp. vii+350. 42s.

[4] *English Landed Society in the Nineteenth Century*, by F. M. L. Thompson. Routledge and Kegan Paul. pp. xiii+374. 45s.

[5] *English Literary Criticism: Romantic and Victorian*, ed. by Daniel G. Hoffman and Samuel Hynes. N.Y.: Appleton-Century-Crofts. pp. x+322. $2.95.

literary debate. Thus the collection is in some ways misleading to students; but it is useful to have such pieces as Mill's *What is Poetry?* and extracts from George Eliot's *Natural History of German Life* made thus accessible. A notable omission from this book is E. S. Dallas, and a useful article on this neglected critic by R. A. Forsyth is welcome. 'The Onward March of Thought and the Poetic Theory of E. S. Dallas' (*BJA*) notes the pre-occupation of early Victorian critics with the problem of 'accommodating the predominantly Romantic theory of the time to the hard-headed claims and standards of science'. Dallas's answer was the abandonment of the Aristotelian mimesis as the basis of criticism in favour of a scientific scale based on the pleasure principle. In this way, he argued, definite standards of aesthetic values could be established. *The Gay Science* was, as Forsyth points out, a notable plea for serious psychological research.

R. H. S. Crossman writes on 'Walter Bagehot' in *Encounter*. Norman St. John-Stevas confirms the authorship of a review in 'Bagehot on Tennyson' (*TLS* 26 April), and, with R. H. Tener, notes a review of the second edition of *Festus* in 'Bagehot and Bailey' (*TLS* 8 February). *Éthique et Idéalisme*, by Charles le Chevalier,[6] is primarily a study of Bosanquet, but there are chapters on T. H. Green and F. H. Bradley, with more general comment on 'the Presence of Coleridge' and John Ruskin.

Northrop Frye has collected four papers on Romanticism by American writers.[7] They are: 'English Roman-

ticism: The Spirit of the Age', by M. H. Abrams; 'The Fate of Pleasure, Wordsworth to Dostoevsky', by Lionel Trilling, tracing changes in the meaning of the word; René Wellek, in 'Romanticism Re-examined', surveys the numerous attempts to define Romanticism, and concludes that those that are of value 'all see the implication of imagination, symbol, myth and organic nature, and see it as part of the great endeavour to overcome the split between subject and object'. Frye himself adds an essay on 'The Revolutionary Element in Romanticism'.

The theme of a book by Allan Rodway[8] is that Romantics are 'as much made as born', or rather that 'the milieu probably encouraged one type of genius and inhibited another'. Thus, the principal factor in the Romantic movement (whose limits are placed between 1750 and 1850) was the social environment. Rodway sees this as a general conflict between order and anarchy, a conflict that raged as much within the individual bosom as in society at large. Social stresses induced a sense of isolation in the individual, and this isolation caused Romantic tendencies to develop in one of two directions, either 'radical' or 'reactionary'. Carlyle was the type of reactionary Romantic; but because 'all our best poets in their best periods' have been radical, only this branch is discussed. Rodway passes rapidly in review all candidates for the title 'Romantic' from Thomson onwards, and, unlike Wellek, concludes that all are united only in that they were victims of an 'Outcast complex'. Among the 'pre-Romantics', however, the complexity stemmed from the fact that they were secretly enamoured of the orthodoxy against which they were in revolt,

[6] *Éthique et Idéalisme*, by Charles le Chevalier. Paris: J. Vrin. pp. 190.

[7] *Romanticism Reconsidered: Selected Papers from the English Institute*, ed. by Northrop Frye. Columbia U.P. pp. ix+144. 28s.

[8] *The Romantic Conflict*, by Allan Rodway. Chatto & Windus. pp. x+256. 30s.

whereas the 'Romantic radicals' possessed an 'imaginative audacity' impossible earlier. The second part of the book deals with individual poets— Smart, Chatterton, Cowper, and the major Romantics. Rodway's preoccupation with the social conflict theme leads to some individual literary judgements; for example, an unusual elevation of Shelley's political satires. Byron fits the pattern much more neatly, and the section on him is possibly the best in a book that is rather overfull of stimulating ideas.

The Romantic Ventriloquists, by E. E. Bostetter[9] (the title is borrowed from Coleridge), is a study of a number of unfinished poems in each of which the poet 'made his most determined effort to solve the aesthetic and philosophical problems that confronted him'. The book's concern is thus with the nature of the Romantic ethos. The poems are The Recluse, Kubla Khan and Christabel, Hyperion and The Fall of Hyperion, The Triumph of Life, and Don Juan. Each of these poems, says the author, breaks off at a memorable dramatic point, leaving the reader with a sense of high endeavour frustrated by insuperable difficulty. Like Rodway, Bostetter emphasizes the isolation of the poets, whose principles are at variance with their social environment. Unlike Rodway, however, he maintains that, far from deriving new 'imaginative audacity' from their isolation, they shrank back in bewilderment and disillusion 'to a traditional and orthodox syntax'. Only Byron was exempt from the general dismay, for he 'discovered a source of artistic power' in the 'comic expression of a disintegrating syntax' —an argument similar to Rodway's.

[9] The Romantic Ventriloquists: Wordsworth, Coleridge, Keats, Shelley, Byron, by E. E. Bostetter. Washington U.P. pp. xii+351. $6.75.

Another variation on the theme of Romantic conflict is supplied by B. R. Godfrey, who maintains, in 'Imagination and Truth: Some Romantic Contradictions' (ES), that Wordsworth and Coleridge were perplexed by the fact that their critical insistence 'that art must truthfully mirror Nature' was contradicted by their practice as poets.

By 'The Theme of the Disappearance of God in Victorian Poetry' (VS) J. Hillis Miller means the 'withdrawal of God from the world', not necessarily disbelief in Him. His concern is with how the poets (Arnold, Browning, Tennyson, and Hopkins, in that order) reacted to the fact of this withdrawal. Only Browning gives 'hints and anticipations of the recovery of Immanence', to be effected through the rejection of 'twenty-five hundred years of dualism'. Miller's book of the same title, published by Harvard U.P., and dealing with De Quincey, Browning, Arnold, Emily Brontë, and Hopkins, has not been available for review. W. A. Madden traces 'The Victorian Sensibility' (VS) through the 'slowly changing relationship between the "public" and "private" voices' of poets and writers. Patricia Merivale has an entertaining article on 'The "Death of Pan" in Victorian Literature' (VN), giving the interpretations of Elizabeth Barrett, Robert Browning, Edmund Gosse, James Thomson, and others to the well-known story from Plutarch. John A. Lester considers 'The Consolations of Ecstasy' (ELIT) as a literary theme.

The importance of nineteenth-century periodicals has never been in doubt, but there is still a wide field there for the editor and researcher. Walter E. Houghton, in 'Reflexions on Indexing Victorian Periodicals' (VS), gives some encouraging glimpses of the forthcoming Wellesley

Index, and enumerates some of the difficulties that the task of compiling it entails. In the meantime studies of individual periodicals accumulate. Esther R. Houghton writes on 'The British Critic and the Oxford Movement' (*SB*). The founding of *The Cornhill Magazine* is discussed by Peter Smith, and Cyprian Blagden traces the history of Longmans' Magazine from 1881 to 1905, both articles in *REL*.

There is news of *The Dublin Review*, *Atlantis*, *The Rambler*, and other Catholic journals in Hugh Mac-Dougall's book on Lord Acton,[10] which, though slim, touches on many aspects of the Catholic Revival. Its main concern, however, is with the reasons for Acton's 'loss of sympathy for virtually all his Catholic contemporaries', including Newman. His moral view of history led him to condemn the Ultramontanes unreservedly, and his ardent espousal of liberal ideas completed his estrangement.

Sir Gavin de Beer has written a study of Darwin[11] that is at once scholarly and entertaining, and which provides a comprehensive account of the climate of scientific opinion from before the voyage of H.M.S. *Beagle* in 1831 until Darwin's last published work in 1881. Darwin's career is traced in lively detail; the controversies surrounding the publication of *The Origin of Species* are particularly well chronicled. One of Darwin's correspondents was Asa Gray, the American botanist who championed Darwin against Agassiz. *Darwiniana*, Gray's collected papers, have been edited by A. H. Dupree.[12] The title of his most considerable essay, 'Natural Selection not Incompatible with Natural Theology', suggests Gray's point of view, and he urged Darwin to put more stress on design. As de Beer records, Darwin replied that to do so would entail the suggestion that different sorts of pigeons have been developed specifically for the gratification of pigeon-fanciers. Gray took little part in the subsequent debates, and his papers were already out of date when they were first collected in 1876. An account of the origin and progress of the Anthropological Society, 1863 to 1871, is given by J. W. Burrow in 'Evolution and Anthropology in the 1860's' (*VS*).

Eric Newton's study of Romanticism in painting[13] seeks to realign the boundaries between 'classical', 'romantic', and 'realist' (or 'extrovert') art by suggesting a central position in which all three are present. His purpose is 'to examine and define the different kinds of Romanticism' by assessing their position relative to this centre of indifference. In effect, however, the categories of Romanticism that he uses—mystery, the abnormal, conflict—are familiar enough. He has some interesting things to say about Turner, Constable, Courbet, and about the P. R. B., who 'knew exactly what they wished to avoid, but never succeeded in stating logically what they wished to achieve'. For them the Imagination was 'the grand highway to truth' —a statement that Newton does not amplify. 'Literary Romanticism' he sees as being 'specially concerned with sinister or exotic aspects of sex'; Keats is a 'nostalgic' poet, pursuing a dream. There is a quaint odour of the 'nineties lingering in the ideas in this rather slight study.

'More exciting things happened in

[10] *The Acton-Newman Relations*, by Hugh MacDougall, O.M.I. Fordham U.P. pp. xi+109. $5.

[11] *Charles Darwin*, by Gavin de Beer. Nelson. pp. xi+290. 21*s*.

[12] *Darwiniana*, by Asa Gray, ed. by A. Hunter Dupree. Harvard U.P. pp. xxiii+327. $5.

[13] *The Romantic Rebellion*, by Eric Newton. Longmans. pp. 224. 30*s*.

book design between 1837 and 1890 than in any other comparable period in the history of the world's printing: and most of them happened in London.' With this challenging remark Ruari McLean opens his study of Victorian book-production,[14] and proceeds to make it good. The substitution of machine processes for the old craftsmanship not only produced more printed books, it radically altered their appearance. Cloth-binding, tooled on the spine, came in in the 1830's and rapidly became general. Baxter prints appeared in 1836, and although Baxter himself abandoned book-illustration, Charles Knight was soon producing colour-illustrated books for the popular market. The Chiswick Press, the work of Owen Jones and Noel Humphreys, Chromolithography, the association of Joseph Cundall and Birkett Foster, the development of wood-block colour-printing, and numerous other factors lend authority to McLean's opening statement. The book is charmingly and nostalgically illustrated; but the colours seem somewhat subdued when compared with their resplendent originals.

(B) POETRY AND DRAMA

No edition of *Lyrical Ballads*, giving all the poems in both volumes, has appeared since that of G. Sampson in 1903, and a new edition[15] presenting the text as it appeared in 1798 and 1800, together with the variant readings of 1802 and 1805, is most welcome. Much has happened in

Wordsworth and Coleridge studies since 1903, and the relevant material is admirably summarized by the editors in their Introduction and Notes. Some contemporary reactions to the first appearance of the poems are usefully given in an appendix. A notable feature of the edition is the scholarly correlation of the different versions of the Preface. All who teach English literature of the period will have felt the need of a volume such as this, which will retain its authority for a long time to come. Donald Davie has made a selection of Wordsworth's poems to be used in schools,[16] adding a useful Introduction and Notes.

Two articles draw attention to the eighteenth-century antecedents of *Lyrical Ballads*. A. M. Kinghorn, in 'Literary Aesthetics and the Sympathetic Emotions—A Main Trend in Eighteenth-Century Scottish Criticism' (*Studies in Scottish Literature*), follows the movement towards simplicity in verse, and W. Powell Jones, in 'John Aikin on the Use of Natural History in Poetry' (*Journal of Aesthetics and Art Criticism*), sees the developing interest in natural history as a factor leading to Wordsworth's landscapes and Coleridge's Albatross.

'Because he was preoccupied with what the mind does with the materials offered by the senses, Wordsworth shows a predilection not only for the word "image" but for the word "form", and, to a less extent, the word "shape";' Colin Clarke's study of the poet,[17] from which this statement is taken, shows by an examination of passages from *Tintern Abbey*, *The Prelude*, and the '*Immortality*' *Ode*, that Wordsworth habitually uses

[14] *Victorian Book Design and Colour Printing*, by Ruari McLean. Faber & Faber. pp. xvi+182. 45s.

[15] *Lyrical Ballads: The Text of the 1798 Edition with the Additional 1800 Poems and the Prefaces*, by Wordsworth and Coleridge, ed. with introduction, notes and appendices by R. L. Brett and A. R. Jones. Methuen. pp. 1+339. 42s.

[16] *Selected Poems by William Wordsworth*, ed. by Donald Davie. Harrap. pp. 160. 6s. 6d.

[17] *Romantic Paradox: An Essay on the Poetry of Wordsworth*, by Colin Clarke. Routledge & Kegan Paul. pp. 101. 14s.

these words equivocally. This illustrates the fact that his 'conviction that the natural world is solid and substantially "other" than the mind that contemplates it, had to come to terms with his conviction that what we perceive is inevitably mind-dependent'. Thus Wordsworth's 'language in *The Prelude* and elsewhere embodies a more subtle play of the mind than is usually conceded'.

A number of addresses given during the Wordsworth Centenary activities in 1950 at Cornell and Princeton have been collected by Gilbert T. Dunklin.[18] Douglas Bush presents a 'Minority Report' on the theme that 'much of the poetry we have cherished was the outpouring of a too simple harmony of soul'. Frederick A. Pottle, arguing from *I wandered lonely as a cloud* on 'The Eye and the Object in the Poetry of Wordsworth', deals with the theme treated more fully by Clarke in the book just noticed. Earl Leslie Griggs looks once more at 'Wordsworth through Coleridge's Eyes', and John Crowe Ransom supplies some general 'Notes Towards an Understanding of Poetry' derived mainly from Wordsworth's remarks on poetic diction. Other essays are by B. Ifor Evans on 'The European Problem', by Lionel Trilling on 'Wordsworth and the Iron Time', which finds a 'Judaic quality' in him, and finally by Willard L. Sperry on 'Wordsworth's Religion'—a theme that, indeed, underlies most of the essays in the collection.

Lionel Stevenson, in 'The Unfinished Gothic Cathedral: A Study of the Organic Unity of Wordsworth's Poetry' (*UTQ*), notes that 'while Southey and Scott were turning out narratives of derring-do in the tradi-tional moulds, Wordsworth grappled with the problem of drawing an exact and complete map of his own mind'. The main attempt at this, *The Recluse*, although successful with more serious matters, was in a form 'gravely deficient for communicating other types of feeling', which were supplied by the shorter poems.

G. H. Hartman, in an interesting article on 'Wordsworth, *The Borderers*, and "Intellectual Murder"' (*JEGP*), points out that 'full consciousness of self, according to *The Borderers*, is born of betrayal', and is 'linked with the unwitting commission of a crime against nature'. The question thus posed by 'Wordsworth's problem play' is: can consciousness therefore yield true moral judgements? Albert Gérard writes on 'Symbolic Landscape in Wordsworth's *Tintern Abbey*' (*Publications de l'Université de l'Etat à Elisabethville*). Hans Combecher contributes 'William Wordsworth: *The Solitary Reaper*: Eine Deutung' (*NS*).

Herbert Lindenberger's book on *The Prelude*[19] is 'a series of related essays, each designed to approach the poem from a single direction'. The first three chapters deal with the language and style of the poem, noting its observance of older ideas of decorum, and examining what Lindenberger calls the 'landscape of re-enactment' by which Wordsworth was able 'not merely to portray the interworkings of discernible objects, but to create a lively interplay of what we would normally call abstract concepts'. A chapter on 'The Possibility of a Long Poem' considers *The Prelude* in the wider context of nineteenth- and twentieth-century criticism. Discussion of the subject-matter of the poem is divided into

[18] *Wordsworth Centenary Studies Presented at Cornell and Princeton Universities*, ed. by Gilbert T. Dunklin. Hamden, Conn.: Shoe String P. pp. xii + 169. $4.75.

[19] *On Wordsworth's Prelude*, by Herbert Lindenberger. Princeton U.P. pp. xix + 316. $7.50.

three parts: 'time-consciousness, 'visionary aloofness', and 'the non-visionary books'. J. F. Danby's *William Wordsworth: The Prelude and Other Poems*[20] is a brief introduction to the poet. Giving 'A Reading of *The Prelude* Book V' (*MLQ*), W. G. Stobie argues that Wordsworth does not depart in the Book from his stated theme 'that the world of books is a force second only to that of Nature in forming and developing the human mind'. But he does insist that books must be approached as one approaches Nature, and should not be presented in a system of controlled reading.

Lionel Trilling writes on 'Wordsworth's *Ode: Intimations of Immortality*' (*Explication as Criticism*), and Karl Kroeber gives 'A New Reading of *The World Is Too Much With Us*' (*SIR*).

'Socrates' pose of simplicity is a device by which the artist reminds us of one danger of abstract thinking. Wordsworth, too, uses simplicity as a device for reminding us of this same danger,' says Gayle S. Smith in 'Wordsworth's Socratic Irony' (*Personalist*). Writing on 'Wordsworth's "Thought" and his "Verse"' (*CE*), T. H. Jackson argues that 'he too often attempted to fuse and suffuse a mechanical poetic with an emotional incandescence which it could not bear'. His point is similar to that of B. R. Godfrey, mentioned above.

R. S. Woof supplies some information about 'Wordsworth's Poetry and Stuart's Newspapers: 1797–1803' (*SB*); W. P. Albrecht looks at 'Hazlitt on Wordsworth: The Poetry of Paradox' (*Six Studies*); and Oswald Doughty reviews 'The Reception of Wordsworth by his Contemporaries' (*EM*).

A. C. Partridge contributes 'Unpublished Wordsworthiana: The Continental Tour of 1820, described in Mary Wordsworth's Journal' (*ESA*). J. R. Watson makes a correction to his 'Wordsworth and Constable' (*RES*. See *YW* xliii. 226). In *The Emerson Society Quarterly* occur two notes on Wordsworth: 'Wordsworth and Bishop Donne', by K. W. Cameron; and 'Wordsworth and the Americans: Two new Letters and Visits, 1844', by Mark L. Reed.

Although it has not been overlooked, the influence on the English Romantics of Wieland's *Oberon* has never been stressed and remained undefined. Werner W. Beyer, who has been interested in the subject for many years, has brought his findings together in a book[21] to prove this influence to have been pervasive. His main concern is with Coleridge, who was engaged in a translation of *Oberon* in 1797. Beyer acknowledges the general debt to Livingston Lowes as a pioneer in tracing influences on Coleridge, but claims that there are certain omissions in *The Road to Xanadu* that can be supplied only by paying due attention to *Oberon*. For example, Lowes saw the origin of *The Ancient Mariner* as 'a queer jumble of fortuitous suggestions', and paid little heed to the shaping spirit that made them a poem. Beyer is able to show that, not only in general structure but also very largely in machinery and incident, there is a parallel with *Oberon* which suggests conscious imitation. Similar parallels are to be found with *Kubla Khan* and *Christabel*. In a series of appendixes Beyer finds traces of *Oberon* in Wordsworth, Southey, Byron, and Peacock's *Rhododaphne*. Curiously,

---

[20] *William Wordsworth: The Prelude and Other Poems*, by J. F. Danby. Edward Arnold. pp. 61. 10*s*. 6*d*.

[21] *The Enchanted Forest*, by Werner W. Beyer. Oxford: Basil Blackwell. pp. xiv+275. 35*s*.

Shelley and Keats (though both are mentioned) were apparently immune to the contagion. (Reviewed as 'Herr Kubla?', *TLS*, 5 December.)

Another approach to the question of conscious artistry in Coleridge's poetry is Max F. Schulz's study of its variations in tone.[22] Schulz finds eight 'voices' there, voices in which Coleridge purposefully sought to 'transform his experience into communicable form' without at the same time 'reducing the experience to a sequence of laboured comments'. The first two voices, those of 'Farrago' and 'Prophecy', belong to the early period, although the latter is still to be heard in the *Hymn Before Sun-rise* in 1802. The third voice is that of *The Ancient Mariner* and *Christabel*, in which Coleridge used the ballad form 'as a species of ventriloquism', as he said, to affect simplicity. Only in *The Ancient Mariner*, however, was he able to achieve the 'unique fusion of balladic and lyric impulses' required for success; the 'Ventriloquism' voice was uncongenial to him, in fact, and hence his many false starts in it. Not so the 'Conversation' voice. Here his 'response to a short-lived domestic happiness and his philosophical belief in the oneness of life helped him to transform the topographical poem . . . into a record of friendly discourse or silent musing'. Schulz examines the relevant poems, notably *Frost at Midnight*, to show, not only how Coleridge improved on Cowper's 'divine chit-chat', but also how 'the oscillation of thought coincides perfectly with the curve of emotion to form a controlled and unified pattern of alternating meditation and description'. Each poem has an 'artful order' of controlled imagery 'organic to this

centrality of belief'. But the art is concealed beneath 'a relaxed, conversational blank verse and a random association of ideas'. Although most of the poems in the 'Dream' voice, in which Coleridge consciously imitated the unconscious technique of dreams, belong to the period after 1802—beginning with *A Day Dream* ('My eyes make pictures . . .'), *Kubla Khan* is a notable exception. However, it 'differs in degree from the later poems of the same type' because 'in it dream and reality remain essentially separate'. The 'I' of the poem contemplates and speculates about the vision. Of the later voices, the 'Confession' one 'forms a melancholy antiphonal to the happiness of the conversation poems and the serenity of the dream poems', and the 'Improvisation' voice is the mode of those later experiments which, though interesting, do not enlist our sympathy. The great merit of this important book is its flexibility, by which the author avoids too rigid an adherence to his categories, and points out that the various voices may be heard in concert in many poems. The broad scheme, however, follows a chronological development.

The following notes appeared in *NQ*: 'Coleridge's Light-Sound Theory' by D. B. Schneider, with an answering comment by J. B. Beer in 'Coleridge and Boehme's *Aurora*'; 'An Unpublished Poem by Coleridge', in which W. Braekman prints some *Lines* addressed to J. May; 'Unpublished Coleridge Marginalia in a Volume of John Donne's Poetry', by Kay Davis; 'Coleridge's "Debt" to Dryden and Johnson', by Max F. Schulz; and 'Coleridge: Brother Edward's Wife', by Lucyle Werkmeister.

In 'The Influence of Wordsworth on Coleridge (1795–1800)' (*UTQ*), A. M. Buchan suggests that 'the familiar notion that the presence of

---

[22] *The Poetic Voices of Coleridge: A Study of his Desire for Spontaneity and Passion for Order*, by Max F. Schulz. Wayne State U.P. pp. 233. $7.50.

Wordsworth stimulated Coleridge to write poetry may have to be laid aside'. Oswald Doughty gives an account of Coleridge's relations with Bowles in 'Coleridge and a Poet's Poet' (*EM*). R. S. Woof writes on 'Coleridge and Thomasina Dennis' (*UTQ*), publishing some correspondence of the governess to Josiah Wedgwood's two children, who met Coleridge frequently in 1798 and 1799. She makes some perceptive comment on him, and also provides evidence of the reaction of one well-versed in contemporary literature to *Lyrical Ballads*.

Ward Pafford maintains that 'Coleridge's Wedding-Guest' (*SP*) is of great importance to the poem as the counterpart of the Mariner himself. G. S. Smith, making 'A Reappraisal of the Moral Stanzas in *The Rime of the Ancient Mariner*' (*SIR*), argues that these stanzas give a perspective to the vision as experienced by both the Wedding-Guest and the Mariner. In 'Keys to "Kubla Khan"' (*ES*) Richard Gerber suggests some sources and echoes in the poem—'Cybele', for example, may unconsciously have suggested 'Kubla'. G. M. Ridenour examines nine poems in 'Source and Allusion in Some Poems of Coleridge' (*SP*), and suggests possible correspondences with Boehme and others. D. B. Schneider writes on 'The Structure of "Kubla Khan"' (*ANQ*). Charles S. Bouslog argues, in 'Structure and Theme in Coleridge's *Dejection: An Ode*' (*MLQ*), that in spite of its intractable subject-matter and lack of structure the poem 'almost succeeds'. Lucyle Werkmeister discusses 'Some Whys and Wherefores of Coleridge's *Lines Composed in a Concert Room*' (*MP*).

In '*Coleridge Unlabyrinthed*' (*UTQ*) George Whalley reviews the editorial work already accomplished on Coleridge's writings, and that still to be done. He believes that, when it is complete, we shall be faced with 'the possibility that Romantic art (when not degenerate) is a genuine counterpart to Classic art rather than a more or less deplorable falling from grace'.

Paul Kaufman draws attention to 'Chatterton's Brother-Poet, William Roberts' (*PBSA*). Roberts died in 1806, aged nineteen. His *Poems and Letters* were published by Southey in 1811.

Paul West has published a collection of critical essays on Byron[23] that includes Wilson Knight's essay on 'The Two Eternities', from *The Burning Oracle*, 'Guilt and Retribution in Byron's Sea Poems' by Bernard Blackstone, and 'The Metamorphosis of Satan' from *The Romantic Agony* by Mario Praz. Paul West himself contributes an essay on 'The Plays', from *Byron and the Spoiler's Art*. Byron's satires are the subject of the remaining essays, with Guy Steffan on 'The Devil a Bit of Our *Beppo*!', an account of the writing of the poem, with an examination of the manuscript and revisions, and the passage on 'Byron's Satire' from *Revaluation* by F. R. Leavis. 'Byron the Improver' is abridged from W. W. Robson's Chatterton Lecture, and '*Don Juan*: A Thousand Colours' is taken from Guy Steffan's introductory volume to the Variorum Edition of the poem. Helen Gardner, in an essay on *Don Juan*, sees the general import of the poem to be that, although most men are fools, not all are knaves. Consequently the satiric edge is often blunted by concessions to the victims. George M. Ridenour quotes 'Carelessly I Sing' from the eighth Canto as the title of an essay on the versification of the poem. Three studies of Byron's character, by Gil-

[23] *Byron: A Collection of Critical Essays*, ed. by Paul West. Englewood Cliffs, N.J.: Prentice-Hall. pp. vii + 175. $1.95.

bert Highet, Bertrand Russell, and John Wain conclude this useful collection.

M. H. Butler makes 'An Examination of Byron's Revision of *Manfred*, Act III' (*SP*), finding there 'a key to interpreting the drama as an eclectic, theological and philosophical treatment of man's eternal struggle'. Frederick L. Beaty describes 'Byron's Concept of Ideal Love' (*KSJ*) as a 'physical and spiritual union requiring innocence, youth, self-sacrifice, intense passion, and independence'. W. C. Childers finds a pun on the name of Pye, the Poet Laureate, in 'The Dedication of *Don Juan*' (*KSJ*). Robert Mortenson suggests 'Another Continuation of *Don Juan*' (*SIR*); and C. N. Stavrou writes on 'Religion in Byron's *Don Juan*' (*SEL*).

K. T. Borrow and Dorothy Hewlett find 'A Link with Australia' (*KSMB*) in the memoirs of Marshall MacDermott, printed in Adelaide in 1871. MacDermott was stationed in Cephalonia while Byron was there in 1823. He gives a version of Kennedy's attempt at Byron's conversion. When he returned to England on leave, Byron entrusted him with the manuscript of the last three Cantos of *Don Juan* to give to Hobhouse. In 'Byron's Cousin Trevanion' (*ES*) David Bonnell Green gives further details in support of Sir Gavin de Beer's note on him (see *YW* xliii. 232).

Ernest J. Lovell, whose own compilation of Byronic records in *His Very Self and Voice* has put us in his debt, has written a biography of another recorder of Byron's conversation, Thomas Medwin,[24] who also wrote a life of Shelley, his cousin. After the deaths of the two poets, Medwin was furiously attacked by

the families and friends of each. Hobhouse, who had assisted at the burning of Byron's own *Memoirs*, sought to discredit Medwin's *Conversations of Lord Byron*, and Mary Shelley, convinced (without reading the book) that his *Life* would sully Shelley's name, tried to restrain Medwin from publishing it. Medwin, whose tastes invariably exceeded his income, pointed out that such a course would involve him in considerable loss, and he asked the now comfortably-circumstanced Mary for an indemnity. Mary then put it about that Medwin had tried to extort money from her, and this view of him has been perpetuated. Lovell presents him, if not as a man of spotless virtue, at least as one of honest merit much abused. The truth seems to lie between the two, for whereas Medwin certainly gave no cause for offence either to Shelley's memory or to Mary in his *Life of Shelley*, his private conduct was sufficiently unconventional to sustain the reader's interest in his biography.

Richard Levin writes on 'Shelley's *Indian Serenade*: A Re-Revaluation' (*CE*). 'The mystery of *Julian and Maddalo* centres on the identity of the Maniac,' says G. M. Matthews in '*Julian and Maddalo*: The Draft and the Meaning' (*SN*). Examination of the drafts of the poem suggests that he is 'a *sermo pedestris* kind of Prometheus, written down to the domestic level'. He typifies the situation of those poets who 'become such by virtue of their special vulnerability to suffering'. D. J. Hughes, in 'Potentiality in *Prometheus Unbound*' (*SIR*), argues that the poem is more philosophical than political in its implications. Joseph Raben considers the question 'Why the Indian Caucasus?' in *KSJ*. His answer is that Shelley had been told that the Hindu Kush was the heart of all mountain

---

[24] *Captain Medwin: Friend of Byron and Shelley*, by Ernest J. Lovell. Macdonald. pp. ix + 348. 40s.

s

systems, and that the Golden Age had been a reality there, with possibly the subsequent 'enslavement and emancipation that foreshadowed universal freedom'. Raben also writes on 'Milton's Influence on Shelley's Translation of Dante's *Matilda Gathering Flowers*' (*RES*); and Jean de Palacio discusses his method of translation in 'Shelley, Traducteur de Dante: Le Chant xxviii du *Purgatoire*' (*RLC*). Donald H. Reiman, in 'Shelley's *The Triumph of Life*: The Biographical Problem' (*PMLA*), contests the view of G. M. Matthews (*YW* xlii. 230 and xliii. 234) that the poem's sombre tone should be attributed to the influence of Jane Williams. In *KSJ* he reviews 'Shelley in the Encyclopaedias'.

Louise Schutz Boas gives details of *Shelley and Mary* in *TLS* (14 November). A description of a copy of the book is given in the same journal (12 December) by Anne Lee Michell, a granddaughter of Richard Garnett. Herbert Huscher prints 'A New Viviani Letter' (*KSMB*). J. T. Brown discusses 'Some Shelley Forgeries by "Major Byron"' (*KSMB*).

It has been an outstanding year for Keats studies, with two remarkable critical biographies and many other works. Aileen Ward's biography[25] is intended in some measure to represent a milestone, marking a stage in the development of our knowledge of the poet. It is far more than this, however. As the author says, 'A new biography of Keats should attempt more than to present new information or synthesize recent criticism: it should try to convey a new sense of the meaning of his life.' Accordingly, she presents, often with rare insight, 'the inner drama of his creative life'. Her criticism of the poems generally aims to reveal his developing understanding of the nature of poetry. Thus *Endymion* is a key work, and the poem is examined very fully, first as a myth through which Keats 'attempted to state, however gropingly, his belief in the necessity of growth, . . . the impossibility of regression into innocence', then as an experience personal to the poet which demonstrated this, bringing the realization that 'that which is creative must create itself'. In the criticism of the later poems the biographical aspect is even more evident, so that in a way the personality of the poet is presented in the setting of the poetry. It is a book of wide and meticulous scholarship, and the great story it has to tell is powerfully and movingly told. W. Jackson Bate's very different book[26] is an exhaustive work—so exhaustive indeed that it would be misleading to suggest a theme for it. Yet if one aspect of Keats's life and thought receives more emphasis than another, it is Keats's intense awareness of the greatness of the past, and its contrast with his own day. In this *Endymion* again is the key work, for the writing of the poem set Keats thinking along these lines. 'It was only during the winter of 1817, as he was finishing *Endymion*,' says Bate 'that he may have begun to feel consciously that this poetry of the past, to which he was attaching so much of his idealism, might be different—in a more fundamental way than he had suspected—not only from what he was writing himself at the moment . . . but from what his contemporaries, even Wordsworth, were doing.' In a chapter called 'The Emergence of a Modern Poet' Bate pays close attention to the contrast in Keats's mind, which the writing of *Endymion* had suggested, between Milton and Wordsworth.

[25] *John Keats: The Making of a Poet*, by Aileen Ward. Secker & Warburg. pp. xii+450. 50s.

[26] *John Keats*, by Walter Jackson Bate. Harvard U.P. pp. xvii+732. $10.

Milton, he reflected, 'did not think into the human heart as Wordsworth does'. The first-fruits of these reflections, recorded in the 'Chamber of Maiden Thought' letter to Taylor, was *The Ode To Psyche*, which was to 'create something of a prototype for the greater lyric of the past century and a half'. Thus, the emphasis in this book is on Keats's position as a major poet, instituting a new era in poetry. However, more general biographical aspects are not neglected, for, as Bate says, although material for the early years is rather meagre, there are times later on 'when we can follow him week by week'. A third book, by Joanna Richardson,[27] is sub-titled 'A Study of Keats and his Friends', but in fact Keats is present only in spirit. The book concerns the later lives of Brown, Severn, and Dilke, and their posterity.

David B. Barron writes on '*Endymion*: The Quest for Beauty' (*American Imago*), and in 'A First Edition of *Endymion*' L. A. Marchand describes a copy (*Rutgers University Library Journal*). In 'Keats and the Metaphor of Fame' (*ES*) J. L. Mahoney discusses Keats's attitude to fame as expressed in his letters and the sonnets. Jack Stillinger argues that the additional lines and stanza in the Woodhouse manuscript of the poem should be restored to 'The Text of *The Eve of St Agnes*' (*SB*). Martin Halpern, in 'Keats's Grecian Urn and the Singular "Ye"' (*CE*), maintains that the Urn is being addressed in the last two lines of the poem. Dwight E. Robinson considers the possible influence on Keats of Wedgwood ware in 'Ode on a "New Etrurian" Urn' (*KSJ*). G. W. Whiting suggests that Keats may have been influenced by Charlotte Smith's *Farewell to a Night-*

ingale (*KSJ*). In 'The Idea of Progress in Keats's *Hyperion*' (*Philologica Pragensia*) Karel Stěpaník gives a Marxist interpretation of the two *Hyperions*.

In 'Keats and the Countryside' (*KSMB*) Katharine M. R. Kenyon shows 'how rooted in the very being of Keats was the reality of country life and Nature'. A. W. Jarvis draws attention to the Rev. Midgley John Jennings in 'A Cousin of John Keats' (*KSMB*). L. H. Kendall, Jr., prints a new letter about Keats from John Murray to J. W. Croker (*KSJ*).

In Edmund Blunden's 'Barry Cornwall and Keats' (*KSMB*), Keats plays much the smaller part.

Thomas Hood is the subject of a short study by Laurence Brander[28] which is chiefly biographical, but has some comment on the background to the best-known poems. It is chiefly interesting for its account of Hood's journalistic career. A full biography of Hood by J. C. Reid has not been available for comment. The 'Corrections in some Letters of Thomas Hood' are supplied by P. F. Morgan (*NQ*).

Eric Robinson and Geoffrey Summerfield write on 'John Taylor's Editing of Clare's *The Shepherd's Calendar*' (*RES*).

Writing on 'Theme and Imagery in the Poetry of T. L. Beddoes' (*SN*), C. A. Hoyt says that *The Improvisatore* contains his themes 'already set out in something like their permanent order'. They are 'contending fathers and sons, sweet passive women, and the grinning Death's-Head that waits to claim both victor and vanquished'. By the time he wrote *Death's Jest Book* 'Beddoes was able to sympathize with the father, and to see the conflict from both sides'. In the same journal

---

[27] *The Everlasting Spell: A Study of Keats and His Friends*, by Joanna Richardson. Cape. pp. 256. 35s.

[28] *Thomas Hood*, by Laurence Brander. Writers and their Work, No. 159. Longmans. pp. 44. 2s. 6d.

D. W. Donne prints 'Eight German letters from T. L. Beddoes to Leonard Tobler'.

In *NQ* T. B. Braumbaugh prints 'A Landor Letter', and Anne Lohrili dates 'The First Publication of Landor's *Diana de Poictiers*' as June 1858, in *Household Words*.

A study of 'The Conserving Myth of William Barnes', by R. A. Forsyth (*VS*), deals not only with Barnes's poetry, with its objective but meaningful presentation of rural life, but also with his social and economic teaching, expressed in *Views of Labour and God* (1859), which 'constituted a rejection of the concept of "economic man"'. His poetry embodied this view.

Nicholas Barker suggests that 'A Very Famous Line' in Burgon's *Petra* was borrowed from Samuel Rogers (*TLS*, 26 June).

Morton Luce's *Handbook* to Tennyson was last revised in 1914, and is restricted to the poems printed in the Macmillan one-volume edition. George O. Marshall has now produced a new book,[29] in which widely scattered information has been assembled and presented 'systematically, poem by poem, as each appeared in a volume in the poet's lifetime'. This scheme presents difficulties of many kinds, not least being the problem of Tennyson's revisions. But these difficulties have not proved insuperable, and the resulting volume gives all the necessary bibliographical details, supplemented by biographical material. Contemporary criticisms of the poems have been noted where these were outstanding or significant. Hallam Tennyson's *Memoir* and the Eversley edition have inevitably been the main sources of information, but the Notes contain reference to very many other sources, past and present.

[29] *A Tennyson Handbook*, by George O. Marshall, Jr. N.Y.: Twayne. pp. 291. $6.00.

Patricia M. Ball contributes a short article on 'Tennyson and the Romantics' (*VP*).

B. N. Pipes, Jr., considers Tennyson's use of lightning in 'A Slight Meteorological Disturbance: The Last Two Stanzas of Tennyson's *The Poet*' (*VP*). R. B. Hovey offers 'Tennyson's *Locksley Hall*: A Re-interpretation' (*Forum*, Houston), and W. D. Templeman reviews the poem's reputation in 'A Consideration of the Fame of *Locksley Hall*' (*VP*). George O. Marshall examines 'Tennyson's *Ulysses* 33–43' (*Ex*), and John Pettigrew analyses what he calls 'one of the few Victorian poems to excite almost universal admiration' in 'Tennyson's *Ulysses*: A Reconciliation of Opposites' (*VP*). T. J. Assad looks at 'Tennyson's *Break, Break, Break*' (*TSE*), and E. P. Vandiver examines 'Tennyson's *Tears, Idle Tears*' (*Ex*).

'From being hailed as a noble poem of faith despite its admixture of doubt, *In Memoriam* came to be defended as a moving poem of doubt despite its unconvincing faith,' says Carlisle Moore in 'Faith, Doubt and Mystical Experience in *In Memoriam*' (*VS*). He argues that both faith and doubt are integral to the poem, which follows the pattern of religious conversion. Doubt remains, but the 'trance-like experience of Section XCV . . . provides a nexus between the disparate elements of doubt and faith. . . . Beginning with doubt and fear, Tennyson ends with doubt and hope.' James G. Taaffe examines 'Circle Imagery in *In Memoriam*', and L. Metzger claims that Tennyson continues Goethe's 'humanistic optimism' in 'Some Parallels between Goethe's *Faust* and Tennyson's *In Memoriam*' (both *VP*). Christopher Ricks writes on 'The Variants of *In Memoriam*' (*Lib*).

'The resolutions of conflict in *Maud* and *In Memoriam* have always seemed weaker than the conflict from which they come,' says William Cadbury in 'The Utility of the Poetic Mask in Tennyson's *Supposed Confessions*' (*MLQ*). He points out that this poem 'ends in despair for the confessor, but by virtue of the mask, that despair is not the reader's'. In 'Tennyson's *Oh*! *That* '*Twere Possible:* A Link between *In Memoriam* and *Maud*' (*PMLA*) George O. Marshall examines the variations between the version of the poem sent to Milnes in 1837 and that in *Maud* in 1855, together with the early draft as it occurs in J. M. Heath's Commonplace Book, where it is dated 1833. He concludes that the poem was part of 'Tennyson's immediate poetic response to Hallam's death'. The points made in these two articles are paralleled in a book on *Maud* by Ralph William Rader,[30] who puts, however, a different interpretation on them. '*Maud*, which meant so much to the poet who read it so passionately and which contains poetry as lovely and technically perfect as any he wrote, has generally been judged to be an imperfect work of art,' says Rader. Considering why this should be, he begins with the supposition that both *Maud* and *Locksley Hall*, despite the poet's vehement assertion to the contrary, are 'in part the poetic expression of some of the facts of Tennyson's early life'. The central situation of both poems recurs with unusual frequency in his poetry, and Rader concludes that it is connected with Tennyson's regard for Rosa Baring, to whom he turned when 'spiritually adrift' after Hallam's death, and who married another in 1838. Also reflected are his affection for Sophy Rawnsley, and for Emily

[30] *Tennyson's Maud: The Biographical Genesis*, by Ralph William Rader. California U.P. and O.U.P. pp. x+155. 36s. $5.50.

Sellwood, who refused him in 1848, although relenting a year later. But, says Rader, 'it is not the fact that the poem was drawn from Tennyson's own experience which caused the trouble [with *Maud*], but the fact that, because he was not emotionally free from that experience, he saw it in inadequate perspective.' J. Philip Goldberg finds in *The Princess* and *Maud* respectively 'Two Tennysonian Allusions to a Poem by Andrew Marvell' (*NQ*)—that is, to *The Nymph Complaining*.

In 'The Moral Paradox of the Hero in *Idylls of the King*' (*ELH*) Clyde de L. Ryals argues that 'Launcelot's and Guenevere's sin is . . . not the cause but the symptom of what is wrong in Camelot'. The impossible vows that Arthur has imposed have created 'the condition which causes guilt and madness throughout his order', because they have diminished individual responsibility. This view is challenged by Stanley J. Solomon in 'Tennyson's Paradoxical King' (*VP*). He contends that Ryals 'ignores the poet's . . . firm belief in social order and the importance of the Head of State in upholding the framework'. Boyd Litzinger examines 'The Structure of Tennyson's *The Last Tournament*' (*VP*). Tennyson's treatment of Becket is compared with Eliot's by Louise R. Rehak in 'On the Use of Martyrs' (*UTQ*).

In *NQ* P. L. Elliott compares '*The Charge of the Light Brigade*' with Russell's reports of the battle to *The Times*, and Christopher Ricks comments in a letter. E. W. Hunter writes on 'Tennyson and Juvenal'. R. W. Rader contributes some information about 'Tennyson's "Strange" Father' from the comments of a Lincolnshire neighbour. More news of the Tennyson family comes from Sir Charles Tennyson, whose 'The Somersby Tennysons' is issued as a supplement to *VS*. An account of the poet's six brothers and four sisters, much of it is drawn from Sir Charles's own recollections; it presents fascinating glimpses of this extraordinary family. The 'black blood', active in the eccentricities of Frederick and the neurosis of Charles, reappeared in the younger brothers. It is represented here, for example, by some gloomy verses by Edward. The sisters, though 'other-worldly', escaped the gloom, although Hallam's death dealt Emily 'a blow which time could never efface'. This essay is the first publication of The Tennyson Society, whose formation is announced in *TLS* (14 June). Included in the supplement is a catalogue of the Frederick Tennyson Collection at Indiana University, compiled by Rowland L. Collins, who also lists the Tennyson items at Princeton in 'Tennyson's Original Issue of Poems, Reviews, etc., 1842–1886' (*Princeton Library Chronicle*).

Since Jones called him an 'agnostic' in 1891, Browning has been accused repeatedly of anti-intellectualism. A readjustment of this view is proposed by Norton B. Crowell in a book[31] seeking to present Browning's central theme in a new light. Browning certainly insisted on the limitations of the intellect, but it is misleading to suggest that he did so in order to exalt the claims of the emotions as a guide, or in any way to separate them from the mind. On the contrary, the interdependence of the 'Three souls that make up one soul' to which St. John refers in *A Death in the Desert*, that is, the body, mind, and spirit, is the true lesson to be drawn from Browning's poetry. The 'involved ratiocinations of Blougram, Prince Hohenstiel-Schwangau, Sludge and Don Juan' may lead us to 'doubt the ability of the

[31] *The Triple Soul: Browning's Theory of Knowledge*, by Norton B. Crowell. New Mexico U.P. pp. xiv+235. $5.50.

mind to make a valid moral choice', but this is because there this triple control is not exercised. Isolated, as in these cases, the mind cannot make a true judgement. Thus 'Browning's poetry, from *Pippa Passes* to *Asolando*, gives a coherent and steady vision of the need for order and wholeness in a man's life.' This thoughtful book presents some interesting comment on all the major poems. William Whitla's *The Central Truth: The Incarnation in Browning's Poetry*, published by Toronto U.P., has not been available.

'The Browning worth bothering about is not the man who wrote hectoring uplift and a jungle of turgid argument. Under the rubbish there is a tough but honest doubter struggling to get out,' says David Page in 'And So Is Browning' (*EC*). Many attempts have been made to rescue different Brownings from the rubbish, of course; but one feels that the distorted bundle of anxiety and 'sexhate' whom Page resurrects would have been better left where he was.

J. C. Maxwell contributes a short note on 'Browning's Concept of the Poet: A Revision of *Pauline*' (*VP*). Notes on '*Soliloquy of the Spanish Cloister*', by Lucy Fryxell and Virginia Adair, and by Roger L. Slakey occur in *Ex*. Patrick W. Gainer adds one in *VP*, suggesting that 'Hy, Zy, Hine' is a mocking of the Angelus bell, and T. C. Kishler also has a note on the poem in *VP*. In 'A Further reading of *Count Gismond*' (*SP*) Sister Marcella Holloway, agreeing with Tilton and Tuttle (*YW* xliii. 237), argues that 'Gismond was no gentle knight, but a true brother to the Duke of Ferrara'. George Monteiro, in 'Browning's *My Last Duchess*' (*VP*), suggests that the Duke told the story in order to exhibit himself as Neptune taming a seahorse. John W. Willoughby argues that 'Browning's

Childe Roland to the Dark Tower Came' (*VP*) is not an allegory 'but a plumbing of the unconscious mind projecting itself in the action of the poem'. C. C. Clarke writes on 'Humor and Wit in *Childe Roland*' (*MLQ*). In 'Caliban's Mind' (*VP*) John Howard rejects the theory that the poem is a satire on the growth of scientific doubt. Wilfred L. Guerin discusses the 'Irony and Tension in Browning's *Karshish*' (*VP*)—tension, that is, between zeal and caution, science and faith. R. D. Altick sees 'criticism of the Grammarian's waste of life' as the central theme of '*A Grammarian's Funeral*' (*SEL*). David Fleisher writes on '*Rabbi Ben Ezra*, 49–72: A New Key to an Old Crux' (*VP*). Conrad Balliet in the same journal argues, in a note on '*Growing Old* along with *Rabbi Ben Ezra*', that Arnold's poem was certainly an answer to Browning's.

Philip Drew makes a general survey of 'Browning's *Essay on Shelley*' (*VP*). In 'Browning's Music Poems: Fancy and Fact' (*PMLA*) George M. Ridenour suggests that Browning used a 'strong sense of the weakness of language in developing the meaning of his poems'. He expanded Shelley's 'varied approximation' approach to meaning to its ultimate implication in *The Ring and the Book*, and he also found the analogy of music helpful in 'fixing' the multiplicities of meaning without distorting them. R. D. Altick supplies some suggestions for new notes in 'Memo to the Next Annotator of Browning' (*VP*). W. M. Ryan tackles the problem of 'The Classification of Browning's "Difficult" Vocabulary' (*SP*).

In 'Browning and the Harriet Westbrook Shelley Letters' (*UTQ*) W. O. Raymond argues, against Betty Miller, that Browning did not read these letters before writing his essay on Shelley. Warner Barnes describes 'The Browning Collection' at the University of Texas (*Texas Library Chronicle*).

G. B. Tennyson contributes 'Carlyle's Poetry to 1840: A Checklist and Discussion, a New Attribution and Six Unpublished Poems' (*VP*).

Carl J. Weber comments on 'The "Discovery" of FitzGerald's *Rubaiyat*'—by Whitley Stokes (*Texas Library Chronicle*). S. Gittleman finds 'An Early Reference to FitzGerald's *Rubaiyat of Omar Khayyam* in Germany' (*NQ*), and comments on 'John Hay as a Critic of *The Rubaiyat of Omar Khayyam*' (*VN*).

Etienne Gilson makes an appreciation of a review by Patmore in *The National Review* in 1860 in 'Coventry Patmore et Maire Biran'. See *PMLA* 'Maire de Biran' (*Studi francesi*).

The censure and subsequent neglect of Clough's poetry were unjust and protracted, but generous amends are now being made. Following Lady Chorley's book (*YW* xliii. 238) comes Walter E. Houghton's 'essay in revaluation'[32] which carries the process of rehabilitation farther. Houghton begins with a review of Clough's many detractors, and proceeds to restore his reputation on the very points for which he was most condemned. *The Bothie*, although 'it has lost the contemporary appeal of its realism and its radical ideas', remains fresh for 'its masterly fusion of plot, character, setting and ideas; its suggestion . . . of a broad picture of life, at any rate, youthful life'. Clough's 'Bothiaics' are no longer an issue, but Houghton puts in a word for their flexibility. In *Amours de Voyage* the charm of the *Bothie* gave place to a penetrating study of contemporary attitudes and 'ambivalent feelings about art, heroism and love'.

[32] *The Poetry of Clough*, by Walter E. Houghton. Yale U.P. pp. xii+236. 37*s.* 6*d.* $5.00.

Where Philip in *The Bothie* had been straightforward, Claude in *Amours de Voyage* is complex. This is reflected in the tone of the poem, and 'in less than a year, Clough's art has gained the sophistication of the great novelists; *Amours de Voyage* is a minor masterpiece', says Houghton. *Dipsychus*, as the text now stands, has two conspicuous flaws: the incongruity of *Dipsychus Continued*, and the uncertainty concerning the intended order of scenes iv-vii. Houghton generally accepts the text of the 1951 editors, but argues against the inclusion of *Dipsychus Continued* with the main poem. Thus *Dipsychus* is inferior to *The Bothie* and *Amours de Voyage* in form, although surpassing both in content. Houghton's critique of the poems is the best thing in the book. Less convincing is his attempt to present Clough as, in his shorter poems, a master of Augustan control, an attempt that Houghton makes partly to account for the insensitivity of the Victorians to his poems. Writing on *Mari Magno*, too, Houghton protests a little too much that concessions to 'Victorianism' are necessary for 'the high quality of the best tales' to appear. As always, Houghton's wit and fluent writing add to the quality of the book. (Reviewed by Kenneth Allott in *EC*, 1964). Clyde de L. Ryals suggests 'An Interpretation of Clough's *Dipsychus*' (*VP*) as 'a satire—of a gentle sort to be sure—on the author himself, on the anguish he suffered during the process of growing up, and on Romantic metaphysics'. Michael Timko discusses Clough's 'positive naturalism' in 'The Satiric Poetry of Arthur Hugh Clough' (*VP*). David Bonnell Green prints new letters between 'Arthur Hugh Clough and the Parkers' (*NQ*), that is, the editor of *Fraser's* and his father, the publisher. Howard Fulweiler writes on 'Mer-

men and Mermaids: A Note on an "Alien Vision" in the Poetry of Tennyson, Arnold and Hopkins' (*VN*), suggesting the influence of Tennyson's two poems in the 1830 volume; and in 'Matthew Arnold: The Metamorphosis of a Merman' (*VP*) he suggests that *The Neckan* and *The Forsaken Merman* hold both private and public comment by Arnold.

Several studies have recently been made of Arnold's relation to the Romantics, but the theme has not been exhausted. Leon Gottfried's book on the subject[33] explores in detail the influence of the major Romantics on Arnold's critical and social thought, as well as on his poetry. Although 'there was more fundamental disagreement than agreement' between them, Arnold's ideas as well as his verse were permeated by Wordsworth's influence. Not so the other Romantics; yet 'it was impossible for a poetically sensitive lad of Arnold's generation to escape the reverberations of Byron's unparalleled popularity', and the young Arnold certainly did not. But it was a selective influence; although at first the contemplation rather than the action attracted him, in Arnold's mature poetry there remained 'a shadow or submerged image' of Byron as 'the type of impetuous, violent action and undivided will'. Keats's influence was of a far more negative sort, as 'something to be avoided'. Yet the energy of Arnold's resistance to it betrayed the power it exerted on him, and the influence itself can be seen in isolated passages. Shelley and Coleridge were never considered by Arnold as important poets; yet strong suggestions exist of Shelley's influence on his poetry, whereas that of Coleridge, at best, 'was merely

[33] *Arnold and the Romantics*, by Leon Gottfried. Routledge & Kegan Paul. pp. x+277. 40*s*.

general and diffuse'. Cut off by 'conditioning' from most English poetry beyond the Romantic tradition, Arnold was not well equipped for his self-appointed task of reforming the taste of his age. Hence his wooing of the Continental poets. But he was also separated from the Romantics by the inability to believe in the power of the imagination, so that his own poetry is 'inevitably most moving when it deals with the alienation and incompleteness of modern man'. This was Arnold's own Romanticism; it was also the source of his insensitivity to his predecessors. (Reviewed by Basil Willey in *CQ*). U. C. Knoepflmacher traces Wordsworth's influence on Arnold in 'Dover Revisited' (*VP*).

Robert A. Greenberg, in 'Arnold's Mournful Rhymes: A Study of *The World and the Quietist*' (*VP*), sees the poem as 'Arnold's apology in behalf of the kind of debating poetry he himself has been writing', and to which he had objected in the 1853 Preface as 'the dialogue of the mind with itself'. Kenneth Allott discusses 'Arnold's Tyrian Trader' in *TLS*, 18 October, and E. E. Stevens also writes under this title in *VN*, suggesting *Ezekiel* and *Isaiah* as sources of the image. Kenneth Allott also suggests, in 'Matthew Arnold's, *The New Sirens* and George Sand' (*VP*), that Arnold reprinted the poem in 1876 as a tribute to George Sand, who died that year. R. L. Brooks discusses 'The *Strayed Reveller* Myth' (*Lib*), finds 'A New Source for Matthew Arnold's *Sohrab and Rustum*' in Hugh Murray's *Travels of Marco Polo* (*PQ*), and writes a short note (*RES*) on 'The Genesis of Matthew Arnold's "Thyrsis"', suggesting a timetable for the writing of the poem. J. L. Mazzaro writes on 'Corydon in Matthew Arnold's *Thyrsis*' (*VP*). M. G. Sundell writes on 'The Intel-

lectual Background and Structure of Arnold's *Tristam and Iseult*' (*VP*), and in 'The Unity of Arnold's *Tristram and Iseult*' (*VP*) J. L. Kendall claims that the Merlin story is not the coda usual in Arnold's verse narrative, aimed to set the poem in perspective, but is meant to present 'symbolically the truth that has been adumbrated dramatically'. Park Honan makes 'an examination of Arnold's experiments in verse discord' in 'Matthew Arnold and Cacophony' (*VP*).

R. H. Super presents 'Documents in the Matthew Arnold–Saint-Beuve Relationship' (*MP*), and P. F. Mattheisen and A. C. Young print 'Some Letters of Matthew Arnold' to Edmund Gosse (*VN*). R. L. Brooks notes 'Some Unaccomplished Projects of Matthew Arnold' (*SB*). George Monteiro prints three new letters between 'Arnold and John Hay' (*NQ*). T. J. Brown writes on Arnold in the 'English Literary Autographs' series in *BC*.

A. A. Adrian argues the case for William Bell Scott's *Rosabell* (later *Mary Anne*) as 'The Genesis of Rossetti's *Found*' (*TSLL*). Jon Bracker gives some 'Notes on the Texts of Two Poems by Dante Gabriel Rossetti' (*Texas Library Chronicle*). J. F. Vogel discusses 'Rossetti's *House of Life* lxxxvii' (*Ex*). In 'Rossetti's *Rose Mary*: A Study in the Occult' (*VP*) Clyde K. Hyder gives sources for the esoteric lore in the poem, and indicates Rossetti's inventive powers.

In 1958 Lona Mosk Packer published an *examen* of *Goblin Market* (*YW* xxxix. 246), suggesting that the poem had been prompted by the pangs of Christina Rossetti's disprized love for William Bell Scott. This is the theme of the same writer's new biography of the poetess,[34]

[34] *Christina Rossetti*, by Lona Mosk Packer. California U.P. and C.U.P. pp. xx+459. 65s.

in which she argues that this love for Scott 'not only affected her creative capacity, leaving a deep mark on her poetry, but crucially shaped her life, developed her character, and finally made her the woman she eventually became'. These are far-reaching claims, especially as they are admittedly based on 'a detailed and carefully constructed edifice of indirect evidence', or, more simply, conjecture. The argument is ingenious, and proceeds from a sensitive reading of the poems in their relation to the activities of the two supposed lovers. It is not, however, conclusive, and further doubt is thrown on its validity by a review of the book by W. E. Fredeman in *VS*. Fredeman had the advantage, denied to Professor Packer, of access to Scott's letters to Alice Boyd, and to the latter's diaries, a mass of tangible evidence that enables him flatly to contradict some of Professor Packer's most crucial suppositions. Professor Packer, who did not claim to advance more than 'a tentative hypothesis', continues to produce evidence in support of it (*TLS*, 24 December, 1964). Apart from the biographical aspect, her book is a notable addition to studies of Christina Rossetti and the whole Pre-Raphaelite movement. It is full of information, and the criticism of the poems is always of interest. While writing the book Professor Packer discovered a cache of more than a hundred and fifty letters by and about the Rossettis in the files of Macmillan, Christina's publisher. The majority of these had never been published, and she has now issued these in a separate volume.[35] A short biographical sketch of Christina Rossetti appears in *Shining*

Lights, by Margaret Cropper,[36] where she figures as an 'Anglican Saint'. In 'William Michael Rossetti and the Quilter Controversy: "Gospel of Intensity"' (*VS*) Professor Packer reviews the attack on Swinburne, Pater, and Burne-Jones by Harry Quilter in *Macmillan's Magazine* in 1880, and W. M. Rossetti's reply. In *UTQ* she compares 'Swinburne and Christina Rossetti: Atheist and Anglican'.

Mother Angela Carson writes on 'Morris's Guenevere' (*PQ*). John W. Morris finds 'The Germ of Meredith's *Lucifer in Starlight*' in *The Ordeal of Richard Feverel* (*VP*); and in 'Meredith and the Wilis' (*VP*), Carl H. Ketcham finds a link between *Phantasy* and *Giselle*.

Wendell Stacy Johnson examines Swinburne's mixed feelings towards Carlyle in 'Swinburne and Carlyle' (*ELN*), concluding that he may have owed Carlyle more than he knew. A. H. Ehrenpreis gives an account of the unfulfilled project of 'Swinburne's Edition of Popular Ballads' (*PMLA*). R. L. Peters considers 'Swinburne's Idea of Form' (*Criticism*).

In 'Swinburne and Symonds: An Uneasy Literary Relationship' (*RES*) P. M. Grosskurth gives an account of their brief friendship. Symonds's attitude changed from disapproval to passionate admiration, and ended in disillusionment. Swinburne was 'always slightly condescending to a man whom he did not regard very highly'.

J. J. McGann writes on 'James Thomson (B.V.): The Woven Hymns of Night and Day' (*SEL*). Anne Ridler has prepared an edition of Thomson's poems and selected letters.[37]

---

[35] *The Rossetti-Macmillan Letters*, ed. by Lona Mosk Packer. California U.P. and C.U.P. pp. xxi+165. 35*s*.

[36] *Shining Lights: Six Anglican Saints of the 19th Century*, by Margaret Cropper. Darton, Longman & Todd. pp. xi+192. 25*s*.

[37] *Poems and Some Letters of James Thomson*, ed. by Anne Ridler. Centaur. pp. xiv+278. 35*s*.

John Edward Keating's *The Wreck of the Deutschland: An Essay and a Commentary*, published by Kent State U.P., Ohio, has not been available for review.

Comparing 'George MacDonald's *A Manchester Poem* and Hopkins's *God's Grandeur*' (*Personalist*), R. L. Chamberlain points out that MacDonald's theme, that 'God's presence shines through the world that "progress" has soiled and darkened', is also Hopkins's. George E. Montag writes on 'Hopkins's *God's Grandeur* and "The Ooze of Oil Crushed"' (*VP*). T. K. Bender expounds the same poem in *Ex*. Also in this journal Sister Robert Louise examines *Spring and Fall: To a Young Child*, and Sister Mary Dominic Stevens writes on *That Nature is a Heraclitean Fire*. Joseph E. Grennen comments on the 'immortal diamond' in this poem in 'Grammar as Thaumaturgy' (*Renascence*). In 'Hopkins' *The Windhover* Viewed as a Nature Poem' (*Renascence*) Br. Francis Greiner makes a plea for a straightforward reading of the poem. Eugene R. August discusses the meaning of 'Hopkins' "dangerous fire"' in *The Windhover* (*VP*). W. McQueen makes a comparison between '*The Windhover* and *St Alphonsus Rodriguez*' (*VN*). In 'The Silent Sonnet: Hopkins' *Shepherd's Brow*' (*Renascence*) Sister M. M. H. Campbell argues that Gardner was wrong to call the poem cynical. In 'Sound and Sense in a Line of Poetry' (*BJA*) David I. Masson considers line 5 of stanza 15 of *The Wreck of the Deutschland*.

Carolyn B. Norris writes on 'Gerard Manley Hopkins in his Sermons and His Poetry' (*NQ*), and on 'Fused Images in the Sermons of Gerard Manley Hopkins' (*TSL*).

George Herman expounds 'Henley's *Space and Dread and the Dark*' (*Ex*). J. M. Munro discusses 'Arthur Symons as Poet: Theory and Practice' (*ELIT*); and a full-length biography and criticism of Symons has been prepared by Roger Lhombreaud.[38]

A few years ago Evelyn Hardy and Robert Gittings edited *Some Recollections*, by Emma Hardy, together with 'some relevant poems by Thomas Hardy' (*YW* xlii. 255). All Hardy's poems to and about his first wife have now been edited by Carl J. Weber, together with a biographical Introduction on 'Hardy's Cornish Romance'.[39] Weber has also collected and edited seventy-four of Hardy's letters to her, to which he has added an Introduction and Epilogue, setting them in their biographical context.[40] W. M. Parker prints some new letters in 'Hardy's Letters to Sir George Douglas' (*English*). Roy Morrell, in '*The Dynasts* Reconsidered' (*MLR*), argues that Hardy did not intend to represent the Great Will as frustrating all human effort, for 'whenever it happens that the Great Will is in equilibrium' then individual wills are free. A study of *The Dynasts* by Harold Orel, published by Kansas U.P., has not been available for review. J. O. Bailey writes on 'Evolutionary Meliorism in the Poetry of Thomas Hardy' (*SP*).

Henry Mayhew is best known for *London Labour and the London Poor*, but his literary activities were manifold, and J. L. Bradley gives a brief glance at his first play *The Wandering Minstrel*, put on at the Fitzroy Theatre in 1834, in 'Henry Mayhew: Farce Writer of the 1830's' (*VN*).

[38] *Arthur Symons as a Poet: A Critical Biography*, by Roger Lhombreaud. Unicorn. pp. 333. 42s.

[39] *Hardy's Love Poems*, ed. with Notes and an Introduction on Hardy's Cornish Romance, by Carl J. Weber. Macmillan. pp. xvi+253. 30s.

[40] '*Dearest Emmie*': *Thomas Hardy's Letters to his First Wife*, ed. by Carl J. Weber. Macmillan. pp. xvi+112. 21s.

In 'Melodrama—Then and Now: Some Possible Lessons from the Nineteenth Century' (*REL*) Jerome Hanratty compares *Black-Eyed Susan* and other plays with the 'dodo-drama' of today, finding a notable decline in thought and language. Charles H. Shattuck has produced 'an attempt to reconstruct Macready's 1842 production of *King John* at Drury Lane',[41] and Martin Neisel comments on this in 'Perspectives on Victorian and Other Acting: The Actor's Last Call, or, No Curtain like the Shroud' (*VS*).

An article called 'W. S. Gilbert: An Anniversary Survey', first published in *TN*, 1961 (*YW* xlii. 236), has been re-issued together with the Checklist of a W. S. Gilbert Exhibition held in New York the same year.[42] The exhibition was impressive, covering every aspect of Gilbert's literary output, and containing rare items, all from the Pierpont Morgan Library.

A collection of essays and extracts about Ibsen has been edited by J. W. McFarlane.[43] It is cast in the form of a debate between those who have held the Shavian view that the plays are 'illustrations of a thesis, expressions of opinion, exercises in moral persuasion', and the school that 'denied that Ibsen had any interest in the propagation of ethical notions, and stressed instead his preoccupation with the technical difficulties of dramatic composition'. Most of the extracts are short, and they are too numerous for individual mention; but most well-known writers on Ibsen, past and present, are represented.

Two articles in *MD* stress the unique quality of the comedy in *The Importance of Being Earnest*. H. E. Toliver, in 'The Importance of Sincere and Studied Triviality', claims that the burlesque in the play is 'absorbed into a special kind of comic order . . . not quite like any other English comedy'. Arthur Ganz, writing on 'The Meaning of *The Importance of Being Earnest*', says that it is the 'absolute faith in pure aesthetic form that makes the Wildean dandy unique, and because it is dominated by him *The Importance of Being Earnest* is a unique play'. A. H. Nethercot, in 'Prunes and Miss Prism' (*MD*), compares Wilde's governess with Mrs. General in *Little Dorrit*. Richard Ellmann, in 'Romantic Pantomime in Oscar Wilde' (*Partisan Review*), says that 'it is easy to guess what efforts to free himself lay behind the recurrent and dominating interest on the part of Wilde's characters in giving themselves away'. In *TLS* (6 September) J. Lees-Milne wrote on 'Wilde's *De Profundis*', and a lengthy correspondence followed. H. Montgomery Hyde unfolds the painful story of Wilde's imprisonment.[44] He was given access to the Home Office files on Wilde, and so was able to bring much new material to the book.

'The selfish youth who goaded Wilde to his doom, and afterwards abandoned him, is an artfully created myth,' says Rupert Croft-Cooke in a biography of Lord Alfred Douglas.[45] Douglas himself was partly responsible for the myth, which has per-

[41] *William Charles Macready's King John: A Facsimile Prompt-Book*, ed. by Charles H. Shattuck. Illinois U.P. pp. 75. $6.95.

[42] *W. S. Gilbert: An Anniversary Survey and Exhibition Checklist*, by Reginald Allen. Bibliographical Society of Virginia University. pp. 82.

[43] *Discussions of Henrik Ibsen*, ed. by J. W. MacFarlane. Boston: Heath. pp. vii+110.

[44] *Oscar Wilde: The Aftermath*, by H. Montgomery Hyde. Methuen. pp. xxi+221. 30s.

[45] *Bosie: The Story of Lord Alfred Douglas, his Friends and Enemies*, by Rupert Croft-Cooke. W. H. Allen. pp. 414. 35s.

sisted at least since the unpublished portions of *De Profundis* became known during Douglas's action against Arthur Ransome. Croft-Cooke sets out the evidence with the partiality of a friend of twenty-five years. The myth vanishes, and in its place appears a young man, impulsive and ill-advised certainly, but whose behaviour 'shows the highest courage and loyalty and is in stark contrast with that of Wilde's other friends'. Apart from the material on Wilde, the book has much information on the literary scene before 1914.

Bernard Shaw is an interloper in this chapter, but hospitality must be extended to a book on him by Martin Meisel,[46] since the larger part of it is concerned with the nineteenth-century theatre, although seen through Shaw's eyes. In effect, the book is a thorough examination of the popular theatre during the latter half of the century. Meisel looks not only at a great many plays, but also at types of characters, modes of acting, and every aspect of the theatre. He begins at the Theatre Royal, Dublin, in the 1860's, where a link existed with a still earlier age in the person of Barrie Sullivan, who, in Shaw's words, was 'the last of the race of heroic figures which had dominated the stage since the palmy Siddons-Kemble days'. In the eighties and nineties the situation in London was extremely complex, in which 'reactionary bursts of primitive melodrama jostled polite comedies, "problem plays", matinee experiments, and full-scale productions of Ibsen, Suderman, Henry James, Barrie and Oscar Wilde'. All these are fully discussed, and their influence on Shaw, and the use he made of them, is skilfully revealed in this very able and informative study.

(C) NOVELS AND NOVELISTS

Specific themes and motifs in the nineteenth-century novel are studied in a number of books and articles. In his book on the Newgate novel[47] Keith Hollingsworth classifies the products of a school loosely defined by those contemporary critics who used the term contemptuously to denigrate the kind of fiction they considered socially dangerous, tending, that is, to familiarize the public with various aspects of vice and crime. Hollingsworth himself does not press any particular thesis concerning cause and effect between early Victorian social movements and the accompanying fiction, but restricts himself, after brief chapters of definition and historical background, to extensive exposition of the themes of *Paul Clifford*, *Eugene Aram*, *Rookwood*, *Oliver Twist*, *Jack Sheppard*, and *Catherine*. Nor does he offer in his critical accounts of the novels any satisfactory reasons for the Victorian novelists' almost obsessive preoccupation with the theme of violence, though in his conclusion he does point to the basic differences between Dickens's imaginative grasp of his subject and Thackeray's more rational approach. He also disentangles the complicated skein of controversy and quarrelling which wasted the energies of Ainsworth, Dickens, Bulwer, and Thackeray for almost twenty years.

Louis James studies the voluminous literature aimed primarily at the Victorian working-class reader.[48] In 1840 there were approximately eighty cheap periodicals, two-thirds of which

[46] *Shaw and the Nineteenth-Century Theater* by Martin Meisel. Princeton U.P. pp. xii + 477. 43s. $7.50.

[47] *The Newgate Novel, 1830–1847: Bulwer, Ainsworth, Dickens, and Thackeray*, by Keith Hollingsworth. Wayne State U.P. pp. 279. $7.95.

[48] *Fiction for the Working Man, 1830–1850*, by Louis James. O.U.P. pp. xiv + 226. 35s.

cost a penny and none more than twopence. Of these, twenty-two were given over entirely to fiction, and by 1850 this number had increased to sixty. The novelists dealt with most fully are J. F. Smith, J. M. Rymer, Pierce Egan, and G. W. M. Reynolds, though James's best chapters are those which trace the influence upon these writers of their better-known contemporaries. For instance, he shows how the combined traditions of the Tale of Terror and the Historical Novel culminate in the implausible, paradoxical Domestic Romance, and he is particularly interesting on the subject of the many plagiarisms of *Pickwick*, where the nature of the emendations to the original indicate precisely the attitudes and interests of the readers. The book contains a checklist of Penny-Issue novels not listed in Montague Summers's *Gothic Bibliography*. Another book which, because of the nature of its thesis, is most interesting on the subject of minor novelists, has been reissued.[49] Henkin claims that 'What the scientific inventions and discoveries of today— relativity, cosmic rays, atom smashers—are contributing to the imaginative literature of today, the theories of evolution and natural selection alone contributed to the imaginative literature of the Victorian era.' In fact they probably contributed more, prompting the imaginations of one or two major Victorian writers, though their immediate impact is to be seen most clearly in the mass of second-rate fiction.

Seeking to account for the relative failure of proletarian novelists in the nineteenth century, John B. Mitchell proposes, in 'Aesthetic Problems of the Development of the Proletarian-Revolutionary Novel in Nineteenth Century Britain' (*ZAA*), that 'it was because of the still relative poverty of their grasp of the new working-class reality as a relatively permanent, historically "right", humanly valid mode of human existence'. He examines in some detail *Sunshine and Shadows*, by Thomas Martin Wheeler. Another form of propaganda novel is dealt with by Irene Bostrom in 'The Novel and Catholic Emancipation' (*SIR*). Even before the advent of the avowed anti-Catholic propaganda novel in the 1820's, the decade when the Irish emancipation question came to a head, there had been indirect propaganda in the depiction of Catholics in Gothic romances and historical novels. The novelists whose work is discussed include Ireland, William and Horace Smith, Scott, and Anna Eliza Bray. In a study of 'Music in the Victorian Novel' (*KR*), D. J. Smith comes to the conclusion that, though music was not one of the major areas of expression of the Victorian spirit, it left a small but vivid impression on the work of the novelists of the time, particularly that of George Eliot, Butler, and Hardy.

There is considerable overlapping between the two volumes of the Oxford History of English Literature which together cover the period 1789–1832[50, 51] Renwick deals with the Gothic Horror novelists, Maria Edgeworth, Jane Austen, and the early Scott; Jack has chapters on the Waverley Romances, Peacock, and the minor novelists, and also discussions of Hazlitt, Lamb, De Quincey, and other writers of miscellaneous prose. The result of this shared responsibility for a relatively short

---

[49] *Darwinism in the English Novel, 1860–1910: The Impact of Evolution on Victorian Fiction*, by Leo J. Henkin. New York: Russell & Russell. pp. 303. $7.50.

[50] *English Literature 1789–1815*, by W. L. Renwick. O.U.P. pp. viii+293. $7.00.
[51] *English Literature 1815–1832*, by Ian Jack. O.U.P. pp. xii+643. $11.50.

period of history is a serious, almost catastrophic, lack of proportion in the space given to various writers. Jane Austen, for example, considered by Renwick to be, like Chaucer, too tempting a subject of discourse, is treated at about the same length that Jack gives to John Galt. It is worth recalling that H. S. Bennett, in the second volume of the Oxford History, made no effort to resist the temptation to write about Chaucer, and in fact spent more than sixty pages on him. Here Jane Austen gets eleven. On the other hand, it is true that there is no shortage of criticism of the major novelists of this period, and one is glad to have in these histories relatively detailed discussions of the work of minor authors.

In his introduction to a new volume of essays[52] Ian Watt claims that 'In general, the criticism of Jane Austen in the last two decades is incomparably the richest and most illuminating that has appeared.' This claim is well substantiated by the quality of work in the rest of the book, where one can find Lionel Trilling's essay on *Mansfield Park*, together with a dissenting view by Kingsley Amis, two opinions of the irony in *Pride and Prejudice* delivered by Reuben Brower and Marvin Mudrick, critical assessments of *Emma* by Mark Schorer and Arnold Kettle, and D. W. Harding's well-known essay, 'Regulated Hatred: an Aspect of the Work of Jane Austen'. The collection would have been even better had some way been discovered of abridging part of Mary Lascelles's book, or of persuading Q. D. Leavis to allow her work on Jane Austen to be reprinted.

Published under the title of the notebook's opening story, 'Love and Freindship', Jane Austen's *Volume*

the Second was printed in 1922, and was included subsequently in the Oxford *Jane Austen* in 1954. Now a new text has been published[53] following the manuscript as closely as possible in its final corrected and revised form. The volume contains works dated between 1790 and 1793, including, besides the story already mentioned, *Lesley Castle, The History of England, A Collection of Letters*, and other *Scraps*.

Robert Liddell's new book on Jane Austen[54] has been made necessary, the author claims, because the Oxford and Cambridge critics have been too little aware of each other's work. In his turn, Liddell seems hardly cognisant of what has been happening in this field recently in America. He ignores most of the critics in Watt's collection, and cites Edmund Wilson only to make an unconvincing example of him. Whilst this book is written with charm and urbanity, there is little in it in the way of fresh critical insights.

In reviewing 'Jane Austen's Critics' (*CQ*), Joseph Cady and Ian Watt conclude that most criticism of her work 'can be considered as the resultant of particular historical and cultural influences as they were modified in individual temperaments; attitudes towards imagination, society, religion and sex having had the main determining roles'. Cynthia Griffin discusses 'The Development of Realism in Jane Austen's Early Novels' (*ELH*), finding that in her earliest work Jane Austen defines the real world in a negative way by contrasting it with the worlds of bad novels. In *Sense and Sensibility* she begins to delineate reality more positively, though

[53] *Volume the Second*, by Jane Austen. Ed. by B. C. Southam. O.U.P. pp. xii+236. 21s.

[54] *The Novels of Jane Austen*, by Robert Liddell. Longmans. pp. xiii+174. 25s. $5.50.

[52] *Jane Austen: A Collection of Critical Essays*, ed. by Ian Watt. Englewood Cliffs, N.J.: Prentice-Hall. pp. vi+184. $1.95. 16s.

mechanically, through the contrasted development of opposed viewpoints. In *Pride and Prejudice*, however, the 'formulaic stiffness' is finally left behind, though the brilliance of this novel derives directly from the experimentation of the early work. In an article on '*Emma* and the Parodic Point of View' (*NCF*), Edward M. White argues that even in a novel as late as *Emma* the false world of literature is used as an instrument for illustrating the 'real' world of the novel. As White points out, behind the subtleties and ironies of all good parody lies the basic premise that literature is not life.

Alexander Welsh sets out, in his new book on Scott,[55] to account for the prevalence of the passive hero in the Waverley novels. The result is a thematic study centring on the relations of property, anxiety, and honour. The typical hero of Scott's novels is, to quote one of them, 'a thing never acting but perpetually acted upon'. Scott himself recognized the recurrence of such figures in his work when he came to review his own fiction in *The Quarterly*, and often created a conventional 'dark hero' to balance against such a character. These two then come to represent the thematic polarities which have been noticed by many critics of the Waverley novels: society and the individual, present and past, sense and sensibility, Hanoverian and Stuart. Welsh tests his thesis in detailed discussions of *The Heart of Midlothian*, *Rob Roy*, and *Old Mortality*. An unaltered and unabridged reprint of the last (1910) edition of the Scott Dictionary has been published.[56]

It contains identifications and descriptions of some 2,836 characters, as well as glossary notes where necessary, and chronological notes on each of the Waverley novels.

Several articles have appeared on a variety of aspects of Scott's life, fiction, and criticism. In 'Sceptred Kings and Laureled Conquerors: Scott in London and Paris, 1815' (*NCF*), Edgar Johnson prints an extract from his forthcoming biography in which he traces Scott's own triumphal tour round the dining-tables of London, the battlefield at Waterloo, and the sights of occupied Paris. In a speculative article on 'What Scott Meant to the Victorians' (*VS*), John Henry Raleigh accounts for his continuing appeal throughout the nineteenth century by reference to the realism and the expansiveness of the Waverley novels.

Arguing that critics in the past have applied valid critical premises faultily in connexion with Scott's work, Francis R. Hart, in '*The Fair Maid*, Manzoni's *Betrothed*, and the Grounds of Waverley Criticism' (*NCF*), sees *The Fair Maid of Perth* as a book about 'the complex natures of courage and its opposite, and the conflicting demands of peace and honor upon both the coward and the brave man'. He claims that the logic of Scott's theme is clearer than Manzoni's, and that the form of *The Fair Maid* is thus more coherent than the more arbitrary structure of events in *I Promessi Sposi*. D. D. Devlin, writing on 'Scott and *Redgauntlet*' (*REL*), views the novel as an attempt to answer the question, 'What qualities of mind and character are necessary to reconcile a deep love of the past with successful living in the present?' Scott's answer is defined dramatically largely through the activities of the comic characters. Finally there is an essay by John Lauber,

[55] *The Hero of the Waverley Novels*, by Alexander Welsh. Yale U.P. pp. xiv+327. $6.

[56] *A Dictionary of the Characters in the Waverley Novels of Sir Walter Scott*, by M. F. A. Husband. New York: Humanities Press, 1962. pp. xvi+287. $7.50.

'Scott on the Art of Fiction' (*SEL*), piecing together Scott's theory of the novel from scattered comments in his reviews and from his *Lives of the Novelists*. Lauber discovers, as one might have expected, that Scott's concepts of fiction are firmly based on the neo-classic principle of 'Imitation', and his concern, therefore, is usually with subject-matter rather than with technique.

Peacock's novels have been published in two volumes[57] with a biographical introduction and extremely useful notes by David Garnett, and in the 'Writers and their Work' series, J. I. M. Stewart contributes an interesting essay on Peacock's fiction.[58] Whilst *Headlong Hall* is made the chief focus of attention, there are also interesting comments on *Melincourt* and *Nightmare Abbey*, and even such works as the *Memoirs of Shelley* and *The Four Ages of Poetry* are not completely neglected.

Emily Brontë has attracted little attention during the year, though Wade Thompson has a piece on 'Infanticide and Sadism in *Wuthering Heights*' (*PMLA*) in which he presents a corrective to the conventional views of 'generations of readers' who believed that they were reading 'a beautiful, romantic, and indeed glorious love story'. In fact, he says, the love story begins and ends in perversity, the love between Catherine and Heathcliff being constantly overshadowed by the threat of infanticide, and culminating, not in a mature relationship, but only in revenge on the following generation.

'Women Without Men at Cranford' (*EC*) is an attempt by Martin Dodsworth to find the effective principle of unity in Mrs. Gaskell's novel. The book is seen as a 'kind of trimmed and tidied dream' in which the author's hostility to the male sex struggles against her awareness of the pointlessness of such antagonism in the predominantly masculine society of her day.

Raymond Maitre's study of Disraeli[59] concentrates primarily, in typically French fashion, on the analysis of his literary personality, and the examination of the works is conducted somewhat mechanically, though with great thoroughness. In addition to painstaking descriptions of each of the novels, Maitre also has detailed sections on Disraeli's philosophy, political views, morality, humour, style, and literary techniques.

Easily the most important service to students of Thackeray this year is the publication of Geoffrey and Kathleen Tillotson's edition of *Vanity Fair*.[60] The text published is that of the 1853 edition incorporating Thackeray's latest revisions and containing all the plates from the first edition, as well as a representative few of the incidental illustrations. In their Introduction, after a full discussion of Thackeray's narrative techniques, the editors give an excellent account of the planning and writing of the novel, and of its mode of publication. Finally, three appendixes discuss the manuscript, and print earlier versions of Chapter Six and a number of passages not in the printed text. Geoffrey Tillotson's book on Thackeray, first published in 1954, has also been re-issued as a paperback.[61]

[57] *Thomas Love Peacock: The Complete Novels*, ed. by David Garnett. Rupert Hart-Davis. 2 vols. pp. xxii+982. 16s. each.

[58] *Thomas Love Peacock*, by J. I. M. Stewart. Longmans, Green & Co. (Published for the British Council and the National Book League.) pp. 36. 2s. 6d.

[59] *Disraeli: Homme de Lettres*, by Raymond Maitre. Paris: Didier. pp. 463.

[60] *Vanity Fair: A Novel Without a Hero*, by W. M. Thackeray. Ed. by Kathleen and Geoffrey Tillotson. Methuen. pp. xli+680. 32s. 6d. (Paperback, New York: Houghton Mifflin. $2.25.)

[61] *Thackeray the Novelist*, by Geoffrey Tillotson. Methuen. pp. xv+311. 12s. 6d.

T

Writing on 'Contrast as a Principle of Structure in *Vanity Fair*' (*NCF*), Myron Taube claims that the novel's organization is determined, not as in the work of Dickens or Collins by continuity of action, but by the contrast of characters and the actions they perform. The most obvious structural contrast is that between the congruent triangles of the Amelia and Becky stories, though a further series of contrasts describes the conflicts between parents and children in different generations. In 'The German Sections of *Vanity Fair*' (*NCF*), John K. Mathison points out that at the end of the novel the theme is clarified by allusion to certain experiences of the various travellers. What is wanting in English society is revealed through the tourists' encounters with German musical and literary culture. Other notes on *Vanity Fair* include Myron Taube's 'Thackeray at Work: The Significance of Two Deletions from *Vanity Fair*' (*NCF*), and 'Misunderstandings About Becky's Characterization in *Vanity Fair*' (*NCF*), by Andrew von Hendy. Myron Taube also has an interesting general article on Thackeray's style called 'Thackeray and the Reminiscential Vision' (*NCF*). As a direct consequence of his unfortunate marriage, and particularly after what Thackeray called his 'year of pain and hope . . . and bitter tears' (1840–41), his prose style changed quite radically, becoming disengaged in tone and reminiscential, culminating in a final blend of Horatian satire and Christian morality. Another essay which finds occasion to analyse Thackeray's tone of voice is 'Thackeray on War' (*VN*), by Eric Solomon. The attacks on war in Thackeray's parodies and fiction recur throughout his work from the late 1830's until the end of his life, delivered with a savage anger quite unlike his usual controlled irony.

Solomon describes his parodies of Fenimore Cooper, Scott, Charles Lever, and Dumas, as well as discussing *Barry Lyndon*, *Vanity Fair*, and *Henry Esmond*. In a general defence of the novelist, David H. Stewart identifies and attempts to dispose of 'Thackeray's Modern Detractors' (*PMASAL*), classifying them as Aristocrats, Psychologists, Victorian Repudiators, and Critical Formalists. Lastly, Henry Summerfield edits 'Letters From a Club Arm-Chair: William Makepeace Thackeray' (*NCF*), six of the novelist's contributions to the *Calcutta Star* between 1843 and 1845 consisting chiefly of political commentary on such topics as the Peel ministry and the Irish question.

Dickens continues to attract a massive and varied criticism. One of the more interesting recent books on his fiction is Mark Spilka's essay relating Dickens to Kafka through their common approach to the conflict between home and society and their common feeling for the grotesque.[62] Dickens and Kafka are unable to move freely, like other novelists, from infantile to adult perspectives; their sensibilities are fixed, says Spilka, at childhood levels of perception as if by permanent psychic damage. He therefore examines their psychological backgrounds in the early chapters of his book, using for documentation *Metamorphosis* and *David Copperfield*. He then goes on, after an interesting general discussion of the Grotesque as a genre, to his major comparative analyses of *Bleak House* and *The Trial* and *David Copperfield* and *Amerika*. The justification for this kind of critical approach is well presented in Spilka's own conclusion, where he says that

[62] *Dickens and Kafka: A Mutual Interpretation*, by Mark Spilka. Indiana U.P. and London: Dobson. pp. 315. $7.50. 45*s*.

'the lines of continuity between our cheerful, readable Victorian forbears and our neurotic, difficult moderns are thick and strong. Granting this, we may lump together the fiction of two centuries as mere private spleen . . . or we may explore their fiction for the severe disruptions it exposes, and for the variety of means by which creative artists mend them.' Spilka's book is an intelligent attempt to follow the latter course.

Philip Collins's new book on Dickens[63] attempts to show some of the processes of Dickens's imagination by comparing what he had actually observed in various schools with the fictional episodes based on these memories. Collins concludes that Dickens was a Romantic Primitivist in his attitude to education; 'none of his characters who have received much education . . . enjoy a richer quality of life as a result'. In the course of his study Collins has sections on schoolmasters, schoolmistresses, child heroes, and Dickens's relations with his own large family of children. Collins has also published a separate essay on the subject of Dickens and adult education,[64] in which he discusses his actual contacts with the world of adult education through the readings he gave at various Mechanics' Institutes, as well as his published ideas on the subject.

Ivor Brown has produced a general work which seeks to relate Dickens to his Victorian background.[65] Whilst the book contains much of interest, it seems somewhat uncertain in its aim, shifting rather uneasily back and forth between the world of Dickens's novels and that of nineteenth-century London, thus confusing history, biography, and criticism.

A symposium on Dickens criticism[66] produced what one of the contributors rightly called a night of 'critical high jinks' in Boston, during which the five scholars rarely came to grips with each other's views, an exception being in their rehearsed analysis of Wemmick's character in *Great Expectations*. The discussion proper is preceded by general papers by each of the symposiasts. Of three interpretative studies of *Great Expectations*, George Levine's 'Communication in *Great Expectations*' (*NCF*), articulating a thesis similar to Spilka's is the most convincing. Dickens recognizes and treats the failure of the individual's relation to Victorian society, and even man's relation to man is, in this novel, shown to be at best idiosyncratic and irrational. Joseph A. Hynes, in an extensive study of 'Image and Symbol in *Great Expectations*' (*ELH*), argues that the novel is constructed of sets of images and symbols which are misvalued by the characters for most of the book and only properly re-read at the conclusion. Writing about 'The Conclusion of *Great Expectations* as the Fulfillment of Myth' (*Personalist*), William H. Marshall presents a somewhat turgid account of the implications of Dickens's revised ending, obscuring his meanings with such sentences as this: 'Soap is the instrument by which Jaggers removes the marks of evil from his hands and therefore the symbol of reality from the self, leaving nothing—the good.' Philip Hobsbaum, discussing 'The

[63] *Dickens and Education*, by Philip Collins. Macmillan. pp. viii+258. 40s.

[64] *Dickens and Adult Education*, by P. A. W. Collins. Leicester: Vaughan College Papers, No. 7, 1962. pp. vi+34.

[65] *Dickens in his Time*, by Ivor Brown. Nelson. pp. 248. 25s.

[66] *Dickens Criticism: Past, Present and Future Directions*, A Symposium with George H. Ford, Edgar Johnson, J. Hillis Miller, Sylvère Monod, Noel C. Peyrouton. Cambridge, Mass.: The Charles Dickens Reference Center, 1962. pp. x+64.

Critics and *Our Mutual Friend*' (*EC*), comes to the conclusion that those with a poor opinion of the novel—James, Orwell, Chesterton, Gissing—are the ones who think it offers no more than the plot and character appeal with which minor Victorian novels have familiarized us. Richard A. Lanham is certainly not one of these detractors. In his essay, '*Our Mutual Friend:* the Birds of Prey' (*VN*), he offers an interpretation of the novel as a profound work of social criticism on the subject of predation—a satiric allegory in which the many predators have a definite thematic function.

Two other pieces on individual novels should be mentioned. William Axton shows how Dickens's prose style contributes to 'Tonal Unity in *Dombey and Son*' (*PMLA*), paying particular attention to the imagery of the sea and voyaging; and Trevor Blount, analysing 'The Graveyard Satire of *Bleak House* in the Context of 1850' (*RES*), suggests that though Dickens is not using his material primarily for the purpose of documentation or propaganda, his satire on contemporary burial-ground abuses did materially aid the cause of sanitary reform. Treating a general theme in 'Charles Dickens: the Pursuer and and Pursued' (*VN*), Warington Winters relates those numerous passages in Dickens's fiction where a character is pursued at night in the vicinity of a church or graveyard to an incident in the novelist's childhood, narrated in 'Lying Awake'. Finally there are a number of interesting items in *The Dickensian:* 'Dickens on Ghosts: an Uncollected Article', with Introduction and Notes by Philip Collins; 'Dickens on Chatham: an Uncollected Piece', again with an Introduction and Notes by Philip Collins; 'Dickens and Latitudinarian Christianity', by Archibald C. Cool-

idge, Jr.; and 'Bird Imagery in *Bleak House*', by Cynthia Dettelbach.

Two papers examine separate aspects of the composition of Trollope's *The Way We Live Now*. P. D. Edwards, in 'Trollope Changes his Mind: The Death of Melmotte in *The Way We Live Now*' (*NCF*), writes about his discovery among Trollope's manuscript papers in the Bodleian of what appears to be a rejected plan for the novel in which two chapters were given over to a trial. For some reason Trollope decided upon a more summary dismissal of his chief character. In 'Anthony Trollope and the Calendar of 1872: the Chronology of *The Way We Live Now*' (*NQ*), Bert G. Hornback works out the novel's time scheme with great thoroughness. Examining 'The Uses of the Village: Form and Theme in Trollope's *The Vicar of Bullhampton*' (*NCF*), William Cadbury claims that the suspense in this novel is derived for the reader by his recognition of an emerging pattern of ethics. In form the novel is neither panoramic nor intensive, but limited, working by synecdoche to make the reader aware of the social macrocosm. It is a form which attempts to combine the high seriousness of the intensive type of novel with the geniality and spirit of the panoramic novel. M. A. Goldberg, without defining the novel's form, studies another of Trollope's novels as a reflection of mid-Victorian society; in 'Trollope's *The Warden:* A Commentary on the "Age of Equipoise"' (*NCF*) he suggests that here Trollope captures the true spirit of the fifties—peace, quietude, equipoise, stability, and compromise. Willam Cadbury has a more general article on Trollope, 'Shape and Theme: Determinants of Trollope's Forms' (*PMLA*), in which, by pairing several different novels to see how differences first of shape and then of theme may form the basis for a satisfactory classification of the works, he challenges an earlier attempt at classification by John Dustin (*YW* xliii. 247).

There is one essay on Charles Kingsley which deserves mention. This is John O. Waller's piece on 'Charles Kingsley and the American Civil War' (*SP*) in which the author seeks to chart Kingsley's growing sympathy, during the war, for the Confederate cause. In the course of his essay he examines the theme of Kingsley's novel of 1857, *Two Years Before*.

A volume in the 'Studies in English Literature' series provides a study of one of the major works of nineteenth-century fiction.[67] '*Middlemarch* resists formulation,' says Daiches in the concluding paragraph of his essay; its rich contradictoriness suggests the many-sidedness of life and the variety of its possible norms. He has, therefore, resisted the temptation to force the novel into a critical strait-jacket of his own devising, though the effort has cost something in terms of clarity of exposition. Within the limited space allowed, however, he does manage to suggest the complexity of the novel's structure and its main moral themes, as well as to chart the many shifts in George Eliot's tone.

Various aspects of structure and theme and the literary influence of *Middlemarch* are dealt with in four articles. Neil D. Isaacs, in '*Middlemarch*: Crescendo of Obligatory Drama' (*NCF*), sets out to establish the novel's governing structural principle as the alternation of two types of scene borrowed from the science of dramaturgy. Conglomerate scenes, of which there is at least one in each book, are used to bring many

characters together at one time and place, while obligatory scenes present the inevitable confrontations of pairs of major characters. Suzanne C. Ferguson, in 'Mme. Laure and Operative Irony in *Middlemarch*: A Structural Analogy' (*SEL*), examines the brief episode in Chapter XV where Lydgate's lack of insight with the actress prepares for his bad judgement in connexion with Rosamond. 'Some of our unresolved difficulties in understanding Dorothea stem from George Eliot's almost metaphysical conception of the place of woman in what we may call "the universal scheme of things", a conception she tried to transmute into aesthetically acceptable fiction.' Such is the burden of Lloyd Fernando's 'George Eliot, Feminism and Dorothea Brooke' (*REL*). He claims that she came as close in this novel as she was ever to do to presenting both the moral ideal and the artistic reality. In 'Isabel, Gwendolen and Dorothea' (*ELH*), George Levine finds that the figures of Dorothea and Casaubon are at work in James's *Portrait of a Lady*. He examines the affinities of the two books, discovering a variety of more or less important parallels, whilst at the same time bringing out some of the essential differences between the characteristic Victorian novel and that pioneered by James.

Patricia Thomson writes on the literary relationships of 'The Three Georges' (*NCF*)—George Eliot, G. H. Lewes, and George Sand. In an interesting paper on 'George Eliot and the Limits of Victorian Realism' (*Philologica Pragensia*), Ian Milner identifies and accounts for the idealizing tendency in George Eliot's art, seeing it as a limiting disability in a realistic novelist who, in other respects, succeeds in rendering the human personality with 'a plastic substantiality, a psychological

---

[67] *George Eliot: Middlemarch*, by David Daiches. (Studies in English Literature, 11.) Edward Arnold. pp. 72. 6s.

complexity and a truth to type that put her well beyond the compass of her contemporaries'. The same author has another article on 'The Genesis of George Eliot's Address to Working Men and its Relation to *Felix Holt, The Radical*' (*Prague Studies in English*). Other articles of interest on George Eliot include A. Katona's study of *Adam Bede* and *The Mill on the Floss*, 'Problems of Adjustment in George Eliot's Early Novels' (*Acta Litteraria*), and Irving H. Buchen's note about George Eliot's implicit comment on Arthur Donnithorne's relations with Hetty, 'Arthur Donnithorne and *Zeluco*: Characterization via Literary Allusion in *Adam Bede*' (*VN*). Finally, in an essay on Chaucer, Milton, and George Eliot,[68] Willene van Loenen Pursell describes in detail the attitudes of various characters in *Middlemarch* towards the idea of romantic love.

Phyllis Bartlett's pamphlet on Meredith[69] consists of a competent summary of his fiction and poetry, though, of necessity, where a writer of Meredith's dimensions is concerned, the treatment of much of his work remains rather sketchy, detailed criticism having to be sacrificed to history and the brief exposition of themes and plots. Discussing 'George Meredith, Sun-Worshipper, and Diana's Redworth' (*NCF*), Harvey Kerpneck comes to the conclusion that the sun is used in *Diana of the Crossways* as a synonym for the elemental values and for 'a particular, topical human situation, where it betokens hope, progress, the finest

future Meredith could envision for his creations'. John W. Morris, in 'Inherent Principles of Order in *Richard Feverel*' (*PMLA*), seeks to account for the seeming lack of unity in the novel, and discovers three principles of order operating in it: a generic archetype (New Comedy), a harmony of parts, and a metaphoric base of language. But these principles together do not finally determine its form, and the novel never achieves its artistic potential. Two papers in *RES* examine revisions of Meredith's novels: L. T. Hergenhan, in 'Meredith's Revisions of *Harry Richmond*', expounds the critical implications of Meredith's deletion of several chapters; and Gillian Beer, in 'Meredith's Revisions of the *The Tragic Comedians*', offers a table of variants between the manuscript in the Altschul Collection at Yale and the first edition.

Of the essays on Hardy reprinted in Albert Guerard's collection,[70] perhaps the most difficult of access is Donald Davidson's on 'The Traditional bases of Thomas Hardy's Fiction' in which he likens the characteristic Hardy novel to a ballad or an oral tale. Hardy, he says, creates a world 'in which typical ballad heroes and heroines can flourish with a thoroughly rationalized "mythology" to sustain them'. There are also pieces on the major novels or general issues in his fiction by A. Alvarez (*Jude*), John Paterson (*Mayor of Casterbridge*), Dorothy van Ghent (*Tess*), Morton Zabel, John Holloway, Albert Guerard, and D. H. Lawrence.

George Wing, in his new book on Hardy in the 'Writers and Critics' series,[71] centres his study on the

---

[68] *Love and Marriage in Three English Authors: Chaucer, Milton and Eliot*, by Willene van Loenen Pursell. (Stanford Honors Essays in Humanities.) Stanford, Calif. pp. 58.

[69] *George Meredith*, by Phyllis Bartlett. Longmans, Green & Co. (Published for the British Council and the National Book League.) pp. 44. 2s. 6d.

[70] *Hardy: A Collection of Critical Essays*, ed. by Albert J. Guerard. Englewood Cliffs, N.J.: Prentice-Hall. pp. 180. 16s.

[71] *Thomas Hardy*, by George Wing. Oliver & Boyd. N.Y.: Grove Press. pp. 119. 5s. 95c.

theme of sexual betrayal. He writes well on all the novels, though he is particularly good on the less fashionable novels such as *Under the Greenwood Tree* and *Far From the Madding Crowd*. In order to avoid what he calls the 'inelastic technicalities' of current criticism, however, Wing invents some curious critical terms of his own.

C. J. Weber, in his preface to his new collection of Hardy's letters,[72] says quite rightly that 'It will, of course, not do to expect too much of Hardy's letters.' They contain little if any literary appeal, though, again as Weber mentions, they do help us to arrive at an understanding of the atmosphere at Max Gate, and will be a useful adjunct to the projected edition of poems about Emma.

Perhaps the most interesting of the general essays on Hardy's fiction to appear this year is Richard Beckman's 'A Character Typology for Hardy's Novels' (*ELH*). Hardy's characters, he claims, may be related to each other systematically in terms of their responses to the ironic world he creates, and form together a logically complete set of archetypal human natures. Beckman tests his thesis in an analysis of *The Mayor of Casterbridge*, a novel that derives its structure and meaning from thematic interrelationships of the characters who manifest these various types of response. Restricting himself to minor fiction, James F. Scott discusses 'Hardy's Use of the Gothic: An Examination of Five Representative Works' (*NCF*). The pieces he chooses to illustrate Hardy's subtle probing of abnormal states of consciousness are *The Withered Arm, The Committee-Man of the Terror, Barbara of the House of Grebe, The Doctor's Legend*, and *Desperate Remedies*. In 'Hardy's

Mayor and the Problem of Intention' (*Criticism*), Robert B. Heilman sets out to answer the question, 'Do the interpolated statements in this novel about the world and people "square" with what the narrative texture is doing or saying?' In fact he discovers a 'sharp hiatus' here, but also concludes that Hardy's characters are 'truly impressive when they are, as it were, acting on their own instead of standing still and submitting to his pedagogical pointer and his theoretical anatomizing'. Howard Babb demonstrates the number and variety of the relationships that Hardy creates between 'Setting and Theme in *Far From the Madding Crowd*' (*ELH*). His chief devices have to do with the naming of characters and with the commentary on the main figures provided by the material world. The impact of anthropology on Hardy's work is discussed by Elliott B. Gose, Jr., in 'Psychic Evolution: Darwinism and Initiation in *Tess of the D'Urbervilles*' (*NCF*); and William H. Marshall analyses Tess's unconscious motivation prior to the murder in 'Motivation in *Tess of the D'Urbervilles*' (*RLV*).

Swinburne's two novels have been published in one volume together with a long and interesting, though digressive, critical study by Edmund Wilson,[73] in which he praises *Love's Cross Currents* for its restraint and psychological subtlety, and discusses its derivation from Laclos's *Les Liaisons Dangereuses*.

Jacob Korg has published two books in connexion with George Gissing. Whilst his biography[74]

[72] *Dearest Emmie: Thomas Hardy's Letters to his First Wife*, ed. by Carl J. Weber. Macmillan. pp. xvi+111.

[73] *The Novels of A. C. Swinburne: 'Love's Cross Currents', 'Lesbia Brandon'*, with an Introduction by Edmund Wilson. New York: Farrar, Straus & Cudahy. pp. 377. $6.50.

[74] *George Gissing: A Critical Biography*, by Jacob Korg. University of Washington Press. pp. vii+311. $6.75.

contains rather too much pedestrian criticism of the novels, it also does a good deal to fill out the real literary background of *New Grub Street*. As for the Commonplace Book,[75] Korg himself says that it 'can claim only the sort of general relationship to Gissing's novels which is natural to texts written by the same author', though it is of course the actual counterpart of the Ryecroft Papers in Gissing's novel. It is supposedly for this reason that Korg edits the book after the fashion of Gissing's purported editing of Ryecroft's diary, classifying the material under such heads as Women, England, Words, and Religion. Discussing 'Gissing's Feminine Portraiture' (*ELIT*), Pierre Coustillas relates Gissing's ideas about women expressed in his fiction to pertinent biographical data.

Two other pieces on late nineteenth-century fiction in *English Literature in Transition* deserve mention. Wendell Harris writes about 'Hubert Crackanthorpe as Realist', examining Crackanthorpe's stories published throughout the nineties, and coming to the conclusion that in them a sense of disillusionment is always lurking in the wings, even during the more romantic and ideal scenes of life. In 'George Moore and the Dolmetsches', Sara Ruth Watson analyses the true significance of the friendship between Moore and Harold Dolmetsch, in particular with reference to Moore's novel *Evelyn Innes*, which helped the revival of Renaissance and Baroque music.

C. Heywood has three articles on the subject of Miss Braddon's borrowings from and influence on her contemporaries. These are: 'Miss Braddon's *The Doctor's Wife*: An Intermediary Between *Madame Bovary* and *The Return of the Native*' (*RLC*); '*The Return of the Native* and Miss Braddon's *The Doctor's Wife*: A Probable Source' (*NCF*); and 'Flaubert, Miss Braddon, and George Moore' (*CL, 1960*).

'At the time [Dodgson] died *Principia Mathematica* was thirteen years in the future, Benjamin Lee Whorf was nine months old and the new mathematics was safely on the other side of the channel. Yet in the Alice books he effectively anticipates the modern viewpoint of semeiotic relativity.' This is the burden of Daniel F. Kirk's conclusion to his study of Lewis Carroll's concern for and use of language,[76] a study based on all of Carroll's works, but particularly on *Alice in Wonderland*, his 'richest and most exciting semeiotic expression'.

Writing on '*The Way of All Flesh*: The Dual Function of Edward Overton' (*TSLL*), William H. Marshall claims that Overton's function in the novel is more than merely one of unifying aesthetically the elements of Pontifex's story and the meaning it has for himself. Overton represents the philosophy of relativism, towards which Ernest's development is tending, in such a way that it becomes, ironically, a kind of absolute itself. William T. Noon, discussing 'Three Young Men in Rebellion' (*Thought*), compares Butler's indictment of Victorian England with similar attitudes and themes in the work of James Joyce and J. D. Salinger; and in another piece of comparative criticism, 'The Imperial Posture and the Shrine of Darkness: Kipling's *Naulahka* and E. M. Forster's *A Passage to India*' (*ELT*), Stanley Cooperman

---

[75] *George Gissing's Commonplace Book*, ed. by Jacob Korg. New York: The New York Public Library, 1962. pp. 69. $2.50.

[76] *Charles Dodgson: Semeiotician*, by Daniel F. Kirk. (University of Florida Monographs: Humanities No. 11.), 1962. pp. 77.

claims that Kipling's hero, Tarvin, 'confronts the very same ultimate *nada* in the shrine of the "Cow's Mouth" as Forster's Mrs. Moore and Miss Quested do in the Marabar caves; in both books there is the sudden intrusion of timelessness, the horror of absolute vacuum in which human ambition, love, hate, even religion vànish as undifferentiated particles down an eternal drain.'

(D) SELECTED PROSE WRITERS

Two major studies examine characteristic modes of thought and expression in the nineteenth century. J. Hillis Miller takes the work of five writers—De Quincey, Browning, Emily Brontë, Arnold, and Hopkins —whose typical Romantic response to the withdrawal of God justifies their juxtaposition here.[77] They all find the disappearance of God intolerable and refuse either piously to accept the situation or to adopt the alternative philosophies of Humanism, Perspectivism, or Nihilism. Instead, working on the central assumption of Romanticism, that the artist can create alone a marvellous harmony of words which will integrate man, nature, and God, they continue to make 'heroic efforts to recover immanence in a world of transcendence'. Miller does not merely treat each of these writers as illustrative matter for a thesis on the nineteenth-century religious consciousness. His prime concern is with literary criticism, and every chapter contains new and original critical insights. For example, in his section on Emily Brontë, he not only provides an extremely subtle and complex reading of *Wuthering Heights*, but also deals in detail with the implications of the joint creation of the world of Gondal —a visionary world against which *Wuthering Heights* was, in a sense, a treason.

Morse Peckham's book[78] also deals with nineteenth-century romanticism, and more particularly with the means by which its artists sought to account for individual identity. He traces four stages in this search—the discovery of analogy from man to nature, Transcendentalism, Objectivism, Stylism—and documents his ideas by reference to the works of no fewer than forty writers, musicians, and painters. In such a vast gallery it is not surprising that some of the characters are treated somewhat cursorily, so that, while *Sartor Resartus* is dealt with at length, Peckham's judgements on Scott and Disraeli suffer from the over-simplification forced upon him by the need for compression. The kind of generalization he is forced to make can be illustrated by his statement that 'in Scott's novels the main characters are stereotypes from the theatre and from earlier fiction; they simply serve the conventions of the novel'. Or this from his one paragraph on Disraeli: 'The climax of his career was the creation of universal manhood suffrage and of the British Empire, the attempt to extend social responsibility to all classes, and the effort to create an impersonal supernatural transcendental authority.'

Richard Haven analyses 'The Romantic Art of Charles Lamb' (*ELH*), examining two essays, 'Old China' and 'The Old Benchers of the Inner Temple', and concluding that here, as in Romantic poems, we are presented not with a rationally ordered sequence of ideas, but with a psychologically ordered moment of

[77] *The Disappearance of God*, by J. Hillis Miller. The Belknap Press of Harvard U.P. pp. ix+367. $7.50.

[78] *Beyond the Tragic Vision: The Quest for Identity in the Nineteenth Century*, by Morse Peckham. New York: George Braziller, 1962. pp. 380. $7.50.

consciousness. Daniel Mulcahy also examines Lamb's art in 'Charles Lamb: The Antithetical Manner and the Two Planes' (*SEL*). Lamb's typical technique in the *Essays of Elia* is, he says, to weave reality with illusion to present the two sides of any question, thus reflecting his determination never to take a stand on a half-truth which might deny the just claims of a conflicting truth. In *HLQ* David Bonnell Green prints 'Three New Letters of Charles Lamb'.

Gertrude Himmelfarb has collected eleven of Mill's essays on Politics and Culture,[79] including those on Bentham and Coleridge, as well as several pieces on the subject of reform, and his long essays on *The Spirit of the Age, Theism*, and *Civilization*. In her introduction to the volume she describes Mill's 'mental progress', culminating in his final retreat from radicalism and rationalism.

Two more volumes in the massive edition of Newman's Letters and Diaries have been published.[80, 81] Subtitled 'Birmingham and London' and 'Papal Aggression', they cover the important three years subsequent to Newman's founding of the two Oratories in London and Birmingham. Throughout most of the earlier volume we see Newman immersed in the problems brought about by the division of the Oratorians into two groups, and, in particular, endeavouring to cope, in letter after letter, with the various manœuvres of his chief correspondent, the leader of the London House, F. W. Faber. At the same time Newman continued to insist on the importance of the literary and intellectual life for the Oratorians, and brought out himself the *Discourses to Mixed Congregations* and the *Lectures on Certain Difficulties felt by Anglicans*. Probably the most dramatic, if not the most important, event in the period covered by the later volume was Newman's denunciation, in the fifth of his *Lectures on the Present Position of Catholics in England*, of Giacinto Achilli, the ex-Dominican who was at that time lecturing to English audiences about the Roman Inquisition. Achilli's libel action against Newman and the preparations for the trial are covered in letters and an Appendix. This volume ends with Newman preparing his lectures 'On the Scope and Nature of University Education', which he was to deliver the next year as the first rector of the Catholic University of Ireland. An extended analysis of Newman's *Discourses on the Idea of a University* has been published[82] in which Fergal McGrath first considers the main events and trends which influenced Newman, before going on to expound Newman's own ideas about Liberal Knowledge and to compare these with the views of later writers on the subject.

Surprisingly, there has never been a full length biography of Keble. Georgina Battiscombe now makes public a life, the lines of which it must have been extraordinarily difficult to trace.[83] She writes most interestingly

[79] *Essays on Politics and Culture*, by John Stuart Mill. Edited and with an Introduction by Gertrude Himmelfarb. (Anchor Books.) Doubleday. pp. xxiv+456. $1.95.

[80] *The Letters and Diaries of John Henry Newman*, ed. by Charles Stephen Dessain. Vol. XIII: Birmingham and London, January 1849 to June 1850. Nelson. pp. xiv+520. 70s.

[81] *The Letters and Diaries of John Henry Newman*, ed. by Charles Stephen Dessain and Vincent Ferrer Blehl, S. J. Vol. XIV: Papal Aggression, July 1850 to December 1851. Nelson. pp. xviii+555. 70s.

[82] *The Consecration of Learning*, by Fergal McGrath, S. J. Dublin: Gill and Son. pp. x+341. 35s.

[83] *John Keble: A Study in Limitations*, by Georgina Battiscombe. Constable. pp. xix+395. 45s.

about Keble's Oxford career, and of course his activities in the Oxford Movement, though she is less happy when dealing with Keble's literary projects.

Thomas Pinney has edited twenty-nine of the sixty or more articles positively attributed to George Eliot.[84] As well as the seven essays which she herself revised for publication in 1884, here printed in their original form, Pinney also reprints eleven articles for the first time, and one short piece, 'Notes on Form in Art', he publishes for the first time. The collection tries to demonstrate George Eliot's mind in the full variety of its range, dealing with such disparate topics as 'Servant's Logic' and 'The Future of German Philosophy', Heine's wit and the moral of the *Antigone*. The book also contains a bibliography of Periodical Essays and Reviews which can be definitely attributed to George Eliot, and a list of such Articles which have been wrongly or doubtfully attributed to her.

The third volume of R. H. Super's edition of Matthew Arnold's prose works[85] contains the first series of *Essays in Criticism, On the Study of Celtic Literature*, and four minor critical essays that Arnold did not see fit to reprint. This volume is edited with the scholarly fullness characteristic of the earlier ones. Arnold's own selection from his prose work, made in 1880 and never before reprinted, has been edited by William E. Buckler.[86] Arnold divided his works

into three sections, Literature, Politics and Society, and Philosophy and Religion, and, as Buckler says in his Introduction, 'It is curious to see such a man, at the very height of his career, confidently cutting himself down to size.' Whilst this selection is obviously not a substitute for the works themselves, it forms an invaluable and uniquely authoritative 'idea-index' to Arnold's thought.

Taking in turn five of the major Romantic poets, Leon Gottfried documents and analyses Matthew Arnold's critical relations with Wordsworth, Byron, Keats, Shelley, and Coleridge, using for his purpose both Arnold's criticism and his poetry.[87] On the whole, Gottfried is inclined to blame Arnold's lack of sympathy for the Romantics on his inadequate critical premises, which placed too much importance on the qualities of power and breadth of achievement in poetry, and he seems to concur with Jacques Barzun in deploring the fact that the poetry of the Romantics should have come to us filtered through Arnold's 'sentimental critical taste'. This book throws a good deal of light on the bases of Arnold's criticism. Three articles discuss various aspects of Arnold's prose writings. Sidney M. B. Coulling has two articles dealing with the history of the composition of two of Arnold's best-known works, 'The Evolution of *Culture and Anarchy*' (*SP*), and 'The Background of *The Function of Criticism at the Present Time*' (*PQ*), whilst Henry Ebel examines another of Arnold's essays in 'Matthew Arnold and Marcus Aurelius' (*SEL*).

Norman St. John-Stevas contributes a good essay on Bagehot to

[84] *Essays of George Eliot*, ed. by Thomas Pinney. Routledge & Kegan Paul. pp. xii+476. 45s.

[85] *Matthew Arnold: Lectures and Essays in Criticism*, ed. by R. H. Super. Vol. III of The Complete Prose Works of Matthew Arnold. Univ. of Michigan Press, 1962. pp. vi+578. $9. 55s.

[86] *Passages from the Prose Writings of Matthew Arnold*, selected by the author. Ed. by William E. Buckler. Vision Press. pp. xx+235. $6. 25s.

[87] *Matthew Arnold and the Romantics*, by Leon Gottfried. Routledge & Kegan Paul. pp. x+277. 40s.

the 'Writers and their Work' series,[88] in which he both expounds Bagehot's literary predilections and amply illustrates his incisive, witty style based largely on 'duomania'—a passion for polarities that can be traced back to a fundamental division in Bagehot's own character, between the sardonic, experienced man of the world, and the other, less well-known, passionate and mystical man, of whom we catch only very occasional glimpses in the essays.

In an attempt to focus attention on what is of permanent importance in Ruskin's writings, John D. Rosenberg concentrates all his attention in his book on the five works 'which most richly display the temper of Ruskin's mind'—*The Stones of Venice*, *Modern Painters*, *Unto This Last*, *Fors Clavigera*, and *Praeterita*.[89] While few would dispute the importance of these particular works, the dangers of over-simplification in such an approach are apparent. Even if Rosenberg does not fully succeed in establishing all his general points, though, his analysis of the works he treats is always acute. Quentin Bell, who has written a general study of Ruskin for the 'Writers and Critics' series,[90] was faced with an even more difficult task. As Ruskin grew older, he confessed himself to be 'almost sick and giddy' with the confused things in his head, 'trains of thought beginning and branching to infinity', and it is not surprising that Bell has difficulty in imposing order on Ruskin's life and voluminous work in one hundred and twenty pages. The method he adopts is not very different from Rosenberg's,

except that the emphases are placed rather differently, and Bell is content to conclude his essay with the warning that, properly to enjoy Ruskin's genius, the reader must be prepared, 'like Alice through the Looking-Glass, to turn his back upon his destination before he can reach it'.

The author of a new study of the Darwin-Butler controversy[91] calls herself a psycho-biographer. She charts the development of Butler's initial enthusiasm for Darwin's theories and his subsequent disillusion and bitter denigrations of Darwin. She claims that the whole episode throws light on the oedipal relationship in the lives of two exceptional individuals, and especially on the father-son part of it. The controversy was, she says, the medium through which Butler attempted to rid himself of Darwin if he could not accept or subjugate him. Another central document in this general field has also been re-issued this year—Gosse's 'genuine slice of life', composed of what he himself calls an 'extraordinary mixture of superficial comedy and essential tragedy'.[92]

Asa Briggs has edited an excellent selection of William Morris's Writings and Designs.[93] Some indication of the book's variety can be given by listing the various section headings: Autobiography, Romance, Commitment, Socialism, Utopia, Protest, and Rest. Briggs calls his collection an Introduction, and it will serve as such, though the care and skill with which the selection has been made will give

---

[88] *Walter Bagehot*, by Norman St. John-Stevas. Longmans, Green & Co. (Published for the British Council and the National Book League.) pp. 42. 2s. 6d.

[89] *The Darkening Glass: A Portrait of Ruskin's Genius*, by John D. Rosenberg. Routledge & Kegan Paul. pp. xiii+274. 30s.

[90] *Ruskin*, by Quentin Bell. (Writers and Critics Series.) Oliver & Boyd. pp. 120. 5s.

[91] *The Quest for the Father*, by Phyllis Greenacre. (The Freud Anniversary Lecture Series.) International Universities Press. (Bailey Bros. & Swinfen.) pp. 128. 27s.

[92] *Father and Son*, by Edmund Gosse. W. W. Norton. pp. 250. $1.25

[93] *William Morris: Selected Writings and Designs*, ed. by Asa Briggs. Penguin Books, 1962. pp. 308. 7s. 6d.

it the status of a representative anthology.

Roger Ricklefs, in the Introduction to his selection from Stevenson's prose works,[94] claims much more for his anthology, though the pieces he chooses scarcely justify his claim that, 'if these writings derive diversity from their author's complex mind, they gain unity from the constant originality and brilliance of his style'.

Erik Frykman makes a contribution to a very minor aspect of nineteenth-century literary history in a study based on the lecture notes of the first holder of the Chair of Rhetoric and Belles Lettres in the University of Edinburgh.[95]

[94] *The Mind of Robert Louis Stevenson: Selected Essays, Letters, and Prayers*, ed. by Roger Ricklefs. Thomas Yoseloff. pp. 127. $3.95.

[95] *W. E. Aytoun: Pioneer Professor o, English at Edinburgh*, by Erik Frykman. (Gothenburg Studies in English, 17.) pp. 139. Sw. Kr.20 (sewn), 27 (cloth).

XIV

The Twentieth Century

MARGARET WILLY and HOWARD SERGEANT

In this chapter books are noticed by Margaret Willy, articles by Howard Sergeant

BOOKS

1. THE NOVEL

It is chiefly to satisfy their instinctive curiosity, affirms Paul West in the preface to his study of the modern novel,[1] that readers turn to fiction rather than to poetry or philosophy. This curiosity is of three main kinds, which might be defined as social, psychological, and cosmic; and Mr. West's primary concern is with 'the novelist's effort to bring psychology back into proportion with manners, and to augment these two with a view of man in the abstract'. After discussing general principles of fiction, he admirably succeeds in communicating 'something of the adventure of comparing one national tradition with another' in his consideration of the permutations of the form in England (starting with George Moore), France, the United States, Germany, Italy, Spain, and Russia. The chief danger of this type of survey, which encompasses so vast a range of material within a comparatively small space, is degeneration into a superficial catalogue of titles and authors which fails to explore any of its ideas in much depth. West triumphantly avoids this in his lively and lucid study, handling an immense subject with ease, authority, and considerable critical penetration.

The modern novel is also considered by Anthony Burgess in his concise, astringent essay[2] issued as a supplement to *British Book News*. He writes only of novelists who have published work during the early 60's—both established authors such as Waugh, Snow, Compton-Burnett, and the younger 'angry' group of the 50's, and new-comers like the emerging West Indian and Nigerian novelists. He notes, however, that the period has been 'remarkable less for the emergence of new talent than for the re-emergence of old' (Huxley, Isherwood, Priestley, and Richard Hughes). As always in this series, there is an excellent bibliography.

C. B. Cox in *The Free Spirit*[3] quotes L. P. Hartley's views, in his essay *The Novelist's Responsibility*, on the devaluation of the individual in fiction, as in life, since the last war. The introductory chapter to this study of liberal humanism in a small group of selected novelists poses the problem of the modern liberal's dilemma: the conflict between admiration of active idealism, on the one hand, and on the other an unwillingness to become involved in commitment to any cause which may impinge on his belief in individual liberty. Cox then proceeds to examine

[1] *The Modern Novel*, by Paul West. Hutchinson. pp. xiii+450. 50s.

[2] *The Novel Today*, by Anthony Burgess. Longmans. (For the British Council and the National Book League.) pp. 56. 2s. 6d.

[3] *The Free Spirit: A Study of Liberal Humanism in the Novels of George Eliot, Henry James, E. M. Forster, Virginia Woolf and Angus Wilson*, by C. B. Cox. O.U.P. pp. 195. 25s.

George Eliot as 'conservative-re-former', and Henry James's search for the good life through the art of personal relationships; Forster's place in the liberal tradition, 'proclaiming the values of freedom, humanitarian-ism, progress, and intelligence', and yet constantly exploring through his comic art 'the flaws that appear when these ideals are put into practice'; Virginia Woolf as a lonely experi-mentalist whose 'quest of the free spirit could bring no certain or lasting solutions'; and the pessimism of Angus Wilson's savage irony in his novels and short stories. Cox's con-cluding chapter is a short survey of the modern novel—in particular the work of D. H. Lawrence, William Golding, and John Wain—as it ex-presses present-day attitudes to the humanist situation.

Frederick C. Crews's book[4] provides another, more detailed exploration of Forster's humanism: in particular of the 'perils' inherent in a belief in the supreme value of 'the life of affec-tionate personal relations, disengaged from political and religious zeal by means of a tolerant eclecticism'. Al-though Forster's individualism seems 'to imply a rejection of every estab-lished tradition', it is shown to be in fact firmly rooted within that of nine-teenth-century liberalism. Crews be-gins with the biographical origins, in both his family background and his years at Cambridge, of his subject's ideas. He then scrutinizes in each of the five novels in turn Forster's use of symbolism; his sense of the comic, and that ironical style 'unsparing in its probing of shams and half-truths'; and the scepticism and melancholy culminating in that 'masterpiece of pessimism', *A Passage to India*, with its theme of the 'incongruity between aspiration and reality'. Here Crews sees most clearly reflected Forster's acceptance of the ironies and dis-appointments resulting from a philo-sophy which places its trust in this world—an acceptance which is, finally, the dominant theme of all his novels.

Moral values and attitudes in fiction also preoccupy Robert Bloom in his study of the novels of Joyce Cary.[5] He feels that while Cary's in-determinate cast of mind greatly en-riches his work, giving depth and complexity in its sense of the varied possibilities of human experience, it has also been responsible for the com-parative neglect by leading critics of the sixteen novels he published be-tween 1932 and 1959. Bloom first con-siders Cary's outlook as expressed in his non-fictional work, then surveys all the novels in an attempt to show how his individual view of reality affected the form and substance of his fiction. The most detailed analysis is reserved for Cary's second trilogy; and these three first-person narra-tives, *Prisoner of Grace*, *Except the Lord*, and *Not Honour More*, serve as the main texts for an exploration of the shortcomings and the value of the indeterminate vision.

Dorothy Brewster's opening bio-graphical sketch in her monograph on Virginia Woolf[6] brings out well the influence upon her fiction of her sub-ject's omnivorous reading, of her in-tellectually stimulating environment, and of both London and the sea. A section is devoted to the critical essays in *The Common Reader*, whose wide-ranging voyages of discovery well communicate the author's zestful sense of the adventure of reading. But

[4] *E. M. Forster: The Perils of Humanism*, by Frederick C. Crews. O.U.P. and Prince-ton U.P., 1962. pp. 187. 25s.

[5] *The Indeterminate World: A Study of the Novels of Joyce Cary*, by Robert Bloom. O.U.P. and Pennsylvania U.P. pp. xv+212. 40s.

[6] *Virginia Woolf*, by Dorothy Brewster. Allen & Unwin. pp. 184. 20s.

the main body of Mrs. Brewster's book summarizes the plot and theme of each of Virginia Woolf's novels in turn, as it reflects her conception of the nature of reality and the difficult task of maintaining a balance between inner and outer worlds. Although the ground covered in a short book necessarily precludes much closeness of critical analysis, this is a sound and thorough introduction which includes some illuminating quotations from unpublished letters and from Leonard Woolf's autobiography, and a useful bibliography.

A. D. Moody's essay[7] is also devoted mainly to critical readings of Virginia Woolf's novels, and her non-fictional output—although at least as considerable as that of her novels—is mentioned only incidentally. The author concentrates on the technical innovations employed to express Virginia Woolf's vision of life, and on her penetrating diagnosis of the sickness of contemporary 'civilization' as represented by the upper-middle-class intellectual and professional society to which her own experience was limited.

Eloise Knapp Hay in her book on the political novels of Conrad[8] sees a striking similarity between Virginia Woolf's Mrs. Ramsay in *To the Lighthouse*, and Conrad's Mrs. Gould in *Nostromo*: each 'very much the earth-mother figure, providing relief rather than solutions, warmth rather than light'. This study, which incorporates the results of wide reading and research into original manuscripts, unpublished documents, and sources not available in English, traces the origin and development of the politi-cal theme through five novels—*The Rescue, Heart of Darkness, Nostromo, The Secret Agent*, and *Under Western Eyes*. Emphasis is laid on the importance of Conrad's Polish background, and the author suggests that for him politics was less an activity than an integral part of life. His preoccupation with human isolation is, she concludes, 'both cause and result of his strong sense of man's necessary involvement in social effort'.

The work of Joyce continues to engage much attention from scholars and critics. David Hayman has edited and annotated a text of *Finnegans Wake*[9] which includes the reproduction of nine formidably emended facsimile pages from the novel, and—by means of different typographical devices—shows up to five layers of the author's additions and substitutions. The editor's introduction covers the progress of the work, Joyce's mastery of language, his methods of composition and revision, and his sources. A catalogue of *Finnegans Wake* manuscripts in the British Museum completes an important contribution to Joyce research, which illuminates both the textual evolution of an influential work and the processes of its creator's imagination.

A necessary companion volume for the serious student of Joyce is Clive Hart's concordance to *Finnegans Wake*.[10] Affirming that 'the book is no simple linguistic puzzle to be untangled once and for all', Hart believes that its content is still a long way from being exhausted, and that any concordance 'is doomed to be a Work eternally in Progress'. He looks forward to the appearance of a much more ambitious work—a complete

[7] *Virginia Woolf*, by A. D. Moody. (Writers and Critics Series.) Oliver & Boyd. pp. 119. 5s.

[8] *The Political Novels of Joseph Conrad*, by Eloise Knapp Hay. Chicago U.P. pp. x+350. 45s.

[9] *A First-Draft Version of Finnegans Wake*, ed. by David Hayman. Faber. pp. 330. 45s.

[10] *A Concordance to Finnegans Wake*, by Clive Hart. O.U.P. and Minnesota U.P. pp. 532. 100s.

dictionary of *Finnegans Wake*. Meanwhile his own compilation, planned to help the reader 'trace the symbolic and thematic development of the intertwining verbal motifs out of which the book is constructed', provides a valuable interim report on the richness of Joyce's resources of vocabulary and the ingenuity of his manipulation of language.

In his short essay *Stephen Ego*[11] G. S. McCaughey examines the character of the hero in *Portrait of the Artist as a Young Man*, and refutes the too frequent assumption that this is a subjective self-portrait. The opinions about art and life expressed by Stephen are, he stresses, not necessarily those of Joyce himself, and the 'portrait' is in his view a maturely and ruthlessly objective one.

Julian Moynahan's chief concern in his survey of the fiction of D. H. Lawrence[12] is with its literary qualities—the author's style, creation of mood and atmosphere, themes, and narrative conventions—rather than its prophetic message or moral significance. Without ignoring the lapses in technique, taste, and insight in the worst of Lawrence's work, Moynahan concentrates on the best. He examines Lawrence's search for form in *The White Peacock*, *The Trespasser*, and *Sons and Lovers*, and his discovery of it in *The Rainbow* and *Women in Love*. The chapters on what he feels to be Lawrence's most unsuccessful work, *Aaron's Rod*, *Kangaroo*, and *The Plumed Serpent*, are entitled 'The Breaking of Form'. *The Lost Girl* and *Lady Chatterley's Lover* are considered in the section 'The Deed of Life' (Lawrence's own words when writing of the second

book), and the final part is devoted to the most successful of the short stories.

Eugene Goodheart's book[13] supplies a useful complement to Professor Moynahan's, in that it deals less with Lawrence as artist than as visionary—the preacher of a revolutionary utopianism uncompromising in its rejection of social life as a condition of salvation. Goodheart sees in his subject a 'tablet-breaker' in the line of writers like Blake, Nietzsche, and Dostoevsky, who shared a comparable attitude towards orthodox Christian tradition. More attention than usual is paid to novels like *Aaron's Rod* and *Kangaroo*, as well as to an interpretation of *The Man who Died* which considers Lawrence's response to the story and personality of Christ.

In his monograph on Hardy[14] George Wing attempts to redress what he calls the 'recent gross underestimating of the importance of Hardy's prose fiction'. This work, he feels, is as immediate in its appeal for us today as it was relevant when *Tess* and *Jude* made their first impact on Victorian sensibilities and ideas of morality. Wing examines the novels and short stories in some detail, beginning by relating their obsession with sexual mischance, bitterness, and betrayal to the known biographical facts about a singularly reticent personality, devoting one chapter to the 'wintry harvest' of the poems, and ending with a consensus of critical opinion from Hardy's time to our own.

In the same series, David Pryce-Jones's study of Graham Greene[15]

[11] *Stephen Ego*, by G. S. McCaughey. pp. 9. (Publisher and price not given.)
[12] *The Deed of Life*, by Julian Moynahan. O.U.P. and Princeton U.P. pp. xxi+229. 30s.
[13] *The Utopian Vision of D. H. Lawrence*, by Eugene Goodheart. Chicago U.P. pp. ix+190. 37s. 6d.
[14] *Hardy*, by George Wing. (Writers and Critics Series.) Oliver & Boyd. pp. 119. 5s.
[15] *Graham Greene*, by David Pryce-Jones. (Writers and Critics Series.) Oliver & Boyd. pp. 119. 5s.

U

traces through all the major novels the pattern of their recurring pre-occupations—such as the corruption of innocence—and the development of their author's technical skill. It also examines the relevance of Greene's religious ideas to the plays *The Living Room* and *The Potting Shed*, and devotes a separate chapter to the 'entertainments'. Summing up with a close scrutiny of Greene's attitude to experience, Pryce-Jones detects in his writing from *The End of the Affair* to *A Burnt-Out Case* an 'element of religious dehydration' which leads him to the conclusion 'that religion as a source of inspiration for further novels has run dry'.

The first full-length consideration of L.P. Hartley to be published, Peter Bien's book[16] concentrates mainly on the *Eustace and Hilda* trilogy (where he makes much use of Freudian dream-analysis), *The Boat*, and the symbolism of *The Go-Between*. Bien is especially interested in the conflict in these novels between moral and aesthetic elements; and he also considers Hartley's strong vein of fantasy as it contributes to the achievement of his artistic goal—'to heighten the mystery of existence while still remaining true to ordinary life'.

Although Laurence Brander's guide to the work of Somerset Maugham[17] includes a chapter on the plays, and one each on his travel books, personal writings ('the most practical literary autobiography since Trollope'), and his criticism, it is on the author's achievement as a writer of fiction that its main emphasis falls. All Maugham's diverse interests, says Brander, 'have served one end, story-telling in one form or another'—both as a master of the art of the short story and as a highly skilled and gifted novelist. His subject's 'robust commonsense', and a comic talent often sardonic, with 'a hard edge of Gallic wit to it', are stressed in this crisp and lucid assessment.

This year's new novels include another of Ivy Compton-Burnett's inimitable exposures of humbug in a claustrophobic family setting.[18] The theme of this grim comedy in which a sister is closer to a man than his wife, and a bewildering tangle of relationships is created by the sexual peccadilloes of a prolific and incorrigible paterfamilias, is whether 'a gifted person owes as much to other people as an average one'. Hereward, the hero, does not think so; and his secure conviction that his talent as a popular novelist explains and justifies all is the mainspring of the action. There is no diminishing of Miss Compton-Burnett's power in her dry mockery of pomposity, cliché, and sententious platitude, through the stylized dialogue in which eavesdropping butler, wryly amused grandmother, and *sotto voce* Chorus of children all speak alike.

By now equally familiar is the world of bibulous exploit and amorous manœuvre and mishap created by the novels of Kingsley Amis. The hero of his latest,[19] luckless as ever, is an overweight, self-indulgent publisher on a business trip to the States, and an aggressive and unrepentant hater of all things American. Transatlantic publishing politics, literary parties, and life on the campus are the targets here, although their English antagonist is ridiculed no less mercilessly than they. It is difficult to see what the introduction of Roger's lapsed Catho-

---

[16] *L. P. Hartley*, by Peter Bien. Chatto & Windus. pp. 288. 30s.

[17] *Somerset Maugham: A Guide*, by Laurence Brander. Oliver & Boyd. pp. 222. 30s.

[18] *A God and His Gifts*, by I. Compton-Burnett. Gollancz. pp. 224. 18s.

[19] *One Fat Englishman*, by Kingsley Amis. Gollancz. pp. 192. 18s.

licism adds to the picture, beyond transitory twinges of guilt. This is the first time an Amis hero has been permitted the indulgence of religious feelings, however fleeting, and it strikes an oddly incongrous note.

Iris Murdoch's new novel[20] is one of her strangest. Nominally the setting is a contemporary one; but the stilted and curiously courtly dialogue and a plot which is pure melodrama, leaving a stage as littered with corpses as the end of *Hamlet*, scarcely achieve credibility on a naturalistic level. Miss Murdoch's language is, however, more than usual that of symbol and parable. Her Gothic fairy-tale of a captive beauty in a castle, waiting to be awakened and rescued at the end of a seven-year spell, is a fantasy of the spiritual life; and through it she explores the nature of freedom and willing imprisonment, of suffering, expiation and the idea of the scape-goat, and the whole conflict between the powers of good and evil. It is all, however, too ambiguous to be satisfying—not least in the delineation of the central figure. Both the verisimilitude of the story and the human reality of the characters seem—in the author's own phrase—'paralysed by an allegory'.

2. SHORT STORIES

Comparatively few studies have been made of the art of the short story, and these are the more valuable when—like Frank O'Connor's[21] —they are written by a distinguished practitioner in that medium. Proceeding from his belief that the short story exhibits 'an intense awareness of human loneliness', and comparing its techniques with those of the novel,

the author examines the methods and characteristics of many leading exponents of the form. He admires Tchekov—whom he considers side by side with the other Russian pioneers Gogol and Turgenev—far more than Maupassant, but does rather less than justice to one of Tchekov's most ardent disciples, Katherine Mansfield. Other chapters in this invigorating critical survey are devoted to Joyce's use of language in *Dubliners*, to the work of Kipling, D. H. Lawrence, and A. E. Coppard, and to some American writers like Hemingway and Salinger.

Also the author, some years ago, of an admirable study of the modern short story, H. E. Bates is one of its most prolific exponents. The scope of his latest collection[22] is indicated by its title. It consists of thirty-five stories covering the same number of years, and taken from more than twenty books: ranging from *The Flame*, first published in 1926 when the author was twenty, to the generous selection from one of the finest volumes of his maturity, *The Daffodil Sky*, and stories published as recently as 1961. Henry Miller, who—somewhat unexpectedly—contributes a preface, likens Bates's work to that of Giono, and speaks perceptively of his painter-like quality in description of nature, his feeling for the femininity of women, the robustness of his humour, his treatment of pain, and the naturalness of his dialogue.

Containing about the same number of stories, and also drawn from past volumes, William Sansom's collection[23] is introduced by Elizabeth Bowen, who describes the author as 'a short-storyist by birth, addiction

[20] *The Unicorn*, by Iris Murdoch. Chatto & Windus. pp. 319. 21s.
[21] *The Lonely Voice: A Study of the Short Story*, by Frank O'Connor. Macmillan. pp. 221. 21s.

[22] *Seven by Five*, by H. E. Bates. Michael Joseph. pp. 454. 25s.
[23] *The Stories of William Sansom*, with an introduction by Elizabeth Bowen. Hogarth Press. pp. 422. 25s.

and destiny'. This collection is a tribute to Sansom's virtuosity, and admirers of his highly idiosyncratic talent will find most of their cherished stories here: from the almost intolerable suspense of *The Vertical Ladder*, *Among the Dahlias*, and *Various Temptations*, and the atmospheric compulsion of pieces such as *Pastorale*, *My Little Robins*, and *Gliding Gulls*, *Going People*, to the humours of *The Three Dogs of Siena* and *A Contest of Ladies*.

While Sansom is a master of fantasy, the realist Graham Greene is seldom associated with the idea of this *genre*. In *A Sense of Reality*,[24] therefore, he surprises his readers with some unexpected departures. In the longest of these four stories, a *conte* entitled *Under the Garden* which occupies more than half the book, a dying man revisits the strange, haunting dream-country discovered long ago by his seven-year-old self in passionate revolt against his mother's fanatical rationalism. Probably the best of the four, *A Discovery in the Woods* looks ahead to envisage, in a chilling yet poignant mood of prophecy, an adventure of the stunted children of the post-atomic age, where a small girl weeps bitterly 'for a whole world lost'.

The setting of the stories in *The Ragman's Daughter*[25] is the industrial Midlands, in and around Nottingham, which Alan Sillitoe has used in his earlier books. Most of his characters—children of mean streets, factory-workers, deserters, rag-and-bone-men—are familiar with the inside of a prison cell or borstal, and still in defiant revolt against authority in the form of police or probation officer. His subjects range from the

adventures of teenagers avid for 'kicks' through sex and stealing, in the title story, to different expressions of escapism in a breaking marriage in the longest one, *The Magic Box*, and his tough realism is tempered always with sympathetic understanding.

Another notable teller of tales, V. S. Pritchett in his new book[26] brings together three linked *novellas* which recount the tempestuous marital differences of the pilot and racing motorist, 'Noisy' Brackett, and his flamboyant wife Sally, as seen by the local baker who is enamoured of her charms. These well demonstrate Pritchett's continuing flair for delineating the exuberant drolleries of human behaviour, especially of the seedier sort.

3. POETRY

The death of Wilfred Owen only a week before the Armistice was a major loss to English letters. With his deep compassion for human suffering and the technical mastery which have made his work a seminal influence on twentieth-century poetry, he was incomparably the maturest poet to emerge from the First World War. Thus it is timely that the eve of the fiftieth anniversary of that war should have been marked by the publication not only of a new edition of his collected poems, but of the first instalment of an autobiography which adds much to our knowledge of his youth.

Basing his edition of the poems[27] on a close study of the manuscripts in the British Museum and elsewhere, C. Day Lewis has added to the original contents a selection of

[24] *A Sense of Reality*, by Graham Greene. Bodley Head. pp. 140. 15s.
[25] *The Ragman's Daughter*, by Alan Sillitoe. W. H. Allen. pp. 190. 16s.

[26] *The Key to My Heart: A Comedy in Three Parts*, by V. S. Pritchett. With drawings by Paul Hogarth. Chatto & Windus. pp. 107. 15s.
[27] *The Collected Poems of Wilfred Owen*, ed. with an introduction and notes by C. Day Lewis. Chatto & Windus. pp. 191. 21s.

juvenilia and some other unpublished pieces. The poet's own variants—which include four facsimile drafts of *Anthem for Doomed Youth*—are given, as well as indications of differences in this text from that of earlier editions. Day Lewis's perceptive introduction, which discusses Owen's poetry and early life, makes use of the poet's unpublished letters to his family, and Blunden's *Memoir* to the edition of 1931 is reprinted as an appendix.

Whetted by this biographical material, the reader's desire to know still more about Owen's formative years is partially satisfied by the first volume of a projected trilogy of memoirs by his artist brother, Harold.[28] Inevitably the author is himself the central figure in this remarkably vivid and intimate picture of family life during the last decade of the nineteenth century and the first of the twentieth. But the many episodes and anecdotes from which the personality of Wilfred emerges—moody and morose, struggling doggedly against the family's material vicissitudes to realize potentialities sensed in himself even then—provide a rewardingly full portrait of the poet as a boy.

The sombreness of temperament in another poet of the First World War whose talent was both brought to fruition and abruptly cut off by it is described by Vernon Scannell in his excellent short study of Edward Thomas.[29] A lonely individual, haunted by melancholy and self-doubt, Thomas was nevertheless capable, like Owen, of an ironic wit and the sudden mood of gaiety. Scannell brings out well the un-flinching emotional honesty of his solitary quest for self-knowledge through his poetry, the fine unobtrusiveness of his craftsmanship, and his gift for delineating 'minute details of natural phenomena with microscopic clarity'.

A contemporary of Thomas whose nature poetry also possesses the qualities of simplicity, freshness, and precision, W. H. Davies is the subject of a satisfyingly solid critical biography by an American scholar, Richard Stonesifer.[30] As well as outlining the facts of Davies's career, and his startling rise to fame from the obscurity of a tramp's life in England and America, it vividly recreates the quirks of personality remembered by the many friends from whom Stonesifer sought opinions and recollections. The second part of the book is devoted to an assessment of Davies as a prose-writer, as a poet of nature and of love, and as a humanitarian poet.

More biographical reminiscences, in which Sir Osbert Sitwell draws an engaging portrait of his friend, preface the reissue of Davies's *Collected Poems*.[31] Their first edition, published in 1942, contained 636 poems; to these have been added a further 113, so that the present volume includes all the poems Davies is thought to have published.

In his study of one specific aspect of the work of Eliot, Yeats, and Pound,[32] George T. Wright also explores the whole question of 'impersonality' in modern poetry. A necessary distinction is drawn between voice of the poet himself and that of

[28] *Journey from Obscurity: Wilfred Owen, 1893–1918. Memoirs of the Owen Family: I. Childhood*, by Harold Owen. O.U.P. pp. xiii+274. 30s.
[29] *Edward Thomas*, by Vernon Scannell. Longmans. (For the British Council and the National Book League.) pp. 36. 2s. 6d.
[30] *W. H. Davies: A Critical Biography*, by Richard J. Stonesifer. Cape. pp. 256. 35s.
[31] *The Complete Poems of W. H. Davies*, with an introduction by Osbert Sitwell. Cape. pp. 630. 25s.
[32] *The Poet in the Poem: The Personae of Eliot, Yeats, and Pound*, by George T. Wright. C.U.P. and California U.P. pp. xiv+167. 12s. 6d.

his *persona*, or dramatic speaker. This Wright sees as a device not for obscuring the poet's real self, but for making statements which would be impossible through explicit self-expression. The different ways in which the poet can be present in his poem, and the variety and effectiveness of *personae* as a structural element, are demonstrated through illuminating analyses of their use by his three chosen writers.

Pound is one of the poets discussed by R. G. Howarth in two short commentaries[33] reproduced from *Some Modern Writers* (1940) which is now out of print. His other subject is the imagery and ideas of Edith Sitwell. In the light of the *Cantos* which have appeared since 1940 and of Dame Edith's later achievement—her most important work appeared after that date—these essays must necessarily seem an incomplete appraisal.

The new edition of T. S. Eliot's *Collected Poems*[34] brings together in a single volume the whole range of his work from *Prufrock* to *The Four Quartets*. With the addition of a few 'occasional verses' not hitherto collected—which include that for Walter de la Mare written for the volume of tributes presented to him on his seventy-fifth birthday—these are all the poems to the end of 1962 which the author wished to preserve.

Eliot's achievement as man of letters, critic, satirical and devotional poet, and dramatist, is succinctly summarized in the monograph by Northrop Frye.[35] Unlike critics who profess to perceive a sharp division between the Eliot of *Prufrock*, *The Waste Land*, and *The Hollow Men* and the later poet of *Ash Wednesday* and *The Four Quartets*, Frye regards 'the structure of his thought and imagery as a consistent unit', showing a change only in content, not of attitude.

In his study of Yeats[36] in the same series Peter Ure devotes equal attention to the poems and the plays, for he regards the latter as an essential part of Yeats's achievement, which cannot be truly assessed without them. Between his biographical introduction and a closing chapter on 'Yeats and the Critics' Ure traces a development whose central theme is seen as a quest for 'unity of being'. It was this which led Yeats through the intricacies of magic and spiritualism, Eastern and Neo-Platonic philosophy, history, folk-lore, and visionary art, to become the major poet of this century.

Eliot is represented by *Marina*, and Yeats by *Easter 1916*, among the twenty poems in *Modern Poetry*[37] subjected to close analysis by C. B. Cox and A. E. Dyson. These range widely in time and mood, from Hardy's *After a Journey* and de la Mare's *The Listeners* to Muir's *The Horses*, Larkin's *At Grass*, and Wain's *On the Death of a Murderer*. Teachers of modern poetry should find this a useful volume, for it exemplifies the editors' belief that the function of practical criticism is not the destructive depreciation which robs the reader of delight in a poem, but that constructive appraisal which can only intensify his enjoyment.

In his lively monograph of Dylan

---

[33] *Two Modern Poets: Ezra Pound and Edith Sitwell*, by R. G. Howarth. Reproduced under the auspices of the Editorial Board, University of Cape Town. pp. 95.

[34] *Collected Poems 1909–1962*, by T. S. Eliot. Faber. pp. 240. 21*s*.

[35] *T. S. Eliot*, by Northrop Frye. (Writers and Critics Series.) Oliver & Boyd. pp. 106. 5*s*.

[36] *Yeats*, by Peter Ure. (Writers and Critics Series.) Oliver & Boyd. pp. 129. 5*s*.

[37] *Modern Poetry: Studies in Practical Criticism*, by C. B. Cox and A. E. Dyson. Arnold. pp. 168. 10*s*. 6*d*.

Thomas[38]—whose *Fern Hill* is scrutinized by the editors of the preceding volume—T. H. Jones considers that the 'legend', created partly by the poet himself and partly by the sensationalism of modern publicity, has done much to obscure the real quality of his work. The purpose of Jones's study is thus to redress the distortions of both undiscriminating enthusiasm and blinkered antagonism. Vividly relating Thomas to his Anglo-Welsh background, it presents a balanced and discerning assessment of his talents as poet, dramatist, storyteller, and broadcaster.

Dylan Thomas is—like Hopkins—a poet whose work frequently baffles, yet richly repays wrestling with its initial difficulties. In his *Readers' Guide*,[39] which opens with the bold affirmation that 'Thomas wrote sixteen great poems . . . Few poets have written so many', William York Tindall offers a detailed elucidation of the complexities of style and imagery which can so easily daunt the newcomer to Thomas's writing. After touching, in his introduction, upon Thomas's impact on American audiences, and considering the major shaping influences on his work, he proceeds to a poem-by-poem critical interpretation of each volume, often shedding fresh light on some of the more obstinate obscurities.

A disciple of Tindall's 'creative process of explication', H. H. Kleinman in his study[40] confines himself to a narrower field in his equally close scrutiny of the imagery of Dylan Thomas's religious sonnets—the *Altarwise by Owl-light* sequence published in the *Twenty-Five Poems* of 1936. Kleinman claims that he has been careful 'not to ascribe to Dylan Thomas an erudition which he himself would have denied'. Many readers may nevertheless find it hard to accept the amount of esoteric learning and lore which is credited to a twenty-one-year-old poet grappling with a still very imperfectly realized mastery of his medium.

Based on his Elliston Lectures in Poetry delivered at the University of Cincinnati in 1962, John Press's penetrating critical survey[41] of the poetic scene in Britain over the past twenty years excludes the work of such poets as the Auden group and Dylan Thomas, whose reputations were firmly established by 1939, in order to concentrate on poets who had published no volume and who were still under the age of thirty at that date. Press regards 1939 as the end of a poetic epoch—that inaugurated by Pound, Eliot, and Yeats—and finds that the poetry written since has its own distinguishing characteristics. Among these, he suggests, two contrasting lines of development are plainly discernible: that of 'argument'—under the obvious influences of Eliot, Empson, and Auden—and of 'incantation', whose origins are harder to trace. The author then considers in detail, under such headings as 'Provincialism and Tradition', 'The Meaning of a Landscape', and 'Metaphysics and Mythologies', the work of twenty poets prominent in the period since the Second World War—including writers as divergent in technique and approach as Amis and Hughes, Barker and Larkin, and Davie and Watkins.

---

[38] *Dylan Thomas*, by T. H. Jones. (Writers and Critics Series.) Oliver & Boyd. pp. 118. 5s.

[39] *A Reader's Guide to Dylan Thomas*, by William York Tindall. Thames & Hudson, 1962. pp. 317. 25s.

[40] *The Religious Sonnets of Dylan Thomas: A Study in Imagery and Meaning*, by H. H. Kleinman. C.U.P. and California U.P. pp. xii + 153. 30s.

[41] *Rule and Energy: Trends in British Poetry since the Second World War*, by John Press. O.U.P. pp. x + 245. 25s.

Of this year's crop of modern poetry anthologies, the latest volume of *Poems of To-day*[42] covers the longest time-span, containing 140 poems written between 1947 and the end of 1961. Nearly eighty poets are represented, from the last work of such older writers as de la Mare and Muir, through the continuing development of poets like Auden and Graves, to selections from the many whose names were unknown in 1947 and who have established their poetic reputations during the past decade.

Also the first anthology in its series to be assembled by a single compiler, Lawrence Durrell's P.E.N. anthology[43] is described by its editor as 'a log-book of the year's work in poetry'. Unevenness of quality is perhaps inevitable where selection is confined to so short a period—and in a volume where little-known writers rub shoulders with those who, like Dame Edith Sitwell, responded to a personal invitation to contribute. While there is good work here, there is too much that is scarcely worth preserving in book form. Certainly it is not possible, as Durrell hoped, to discern any 'general pattern and shape'.

When the original *New Lines* appeared in 1956, introducing those writers who became known to the poetry-reading public as 'The Movement' and representing a vigorous reaction against romanticism, it sparked off one of the most spirited literary controversies of recent years. Now Robert Conquest, answering the critics of his first selection in his provocative introduction to the

second,[44] justifies his original position and the historical place of the poetry he approves in the central tradition. He admits, however, to having previously gone 'further than was strictly necessary in excluding some types of verse'. This relinquishment of 'exclusionist theories' has resulted in a volume considerably broader in scope than his last. Eight of the original contributors appear in the company of sixteen new ones, including some whose names—Hughes, Thwaite, Scannell, and Blackburn—were certainly not associated with the first group, and others, like John Fuller and Laurence Lerner, to whom recognition has come since 1956. There are still, however, notable omissions. Surely R. S. Thomas fulfils Conquest's desideratum of 'following the central principle of English poetry, and uses neither howl nor cypher, but the language of men'.

One of the new-comers to *New Lines— II*, Edward Lucie-Smith is both a contributor to and co-editor of *A Group Anthology*.[45] Formed in Cambridge in 1952 under the chairmanship of Philip Hobsbaum, the 'Group' now meets weekly in London, with Lucie-Smith as chairman, for critical analysis of the previously circulated poems of a member. The editors interestingly outline the function and practical usefulness of the group; and the sixty-eight poems here—selected from approximately 3,000 discussed in this way—include both the work of those still comparatively unknown and that of more familiar writers such as George Mac-Beth, Peter Redgrove, and Peter Porter.

The ten poets whose work is anthologized in Maurice Wollman's

[42] *Poems of To-Day: Fifth Series*, compiled for The English Association by Margaret Willy. Macmillan. pp. xix + 172. 13s. 6d.

[43] *New Poems 1963: A P.E.N. Anthology of Contemporary Poetry*, ed. by Lawrence Durrell. Hutchinson. pp. 160. 21s.

[44] *New Lines—II*, ed. by Robert Conquest. Macmillan. pp. xxix + 136. 21s.

[45] *A Group Anthology*, ed. by Edward Lucie-Smith and Philip Hobsbaum. O.U.P. pp. xv + 127. 21s.

selection for schools[46] belong to no one group or movement, and are of widely varying ages. They are 'contemporary', says Wollman, in the sense that 'they face the forces and values of life today and make poetry from them', posing questions that 'are fundamental to present-day life'. The writers represented are Blackburn, Enright, Graves, Gunn, Hughes, Kavanagh, MacNeice, Scannell, Hal Summers, and R. S. Thomas; and the work of each is prefaced by a brief biographical and critical foreword.

The prevailing mood of Louis MacNeice's last volume[47] is one of disenchantment. His disillusion amounts at times to cynicism (*Greyness is All* or *New Jerusalem*), and he is increasingly preoccupied with the themes of lost childhood, as in the moving *Soap Suds* and *Round the Corner*, and of death: *Charon* is one of the most powerful poems he ever wrote. Yet these, with his precise evocation of place (*October in Bloomsbury* and *Goodbye to London*) and the familiar thumb-nail portraits of people, are all characteristic of his earlier work; and they have combined here to produce one of his maturest and most memorable books.

Christopher Hassall's is also a posthumously published volume,[48] which takes its title from the opening sequence of forty sonnets. These form not only a topographical poem about Canterbury and the surrounding country—Bell Harry is the local name for the central tower of Canterbury Cathedral—but also an elegy in memory of Frances Cornford, and a chapter of spiritual autobiography written in a mood of Wordsworthian reflection. The second half of the

book contains a group of miscellaneous poems in the discursive manner and traditional idiom of Hassall's earlier work.

Another farewell to poetry is taken in James Kirkup's 'Last and First Poems'.[49] His 'refusal to conform' seems a curious reason to offer for bringing his poetic career to a close, for this volume shows no striking evidence of nonconformity nor original departures from familiar ideas and verse techniques. As his publishers observe, Kirkup 'has always written in the main stream of English contemplative, lyrical, and satiric verse'. The book contains some recent unpublished poems and a selection of hitherto unpublished early ones, pictorial pieces about Malaya and Japan, and translations from Baudelaire, Valéry, and other French writers.

A Round of Applause[50] is one of two contributions by Scots to 'The Phoenix Living Poets' series. Norman MacCaig's work abounds in images from his native landscape: of loch, stream, and 'the sound of slapstick water / Perpetually falling downstairs'; startled heron and rising eiderduck, plump, grunting ptarmigan and the buzzard 'riding a crinkle in the air'; herring-baskets and fishing dinghies by the pier where 'A gull slews in with icefloes in his eyes'. These are employed not merely for straightforward visual scene-painting, effective as this is in such poems as *Spraying Sheep* and *Byre*. Far more frequently the poet uses them to convey his metaphysical sense of paradox; and he probes the enigma of existence, in which he sees the contradictions in the mind and experience of man echoed in the natural world, with an arresting

[46] *Ten Contemporary Poets*, ed. by Maurice Wollman. Harrap. pp. 176. 6s. 6d.
[47] *The Burning Perch*, by Louis MacNeice. Faber. pp. 58. 12s. 6d.
[48] *Bell Harry, and Other Poems*, by Christopher Hassall. Longmans. pp. 43. 21s.
[49] *Refusal to Conform: Last and First Poems*, by James Kirkup. O.U.P. pp. xi+121. 25s.
[50] *A Round of Applause*, by Norman MacCaig. Chatto & Windus, 1962, pp. 64. 12s. 6d.

verbal economy and often an ironic wit.

Sydney Tremayne is a contemplative poet of quiet integrity and a fine, fastidious craftsmanship. In his fourth book,[51] which shows a steadily maturing development from, yet unity with, his earlier work, he explores the recurring themes of silence and solitude, separateness and identity in love, and a patient, listening receptivity. He too illumines this inner world with the clarity of a northern light and through images of river, seashore and mountain and the flight of birds; and also through the life of nature observed with a precise and loving eye from the lonely hilltop house where he lives.

John Lehmann's collection[52] contains all he wishes to preserve from his work written over the past thirty-three years. Grouped under seven subject-headings, such as 'Perturbations of War' and 'A Mediterranean Sequence', the poems are presented largely in chronological order. Although the author has omitted a number from his last volume, thirty are included which have not previously appeared in book form, as well as some prose experiments like the war-time *Vigils* published 'in the hope that they will be regarded as equally valid poetic expression'.

Another volume of collected poems which spans a writing career—and covers largely the same period as Lehmann's—*The Doors of Stone*[53] also consists of all that its author cares to retain of his past work. F. T. Prince's *Soldiers Bathing* is considered by many critics to be one of

the finest poems to come out of the Second World War. Few of the others in this collection rise to that level. The interest here lies less in any distinctive style than in the unusualness of the subjects—from the Browningesque monologue *The Old Age of Michelangelo*, and the long poem on the fate of Strafford, to a piece suggested by a song composed by Richard Coeur de Lion in captivity, and another by the verses of the thirteenth-century poet Jean Bodel written in farewell to his friends after he had become a leper.

An older poet whose work has attracted attention in the periodicals, F. Pratt Green in *The Skating Parson*[54] also shows a pleasing freshness and originality in his choice of subject, as well as considerable technical virtuosity. His poems range in mood from the coolly cryptic, ironical wit of *Meteorology*, *Chinese Restaurant*, or *Sonnets for a New Decade* to the deeply experienced compassion of *You Can't Teach the Heart not to Stare* and *Spastics*; from the light-hearted exuberance of the portrait of a Welsh backslider from the chapel, or of *Hurray for the Cliché*, to such serious religious poems as *The Ship* and *My Hour is Not Come*.

Anthony Thwaite is one of the best of our younger poets, and a number of the poems in *The Owl in the Tree*[55] are included in the anthologies already mentioned. His material is that of everyday life. What is so impressive is the way in which this poet's poised assurance of technique disciplines a sensibility perpetually attuned to the pitiable helplessness of the human predicament. Thwaite is never unaware of the imminence not only of

---

[51] *The Swans of Berwick*, by Sydney Tremayne. Chatto & Windus, 1962. pp. 48. 10s. 6d.

[52] *Collected Poems, 1930–1963*, by John Lehmann. Eyre & Spottiswoode. pp. 128. 18s.

[53] *The Doors of Stone*, by F. T. Prince. Hart-Davies. pp. 128. 21s.

[54] *The Skating Parson, and Other Poems*, by F. Pratt Green. Epworth Press. pp. 69. 10s. 6d.

[55] *The Owl in the Tree*, by Anthony Thwaite. O.U.P. pp. 59. 18s.

death, but of all the hovering catastrophes which threaten the vulnerability of the most apparently secure and protected existence.

Jon Stallworthy in his second volume[56] uses largely traditional forms and a deceptive simplicity of tone. He writes much about the intense imaginative experiences of childhood and youth; but there are also many more objective poems—the vividly visual Indian pieces, *Toulouse Lautrec at the Moulin Rouge*, *Galatea*, *Jonathan Swift before his Mirror*, and the two fine poems about Yeats. Stallworthy indeed often sounds a very Yeatsian note, as in, for example, his *Letter to my Sisters*; and he has a gift for striking out the memorable image or phrase ('The blinding signature of God', or such a climactic line as 'And Grendel's shadow growing on the wall').

Also a second book, Patricia Beer's collection[57] confirms the talent recognized by many critics of her first, and consolidates her reputation as a poet with a strongly individual power of utterance. As in the earlier volume there recurs here, in poems like *Vampire*, *Ballad of the Red-Headed Man*, and *The Other Mariners*, that incantatory magic and quality of 'otherness' found in both Coleridge and de la Mare. The controlled compassion of Miss Beer's magnificent poem on the death of a nun places it in the same class as Dylan Thomas's elegy on Ann Jones.

In his fourth collection[58] Michael Hamburger explores different facets of experience by projecting himself into a number of varying situations and 'modes of knowing': those of the Arctic explorer, the bird watcher, the blind man, the old woman, the infant, and—in *Words*—of the poet. This writer's magnanimity and maturity of attitude are illustrated by *In a Cold Season*, his long poem on Eichmann, murderer of millions including the author's own grandmother.

Many of the poems in Charles Tomlinson's 'Peopled Landscape'[59] are inspired by music, sculpture, and the work of other poets. He deals much in the impalpable and the abstract; and the fact that these are too seldom embodied in concrete images or imaginatively transmuted accounts for the over-all impression of dullness and flatness left in his book. This is heightened by metrical eccentricities which make his rhythms too often resemble those of chopped-up prose.

In his third book[60] Peter Redgrove continues to find affinities between the activity of man and that of nature. He is in fact at his vigorous and individual best when writing of the human mood in tune or at war with the elements, in a world of stormy wind, rain, fog, and most of all in that cold weather—'Crisp-flaring turf, stiff marsh, gagged stream, / Paths the skidding ferrule will not prick'— which best suits his private climate of mind.

The recipient, like Redgrove, of an E. C. Gregory Award, Donald Thomas devotes the first section of his book[61] to crisply observed portraits of places, from Madrid, Tangier, and the English cemetery at Florence to the West Riding and the English seaside resort with 'pale Nash terraces' and wrought-iron balconies,

[56] *Out of Bounds*, by Jon Stallworthy. O.U.P. pp. viii+62. 15s.
[57] *The Survivors*, by Patricia Beer. Longmans. pp. 34. 18s.
[58] *Weather and Season*, by Michael Hamburger. Longmans. pp. 64. 18s.

[59] *A Peopled Landscape*, by Charles Tomlinson. O.U.P. pp. 51. 16s.
[60] *At the White Monument*, by Peter Redgrove. Routledge & Kegan Paul. pp. 57. 12s. 6d.
[61] *Points of Contact*, by Donald Thomas. Routledge & Kegan Paul. pp. 65. 12s. 6d.

where 'Death and dissection meditate/ The little knives laid out for tea'. 'Myths', ancient and modern, occupy his second section, and display the same dry, cool accomplishment and clarity of outline.

To those familiar with the charged energy of Ted Hughes's work, his latest collection[62] will seem curiously uncharacteristic. Forsaking his animals of actual experience, he turns in these twenty-three poems to a world of fantastic moon creatures and plants (given bizarre shape in the illustrations by R. A. Brandt). The macabre element is not genuinely sinister; and it is difficult to resist the suspicion that these pieces are really mainly for children, who will undoubtedly enjoy them more than do parents and others who admire Hughes's serious poetry.

4. DRAMA

The dramatic revival of H. H. Anniah Gowda's title[63] is that of the Edwardian and Georgian eras after the decline of English poetic drama during the nineteenth century. Gowda provides fully documented appraisals of the various influences— religious themes, ancient myth and legend, current philosophical ideas, and the techniques of the Japanese Noh drama—on more than a hundred plays of the period. The dramatists range from Bridges, Stephen Phillips, Bottomley, Masefield, Hardy, Flecker, Binyon, and Drinkwater to Yeats and Eliot.

A symposium which contributes substantially to the playgoer's understanding of what is afoot in the modern theatre of ideas, *Experimental Drama*[64] is based on a series of ten University of London extension lectures, with one exception—Katharine J. Worth's essay on 'Avant Garde at the Royal Court Theatre: John Arden and N. F. Simpson'. This and Dr. Worth's other contribution on John Osborne, the two papers by the editor on 'The Playwright and His Theatre, 1945–1962' and on some Irish dramatists, and others—all by distinguished critics—on some postwar experiments in poetic drama, and on the work of Fry, of Robert Bolt and John Whiting, of Pinter, Becket, and Wesker, and on the 'regional realism' of dramatists like Shelagh Delaney, make up a lively and stimulating picture of the contemporary playwright's part in—to quote W. A. Armstrong—'the perennial struggle of the human imagination against religious complacency, moral apathy, and social conformity'.

Bamber Gascoigne's satisfyingly informative survey of international drama in the twentieth century[65]— praised as 'the best introduction to the subject yet written', and reviewed at length in the last volume of *YW*— is now available in a cheaper edition in Hutchinson's University Library.

In his account of Bernard Shaw's work[66] C. B. Purdom aims not only to discuss the dramatist's leading ideas and to give critical judgements on the plays, but also to communicate something of the personal excitement and exhilaration experienced since his first enthusiastic encounter with them at the Court Theatre early in this century. He surveys his subject under three headings—biographical, criti-

---

[62] *The Earth-Owl and Other Moon-People*, by Ted Hughes. Faber. pp. 46. 15s.

[63] *The Revival of English Poetic Drama*, by H. H. Anniah Gowda. The Literary Half-Yearly Publication of the University of Mysore. pp. xvi+322. 45s.

[64] *Experimental Drama*, ed. by William A. Armstrong. Bell. pp. 223. 16s.

[65] *Twentieth-Century Drama*, by Bamber Gascoigne. Hutchinson. pp. 216. 15s.

[66] *A Guide to the Plays of Bernard Shaw*, by C. B. Purdom. Methuen. pp. 344. 35s.

cal, and scene-by-scene description of the plays and their characters from *Widowers' Houses* to *Buoyant Billions*. His guide is especially useful for its notes on the original productions—mostly performed under Shaw's own direction—and its hints to future producers.

Twelve of Yeats's later plays are considered by Helen Hennessey Vendler,[67] who relates their language and symbolism to that of the poet's strange and original prose work, *A Vision*, whose substance he claimed to have received from supernatural sources. Mrs. Vendler does not regard either this book, congested with psychic phenomena, or the author's plays, as of equal importance with the lyric poetry: 'not even the most admiring critic,' she affirms, 'could swallow *A Vision* whole'. She does nevertheless feel that both deserve a better hearing than they have had, and that some knowledge of the 'mystic geometry'—Yeats's own phrase— of *A Vision* is essential to an understanding of the last plays. The first half of her book examines in detail Yeats's elaborate 'system' for representing human experience, both personal and historical, and lays especial emphasis on its symbolic statements about aesthetics and the nature of the creative process. Each of the selected plays is then discussed in the light of her interpretation of *A Vision*. Mrs. Vendler is a highly intelligent and discriminating critic, whose treatment of a difficult but key work succeeds in genuinely elucidating its mysteries.

Yeats's views on the future of English poetic drama are examined, with copious quotation of passages on the subject from his essays and auto-biographies, in an article by Vinod Sena.[68]

The debt owed by Yeats to Synge, his collaborator in the heyday of the Abbey Theatre and one of the foremost figures of the Irish literary renaissance, is outlined in an appendix to T. R. Henn's edition of all Synge's plays and published poems.[69] After a general introduction on the dramatist and the language and rhythm of his plays, Henn deals with each, and with the poems and translations, in a short separate essay. These admirably fill in the background of local meanings, people, and places which, as a compatriot familiar with the Synge country, Henn is well equipped to provide; and there are very full textual notes and a useful bibliography.

According to Carol H. Smith, in her discussion of the principles underlying Eliot's plays,[70] his dramatic theory and practice are rooted in his concept of the need for order in art as in religion. Surveying the plays from *Sweeney Agonistes* to *The Elder Statesman*, she perceives a clear connexion between the poet's religious perspective—a movement away from 'despair at the disorder of the natural world to his acceptance of a supernatural order which gives meaning and unity to the world's apparent chaos'—and his views on art and drama. Eliot's endorsement of classicism is seen as 'an effort to require of art a form which could order experience, just as a religious interpretation of existence could order the world of nature. In fact, art's function

[67] *Yeats's 'Vision' and the Later Plays*, by Helen Hennessey Vendler. O.U.P. and Harvard U.P. pp. 260. 35*s*.

[68] In *An English Miscellany*, edited by Rajiva Verma and Yashoda N. Singh. St. Stephen's College, Delhi. pp. 79. *Rs*. 1.

[69] *The Plays and Poems of J. M. Synge*, ed. by T. R. Henn. Methuen. pp. xi+363. 42*s*.

[70] *T. S. Eliot's Dramatic Theory and Practice*, by Carol H. Smith. Princeton U.P. pp. ix+251. $5.50.

became for Eliot the microcosmic reflection of divine order.'

Hans Itschert's monograph on Christopher Fry[71] concentrates on a detailed analysis of the three religious festival plays—*The Boy with a Cart*, *Thor with Angels*, and *A Sleep of Prisoners*—in order to discover what common features these share, and to demonstrate their effectiveness as works for the stage rather than to examine their imagery or message.

John Osborne's impulse to shock his audiences into attention is nowhere plainer than in his two *Plays for England*,[72] produced at the Royal Court Theatre in 1962. *The Blood of the Bambergs* is not only a satire on a royal wedding, but mocks the whole mystique of monarchy; while *Under Plain Cover* was declared by one leading critic to have 'for the first time [brought] Genet into England'.

5. GENERAL

Few writers could be better qualified to examine the relationship between modern life and art than a poet of Stephen Spender's generation, experience, and intense awareness of the challenge of contemporary history. In his exploration of this theme[73] he is mainly concerned to trace the ways in which the creative artist since the Industrial Revolution has reacted to the pressures of his world, and attempted to come to terms with a rapidly and radically changing environment. He shows writers like Gerard Manley Hopkins, D. H. Lawrence, and Virginia Woolf confronting the past with the present—which

he conceives to be the fundamental aim of modernism—through forms, idioms, and sensibilities which are essentially the product of their own time. Among the other aspects of a complex situation which he probes so perceptively in this thought-provoking study are the much-discussed 'two cultures' of poetry and science, and our present impoverishment by 'the application of the prose principle to poetry'; the growing intrusion, over the past two decades, of the critical intellect upon the creative imagination.

John Wain's volume of literary criticism[74] is his first since *Preliminary Essays* won the Somerset Maugham Award in 1958. Not all his subjects are modern ones, but the latter provide the material for some of his most stimulating and provocative reflections. He writes on Hopkins, a poet 'unaccountably born out of his time', on four contemporary critics (Eliot, Edmund Wilson, R. P. Blackmur and Cyril Connolly), on Betjeman (the vogue for whose work he regards as 'merely one more sign that the mass middle-brow public distrusts and fears poetry'), and on Orwell. The longest and most interesting piece is a consideration of 'The Conflict of Forms in Contemporary English Literature'. Readers may quarrel with Wain, but few will be able to deny the astringent liveliness of his vigorous, inquiring mind.

In his study of existentialism in modern literature[75] the Professor of English at Washington State University considers the sense of disturbance and crisis in the novels and plays of a number of writers—Ibsen, Kafka, Eliot, Arthur Miller, James

[71] *Studien zur Dramaturgie des 'Religious Festival Play' bei Christopher Fry*, by Hans Itschert. Tübingen: Max Niemeyer. pp. 254. DM. 32.

[72] *Plays for England*, by John Osborne. Faber. pp. 136. 12s. 6d.

[73] *The Struggle of the Modern*, by Stephen Spender. Hamish Hamilton. pp. xiii+266. 25s.

[74] *Essays on Literature and Ideas*, by John Wain. Macmillan. pp. xi+270. 30s.

[75] *Existentialism and Modern Literature*, by Davis Dunbar McElroy. Philosophical Library, New York. pp. xi+58. $3.75.

T. Farrell, and William Faulkner—and their views on the place of man in the modern world.

Graham Hough's investigation of the function of literature in our present intellectual economy[76] consists of six Third Programme talks given during 1962 and 1963. Drawing on a quarter of a century's experience of lecturing on English in universities, he writes less from the standpoint of the author in society than that of the reader, critic, and teacher. The authority of organized religion has, he believes, been largely replaced for much of the population by philosophies and patterns of conduct supplied by such works as *Lady Chatterley's Lover*, *The Catcher in the Rye*, and *Look Back in Anger*; and there has been a general tendency to look to literature as a monitor and a guide to the solution of moral problems. Affirming that 'the work of imaginative literature is a thing in itself, worth having for its own sake, and that its value as a social or moral force outside itself is only incidental', Hough likewise rejects that 'moral censor' which 'restricts the range of our imaginative experience and . . . narrows and frustrates the free range of literary curiosity and appreciation'. For him the true function of criticism should be to clarify for each new intellectual generation of readers its own relation to the great works of the past; and he feels that 'to keep going the lively current of ideas, the fruitful and enjoyable meeting of minds', is one of the marks of a civilized society. In his chapter 'A Programme for Literary Education' he pleads for a radical revision of our system of higher education which would enable a broadening of the range of reading among young people.

The cogency of Hough's arguments and the crispness of their expression make this a most stimulating and salutary study.

Another vigorously individual educationist, Sir Herbert Read is represented in this role by three recent essays in the anthology of his work[77]—some of it hitherto unpublished—which has been assembled to commemorate his seventieth birthday. Two opening sections of verse, containing a generous selection of shorter lyrics and the dramatic dialogue, *Moon's Farm*, in its entirety, are followed by fifteen very characteristic essays. These not only display the full range of Sir Herbert's activity as literary and art critic and social philosopher, but clearly demonstrate what Allen Tate in his introduction calls his 'synthesis of romantic intuition and intellectual order'.

In his 'dual portrait' of Lawrence of Arabia and his senior, even more famous namesake, George Bernard Shaw,[78] Stanley Weintraub shows how their friendship was based on mutual respect and admiration; and how in some ways the younger Shaw was regarded by the elder in the relation of a son. They were introduced by Sydney Cockerell in 1922, and their association lasted until the younger man's untimely death on the motor-cycle which, ironically, the Shaws had provided. Weintraub traces their interlinking story through the dozen-odd years of its duration, with quotations from many unpublished manuscripts, documents, and letters.

The annual Presidential Address of

[76] *The Dream and the Task: Literature and Morals in the Culture of Today*, by Graham Hough. Duckworth. pp. 103 15s.

[77] *Selected Writings: Poetry and Criticism*, by Herbert Read. With a Foreword by Allen Tate. Faber. pp. 406. 42s.

[78] *Private Shaw and Public Shaw: A Dual Portrait of Lawrence of Arabia and George Bernard Shaw*, by Stanley Weintraub. Cape. pp. xvi+302. 30s.

the English Association[79] provided the lecturer with an opportunity for a retrospective glance at an era which was, he affirms, 'something more than a Victorian tail-piece'. After sketching in the social and political background, Sir Sydney proceeds to the poets (his choice of a representative Edwardian is Walter de la Mare), the theatre (Shaw, Granville-Barker, and Galsworthy), the novels of Wells and Bennett, and Chesterton's *The Napoleon of Notting Hill*. But 'if one were seeking for a single guide to the Edwardian era', he feels, 'it would be difficult to find anyone half so comprehensive or half so arresting as Max'.

A figure equally representative of the Georgians is the subject of Patrick Howarth's biography.[80] As the creator of *The London Mercury* J. C. Squire was at the centre of literary London in the 20's, and a generous friend to many now established writers who were his protégés in their struggling youth. As Howarth justly observes, it was as an editor that Squire's 'outstanding contribution to English literature was made'. His biographer's claim that 'the years from 1910 to 1925 produced one of the greatest flowerings of the English lyric in history' may strike many readers as excessive. Few, however, will fail to appreciate the justness of Howarth's appraisal of Squire's many-sided personality—not only as editor, but as brilliant parodist, captain of the comic literary cricket team (the Invalids) satirized by A. G. Macdonell in *England their England*, and as the one largely influential in saving Stonehenge from the vandals. This man's unfulfilled potentialities and the tragic deterioration of his last years, when he fell victim to bankruptcy, alcoholism, and loneliness, are delineated with candour and compassion.

In her critical biography of Flora Annie Steel,[81] Daya Patwardhan classes her subject with Kipling as one of the two greatest Anglo-Indian writers. After a detailed consideration of Mrs. Steel's life and personality, and of her novels and short stories set in the period between 1867 and 1929, her biographer compares her work and attitude towards India and its people with those of Kipling and Forster. Mrs. Patwardhan sees Mrs. Steel as an embodiment of the liberal Victorian spirit, but concludes that the value of her work is ultimately greater on historical than on literary grounds.

ARTICLES

1. GENERAL

In 'A Question of Tone' (*CQ*) Richard Hoggart discusses some of the problems in autobiographical writing which arise from the writer's sense of audience, and puts forward claims of a sociological nature. Since there are few formal rules for this type of literature, most autobiographers today habitually make use of conventional but artificial styles (exemplified under such designations as 'the poeticized-shimmer', the engagingly-unbuttoned, false gentility, and vicarious toughness) in order to produce what has become widely acceptable to an undiscriminating

[79] *Edwardian Retrospect*, by Sir Sydney Roberts. O.U.P. (for the English Association) pp. 16. 5s.

[80] *Squire: Most Generous of Men*, by Patrick Howarth. Hutchinson. pp. 308. 35s.

[81] *A Star of India* (*Flora Annie Steel, Her Works and Times*), by Daya Patwardhan. With a Foreword by V. de S. Pinto. Poona: A. V. Griha Prakashan. pp. iv+219. Rs. 16.

audience. The danger of paying too much attention to such a public is intensified where there is an assumed social gap between the readers and the autobiographical material. So much is this the case that writers who originate from the working classes find it difficult to avoid dropping 'into harshness or sentimentality', and, in the absence of more appropriate models, tend to fall back upon the traditional tones and manners of other social groups. The objection to these literary devices is that 'life is being seen through a retrospective haze'. Whilst serious autobiographers should certainly aim at a distinctive style which will fully express their own personalities, it should at the same time be incumbent on them to adopt some formal discipline more conducive to 'great honesty and greater patience'.

More concerned with ideas than styles in 'Tragic Resignation and Sacrifice' (*CQ*), Raymond Williams observes that, although the 'rhythm of sacrifice' still retains a hold at the centre of Christian belief, for Western civilization as a whole it has lost significance in its original form, in which a man is killed so that others may live. Heroes today are to be regarded, not as martyrs, but as victims or scapegoats; and their tragic deaths, far from resulting in a general renewal of life, merely accentuate the communal burden of guilt. Unlike most modern tragedy, however, *Murder in the Cathedral*, *The Cocktail Party*, and *Doctor Zhivago* all appear to be based to some extent on the early conception of sacrifice, and though the precise nature of the sacrifice may be dependent upon the particular context, the three central characters are presented as martyrs rather than victims. Yet if the sacrifice in *Murder in the Cathedral* is both a redemption and a conversion, that in *The Cock-*

tail Party can only be described as a tragic resignation, since it does nothing to redeem the world in which it takes place, but serves to ratify the world as it is. *Doctor Zhivago*, on the other hand, fuses the Christian idea of redemption with the Marxist view of history.

Citing *The Cocktail Party* to illustrate an altogether different point in 'The Passing of Puritanism' (*CQ*), John Wren-Lewis contends that the Romantic and Puritan tradition of world-denial and the Classical and Catholic tradition of world affirmation are but two sides of the same coin, and that both traditions are, in fact, other-worldly and escapist. The former, often presented in terms of entertainment to find expression today, seeks to uphold personal values by pronouncing the external world corrupt; whilst the latter, postulating the idea of a transcendent Power which has ordained the natural order, insists that human values be adapted to that order. Yet religion originated in the recognition of value in personal life. Our greatest need, therefore, is a new kind of affirmation of the basic religious impulse, 'which refuses to accept the conflict between personal values and organic life . . . and sets out to resolve it by changing the workings of nature so as to make the physical world subserve personal values instead of overriding them'.

In 'Art, Entertainment and Religion' (*QQ*), Louis Dudek looks at the problem from another angle. Believing Puritanism to be the natural expression of Christianity in its extreme form, he arraigns our religious tradition for the separation of art and entertainment so peculiar to Western culture. As Christianity has always been antipathetic to art based on enjoyment, it is responsible for the divison between serious art and superficial entertainment. For though

x

it is true that in the twentieth century we have virtually abandoned the Christian ethic, in doing so we have rejected most of the values for which it stood, and our entertainments are largely devoted to the commercial exploitation of pleasure. As a return to the old exclusive morality is no longer possible for us, we must find a 'new aesthetic of life' by which to establish 'some kind of new relationship between the demands of pleasure and the serious convictions of man'. Until we have reached a total acceptance of life and death, and all that they imply, we shall not have the art and religion we need, exhibited in a 'union of the artistic and the entertaining'.

2. THE NOVEL

The extent to which Joseph Conrad made use of material from his own personal experience in his writing has been the subject of critical discussion for some time. In 'Conrad and the S.S. *Vidar*' (*RES*) Norman Sherry examines some of the facts relevant to the period during which Conrad served as first mate in the S.S. *Vidar* (August 1887 to January 1888) and arrives at the conclusion that not only did Conrad draw heavily upon personal experience and observation in his Malayan novels, but that, except when the material was designed to have dramatic or symbolic significance, his characteristic method was to present factual details from his own past without disguise or alteration.

Carlisle Moore, on the other hand, concentrates upon the experience of Conrad the writer rather than Conrad the seafarer in 'Conrad and the Novel as Ordeal' (*PQ*). Asking why Conrad placed his heroes in 'bewildering and frustrating predicaments' and watched how they reacted to the strain, Moore endeavours to answer his question by showing that

Conrad's preoccupation with the ordeals of his characters was due, not to a guilt-complex arising from his 'desertion' of Poland, nor his experiences at sea, but to his painful struggle for success as a writer. For his novels are much more important as studies of moral and psychological behaviour than as adventure stories of the sea. His accounts of moral failure and success and his studies of man under psychological stress can profitably be regarded as 'emblematic re-enactments of his own harrowing problems as a writer in England'.

In 'Conrad's *Karain* and *Lord Jim*' (*MLQ*) Bruce M. Johnson maintains that Conrad's story, *Karain, a Memory*, begun in 1897 and published in *Tales of Unrest*, cleared some of the intellectual and emotional ground for *Lord Jim*. Resemblances, both in motif and characterization, can be discerned between the short story and the later novel, but perhaps the most significant of the affinities between the protagonists is the way in which they contribute in each case to the main theme of illusion.

Similarly, in '*The Nigger of the Narcissus* and the MS. Version of *The Rescue*' (*ES*), René Kerf points to resemblances in nautical setting, imagery, and characterization between the two volumes to which his title refers. Although *The Rescue* did not appear until twenty-two years after the publication of *The Nigger of the Narcissus* (1898), the first three parts were actually written between 1896 and 1899, so that, to some extent, the earlier publication drew upon the original text of the other.

Although Ford Madox Ford was obviously dedicated to the craft of letters, and derived enormous benefit from his friendship and collaboration with such a serious novelist as Conrad, he produced little of real value until he reached middle-age; and, as

A. G. Hill observes, in 'The Literary Career of Ford Madox Ford' (*CQ*), if he was late in reaching the height of his powers, he did not remain there for long. In the belief that the sudden maturing of Ford's vision just before and immediately after the First World War can be explained only by reference to his personal history, Hill relates what can still be ascertained about Ford's private and public life to his novels, laying particular stress upon the effects of his liaison with Violet Hunt and his experience during and after the war. The outcome was a new attitude towards the moral dilemmas facing 'the man of honour in the modern world'. The Fifth Queen trilogy. *The Good Soldier*, three of the Tietjens novels, and a few poems together provide sufficient evidence of an achievement which will stand the test of time as well as anything else in the twentieth century.

In '*Parade's End;* Where War Was Fairy Tale' (*TSLL*) Ambrose Gordon states that, though Ford was a dedicated modern realist, in his best work he often explored a 'fairy-tale' aspect of experience, and that without this element his realism would have been impoverished. Ford had to find his reality by way of fantasy. According to Gordon, this is particularly true of *Parade's End*, and such experimental books as *The Half Moon*, *Ladies Whose Bright Eyes*, and *The Brown Owl* served to prepare the ground. Though describing life in the trenches in *Parade's End*, Ford 'treated the trenches as though they were fairyland; and, strangely, they came alive and stayed alive'.

The work of D. H. Lawrence continues to engage the attention of critics and scholars, and ingenious theories are still being formulated to account for both the man and his novels. Edward Engelberg, for instance, in 'Escape from the Circles of Ex-perience: D. H. Lawrence's *The Rainbow* as a Modern *Bildungsroman*' (*PMLA*) posits the view that, although *Sons and Lovers*, *The Rainbow* and *Women in Love* can all be regarded as variations of *Bildungsroman*, only in *The Rainbow* was Lawrence completely successful in preserving the balance between conflicting elements so vital to this genre. At the same time, by delineating what the 'relation of the hero to his experience had become in the twentieth century', he was able to demonstrate the possibilities of the *Bildungsroman* for the present age.

In 'Lawrence's Sacred Fount: The Artist Theme of *Sons and Lovers*' (*TSLL*) Maurice Beebe places Lawrence within the 'Sacred Fount' tradition, adhering to the theory that the artist 'must experience life in order to depict it', yet exhibiting in *Sons and Lovers* an unconscious leaning towards the Ivory Tower concept of the artist as an exile from life. The tension set up by these contrasting attitudes is held to be responsible for the richness and ambiguity of the novel; for the protagonist, Paul Morel, is clearly portrayed as an artist by temperament and ability. So that the gradual development of the minor but unifying theme of the liberating power of artistic creativity serves to resolve the conflict and overcome the stalemate between the two major themes dealing with the Oedipus complex and Paul's relationships with Miriam and Clara. Having first lived through the experience, Lawrence transmuted it into art in *Sons and Lovers* and, in doing so, freed himself for the new experience recorded in *The Rainbow*.

In 'Pussum, Minette, and the Africo-Nordic Symbol in Lawrence's *Women in Love*' (*PMLA*), Robert L. Chamberlain lays emphasis upon the symbolic nature of the metaphor of destruction which appears to dominate the novel in question. The innumerable allusions to matters normally confined to an Arctic or African setting, the extensive use of the double-sided image of 'disintegration by heat' and 'annihilation by cold' throughout the volume, and the famous dissertation on death by heat and cold (following Birkin's efforts to destroy the moon's reflection) can all be seen as an attempt to convey in metaphorical language the author's deepest insights, and combine to make *Women in Love* itself a constitutive symbol.

Taking as his starting-point Catherine Carswell's remark that Lawrence might have been a new kind of Dickens of the Midlands if he had so wished, Leo Gurko advances the claim, in '*The Lost Girl*: D. H. Lawrence as a "Dickens of the Midlands"' (*PMLA*), that Lawrence had a curiously well-developed flair for satire, and that his capacity for Dickensian comedy reaches its highest level in *The Lost Girl*. His aptitude for caricature provided the novel with such comic types as Mr. May, the vaudeville impresario who would not have been out of place in *Pickwick Papers*, and his narrative energy supplied the necessary impetus to carry it from one level of experience to another. This Dickensian quality gives *The Lost Girl* a special flavour, despite its structural defects.

The motivating impulse behind Lawrence's *Studies in Classic American Literature* is shrewdly analysed by Douglas Grant in 'Hands up, America!' (*REL*). Grant compares the original essays, as printed in the *English Review* and the *Nation and Athenaeum*, with the drastically revised versions included in the volume; and insists that, whatever object Lawrence may have had in writing the original essays, the *Studies* make it clear that he was, in fact, boldly and

yet coherently 'appropriating' American literature in order to reinforce the personal argument so vital to *Women in Love* and his later novels.

Taking umbrage at Harry T. Moore's introduction to *The Collected Letters of D. H. Lawrence*, F. R. Leavis comments, in 'Lawrence Scholarship and Lawrence' (*Sew*), on what he considers to be basic misconceptions of the editorial function on the part of Lawrence scholars, and complains about the multiplication of 'authorities' as a result of the growth of industrial literary scholarship. Leavis finds especially offensive the tendency of such 'authorities' to accumulate impertinences, 'anti-critical identifications of *personae* and fictive episodes with actual persons and collected facts'.

In 'D. H. Lawrence's War Letters' (*TSLL*) George Panichas refutes the opinions of Graham Hough and Eliseo Vivas on the subject of Lawrence's reaction to the First World War, and asserts that the letters Lawrence wrote during the war were, to him, just as valid and self-revealing a communication of experience as the war memoirs of Sassoon, Blunden, and Graves. Not only do these letters exhibit the total range of Lawrence's response to war, and his contempt for the military spirit, but they show equally clearly the difficulties he had to overcome as a creative artist at an important phase of his development.

In the February (1960) issue of *MP* James R. Thrane published proof of his discovery that the retreat sermons on hell in Joyce's *A Portrait of the Artist as a Young Man* were derived from *Hell Opened to Christians, to Caution Them from Entering into It*, the English translation of a seventeenth-century meditation book by Giovanni Pietro Pinamonti. Under the impression that the 1868 edition of

Hell Opened was the last Victorian printing, however, Thrane assumed this to be the volume utilized by Joyce. James Doherty, in 'Joyce and *Hell Opened to Christians*: The Edition he used for his "Hell Sermons"' (*MP*), points out that there were later editions of the translation and, by a scholarly comparison of the textual variations, establishes that Joyce used the revised edition published in 1889.

H. A. Kelly briefly considers the nature of stream of consciousness writing in 'Consciousness in the Monologues of *Ulysses*' (*MLQ*), and defines it as the endeavour 'to record the thoughts of a character directly, just as they appear in the mind, without narration, description or editing'. Giving Dujardin full credit for producing the first systematic attempt at this kind of writing, and for providing the most competent analysis of the technique involved, Kelly argues that Dujardin's definition, though acceptable in general outline, nevertheless confuses unedited thought with thought that is merely peripheral, and this has given rise to erroneous conceptions of the method. For, obviously, only one element of thought can be recorded at a time, and that element must of necessity be at the centre of attention. Applying various tests, Kelly finds that the works of Henry James, Dorothy Richardson, and Virginia Woolf cannot properly be termed stream-of-consciousness writing because consciousness in these works is described by means of third-person narrative. Similarly, the works of Proust and Faulkner should be excluded from the category since in these cases consciousness is described in first-person narrative, and not recorded directly. Only in *Ulysses* has the method been completely successful.

In 'Dorothy M. Richardson: The Personal "Pilgrimage"' (*PMLA*) Gloria Glikin does not make quite the same distinctions, though she does remark that not until the sixth volume of the *Pilgrimage* sequence, *Deadlock*, did Dorothy Richardson make use of the *direct* internal monologue in order to convey the processes of her mind. Having had access to private documents of Dorothy Richardson, she reveals biographical details previously unknown, and maintains that, since *Pilgrimage* was, in fact, a portrayal of the author's world, it should be examined in the context of her life. Not only did Dorothy Richardson portray herself in the person of the heroine, but also depicted other people from her circle. Gloria Glikin draws comparisons between the aims of Proust, Joyce, and Dorothy Richardson, and holds that 'in dimension *Pilgrimage* has its place beside *À la Recherche du temps perdu* and *Ulysses*'.

Treating *A Passage to India* as a symbolic novel, V. A. Shahane discusses, in 'Symbolism in E. M. Forster's *A Passage to India*' (*ES*), what he considers to be the three divergent currents which, with symbolic and dramatic effect, converge on the central stream to give the novel its organic unity.

Roger L. Chubb, in '*A Passage to India*: The Meaning of the Marabar Caves' (*CLA*), concentrates on the significance of but one of the central symbols, the Marabar Caves, and relates his interpretation to the mental experiences of Mrs. Moore and Adela Quested during and after their visit to the Marabar. The caves represent something which is, in fact, beyond the power of human understanding—the mystery 'behind the existence of conscious spirit in the universe'.

Although Aldous Huxley has disclaimed any deep understanding of musical genius, there can be little doubt that music makes an important contribution to his writing, according to Carlyle King in 'Aldous Huxley and Music' (*QQ*). King discusses Huxley's work, from *Point Counter Point* to *Island*, at some length in search of evidence to support this thesis, and demonstrates by appropriate quotations that Huxley drew upon music for symbols and metaphor, and on several occasions introduced a musical element into his characterization and plot-structure.

In 'Aldous Huxley's *Island*' (*QQ*) D. H. Stewart looks at *Island* from a social rather than a literary standpoint and suggests that, though based on concepts similar to those informing *Brave New World* and *1984*, it goes a good deal further than either of these volumes by exploring the possibilities of a solution to human problems arising out of a combination of modern techniques and primitive virtues. In this sense *Island* can be described as a 'Third Way' book, since it attempts to bridge the gap between East and West, between humanism and science, and between the opposing ideologies of individualism and collectivity.

As a gesture of respect to John Cowper Powys in his ninety-first year, the January issue of *REL* is devoted largely to a consideration of his achievement. In '"Mythology" in John Cowper Powys's Novels' Angus Wilson complains that, though Powys will probably stand with Lawrence and Joyce in the eyes of posterity, his work has never been given the critical attention it deserves. To prepare the way for the scholarly analysis involved in such a task, Wilson concentrates upon the central metaphysic of Powys's greater novels as revealed by an examination of *Wolf Solent* and *Porius*. More appreciative than critical in his approach to the subject in 'The Immortal Bard',

Henry Miller declares Powys's *Autobiography* to be 'the greatest, the most magnificent, of all autobiographies', and *A Glastonbury Romance* to be unique in the whole of English literature. In 'The Happy Introvert' J. B. Priestley refers to Jung's *Psychological Types* and, on the strength of the *Autobiography*, places Powys among the Introverted Sensation Types who 'bring sensations of the outer world into the magical depths of their inner world'. Stressing the fact that Powys comes from the same stock as Cowper and Donne, Dominique Aury, in 'Reading Powys' (translated by Margaret Davies), insists that, although Powys has written few poems, his work is fundamentally poetic. In 'John Cowper Powys: Letter Writer' Iorwerth C. Peate is concerned with Powys's abilities and idiosyncrasies as a correspondent over a period of many years, and remarks that each of the letters has the 'mysterious power of evoking a personal presence and an intimate conversation'. Peate reproduces a letter written in November 1947, which demonstrates Powys's 'Renaissance disregard' for punctilios of fold and spacing. G. Wilson Knight contributes a detailed study of Powys's *Owen Glendower* as a work of art in which a scrupulous regard for historical exactitude is combined with a profound metaphysic, and praises the way in which Powys integrates natural descriptions into the multifarious convolutions of the story. J. C. Powys, maintains Wilson Knight, is 'the greatest master of natural description' in English literature. In 'The Second Brother: A Note on T. F. Powys' Kenneth Hopkins traces the rather different career of the second of the three famous Powys brothers, and compares his achievement with that of both John Cowper Powys and Llewelyn Powys. Though Theodore Francis Powys displays affinities with Bunyan and the Bible, and parallels can be found in Saki for some of his turns of phrase and thought, the unique contribution to his work comes only from himself. Hopkins considers his *Mr. Weston* to be virtually without flaw, and places *Unclay* at the same level. To complete the picture of the Powys brothers, R. C. Churchill discusses the work of Llewelyn Powys in 'Not Least Llewelyn'. Churchill suggests that if, as a novelist, Llewelyn Powys lacked John's rich imagination and Theodore's talent for allegory, his philosophy was logically and realistically superior to that of either of his brothers, and that, as a writer on the English countryside, he is by no means the 'least of the Powyses.'

In 'Evelyn Waugh's Gentlemen' (*CQ*) Bernard Bergonzi takes for his starting-point the generally accepted view of Waugh's fiction as the expression of a personal myth, in which the aristocracy (and Catholic aristocracy in particular) are presented as the custodians of traditional values in a world increasingly threatened by the barbarians, and, whilst accepting this view of the earlier work with some reservations himself, argues that the three novels making up the Crouchback trilogy must completely change our conception of 'Waugh's fictional development'. With the publication of *Unconditional Surrender* and the completion of the trilogy, the 'romantic and aristocratic myth' which has previously dominated Waugh's work is 'totally transformed'. To lend weight to his argument Bergonzi examines Waugh's serious novels in the 'new perspective' provided by the Crouchback trilogy.

Charles G. Hoffman has made excellent use of the James Osborn Collection of Joyce Cary Manuscripts deposited in the Bodleian Library. In 'The Genesis and Development of Joyce Cary's First Trilogy' (*PMLA*) Hoffman reports on his study of the Cary manuscripts, notebooks, and worksheets, and quotes evidence to show that the Gully Jimson trilogy, though the first trilogy Cary published, was neither an accidental discovery of the multiple novel, nor a sudden change of method, but the result of a logical development of Cary's ideas and techniques. It represented a further exploration of Cary's belief that 'all reality is inter-related, but that the individual has only a partial view of reality'. From the various material made available to him by the James Osborn Collection, Hoffman attempts to reconstruct the order in which the first trilogy originated.

Continuing his researches in '*The Captive and the Free*: Joyce Cary's Unfinished Trilogy' (*TSLL*), Hoffman reports that, although only two apparently unconnected novels (*The Moonlight* and *A Fearful Joy*) were published during the eight years which elapsed between the completion of the Gully Jimson trilogy and the commencement of the Chester Nimmo trilogy, an examination of the Cary manuscripts in the Osborn Collection reveals that Cary attempted to write another trilogy which remained unfinished. Two separate versions of this projected work exist and the separate novels were to have been entitled *The Captive and the Free* (not to be confused with the posthumous novel with that title), *Easy Money*, and *Bow Down to Heaven*. Hoffman discusses the relevant material and demonstrates that not only were *The Moonlight* and *A Fearful Joy* related to each other in the author's intention, but that some of the unfinished material was actually used by Cary in the construction of the Chester Nimmo trilogy.

Graham Greene attached to *The*

Heart of the Matter a quotation from Péguy: 'The sinner is at the heart of Christianity . . . No one is as competent as the sinner in matters of Christianity. No one, unless it is the saint.' With this quotation firmly in mind, Robert A. Wichert, in 'The Quality of Graham Greene's Mercy' (*CE*), examines the early novel, *The Power and the Glory*, and the curious travel book, *The Lawless Roads*, in the light of Péguy's attitudes in order to show that in the whole matter of pity and mercy, salvation and sanctity, Greene has close affinities with Péguy. Wichert holds that both authors try to bring 'God's mercy towards man right down almost into the depths of Hell and to lift man's love for God right up into the topmost circle of Heaven'.

Answering the critical comments of James Noxon and John Atkins in his 'The Suspension of Disbelief: Greene's *Burnt-Out Case*' (*DR*), D. J. Dooley considers *A Burnt-Out Case* in relation to the notions of such modern existentialists as Sartre and Camus to define and clarify Greene's religious and aesthetic views.

In 'Graham Greene' (*CQ*) Laurence Lerner sets himself the task of convincing readers that, in addition to being a skilful craftsman, Greene is a writer of vision, and despite Greene's Catholicism, finds a similarity of viewpoint between Greene and the pessimistic type of humanist who visualizes the world as a place of intrinsic evil. Greene depicts the world as Hell, since this is the first step of the argument to faith, along the path from humanism, through disillusion, to belief. Lerner provides an interesting analysis of Greene's novels by dividing his characters into four main groups: the pious, the sinners, the innocents, and the humanists.

Herbert Howarth, commenting upon Lawrence Durrell's feeling for Greece and his antipathy towards Egypt in 'A Segment of Durrell's Quartet' (*UTQ*), endeavours to reconstruct the 'interplay of certain intentions' underlying the Alexandrian Quartet. Howarth suggests that, despite his antipathy to and lack of knowledge of the Egypt of the villages and country estates, Durrell succeeded in bringing the real Egypt to life in English literature for the first time simply by 'lifting his material'; and he provides a fascinating account, complete with quotations for comparison, of the way in which Durrell appropriated and transformed to his own purposes passages from E. W. Lane's 125-year-old *Manners and Customs of Modern Egyptians* and J. W. McPherson's *The Moulids of Egypt*. Beginning to write of Egypt destructively, Durrell transcended his original plan and 'accepted his role as creator'.

In '*Lord of the Flies*: Beelzebub Revisited' (*CE*) Bern Oldsey and Stanley Weintraub point out that if Golding's *Lord of the Flies* is to be described as 'derivative', as some critics have insisted, it is only so in the sense that it falls within the main stream of several English literary traditions, as does *Gulliver's Travels*, Swift's version 'of the primeval savagery and greed which civilization only masks in modern man'. But although Oldsey and Weintraub comment upon the narrative and shrewdly analyse the principal characters, they make no effort to draw explicit parallels, beyond remarking on Golding's Swiftian obsession with physical ugliness and meanness, etc.

David Lodge, in 'The Modern, the Contemporary, and the Importance of Being Amis' (*CQ*), considers the novels of Kingsley Amis in the light of Spender's distinction between 'moderns' and 'contemporaries'.

Lodge finds that, although Amis may have imposed restrictive limits upon his writing by his rejection of the modern mode, his awareness of his limitations, his sardonic sense of literary tradition, and his characteristic use of language, combine to make him 'particularly important'.

In the belief that over the last twenty years Samuel Beckett has applied himself to the task of finding a form that will accommodate the 'mess' of human experience, David H. Hesla, in 'The Shape of Chaos: a Reading of Beckett's *Watt*' (*C*) examines *Watt*, which he regards as the first of Beckett's experiments in a new form. Hesla expresses the opinion that Beckett found the form he needed whilst writing this volume, and that his subsequent work has largely been a refinement and adaptation of this new manner and matter.

3. THE SHORT STORY

John Howard Wills considers *Youth* to be the most seriously underestimated of all Conrad's shorter works, and in 'A Neglected Masterpiece: Conrad's *Youth*' (*TSLL*) he essays a brief assessment of the story, which he claims to be 'an abiding vision of modern man' as well as a perfect blending of form and substance.

In 'Saki's Ironic Stories' (*TSLL*) Robert Drake discusses the stories of Saki which can be said to be dependent upon irony rather than humour, and observes that the irony usually consists in the way the main characters bring about their own downfall by scorning as 'unreal' some aspect of total reality.

Ann Englander points out, in '*The Prussian Officer:* The Self Divided' (*Sew*), that although Lawrence's *The Prussian Officer* has been highly praised, critics have been unable to

agree about the meaning or the subject. She maintains that the confusion in the story is due to the fact that there is an 'unbridgeable gap' between the abstract theory and the concrete struggle, between the general and the particular.

Remarking that Liam O'Flaherty's collections of short stories contain some of his finest work, George Brandon Saul, in 'A Wild Sowing: The Short Stories of Liam O'Flaherty' (*REL*), provides a brief account of the pieces in *Spring Sowing*, *The Tent*, *The Mountain Tavern and Other Stories*, and *Two Lovely Beasts and Other Stories*.

4. POETRY

In 'The Nature and Meaning of Poetry: an English Approach' (*AP*), Howard Sergeant considers poetry as a pattern of experience revealed in a series of words, dynamically related to one another, which reflect in their structure and inter-relationship the poet's and the reader's recognition in one experience of something basic to the nature of all experience. Referring to the future of poetry, Sergeant maintains that whatever synthesis of inner and outer experience may be achieved, it is certain that science cannot be excluded, but will make its proper contribution to the meaning of poetry and to the pattern of values which emerges.

J. O. Bailey traces the development of Hardy's personal philosophy as expressed through his poetry in 'Evolutionary Meliorism in the Poetry of Thomas Hardy' (*SP*). Bailey distinguishes three separate phases— first, the period of bleak pessimism stretching from 1862 to about 1886, when his ideas were shaped by his reading in Darwin, Huxley, Spencer, and Mill; second, the period extending to the completion of *The Dynasts* in 1908, in which the influences of Schopenhauer and Von Hartmann were apparent; and third, the period from 1908 onwards, in which Hardy formulated and expressed in both prose and poetry his interpretation of natural law which he described as evolutionary meliorism. The conclusions reached in the final phase are summarized in his 'Apology' to *Late Lyrics and Earlier*.

Hardy's philosophy is also the subject of '*The Dynasts* Reconsidered' (*MLR*), by Roy Morrell, who claims that the misinterpretation of Hardy's real views has caused confusion and left the poet open to the charge of inconsistency. Morrell attempts to show how Hardy dealt with some of the main concepts derived from evolutionary meliorism in *The Dynasts* in order to establish the validity and consistency of his attitude towards the human situation.

In 'W. B. Yeats, Jonathan Swift, and Liberty' (*MP*) Donald T. Torchiana argues that Yeats's concept of liberty was not only influenced, but inspired, by Swift, but suggests that what Yeats had in mind was a special kind of intellectual liberty, 'fiercely aristocratic and narrowly Augustan— part of the great Irish song against Whiggery'. To support his argument, Torchiana discusses the part Yeats played in the public affairs of Ireland, and compares Yeats's views with those of Swift, whose bitter wisdom 'informed the position that Yeats defended'.

After a brief examination of Yeats's debt to Donne, James L. Allen, in 'Yeats's Use of the Serious Pun' (*SQ*), discusses some examples of a particular kind of ambiguity in Yeats's work, the serious or metaphysical pun.

W. B. Stanford reviews the inaccuracies and inadequacies of Donald R. Pearce's *The Senate Speeches of W. B. Yeats*, and examines some of the wider aspects of the subject in 'Yeats in the Irish Senate' (*REL*). Stanford concludes that, though Yeats may not have been a great statesman or parliamentarian, he took his senatorial duties seriously and in his political thought and action performed some lasting service to his country.

In 'The Hidden Aspect of *Sailing to Byzantium*' (*Ea*) L. C. Parks attempts an analysis of *Sailing to Byzantium* designed to show that its inception and development can best be seen as the expression of Yeats's perennial search for unity, and that in the dialectic set up in the poem itself Yeats drew a valid analogy between art and the Rosicrucianism which dominated much of his life. In the course of his inquiries, Parks reveals that even the form of the poem follows the strict pattern of a Rosicrucian 'initiation into an ideal order of reality', and insists that by its means Yeats succeeded in fusing his aesthetic with an occult idealism. Since this was a lifelong aim of the poet, *Sailing to Byzantium* rightly stands at the centre of his work.

In 'Two of Yeats's Last Poems' (*REL*) Jon Stallworthy examines and compares the various drafts made by Yeats in the composition of *The Long-Legged Fly* and *The Statues*, showing the different stages of development and commenting upon the reasons for the changes made before the poems reached their final state. As Stallworthy constantly relates the drafts at their various stages to other poems and to the ideas held by the poet, the method convincingly demonstrates that 'one poem does light up another', and that to understand part of the *opus* we must read the whole.

Donald T. Torchiana and Glenn O'Malley provide extracts, in 'Some

New Letters from W. B. Yeats to Lady Gregory' (*REL*), from the twenty-three letters acquired by the Deering Library of Northwestern University in 1959. These letters throw fresh light on Yeats's activities in public affairs from 1912 to 1914 and during the autumn of 1920.

It is well known that T. S. Eliot studied Sanskrit and Indian philosophy whilst at Harvard. K. S. Narayana Rao, in 'T. S. Eliot and *The Bhagavad-Gita*' (*AQ*), is concerned with tracing the influence of the *Gita* upon the author of *The Waste Land*, and with examining Eliot's poem, *To the Indians Who Died in Africa*, from an Indian point of view. This poem, in his opinion, is imbued with Indian thought and derives something of its structure from the *Bhagavad-Gita* itself.

Although Edwin Muir's life and career were shaped by the institutions and events of the twentieth century, Alexander Porteous observes in 'The Status of Edwin Muir' (*Quadrant*), that the basis of his sensibility was his experience of the small agrarian community of an island in the Orkneys, where he was born and spent his early childhood. Porteous discusses Muir as critic, teacher, and poet, and claims that if there are any major poets in our own time, Muir must be accounted among them—'the stamp of one fine mind is strongly on all his poems, they are informed by one individual voice . . .'.

V. L. O. Chittick discusses Auden's early political tendencies in 'Angry Young Man of the Thirties' (*DR*). Accepting the Marxist explanation of social conditions and the inevitability of class war, Auden felt that he had a positive contribution to make through the medium of his poetry, only to be disillusioned by his experiences in England and Germany. After his service as a stretcher-bearer in the Spanish Civil War, and his visit to war-torn China, he returned home via the United States. Chittick suggests that one of the changes in attitude which resulted from his taking up residence in America, possibly due to the influence of his reading in the works of Kierkegaard and Niebuhr, was the change from his 'belief in the redemptive power of humanistic love to belief in that of Christian love'. Auden's acceptance of the Christian way of life was confirmed in the Epilogue to his *New Year Letter*, and by this time the poet had substituted 'righteous indignation' for anger.

In 'Louis MacNeice' (*Lond Mag*), Ian Hamilton comments upon the work of another member of the Auden-Spender quartet. MacNeice's reputation survived the thirties more comfortably than those of his colleagues because his 'guilt-ridden perplexity' in the face of fiercely clearcut social obligations has been more acceptable to post-war poets, suspicious of party lines. Hamilton notes that 'two distinct almost antithetical styles' can be discerned in MacNeice's poetry—his 'bright' style, in which the love of bright particulars persists and is given body by the socio-political materials it endeavours to assimilate; and his 'prosy' style, in which MacNeice feels compelled to stand at the centre of his work 'in a confessional stance that does not suit him'. If MacNeice's duties at the B.B.C. encouraged him further towards exploration and discourse, and away from his real gifts, in *Visitations* and *Solstices* he rediscovered much of the earlier concentration and vitality.

Since his death in America Dylan Thomas has become the subject of a growing mythology. R. George Thomas examines his poetry as the work of a Welsh poet in 'Dylan Thomas: a Poet of Wales?' (*English*), and attempts to disentangle the legend from the facts of his life. George Thomas summarizes the poet's early background and deals with some of the factors which may have exercised an influence upon his development. Dylan Thomas's sudden rise to fame on the publication of *Deaths and Entrances* in 1946 is partly accounted for by the new relationship which had been established between the poet and his readers as a result of the shared experience of the Blitz, and 'that deepening interest in the fundamental verities of human experience which seems to accompany wide-scale war'. On the other hand, Thomas's dedication to his craft and the discipline he had learned to impose upon his work began to bring their own rewards. With the aim of conveying the experience of 'an almost instantaneous realization of felt truth', Dylan Thomas seems to have deliberately limited his range of subject to 'the significant themes of birth and fading innocence, love and copulation, the passing of time, and death'.

In 'The Poetry of Keith Douglas' (*CQ*) Ted Hughes points out that, although Keith Douglas is generally regarded as a 'war poet', probably because he failed to survive the Second World War, he offers more than 'just a few poems about war', and every poem he wrote has some special value. Yet in a sense war was Douglas's ideal subject—'the burning away of all human pretensions in the ray cast by death'—and it was war that brought his poetic talent to maturity.

The poetry of Ted Hughes is compared and contrasted with that of R. S. Thomas by J. D. Hainsworth in 'Extremes of Poetry: R. S. Thomas and Ted Hughes' (*English*). Despite a difference in age, both poets came to prominence in the fifties, both are nature poets, and both have been influenced by 'the line of city poets from Donne to Eliot, whose characteristic wit, irony, and sophistication' are seldom to be found in the work of other nature poets. However, the contrast in their use of language is striking—Thomas is quiet and restrained, while Hughes is 'all explosive force', and his violence of language is balanced by the violence in his material. Thomas is a priest and draws his subjects from the everyday lives of his parishioners, Welsh countryfolk. Nevertheless, they share a concern in relating poetry to contemporary society.

Alan Brownjohn, in 'The Poetry of Thom Gunn' (*Lond Mag*), remarks upon the early recognition of Gunn's talent which has placed him in the 'widely acknowledged triumvirate of the best poets to emerge in the fifties', and attempts a new assessment of his poetry. Brownjohn maintains that if action, especially violent action, is Gunn's most characteristic theme, the 'movement' he celebrates is usually purposeless; and this has a crucial bearing on the quality of his poems. Nor has Gunn been entirely successful in breaking away from this constricting technique by taking up syllabics, though there is hope that his change of style may yet release him from his repetitiveness of theme. His ultimate reputation will depend upon his ability to use his considerable talent 'to report on human behaviour patiently and sanely', and most of all to break the hold which 'self-conscious poses' and a very limited 'range of preoccupations' have upon him.

There is a sense in which the poems of any genuine poet can be said to constitute his spiritual autobiography. In 'The Discovery of God's Jazz: The Poetry of Jack Clemo' (*English*) Howard Sergeant insists that this is true in practically every sense in the case of Clemo, for most of his poems are directly concerned with his own religious experience and 'highlight the periods of spiritual crisis'. Sergeant traces Clemo's development through his poetry, from the isolationist position he took up after his conversion, to the point at which he was prepared to repudiate his individualism and seek communion within a 're-vived' Church. Clemo's most revi-talizing influences, at the later stage, have been the visiting American evangelists, Renée Martz and Billy Graham, and the impact of American revivalism is mainly responsible for the remarkable change of outlook expressed in *The Map of Clay*.

5. DRAMA

Observing that nineteenth-century plays have been somewhat neglected, Jerome Hanratty, in 'Melodrama—Then and Now' (*REL*), suggests that the time is appropriate for a re-examination of modern drama in relation to the nineteenth-century theatre to see 'if a more sympathetic appraisal can help us, in any way, to-day'. In this article, Hanratty reviews some of the characteristics of the nineteenth-century play in order to throw fresh light on the established features and trends of twentieth-century drama. In particular, he draws attention to two very strong forms of 'contemporary melodrama'—first, the 'dodo drama', in itself a 'middle-class extension of Victorian drawing-room drama'; and second, the 'kitchen-sink' drama, in which the kitchens of the sixties have been substituted for the drawing-rooms of the thirties. Hanratty discusses the use of language, the treatment of irony, and the attitude towards craftsmanship. Modern dramatists, he says, might do well to pay more attention to the basic consumer-needs and, in order to reach a wider audi-

ence, could learn a great deal from the nineteenth-century rediscovery of Old English folk-humour and way of life 'in all its traditional vigour and overt comedy independent of fashion'.

In 'Bernard Shaw and C. E. M. Joad: The Adventures of Two Puri-tans in Their Search for God' (*PMLA*), John G. Demaray points to the similarity in the philosophical viewpoints of Shaw and Joad. Though Shaw belonged to the 'chim-ney-sweep school' of the history of ideas, and Joad belonged to the 'academy', together they united the vitalism of Nietzsche, the rationalism of Descartes, and the evolutionary theories of the nineteenth century into the 'best of all possible Puritan compromises'. Demaray attempts to trace the development of Shaw's theory of the Life Force, laying great emphasis upon the effect of what he alleges to be Shaw's first sexual experience at the age of 29, when he was seduced by Mrs. Jenny Patterson, a widow in her forties. Unlike Shaw, however, Joad turned to Christianity for the answer to his problems and the resolution of his conflicts. Though profoundly discouraged by the situa-tion in his own age which had ex-perienced two world wars, Shaw re-tained to the end the hope that 'in-telligence might save mankind': but Joad eventually discarded the belief that man might improve through evolution and accepted the Christian view of the corruption of the 'natural' man by Original Sin.

Noting a common confusion be-tween Shaw as a polemical pamphle-teer and Shaw as a successful drama-tist, Michael Quinn presents what he calls a negative view of *Arms and the Man* in 'Form and Intention' (*CQ*). Shaw, he maintains, was essentially a comic dramatist, and though he may have contributed little to a revival of classical comedy, his experience with the comic form is worth the consideration of 'any serious comic dramatist in this country'. *Arms and the Man* serves as a convenient text for study because it was Shaw's first success and is generally regarded as typical of Shaw. Contrary to what the author's preface leads us to expect, *Arms and the Man* is neither a satiric comedy nor a serious comedy in the neoclassical tradition; it belongs in 'the great tradition of English artificial comedy'.

In '*The King's Threshold:* A Defence of Poetry' (*REL*), S. B. Bushrui reconsiders *The King's Threshold*, which he regards as one of Yeats's greatest works. Not only does the play mark an important development in Yeats's theory of poetry, but it indicates the point at which Yeats abandoned passivity for action and 'descended from the realms on high to the world of reality'. Bushrui claims that *The King's Threshold* contains in germinal form all the most striking attributes of the aristocratic system—'Dignity, nobility and reverence . . . based on custom and ceremony, pomp and ritual . . .'—which Yeats spent a lifetime in delineating. Although it expresses Yeats's poetic faith at a comparatively early stage of his career, it made possible the later developments.

Ronald Gaskell's aim, in 'The Realism of J. M. Synge' (*CQ*), is to clarify Synge's conception of reality, to show how that conception was presented in his plays, and to assess its possibilities as drama. Gaskell examines Synge's ideas, as expressed in his work, and without questioning his integrity or sense of reality, implies that his vision was insufficiently dramatic. His indifference to the will, Gaskell insists, makes a 'fully dramatic play virtually impossible'. Synge's use of dialogue and the deficiency of his rhythms are also criticized. Whilst the imaginative force of Synge's plays enables us to come to grips with reality, the plays cannot accurately be described as great drama.

Louise Rouse Rehak makes an interesting comparison between the methods of Tennyson and T. S. Eliot in 'On the Use of Martyrs: Tennyson and Eliot on Thomas Becket' (*UTQ*). Eliot, she contends, makes a virtue of the historical limitation and embodies the concepts of a limited theology in *Murder in the Cathedral*, while Tennyson makes greater use of the ironic opportunities of Becket's career and conceives his *Becket* in terms of a humanistic rather than a supernatural morality. Contrasting the structure, characterization, and diction of the two plays, she reaches the conclusions that *Murder in the Cathedral*, though Eliot's best play, remains outside 'the meaning of our tradition of drama', its innovation leaving no room for future development, but that Tennyson's *Becket* has something of 'our current flavour of the drama of alienation in its ironic texture of relationships'.

Since John Russell Brown suggests that we take a new look at Shakespeare with the knowledge we have gained from the study of modern dramatists, his 'Mr. Pinter's Shakespeare' (*CQ*), might well have been written with Eliot's famous passage in mind—'. . . for order to persist after the supervention of novelty, the whole existing order must be, if ever so slightly, altered . . .'. Brown makes the point that during the last ten years a new kind of drama has emerged which challenges previous conceptions, in the sense that 'development' or argument is conspicuously absent, or rather, that 'exposition' has become both 'development' and 'conclusion'. Most of Pinter's plays, for instance, have minimal plots and little argument, but they 'progressively reveal the inner nature of their characters'. Pinter's various devices keep the audience alert and interested, even if unable to 'get the message'. Referring in turn to *A Slight Ache*, *The Dumb Waiter*, *The Caretaker*, and *The Birthday Party*, as well as to works by Beckett and Ionesco, Brown claims that in ten years the new dramatists have created an audience with new powers of perception, an audience capable of responding to the new art, able to appreciate the almost musical form, whereby 'proportion and tempo accentuate the inner drama', and able to recognize the climactic revelations of character and situation. As this audience helps to make up the audience for Shakespeare's plays, it is possible that this 'discovery about the basic resources of the theatre' may bring about an entirely new response to Shakespeare. It may now be more capable of recognizing Shakespeare's 'progressive demonstration of character and situation within his fables', of rediscovering his subtle method of presenting human nature and his intuitive skill in using the stage 'as a means of viewing deeply and widely'. For in certain aspects Shakespeare's techniques are closer to those of Pinter and Beckett than to dramatists of earlier generations. 'Mr. Pinter's Shakespeare is a discovery that can alter our presuppositions.'

Continuing this fascinating and well-argued theory in 'Mr. Beckett's Shakespeare' (*CQ*), Brown observes that critics and scholars are in general agreement that all Shakespeare's plays manifest a 'fundamental' idea, and tend to assess the quality of the plays according to the presentation of the symbols of that idea. Though the new dramatists have abandoned thematic development and symbolic situations, and

have also rejected ideologies, since they live in a world which includes ideologies, they will inevitably write with some reference to them. It is really a matter of priorities; and in this respect the new dramatists do not place ideas high amongst their 'conscious artistic concerns'. But it is presumptuous to say that dramatic experience can be fully described in terms of pattern and symbol. Shakespeare may have been more confident of the human situation than we are today, but his imagination was rich enough to contain other elements. The unity expressed in symbolic terms is not the only kind of unity, and the plays may have other important aspects yet to be brought out properly. It is these other aspects with which dramatists like Beckett are concerned. In *Waiting for Godot* Beckett has demonstrated that dramatic illusion can present human beings 'as instinctively perceived in relation to each other in time' and simultaneously hint at another 'world of thought by "momentary symbolism"', a world possessing its own conceptual unity. This possibility is important to the modern understanding of Shakespeare, who can still perplex us. Brown believes that Shakespeare discovered this kind of theatrical illusion for himself, and that it explains the apparent ambivalence of some of his plays. Whilst we must give due emphasis to Shakespeare's symbolism, and to his presentation of various concepts, we should also try to assess his achievement 'in the less easily defined plane of his drama's action'.

G. Wilson Knight, in 'The Kitchen Sink' (*Encounter*), also maintains that modern dramatists are breaking new ground, and summarizes their achievements, with references to Arden's *Live Like Pigs*, Behan's *The Quare Fellow*, Beckett's *Waiting for Godot*, Bolt's *A Man for all Seasons*,

Delaney's *A Taste of Honey*, Osborne's *Look Back in Anger*, *The Entertainer*, and *Luther*, Pinter's *The Caretaker*, *The Dumb Waiter*, *The Birthday Party*, and *The Room*, Wesker's *Chicken Soup with Barley*, *Roots*, and *Chips With Everything*, and Whiting's *Saint's Day*, *Penny for a Song*, *Marching Song*, and *The Devils*. He finds that the kitchen-sink dramas help to bring 'new health to the insane paradoxes of a decaying culture', and the dramas of the absurd assist in letting substances break through which are not on any other terms 'assimilable by our sterile sophistication'.

XV

American Literature

G. H. MOORE and T. R. ARP

In this chapter books are noted by Geoffrey Moore, articles by T. R. Arp

1. GENERAL

That 'Bible' of American literature students, *Literary History of the United States*,[1] appears in a third, revised, one-volume edition. The main difference between this and previous editions is that there are two new chapters covering the literature which has been produced since the Second World War. The first sums up the current achievement of older writers, and the second interprets newer authors and 'movements'. Willard Thorp and Robert E. Spiller are responsible for the chapter entitled 'End of an Era', and Ihab Hassan for 'Since 1945'. The 'Bibliography for the General Reader' compiled by Thomas H. Johnson, and included only in the one-volume edition, has been revised and brought up to date by Richard M. Ludwig.

Henry Lüdeke's *Geschichte der Amerikanischen Literatur*[2] has been issued in a second, revised edition. Lüdeke's book does not have the range of the *Literary History of the United States*, but it has all the advantages (and disadvantages) which spring from a one-man point of view.

Lüdeke, whose approach is that of the typical continental Professor of 'Amerikanistik', devotes two-thirds of his book to the period before the twentieth century, and spends almost as much time on Jefferson, Washington, Parkman, and Fiske as he does on Hawthorne, Melville, and Mark Twain. There is a bibliography for each chapter and a substantial index.

Eight American Authors[3] has also been reissued, this time in paperback form at a very reasonable price. It contains an invaluable summary of bibliographies and critical opinions on a group of American writers selected by the Modern Language Association of America as being the most outstanding, namely, Poe, Emerson, Hawthorne, Thoreau, Melville, Whitman, Mark Twain, and Henry James. A bibliographical supplement, covering the period 1955–62 and compiled by J. Chesley Mathews, has been added to the original edition of 1956.

Another revised book is Clarence Gohdes's *Bibliographical Guide to the Study of the Literature of the U.S.A.*[4] This second edition of the *Guide* brings Gohdes's work up to 1963, eliminates obsolete titles, and adds a new section listing the most important

---

[1] *Literary History of the United States: History.* (Third Edition, Revised.) Ed. by Robert E. Spiller, Willard Thorp, Thomas H. Johnson, Henry Seidel Canby, Richard M. Ludwig. New York and London: Macmillan. pp. xxiv+1511. $12.50.

[2] *Geschichte der Amerikanischen Literatur*, by Henry Lüdeke. Berne and Munich: Francke Verlag. pp. 544. S.Fr. 38.50. DM. 33.50.

[3] *Eight American Authors: A Review of Research and Criticism*, ed. by Floyd Stovall. New York: Norton. pp. xii+466. $1.95.

[4] *Bibliographical Guide to the Study of the Literature of the U.S.A.*, by Clarence Gohdes. Duke U.P. and Cambridge U.P. pp. ix+125. 48s.

biographical studies of a hundred selected American authors. The main format, however, is unchanged. There are thirty-five sections, covering the philosophy and general methodology of literary and historical study, as well as chapters on such subjects as 'Biography', 'Magazines', 'Newspapers', 'Fiction', 'Criticism', and 'The English Language in the U.S.' Gohdes's book is a useful addendum to the separate Bibliography volume of the original three-volume *Literary History of the United States*.

Jacob Blanck's *Bibliography of American Literature*[5] proceeds to a fourth book, covering eighteen authors from Hawthorne to Joseph Holt Ingraham. Like the previous volumes, it is an extremely competent piece of work, of interest as much to book collectors as to students of American literature, since it is precise and detailed in its descriptions of binding, typography, and format.

An Analytical Index to 'American Literature', Volumes I—XXX,[6] covers the period March 1929 to January 1959. There is an 'Author-Subject Index' and a 'Book Review Index'. Since *American Literature* has been for thirty years or more the leading magazine for research in its field, this volume is a valuable aid to critical and scholarly study.

Arthur P. Dudden's *The United States of America: A Syllabus of American Studies*,[7] comes in two parts, one devoted to 'Literature, Language and the Arts', and the other to 'History and Social Sciences'. These volumes are based on the required reading for the University of Pennsylvania examination for the Certificate in American Studies. Part I deals with the literary history and language of the United States, presents analyses of major works by Franklin, Hawthorne, Mark Twain, Lewis, Fitzgerald, O'Neill, Faulkner, and Hemingway, and ends with a series of topics on 'The Arts and Related Subjects', which are intended to stimulate discussion in this field. Dudden's method is perhaps too cut-and-dried; but his summaries and condensations of whole areas of study enable the student to get a clearer picture of a subject which—at least in the United States—is 'inter-disciplinary'.

It is becoming more customary to print anthologies of American literature by periods than to embody them in single, hard-bound editions which are difficult to handle. The 'Viking Portable' selection,[8] edited by Milton R. Stern and Seymour L. Gross comes in four paperback volumes. The first is devoted to the period up to 1800, the second, *The American Romantics*, to the period from 1800 to 1860, the third, *Nation and Region*, from 1860 to 1900, and the fourth to *The Twentieth Century*. The size of these new anthologies enables their editors to make a wider and fuller choice than is possible in a one-volume edition. For example, Stern and Gross are able to include not only Bradford, Mather, and Twain, but also John Smith, Nathaniel Ward, Samuel Sewall, and Roger Williams, together

[5] *Bibliography of American Literature*, compiled by Jacob Blanck. Vol. Four: Nathaniel Hawthorne to Joseph Holt Ingraham. Yale U.P. pp. xxii+495. 144s.

[6] *An Analytical Index to 'American Literature', Vols. I—XXX, March 1929—January 1959*, by T. F. Marshall. Duke U.P. and Cambridge U.P. pp. vii+253. $7.50. 60s.

[7] *The United States of America: A Syllabus of American Studies*, by Arthur P. Dudden. Two vols. Pennsylvania U.P. pp. 155, 147. $1.95 each.

[8] *American Literature Survey*, ed. by Milton R. Stern and Seymour L. Gross. *Colonial and Federal to 1800*, pp. xxii+536. *The American Romantics, 1800–1860*, pp. xiv +544. *Nation and Region, 1860–1900*. pp. xxi+531. *The Twentieth Century*, pp. xxi+586. New York: Viking, 1962. $1.75 each.

with extracts from such political writers as Jefferson, Madison, and Hamilton.

Darrel Abel's *American Literature*[9] is neither a history nor an anthology, but a series of analyses and descriptions of the writings of the major American writers. Abel's three books are entitled *Colonial and Early National Writing*, *Literature of the Atlantic Culture* (by which he means Emerson and the Transcendentalists, Hawthorne, Poe, James, Longfellow, Lowell, Melville, and Whitman), and *Masterworks of American Realism*, which covers the work of Mark Twain, William Dean Howells, and Henry James. There is a fourth volume, *Recent American Literature*, edited by Donald Heiney, which is not included in the present series.

Michigan Novels: An Annotated Bibliography[10] is edited by Albert G. Black. It aims to furnish the student of regional American literature with a list of novels about the Michigan region and, more ambitiously, with the special point of view presented by novelists who have concentrated on this part of the world. Black's list, which runs to 303 works, includes not only such well-known local authors as Constance Woolson, but also a host of others whose names have vanished with the period in which they wrote. One novelist of whom few could have heard is Oll Coomes, author of such epics as *Happy Harry, the Wild Boy of the Woods, Long Bear, the Giant Spy*, and *One Armed Alf, the Giant Hunter of the Great Lakes*.

The American Colonial Mind and the Classical Tradition[11] is a survey of what Richard M. Gummere considers an essential element in the development of American culture up to 1800, that is, the interest of the colonists in Greek and Roman ideas. Gummere's approach is both biographical and literary. He deals, for example, in some detail with William Byrd and Samuel Sewall, as being diarists in the ancient tradition, the one from the South and the other from the North; with Logan, Franklin, and Bartram as 'Humanist, Pragmatist, and Platonist'; with Jonathan Boucher ('Toryissimus'); and with Adams and Jefferson. There are also chapters devoted to 'Colonial Reactions to a Classical Education', 'Colonies. Ancient and Modern', and 'The Classical Ancestry of the Constitution'. Gummere's book makes it clear that the division between scholarship and literature, and even more between science and the arts, did not exist for the early colonists.

Nancy Hale's 'discovery' of New England[12] is, although entirely personal, of interest to the student of American literature. Miss Hale was brought up near Boston in an atmosphere of the past. When she was six she was asked to tell what her ancestors had done in the American Revolution, and reports herself as saying, 'I had a great-uncle who was hanged.' Her selection is all the better for not being a standard scholarly collection. In the period 1620–43, for example, she picks not only William Bradford's *Of Plymouth Plantation*, Francis Higginson's *New England's Plantation*, and selections from *The Bay*

[9] *American Literature*, by Darrel Abel. Vol. 1. *Colonial and Early National Writing*, pp. 442. Vol. 2. *Literature of the Atlantic Culture*, pp. 537. Vol. 3. *Masterworks of American Realism*, pp. 370. New York: Barrons. $2.25 each.

[10] *Michigan Novels: An Annotated Bibliography*, by Albert G. Black. Ann Arbor, Mich.: Michigan Council of Teachers of English. pp. 64. $1.50.

[11] *The American Colonial Mind and the Classical Tradition*, by Richard M. Gummere. Harvard U.P. pp. xiii+228. $5.25.

[12] *New England Discovery: A Personal View*, by Nancy Hale. New York: Coward-McCann, Inc. pp. xxiv+549. $9.95.

Psalm Book, but also passages from
Thomas Welde on the subject of
'Anne Hutchinson's Exile' and
Catherine Maria Sedgwick on 'Din-
ner at the Winthrops'. Miss Hale is,
in other words, both sympathetic and
knowledgeable about the history of
her ancestors. Her selection, which is
divided into periods of approximately
twelve to fifteen years, continues
through the nineteenth century up to
modern times. It ends with T. S.
Eliot's 'The Boston Evening Transcript', E. E. Cummings's 'Cambridge
Ladies', Robert Lowell's 'Waking in
the Blue', and J. F. Kennedy's 'New
England Industry'.

In *Ante-Bellum Southern Literary
Criticism*[13] Edd Winfield Parks considers the critical ideas of Thomas
Jefferson, Hugh Swinton Legaré,
Richard Henry Wilde, William Gilmore Simms, Philip Pendleton Cooke,
Thomas Holley Chivers, William J.
Grayson, Henry Timrod, and Paul
Hamilton Hayne. Parks points out
that, although Jefferson regarded
Homer and the Greek dramatists as
literary models, he also wrote a
stimulating essay on English parody.
Legaré was, in the main, a classicist,
but his mind was not closed to the
ideas of Byron. Parks notes the shift,
after the Civil War, from Classicism
to Romanticism, and the way in
which Southern writers made use of
the historical romance in order to
put forward their beliefs about the
South and its future.

Stuart C. Henry's volume of essays
in honour of H. Shelton Smith, entitled *A Miscellany of American Christianity*,[14] contains, among material of
purely theological interest, several

essays on the relationship of religion
to American sociology and literature.
Gordon Esley Finney's 'Some As-
pects of Religion on the American
Frontier' is particularly interesting in
this respect, as also are Stuart C.
Henry's 'Puritan Character in the
Witchcraft Episode of Salem', and H.
Burnell Pannill's 'Bronson Alcott:
Emerson's "Tedious Archangel"'.

Ursula Brumm's interest in religion
and the American scene is well
known. Her book-length study entitled *Die Religiöse Typologie im
Amerikanischen Denken*[15] is concerned
with Samuel and Cotton Mather,
Edward Taylor, Jonathan Edwards,
and Emerson, and, in more detail,
with Hawthorne and Melville. Her
final chapter, dealing with Christ and
Adam as 'types' in American literature, extends R. W. B. Lewis's ideas
on this subject. Miss Brumm has, in
fact, hit upon a most important
theme in American literature, and it
would be interesting to see her work
expanded even further. For example,
Christ-figures and Christ-references
appear not only in Hawthorne, Melville, and the earlier writers mentioned, but also in the work of
novelists as disparate as Scott Fitzgerald and John Steinbeck.

Spirit of a Free Society[16] is a
Festschrift for Senator Fulbright on
the occasion of the tenth anniversary
of the establishment of the Fulbright
programme in the German Federal
Republic. It consists of eleven essays,
of which five are on literary subjects.
H. J. Lang writes on Hawthorne's
ambiguity and Hans Galinsky on
Emily Dickinson, while Alvan S.

[13] *Ante-Bellum Southern Literary Criticism*,
by Edd Winfield Parks. Georgia U.P., 1962.
pp. x+358. $7.50.
[14] *A Miscellany of American Christianity:
Essays in Honor of H. Shelton Smith*, ed. by
Stuart C. Henry. Duke U.P. and Cambridge
U.P. pp. viii+390. $10. £4.

[15] *Die Religiöse Typologie im Amerikanis-
chen Denken*, by Ursula Brumm. Leiden:
E. J. Brill. pp. 195. 22 guilders.
[16] *Spirit of a Free Society: Essays in Honor
of Senator James William Fulbright on the
Occasion of the Tenth Anniversary of the
German Fulbright Program*. Heidelberg:
Quelle & Meyer, 1962. pp. 391. DM. 32.

Ryan, Marvin Spevack, and Cecil B. Williams deal respectively with the poetry of Robert Frost, the Beat Generation, and 'Regionalism in American Literature'.

Another *Festschrift*, this time produced by the American Folklore Society of Philadelphia, is in honour of MacEdward Leach. *Folklore in Action*[17] contains essays by, among others, Tristram P. Coffin on 'The Folk Ballad and the Literary Ballad: an Essay in Classification', and Malcolm G. Lawes, Jr., on 'Anglo-Irish Balladry in North America'.

Although *Varieties of Literary Experience*[18] consists of essays on 'world literature', there are several of interest to students who specialize in American literature. One is Edward Dahlberg's '*Moby-Dick*: An Hamitic Dream', and another Leon Edel's 'How to read *The Sound and the Fury*'. Edel's essay is a brief but valuable attempt to establish some connexion between Faulkner and the reader who, from the first, is entirely uncomprehending.

Myth and Symbol[19] also covers a wide field. Among essays on *King Lear*, on Surrealism, and on Brecht, there are two on American literature: Sister M. Joselyn, O.S.B.'s 'Animal Imagery in Katherine Anne Porter's Fiction', and Alexander C. Kern's 'Myth and Symbol in Criticism of Faulkner's "The Bear"'.

Italian Influence on American Literature[20] is a beautifully produced Grolier Club publication consisting

of an address by C. Waller Barrett and a catalogue of an exhibition of books, manuscripts, and art held between 17 October and 10 December 1961.

Cecil Robinson's *With the Ears of Strangers*[21] is concerned with the image of the Mexican in American literature. Using as examples the work of the chroniclers of the Conquest of Mexico, as well as comments by later writers, Robinson picks out major sources of misunderstanding on the subject. As an epitome of 'the loneliness of triumph', Robinson quotes Archibald MacLeish's 'Conquistador'.

Paul Elmer More's *Shelburne Essays on American Literature*[22] is edited in paperback form by Daniel Aaron, who also contributes an able introduction. Aaron points out that although More never thought of his essays as constituting a history of American letters, they nevertheless tell a story: the development of one literary strain from the Puritans to that 'disconsolate and restless searcher' Henry James. *The Shelburne Essays* deal with the work of Edwards, Franklin, Freneau, Hawthorne, Whittier, Emerson, Thoreau, Whitman, Charles Eliot Norton, and Henry James.

In *Re-Appraisals: Some Commonsense Readings in American Literature*,[23] Martin Green maintains that the major texts of American literature are nowadays not so much over-interpreted as 're-invented'. Green has some blunt things to say about

[17] *Folklore in Action*, ed. by Horace P. Beck. Philadelphia: American Folklore Society, 1962. pp. xii+210.
[18] *Varieties of Literary Experience*, ed. by Stanley Burnshaw. Peter Owen. pp. xvi+446. 45s.
[19] *Myth and Symbol: Critical Approaches and Applications*, ed. by Bernice Slote. Nebraska U.P. pp. viii+196. $1.95.
[20] *Italian Influence on American Literature*. An Address by C. Waller Barrett, 1962. New York: The Grolier Club. pp. 131.

[21] *With the Ears of Strangers: The Mexican in American Literature*, by Cecil Robinson. Arizona U.P. pp. ix+338. $7.50.
[22] *Shelburne Essays on American Literature*, by Paul Elmer More. Sel. and ed. by Daniel Aaron. New York: Harcourt Brace. pp. 280. $2.45.
[23] *Re-Appraisals: Some Commonsense Readings in American Literature*, by Martin Green. Hugh Evelyn. pp. 252. 30s.

'American Literature as a Subject', 'Emerson: the Rejected Leader', 'The Hawthorne Myth: a protest', 'Melville and the American Romance', 'Twain and Whitman: The Problem of "American" Literature', 'Henry James and the Great Tradition', 'Faulkner: the Triumph of Rhetoric', 'Franny and Zooey', 'American Rococo: Salinger and Nabokov', and 'Studies in Classic American Literature'. Sometimes, however, his 'commonsense' method of reading leads to misinterpretation, as when he endeavours to explode 'the Hawthorne Myth' by reading Hawthorne as if he were a realist.

In *American Fiction: The Intellectual Background*[24] D. E. S. Maxwell considers the ideas of Poe, Cooper, Melville, Hawthorne, Twain, and Edith Wharton. In a final chapter he compares modern American fiction with its inheritance. Maxwell's conclusion is that 'classical' discipline and a respect for orthodox values have been as powerful in shaping American fiction as 'romantic individualism'.

2. COLONIAL

A paperback version of *Mourt's Relation*,[25] entitled 'A Journal of the Pilgrims at Plymouth', is edited from the original printing of 1622 by Dwight B. Heath. *Mourt's Relation* is the earliest published account of the coming of the Pilgrims to America and the establishment of Plymouth Plantation—quite simply, a day-by-day journal. There are many conjectures as to the reason for its name. It contains a brief foreword signed by 'G.

Mourt', a man unknown to scholars and historians, who, while explicitly denying authorship, states that he wishes to make the 'relation' which follows more generally known. George Morton has been suggested as the author. Heath maintains that, despite his disclaimer, one Mourt himself might actually have been the author.

Edmund S. Morgan's latest contribution to scholarship on the subject of New England[26] traces the genesis, flowering, and decline of the Puritan ideal of a Church of the Elect in England and America. Historians have generally supposed that the main outlines of the Puritan Church were decided in England and transported to the New World. Morgan suggests that the distinguishing characteristic of the New England ideal—that of a church composed exclusively of true and tested 'Saints'—developed fully only in the 1630's and 1640's, after the arrival of the first settlers in New England. He supports his thesis by a close examination and comparison of Puritan thought in England and America.

Arthur P. Hudson's *Songs of the Carolina Charter Colonists 1663–1763*[27] is interesting for its detail concerning old English and Scottish ballads and songs transplanted to the colonies. There are sections on ballads, love songs, nursery rhymes and religious songs.

Two more volumes of *The Papers of Benjamin Franklin* cover, respectively, the periods April 1, 1755, through September 30, 1756, and October 1, 1756, through March 31, 1758. In

[24] *American Fiction: The Intellectual Background*, by D. E. S. Maxwell. Routledge & Kegan Paul. pp. vii+306. 35s.
[25] *A Journal of the Pilgrims at Plymouth: Mourt's Relation*, ed. with introduction and notes by Dwight B. Heath. New York: Corinth. pp. xxiii+96. $1.45.

[26] *Visible Saints: The History of a Puritan Idea*, by Edmund S. Morgan. New York U.P. pp. ix+159. $4.50.
[27] *Songs of the Carolina Charter Colonists: 1663–1763*, by Arthur Palmer Hudson. Raleigh, N.C.: Carolina Charter Tercentenary Commission, 1962. pp. x+82. 50c.

Volume 6[28] Franklin is shown as one of the leaders in the defence of Pennsylvania against the French and English. When General Braddock was unable to secure transport for his march against Fort Duquesne, Franklin went among the Pennsylvania farmers and recruited the necessary wagons, horses, and drivers. During this period, also, he wrote his parables against persecution and on brotherly love, laying the foundation for his later election to a Fellowship of the Royal Society. In Volume 7[29] we find Franklin in London, beginning his 'second career' as a colonial agent. During the voyage to England he wrote *The Way to Wealth*, his most widely reprinted single composition. In the late fifties he settled down in the congenial atmosphere of London and began the negotiations with the Proprietors of the colonies which were the object of his mission.

Mason L. Weems's *Life of Washington*[30] is edited by Marcus Cunliffe. In a long and informative introduction Cunliffe maintains that Parson Weems's writings have a sort of timelessness. What intrigues us in them is the possibility that, despite himself, he may have conveyed valuable truths about George Washington and the United States. Cunliffe concludes that, 'far from being ruined by his tales, we decide that American history would be thinner without them'.

Two volumes of *Adams Family Correspondence*[31] cover the periods December 1761–May 1776 and June 1776–March 1778. These letters form an unbroken record of the changing modes of domestic life, religious views and habits, travel, dress, servants, food, schooling, reading, health and medical care, diversions, and every other conceivable aspect of manners and taste among members of a substantial New England family. There are about six hundred letters in the two volumes, beginning with a series of hitherto unpublished courtship letters between John Adams and Abigail Smith. Weekly and sometimes daily reports by Adams between 1774 and 1777, and his wife's letters in reply, remind us of the difficulties of raising a family of young children and managing a farm while war is going on not far from your door-step. This superbly-produced edition is sponsored by the Massachusetts Historical Society.

3. EARLY NINETEENTH CENTURY

Volume II of *The Papers of John C. Calhoun*[32] covers the year from 1817 to 1818 and includes 3,000 letters and other documents written by and to Calhoun when he was Secretary of War. He was then an ambitious young man of thirty-five, the last of the five members of Monroe's cabinet to join the Government. Four months later, Congress passed, almost without amendment, a bill which Calhoun had written to reorganize the army staff. On his second day in office, he authorized an offensive mission by the United States across the Georgia

[28] *The Papers of Benjamin Franklin.* Volume 6, 1 April, 1755, through 30 September, 1756. Ed. by Leonard W. Labaree and Ralph L. Ketcham, with the assistance of Helen C. Boatfield and Helene H. Fineman. Yale U.P. pp. xxix+581. $10. 72s.

[29] *The Papers of Benjamin Franklin.* Volume 7, October 1, 1756, through March 31, 1758. Ed. by Leonard W. Labaree and Ralph L. Ketcham, with the assistance of Helen C. Boatfield and Helene H. Fineman. Yale U.P. pp. xxvi+427. $10. 72s.

[30] *The Life of Washington*, by Mason L. Weems. Ed. by Marcus Cunliffe. Harvard U.P., 1962. pp. lxii+226. $4.50.

[31] *Adams Family Correspondence.* Volume I, December 1761–May 1776. Volume II, June 1776–March 1778. Ed. by L. H. Butterfield in association with Wendell D. Garrett and Marjorie E. Sprague. Harvard U.P. pp. xxiii+424, xxi+490. $17.50 the two.

[32] *The Papers of John C. Calhoun.* Volume II, 1817–18. Ed. by W. Edwin Hemphill. South Carolina U.P. pp. xciv+513. $10.

border into Spanish Florida, in order to attack the Seminole Indians. The year chosen for Volume II marks a turning-point in Calhoun's career.

Frank Otto Gatell's book on John Gorham Palfrey[33] describes the career of an early nineteenth-century 'monument to the Puritan idea of rectitude'. Palfrey was an historian, a Harvard man, a Unitarian minister, and a crusader against slavery. Gatell has made use of the Palfrey family manuscripts, among them an unpublished autobiography. In his search for a 'meaning' in Palfrey's life, he does not attempt to make judgements, but rather lets the facts speak for themselves. Palfrey is a type of New Englander the fine flower of which was Henry Adams. The breed still exists, but the original strength of the Puritan tradition has given way to 'the genteel tradition'.

A much more important leader in the Anti-slavery movement was William Lloyd Garrison, who is the subject of a book by Walter M. Merrill.[34] Merrill finds Garrison's life to be of great relevance today, when discrimination against Negroes still constitutes one of America's most pressing problems. However, he is concerned as much with Garrison the man as with the case for which he fought. Merrill argues that Garrison filled a far more important role in abolition than many recent historians have been willing to admit.

Lewis Leary's *Washington Irving*[35] is Pamphlet No. 25 in the University of Minnesota 'American Writers' series. Leary, who is the author of

another contribution to the series on Mark Twain, feels that few writers have successfully stretched a small talent further than Washington Irving. Nevertheless, he appreciates Irving's dexterity, readiness of tongue, and alert recognition of absurdities. He was, in Leary's opinion, America's first, if not her best, romantic historian, a 'iocal colorist' before the term became popular with literary historians, a comic realist before Thackeray, and a caricaturist before Dickens.

Anna Maria Crinò's monograph *Echi, Temi e Motivi nella Poesia di William Cullen Bryant*[36] deals mainly with Bryant's ideas on poetic theory. This is an intelligent study, although it does not present as much of the 'Italian point of view' as one might wish. The chapter entitled 'Il Mondo Poetico di William Cullen Bryant' may be recommended.

Literary Wise Men of Gotham[37] is concerned with the literary pundits of New York during the period 1815–60. John Paul Pritchard examines in detail Edmund Wilson's thesis that New York writers of the nineteenth century were more representative of American thought than their New England contemporaries. Men like James Kirke Paulding, Nathaniel Parker Willis, Samuel Ward, and Gulian Verplanck were men of the world as well as literary critics. Free from the religious restrictions of their New England colleagues, they provided, in the four decades before the Civil War, a body of criticism which, in Pritchard's opinion, helped substantially to guide the course of future American literary development.

John Pendleton Kennedy's *Horse-*

[33] *John Gorham Palfrey and the New England Conscience*, by Frank Otto Gatell. Harvard U.P. pp. x+337. $6.95.

[34] *Against Wind and Tide: A Biography of William Lloyd Garrison*, by Walter M. Merrill. Harvard U.P. pp. xvi+391. $8.75.

[35] *Washington Irving*, by Lewis Leary. (Minnesota Pamphlets on American Writers, No. 25.) Minnesota U.P. pp. 48. 65c. 5s.

[36] *Echi, Temi e Motivi Nella Poesia di William Cullen Bryant*, by Anna Maria Crinò. Verona: Ghidini E Fiorini. pp. 81.

[37] *Literary Wise Men of Gotham: Criticism in New York, 1815–1860*, by John Paul Pritchard. Louisiana State U.P. pp.ix+200. $6.

Shoe Robinson[38] is edited, with an introduction, by Ernest E. Leisy. This book is one of a series of important, but scarce, American books produced under the general editorship of Harry Hayden Clark, of which *Modern Chivalry, Ormond,* and *The Yemassee* have already been published. When the two volumes of *Horse-Shoe Robinson* appeared in 1835 Poe said, 'We feel little afraid of hazarding our critical reputation when we assert that they will place Mr. Kennedy at once in the very first rank of American novelists.' Leisy believes that Poe was right. Robinson brought to the American novel a 'dramatic method' which triumphed over the expository mode of writers like Fenimore Cooper. His romance was tinged with realism and, Leisy believes, his zest in characterization was badly needed in the American novel of his day.

Edith Mettke's *Der Dichter Ralph Waldo Emerson: Mystisches Denken und poetischer Ausdruck*[39] is concerned primarily with Emerson as poet. Having considered Emerson's pronouncements on poets and poetry, however, Miss Mettke proceeds to a detailed analysis of 'Nature'.

Another volume of *The Journals and Miscellaneous Notebooks of Ralph Waldo Emerson*[40] appears under the editorship of William H. Gilman and Alfred R. Ferguson. Volume III (1826–32) covers the years of Emer-

son's preaching, his brief marriage to Ellen Tucker, and his misery after her death. During these years Emerson noted down many ideas for sermons, wrote occasionally about family matters, but commented little on the impact upon him of other people and outside events. The pattern during this period is consistent with that of the earlier journals. Emerson was concerned not so much with the existence of God as with the nature of Christ. In literature he read more of Wordsworth and Coleridge and less of Milton and the Augustans; stylistically, he moved from the bookish rhetoric of his early essays towards the fluency of the later.

The Collected Writings of Walt Whitman are being issued under the general editorship of Gay Wilson Allen and Sculley Bradley. Thomas L. Brasher is the editor of *The Early Poems and the Fiction*.[41] He has collected all known versions and established a definitive text of Whitman's first work, which appeared and reappeared in some twenty magazines and newspapers. His book is chiefly valuable for the fact that it brings together pieces which were for a long time scattered among several posthumous collections, most of which are now out of print. The difficulty of editing arose, not only from searching out, but from identifying, pieces which Whitman wrote but which he did not include in his *Collected Works*.

Prose Works 1892: Volume I (Specimen Days) is edited by Floyd Stovall.[42] *Specimen Days* was originally written and published as newspaper despatches and records, in the

[38] *Horse-Shoe Robinson,* by John Pendleton Kennedy. Ed. with Introduction, Chronology and Bibliography by Ernest E. Leisy. New York and London: Hafner, 1962. pp. xxxii+550. $2.75.

[39] *Der Dichter Ralph Waldo Emerson: Mystisches Denken und poetischer Ausdruck,* by Edith Mettke. Heidelberg: Carl Winter. pp. 154. DM. 19.

[40] *The Journals and Miscellaneous Notebooks of Ralph Waldo Emerson.* Volume III, 1826–32. Ed. by William H. Gilman & Alfred R. Ferguson. Harvard U.P. pp. xvii+398. $10.

[41] *The Collected Writings of Walt Whitman: The Early Poems and the Fiction.* Ed. by Thomas L. Brasher. New York U.P. pp. xxii+352. $10.

[42] *The Collected Writings of Walt Whitman: Prose Works 1892.* Vol. I: *Specimen Days.* Ed. by Floyd Stovall. New York U.P. pp. xx+358. $10.

main, of Whitman's experience as a male nurse during the Civil War. It also contains some nature studies made near Camden after his paralysis in 1873. Stovall has collated the sketches and recorded the variants from Whitman's own 1892 text of *Complete Prose Works*. *Specimen Days* is one of Whitman's most moving works. Written in simple, direct language, it shows the same love for, and understanding of, humanity which characterizes the poems.

4. LATER NINETEENTH CENTURY

The Sut Society's *The Lovingood Papers*[43] for 1963 includes notes by M. Thomas Inge on a personal encounter with George Washington Harris; on 'Sut Lovingood Come to Life', by Milton Ricketes; and on 'Sut Lovingood's Dream', by Hamlin Hill. This collection of essays is dedicated to William Faulkner, who wrote about Sut Lovingood that he 'had no illusions about himself, did the best he could; at certain times he was a coward and knew it and wasn't ashamed; he never blamed his misfortunes on anyone and never cursed God for them.'

David Ross Locke's *The Struggles of Petroleum V. Nasby*[44] is issued in shortened form. This book originally appeared as newpaper articles during the Civil War, and was published under its present title in 1872. The 1872 volume contained 189 letters, 3 lectures, and 23 illustrations. The Beacon edition under review contains approximately one third of the letters,

one of the lectures, and a selection of the original Thomas Nast illustrations. Locke, who died in 1888, was a young radical writer, formerly editor of the Findlay, Ohio, *Jeffersonian*. His 'letters' became famous for their satire of the northern Democrats, although he was opposed to Lincoln's war policies. In 1865 Locke became editor of the Toledo *Blade*, and continued publishing his letters in that paper. They are written in a style similar to that later made famous by James Russell Lowell in 'The Bigelow Papers'. The 'works' of *Petroleum V. Nasby* and other colloquial books of this kind may be considered forerunners of the 'realistic' style of writing which was to be the focus of attention in America in the later part of the nineteenth century. Hamlin Garland's *Main-Travelled Roads*[45] consists of six 'realistic' stories about the Mississippi valley. Thomas A. Bledsoe, the editor of this Rinehart paperback reissue of Garland's best-known work, considers that Garland's very limitations are significant for the rebellion he characterized. He was not only a realist, but a moralist, and Bledsoe finds it 'tragically ironical' that his later prose should be so full of glowing platitudes, which contrast oddly with the taut style of *Main-Travelled Roads*.

Ethel Stephens Arnett's *O. Henry from Polecat Creek*[46] portrays the early life of William Sydney Porter, who became famous as 'O. Henry'. Mrs. Arnett shows how his early years not only shaped O. Henry's personality, but also provided him with characters which he used in his satires. This is a useful addition to our

[43] *The Lovingood Papers: 1963*, ed. by Ben Harris McClary. Published for the Sut Society by Tennessee U.P. pp. 67.
[44] *The Struggles of Petroleum V. Nasby*, by David Ross Locke. Original illustrations by Thomas Nast. Abridged edition. Selected, edited, and with an introduction by Joseph Jones. Notes to the chapters by Gunther Barth. Boston: Beacon. pp. xxvi + 246. $2.45.

[45] *Main-Travelled Roads*, by Hamlin Garland. Ed. with an introduction by Thomas A. Bledsoe. New York: Holt, Rinehart & Winston. pp. xlv + 185. 95c.
[46] *O. Henry from Polecat Creek*, by Ethel Stephens Arnett. Greensboro, N. Carolina: Piedmont. pp. xxi + 240. $5.95.

knowledge of the world-famous humorist who was also a tragic American figure.

Lucy T. Clark has compiled *A Checklist of the Barrett Library Wegelin Collection of Later Nineteenth Century Minor American Poetry*.[47] Her bibliography covers the years 1821–99, and lists the works during that period which were collected by the late Oscar Wegelin. Although it does not pretend to be complete, it is valuable in providing evidence of that 'mob of scribbling women' of whom Hawthorne complained.

The Prentice-Hall paperback collection of critical essays on Emily Dickinson[48] is edited by Richard B. Sewall. It includes contributions by Conrad Aiken, Allen Tate, Yvor Winters, George F. Whicher, Henry W. Wells, Thomas H. Johnson, and Charles R. Anderson. Here also may be found Allen Tate's 'Emily Dickinson' (1932), R. P. Blackmur's 'Emily Dickinson's Notation' (1956), Richard Wilbur's 'Sumptuous Destitution' (1960), and Archibald MacLeish's 'The Private World: Poems of Emily Dickinson' (1961). The theme of the volume is set by the title of John Crowe Ransom's essay—'A Poet Restored'. If there is any qualification to be made about this selection, it is that it is a paean of praise. Even one dissentient voice would have been welcome.

It seems appropriate to begin a commentary on books concerning Mark Twain with a symposium entitled *The Gilded Age: A Re-Appraisal*.[49]

The editor, H. Wayne Morgan, has undertaken to examine the historical facts and interpretations which were available on that period in American history known as the 'Gilded Age'. This is taken roughly to be the years between 1865 and 1890. There is one essay, written by Robert Falk and entitled 'The Search for Reality: Writers and Their Literature', which is of particular interest to students of literature. The other contributors to this collection deal with such topics as 'The Robber Baron in the Gilded Age: Entrepreneur or Iconoclast?' and 'Gilt, Gingerbread, and Realism: The Public and its Taste'.

Douglas Grant's *Twain*[50] is the first book to be written on Mark Twain by an Englishman for a long time. It is divided into three chapters: 'S-t-e-a-m Boat A-comin'!', which deals with Twain's early background; 'The Gigantic Picnic', which is concerned with the years after 'The Celebrated Jumping Frog' went from California to New York; and 'Asking for a Light', which covers the period from 1889 to the end. Grant quotes Howells's description of Twain at the age of fifty—'He glimmered at you from the narrow slits of fine blue-greenish eyes, under branching brows, which grew more and more like a sort of plumage, and he was apt to smile into your face with a subtle but amiable perception, and yet with a sort of remote absence.' This is a good example of the excellent use which Grant makes of quotation and illustration.

Mark Twain's Frontier[51] is a 'textbook of primary source materials for student research and writing'. The editors have provided a map of Mark

[47] *The Barrett Library Wegelin Collection of Later Nineteenth Century Minor American Poetry, 1821–1899*. Compiled by Lucy T. Clark. Virginia U.P. 1962. pp. 107.

[48] *Emily Dickinson: A Collection of Critical Essays*, ed. by Richard B. Sewall. Englewood Cliffs, N.J.: Prentice-Hall. pp. 182. $1.95.

[49] *The Gilded Age: A Re-Appraisal*, ed. by H. Wayne Morgan. Syracuse U.P. pp. vii + 286. $2.95.

[50] *Twain*, by Douglas Grant. Oliver & Boyd, 1962. pp. 120. 5s.

[51] *Mark Twain's Frontier*, ed. by James E. Camp and X. J. Kennedy. Holt, Rinehart & Winston. pp. xv + 269. 16s.

Twain's 'frontier' and divided their material into five sections. In the first there are letters from Twain to his mother, and his brother Orion, together with extracts from *Roughing It* and *The Autobiography of Mark Twain*. The second section deals with Twain's newspaper reporting in Virginia City, the third with mining in California and his apprenticeship in the telling of a 'tall tale', the fourth with his contemporaries' views on him, and the fifth with extracts from Van Wyck Brooks's *The Ordeal of Mark Twain* and Bernard DeVoto's *Mark Twain's America*. This is a most helpful guide for any student of Twain's contribution to literature.

The Prentice-Hall paperback collection of critical essays on Mark Twain[52] is edited by Henry Nash Smith. It includes, among others, essays by Van Wyck Brooks on 'Mark Twain's Humor', by Leo Marx on 'The Lost America—the Despair of Henry Adams and Mark Twain', and by Leslie Fiedler on 'As Free as any Cretur'. Smith also prints W. H. Auden's lively and penetrating comparison of *Huckleberry Finn* and *Oliver Twist*, and Bernard DeVoto's article on Twain's later years entitled 'Symbols of Despair'. This is perhaps the best selection which could have been chosen from the now considerable body of Twain criticism.

Hamlin Hill's reprint of *A Connecticut Yankee in King Arthur's Court*[53] is a facsimile of the first edition. The editor has provided an introduction and bibliography. The

only differences between this and the first edition are that the title page does not have the name of 'Samuel Langhorne Clemens' on it, owing to a quibble by the Estate, and that the book is slightly smaller than the original.

In *Mark Twain and Little Satan*[54] John S. Tuckey is concerned with *The Mysterious Stranger*, believing it to be the most important of Twain's later writings. The story exists in three different drafts, all in Twain's own hand-writing, which were left unfinished when he died in 1910. It was Twain himself, Tuckey believes, who was 'the mysterious stranger'. The role was one which he felt he had to play in order to reveal the limitless power of the creative mind, because, in the end, his art had lost contact with reality.

Sister M. Corona Sharp, O.S.U., has made a fascinating study of the 'evolution and moral value of a fictive character' in *The Confidante in Henry James*.[55] As conceived by James, the role of 'confidante' involved the drawing out of information and interpreting it for the reader. Sister Corona believes that James's use of the 'confidante' relationship constitutes more than a technical triumph, that in fact it plays a great part in unifying some of his most important works. After discussing the 'minor confidante'—for example Mrs. Prest in *The Aspern Papers* and May Bartram in 'The Beast in the Jungle'—Sister Corona proceeds to a study of Madam Merle in *The Portrait of a Lady*, Maria Gostrey in *The Ambassadors*, and Susan Stringham in *The Wings of the Dove*.

[52] *Mark Twain: A Collection of Critical Essays*, ed. by Henry Nash Smith. Englewood Cliffs, N.J. Prentice-Hall. pp. 179. $1.95.

[53] *A Connecticut Yankee in King Arthur's Court*, by Samuel Langhorne Clemens. A Facsimile of the First Edition. With an Introduction and Bibliography prepared by Hamlin Hill. San Francisco: Chandler. pp. xv+575.

[54] *Mark Twain and Little Satan*, by John S. Tuckey. Purdue University Studies. pp. 100. $1.75.

[55] *The Confidante in Henry James*, by Sister M. Corona Sharp, O.S.U. Notre Dame U.P. pp. xxx+305. $6.75.

F. R. Leavis has provided the preface to a selection of Henry James's literary criticism, edited by Morris Shapira.[56] Leavis believes that it is not only in James's Prefaces that we find his most impressive and valuable criticism. As 'George Eliot's successor' he is important for his essays on Maupassant, Balzac, and other European writers. Among the pieces printed in this volume, which run from 1865 to 1914, there are 'Mr. Walt Whitman', 'The Art of Fiction', 'Emerson', 'Gustave Flaubert', 'The Future of the Novel', and 'The New Novel'.

Recollections of Life in Ohio, from 1813 to 1840[57] is a reprint of a book by the father of William Dean Howells. This facsimile reproduction of the first edition is introduced by Edwin H. Cady. In a preface the younger Howells tells us that it was on his suggestion that his father began to set down the facts of his early life. His book is a fascinating account of pioneer life in Ohio by an immigrant Quaker Welshman, who set up a woollen mill, educated himself, lived in a log cabin, opened a grammar school, started a weekly newspaper, and studied medicine.

'*Artie*' and '*Pink Marsh*'[58] is the title of a reprint of two novels by George Ade. *Artie* appeared in 1896 and *Pink Marsh* in 1897. Like Ade himself, the main characters explore Chicago and describe what they see without sentimentality. Mark Twain was enthusiastic about these novels sixty years ago, and James T. Farrell, who introduces them, is equally so today. Ade's appeal does not depend upon caricature or exaggeration; his is a humour of character. William Dean Howells wote of *Artie*, 'I do not believe there is a better story of American town life in the west.'

5. TWENTIETH CENTURY

William C. Brownell's *American Prose Masters*[59] is re-issued by Harvard University Press under the editorship of Howard Mumford Jones. Brownell's book, which originally appeared in 1909, consists of essays on Cooper, Hawthorne, Emerson, Poe, Lowell, and Henry James, and was probably the best assessment of the major nineteenth-century American writers to be written according to the standards of the time. It is as illustrative of the critical temper of the pre-First World War period in American letters as it is illuminating on the subject of the authors with whom it deals.

Another reprint is that of T. K. Whipple's *Spokesman*.[60] Although the essays which comprise this volume were written during the 1920's, one still finds Whipple's opinions quoted approvingly today. At the time that he wrote, the reputations of the people he dealt with (Robinson, Dreiser, Frost, Anderson, Sandburg, Lindsay, Lowell, O'Neill, and Willa Cather) were not yet consolidated. What is surprising, therefore, is how relevant some of his comments still

---

[56] *Henry James: Selected Literary Criticism*, ed. by Morris Shapira. Prefaced with a note on 'James as Critic' by F. R. Leavis. Heinemann. pp. xxiii+349. 30s.

[57] *Recollections of Life in Ohio, from 1813 to 1840* (1895), by William Cooper Howells, with an Introduction by his son, William Dean Howells. A facsimile reproduction, with an Introduction by Edwin H. Cady. Gainesville, Fla: Scholars' Facsimiles & Reprints. pp. xiv+207. $7.50.

[58] '*Artie*' and '*Pink Marsh*'. Two novels by George Ade. Drawings by John T. McCutcheon. Introduction by James T. Farrell. Chicago U.P. pp. xi+224. $3.95. 29s.

[59] *American Prose Masters*, by W. C. Brownell. Ed. by Howard Mumford Jones. Harvard U.P. pp. xx+295. $4.25.

[60] *Spokesman*, by T. K. Whipple. With a Foreword by Mark Schorer. California U.P. and C.U.P. pp. xiii+276. $3.50. Cloth, 28s. Paper, 12s. 6d.

are. In a long introduction Mark Schorer compares Whipple to his friend Edmund Wilson. Like Wilson, he had a strong 'tendentious bias', made up of at least as much social polemic as of disinterested criticism.

Reed Whittemore's Minnesota Pamphlet on *Little Magazines*[61] is, as might be expected, lively and informative despite its mere forty-seven pages. Whittemore, who is a poet of talent and wit and a former editor of *Furioso*, is in a good position to write on the subject he has chosen. He is as informative about the economics of little magazines as he is about their points of view. His essay covers the whole history of his subject from Harriet Monroe's *Poetry (Chicago)* to *Tiger's Eye*.

The St. Louis *Mirror*, which appeared from 1892 to 1920, was not quite a little magazine, but on the other hand, although it came out weekly, it was not exactly a newspaper. Edited by William Marion Reedy, it played a large part in playing down 'the genteel tradition' in the Middle West and in encouraging a certain kind of American poetry. There were few American poets during the twenty years before the First World War to whom Reedy's weekly did not offer hospitality. Among them were Ezra Pound, Edwin Arlington Robinson, Carl Sandburg, Vachel Lindsay, and Edgar Lee Masters, whose *Spoon River Anthology* first appeared in the *Mirror*. Max Putzel[62] gives a colourful description of Reedy's boyhood in St. Louis in the years immediately following the Civil War; but the major part of his book

is devoted to the frenetic literary enterprise and violent debates which took place in the *Mirror*.

William Wasserstrom's book on *The Dial*[63] recaptures the intellectual stir which made that magazine the most significant publication in the arts during the 1920's. Wasserstrom points out how the later *Dial* differed from earlier versions of the magazine and from other 'little' magazines of its time. Its contributors included T. S. Eliot, Edmund Wilson, William Carlos Williams, Thomas Mann, D. H. Lawrence, Yeats, and Picasso. Although the magazine ceased publication in 1929, its views are still quoted today. Wasserstrom has assembled much original material based on interviews and correspondence with Marianne Moore, a former editor of *The Dial*, with Dr. J. S. Watson, Jr., and with Scofield Thayer.

Sylvia Beach,[64] was very much a friend and patron of the arts. A monograph published by the *Mercure de France* contains tributes from T. S. Eliot, Marianne Moore, Archibald MacLeish, Allen Tate, and Malcolm Cowley, as well as from such well-known French writers as André Chamson and Maria Jolas. 'Shakespear & Co.', Miss Beach's bookshop in the Rue de L'Odéon, is best known for its association with James Joyce, but it was also a rendezvous for expatriate literary Americans, as Malcolm Cowley attests.

John M. Bradbury continues to write on Southern topics. This time it is a critical history of Southern literature between 1920 and 1960,[65] to

---

[61] *Little Magazines*, by Reed Whittemore. (Minnesota Pamphlet on American Writers No. 32.) Minnesota U.P. and O.U.P. pp. 47. 65c. 5s.

[62] *The Man in the Mirror: William Marion Reedy and his Magazine*, by Max Putzel. Harvard U.P. pp. xiv + 351. $7.50.

[63] *The Time of the Dial*, by William Wasserstrom. Syracuse U.P. pp. vii + 194. $4.95.

[64] *Sylvia Beach, 1887–1962*. Mercure de France. pp. 172. Fr. 18.

[65] *Renaissance in the South: A Critical History of the Literature, 1920–1960*, by John M. Bradbury. N. Carolina U.P. pp. 222. $5.

which period Bradbury gives the title of 'Renaissance'. His approach is ambitious. After dealing with the 'awakening' of Southern literature in the early 1920's and the first phase of poetry and drama, he turns to the 'new social realism' which developed out of the Fugitive movement. There follow sections on 'The Negro and the New South' and on recent poetry and drama from the Southern states. Bradbury discerns two strands: one of traditionalism (which might be considered essentially Southern), the other of 'protest literature' which has emerged from the problem-ridden South of modern times. In recent Southern literature he sees an intertwining of these two strands.

During the 1920's Donald Davidson, the Southern writer and 'Fugitive' poet, was a book-reviewer for the Nashville *Tennessean*. He saw in this an opportunity of creating a forum for Southern literary opinion which constituted, to some extent, a Southern literary journal. John Tyree Fain has made a selection from Davidson's articles during this period. His book[66] is divided into six sections: 'Southern Fiction', 'Other American Fiction', 'Poetry', 'Critics and Commentators', 'Society and the Arts', and 'Backgrounds of Agrarianism'. As might be expected, Davidson is most interesting on the subject of Southern writers, but his comments on Hemingway, Sherwood Anderson, Sinclair Lewis, and Theodore Dreiser are often penetrating. This collection, although more than of merely 'period' interest, helps to establish the literary background out of which the Fugitives emerged.

Daniel Aaron has edited Robert Herrick's *The Memoirs of an American*

Citizen.[67] This, the most widely read of the many novels which Herrick wrote about Chicago, consists of the self-revelation of Van Harrington, an Indiana farm boy who arrived penniless in Chicago and emerged with his 'bagful of plunder'. The 'period' background here, also, is excellent. Herrick was not writing sensational journalism, nor was he 'muckraking', like Lincoln Steffens and Upton Sinclair. As in the case of Dreiser, he was more interested in dramatizing the moral aspects of Harrington's situation, his succumbing to the spell of 'business', that 'one great American passion'. Aaron's impeccable editing is matched by the format of this interesting addition to the John Harvard Library.

Another reissue is Frank Harris's *The Bomb*,[68] introduced by John Dos Passos. This is the story of the Chicago anarchists who were found guilty of inciting the Haymarket Riot in 1886. The great question of the time was whether they had conspired to murder and actually thrown the bomb which killed eight policemen and wounded sixty. Governor Altgeld thought that they had not, and finally pardoned the two survivors in 1892. *The Bomb* is the first-person account of Rudolph Schnaubelt, the anarchist who disappeared and the one who might have thrown the bomb. In an Afterword, Harris reveals that the character of Schnaubelt is purely imaginary, but that, for the rest, he kept as closely to the facts as he could. In a graphic introduction ('Frank Harris was an objectionable little man. He was sallow as a gypsy. He had bat ears, dark hair with a

---

[66] *The Spyglass: Views and Reviews, 1924–1930*, by Donald Davidson. Sel. and ed. by John Tyree Fain. Vanderbilt U.P. pp. xxii + 262. $4.

[67] *The Memoirs of an American Citizen*, by Robert Herrick. Ed. by Daniel Aaron. Harvard U.P. pp. xxxii + 270. $4.75.

[68] *The Bomb*, by Frank Harris. Introduction by John Dos Passos. Chicago U.P. pp. xxiii + 332. $4.95. 37s.

crinkle in it that grew low on the forehead, and a truculent mustache.') Dos Passos gives colour to Harris's story.

Ring Lardner, one of the more important of American satirists, seems to be less well-known among educated people in Europe than the second-rate Damon Runyon. Walton R. Patrick's book on Lardner[69] attempts to evaluate his literary achievement. Patrick places chief emphasis on Lardner's fiction, and devotes his first chapters to the connected groups of stories which Lardner wrote about 'Bush League' baseball players, about a Chicago police detective, and about two 'wise boobs' who appear as the main characters of Gullible's Travels. He then goes on to examine at some length the stories which appeared in How to Write Short Stories and The Love Nest and Other Stories.

Maxwell Geismar introduces The Ring Lardner Reader.[70] He has organized his selection into six parts in order to illustrate what he sees to be the dominant themes in Lardner's work, and also to describe the social development of the period. The section entitled 'Provincial Life', for example, includes 'You know me Al' and 'Haircut'. In the third section headed 'Success Story, U.S.A.' are to be found 'Champion', 'The Love Nest', and 'Mr. Frisbie'. Under 'The Popular Arts' Geismar prints, among other stories, 'Alibi Ike' and 'The Origin of Football'. In the sixth section, entitled 'Native Dada', there are a number of 'Plays' and the prefaces to How to Write Short Stories (1924), The Love Nest (1926), and The Story of a Wonder Man (1927).

A Middle Western writer who is better-known in Europe than Lardner is Sinclair Lewis. Mark Schorer's mammoth biography of Lewis is followed this year by Vincent Sheean's Dorothy and Red.[71] When Lewis met Dorothy Thompson, at a dinner-party in Berlin in 1927, he was already world-famous for his novel Main Street. He was by then divorced from Grace Hegger, and he and Miss Thompson married at once. Lewis and his second wife constantly wrote to each other, and both kept a diary. The correspondence which Sheean prints tells the story of their marriage from the first small rifts to the final break-up. He has based his book on the Dorothy Thompson Papers, now at Syracuse University Library, and adds to the information supplied by Schorer's biography.

Schorer himself has produced a University of Minnesota pamphlet on Lewis[72] which paraphrases in forty-seven pages the substance of his book. Schorer admits that 'in a strict literary sense' Lewis was not a great writer, but without his writing he feels that one could not 'imagine' modern American literature. His epitaph should be: He did us good.

Wilfried Edener has undertaken an examination of religion in the works of Sinclair Lewis.[73] He prefaces his thesis with some general remarks about religion and the criticism of religion in the United States from the time of Benjamin Franklin to Hamlin Garland, then proceeds to an examination of Lewis's life, and a close

[69] Ring Lardner, by Walton R. Patrick. New York: Twayne. pp. 175. $3.50.

[70] The Ring Lardner Reader, ed. by Maxwell Geismar. New York: Scribner. pp. xxxiv+661. $7.50.

[71] Dorothy and Red, by Vincent Sheean. Boston: Houghton Mifflin. pp. vii+363. $6.95.

[72] Sinclair Lewis, by Mark Schorer. (Minnesota Pamphlets on American Writers No. 27:. Minnesota U.P. and O.U.P. pp. 47. 65c. 5s.

[73] Die Religionskritik in den Romanen von Sinclair Lewis, by Wilfried Edener. Heidelberg: Carl Winter. pp. 240. DM. 26.

study of *Elmer Gantry*, *The God-Seeker*, and other later works.

Another thesis from Heidelberg is concerned with the novel of 'Flaming Youth'. Horst Hermann Kruse considers[74] subject matter and form in a number of novels, including *Flaming Youth*, *I Thought of Daisy*, *This Side of Paradise*, and *The Sun Also Rises*.

A major figure of the period of 'Flaming Youth' was F. Scott Fitzgerald, whom William Goldhurst[75] undertakes to place against the background of his time. Goldhurst's method is to consider the work of four colleagues who influenced Fitzgerald strongly: Edmund Wilson, H. L. Mencken, Ring Lardner, and Ernest Hemingway. He examines in some detail the personal and professional relationships of each with Fitzgerald, pointing out affinities and suggesting where one has influenced the other. There were many significant exchanges of advice and ideas between Fitzgerald and his four friends. This book combines literary criticism, social history, and biography in an unusual and interesting way.

Working with the Fitzgerald manuscripts in Princeton University, Matthew J. Bruccoli[76] has reconstructed seventeen drafts and three versions of *Tender is the Night* in order to answer questions about the novel which have puzzled critics of Fitzgerald. Disappointed by the adverse critical reception of what was intended to be his major novel, Fitzgerald fell to rewriting and rearranging. In 1951, eleven years after his death, his pub-lisher brought out a volume which incorporated Fitzgerald's changes. However, controversy has continued about the merits of the two published versions, and the latest edition restores the original version of 1934. Bruccoli reconstructs various stages in the novel, and comes to his own conclusion about which version is the most valid.

Andrew Turnbull's *The Letters of F. Scott Fitzgerald*[77] brings together for the first time a selection of Fitzgerald's letters, which are full of the drama of Fitzgerald's private life. He has grouped his selection around the people who were closest to Fitzgerald. The book opens with correspondence between the author and his daughter 'Scottie'. Then follow letters to Zelda, and a number addressed to his editor, Maxwell Perkins. Another section consists of letters to Ernest Hemingway which tell us about the other side of this famous friendship. There are also sections devoted to correspondence with, among others, John Peale Bishop, Shane Leslie, Harold Ober, Christian Gauss, Gerald and Sara Murphy, and Mrs. Bayard Turnbull.

The Fitzgerald Reader[78] is divided into four parts. In 'Winter Dreams' the editor, Arthur Mizener, makes a selection from the stories of the 1920's and *The Great Gatsby*. 'The Crack-Up' includes most of the important stories of the early 1930's, plus the first six chapters of *Tender is the Night*. 'Pasting it Together' contains the article with that title, 'The Crack-Up', and 'Handle With Care'. In 'Handling It With Care' Mizener prints the stories in *Afternoon of an*

[74] *Die Romane der 'Flaming Youth'*, by Horst Hermann Kruse. Heidelberg: Carl Winter. pp. 144. DM. 17.50.

[75] *F. Scott Fitzgerald and his Contemporaries*, by William Goldhurst. Cleveland & New York: World Publishing Co. pp. 247. $4.50.

[76] *The Composition of 'Tender is the Night': A Study of the Manuscripts*, by Matthew J. Bruccoli. Pittsburgh U.P. pp. xxv+252. $6.

[77] *The Letters of F. Scott Fitzgerald*, ed. by Andrew Turnbull. New York: Scribners. pp. xviii+615. $10.

[78] *The Fitzgerald Reader*, ed. and with an introduction by Arthur Mizener. New York: Scribners. pp. xxvii+509. $7.50.

Author and the first four chapters of *The Last Tycoon*. In an analytical introduction he correlates Fitzgerald's work in terms of 'thematic and technical progress'. Even though Fitzgerald was extremely tired at the end of his life, he could still see his 'vision'. For all its quietness, his voice is deeply moving.

Between 1905 and 1955 James Branch Cabell published over forty books. Arvin R. Wells's study of Cabell[79] attempts a re-assessment of this now neglected author, whose works, now that *Jurgen* is out of print, can no longer be obtained. Wells believes that Cabell was a serious literary artist, and that his reputation should not depend on the admiration of those who have valued him for his 'special' and precious qualities. Wells is concerned with Cabell's 'comic vision'. He devotes, in fact, four of his eight chapters to the Cabell view of comedy. Cabell's achievement, Wells believes, was the creation of a kind of comedy which treads the line between comedy and tragedy without being tragi-comedy.

Earl Rovit's study of Ernest Hemingway[80] attempts to present Hemingway's work in the round by analysing his style, the way in which he uses narrative, and the kind of theme which recurs most frequently in his work. Rovit's thesis is that the elements of Hemingway's artistic techniques are not only important in themselves, but are essential in the development of the 'overall pattern' of his work. There is, Rovit believes, an 'organic growth' from *In Our Time* to *The Old Man and the Sea*. Not Flaubert or Turgenev, but Emerson and Whitman, seem to be Hemingway's artistic ancestors. Like Faulkner he was concerned with 'the heart in conflict with itself'.

Hemingway par lui-même, by G.-A. Astre,[81] is one of the 'Écrivains de Toujours' series and, like the others, vividly illustrated. Astre establishes Hemingway's background in Oak Park, Illinois, and proceeds to tell the story of his life through to his death in Ketchum, Idaho, on 2 July 1961. Astre's contention is that Hemingway refused to live 'diminué', that he needed to stay faithful to the personality which he had imposed upon himself, and which he understood at the end as being the 'final truth' for him. He wished, Astre believes, to decide his death at a moment when it was 'convenient' to him.

Ernest Hemingway[82] is the title of an Italian publication translated by Salvatore Bottino and based on the pamphlet by Philip Young in the University of Minnesota series. It is indicative of the great interest in American literature which is found today on the Continent, an interest which, judging from the extent to which American literature figures in courses in schools as well as universities, is greater than in the United Kingdom.

Hans W. Bentz's *Ernest Hemingway in Übersetzungen*[83] is a bibliography of translations. The titles of the original works are arranged alphabetically, with their publishers, year of publication, and prices. Bentz's compilation illustrates the variety of languages into which Hemingway's novels and stories have been translated. They

---

[79] *Jesting Moses: A Study in Cabellian Comedy*, by Arvin R. Wells. Florida U.P., 1962. pp. ix+146. $5.

[80] *Hemingway*, by Earl Rovit. New York: Twayne. pp. 192. $3.50.

[81] *Hemingway par lui-même*, by G.-A. Astre. Paris: 'Écrivains de Toujours', Aux Editions du Seuil., 1961 pp. 191.

[82] *Ernest Hemingway*, by Philip Young. Tr. by Salvatore Bottino. Milan: Ugo Mursia Editore, 1962. pp. 75. Lire 600.

[83] *Ernest Hemingway in Übersetzungen*, by Hans W. Bentz. Frankfurt am Main: Hans W. Bentz Verlag. pp. vii+34+5.

include Serbo-Croat, Arabic, Bengali, Korean, Hungarian, Finnish, Tamil, Japanese, and Turkish, as well as the 'usual' languages.

Cleanth Brooks's *William Faulkner: The Yoknapatawpha Country*[84] is a study of Faulkner as a literary artist. Brooks maintains that it is of the utmost importance to Faulkner's contribution that he set his fiction in North Mississippi. This attachment to a particular region gives him, not provinciality, but universality. The stories and novels which are ostensibly about 'Yoknapatawpha Country' have, in fact, a meaning for all of us. Brooks analyses the chief novels with characteristic intelligence and insight. A most helpful feature of this book is the degree of its documentation. The genealogies, especially, are important, as also are such essential pieces of information as the sequence of events in *Absalom, Absalom!* There is a 'Character Index', as well as a very comprehensive ordinary index.

William Faulkner: An Introduction and Interpretation[85] is the title which Lawrance Thompson has given to his contribution to the Barnes and Noble 'American Authors and Critics Series'. Thompson begins by sketching Faulkner's literary career and 'technical innovations', then proceeds to analyse *Absalom, Absalom!, Light in August, Go Down Moses, Sanctuary, Requiem for a Nun, The Hamlet,* and *The Town.* His concluding chapter is concerned with Faulkner's 'moral vision'. He quotes Faulkner on a visit to Japan as saying that the writer must 'show the base, the evil things that man can do and still hate himself for doing it'. Faulkner, Thompson concludes, intended that the 'indirections' of his art should create in his readers an awareness not only of conflicts, but also of the possibilities of greater harmony.

Faulkner's People[86] by Robert W. Kirk, in conjunction with Marvin Klotz, is described as 'a complete guide and index to characters in the fiction of William Faulkner'. It is constructed in the following way. The novels from *Soldier's Pay* (1926) to *The Reivers* (1962) are listed by title, in order of publication. Under each title, all of the named characters who appear or are mentioned in the work are listed alphabetically, together with the number of every page on which the character's name occurs. A concise account of the actions of each character is given, together with a description of that character's salient features. Immediately following the section devoted to the novels appear the named characters in all of Faulkner's stories and sketches. These are also given in order of publication. Characters who carry over from the novels to the stories, or who are handled inconsistently by Faulkner, are marked with an asterisk and discussed in an appendix. Here, also, there are helpful genealogical charts, together with a map of 'Yoknapatawpha Country'. Finally, a complete Index lists every work in which the various characters occur.

The Tragic Mask by John Lewis Longley, Jr.,[87] is a study of Faulkner's heroes. Longley was teaching at the University of Virginia when Faulkner was Writer-in-Residence there, and

[84] *William Faulkner: The Yoknapatawpha Country*, by Cleanth Brooks. Yale U.P. pp. xiv+499. $8.50. 63s.

[85] *William Faulkner: An Introduction and Interpretation*, by Lawrance Thompson. New York: Barnes & Noble. pp. viii+184. Cloth, $3.50. Paper, $1.50.

[86] *Faulkner's People*, by Robert W. Kirk, with Marvin Klotz. California U.P. and Cambridge U.P. pp. xiii+354. $5.95. 48s.

[87] *The Tragic Mask: A Study of Faulkner's Heroes*, by John Lewis Longley, Jr. N. Carolina U.P. pp. ix+242. $6.

was able to ask him many questions about his work. The book begins with a discussion of Faulkner's 'comic heroes' (Gavin Stevens, Byron Bunch, V. K. Ratliff, and Ike Mc-Caslin), proceeds to a discussion of Faulkner's 'social comedy' and 'comedy of extremity', and ends with some ideas on 'Faulkner and tragedy'. Colonel John Sartoris is cited as an example of 'the classic tragic hero', Joe Christmas is 'the hero in the modern world', and Thomas Sutpen is an example of 'the tragedy of aspiration'.

John Faulkner's 'affectionate reminiscence'[88] of his brother Bill is not concerned with the public image of William Faulkner. It is about Faulkner as a boy, growing up in the environment which furnished him with most of the raw material about which he later wrote, and about the man who retained during his life an almost mystical feeling for that environment. The Faulkner who emerges from his brother John's description is one fiercely loyal to his family and old friends while often disagreeing violently with them. He is a man steeped in frontier humour and, to the end, a Southerner who both loved and hated his native ground because it never lived up to what he felt it capable of being. John Faulkner attempts to identify some of the people and places in Mississippi who appear under other names in Faulkner's work—for example, 'From where I sat I could see the section of the Square across which Joe Christmas was led from the jail to the courthouse and where, manacled, he had broken away from his guard and run, chased by Percy Grimm, on his commandeered bicycle.'

In The Hidden God,[89] Cleanth Brooks undertakes a study of Hemingway and Faulkner, as well as of Yeats, Eliot, and Robert Penn Warren. Brooks believes that whatever a writer has to say about mankind, Christianity or culture in general is most significantly explained in his achievement as a literary artist. For that reason he deals in these lectures with the characteristic literary work of each author, rather than with his 'theology' or 'philosophy'. About Hemingway, Brooks concludes that he is perfectly right to confine himself to his own idiosyncratic 'secular terms'. It might be presumptuous, Brooks believes, for the reader to assume that he could go at all along the road that Hemingway's lonely heroes are forced to take. Hemingway's characters are willing to face the fact that most men can learn the deepest truths about themselves only through suffering. Pain and loss are means to a deeper knowledge and to a more abundant life.

Ellen Glasgow and the Ironic Art of Fiction[90] is a paperback reprint of F. P. W. McDowell's study of the Virginia novelist, published in 1960 (YW xli. 294).

There are twelve stories in The Collected Stories of Ellen Glasgow,[91] seven of which, from The Shadowy Third and Other Stories published in 1923, have long been out of print. Four others appeared in magazines during Miss Glasgow's lifetime, and one was still in manuscript at the time of her death. In his introduction,

[88] My Brother Bill: An Affectionate Reminiscence, by John Faulkner. New York: Trident. pp. 277. $4.95.

[89] The Hidden God: Studies in Hemingway, Faulkner, Yeats, Eliot, and Warren, by Cleanth Brooks. Yale U.P. pp. xi+136. 35s. 6d.
[90] Ellen Glasgow and the Ironic Art of Fiction, by Frederick P. W. McDowell. Wisconsin U.P. pp. xi+292. $1.95.
[91] The Collected Stories of Ellen Glasgow, ed. by Richard K. Meeker. Louisiana State U.P. pp. viii+254. $5.

Richard K. Meeker discusses how the stories grew out of Miss Glasgow's childhood and later experiences. He also attempts to trace some literary influences on her work, and to place the stories in the context of Miss Glasgow's achievement as a whole. If she had had her way, he points out, she would have included a volume of short stories in the 'Virginia' edition of her work. Miss Glasgow, Meeker concludes, had all the equipment of a great short story writer except a 'respect for form'.

Ray B. West's Minnesota pamphlet on Katherine Anne Porter[92] is an appraisal of an American woman writer who has also been less appreciated, certainly in Europe, than was her due. West believes that Henry James was Miss Porter's model, although she herself speaks of an early attraction to Sterne. She admired Katherine Mansfield for her 'quiet ruthlessness of judgement', and disliked Gertrude Stein for her 'absence of moral, intellectual and aesthetic judgement'. In a small compass, West manages to include a surprisingly large amount of analysis of the main stories, from *Flowering Judas* to *Pale Horse, Pale Rider*. There is also some discussion of *Ship of Fools*. At the age of seventy-two Katherine Anne Porter announced that she had three more books to write, one of them on Cotton Mather.

The late Richard Chase contributes an unexpectedly favourable Preface to the third printing of the Dell paperback edition of *You Can't Go Home Again*.[93] He believes that critics must put on one side certain clichés and half-truths about Wolfe if they are to discern what is enjoyable in his work. The most injurious notion is that Wolfe's main achievement lay in his being 'a novelist who wrote novels about a novelist writing novels'.

Harry John Mooney Jr.'s study of James Gould Cozzens[94] is published in the University of Pittsburgh's 'Critical Essays in Modern Literature' series. Mooney believes that Cozzens's position in contemporary American literature has been anomalous. Although he was never completely neglected, Cozzens attained wide popularity only after the publication of *By Love Possessed*. Since then he has been both appreciated and condemned for the wrong reasons. Criticism of Cozzens's work is scattered in book reviews and journals, and there have been no successful attempts to interpret his eight novels in the light of the 'principal themes' in his work. Mooney attempts this task. He believes that a large part of Cozzens's current significance lies in his ability to 'expand beyond the capacity of anyone else in his generation the scope and quality of the traditional'.

George Wickes believes that the time has come for a balanced critical appraisal of the work of Henry Miller. He brings together, in his miscellany entitled *Henry Miller and the Critics*,[95] twenty-one opinions about Miller and his work. Among the contributors are George Orwell, Alfred Perlès, Edmund Wilson, Philip Rahv, Lawrence Durrell, and others who knew Miller either in Paris or at Big Sur. The result is both a general survey of critical opinion and a series

[92] *Katherine Anne Porter*, by Ray B. West, Jr. (Minnesota Pamphlets on American Writers No. 28). Minnesota U.P. & O.U.P. pp. 48. 65c. 5s.

[93] *You Can't Go Home Again*, by Thomas Wolfe. With an introduction by Richard Chase. pp. 671. 95c.

[94] *James Gould Cozzens: Novelist of Intellect*, by Harry John Mooney, Jr. Pittsburgh U.P. pp. ix+186. $2.

[95] *Henry Miller and the Critics*, ed. by George Wickes. Preface by Harry T. Moore. S. Illinois U.P. pp. xviii+194. $4.50.

of personal accounts of Miller's career, with some weighting in the latter category. There is a preface by Harry T. Moore and a 'draconian post-script' by Miller himself.

Down These Mean Streets A Man Must Go[96] is the title which Philip Durham has given to his study of Raymond Chandler. Chandler, Durham believes, was a true romantic. He created a modern knight in an atmosphere that was antipathetic to the ideals of knighthood. In Durham's opinion, Chandler's work is in the mainstream of American literature, the broad flow of frontier literature which moved 'from Georgia of the 1830's to California of the 1950's'. This 'mainstream' of American literature produced 'modern morality plays' of which Chandler's works are examples.

Selected Writings of Truman Capote[97] represents the author's choice of his work, and includes six stories from *A Tree of Night*, four from *Breakfast at Tiffany's*, and 'Among the Paths to Eden.' In the non-fiction section there are extracts from *Local Color* and from *The Muses Are Heard*, which is described by Mark Schorer, who introduces the volume, as one of the 'great satiric reports of our time'.

Chester E. Eisinger's *Fiction of the Forties*[98] is better than its rather pretentious chapter headings would lead one to believe. Eisinger divides his subject into six categories: 'The War Novel'; 'Naturalism: The Tactics of Survival'; 'Fiction and the Liberal Reassessment'; 'The Conservative Imagination'; 'The New Fiction', and 'In Search of Man and America'. Although it is not of the standard of Frederick J. Hoffman's *The Twenties*, Eisinger's study is nevertheless of interest as a preliminary essay in the definition of what the forties meant in American literature.

Soon, One Morning[99] is an anthology of pieces by American Negroes written during the period 1940 to 1962. The collection is divided into three parts: essays, fiction, and poems. Langston Hughes writes on 'Moscow Movie', and John Hope Franklin on 'The Dilemma of the American Negro Scholar'. There are stories by, among others, Richard Wright, Ann Petry, Ralph Ellison, James Baldwin, and Katherine Dunham; and Gwendolyn Brooks, Langston Hughes, LeRoi Jones, and Paul Vesey are among the poets. In his introduction, Herbert Hill claims that an 'aesthetic tradition' has now emerged after the previous 'main tendencies' of 'folk tradition' and 'racial protest'.

In studying the influence of American literature in German-speaking Switzerland during the years 1945 to 1950,[100] Gertrud Möhl considers, first, the novel and, second, drama. The expected names appear: Dreiser, Lewis, Hemingway, Faulkner, Steinbeck, and Dos Passos. There is no mention of Fitzgerald, however, or of Thomas Wolfe. On the other hand, there is much about Upton Sinclair, Erskine Caldwell, William Saroyan,

[96] *Down These Mean Streets a Man Must Go: Raymond Chandler's Knight*, by Philip Durham. North Carolina U.P. pp. viii+173. $5.

[97] *Selected Writings of Truman Capote*, ed. by Mark Schorer. Hamish Hamilton. pp. xiv+460. 25s.

[98] *Fiction of the Forties*, by Chester E. Eisinger. Chicago U.P. pp. 392. $7.95. 59s. 6d.

[99] *Soon, One Morning: New Writing by American Negroes 1940–1962*. Sel. and ed., with an introduction and biographical notes, by Herbert Hill. New York: Alfred A. Knopf. pp. 617. $6.95.

[100] *Die Aufnahme Amerikanischer Literatur in der Deutschsprachigen Schweiz während der Jahre 1945–1950*, by Gertrud Möhl. Zurich: Juris-Verlag, 1961. pp. xxiii+114.

and Thornton Wilder. Miss Möhl's consideration of the drama extends to O'Neill, Wilder, Williams, and Miller, but not to William Inge or Edward Albee, or to any of the playwrights of the 30's, such as Maxwell Anderson, Elmer Rice, or Clifford Odets.

Recent American Fiction[101] is a reprint of a lecture given by Saul Bellow at the Library of Congress on 21 January 1963. Concentrating mainly on such contemporary novelists and short-story writers as James Jones, J. F. Powers, John Updike, Philip Roth, and Vladimir Nabokov, he comments on the 'view taken by recent American novelists and short-story writers of the individual and his society'. 'As for the future,' Bellow concludes, 'it cannot possibly shock us since we have already done everything possible to scandalise ourselves.'

In *First Person Singular*[102] Herbert Gold introduces essays by contemporary writers, among them Nelson Algren, James Baldwin, Saul Bellow, Herbert Blau, George P. Eliott, Mary McCarthy, Arthur Miller, William Saroyan, and Gore Vidal. The writers chosen have undertaken to speak out on some topic near to their hearts. Bellow, for example, writes some 'Literary Notes on Khrushchev', Mary McCarthy's topic is 'America the Beautiful: The Humanist in the Bathtub', and Gore Vidal has chosen Barry Goldwater as his subject. Gold's introduction, entitled 'How Else Can a Novelist Say It?', explains the reason for this uneven but very lively collection of personal statements.

The Creative Present[103] consists of attempts by ten well-known critics to evaluate the work of seventeen leading American writers of the post-war generation. Alun R. Jones writes on the fiction of Eudora Welty, Granville Hicks on 'Generations of the Fifties: Malamud, Gold, and Updike', Mark Schorer on 'McCullers and Capote: Basic Patterns', Alan Pryce Jones on 'The Fabulist's Worlds: Vladimir Nabokov', Diana Trilling on 'The Radical Moralism of Norman Mailer', and other critics on James Baldwin, J. D. Salinger, Saul Bellow, William Styron, James Jones, Jack Kerouac, and Mary McCarthy. The fact that both the editors have been on the staff of the *New York Times Book Review* probably accounts for the slightly journalistic quality of the essays. In his introduction Charles Simmons maintains that all the writers dealt with 'seem to have a future'.

The mood of the dedication of *Essays in Modern American Literature*[104] ('For Spook—to help him build an elephant . . .') seems to some extent to be reflected in the essays which follow, one of which is entitled 'That Was No Lady—That Was Jack Kerouac's Girl'. These are unusual pieces, none of which has appeared in print before. John Hague, W. Hugh McEniry, and David W. Marcell write on conservative themes arising from the study of nineteenth-century American literature, but the majority of the contributors deal with the twentieth century. Two interesting studies are 'Imagery and Meaning in *The Great Gatsby*', by

---

[101] *Recent American Fiction*, by Saul Bellow. Washington: Library of Congress. pp. iii+12. 15c.

[102] *First Person Singular: Essays for the Sixties*, ed., and with an introduction, by Herbert Gold. New York: Dial. pp. 254. $5.

[103] *The Creative Present: Notes on Contemporary American Fiction*, ed. by Nona Balakian and Charles Simmons. New York: Doubleday. pp. xx+265. $4.95.

[104] *Essays in Modern American Literature*, ed. by Richard E. Langford, in association with Guy Owen and William E. Taylor. Stetson U.P. pp. 122. $1.40.

Guy Owen, and 'James Gould Cozzens: A Cultural Dilemma', by
Richard P. Adams.

*Images of Truth: Remembrances
and Criticism*[105] is the title of Glenway
Wescott's collection of essays on
some of his contemporaries. Apart
from a general piece on 'Fiction
Writing in a Time of Troubles',
Wescott is concerned with Katherine
Anne Porter, Somerset Maugham,
Colette, Isak Dinesen, Thomas Mann,
and Thornton Wilder.

*I'll Take My Stand: The South and
the Agrarian Tradition*[106] has long
been a centre of controversy in the
United States. Published in 1930, it
consists of essays by 'Twelve Southerners', of which the most important
are perhaps 'Reconstructed but Un-
regenerate', by John Crowe Ransom;
'A Mirror for Artists', by Donald
Davidson; 'Education, Past and Present', by John Gould Fletcher; 'Remarks on the Southern Religion', by
Allen Tate; 'The Hind Tit,' by
Andrew Nelson Lytle; 'The Briar
Patch', by Robert Penn Warren; and
'Not in Memoriam, but in Defense',
by Stark Young. Virginia Rock provides biographical essays for this
'Harper Torchbook' re-issue. In his
introduction, Louis D. Rubin claims
that, as a human document, this
Southern manifesto is still very much
alive. He believes that concerns of
1930 are not only the concerns of 1960,
but will very likely be the concerns of the year 2000 also. However,
to read the original introduction to
I'll Take My Stand with its fierce
attack on 'industrialism'—which it
describes as an 'evil dispensation' to

be thrown off—it is difficult to see
how the attitude of the 'Twelve
Southerners' can be realistically maintained without considerable qualification.

William H. Rueckert's study of
Kenneth Burke[107] is organized in
terms of the main stages of Burke's
development as a critic. Rueckert
considers the 'aesthetic' of *Counter-
Statement*, and proceeds to a detailed exposition and application of
one of Burke's major contributions to
literary criticism: the analysis of
poetry as 'symbolic action'. In a later
chapter he examines 'dramatism'—
which he defines as 'language as the
ultimate reduction'—and Burke's
'dramatistic theory of literature'. The
analysis is highly detailed, and the
bibliography and index comprehensive.

Judging from the appearance of
Studies in J. D. Salinger,[108] there is
likely to develop a Salinger 'industry'.
This paper-bound symposium edited
by Marvin Laser and Norman Fruman contains a variety of studies, a
number of them being based on *The
Catcher in the Rye*. Robert Gutwillig
writes on 'Everybody's Caught *The
Catcher in the Rye*', Charles H. Kegel
on 'Incommunicability in Salinger's
The Catcher in the Rye', Hans Bun-
gert on 'Salinger's *The Catcher in the
Rye*: The Isolated Youth and His
Struggle to Communicate', and Kon-
stantin Chugunov on 'Soviet Critics
on J. D. Salinger's Novel, *The Catcher
in the Rye*'. There are also many
general pieces, notably Mary Mc-
Carthy's 'J. D. Salinger's Closed
Circuit', Charles Kaplan's 'Holden

105 *Images of Truth: Remembrances and
Criticism*, by Glenway Wescott. Hamish
Hamilton. pp. 310.

106 *I'll Take My Stand: The South and the
Agrarian Tradition*, by Twelve Southerners.
Introduction by Louis D. Rubin, Jr. Biogra-
phical essays by Virginia Rock. Harper and
Row, 1962. pp. xxx+384. $2.25. 17s.

107 *Kenneth Burke and the Drama of Human
Relations*, by William H. Rueckert. Minnesota U.P. pp. xiv+252. $6.

108 *Studies in J. D. Salinger: Reviews,
Essays, and Critiques of 'The Catcher in the
Rye' and other Fiction*, ed. by Marvin Laser
and Norman Fruman. New York: Odyssey.
pp. xi+272. $1.95.

and Huck: The Odysseys of Youth', Frank Kermode's 'Fit Audience', and Arthur Mizener's 'The Love Song of J. D. Salinger'. There are, in addition, four 'explications' of 'For Esmé—with Love and Squalor', a checklist of Salinger's work, and suggested topics for writing designed for University students.

The Inclusive Flame[109] is Glauco Cambon's title for his studies of Edwin Arlington Robinson, Wallace Stevens, Hart Crane, William Carlos Williams, and Robert Lowell. Cambon, an Italian scholar, prefaces his studies with an introductory chapter ('Space, Experiment, and Prophecy') devoted to the work of selected nineteenth-century American authors, his attempt being to show how the atmosphere of symbolism which developed at that time in the United States is related to the work of contemporary American writers. The title of his book is taken from his essay on Wallace Stevens, who, says Cambon, gazes at the sun of reality, refracts its 'inclusive flame' into rainbows and then pursues them to the 'boundaries of the invisible'.

Louis Untermeyer's 'reappraisal' of Edwin Arlington Robinson[110] was written when Untermeyer was Consultant in Poetry at the Library of Congress. Untermeyer believes that the sincerity of Robinson's poems lies in their sadness. Robinson met adversity with probity, and refused to soften difficult circumstances with hypocritical moralizing. He made the reader understand the 'unbeaten humanity' of his Miniver Cheevys and Bewick Finzers. Untermeyer's pamphlet contains a bibliography,

and a list of materials in the Edwin Arlington Robinson exhibit on display at the Library of Congress from 15 April to 16 July, 1963.

In *The Poetry of Robert Frost*[111] John Robert Doyle, Jr., analyzes Frost's work under the headings of 'Some Distinguishing Characteristics', 'Raw Materials Into Poems', 'Drama in Many Things', 'Serious But Not Solemn', 'Character Through Dramatic Narratives', 'Lyric Range and Duration', 'Thought In Lyric Form', and 'Attitudes and Ideas'. There is a certain disadvantage inherent in arranging poems under headings in this way which Doyle, for the most part, avoids. The 'thematic' approach leads sometimes to a tendency to move away from the evaluation of a poem as a work of art complete in itself.

William Van O'Connor's Minnesota Pamphlet on *Ezra Pound*[112] covers the whole of the poet's work in the usual (for the series) forty-seven pages. O'Connor, who, apart from his numerous other works, has published a 'Casebook on Ezra Pound', begins with a dramatic quotation from a broadcast made on 7 December 1941. He says, quite rightly, that the style and ideas of the broadcast suggest that Pound had a 'disordered mind'. However, there is a tendency to use this 'degeneration' (the term is F. R. Leavis's) as a stick with which to beat Pound. O'Connor's tentative conclusion is that, if Pound's poetry should 'achieve a place in the permanent canon of English and American poetry, Time will, as Auden says, lay its honors at his feet'.

[109] *The Inclusive Flame: Studies in American Poetry*, by Glauco Cambon. Indiana U.P. pp. viii + 248. $6.95.

[110] *Edwin Arlington Robinson*. A re-appraisal by Louis Untermeyer. Washington: Library of Congress. pp. 39. 25c.

[111] *The Poetry of Robert Frost: An Analysis*, by John Robert Doyle, Jr. Johannesburg: Witwatersrand U.P. New York: Hafner, 1962. pp. vii + 303.

[112] *Ezra Pound*, by William Van O'Connor. (Minnesota Pamphlets on American Writers No. 26.) Minnesota U.P. and O.U.P. pp. 47 65c. 5s.

Sailing After Knowledge[113] is the title of George Dekker's sound and detached study of *The Cantos*. Few poems are so difficult and uneven as Pound's longest work yet, properly related to their context, many of the *Cantos* reveal a depth and beauty which is not apparent on a superficial reading. The problem, as Dekker sees it, is twofold: first, to isolate the 'great' Cantos for special attention, and, second, to illuminate them by making their context meaningful. This he does well.

E P to L U[114] is the title of a small book containing nine letters written to Louis Untermeyer by Pound between 1914 and 1931. This represents a very small proportion of the letters which Pound sent to numerous correspondents during his long writing life, but they form a significant sample. The longest and most significant of the letters is a five-page biographical summary which Pound presented to Untermeyer in Rapallo in 1930.

Donald Gallup's *A Bibliography of Ezra Pound*[115] is a labour of love. Its plan is similar to that of the bibliography of T. S. Eliot published in 1952. Gallup records in detail English and American first editions of Pound's own books, but represents volumes containing only contributions by Pound merely by the actual first edition in book form. A third section of the book is devoted to contributions to periodicals, and a fourth to translations.

Hans W. Bentz's bibliography of T. E. Eliot's works in their foreign translations[116] is prefaced by a photostat of a letter from Eliot himself, congratulating Bentz on his industry. This volume is the fourth in a series entitled 'World Literature in Translations', and was intended as a tribute to the poet on his seventy-fifth birthday. Whereas Bentz's bibliography of Hemingway's works was published as an ordinary printed book, a much less elaborate form has been adopted for the Eliot volume. Bentz points out, in defence, that the Library of Congress, in all its richness, publishes bibliographies in a similar form. His book reveals the very large number of languages into which Eliot's works have been translated, from Bengali to Japanese.

The University of Minnesota pamphlet on *William Carlos Williams*[117] is by John Malcolm Brinnin, the biographer of Dylan Thomas. Brinnin notes that, among his fellow poets of an illustrious generation, Williams has been 'the man on the margin . . . the embattled messiah'. During the years when Eliot, Pound, Stevens, Marianne Moore, and Cummings were conducting their own experiments, Williams was trying a violent new orientation. Brinnin approves Williams's attempt, and records his achievement.

Samuel Hazo's 'introduction and interpretation'[118] of Hart Crane in the Barnes and Noble Series begins, conventionally enough, with a biographical sketch, proceeds to a discussion of Crane's poetic method, then concen-

[113] *Sailing After Knowledge: The Cantos of Ezra Pound*, by George Dekker. Routledge & Kegan Paul. pp. xvi + 207. 30s.

[114] *E P to L U: Nine Letters Written to Louis Untermeyer by Ezra Pound*, ed. by J. A. Robbins. Indiana U.P. pp. 48.

[115] *A Bibliography of Ezra Pound*, by Donald Gallup. Hart-Davis. pp. 454. £6. 6s.

[116] *Thomas Stearns Eliot in Übersetzungen*, by Hans W. Bentz. Frankfurt am Main: Hans W. Bentz Verlag. pp. xiii + 59.

[117] *William Carlos Williams*, by John Malcolm Brinnin. (Minnesota Pamphlets on American Writers No. 24.) Minnesota U.P. and O.U.P. pp. 48. 65c. 5s.

[118] *Hart Crane: An Introduction and Interpretation*, by Samuel Hazo. New York: Barnes & Noble. pp. x + 146. $2.95 cloth, $1.25 paper.

trates on individual poems. Hazo refers to the adulation of Crane by Allen Ginsberg. In his poem called 'Death to Van Gogh's Ear' Ginsberg identifies the suicides of Crane and Mayakovsky as acts capable of regenerating the societies which ostracized them. In opposition, Hazo quotes Peter Viereck's view that Crane, like Vachel Lindsay, came to grief because of an unqualified optimism about human nature. The facts of Crane's life should not, Hazo believes, be allowed to obscure his poetic achievement.

R. K. Meiners's study of the works of Allen Tate is entitled *The Last Alternatives*.[119] Meiners considers his subject under the headings of 'Beginnings and Themes'; 'The Center: Unity and Dissociation'; and 'The Poetic Paradox'. A chapter is devoted to *The Fathers*, another to Tate's poetic style, and yet another to *Seasons of the Soul*. This is the first full-length treatment of Tate's work.

Ralph J. Mills Jr.'s Minnesota pamphlet on Theodore Roethke[120] is a eulogy, but a justified one. Few contemporary poets, Mills believes, can match the daring, the richness, and the freedom of Roethke's best work. He feels that the intensity and clarity of Roethke's vision place him among the finest of modern American poets, able to take his place along with Wallace Stevens, William Carlos Williams, and E. E. Cummings.

Drama Was A Weapon[121] is a study

of the left-wing theatre in New York between 1929 and 1941. During the 1930's the American theatre not only suffered from the effects of the depression, it faced, says Morgan Himelstein, the challenge of the Communist Party, which decided that it must assist in the fight to overthrow Capitalism. The Party organized itself into theatre groups, and there hung above the stage of the Workers' Laboratory Theatre a red banner proclaiming that 'The Theatre is a Weapon'. In a well-documented account, Himelstein describes the details of this rather inflated 'struggle' between the theatre and the Party.

Louis Broussard's *American Drama*[122] is a study of contemporary allegory from Eugene O'Neill to Tennessee Williams. It is Broussard's contention that, in the forty years since O'Neill published *The Emperor Jones* and *The Hairy Ape*, a remarkable number of American playwrights have pursued the theme of twentieth-century man journeying through the confusion of his time. Broussard believes that the origins of this theme lie in the realism of Ibsen, the psychology of Strindberg, the psychiatry of Freud, and the philosophy of Bergson. Whether or not this is true, Broussard's book would be important if only because there is scarcely an American playwright who has not yielded to the temptation to produce his own Everyman.

Eugene O'Neill and the American Critic[123] is a 'summary and bibliographical checklist'. Jordan Y. Miller has assembled all important published

---

[119] *The Last Alternatives: A Study of the Works of Allen Tate*, by R. K. Meiners. Denver: Swallow. pp. 217. $4.50.

[120] *Theodore Roethke*, by Ralph J. Mills, Jr. (Minnesota Pamphlets on American Writers No. 30.) Minnesota U.P. and O.U.P. pp. 47. 65c. 5s.

[121] *Drama Was a Weapon: The Left-Wing Theatre in New York, 1929–1941*, by Morgan Y. Himelstein. Rutgers U.P. pp. xix+300. $6.

[122] *American Drama: Contemporary Allegory from Eugene O'Neill to Tennessee Williams*, by Louis Broussard. Oklahoma U.P., 1962. pp. vii+145. $3.75.

[123] *Eugene O'Neill and the American Critic: A Summary and Bibliographical Checklist*, by Jordan Y. Miller. Hamden, Conn. and London: Archon, 1962. pp. viii+513. $15.

items concerning O'Neill, from his early successes, through the posthumous revival, up to the end of 1959, in a book designed for the student of American drama. He has also written a brief summary of the 'four major points' which he believes contributed to the decline of O'Neill's reputation and its subsequent revival.

Clifford Leech's book on O'Neill in the 'Writers and Critics' series[124] considers the dramatist's work chronologically. This is a detailed account, despite its mere 120 pages. O'Neill was a playwright who had many failures, but the record as a whole is impressive. He had sharp intuitions of human nature and great skill in composing 'patterns of contrast and interrelation'. Leech believes that there is an 'appropriate irony' in the fact that the years in which O'Neill proclaimed so regularly the

[124] *O'Neill*, by Clifford Leech. Oliver & Boyd. pp. 120. 5s.

vanity of hope were the years in which his writing became most alive and his vision of human nature the most moving.

Tennessee Williams's mother's account of her son[125] is 'as told to Lucy Freeman'. Her book tells the story of Williams's father Cornelius, an unhappy and a violent man who terrorized the family; of his sister Rose whose fate was mental illness and a brain operation; of his brother Dakin; and of the playwright himself, with his self-doubts and ultimate triumph. This book is not without its interest, although it is not at all critical in any literary sense. Mrs. Williams publishes for the first time a number of letters which the playwright wrote to her over the years, together with some of his early poetry.

[125] *Remember Me to Tom*, by Edwina Dakin Williams, as told to Lucy Freeman. New York: Putnam. pp. 255. $5.95.

ARTICLES

1. GENERAL

American scholars, and American publishers, are taken to task by William M. Gibson and Edwin H. Cady in 'Editions of American Writers, 1963: A Preliminary Survey' (*PMLA*). The authors point with some shame to the absence of standard editions of major American poets and novelists, for with few exceptions—most notably Emily Dickinson and Sidney Lanier—American writers continue to be presented to the world in piecemeal and unreliable fashion. Gibson and Cady consider the current situation in the light of cost and need, and look with hope towards such projects as the Ohio State edition of Hawthorne.

In 'The American Scholar Today' (*Southwest Review*) Henry Nash Smith takes up Emerson's definition

of the American Scholar in its potential application to contemporary America. He believes that the prophets of our time must be sought in such men as C. Wright Mills, William H. Whyte, Jr., and Paul Goodman, men who document the twentieth-century varieties of authority and conventionality which oppress 'Man Thinking' today.

Larzer Ziff's 'The Literary Consequences of Puritanism' (*ELH*) examines the work of the English Anglican minister, Abraham Wright, whose parody-sermons in the Puritan style clarify the characteristic distinctions between Puritan and Anglican literary tastes. The 'consequences' which Ziff finds well displayed in the work of Henry James ('plain style, passion, allegory'), are the signs of a great shift in the imagination, and support 'such descriptions of the typically American form of fiction as that of the late Richard Chase'.

Gaylord C. LeRoy, in 'American Innocence Reconsidered' (*Massachussetts Review*), analyses the philosophical assumptions underlying such studies of 'American innocence' as R. W. B. Lewis's *The American Adam*, Henry Nash Smith's *Virgin Land*, Leslie Fiedler's *An End to Innocence*, Ihab Hassan's *Radical Innocence*, and Henry Bamford Parkes's *The American Experience*. These writers, LeRoy asserts, have produced unconvincing accounts of American idealism and disillusionment because they have not adequately recognized the distinctions between the subjective attitudes associated with the myth of the frontier and the objective situation—materialism, primarily—which has balked the idealistic impulse towards innocence. The fundamental questions are those which involve the nature of historical causation. LeRoy calls for 'a more rigorous materialism' in the interpretation of the past and the present, one which will avoid the sentimental evasion of the real causes of American disillusionment.

In *Saturday Review*, Alfred Kazin surveys the major fictional accounts of New England, from Hawthorne and Harriet Beecher Stowe to James and Santayana. 'The First and the Last: New England in the Novelist's Imagination' claims that the area is 'the most conceivably distinct place that in America a place can be', displaying an extraordinary example of historical tradition and consistency of character.

While it tends to overlook many important distinctions, and to ignore comparable themes in cis-Atlantic literature, Earl Rovit's brief 'Fathers and Sons in American Fiction' (*YR*) offers the interesting thesis that 'the strategic rejection of the father ... is almost omnipresent in American writing'.

John D. Seelye, in 'The American Tramp: A Version of the Picaresque' (*AQ*), considers the motives and fashions of the 'knights of the road' from the beginning of the nineteenth century.

The tableau of American folkways, often so influential in its literature, is enriched by Gerald Carson's 'The Dark Age of American Drinking' (*VQR*), a vivid and lively description of tippling in the early part of the nineteenth century, before 'alcoholic beverages and the evangelical churches came to a parting of the ways'.

Sidonia C. Taupin's '"Christianity in the Kitchen", or a Moral Guide for Gourmets' (*AQ*) calls our attention to an 1857 cookbook by the wife of Horace Mann which advocates certain culinary practices conducive to temperate, Christian living. As Mrs. Mann put it, 'There is no such prolific cause of bad morals as abuses of diet.' Carl Bode offers a more orthodox approach to American morality in 'Columbia's Carnal Bed' (*AQ*), surveying the few extant books about sex written in America during the nineteenth century. Both pornography and serious books on the subject are extremely rare, but Bode managed to find a sampling in the Kinsey Institute, which he describes with gusto.

In its special 'American Studies' supplement, *AQ* includes Richard E. Sykes's 'American Studies and the Concept of Culture', and a valuable bibliography of 'Selected Writings on American National Character' compiled by Michael McGiffert.

2. COLONIAL

Peter Marshall's 'Travellers and the Colonial Scene' (*British Association for American Studies Bulletin*) is an informative survey of travellers' journals and books between 1750 and 1775, which deserves more auspicious publication than a photographic copy of typescript.

'The Image of the Negro in Colonial Literature' (*NEQ*) presents Milton Cantor's sampling of the few writers who mention Negroes in the seventeenth and eighteenth centuries. Cantor concludes 'that the foundation of pro-slavery and anti-slavery thought was laid in the colonial period'.

In 'The Hazing of Cotton Mather' (*NEQ*), David Levin examines the few reliable sources of information on Mather's childhood. He shows, chiefly, the need for a fresh version of the life of the New England divine, one which will reject fanciful and ill-founded incidents in favour of a more judicious account. Mather has been for too long a useful but innocent victim of those who would propound easy theories of American intellectual history.

Levin's article on '*The Autobiography of Benjamin Franklin:* The Puritan Experimenter in Life and Art' (*YR*), is a critical re-reading of that book, emphasizing Franklin's attempt at self-definition by means of a created *persona*. Franklin employed himself, says Levin, 'as a prototype of his age and his country', and relied on his Puritan background for both method and theme. Without specific reference to Puritan habits of mind, Robert F. Sayre essays a similar reappraisal of the *Autobiography* in 'The Worldly Franklin and the Provincial Critics' (*TSLL*). His purpose is a 'counter-attack' in defence of Franklin directed against D. H. Lawrence, William Carlos Williams, and others. Sayre, like Levin, stresses Franklin's artistry in creating an ironic character as the object of his older and wiser judgement.

Paul R. Baumgartner's 'Jonathan Edwards: The Theory Behind His Use of Figurative Language' (*PMLA*), counters the prevailing notion that for a Calvinist the only justificaton for figurative writing was the accommodation of truth to the fallen nature of man. Basing his analysis on the doctrine of 'the analogy of being', Baumgartner suggests that Edwards considered his figures to be expressive of 'literal truth'.

One of the year's most impressive essays on American intellectual history is Edward H. Davidson's 'From Locke to Edwards' in *JHI*. He traces the 'romance' tradition in American writing to Edwards's discovery and rejection of Locke's 'program for language'. It was his reading of Locke, Davidson says, which helped turn Edwards from 'the major direction of Puritanism in America' (which led to Emersonian optimism) towards 'the dark byways of private consciousness, into those speculative ambiguities of knowing and not knowing, and into the mystery of the imperilled soul forced to know first itself and then some minute and cloudy portion of the outside world'.

3. EARLY NINETEENTH CENTURY

'Caves and Cave Dwellers: The Study of a Romantic Image' (*JEGP*), is Clark Griffith's comparative study of Emerson, Melville, Poe, and Hawthorne in terms of recurring cave and cave-dweller images. His purpose is 'to uncover four Romantic conceptions of experience, and thereby to put a finger on the four major viewpoints of which the American Romantic movement as a whole appears to have been composed'.

Herbert R. Coursen, Jr., in 'Nature's Center' (*CE*), links the attitudes towards nature of Melville, Emily Dickinson, and Henry Adams, documenting 'the movement away from the optimistic analogies of the early Emerson and into the ironic sunlight of later writers'. This movement culminates with Henry Adams, 'who points toward a new century by permitting order to exist merely as man's forlorn dream' opposed by 'the insane nightmare which is Nature's Law'.

Robert A. Bone, in his essay in *AQ* entitled 'Irving's Headless Hessian: Prosperity and the Inner Life', asserts that Irving has the distinction of being the first to explore the recurrent American theme of the inimical effect of prosperity on the life of the spirit. Ichabod Crane, 'confronted with the opulence of the Van Tassels, succumbs to the sins of covetousness and idolatry'. Everett H. and Katherine T. Emerson print fifteen unpublished 'Letters of Washington Irving, 1833–1843' in *AL*. The letters, addressed to Gouverneur Kemble, reveal Irving 'much attached to his family and his own peace and comfort'.

Discussing 'The Importance of Point of View in Brockden Brown's *Wieland*' (*AL*), William M. Manly finds that Brown's novel lies in the tradition of 'those peculiarly American explorations of the tormented psyche which seem ambiguously and resonantly to hover between appearance and reality'. *Wieland* is the first clear example of an American author grasping the dramatic possibilities of 'point of view' in fiction.

NCF prints two essays on James Fenimore Cooper. John J. McAleer's suggests that the 'Biblical Analogy in the Leatherstocking Tales' amounts to 'tentative experiments in symbolism', and Charles O'Donnell's investigates 'The Moral Basis of Civilization: Cooper's *Home* Novels'. O'Donnell believes that *Homeward Bound* and *Home As Found* are 'contrapuntal' novels, not merely linked by their publication date (1837).

Representing as they do a 'retreat' from civilization, and a 'return to an open civilization already far on its way toward corruption', they should be read as two parts of the same novel.

Robert Montgomery Bird's unjustly neglected *Nick of the Woods* is the subject of Joan Joffe Hall's 'An Interpretation of the American Wilderness' in *AL*. Bird's novel, which deals with the struggle in the wilderness between settler and Indian, raises the 'typically American issue' of the moral cost of such a struggle 'to the man who tries conscientiously to be a good Christian'. Bird wrote 'expressly to dispute with Cooper the fundamental nature of the American savage', and his novel has links with Melville's *The Confidence-Man* in its portrayal of an 'Indian-hater'.

In 'The Conscious Art of Edgar Allan Poe' (*CE*), Floyd Stovall briefly insists that Poe's work 'was the product of conscious effort by a healthy and alert intelligence', but James W. Gargano's 'The Question of Poe's Narrators' in the same journal offers generous evidence to support his claim that, 'though his narrators are often febrile or demented, Poe is conspicuously "sane"'. Gargano employs the fashionable critical method which treats Poe's narrators and *personae* as distinct from their creator. Taking as antagonists Aldous Huxley, Yvor Winters, Cleanth Brooks, and Robert Penn Warren, Eric W. Carlson analyses 'Symbol and Sense in Poe's "Ulalume"' (*AL*). Carlson asserts that to read Poe through the 'ironic lenses' of contemporary taste is to risk misreading Poe's meaning. 'Under the surface of Poe's mythic symbolism and sound impressionism,' he says, 'there is a psychological meaning.'

Joseph Schwartz, in 'Three Aspects of Hawthorne's Puritanism' (*NEQ*), documents and supports Yvor Winters's contention that Hawthorne turned his back upon the religion of his ancestors, so that we 'will have to search elsewhere for his metaphysical roots'. Sister Jane Marie Luecke, O.S.B., incisively differentiates between Hawthorne's conscious, wilful villains (such as Roger Chillingworth) and his inadvertent wrongdoers, in her 'Villains and Non-Villains in Hawthorne's Fiction' (*PMLA*).

Fanshawe, Robert E. Gross claims in 'Hawthorne's First Novel: The Future of a Style' (*PMLA*), is valuable to scholars because it displays basic characteristics of Hawthorne's writing as they appear at the beginning of his career. *Fanshawe* reveals 'balanced and concessive syntax, abstract and general diction, the alienation theme, the whole arsenal of moralizing devices, the portentous tone, the grotesquery, the wise announcements, the imagic play, and the static plotting'. Kermit Vanderbilt in *CE* applies a clear critical method to demonstrate 'The Unity of Hawthorne's "Ethan Brand"', and Karl P. Wentersdorf investigates varied sources, ranging from Hawthorne's blissful first year of marriage to his intense memories of *The Tempest* and *Cymbeline*, to account for 'The Genesis of Hawthorne's "The Birthmark"' (*Jahrbuch für Amerikastudien*).

Of many critical studies of *The Scarlet Letter*, the most interesting is Edward H. Davidson's 'Dimmesdale's Fall' (*NEQ*) which claims for the sinning minister damnation in both Puritan and Romantic terms. Davidson believes that Dimmesdale died convinced of his moral freedom in a morally predestined world. He was 'that ultimate criminal in Hawthorne's order of humanity, the outcast of the universe'. Harry R. Warfel's resumé of 'Metaphysical Ideas in

The Scarlet Letter' (*CE*), is a useful summary of widely held attitudes. Dan Vogel, on the other hand, takes a consciously heterodox position in his examination of 'Roger Chillingworth: The Satanic Paradox' (*Criticism*). Chillingworth, Vogel says, is 'purgatorial' in his relation to Dimmesdale, a necessary if unpleasant role for 'the destruction of the flesh, that the spirit may be saved (*Corinthians* v, 5)'.

L. Moffitt Cecil analyses 'Hawthorne's Optical Device' in *AQ*. The novelist's preoccupation with 'ocular perception' is related to the symbolic values inherent in his manipulation of light and colour. In this relationship Cecil sees the germ of a characteristic principle of Hawthorne's narrative technique: 'his frequent practice of presenting the visual experiences of his *personae* as direct and final revelation of character.' In a rather more ambitious vein, John F. Adams concludes from his study of 'Hawthorne's Symbolic Gardens' (*TSLL*) that, 'wherever Hawthorne pictures a garden and a fountain—real or metaphorical—pride, self-sufficiency, and inhumanity are an issue.' Richard C. Carpenter's interest is more particularized in 'Hawthorne's Scarlet Bean Flowers' (*UKCR*, which from 1963 has been re-christened *The University Review*). Carpenter argues for the integrity of the sentimental ending of *The House of the Seven Gables*, basing his claim on a series of horticultural symbols and images 'which place in opposition the sterility and decay of the elder Pyncheons and the promise of the young couple'. He believes that this juxtaposition of symbols makes the optimistic outcome inevitable.

In a note in *AL*, James D. Hart describes the discovery in a manuscript collection at Berkeley of 'Hawthorne's Italian Diary', kept during the author's Italian sojourn of 1858–9.

The manuscript fills in several blanks in the published *Italian Note-Books*. A. M. Baumgartner's '"The Lyceum Is My Pulpit": Homiletics in Emerson's Early Lectures' (*AL*) investigates the effect Emerson's 'Lyceum' experience had on his later works. Baumgartner believes that Emerson was popular in the 'Lyceum circuit' because of his early homiletic training, which in turn had its influence on his style and method in the essays. Emerson's education had established in him such habits as the selection of common rather than novel subjects; an attention to the interests of his audiences; an effort always to be positive rather than negative; and the need for economy in delivery and diction. But most important, Baumgartner says, Emerson was taught to distrust merely logical structures in the effort to be persuasive. Ray Benoit, taking a contradictory stand, discovers the source of Emerson's illogicality in his reading of Plato ('Emerson on Plato: The Fire's Center', *AL*). Though Baumgartner argues that Emerson read Plato too late to have been deeply influenced, Benoit claims that Plato's refusal to choose 'between spirit and matter', seeing each of them as aspects of 'a ground of being higher than both', was a shaping influence in Emerson's technique. Emerson was neither idealistic nor materialistic, but felt that 'only the whole truth could be true at all'. As Benoit puts it, 'if one does not understand the *Timaeus*, he can never understand Emerson'.

In 'Thoreau's Development in *Walden*' (*Criticism*), Paul Schwaber insists that we read Thoreau's work as a spiritual autobiography of those years during which he was occupied in the writing of it. *Walden* is a dramatic rendering of Thoreau's search for self-reliance, joy, freedom —and, 'in a word, excellence'. The book, as was also the case with Thoreau himself between 1845 and 1854, moves from discontent with the times to peace in spiritual strength, so that at the moment Thoreau records his return to society, 'his self-reform is complete'. Robert W. Bradford, in 'Thoreau and Therien' (*AL*), explores some of the sources of Thoreau's ambiguity about the Canadian woodchopper in *Walden*, who was modelled on Thoreau's sometime friend Therien. Analysing the changes which took place between Thoreau's journal entries, the 'First Version' of *Walden*, and the published book, Bradford finds that Thoreau had at first admired Therien for his 'exuberance and innocence', but had hoped that he would grow spiritually. This never occurred, however, and at the end of his life Thoreau rudely renounced Therien's friendship. The result of his disappointment was not only an equivocal portrait in *Walden*, but also an increase in his distrust of democracy. 'Mariners and Terreners: Some Aspects of Nautical Imagery in Thoreau' (*AL*), is Willard H. Bonner's catalogue of two sets of recurring images which Thoreau balanced against each other. Bonner concludes that, for Thoreau, man's proper place was on shore, since no man could remain long in the 'spiritual existence' of the sea.

In his detailed review of Newton Arvin's *Longfellow*, Marius Bewley puzzles over the motives that could have led Arvin to undertake such a study ('The Poetry of Longfellow', *HR*). Bewley finds the book frankly 'downhearted'. Loring E. Hart's 'The Beginnings of Longfellow's Fame' (*NEQ*), reviews the first American critical reception of the poet, and shows that his reputation was established early.

In '*Uncle Tom's Cabin*: The Sinister Side of the Patriarchy' (*NEQ*), Severn

Duvall investigates Southern antagonism to this important novel. He finds
that the strength of the attack arose
from Southerners' reaction to Harriet
Beecher Stowe's debunking of the
social myth of the South. She did not
accept that the slaveholder was a
benevolent patriarch who deserved
the love and respect of his 'family'.

James W. Gargano's 'Technique in
"Crossing Brooklyn Ferry"' (*JEGP*),
demonstrates that Whitman's method
in the poem depends on the 'gradual
magnification of the reoccurring moment with which the poem begins and
ends'. Whitman manages to obliterate
'time, place, and distance here more
successfully than he does in his formal
rationalizations', thus providing the
reader with 'both a doctrine and an
experience, a comforting array of
rather conventional "proofs" and an
emotional escape beyond the constraint of time and place'. Edmund
Reiss's subject, 'Whitman's Debt to
Animal Magnetism' (*PMLA*), has a
wider application. Whitman was
deeply interested in the current vogue
for mesmerism, animal magnetism,
and phrenological investigation, and
relied on these occult sciences for
imagery, assumptions, and ideas.
Animal magnetism, Reiss believes,
was particularly influential in Whitman's conceptions of the poet and the
leader.

In 'The Metaphysics of Indian-
Hating' (*NCF*), Hershel Parker sees
The Confidence-Man, like the rest of
Melville's work, as 'a tragic study of
the impracticability of Christianity'.
The Confidence-Man is 'a satiric
allegory in which Indians are Devils
and the Indian-haters are dedicated
Christians'. Melville's real subject, in
this book as elsewhere, is the hypocrisy of 'the nominal practice of
Christianity'. Allen Guttmann investigates 'Melville's Allusive Art
from *Typee* to *Moby-Dick*' (*MLQ*),

examining the various functions and
estimating the effectiveness of Melville's allusions to sources beyond his
immediate subject. Guttmann believes that Melville undertook a
'literary voyage' in which he 'discovered allusion, recklessly over-used
it, but at length attained a mastery of
it'. Richard Harter Fogle offers a
brief but incisive review of 'Melville's Poetry' (*TSE*), cataloguing his
typical themes, forms, and metres.
Hennig Cohen's 'Wordplay on Personal Names in the Writings of Herman Melville' (*TSL*), is a useful if
somewhat elementary compilation.

'The Shadow in *Moby-Dick*' (*AQ*)
is, to John Halverson, Melville's em-
ployment of the Jungian archetype of
the 'dark brother' *alter ego*, exemplified in the Queequeg-Ishmael friendship, and also in the Pip-Ahab and
Fedallah-Ahab relationships. J. J.
Boies analyses '*The Whale* Without
Epilogue' (*MLQ*), reminding critics of
Moby-Dick that on its first publication as *The Whale* in London, it did
not contain the epilogue in which the
narrator Ishmael explains his survival of the general catastrophe. Such
critics as Lawrance Thompson and
Howard Vincent, who attempt to find
the epilogue thematically relevant, are
mistaken, Boies believes. The addition was doubtless made simply in
response to reviewers' objections that
Melville had allowed his narrator to
die. Boies believes that the book is
thoroughly nihilistic, and that the
epilogue is nowhere prefigured in the
text.

David H. Hirsch outlines 'The
Dilemma of the Liberal Intellectual'
(*TSLL*) as it is presented in Melville's
Ishmael. An investigation of 'The
Historical Chapters in *Billy Budd*'
(*University Review*) reveals to Joan
Joffe Hall the reasonableness of
Claggart's accusations of Billy, and
justifies Vere's hanging of him. But

even more important, her comparison of both Billy and Captain Vere with contemporary accounts of Nelson at Trafalgar demonstrates an economy of narrative method which she finds 'unique to *Billy Budd* in Melville's work'.

The most intriguing new field of Melville scholarship investigates his awareness of political theory and contemporary political activity. Ray B. Browne's '*Billy Budd*: Gospel of Democracy' (*NCF*), seems to push the subject farthest when he reads the *novella* as a political allegory with literal reference to the conflict between Edmund Burke and Thomas Paine. Captain Vere, Browne asserts, is 'in fact Melville's antagonist', and the book, 'instead of demonstrating the irresistible triumph of political evil, of conservatism, insists on the opposite: that the Veres (and Claggarts) prevail only in the short run, never in the long'. Melville, he insists, 'casts his hope with the people', who will inevitably inherit the earth. In a subsequent issue of *NCF*, Browne's Purdue University colleague, Bernard Suits, publishes an orthodox rejoinder. The historical evidence submitted by Browne, Suits believes, is not strong enough 'to compel the rejection of an interpretation incompatible with Browne's interpretation'. Alan Heimert, less ingenious than Browne, and more attentive to historical probabilities, offers an extensive list of echoes in *Mardi* and *Moby-Dick* of the current political issues of the 1840's ('*Moby-Dick* and American Political Symbolism', *AQ*). Heimert documents, in particular, contemporary references to imperialism and slavery, drawing on political oratory and its recurring images— 'the ship of state', for example, and even numerous references to Ahab as an 'expansionist' king of Samaria. For his portrait of Captain Ahab,

Heimert feels, Melville is indebted both to adverse descriptions of John C. Calhoun and to dedicated partisanship of American imperialism.

4. LATER NINETEENTH CENTURY

In 'Mark Twain: Reflections on Religion' (*HR*), Charles Neider presents the first printing of five suppressed chapters of Twain's *Autobiography*. As Twain reported to Howells, they are 'fearful things'. But, he adds, 'I got them out of my system, where they had been festering for years.' An amusing account of less fearful things is C. Merton Babcock's 'Mark Twain's Seven Lively Sins' (*TQ*), a collection of Twain anecdotes. The sins he lists are gambling, smoking, drinking, swearing, lying, loafing, and stealing. Jim Hunter's 'Mark Twain and the Boy-Book in 19th-Century America' (*CE*), estimates the importance of Twain as a writer for and about boys. Twain was an example of the 'Romantic and distinctly American faith in childhood' which continues strongly today, and which helps explain some characteristically American attitudes and actions. Although Hunter does not attempt to document his assertion that such a faith is 'distinctly American', he writes with great sympathy about Twain. In a more scholarly article, Hamlin Hill establishes the relationship between Twain's 'Audience and Artistry' (*AQ*), tracing the influence on Twain of the sale of his books by subscription, and asking himself what kind of audience bought subscription books. He concludes that it was composed of 'Midwestern mechanics and farmers', who were thought to demand size, fact rather than fiction, topical material, and 'an odd mixture of sensationalism and moralizing'. But Mark Twain was himself a Midwesterner, and Hill thinks that he consciously constructed his subscription books 'to appeal to the tastes of a reader much like himself', so there was no real question of compromising his artistic aims.

In '"The Jumping Frog" as a Comedian's First Virtue' (*MP*), Paul Baender argues that in this early story Twain was consciously manipulating the tradition of Southwestern humour after its vogue had passed. He was not, as some readers have insisted, naïvely displaying his immersion in the locale of the story.

The appearance of Henry Nash Smith's *Mark Twain: The Development of a Writer* is the occasion for several lengthy review articles. William Van O'Connor's, in *NCF*, is a straightforward attack on the 'Twain industry', which he considers 'the last refuge of the old Parringtonians'. Smith's book, O'Connor believes, is representative of 'the whole Twain mystique'. Twain scholars, he says, have 'rules' other than those which apply to a true novelist. Those who see Mark Twain as the great American writer, O'Connor concludes, suffer from 'deficient literary sensibilities and insufficient critical acuteness'. O'Connor's position is supported by Robert A. Wiggins in 'Pudd'nhead Wilson: "A Literary Caesarean Operation"' (*CE*). Wiggins contradicts F. R. Leavis by exhibiting the deeply flawed structure and characterization of the novel.

On the other hand, Louis D. Rubin, Jr., in another review of Smith's book ('Mark Twain and the Language of Experience', *Sew*) has little to say for or against Twain, but is enthusiastic about Smith's methodology. He finds that Smith adapts Erich Auerbach's emphasis on language and structure, and sees in this a source of great critical power. Smith's contribution

to American studies, Rubin feels, is his 'demonstration of the way in which for Twain the problem of idea and image, of form and meaning, is always one of fictional technique'.

In 'Emily Dickinson's White Robes' (*Criticism*), J. S. Wheatcroft comes to the conclusion that Miss Dickinson used the traditional symbol of white garments in two distinct ways, first as indicating death (as in the case of frost and snow), and, second, as signifying innocence, marriage, and immortality. Combining these two uses, she created the composite figure of 'death, unfulfilled love for an earthly lover, and love consummated with a divine lover'. On occasion Wheatcroft seems willing to assume that garments of an unspecified colour were white in the poet's imagination, thus weakening an interesting analysis. In 'The Indefatigable Casuist' (*University Review*), Thornton H. Parsons points out the well-established fact that much of Emily Dickinson's poetry deals with deprivation, and that she had worked out an emotional compromise which enabled her to find spiritual compensation in loss—even though she denied traditional Christian doctrines. With perhaps too few examples, Suzanne M. Wilson describes 'Structural Patterns in the Poetry of Emily Dickinson' (*AL*). Basically Emily Dickinson worked in a homiletic form, with three variations which grew more complicated as her writing career proceeded. It is improper to think of her as merely 'automatic' or 'instinctive' in her art, Miss Wilson says, since the 'pattern of experiment with this basic organization indicates design and manipulation, and these indicate conscious artistry'. William R. Manierre's 'E.D.: Visions and Revisions' (*TQ*), is a close examination of the editorial changes which were made on the first publication of Emily Dickinson's poems. Manierre displays considerable rancour about reprints which have appeared since T. H. Johnson's scholarly edition of 1955, yet which continue to use the flawed first publication versions.

By far the most important article on Emily Dickinson, and one which threatens to undermine the reliability of one of the few 'standard' editions of an American author, is Edith Perry Stamm's 'Emily Dickinson: Poetry and Punctuation' (*Saturday Review*). The apparently eccentric punctuation of Emily Dickinson's manuscript poems seems to have been based on a popular system of rhetorical or elocutionary symbols. These were used to direct the reader in his oral delivery of the poem, and more significantly, to indicate precisely the tone the poet desired to achieve. Thus T. H. Johnson's use of the dash as the single representation of various distinct symbols in his 1955 edition does not capture the real intention of Emily Dickinson.

Robin Magowan, in 'Pastoral and the Art of Landscape in *The Country of the Pointed Firs*' (*NEQ*), compares Sarah Orne Jewett's performance in that small classic to literary pastoral, and to landscape painting, particularly that of J. F. Millet and Miss Jewett's fellow Maine artist Winslow Homer.

William T. Stafford, in 'Literary Allusions in James's Prefaces' (*AL*), displays Henry James's 'critical mind working at its finest pitch' by defining the functions of his allusions. Most important are the novelist's references 'to those writers whose works represent precedents James specifically wishes to avoid, and to those whose works embody precedents, techniques, and accomplishments he hopes to emulate or forward'. George Levine's 'Isabel, Gwendolen, and Dorothea' (*ELH*) argues for James's indebtedness to George Eliot for the characters of Isabel Archer and Gilbert Osmond in *The Portrait of a Lady*. They are modelled not only on Gwendolen Harleth and Henleigh Grandcourt in *Daniel Deronda*, as has been pointed out already, but also on Dorothea Brooke and Edward Casaubon in *Middlemarch*. Referring to 'Hyacinth's Fallible Consciousness' (*MP*) in her reading of *The Princess Casamassima*, Sister Jane Marie Luecke, O.S.B., claims that the moral realism of the novel rests on the chief character's flawed perception. The novel achieves its significantly human vision from the 'dangerous' susceptibility of Robinson's consciousness to see 'only what it wants to see'. In 'The Turn of the Screw and Alice James' (*PMLA*), Oscar Cargill repudiates his well-known 'Henry James as Freudian Pioneer'. This *novella*, Cargill concedes, *is* concerned with the madness of the governess, which was suggested to James by the mental illness of his sister Alice. To protect her, however, James had to disguise this 'germ', so his preface denies what his story contains.

The Sacred Fount seems currently to be the fashionable puzzle to Jamesians, and a number of readings have been made available. Tony Tanner, in 'Henry James's Subjective Adventurer' (*E & S*), sees the novel as James's contribution to the long debate over 'the question of the relationship between vision and fact'. James's notion of 'non-participatory speculation' is related, Tanner thinks, to the traditional idea of the artist as 'a man who creates forms which might be truer than the truth'. Jean Frantz Blackall defines '*The Sacred Fount* as a Comedy of the Limited Observer' (*PMLA*), finding in it 'the irony of the discrepancy between the insight or knowledge of an intelligent but not infallible observer and the things he contemplates'. The narrator, she maintains, has 'his head perpetually in a theoretic, psychologic cloud'. In his suggestive reading of the novel, entitled '*The Sacred Fount*: "The Actuality Pretentious and Vain" vs. "The Case Rich and Edifying"' (*MFS*), Parker Tyler finds it a fairly explicit symbolic account of James's attitude towards his audience, his imagination, and his work. Robert J. Andreach, however, sees in the novel an example of 'The Existential Predicament' (*NCF*). He insists that the book is successful, but must be understood in terms of the dichotomy 'between the real experiencing of the world and the logical apprehension of the world'.

In '*The Awkward Age, The Sacred Fount*, and *The Ambassadors*: Another Figure in the Carpet' (*NCF*), Julian B. Kaye maintains that James's *The Ambassadors* is more closely related to the two novels which preceded it (which are 'preliminary sketches' for it) than to *The Wings of the Dove* and *The Golden Bowl*. Lotus Snow's '"A Story of Cabinets and Chairs and Tables": Images of Morality in *The Spoils of Poynton* and *The Golden Bowl*' (*ELH*) links the characters of perceptive figures like Fleda Vetch and Prince Amerigo to the *objets d'art* presented in the two novels. Of the characters, she says that 'the measure of their esthetic value is their morality, and the measure of their morality is the intelligence and the intensity of their perception'.

The publication of the third volume of Leon Edel's biography of Henry James receives some important critical commentary. Frederick J. Hoffman's 'The Expense and the Power of Greatness' (*VQR*) is frankly a series of reflections on the author which the biography has provoked. Edel's continuing edition of James's tales, on the other hand, receives a very acute analysis by Herbert Ruhm ('The Complete Tales of Henry James', *Sew*). Ruhm strenuously objects to Edel's editorial policies, accusing him of suppressing in his textual notes his already published awareness of major and important revisions which are glossed over in this edition. Ruhm also calls into question Edel's choice of revised versions of the stories made at various times in James's career. These are presented in the chronology of the first magazine publication, as if they represented the development of the writer. *Sew*'s 'Note on Contributors', incidentally, announces that Ruhm is at work on a 'variorum edition of all the fiction of Henry James'.

In '*The Education of Henry Adams* Reconsidered' (*CE*) Herbert F. Hahn concludes that Adams was not a pessimist, but an ironist who defied the modern world and offered 'human thought' as 'the point of view with which to face that world without despair'. More impressively, James K. Folsom traces 'Mutation as Metaphor in *The Education of Henry Adams*' (*ELH*). From this recurrent metaphor, he derives a very satisfactory explanation of the final chapters of the book in terms of Adams's interest in the new force which will supplant 'the Dynamo'. This force Adams symbolized by 'the X-Ray'. In examining Adams's attitude towards it Folsom accounts for the apparent lapse of theme and tone in the final paragraph of the autobiography.

Malcolm Bradbury and Arnold Goldman treat Stephen Crane as a 'primitive Hemingway' in 'Stephen Crane: Classic at the Crossroads' (*British Association for American Studies Bulletin*). In *The Red Badge of Courage* Crane opened up a new and subsequently recurring situation to

American fiction: that of intellectuals at the crossroads, giving themselves up to the incomprehensible, 'losing their souls in the flux of things', in R. W. Stallman's phrase. A similar claim is made by William B. Dillingham in 'Insensibility in *The Red Badge of Courage*' (*CE*), though Dillingham refrains from calling Henry Fleming an 'intellectual'. Relying rather heavily on C. C. Walcutt's *American Literary Naturalism*, he documents Crane's definition of courage, which 'is by its nature sub-human'. In order to be courageous, Crane believed, a man in time of danger must abandon the highest of his human faculties, reason and imagination, and 'act instinctively, even animalistically'. George W. Johnson examines 'Stephen Crane's Metaphor of Decorum' (*PMLA*), seeing it as a continuing reliance on gentility in tone and phrasing. Harold R. Hungerford proves by historical deduction that Crane had in mind a particular battle, Chancellorsville, in *The Red Badge of Courage* ('"That Was at Chancellorsville"', *AL*). Harland S. Nelson's estimation of 'Stephen Crane's Achievement as a Poet' (*TSLL*) challenges Daniel G. Hoffman's preference for Crane's more 'modern' poems. Defending Crane's simple 'parables', Nelson claims that his talent was for the slighter things 'where his control is most sure'.

A special number of *MFS* on 'American Realists' contains articles on Stephen Crane, Harold Frederic, Theodore Dreiser, William Dean Howells, Ernest Hemingway, and Frank Norris. Though the issue is not particularly unified in its point of view, it is a valuable collection of readings and reassessments of such novels as *The Rise of Silas Lapham*, *Sister Carrie*, and *The Octopus*.

5. TWENTIETH CENTURY

Philip Roth discusses 'Writing About Jews' in *Commentary*, answering attacks on his portrayals of unpleasant Jewish characters. He summarizes the nature of his antagonists' arguments thus: 'I had told the Gentiles what apparently it would otherwise have been possible to keep secret from them: that the perils of human nature afflict the members of our minority.' Roth's defence is that he is neither a sociologist nor an apologist, and that people who can read fiction would not expect him to be.

Randall Jarrell's 'Fifty Years of American Poetry' (*Prairie Schooner*) is an address delivered at the National Poetry Festival sponsored by the Library of Congress. It aims at summarizing the twentieth-century poetic themes and methods, and has little of the customary Jarrell bite, except at the expense of Yvor Winters and Richard Eberhart and their followers. Jarrell seems to have revised his earlier estimation of Wallace Stevens.

'The Nineteen-Thirty Agrarians' (*Sew*) is Edward M. Moore's sympathetic reappraisal of the Southern Agrarian movement, on the occasion of the re-issue of their manifesto *I'll Take My Stand*.

Tony Tanner, in 'Pigment and Ether: A Comment on the American Mind' (*British Association for American Studies Bulletin*), documents an American tendency to 'oscillate between particulars and vague generalizations', best defined in the Transcendentalists, but of relevance when studying Melville, Sherwood Anderson, Dos Passos, and Salinger.

Paul S. Boyer's 'Boston Book Censorship in the Twenties' (*AQ*) claims that the issue of censorship became, for both the censors and their critics, an 'escape from a real confrontation with the problems which the turbulent decade presented'.

The October 1963 issue of *REL* contains articles by British critics on various aspects of American literature, including two on Saul Bellow: Malcolm Bradbury's evaluation of Bellow's place in the Naturalist tradition, and Geoffrey Ran's 'reading' of the novels in chronological order. Michael Millgate contributes a study of Faulkner's extensive revisions of *Sanctuary* from galley proofs, and Geoffrey Moore provides a structural analysis of Hemingway's *The Sun Also Rises*.

In a different vein, less specifically concerned with literary matters, *TQ* prints a symposium on 'Individualism in 20th Century America'. In addition to Frederick J. Hoffman's 'Dogmatic Innocence: Self-Assertion in Modern American Literature', it presents contributions from the fields of politics, anthropology, economics, and history.

In 'Mr. Booth's Quarrel with Fiction' (*Sew*), Peter Swiggart examines Wayne C. Booth's much praised *The Rhetoric of Fiction*. He finds the author lacking in sensitivity to fictional techniques, and willing to ride rough-shod over post-Jamesian critics in order to promulgate a theory of morality in fiction. Booth is far more anxious, Swiggart says, to establish the function of rhetoric as a kind of moral communication than to explore disturbing complexities either in what is to be communicated or in the way in which such communication is to be achieved. Swiggart believes that 'it becomes evident that Mr. Booth is willing to associate rhetoric not with communication *as such*, but only with communication of simple moral beliefs to an audience limited both by intelligence and by training.'

Richard Lehan's 'Dreiser's *American Tragedy*: A Critical Study' (*CE*) is a brief but ambitious attempt to give the novel the kind of reading which Lehan claims it has not had except in F. O. Matthiessen's book-length study of Drieser's works. 'The Imagery of Dreiser's Novels' (*PMLA*) is William L. Phillips's effort to show that a close reading of Dreiser's novels reveals complex patterns of imagery, sometimes the result apparently, of conscious manipulation, and sometimes of an unconscious compulsion to say things in a particular way.

W. R. Irwin describes 'The Comic Spirit' (*AL*) in Robert Frost's poetry, defining its sources and workings. The chief sources he detects are human idiosyncrasies or discord, and menacing images or situations, to which man opposes 'a cheerful unwillingness to be dismayed'.

In 'Vision and Reality: A Reconsideration of Sherwood Anderson's *Winesburg, Ohio*' (*AL*), Epifanio San Juan, Jr., refutes the critics, Lionel Trilling and Alfred Kazin among them, who denigrate Anderson's power of thought and language. San Juan examines Anderson's method of characterization and the values it upholds, his handling of patterns of imagery, the rhythm of his prose, and his modes of irony.

Richard Eberhart discusses an important topic in 'Emerson and Wallace Stevens' (*Literary Review*—which prints 'Stevens' as 'Stephens' on its cover), but his tone and diffuse critical method rob his statement of the force it might have had. On the basis of a rather casual reading of a few passages from the two writers, Eberhart claims Stevens as a Transcendentalist. Much more valuable is the 'Checklist of Stevens Criticism' (*TCL*), compiled by Jackson R. Bryer and Joseph N. Riddel.

Benjamin T. Spencer's essay on

'Doctor Williams' American Grain' (*TSL*), is an account of William Carlos Williams's life-long efforts to define and create an original literature that would both spring from and be relevant to American conditions. Spencer decides that Williams derived his ideas from 'three interrelated yet distinct Americas—what may be termed the Platonic, the unconscious, and the cultural'.

Alan Holder traces Ezra Pound's treatment of Henry James over the years in his 'The Lesson of the Master: Ezra Pound and Henry James' (*AL*), an essay which reveals both Pound's misreading of 'the master' and his strong sense of identity with him. William NcNaughton sprinkles his analysis of 'Ezra Pound's Meters and Rhythms' (*PMLA*), with quotations in Greek, Latin, Chinese, and Italian, but his emphasis on Pound's awareness of quantity in English verse is important. Myles Slatin writes 'A History of Pound's Cantos I–XVI, 1915–1925' (*AL*), following the poet in his published and unpublished letters, and in the published versions of the early Cantos. Searching for a definition of the poem's form, Slatin compares earlier drafts and remarks about the Cantos with the London edition of *Seventy Cantos*. He believes that Pound began his poem more in the manner of Byron composing *Don Juan* than in the manner of Milton beginning *Paradise Lost*. The result is 'an "action" poem, dedicated to and modeled upon experience', for which 'there can be no ending'.

In 'T. S. Eliot and F. H. Bradley: A Question of Influence' (*TSE*), E. P. Bollier undertakes an important review of the whole problem of Bradley's influence on the poet in the light of what scepticism meant to Bradley, and how Bradley's sceptical thought affected Eliot and his work.

Joseph P. O'Neill, S. J., analyses *Mourning Becomes Electra* as an example of 'The Tragic Theory of Eugene O'Neill' (*TSLL*), comparing the play with the *Oresteia* in his attempt to explicate the differences between the ancient and the modern concepts of tragedy. O'Neill's indebtedness to Thoreau for the character of the absent Simon Harford in *A Touch of the Poet* is well known, but in 'Eugene O'Neill's Debt to Thoreau' (*JEGP*), Mordecai Marcus provides further evidence: Harford's mother is Thoreau's mother, and Cornelius Melody, the protagonist, is modelled on Hugh Quoil, mentioned by Thoreau in *Walden* and in his Journals. The references to Thoreau in a play concerned with the betrayal of ideals by materialistic ambition suggest to Marcus 'the depth and bitterness of O'Neill's feelings about the betrayal of American life by materialism'.

Throughout his career Archibald MacLeish has been seeking a metaphor by which to give meaning to the modern age, Eleanor M. Sickels claims in 'MacLeish and the Fortunate Fall' (*AL*), and he found it finally in the Christian myth. MacLeish's Fall, though fortunate and even triumphant, is not Milton's, Miss Sickels maintains. It is fortunate because without it man is a mere animal, not because it made way for a Saviour who died for the elect. MacLeish's redemption is 'in all human good achievement, and in the very yearning for the infinite which caused the Fall'. Sheldon N. Grebstein agrees, and in '*J.B.* and the Problem of Evil' (*University Review*), he defines MacLeish's philosophical position as 'agnostic humanism'. MacLeish believes in human greatness 'without divine origin or justification'.

Daniel Curley's 'Katherine Anne Porter: The Larger Plan' (*KR*), is a résumé of her work, culminating in a regretful judgement of *Ship of Fools*. In this novel Miss Porter seems to have undertaken all the things least likely to succeed for her, all the devices and attitudes that have in the past failed her. *Ship of Fools*, Curley says, is 'a denial of the very Realities on which her successes have always depended'.

F. Scott Fitzgerald, with Henry James and William Faulkner, seems to be most attractive to critics of modern American fiction. Arthur Mizener, in 'The Voice of Scott Fitzgerald's Prose' (*E & S*), traces the writer's career in terms of his 'tone of voice', since 'Fitzgerald's prose is the best measure we have of his sensibility at any given moment in his career'. Mizener carefully distinguishes between Fitzgerald's 'fully realized attitudes and the ones he could not find a wholly convincing voice for'. *The Great Gatsby* continues to be the most popular subject for analysis, and in 'A Study in Literary Reputation' (*New Mexico Quarterly*), G. Thomas Tanselle and Jackson R. Bryer collect a series of references to the novel indicating the stages of its reputation. What they document is 'a case study in the workings of literary evaluation —of the critical snowballing process by which a work becomes established as a classic'. They find the lesson disturbing, because they feel that this process has become mechanical, and that a great deal of energy may have been misdirected. A word to the wise, perhaps, but Howard S. Babb undertakes to relate '*The Great Gatsby* and the Grotesque' (*Criticism*), and Sister M. Bettina, S.S.N.D., defines the particular type of imagery used by Fitzgerald to achieve his 'ironic double vision' in 'The Artifact in Imagery: Fitzgerald's *The Great Gatsby*' (*TCL*).

'In Praise of Scott Fitzgerald' (*CQ*),

by John Lucas, seems to be advocating a similar critical elevation of *Tender Is the Night*, which Lucas examines with some particularity in order to prove it a great novel.

Seymour L. Gross offers an analytic reading of 'Fitzgerald's "Babylon Revisited"' (*CE*), as evidence of the writer's horror as he sees the 'nightmare of irrevocable loss'. Jackson R. Bryer, notwithstanding his strictures on the reputation of *The Great Gatsby*, is responsible for 'F. Scott Fitzgerald: A Review of Research and Scholarship' (*TSLL*).

CE's November issue, devoted to contemporary fiction, contains three articles on William Faulkner: John K. Simon's 'What Are You Laughing At, Darl?', a study of madness and humour in *As I Lay Dying*; Thomas E. Connolly's useful 'Skeletal Outline of *Absalom, Absalom!*', keyed to the widely available Modern Library edition; and William J. Sowder's examination of 'Lucas Beauchamp as Existential Hero' in *Intruder in the Dust*. Richard P. Adams's 'The Apprenticeship of William Faulkner' (*TSE*), is a long and fruitful summary of literary influences, from the Bible and Shakespeare to Conrad and *The Golden Bough*. In 'Faulkner and Sartre: Metamorphosis and the Obscene' (*CL*), John K. Simon claims that these two writers share a technique which is of far less limited scope than is sometimes believed. Their common imagery points to a certain personal affinity, as well as to the 'common predilection of the contemporary period for sudden metamorphoses of matter'. Richard E. Fisher's 'The Wilderness, the Commissary, and the Bedroom: Faulkner's Ike McCaslin as Hero in a Vacuum' (*ES*), asserts that Ike does not sufficiently reveal to others the experience that has made his own limited heroism possible. Fisher says that his teaching is unsatisfactory because his understanding is incomplete.

John T. Flanagan attempts to pick out 'Faulkner's Favorite Word' (*Georgia Review*). In this brief survey of Faulkner's peculiarities of diction and syntax, Flanagan decides that 'implacable' is the most Faulknerian word, reverberating in theme and tone throughout the novels. Examining in detail Faulkner's allusions to ancient mythology, Lennart Bjork concludes that Faulkner has successfully fused 'the three major Western cultures—the Greek, the Hebrew, and the Christian' ('Ancient Myths and the Moral Framework of Faulkner's *Absalom, Absalom!*', *AL*). Neil D. Isaacs offers an extended and perceptive reading of the short story 'Wash' in his 'Götterdämmerung in Yoknapatawpha' (*TSL*). *Sew* reprints Allen Tate's *New Statesman* article on the death of Faulkner, an 'obituary of a man I did not like, but of a writer who was the greatest American novelist after Henry James'.

In 'Hart Crane's Doubtful Vision' (*CE*), Gordon K. Grigsby attempts to free Crane of the charge of incapacity in working out his ideas in The Bridge. The poem's 'vacillation', its dialectical development, its ironic juxtapositions, Grigsby believes, are fully intended. Crane was trying for a difficult rather than an easy beauty, 'a complex rather than a synthetic coherence'.

In 'Discipline the Saving Grace: Winters' Critical Position' (*Renascence*), Robert Kimbrough attempts to trace Yvor Winters's transfer of allegiance 'from Aristotle to Aquinas', an event which he says took place about 1930. Alan Stephens's critical estimate of '*The Collected Poems* of Yvor Winters' (*TCL*), is that the hundred or so poems Winters has chosen to publish as the corpus of his work comprise a deliberate, formal arrangement. The poems are intended to show a development from the early and vigorous free verse poems to the last poems, which are 'simplified and hardened, barer in style'.

Robert Penn Warren sketches in his own fictional sources from Louisiana politics and folkways in '*All the King's Men:* The Matrix of Experience' (*YR*), and *SAQ* prints a symposium on Warren in one issue, including Madison Jones's 'The Novels of Robert Penn Warren' and M. L. Rosenthal's 'Robert Penn Warren's Poetry', both of which conclude that Warren's ambition has outstripped his talents in each *genre*. John Hicks contributes an essay on Warren's criticism, pointing out his affinities with the New Humanists, and his lack of any real development as a critic despite his firm sense of 'the organic qualities of art'. 'The Burden of the Literary Mind: Some Meditations on Robert Penn Warren as Historian', by William C. Havard, is primarily concerned with *The Legacy of the Civil War*, but also investigates certain historical implications in Warren's fiction.

Robert B. Holland sets out, in 'Dialogue as a Reflection of Place in *The Ponder Heart*' (*AL*), to show how the structure of the dialogue of Eudora Welty's characters is 'a vocalization of the design of the culture in which they move'. 'The Necessary Order' (*Jahrbuch für Amerikastudien*), is Klaus Lubbers's revaluation of the achievement of Carson McCullers. Lubbers offers a chronological interpretation of themes and structures in Mrs. McCullers's five novels. Wayne D. Dodd discusses 'The Development of Theme Through Symbol in the Novels of Carson McCullers' in *Georgia Review*. He feels that her characters are doomed by 'the discreteness of individuals from each other and from God himself', and that all efforts to achieve harmony in the world must fail because the quest is inevitably self-centred.

'Flannery O'Connor's Way: Shock, with Moral Intent' (*Renascence*), by Maurice Bassan, attempts to prevent the author from being lost in obscurity because of the indifference of critics. She is, Bassan maintains, as distinguished a minor writer as Sarah Orne Jewett. Jonathan Baumbach, limiting himself to a close reading of Flannery O'Connor's first novel, *Wise Blood*, writes of 'The Creed of God's Grace: The Fiction of Flannery O'Connor' (*Georgia Review*). He claims that in all her fiction the author explores an apparently Godforsaken, but finally redeemed world of corrosion and decay. Despite her somewhat solemn concerns, Baumbach says, at her best her fiction is mordantly comic.

Alwyn Berland's estimate of 'The Fiction of Shirley Ann Grau' (*C*), is that her vision is essentially a mimetic one. Her characters behave as they do, Berland claims, because a firm centre of vision is missing from her fiction.

Joseph N. Riddel, in '*A Streetcar Named Desire*—Nietzsche Descending' (*MD*), judges Tennessee Williams's play a failure in its overabundant intellectualism, its aspiration to say something about man and his civilization, and its often contradictory exploitation of ideas. But Williams is not the only contemporary dramatist to be set upon by the academic critics: Joseph A. Hynes attacks Arthur Miller's theory of tragedy and the plays which exemplify it in 'Arthur Miller and the Impasse of Naturalism' (*SAQ*). Naturalism and tragedy, Hynes says, are inherently incompatible. James W. Douglass aims his fire more particu-

win 'is a premonitory prophet, a larly at 'Miller's *The Crucible:* Which Witch Is Which?' (*Renascence*). He finds that, though they are distinct in their points of view, both Miller and the Salem judges are extreme and dangerous in their absolute moral values. Miller merely cries 'witch' at the judges, Douglass says, and one witch hunt is as bad as another.

David D. Galloway's 'Nathanael West's Dream Dump' (*C*), chronicles West's discovery that for him Hollywood contained 'both an instant symbolism and a microcosm of his favorite subjects: the ignoble lie, the world of illusion, the surrealistic incongruities of the American experience'. *The Day of the Locust*, Galloway claims, was a clear influence in both theme and style on Fitzgerald's *The Last Tycoon*. T. G. Rosenthal makes a case for James T. Farrell's *Studs Lonigan* trilogy as an attempt to take the personal element out of tragedy. It is at least a partial fulfilment of the 'search for an American tragedy' because of the American tendency to value society and the group above the individual ('Studs Lonigan and the Search for an American Tragedy', *British Association for American Studies Bulletin*). In addition to his article on Saul Bellow and the naturalist tradition in the American literature number of *REL*, Malcolm Bradbury writes more extensively on 'Saul Bellow's *The Victim*' in *CQ*. This 1947 novel, Bradbury claims, most clearly reveals the typical pattern of Bellow's work, which is the attempt to assert an individual act of will against the deterministic forces of environment.

Colin MacInne's 'Dark Angel: The Writings of James Baldwin' (*Encounter*), is an extended survey and analysis of Baldwin's fiction and essays. MacInnes decides that Bald-

fallible sage, a soothsayer, a bardic voice—"not a novelist"'. In a critical evaluation of the work of William Burroughs ('The Subtracting Machine', *C*), Ihab Hassan concludes that, despite his 'apocalyptic gifts', Burroughs remains 'a satirist more than a visionary, an ironist more than a prophet, an allegorist more than a poet'.

Jonathan Baumbach is informative in 'The Economy of Love: The Novels of Bernard Malamud' (*KR*), though he tends toward sophisticated myth-hunting—not altogether inappropriate for this novelist.

The Fall number of *C* is given over to essays on John Hawkes and John Barth. It includes an introductory comparative study by Alan Trachtenberg which finds the two novelists sharing the role of 'fabulists, for whom the traditional realism of the novel is worn out'. They prove together that the novel is still an energetic form, that experiment is not dead. Also included is an excellent study of Hawkes's prose style by Albert J. Guérard, and bibliographies compiled, once again, by Jackson R. Bryer.

Index I. Authors

Index II. Authors and Subjects Treated

DATE DUE